PHONEMICS: A TECHNIQUE FOR REDUCING LANGUAGES TO WRITING

PHONEMICS

A Technique for Reducing Languages to Writing

by

KENNETH L. PIKE

ANN ARBOR

THE UNIVERSITY OF MICHIGAN PRESS

Thirteenth printing 1976
Copyright © by The University of Michigan 1947;
renewed © by Kenneth L. Pike 1975
ISBN 0-472-08732-0
Published in the United States of America by
The University of Michigan Press and simultaneously
in Rexdale, Canada, by John Wiley & Sons Canada, Limited
Manufactured in the United States of America

FOREWORD

In 1943, at the time of the publication of Kenneth Lee Pike's Phonetics, two other books by him were announced as in preparation. The pressure of a variety of special demands arising from the national war effort has delayed the completion of these books. Important for those demands was the contribution Dr. Pike made to the materials for the teaching of English as a foreign language produced by the English Language Institute of the University of Michigan. The basic research he carried forward as part of this program resulted in his book Intonation of American English, published by the University of Michigan Press in 1945.

In spite of heavy practical duties the work upon the two books announced in 1943 went steadily forward and they have developed and matured with the delay. Both books provide necessary supplements to the earlier volume, Phonetics if one would grasp with some completeness the approach of modern linguistics to the study of vocal sounds. Tone Languages, deals with the nature of tonal systems and provides a technique for the analysis of significant tonal contrasts. The new material here on two languages never before reported provides, not a sampling, but a thoroughgoing dealing with all the pertinent evidence, including an extensive analysis of tone sandhi and tone fusion.

Phonemics is more directly the counterpart of Phonetics. In Phonetics the end sought was the establishing of a technique of description which could deal with the nature and formation of all sounds whether these sounds are used in language or not. Practically it sought a means to describe sounds in terms of movements of the "vocal apparatus," in terms of articulatory formulas. In Phonemics the end sought is the establishing of a satisfactory technique for discovering the pertinent units of sound in any language and organizing them for an alphabet writing.

Much discussion has centered upon the nature of the "phoneme" and many have attempted to define it - some as a "psychological unit," others as a "class of sounds." Dr. Pike furnishes a very practical and scientifically sound approach by carefully stating the assumptions upon which he proceeds and then leading the reader step by step through the intricate problems involved in arriving at the phonemes of a language. Practically, then, "a phoneme is one of the significant units of sound arrived at for a particular language by the analytical procedures developed from the basic premises...." Phonemic analysis thus seeks to arrive, not simply at the phonetic character of the separate sound units, but at the structure of the sound system of a language. Phonemic analysis is a fundamental step in the modern structural approach to linguistic study.

This book has grown out of more than a decade of experience investigating, in the field, a great variety of diverse languages. The premises underlying the phonemic procedures here set forth rest upon that experience. They are assumptions concerning general characteristics of language; but the generalizing is based upon an unusually wide range of first-hand observation.

In addition to these years of experience in various linguistic communities, Dr. Pike has devoted part of each year to training other field workers to make structural analyses of languages. The validity of his premises and the usefulness of his procedures have been constantly put to the test of practical application. This book, therefore, with its step by step approach and many specific illustrations, brings the materials of one of the most important divisions of modern linguistic study within the grasp of the reader without special technical training.

Charles C. Fries

The present volume is a revision and expansion of one of the same title which appeared in mimeographed form in 1943. The book has gone through successive revisions each year and been tested in the classroom[1] with about 1000 students since that time. The purpose of the material has been to give to the student a methodology for reducing languages to writing, and to do so by means of graded exercises in language analysis. It appeared to me that phonemic theory was in an advanced state but that the actual teaching presentation of these theories to beginners was handicapped by lack of drill material for classroom use. In order to supply this need, the book was so arranged that presentation of theory was accompanied by data to which these principles could be applied. The student who has worked through exercises of this type is much better prepared to solve actual difficulties which he meets in the field than he would be if he had heard about such solutions but had not had an opportunity to try to work them out in miniature.

The choice of material for the phonemic exercises was not an easy one. If, for example, an investigator states that such and such a sound occurs in certain positions in words whereas a different but phonetically similar sound never occurs in these same positions, the reader assumes that the investigator has studied all the data before asserting the absence of the second of these sounds from the environments mentioned. In essence then, the phonemic procedures demand the presentation of all the data of the language being examined before valid conclusions can be drawn. This principle came into conflict with the desire to have a wide variety of problems included. It was impossible to present a great number of different languages and at the same time to guarantee that all the phonemic data for each were presented, since too few languages have been adequately described phonemically and since the bulk of the volume would then have exceeded the limits of practicality, while the amount of time required for a student to work out the distributions of sounds of complete problems is so great that the actual practical limitations of classroom time would prevent him from solving many such problems. Nevertheless, one of the aims of the book was to present a large enough number of problems that by the time the student had worked them all

he would have a fair idea of the range of sound systems which might be encountered.

In the face of this dilemma I early began (about 1937) to dictate to the class various Hypothetical Language Problems with the statement to the student that he was to assume that these problems represented all the data of these "languages" and that he must arrive at phonemic solutions of those data and of those data alone, since no other information was known about these languages. This allowed him to make statements of the absolute distribution of sounds and reach conclusions even where arguments from silence were necessary. At the same time it made it possible to keep the problems short so that many types of language situations could be presented in the space and time available. These hypothetical languages were so constructed that each reflected in condensed form some kind of actual or potential language situation. Each was treated as a separate hypothetical language. Soon they were called Dialects of Kalaba.[1]

Repeatedly during succeeding years the attempt was made to utilize actual language material. In each case, however, the effort proved abortive because of the difficulty mentioned, namely, that all of the data could not be presented in a brief space and yet make a simple, brief, accurate exercise. In 1946, however, a modified type of problem was worked out which partially overcame this difficulty. Rather than asking the student to handle the full procedure for the analysis of all the phonemes of the language, the directions required the student merely to analyze some one or more parts of the phonemic system. Any data which he needed for this purpose were supplied him. The material for one of these problems was chosen from an actual language and presented in an abbreviated form. Since, however, the data were essentially incomplete, a thorough phonemic analysis applied to them would not yield a true picture of the structure of the entire phonemic system of the language. The conclusions derived from the data were claimed to be valid only for those parts of the material for which directions were supplied.

---

[1]In the sessions of the Summer Institute of Linguistics at the University of Oklahoma in Norman, Oklahoma, and at Caronport, Saskatchewan, Canada, as well as (1945) at the Linguistic Institute sponsored jointly by the Linguistic Society of America and the University of Michigan at Ann Arbor, Michigan.

[1]The name grew out of simple dictation exercises in which the teacher would pronounce syllables such as [ka], [la], [ba], versus [kʼa], [ɬa], [ᵐba], and so on, in which the student had to find the phonetic or phonemic contrast. After a sufficient number of problems of this nature were utilized, the name followed almost inevitably. No such label is essential, of course, but it has proved helpful in simulating a field atmosphere in the classroom.

Items of this kind were called Restricted Language Problems. Several different restricted language problems could be
chosen from any one actual language and could
be presented in different parts of the volume. In order that the student might not be
confused by an apparently different system
for the same language found in different
parts of the book, these items were called
Restricted Chontal A, Restricted Chontal B,
Restricted Chontal C, and so forth. Furthermore, care was taken that in any one of the
problems none of the data would lead to erroneous analysis of any of the phonemes in the
language. Restricted Problem C might, for
example, contain further phonemes or types of
phonemic problems which were not encountered
in Restricted Problem A of the same language,
but the solution of Problem C would not contradict the analysis of Problem A nor violate
conclusions which one would have reached on
the field. In this way actual language material has been presented within the graded
sequence of the volume without violating phonemic procedures or the data of these languages. A few problems are also presented
which attempt to give in condensed form, but
in exercises much more involved than the ones
earlier in the book, samples of all of the
most important data concerning the phonemic
systems of a few languages as complete units.

In order for the procedures to be
applied to the material, the data in this
volume had to be written accurately. On the
field, however, the student's first notes
would be certain to contain many errors and
omissions. The procedures had to be so designed that these errors would be discovered
in the normal course of the investigation.
In this respect then, it was difficult to
make the phonemic exercises parallel the
field procedures. To solve this difficulty,
problems here are first assumed to be without
error in phonetic recording; with them the
student learns the handling of accurate phonetic data. After these problems a different type is presented in which the data are
assumed to be incomplete and inaccurate. In
these latter cases the student is expected to
discover items which appear suspicious and
which he would, were he in the field, double-
check with his informant. It is assumed that
the student who is able to discover suspicious items in his data will, upon checking
them with the informant, be able to ascertain with some certainty whether or not he
actually heard correctly. By finding these
errors he can then correct his data and apply
the regular procedures to them.

In order to have a volume of exercises which could be worked successfully by
students, it is evident also that the exercises must be graded in difficulty and that
the theory must be introduced gradually in
such a way that the student can tackle a
problem with the assurance that it is solv-
able within the theory as it has been so far
presented to him. These requirements demand
a Step-by-Step Procedure which combines acceptable phonemic theory with a progressive

presentation of it. A procedure first presented must not be dependent for its application upon principles given later on. Such
a progression can by no means be taken for
granted in an analysis which in some respects
must be circular; that is, many phonemic conclusions are based, not upon absolute data
as such, but upon the correlation and interrelationships of data or upon the observation of the effect of a total structure ex-
erting a pressure upon the interpretation of
some one point of that system. Nevertheless,
a step-by-step procedure was a prerequisite
to the usefulness of the volume. Over a period of several years various types of sequences of presentation of material were attempted and those discarded which were not
effective. Their more successful characteristics have been retained as subdivisions of
the present order of materials.

Thus in 1941 the approach centered
around extensive charting in order to locate
segments in mutually exclusive positions;
now the charting is utilized in substantiating hypotheses of distribution--yet the early
list of positions is preserved at the Working
Outline for Determining Distribution of Phonemes in Phonological and Grammatical Units
(pp. 182-184). In 1942 the approach emphasized that every phone was a phoneme unless
it was accounted for in one of various ways;
the progression no longer centers on this
attack on the data, but it is preserved as
part of the procedure for handling nonsuspicious segments (p. 71). In 1943 procedures
were classified as to techniques which either
separate the segments into distinct phonemes,
or unite them into single phonemes, or interpret them as phonetically complex single phonemes, and so on. This type of division
still can be seen as it is reflected in the
subdivision of the longer procedures (see,
for example, p. 84), or in chapter headings
(compare Chapter 12).

It became evident, however, that the
procedures needed to be explained in terms
of the reasonable assumptions underlying
them if the students were to understand them
readily. Otherwise, they appeared to be ut-
terly arbitrary and without legitimate cause
for usage, with no practical goal or justification. This was especially true for those
students who had already been working in the
field and had been utilizing certain types
of alphabets which were in part nonphonemic.
If these students were to be persuaded of
the validity of phonemic procedures, they had
to have some type of explanation which would
appear to them to be valid. It was with
people of this background in mind that the
initial presentation of the three or four
phonemic premises as given in the present
revision was developed in 1945. To be sure,
these premises do not cover all possible assumptions under which phonemic procedures
operate, and the careful reader will see various sub-assumptions contained tacitly or ex-
plicitly in them. Nevertheless, as a practical device they proved sufficiently compre-
hensive to serve as a point of reference for

explaining and justifying the procedures and to serve as a point of departure from which all the procedures might be developed in a progressively graded series. In this way the student has to remember only a very few general principles; in terms of these basic principles he can be made to understand the entire course. As an actual classroom procedure this presentation in terms of initial premises with procedures springing from them has proved much more teachable than earlier editions of the volume which worked directly from the procedures without such an orientation.

One of the goals of the procedures is to have them so arranged that they would serve to solve the problems in the book but, further, that this procedure could also be followed point by point on the field with a probable measure of success resulting therefrom. As a part of the course of the Summer Institute of Linguistics for the past several years, there has been a ten-day field investigation for each of the students. During this time he is expected to apply the procedures as they are given here and to present the materials gathered in that way. Data obtained in this fashion is, of course, incomplete, but the experience so gained has demonstrated that the procedures presented here are applicable in the order presented. Further observation of some of the graduates of earlier years has been possible over extended periods of time; here again it appears that the procedures, though by no means capable of working themselves, are nevertheless helpful.

Even though the statement and sequence of the assumptions have been freshly worked out here for the special purpose of building procedures upon them, it will be seen that many of the phonemic premises are not in essence new: the modification of sound types by their environment, the free fluctuation of material, and the interpreting of sound types in sequences in various ways, have all been pointed out by earlier writers.[1] It is to be regretted that we do not have a statement of the history of phonemic theory, or that a critical review of the literature can not be given here. However, it is scarcely pertinent to the purpose of this volume. Nevertheless, in various places throughout the discussion conflicting theories of analysis have been referred to; at some later date it may be possible to add a separate chapter surveying the literature.

Even though most of the principles of phonemics utilized in this book can already be found in the technical literature, certain contributions are here made to the field. Since they had to occur along with the practical presentation for the beginner, some of these are not written in such a way that they are convenient of access to the technician. Nevertheless, the phonemic theorist will be especially interested in Chapter 4, in which much of the theory is gathered together. In that chapter he should notice the discussion of phonetic versus phonemic syllables; close-knit syllable nuclei; suprasegmental phonemes; grammatical prerequisites to phonemic analysis; the source of phonemic premises; and relative quality. A certain amount of hitherto unpublished research data appears also in the Restricted Language Problems.

Many valuable data have never reached technical periodicals, even though they are in the files of investigators, simply because certain observers were untrained in the written presentation of scientific materials. It is hoped that the discussion of Descriptive Procedures will result in a higher percentage of such facts being made available. If many lay workers in the field should but learn the rudiments of linguistics and the essentials of a routine description of the results of their investigations, they could provide accurate and adequate surveys of sounds, sound types, sound sequences, and record texts in the vernacular.

[1] Some of the materials which are the most helpful for the understanding of phonemic principles are Edward Sapir, "Sound Patterns in Language," Language, I (June, 1925), 37-51; Leonard Bloomfield, Language, Chapters V-VIII (New York: Henry Holt and Company, 1933); Morris Swadesh, "The Phonemic Interpretation of Long Consonants," Language, XIII (January-March, 1937), 1-10; also, the same author, "The Phonemic Principle," Language, X (June, 1934), 117-29. For procedures of phonemic analysis--somewhat distinct from the theory of analysis as such --one should see also Morris Swadesh, "A Method for Phonetic Accuracy and Speed," American Anthropologist, XXXIX (October, 1937), 728-32; also Jules Henry, "A Method for Learning to Talk Primitive Languages," American Anthropologist, XLII (October-December, 1940), 635-41; and Carl Voegelin, "Anthropological Limits of Language," Proceedings of the Indiana Academy of Science, XLVI (1937), 57-64; Bernard Bloch, and George Trager, Outline of Linguistic Analysis (Baltimore: Linguistic Society of America, 1942). In the article by Sapir, the argument and demonstration are handled in terms of two hypothetical phonetic systems which have similar sounds but a different systematic arrangement of these sounds into phonemes; for hypothetical language problems constructed on these data, see p. 156. Apart from the examples in the present volume this is the only treatment I have seen which makes large use of hypothetical languages for phonemic analysis. For teaching morphological analysis similar types of problems are used by my colleague, Eugene A. Nida, in his Morphology: The Descriptive Analysis of Words, University of Michigan Publications in Linguistics, II (Ann Arbor: University of Michigan Press, 1946).

Those persons who expect to utilize phonemic techniques for reducing to writing languages which have hitherto been unwritten will find that the material presented, though appearing to them to be highly technical, is prepared with practical goals in view. The section on Orthographical Procedures is designed to show them the specific application of phonemic theory to the formation of alphabets to be used in the preparation of vernacular literatures.

Before the student can adequately handle a phonemic analysis he needs to be able to hear, produce, and transcribe sounds. A phonemic book, therefore, must have as a prerequisite a study of phonetics. In order to furnish some of these data within the confines of the present volume, a section on phonetics has been given which is designed chiefly to allow the student to produce, hear, and transcribe the sounds utilized later in the problems. It does not give illustrations of these sounds in various languages nor discuss the particular shades of sounds which occur in any particular language. For these the student can consult other texts. If, however, he can handle the material given here he should be prepared to understand the phonemic procedures and to carry on work in the field. The theory of the phonetic data presented is based upon my volume, Phonetics: A Critical Analysis of Phonetic Theory and a Technic for the Practical Description of Sounds.[1]

The exercise material in phonetics is based upon experience in the classroom. Various new drill types are given, in addition to many old ones which may be found in current phonetic literature. The drills on tone should be preceded by practice in intonation since the analysis and control of one's own intonation is the best approach to a study of tone. For this material one may see The Intonation of American English.[2] If one wishes further details for the theoretical analysis of tone than are presented in this volume, one may consult Tone Languages.[3]

The presentation of the earlier editions of the volume was made possible by funds supplied by the Summer Institute of Linguistics of Glendale. In 1946 a complete rewriting of the manuscript was accomplished as part of the work undertaken as Lloyd Post-Doctoral Fellow of the University of Michigan. The phonetic and phonemic staffs of the Summer Institute of Linguistics have provided material for the Restricted Language Problems; each of these contributions is acknowledged in the appropriate place in the text. Miss May Morrison contributed greatly to the volume by typing various drafts of it and influencing the mechanical features of presentation of the problems. Donald Stark constructed a large percentage of the Kalaba Problems. It has been from my wife, however, that I received the initial stimulus to commit to writing these problems and procedures, and from her I have received much searching and helpful criticism; the attempt to build these procedures around a limited number of phonemic axioms was initiated by her.

K.L.P.

---

[1] University of Michigan Publications in Language and Literature, XXI (Lithographed Edition, Ann Arbor: University of Michigan Press, 1944).

[2] Kenneth L. Pike, University of Michigan Publications in Linguistics, I (Ann Arbor: University of Michigan Press, 1945). For supplementary classroom material, designed to be used with these volumes, see Eunice V. Pike, Dictation Exercises in Phonetics (Glendale: Summer Institute of Linguistics, 1946).

[3] Kenneth L. Pike (Ann Arbor: University of Michigan Press, 1948).

CONTENTS

Chapter

PART II. ANALYSIS AND DESCRIPTION
OF PHONEMIC UNITS

ANALYTICAL PROCEDURES

A P P E N D I X

ADDENDA AND ERRATA
(July, 1949)

These addenda and errata provide the student with a number of additional phrases and references--as well as with a few corrections--which should prove helpful, according to those who have used this textbook during the past two years. Before beginning serious study of the phonemic procedures, the reader would do well to enter the changes and additions in the text itself, since they clarify a number of points which at present appear difficult to understand. Misprints and solecisms that do not materially hinder understanding of the text are not listed.

The letter "a" or "b" after a page number refers to the first or second column on the page; "n" indicates a footnote.

Inside front cover.--Add the [l] sounds; see p. 70 for missing symbols.

Page 7.--Draw a hyphen through the varieties of [g] which occur in the central section of the page (flat central fricatives).

Page 10, Fig. 7.--Under the segment [o], lower the hyphens to relaxed position, and add ```` under the [o] in high frictionless position.

Page 14a.--At the end of the footnote continued from the preceding page, add: See pp. 128-30.

Page 20a, last paragraph, line 14.--Change "mouth" to: nose.

Page 38b, Fig. 32.--For delayed glottal release, extend the solid line which indicates glottal closure farther to the right under the segment [tˀ] (but without arrows superimposed on it), and then lower it to vibrating position.

Page 41, Figs. 34 and 36.--Delayed releases may be diagramed for back tongue position analogous to the delayed release just indicated for the velic in Fig. 32.

Page 45.--Substitute slant lines for all brackets in chart here and on inside back cover.

Page 59b, first full paragraph, line 5.-- After [t], add: [k]; after [b], add: [d].

Page 60a, first full paragraph, line 33.-- Change "second" to: third.

Page 61b, last paragraph, line 7.--After "(3) Phonemes exist," add: See also p. 64bn.

Page 62b, second full paragraph, line 18.-- After "some morphemes," add: or morpheme sequences.

Page 64b.--After first paragraph, add: See also p. 160bn.

Page 69b.--At end of first full paragraph, add: See also p. 94a, second full paragraph, and p. 119a.

Page 70.--Circle all voiceless nasals. Draw a circle also around [ə], [ʌ], and [a]. Raise the line which passes directly under [I] so that it passes directly over it instead. Make these changes also in the chart on the inside front cover.

Page 71a.--In line preceding footnote, change all brackets to slant lines; do this also for nonsuspicious segments listed on pp. 74a, 77a, 80b, 85a.

Page 72a.--Delete Problem 4.

Page 73a, Problem 5, Phonetic Data.--Add dot under k in [ksama].

Page 73b, line 2.--After the words "with those segments," add: or suprasegmental characteristics.

Page 73b, fourth full paragraph, line 10.-- After the words "in those environments," add: and therefore we deduce that one of these environments is responsible for the difference between the suspicious segments.

Page 73b, end of fifth full paragraph, just before Concluding Procedures.--Add: (i.e. in environments which are similar but nonconditioning in respect to the point at issue).

Page 74a.--Add dot under k in list of nonsuspicious segments.

Page 76b, end of first full paragraph.--Add: If one of two phonetically analogous sets of suspicious pairs of sounds in a problem acts like the other set, the description of the action of the two sets may often be combined for conciseness; e.g. if [d] and [g] (in a problem a bit more expanded than this one) were both to occur before [v], [z], and [ǥ], one might say that 'voiced stops occur only before voiced nonvocoids, whereas voiceless stops never occur in that position.' If only one set of suspicious segments is involved, then a generalized statement (such as the one in the text) may be used, or the specific segments may be listed.

Page 77a, line 3 of last paragraph above the footnotes.--Change "p. 72" to: p. 73.

Page 78b, Problem 15.--Change šǫti to: šǫvi.

Pages 78-79.--Add: Note to teachers: The short problems 10 and 11 are more difficult to handle than are problems with more data.

Page 80b, Phonetic chart.--Add u to phonetic chart and to list of nonsuspicious segments.

Page 84a, next to last paragraph.--Add the following footnote at the underlined word "only": Note that in many contexts the word "always" cannot be substituted for the word "only" without resulting in ambiguity or error.

Page 84b, end of second full paragraph.--Add: Note: One can reach a tentative conclusion that the submembers of a hypothesized phoneme are mutually exclusive, by the negation of the separating procedures-- but one must check with the specific uniting procedures (with charts, etc., of Procedure I-C) to substantiate this conclusion. Similarly, one can reach a tentative conclusion as to the existence of phonemic contrast between two segments, by the negation of uniting procedures--but in order to avoid serious possibilities of error arising from a negated hypothesis of mutual exclusiveness which is incomplete or inaccurate, one must check this conclusion of contrast by using the specific

procedures of I-A and I-B for finding contrast. When the result of separating procedures is negative, and the result of uniting procedures is also negative, one should reëxamine the hypothesis of mutual exclusiveness to see if it can be refined so as to be in accordance with all the facts.

Page 85b, first chart, first column.--After "Submembers of," add: hypothesized phoneme. Do this also on pp. 88a, 92b, 93a.

Page 85b.--Preceding "Concluding Procedures," change "Phonemic norm" to: Phonetic norm of the phoneme.

Page 86a, second full paragraph of type, line 5.--After "occur," add: exclusively.

Page 86b, first line.--At word "exclusive," add a footnote: This statement must be modified, in reference to material that appears later in the book, to allow for two segments united in free fluctuation (Procedure III) or in sequence (Procedure IV-B). Furthermore, these two conditions may not constitute evidence strong enough to warrant uniting segments if there results a sharp break in the symmetry of the system (cf. Discussion, p. 137a).

Page 88a, third full paragraph of type, line 4.--At "NORM," add a footnote: The norm is also considered to be one of the submembers of the phoneme.

Page 88b, second full paragraph.--Underline the first part of the first sentence (i.e.: "A chart ... have been eliminated"). Underline the third sentence (beginning "Utilize only ..."), and add the following: It is permissible--or, possibly, preferable--to choose in a related fashion the labels for the rows and columns of the chart, i.e., to mention only those phonetic characteristics which are essential for distinguishing the various types of sounds. On p. 85b, in the Chart of phonetic norms of the phonemes, this would imply the deletion of the words "unaspirated" (from "Voiceless unaspirated stops"), "Voiceless" (from "Voiceless fricatives"), and "unrounded" and "rounded" (from "Front unrounded" and "Back rounded"); on p. 123a it would imply the deletion of "Voiceless" (from "Voiceless stops"), "Voiced" (from "Voiced nasals" and "Voiced laterals"), and "close," "open," "unrounded," and "rounded" (from the labels for the vocoids).

Page 88b, third full paragraph.--Underline the second sentence.

Page 92b, next to last paragraph, line 10.-- Replace [k] with [ḳ].

Page 94a, second full paragraph.--Underline last sentence (beginning "If two pairs ..."), and add: See pp. 69b and 119a.

Page 95a, last paragraph, lines 9-10.--Delete "at the same place in the procedure" and substitute: just before or within the concluding procedures.

Page 96a, second paragraph, line 13.--After "CONDITIONED SUBSTITUTION of," add: full. In lines 14-15, after "nonphonemic conditioned occurrence," add: (or substitution).

Page 99a.--Delete problems 56 and 57.

Page 101a, Problem 66, third line from end of data.--Change gedon to: geḍon. In next to last line of data, change nabob to: naḅoḅ.

Page 101b, Problem 68.--Change all r symbols to: ṛ.

Page 102b, Problems 71, 72, 73, and p. 103a, Problem 74.--In Directions, change "Procedure 3" to: Procedure IV.

Page 103a, Problem 75.--Add: [ḅukli] 'pebble.'

Page 111a, end of footnote.--Add: p. 56.

Page 112a, Problem 99.--Change Directions to read: How many phonemes of stress are there here? Of tone? Of length?

Page 119a, Problem 115, first word of data.-- Change [pap] to: [paṗ].

Page 120a, Problem 118.--Delete problem, or place it in Chapter 12.

Page 122a, first paragraph of type, line 12.-- After "fluctuation occurs," add: and state any restricted environments in which the segments occur without perceptible fluctuation.

Page 122b, end of short paragraph beginning "[t] and [d]."--Add a footnote: A slightly different format occasionally has some advantages (and is required in the statement of environments in which segments occur without perceptible fluctuation):
> [t] and [d] are submembers of a single phoneme, fluctuating freely between vowels word medially; of these submembers, only [t] occurs word initially.

Page 131a.--To title of list at bottom of column, add a footnote: For three-segment sequences, see p. 136a.

Page 131a, next to last short paragraph.-- After [gw], add: [ku].

Page 131b, last line.--Delete the underlining from this line, and from the first two lines of the next page. Then underline the phrase, just preceding this parenthesis, which reads: note certain types of nonsuspicious sequences, which are probably sequences of two phonemes.

Page 137a, end of first full paragraph.-- After "distributional facts," add: When pressures are equally balanced, choose the analysis which parallels the phonetic data, separating a sequence into two or more segments; this tends toward economy of symbols and fewer postulated phonemes.

Page 137a, end of footnote.--Add: Note to teachers: It has proved convenient to teach Procedure IV-A before I-A, for then the terms "consonant" and "vowel" are understood in relation to "nonvocoid" and "vocoid." Furthermore, this illustrates clearly and early the necessity for phonemic theory. Procedure IV-B can also be taught early with profit provided students have previously been instructed in the phonetic nature of affricates, and so on.

Page 138b, Solution to Problem 154.--Change (or /mot/) to: (or /mōt/).

Page 141b, end of first full paragraph.-- Add: or chosen so as to give the simplest morphological statement; cf. also p. 149a.

Page 150a, Problem 170, Directions, line 1.-- Change "predominant" to: nonsuspicious.

Page 159b, next to last line above footnotes.-- Change suM to: zuM.

Page 160b, line 10.--After "unless it is," add: consistently; after "represented," add: at every occurrence.

Page 161a, footnote 1, first paragraph, line 8.--After "Analysis," add: See Word, III (Dec., 1947), 155-72. (For an opposite opinion, see the review by C. F. Voegelin, International Journal of American Linguistics, XV [Jan., 1949], 75-85, and see Charles F. Hockett, "Two Fundamental Problems in Phonemics," Studies in Linguistics, VII, 2 [June, 1949], 29-51.)

Page 161b, footnote, section (3), line 10.-- After "identification of," add: some morphemes or close-knit sequences of.

Page 164a-b.--In the numerals marking intonation add a degree sign before each 2.

Page 164b, Problem 213, second column of data, second line.--Change [ki] to: [bi].

Page 165a, Problem 214, next to last utterance.--Change "blue" to: big.

Page 165b, line 5.--Change "'I'" to: 'my.'

Page 166b, Problem 216, last utterance.--Replace [tiso'mappo'los'sapol] by: [tiso'map'mosal'sapol].

Page 168b, section (1), lines 4-5.--After "symbolized," add: uniformly at every occurrence. At the end of the sentence, add: and these must be uniformly symbolized; cf. p. 160a-b.

Page 169b, Problem 225, last item in second column of data.--Change [isaxut] to: [išaxut].

Page 170a, Problem 228, second column of data.--Change [nap] to: [náp]; last word of data, change [kuku] to: [kūkú].

Page 172a, line 3.--Add stress mark before šą̆ą̀ to make it: 'šą̆ą̀.

Page 187a, section B2a, last line.--Change "final" to: medial.

Page 225a.--Add a footnote to column on Suggested Orthography: I have heard indirectly, since this text was originally written, that social pressures have proved so strong (cf. pp. 211b-214) that it is advisable to use "c" and "qu-" (as in the Spanish) for /k/, and to use "k" for /k/.

Page 239a, above last entry.--Add: Grammatical prerequisites, 62b-63a, 89-92, 159-168.

Page 242a, entry entitled "LIQUID."--Delete: [n].

Page 242b, entry entitled "MORPHOLOGICAL PROCESS."--After "type of," add: meaningful.

Page 243b, entry entitled "Nida."--Add: ix(bn), 167an.

Page 245b, entry entitled "PHONEME," line 8.--After "unit," add: or unless it comprises two phonemes.

Page 245b, above next to last entry.--Add new entry: PHONEMIC: Pertinent to the contrastive phonological systems of a language. Elements are sometimes phonemic without being themselves full phonemes (e.g. length of vowel may early be called "phonemic" in a language in which phonetically long vocoids are later analyzed as homorganic sequences of two short vowel phonemes).

Page 249a, above entry SECONDARY ARTICULATOR.--Add new entry: Sapir, ix(bn), 156.

Page 250a, above entry STATIC DIAGRAM.--Add new entry: Statement: See Descriptive Statements.

Page 254b, entry entitled "Zoque."--Add: 202b-206.

Part I

ANALYSIS AND PRODUCTION

OF PHONETIC UNITS

PHONETIC SYMBOLISM

THE VALUE AND BASIS OF FORMULAS FOR SOUND PRODUCTION

Language consists of systematized vocal noises. These noises are made in the mouth, nose, and throat, and are organized into words and phrases for communication. In order to study a language that is new to him, an investigator must study the vocal noises.

These vocal sounds are produced by movements of parts of the mouth, nose, throat and lungs. Within the vocal apparatus there are only a few parts such as lips and tongue which can move. If one can master the general types of movement which these parts can undergo, and the combinations of their movements, one can then pronounce the sounds of any language since sounds of all languages are produced by combinations of these variables.

Similarly if one can create formulas to represent these movements it follows that one can with them represent graphically the sounds of any language since the sounds are caused by the movements of the vocal parts. A phonetic alphabet constitutes a series of such formulas. For example, the letter "b" represents a movement of the lungs which thrusts air upward and outward through the throat, past the vibrating vocal cords, into the mouth; the symbol shows further that in the mouth the air stream is temporarily but completely interrupted by a closure of the passage through the nose, and by a closure at the lips of the passage through the mouth.

Courses in practical phonetics are designed to study the several variables of movement in terms of their effect upon the production of sounds. Students listen to various kinds and sequences of sounds and learn to reinterpret them in terms of the vocal mechanisms which produce them, and to symbolize them in formulas which consist of letters of the alphabet.

PRODUCTIVE AND CONTROLLING MECHANISMS FOR SOUNDS

It proves difficult or impossible to describe the flavor of a pumpkin pie in such a way that one who has never eaten that kind of a pie may know what it tastes like. One must content oneself with comparing it to other similar flavors, or one must describe it by means of a recipe in which the description is not one of taste as such, but of the raw materials entering into the pie, plus the procedure for combining and cooking them. In practical phonetic work one must follow a similar procedure. Frequently the most adequate available description of a sound, for the purpose of learning to produce it, is a definition which tells a student how to make that sound, rather than telling him what constitutes its acoustic properties. It is this type of definition which will appear most frequently throughout succeeding sections of this material.

Although sounds may be made by percussion, or by vibrating strings, or by other means, the large majority of vocal sounds are made by a moving column of air passing through a narrow orifice in the mouth, nose, or throat. An air column to be set in motion within the vocal cavities must have something pushing or pulling it, but once it is moving it can be controlled at its outlet, just as a stream of water from a hose may be controlled by a nozzle. In addition, there may be further interferences with the air stream between its point of origin and its point of escape.

There are several ways in which an air column may be set in motion. The walls of the lungs may contract so as to force air outward. In this event the lungs may be called an INITIATOR of the air stream. All normal English sounds are produced in this way. There can be, however, other places at which an air stream is begun. The tongue can be pressed against the top of the mouth and then, while retaining its contact, moved backwards so as to create a suction in the mouth, and to cause air to rush inward to fill in the partial vacuum; this is the same mechanism which one uses in sucking water up into a straw. If the vocal cords are made to close the passage to the lungs, and the larynx is raised, the air in the throat is compressed and forced out through the mouth or nose. Air columns set in motion by each of these initiators are found in speech, so the student of languages should be ready to recognize which initiator is the source of the air stream for any particular sound. The quality of the sound will be affected by the manner in which its air stream is initiated.

The direction of the air stream likewise affects the sound. If suction is created, causing an ingressive air stream, the acoustic results are considerably different from those produced when an egressive air stream is caused by pressure from one of the initiators. In Figure 1 notice that an arrow indicates that the tongue is moving inward, causing an ingressive air stream.

The parts which modify and control the air stream are either movable or stationary. The movable parts include the lips, jaw, tongue, velum (i.e., soft palate, uvula,

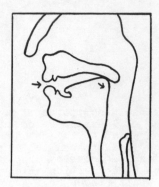

Fig. 1. Ingressive
Air Stream to the
Mouth

velic (i.e. nasal side of the soft palate),
vocal cords, and other less important items.
The tongue is so very flexible, however,
that it is convenient to describe it in
several parts: the tip, the blade (i.e. the
part directly behind the tip), the middle
part, the upper back part of the tongue, and
the root of the tongue (facing the back wall
of the throat). When these movable parts
affect the air stream they may be called
ARTICULATORS:

　　　Stationary parts of the vocal apparatus serve as convenient points of reference for indicating the movement of the
flexible ones. The stationary parts include
the teeth, the alveolar arch (which is behind the upper teeth), the hard palate, and
the back wall of the pharynx. When an articulator in controlling the air stream
touches another articulator or one of these
stationary parts, it is convenient to call
the junction or near junction of the two a
POINT OF ARTICULATION and to describe sounds
containing such productive characteristics
as bilabial, velar, uvular, glottal, and so
on, or labiodental, interdental, dental.
Usually the articulator is flat from side to
side, but it may be slightly grooved or with
the air escaping centrally over the center
of the tongue, or laterally over the sides
of the tongue. For these different articulators and certain pertinent stationary
parts of the vocal mechanism see Figure 2.

　　　The moving air stream may be affected by the movable parts in various ways.
The two escape cavities (the mouth and the
nose) may be closed off so that the air
stream is completely dammed up, or stopped,
as in [p] and [t], or less frequently the
air stream may be completely interrupted by
a single closure in the throat. On the
other hand, one of the two escape cavities
may be closed off and the air diverted out
the other in a continuous stream. Even
while the air is escaping outward through
one of the cavities, some articulator may
reduce the opening partially, so that the
air stream is considerably impeded and audible friction is created at that point. In
[f], for example, the friction is noticeable

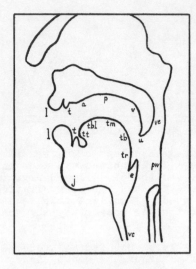

Fig. 2. Points of Refer-
ence in the Vocal
Apparatus
l, lips; t, teeth; a, al-
veolar arch; p, palate;
v, velum; u, uvula; ve,
velic; tt, tongue tip;
tbl, tongue blade; tm,
tongue mid; tb, tongue
back; tr, tongue root; j,
jaw; pw, pharynx wall; vc,
vocal cords, e, epiglottis.

at the junction of the upper teeth and lower
lip. The interruption of the air stream,
however, may be less severe so that there is
little or no audible friction at the point
of partial closure.

　　　One of the most important types of
interruption occurs in the throat and is
caused by the rapid opening and closing of
the vocal "cords" (somewhat like two lips)
in such a way that a characteristic vibration called VOICING is added to sounds like
[o], [v], and [b], in contrast with the
voiceless sounds [h], [f], and [p]. In the
voiced sounds the contrast between those
which have a strong local friction, such as
[v], and those with no audible friction,
such as [e], is very great, and usually is
easy to recognize. In voiceless sounds this
difference is less easy to hear, because even
in the most open types a very light friction
may be heard, as of the air blowing through
an open tube. However, it is convenient to
speak of the voiceless ones as frictionless
when they have no strong local friction, even
though a little of this cavity friction may
be present.

　　　One of the most important distinctions in sound types is that between
sounds which have the air escaping from the
mouth over the center of the tongue but with
no strong local friction in the mouth (even
though friction may at times occur elsewhere
during the sounds) and those sounds which do
not. The former sounds, such as [o], [e],
[u], [w], and [r] may be called conveniently

CENTRAL RESONANT ORALS, or VOCOIDS. The others, including sounds which have local friction in the mouth or which do not have air escaping through the mouth at all may be called NONVOCOIDS.

In general the syllabic vocoids are written with ordinary or special "vowel" letters such as "a" and "ɔ". For the specific symbols[1] for the voiced vocoids see Chart 1.

in size, such as "A" and "Ɔ".

The nonsyllabic vocoids may be represented by the same symbols as the syllabic ones, except (1) that it frequently is convenient to raise them above the line, as "xᵃ", "xᵓ", "xᴬ", etc., and (2) that nonsyllabic [i], [u], and [ɹ] may optionally be written as "y", "w", and "r" respectively, and (3) voiceless nonsyllabic vocoids of various timbres may optionally be written "h"

Chart 1. Symbols for Voiced Syllabic Vocoids

		Front		Central		Back	
		Unrounded	Rounded	Unrounded	Rounded	Unrounded	Rounded
High	close	i	ü	ɨ	ʉ	ï	u
	open	ʟ	ü			ï	ʊ
Mid	close	e	ö	ə	ɹ²	ë	o
	open	ɛ		ʌ			
Low	close	æ	ö				ɒ
	open	a		ɑ			ʋ

The phonetic charts and the paragraphs given here contain a number of symbols which constitute formulas for many sounds produced by the various speech articulators and initiators. Some of the technical terms on these charts will appear presently, but observe that many of the details have already been explained. The charts are suggestive of the possibilities, but by no means complete.

Voiceless vocoids may be written with capital letters, or letters extra-large

until a phonemic analysis demonstrates whether they should be classed as vowels or consonants, but they may optionally be written with large or capital vocoid letters. The light cavity friction heard during [h] is not of a strong local type and not sufficient to remove it from the vocoid class.[1]

A pharyngeal voiceless fricative may be written [ħ]; it is a vocoid however, since it has no friction in the mouth. Similarly a voiced vocoid with added audible friction at the glottis may be written as [ɦ]; it is traditionally called "voiced h."[2]

---

[1]The symbols used in this book are chosen or created for typing or because of traditional usage, especially Americanist usage. For the alphabet of the International Phonetic Association see the Appendix.

It should be noted that it is more or less immaterial what alphabet is used in rough phonetic field notes, since the alphabet for publication must be modified in accordance with a phonemic analysis of the particular language and the orthographic tradition of the area being represented or the journal to which an article is being submitted.

[2]With retroflexed or retracted tongue formation.

---

[1]When [h] functions as a consonant phoneme (in circumstances to be discussed in Part II), it is traditionally listed as a voiceless glottal fricative on the consonant chart. Similarly, when [i] and [u] are phonemically consonants, a line of "semivowels," or nonsyllabic vocoids, may be added to the consonant chart, with [y] classed as palatal and [u] as bilabial.

[2]When these function phonemically as consonants, they may be added to the consonant chart: [ħ] as a voiceless pharyngeal fricative; [ɦ] as a voiced glottal fricative.

Nonvocoids are, in general, written with ordinary or special "consonant" letters such as "p", "l", and "p". For the specific typical symbols for sounds with egressive lung air see Chart 2. Where symbols exist for the voiced sounds, the same symbols underlined or the corresponding capital letter indicates voicelessness.

Nonsyllabic nonvocoids produced by an air stream other than that escaping from the lungs can be represented by the symbols given on Chart 2 plus the following modifications, (in which C represents any nonvocoid, V any vocoid).

Ingressive lung air: C ←

Egressive pharynx air: Cᵠ

Ingressive pharynx air: Cˤ

Egressive mouth air: C ᐟ

Ingressive mouth air: Cˏ

Syllabic nonvocoids can be symbolized by a vertical stroke underneath the letter: e.g. ļ.

Further symbols for showing methods of indicating additional sound types:

Local Modification:

    Fronting: Ç ,   Vˏ

    Backing: Ç ,   V ᐟ

    Raising: V^

    Lowering: Vᵛ

Additional Articulation:

    Labialization   Ç (one segment), or
    or rounding: Cᵂ (two segments)

    Palatalization: Ç or C⁽ⁱ⁾ (one segment), or Cʸ (two segments)

    Velarization: C⁽ᵘ⁾

    Nasalization: Ç , Ṽ (or Cⁿ , Vⁿ)

    Pharyngealization: ₵

Strength of Articulation:

    Fortis: Ç ,   Ṿ

    Lenis: Ç ,   Ṿ

Fricative Articulation: Ç

Nonvocoid Without Audible Release: Vᶜ

Special Symbols for Voicelessness:

    Underlining (italics): C , V

    Capitals: M , N

Subcircle: C̥ , V̥

Special Symbol for Voicing: C̬

Temporary Doubt in Transcription: C̰ , V̰

Certainty of Transcription: C̲ , V̲

Stress:

    Primary: 'C (or V́)

    Secondary: ˏC (or V̀)

Length:

    Long: [:] or [·]

    Short: (unmarked)

    Half-long: [·] (raised dot)

Relative Pitch:

    High: V́ , or V¹

    Mid: V̓ , or V²

    Norm: V̄ , or V³

    Low: V̰ , or V⁴

    Slightly Higher then "High": 1+

    Slightly Higher than "Mid":   2+

    Slightly Lower than "High":   1-,
                              and so on

Pause:

    Tentative, or short: [|]

    Final, or long: [||]

Phonological or Grammatical Borders:

    Syllable Division: [(CV).(CV)] (low
                                  dot)

    Morpheme Division or Compounding:
                CV-CV (hyphen[1])

    Word Division (or Utterance Division):
                CV CV (space)

    Proclisis or Enclisis: CV--CVCV
                (dash), or CV-CV (hyphen)

    Exercise 1. For the sounds [p],
[pᵠ], [s], [m], [o], [l], [r], [z←],
[u] state the following:

        (a) Air mechanism used
        (b) Direction of the air stream

---

[1]Hyphen should be used for only one of the purposes suggested here, in any one set of data. If two symbols are needed in the same context, use a dash for one of them.

Chart 2. Symbols for Nonsyllabic Norvocoids with Egressive Lung Air

General Type of Norvocoid		Bilabial	Labio-Dental	Inter-Dental	Alveolar	Retro-flex	Alveo-Palatal	Retro-flex	Palatal	Velar	Back Velar	Uvular	Phar-yngeal	Glottal
Stops														
One-segment Unaspirated	vl.	p		t̪	t	ṭ			kᶜ	k	ḳ (q)		ʞ̈	ʔ
	vd.	b		d̪	d	ḍ			gᶜ	g	g̣ (G)			
Two-segment Aspirated	vl.	pʰ (pˊ)			tʰ (tˊ)					kʰ(kˊ)				
	vd.	bʰ (bˊ)			dʰ (dˊ)					gʰ(gˊ)				
Affricated	vl.	pɸ		t̪θ	ts (¢)		tš (š)			kx				
	vd.	bβ		d̪ð	dz (ʒ)		dž (ǰ)			gɣ				
Laterally released	vl.				tɬ (ƛ)									
	vd.				dl (λ)									
Fricatives														
Central Flat	vl.	ɸ	f	θ	θ̠			θ̣	ᶍ	x	x̣	x̣		
	vd.	β	v	ð	ð̠			ð̣	ɣ̟	ɣ	ɣ̣			
Grooved	vl.	w̥+			s	ʂ̣	š	ʂ̣						
	vd.	w+[2]			z	ʐ̣	ž	ʐ̣						
Lateral	vl.				ɬ (ƛ)									
	vd.				l̲ (λ)									
Frictionless														
Nasal	vl.	m̥ (M)			n̥ (N)	ṇ̥	ñ̥ (Ñ)			ŋ̥ (Ŋ)				
	vd.	m			n	ṇ	ñ			ŋ				
Lateral	vl.				ɬ̥ (L)	ḷ̥	ʎ̥ʸ							
	vd.				l	ḷ	ʎ							
Vibrants														
Flapped	vl.	ɾ̥			ř̥	ᵳ̥								
	vd.	ɾ			ř	ᵳ								
Trilled	vl.	ʙ̥			r̥̃							ʀ̈		
	vd.	ʙ			r̃									

[For h, ḥ, and ḫ, see footnotes, p. 5]

[1] Parentheses enclose optional symbols.

[2] For [w], [y], [r], and their voiceless counterparts, see p. 5.

(c) Status of the vocal cords
    (Vibrating or not vibrating)
(d) Status of the nasal passage
    (open or closed by the velic)
(e) Status of the air stream
    (completely or partially im-
    peded; if partially impeded.
    state whether with local
    friction or without it)
(f) Place of impedance of air
    stream

Exercise 2. For those nonvocoid
sounds in Exercise 1, give technical
names, with characteristics represented
in the following order:

(a) Voicing or Voicelessness
(b) Point of articulation
(c) Aspiration (if present)
(d) Shape of articulator (if
    other than flat or normal)
(e) Impedance or exit type
(f) Direction of air stream
(g) Air mechanism used

Samples: [f⁹] is a voiceless, labio-
dental, fricative with egressive pharynx
air (aspiration and shape omitted); [ŋ]
is a voiced, velar, nasal with egressive
lung air.

Exercise 3. For the vocoids [u],
[i], [ü], [a], [o] give technical names,
with characteristics represented in the
following order:

(a) Voicing
(b) General tongue height (high,
    mid, low)
(c) Specific tongue height
    (close, open)
(d) General tongue placement
    (front, central, back)
(e) Rounding
(f) General modified character
    (retroflexed, nasalized)
(g) General character (vocoid)
(h) Direction of air stream
(i) Air mechanism used

Samples: [e] is a voiced, mid, close,
front, unrounded, vocoid with egressive
lung air; [Ɔ⁺] is a voiceless, low,
close, back, rounded, nasalized vocoid
with ingressive lung air.

STATIC DIAGRAMS FOR SOUNDS

The general position of the initiator
and articulators for sounds can oftentimes
be indicated conveniently by diagrams of the
face which show the position of the vocal
apparatus at the most crucial part of the
sound. These diagrams are of a STATIC type
in that they portray the mechanism as if it
were stationary during sound production.

In Figure 3 notice the contact of
the tip of the tongue with the alveolar arch
at the time when the egressive air from the
mouth is interrupted during the pronunciation

of [t]. Notice also that the velic closes
off the nasal passage and that the vocal
cords are not vibrating.

In Figure 4 the wavy line in the
throat indicates that the vocal cords are
vibrating; the closure of the lips indicates
that no air is escaping from the mouth.
With the velic down, however, air is allowed
to pass through the nose so that the sound
segment diagrammed here is [m].

Exercise 1. Draw face diagrams of
[p], [pʔ], [pˤ], [p<]. Indicate the
direction of the air stream with an
arrow; for pulmonic air stream place
the arrow below the glottis; for pharyngeal, through the glottis; for oral,
on the tongue.

Exercise 2. Draw face diagrams for
[k], [g], [f], [z]. If no air escapes
past a given articulator, make that articulator actually touch the other side
of the air chamber (point of articulation). If air does escape, indicate
it by leaving a space between articulator and point of articulation. Be
sure to make the velic either closed or
open. Indicate voicing with a wavy line
at the glottis. Draw diagrams such as
those used for Figure 3, or utilize face
diagrams which are duplicated beforehand,
with moveable potential articulators
ready to be filled in by hand.[1] Compare
Figure 5.

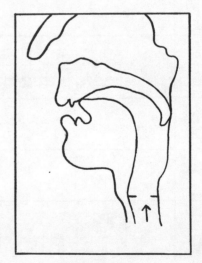

Fig. 3. [t]

---

[1]For the suggestion of giving the
student partially prepared face diagrams,
rather than requiring him to draw the entire
figure, I am indebted to Dr. Fred B. Gerstung
of Wheaton College.

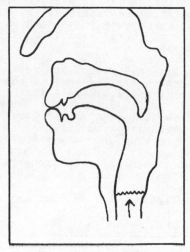

Fig. 4. [m]

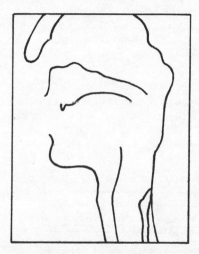

Fig. 5. Sample Static
Diagram to be Completed
by the Student

SEQUENCE DIAGRAMS FOR SOUNDS

Sounds are not caused by fixed positions of the vocal apparatus in the way
that the previous diagrams might seem to indicate. Actually these positions are very
fluid, with no time during which all the articulators are at rest. The movements flow
into one another in a smooth combination.
There is considerable overlapping movement
since the movements of the articulators of
the first sound tend to anticipate those
movements which will be consummated in the
second, and so on. For this reason the static
disgrams are best supplemented with SEQUENCE
types which show in a very rough way the
manner in which these articulations fade into
one another.

A sequence can be constructed by

utilizing a pair of parallel lines, one of
which symbolizes complete contact of an articulator with its point of articulation and
complete closure of the outlet at that point.
The other line, the bottom one, symbolizes
an articulator which is released or removed
from its point of articulation in such a way
as to leave the passage unimpeded at that
point. In Figure 6 notice that for [aiai]
the middle part of the tongue is approximately at the bottom of the mouth during the
production of [a], so that the passageway
through the mouth is open wide. This fact
is symbolized by the broken line which is
low in the diagram during that sound. For

Complete Closure
of Passageway: [a]   [i]   [a]   [i]

Movement of the
Articulator:

Complete Open-
ness of Passage-
way:

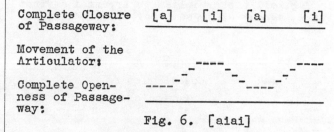

Fig. 6. [aiai]

Symbol for Middle of the
Tongue: ----

[i], however, the tongue is raised considerably and the passageway in the mouth is
narrowed, as the rising broken line indicates.

One cannot identify the exact border
between two sounds, since the movements slur
gradually into one another. One can make a
vague identification of the central moment
of the sound, however, by choosing the point
at which a moving articulator most closely
approaches its point of articulation (the
CREST or peak of movement), or by choosing
as the center of the sound that moment at
which a moving articulator is farthest from
its point of articulation (the TROUGH of
movement). In Figure 6 the crest of movement
for [i] produces a center of sound. The
trough of movement for [a] also produces the
center of a sound. From these statements it
follows that, within the limits of perception,
every movement of an articulator constitutes
a new sound when it reaches its crest or
trough, except that one sound, only, will be
created if two movements reach their centers
simultaneously.

The articulators are not all of equal
value in controlling the basic quality of the
sound. It proves convenient to classify them
as follows: PRIMARY articulators, those in
the mouth; SECONDARY articulator, the velic
in the nasal cavity; TERTIARY articulators,
those in the throat, including the vocal
cords. Thus in [b] the labial closure would
be primary and the vocal cord vibration
tertiary. When two articulators are acting
simultaneously in the mouth both of them
would be primary, but if one of them has a
lesser degree of closure it would be less
important to the final formation of the

quality of the sound and would here be considered subprimary. Thus in an [s] accompanied by rounded lips the articulation at the alveolar arch would be primary and the labial articulation would be subprimary.

The DEGREES OF CLOSURE within any one passageway may be given in descending order as follows: first, the greatest degree of closure is that which blocks the passageway completely; second, the next degree of closure is that which partially blocks the passageway and produces a strong audible friction at that point; third is that degree of closure which produces (very little or) no audible friction at the point of articulation. In Figure 7 the symbolism is arranged so that these degrees of closure may more readily be

division indicates the relaxation of the articulators indicated within it, or the openness of the passageway in which such articulators occur.[1] There is no local friction in these instances.

In Figure 7 notice the action of the lips in [abop]. For [b] and [p] the lips are closed but unrounded, whereas for [o] they are rounded. For [a], however, the lips are symbolized as further open and unrounded. The vocal cords are symbolized as being partially open when they are vibrating, since the general acoustic effect is that of an uninterrupted continuant even though the vocal lips are actually opening and closing.

In Figure 8 notice that the velic

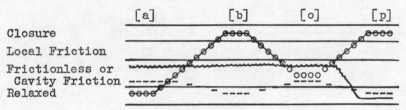

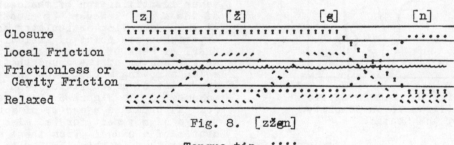

Fig. 7. [abop]

Lips unrounded ⊖⊖⊖⊖
Lips rounded ○○○○
Tongue mid ----
Vocal cords:
  Vibrating ∿∿∿
  Not vibrating ——

Fig. 8. [zžgn]

Tongue tip ····
Tongue blade ‚‚‚‚
Tongue back ˎˎˎˎ
Velic ''''
Vocal cords:
  Vibrating ∿∿∿

indicated. Any symbol which falls in the upper subdivision indicates complete closure of some passageway by the articulator indicated. A symbol occurring in the second subdivision indicates that there is strong local friction at the point of articulation and by the articulator symbolized. In the third subdivision the articulators are far enough from their points of articulation so that no local friction is caused by them, but at the same time the quality of sound is influenced in items like [i], [a], [o], by the degree of closure of the passageway. The lowest sub-

leaves the nasal passage open for [n] but closed for [zžg]. Notice also that the

---

[1]Occasionally it is convenient (as in Fig. 7 for [---] during [b] and [p]) to drop the symbolization of an articulator to the lower part of the diagram if that articulator is relatively open, frictionless, not under attention, or seems nonpertinent to the production of the major acoustic characteristics of a sound. These diagrams are schematic, and are not intended to be precise or "accurate."

tongue blade causes friction for [ž] rather
than the tongue tip as for [z], and that the
back of the tongue rather than the front
part causes friction for [g].

It should be emphasized that this
symbolism is highly arbitrary and makes no
attempt to indicate the minutiae of the articulation. The symbolism is nevertheless adequate to be of great value in helping the
student to understand how sounds are produced
and how the articulators act during them, as
well as in showing him the manner in which
the sounds slur into one another.[1] For
general usage, the exact point of articulation need not be indicated in these diagrams, but just the general region of articulation and the more important movements.

A single sound caused by the movement of a single articulator (or the synchronous movement of several articulators) may
be called a sound SEGMENT. In the sequence
[iaoaio], one can notice that the total
number of occurrences of segments is six,
but that the number of kinds of segments is
fewer--in this case three. In language one
must be prepared to recognize not only sounds
of different qualities, but one must also be
able to cut a continuum of sound into its
total number of successive segments. One
can illustrate the difference between kinds
and numbers of segments by the diagram of a
pie which is cut into five pieces, three of

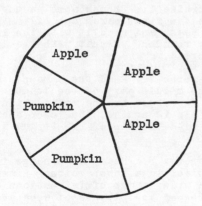

Fig. 9. Numbers and Kinds of
Segments Illustrated by a Pie
Plate Holding Two Kinds of Pie

Total number of occurrences of
segments: 5. Number of kinds
of segments: 2.

which are apple, but in which two of the
pieces of apple pie have been removed and
pumpkin pie substituted. In the pie as it
then stands the total number of occurrences
of segments of all types is still five even
though there are two kinds of segments. See
Figure 9.

---

[1]Foreshadowing Premise 1, of the presentation of phonemics.

Exercise 1. Draw segment diagrams[1]
showing the following items:

    (a) The vocal cords for [amtepzg]
    (b) The velic for [dgnefma]
    (c) The tongue back for [gaksuvo]
    (d) The lips for [apfpdm]
    (e) The tongue mid for [tiθega]
    (h) The tongue tip, vocal cords,
        and velic for [tʰa], [ta],
        [da].

Note the following key for symbols
to be used in diagramming.

KEY

Lips rounded   oooo
*Lips unrounded   ⊖⊖⊖⊖
Tongue tip ····
Tongue blade ⁄⁄⁄⁄
**Tongue mid ----
Tongue back ＼＼＼＼
Tongue sides ⌄⌄⌄⌄
Velic ⫶⫶⫶⫶
Vocal cords:
   Vibrating 〰〰
   Not vibrating ——

   * or labio-dental
  ** or somewhat front,
     as for front vowels

Exercise 2. Draw sequence diagrams
for the next paragraph, as pronounced in
your dialect of English. Symbolize all
articulators which were indicated in the
key in the preceding exercise. First,
write above the top line the phonetic (or
phonemic) symbols transcribing the phrase
or word to be charted. Then indicate the
movement of any one articulator throughout the entire phrase; following which
symbolize a second articulator, and so on.

---

[1]It will save class time or homework
time if the teacher has duplicated blanks
ready to be filled in.

PHONETIC EXERCISES FOR PRONOUNCING SOUND TYPES

MIMICRY

The student should be ready to mimic the speakers whom he hears. Every inflection, every lip movement, every tongue movement, every gesture--oral and non-oral--should be repeated by the student with as much fidelity as he can attain. He may "feel queer" in attempting to mimic but he should remember that he has a choice: (1) he may choose to appear queer to himself but less queer to the native because of the accurate reproduction of the sounds, or (2) he may choose to appear natural to himself but seem to the native speakers of that language to be very queer and "foreign" because of his carry-over of English sounds to the other language. In adult society within a single language group it is likely to appear highly discourteous for one person to mimic another, but when different languages are involved the speakers of the one are highly pleased when a foreigner attempts to speak their language flawlessly. The mimicry of foreign speakers with scrupulous attention to detail is socially commendable rather than rude. The student should take every opportunity, therefore, of trying to mimic native speakers, taking care to reproduce their sounds as accurately as possible.

It is also advantageous, although in this case socially unacceptable, to mimic the way in which foreigners speak English. If an English speaker can pronounce English so that it sounds the way it does when used by the speaker of a certain foreign language, the probability is that he will be able thereafter to speak the foreign language with a fairly acceptable pronunciation.

Mimicry of this type may be achieved strictly by trial and error. There is, however, a type of deliberate imitation which may be called EXPERIMENTAL MIMICRY. It is not necessary for the student to utilize blind mimicry which consists of the repetition of sounds endlessly until he gets them correctly. It is possible for him to practice his mimicry in another fashion. When he notices that he has failed to mimic a vowel correctly, for example, he may deliberately experiment with modifications of his tongue position or lip position or throat formation to see if by so doing he can come closer to the desired sound. By such a judicious and deliberate modification of sound he may save himself a great deal of time and actually get better results than he could otherwise.

Exercise 1. Attempt to mimic the speech of some foreign language which is accessible to you.

Exercise 2. Mimic the English of some foreigner who carries into his English speech the pronunciation habits of his native language.

Exercise 3. Repeat Exercises 1 and 2, adding mimicry of gestures.

In addition to attempting to mimic the individual sounds of a language, the student should be prepared to mimic the general patterns of the voice quality. This may be termed STYLE MIMICRY, and it can be subdivided into several general types.[1] Some of these characteristics are the following: general rounding of the lips, whether rounded, or somewhat spread, or with marked variation from spread to rounding; general tongue position, from front to back; general preciseness or laxness of articulation; the general tensity of the vocal cords; general breathiness or clarity of speech; the circumstances under which the general height of the voice may be raised; and so on.

Exercise 1. Choose some passage, for example the first paragraph of the preceding page, and read it with the lips heavily rounded. Repeat with the lips wide spread.

Exercise 2. Read the same passage with the middle part of the tongue thrust far front in the mouth while the tongue tip is against the lower teeth. Repeat with the tip of the tongue curled upward.

Exercise 3. Read the passage in a high voice; in a lower voice. Repeat, using a wider range of inflections or gaps between the pitches of separate syllables.

Exercises of this type can be very important. Practice with the front tongue position is especially helpful for American students since many languages which they may have to learn have a tongue position farther front than does English. Spanish would be one of that number.

Another highly important characteristic of good pronunciation consists of

---

[1]For further reference to them see Kenneth L. Pike, The Intonation of American English, University of Michigan Publication in Linguistics, I (Ann Arbor: University of Michigan Press, 1945), 99-103.

rhythmic types. In English one tends to hear STRESS-TIMED RHYTHM in contradistinction to a SYLLABLE-TIMED RHYTHM. In the syllable-timed type the syllables themselves tend to be more or less equally spaced and come at approximately even recurrent intervals. As a result of the syllable timing the vowels are likely to be clear cut and precisely articulated. In stress timing, on the other hand, some of the vowels may be drastically reduced in time and their precision of articulation and distinctive quality may be obscured. Since in this rhythmic style there is a tendency for the stressed syllables to occur at more or less evenly spaced intervals in time, and since between two such stresses there may be an indeterminate number of syllables, then if only one syllable comes between the stresses, it will be likely to receive more time, emphasis, and clarity than will three or four unstressed syllables if they all occur between the same two stresses. Compare, for example, the following sentences:

The 'teacher 'came.
The 'teacher is the one who 'came.

If now the length of time between the stressed syllables teach- and came is kept the same, then the syllables -er is the one who are more rapid than the -er of the first sentence. This jamming together of syllables modifies the quality of the vowels.

Exercise 1. Read some passage using syllable-timed rhythm. With a pencil, tap rapidly and evenly in pronouncing one syllable per tap of the pencil, and give to each syllable a certain amount of emphasis or stress. If a metronome can be obtained it may be easier to work with it.

Exercise 2. In the same paragraph mark stresses on syllables which should receive special attention and emphasis in the reading of normal English prose. Then tap regularly, but more slowly than before, or use a metronome. Pronounce a stressed syllable at each beat. Jam all extra syllables together fast enough to be able to keep the stresses evenly timed.

For American students the exercise in syllable timing is exceedingly important inasmuch as they are likely to jam together syllables of foreign languages which use timing different from that of English. For many foreigners speaking English, on the other hand, the exercise on stress timing is very helpful indeed, since it aids them to obtain a rhythmic handling of data according to recurrent stresses, and so procures automatic obscuring of the vowel qualities.[1]

---

[1]It frequently proves easier for a foreigner learning English, to obtain certain obscure English vowels by rhythm practice than by studying obscure vowels as such.

If a person can make various general adjustments of organic position and rhythmic style, such as the types just discussed, he can control with a few conscious adjustments a large number of additional specific modifications which follow automatically from these general ones. If, on the contrary, he tries to modify all consonants by thinking of each consonant in turn, he will find it impossible because the rate of speech of any language is too fast to allow him to do so. It is easier to adopt a general front tongue position than to try to front each sound individually. Basic adjustments can be consciously maintained and thereby bring with them mechanically any important modifications of sounds.

Practice in directed mimicry of this type and in general phonetic exercises such as are proposed in this volume lead to FLEXIBILITY of pronunciation. When the student meets a difficult sound which he cannot analyze, or whose differences from English are sufficiently minute to escape his attention, he may nevertheless pronounce the sound satisfactorily if, over a period of time, he has deliberately developed his capacity to mimic. General mimicry ability engenders general flexibility, and general flexibility allows for minor adjustments which are even more detailed than those which the student can handle analytically.

Sometimes students get the false impression that the best way to learn the difficult sounds of a particular language is to concentrate on them and to ignore any sounds which are similar to those in his own language or which do not occur in either language. This is an unfortunate impression. Even after the student has made all the major adjustments which he can handle consciously and easily, there may still remain dozens of minor adjustments needed. The best chance he has for making these is to have acquired a flexibility in pronunciation and a capacity for accurate mimicry developed by studying a wide variety of sounds.

VOCOIDS

A vocoid[1] is a sound which has air escaping (1) from the mouth, (2) over the center of the tongue (that is, not lateral),

---

[1]The value of utilizing the term "vocoid" instead of "vowel" here is the following: Certain sounds such as [i], [u], [ü], [r], and [h] may in some language occur in structural positions in sequences of sounds in the syllable or word, which are also occupied by sounds such as [t], [s], and [l]. In other languages the [i], [u], and so on, may occur in structural positions which are also occupied by [a], [o], [e]. In the first instance, [i], [u], [ü], [r], [h] are functioning as consonants. In the second instance they are functioning as vowels. Since the sounds themselves, as

(3) without friction in the mouth (but friction elsewhere does not prevent the sound from being a vocoid).

Exercises are needed for learning to pronounce[1] various types of vocoids.

---

such may be the same in each of the two instances, it is advantageous to utilize the term vocoid to represent the sounds in their phonetic character without regard to their distribution in sequences or their usage as consonants or vowels. In this way the inconsistency is avoided which would otherwise be introduced by using the term "vowel" to represent both the phonetic nature of the sounds and their phonemic distributional characteristics.

The inconsistency which would result from using the terms "vowel" and "consonant" in two ways, one phonetic and the other phonemic, can be seen in the following statement: "In Language A there are vowels and consonants [phonemic use of the terms]. Some of the vowels [phonetic use of the term] are vowels [phonemic use] and some of the vowels [phonetic use] are consonants [phonemic use]. Some of the consonants [phonetic use] are consonants [phonemic use] and some of the consonants [phonetic use] are vowels [phonemic use]." In the usage of the terms in the present volume, with vocoid restricted to phonetic use only, and vowel to phonemic use only, this same sentence might be reworked in some such way as follows: "In Language A there are vowel phonemes and consonant phonemes whose classification in one or the other of the two groups is determined by characteristics of their permitted distributions in sequences of sounds in larger structural units such as syllables or words. Most of these vowels are phonetically vocoids (such as [a], [e]), although one of two are phonetically nonvocoids (e.g. fricative [ɨ], which is syllabic and functioning as a vowel). Most of the consonants are nonvocoids (e.g. [p], [s], [m]), but a few are vocoids (e.g. nonsyllabic voiced [i] written as [y], and nonsyllabic voiceless [i] written as [h])."

[1]For learning to transcribe vocoids from dictation, the student needs a teacher or a colleague to dictate them to him. Items for dictation practice may be found in Eunice V. Pike, Dictation Exercises in Phonetics, (Glendale: Summer Institute of Linguistics, 1946).

Drills may be of three general types: PRODUCTION DRILLS for actually learning to make a sound, DIFFERENTIAL DRILLS for learning to tell them apart, and SKILL DRILLS for learning to hear them and produce them in difficult sequences of sounds. The drills suggested in this section are largely of a production and differential type. For obtaining further facility in the pronouncing of these sounds and the recording of them the student should dictate

Some[1] of them prove very difficult for speakers of English yet are highly important for the accurate pronunciation of the languages which contain them. If the student has achieved general ability for mimicry as described in the preceding paragraphs, the task of learning specific vocoids will be much easier.

Segmental Modification of Vocoids

Vocoids may be modified in quality, by the simultaneous change in some articulator. This is SEGMENTAL modification. Vocoids may also be modified by a change in pitch, or intensity, or length. This is SUPRASEGMENTAL modification.

Lip Modifications of Vocoids

Some vocoids have the lips rounded during their pronunciation. If the opening is large they are only slightly rounded. If the opening between the lips is small and

---

to one of his colleagues and receive dictation from his colleague in return, utilizing sequences of sounds in which these various types are mixed up and put in awkward combinations rather than being in simple syllable formations.

In taking dictation one hears certain sound combinations which appear clear to him. On the other hand, he is likely to find combinations of which he is doubtful. In order to keep in mind those sections which need further checking because he has not been certain of them at the first recording, it is convenient to put a wavy underline under any sound or sequence of sounds of which he is in doubt, e.g. [asa]. If, on the other hand, something appears surprising, but certain, he can indicate that he is sure of the sound or sequence of sounds by a double underline, e.g. [asa]. This is important when one comes to taking actual language material (1) since he can then concentrate on the more difficult parts, and (2) since he will not base theoretical conclusions of distribution and phonemic interpretation upon his more doubtful materials, and (3) since, when he at some later time finds the source of the difficulty, he can return and check in his data those points where the problem previously arose without being solved. In this way he can correct his material faster than he would otherwise be able to do.

[1]Various exercises similar to some of these are current in available literature on practical phonetics. Note especially Henry Sweet, A Primer of Phonetics, Third Edition (Oxford: Clarendon Press, 1906); Daniel Jones, An Outline of English Phonetics, Sixth Edition (New York: E. P. Dutton and Co., 1940); G. Noël-Armfield, General Phonetics, Fourth Edition (Cambridge: W. Heffer and Sons, 1931).

round the vocoids are heavily rounded. On the other hand, the lips may be unrounded or spread (See Figure 10) so that they are parallel to each other. In this case the opening between the lips is flat.

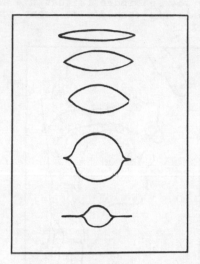

Fig. 10
Degrees of Lip Rounding

Exercise 1. In the following English words, which vowels are rounded? less heavily rounded? unrounded? Use your mirror to help you to answer the questions:

bought   beat
bait   boot
but   bit
bite

Exercise 2. What do you observe about the lip movement in the words bout and boat? Are the lips constantly rounded or unrounded, or do they become more or less rounded during the pronunciation of the vowels? How do these compare with your pronunciation of the words bought and boot?

Exercise 3. Pronounce slowly the vocoid a of the English word ma. Then while pronouncing the vowel, round the lips slightly until they are nearly closed but do not change the position of the tongue. Observe the lip change, in a mirror, and note the change in sound.

Exercise 4. Pronounce the vowel i as in beat.[1] Continue the sound and round the lips. Be very careful not to

change the position of the tongue. The vowel which results from this exercise is [ü]. If you have difficulty with it, try saying wiwiwi very fast while keeping the tongue position far front; or say [u], continue the sound, then while watching in a mirror to see that the lips remain rounded, deliberately push your tongue forward in the mouth.

Exercise 5. Pronounce the vowel u of boot. Continuing the sound, unround the lips but do not change the position of the tongue. By this exercise [u] should be changed into [ɨ].

Exercise 6. If you have difficulty pronouncing [ɨ], say [u], with a pencil hold the tongue back in the mouth and unround the lips as for [i]. Then pronounce [u] and with the fingers pull the corners of the lips apart.

Exercise 7. Take an English sentence pronouncing the syllables one after another. For each syllable, maintain the tongue position which you would normally have for the vowels, but round the lips sharply. Then repeat the syllable making the lips widespread.

Exercise 8. With a companion, practice mimicing rounded and unrounded vowels of all types and with different degrees of rounding. Note Figure 11 to see the unrounding and rounding of the lips in [uiu].

Tongue Modifications of Vocoids

The tongue can be moved somewhat from front to back in the mouth. Sounds pronounced with the tongue farther front differ from those which are pronounced with the tongue farther back.

all. The student should not, therefore, assume that the vocoids to be practiced are to be limited to those he uses in his own English speech. Starting from his own speech, which may differ from that of other students, he should rather learn by these exercises to modify the vocoids in various ways and to make them nonglided rather than dipthongized. By doing so, he can then achieve mimicry of any of the vocoids, regardless of the point from which he begins to learn them.

One of the most interesting schemes for indicating vowel quality and one of the most helpful on the practical level is that of the "Cardinal Vowels" of Daniel Jones. He sets up a chart indicating extreme vowel positions and has the sounds produced at these positions, illustrating them on phonograph records. Deviations from these norms can then be designated on charts. For a description of this technique see Daniel Jones, An Outline of English Phonetics, Sixth Edition (New York: E. P. Dutton and Co., 1940), Chapters VIII, XIV.

---

[1] The vocoid [i] has been illustrated as being approximately the sound in the English word beat. This type of definition by way of illustration is highly unsatisfactory inasmuch as speakers of English do not all pronounce their words in the same fashion. Some speakers pronounce the vowel of that word with no perceptible glide at

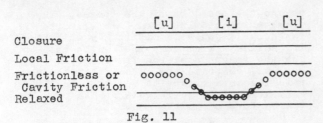

	[u]	[i]	[u]
Closure			
Local Friction			
Frictionless or Cavity Friction			
Relaxed			

Fig. 11

Lip Movement for [uiu]

Exercise 1. While keeping the lips spread wide apart, begin by pronouncing the vowel [i], continue the voicing for the sound and deliberately move the tongue back farther into the mouth, or push it back with a pencil, producing [ɪ]. Be sure that the tongue stays up high in the mouth, however, and does not drop down toward a low or central position. Reverse this procedure by slurring gradually from [i] to [ɪ].

Exercise 2. Slur slowly as before but this time stop the tongue movement when it gets halfway back to [ɪ] from [i] or halfway forward toward [i] from [ɪ]. This should produce the sound [ɨ], with an INTERRUPTED-SLUR drill.

Exercise 3. Again, have a slow slur from [i] towards [ɪ] but interrupt the slur halfway to [ɨ] so that you obtain [i] in a slightly backed variety, that is [i⁾].

Exercise 4. By exercising with interrupted slurs try to produce as many degrees of different vowel qualities between [i] and [ɪ] as you can.

Exercise 5. Some students find it easier to use a BRACKETING EXERCISE rather than one with interrupted slurs. In the bracketed type the vowels are pronounced in a clear-cut way with no gliding. First the front vowel is pronounced, then the back vowel, and then the student attempts to pronounce a variety in between the two. This is especially effective if the student is mimicing the instructor. Practice the following series of bracketed sets: [i, ɪ, ɨ]; [i, ɨ, ɨ<]; [i, ɨ<, i⁾]. Construct other such sets and pronounce them.

For practical phonetic drills of this type and for general descriptive terminology it is convenient to call [i] a FRONT vocoid and [ɪ] a BACK vocoid. If you will look at your mouth in a mirror during the pronunciation of these sounds you will notice that the tongue tip is quite front in the mouth even during the pronunciation of the back vowel [ɪ], and you might inquire as to why the [ɪ] is still called a back vocoid. The answer is that a phonetic statement of this type assumes that classification will be made in terms of the highest point of the

tongue.[1] Turning to your mirror again, you may observe that the tongue as a whole, including the highest part, is farther back for [ɪ] than for [i].

Notice in Figure 12 that the top of the tongue is diagrammed more front for [i] than for [ɪ].

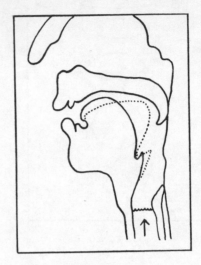

Fig. 12
Tongue Position for [i]——
Tongue Position for [ɪ] and
[u] ····

Exercise 1. Use interrupted slurs to start from the back rounded vowel [u] to glide toward the front rounded vowel [u], making as many different stages of sound as you can.

Exercise 2. Practice a bracketing exercise with [u, ü, ʉ]; [ü, ʉ, ʉ<]; etc.

Exercise 3a. If you have difficulty pronouncing [ü], begin by pronouncing the vowel [i] and then with the fingers deliberately pull the lips to rounded position.
3b. Or say [u]; watch in a mirror to

___

[1]As a matter of fact, the assumption cannot be justified. It is not just the highest point of the tongue which determines the vowel quality but the entire contour of the tongue tip, tongue body and root of the tongue, as well as the shape of the throat passages and the position of the lips, and so forth. Nevertheless it proves convenient for practical purposes to utilize a description in terms of this assumption. The inaccuracies which it certainly entails are not sufficiently great to prevent the student using the nomenclature and chart as convenient points of reference for learning to pronounce and write the sounds. With the systems of sample pronunciations from his instructor he is able to make a correlation between the acoustic quality of the sounds and this type of classification.

see that the lips do not move and then push the tongue front until you feel the tip of your tongue against your front teeth.

Just as there are degrees of tongue placement from front to back, so there may be degrees of tongue placement from HIGH to LOW. That is, the tongue may be closer to the top of the mouth or may be lowered within the mouth. Frequently the lowering of the tongue is accomplished by a lowering of the jaw, but this is not necessarily the case. Since the mouth tends to be more closed for the high types than for the low types, a high vocoid is said to be CLOSER than a low vocoid and a low vocoid is OPENER than a high one. The vocoid [i] of English beat, for example, is higher than the vocoid [æ] of English bat. (See Figure 13.)

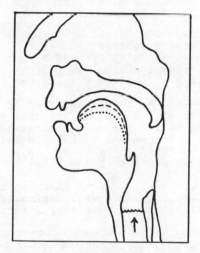

Fig. 13
Tongue Position for [i] ——
Tongue Position for [e] ----
Tongue Position for [æ] ....

Exercise 1. Slur slowly from [i] to [æ]. Repeat, in reverse.

Exercise 2. Use interrupted slurs to start from [i], gliding toward [æ] but stopping at [e]. Repeat by stopping halfway between [i] and [e].

Exercise 3. By using interrupted slurs make as many different sounds between [i] and [æ] as you can.

Exercise 4. By using bracketing exercises, try to get as many divisions as you can between [i] and [æ], that is [i, æ, e]; [i, e, e˅]; [i, e^, i˅], and so on.

Exercise 5. Did you find the sounds [ɛ] and [ɩ] of English bet and bit within the types which you made between [i] and [æ]?

Exercise 6. If you have difficulty making lowered varieties of [e] or [æ], pronounce [e] and [æ] in your normal

way and lower the jaw deliberately. Reverse these directions to get closer varieties of the same sounds or other sounds.

The sounds [i] and [æ] tend to be somewhat TENSE. The sounds [ɩ] and [ɛ] of bit and bet tend to be LAX. It is this fact which allows one at times to slur from [i] to [æ] without going through the vocoid qualities of [ɩ] and [ɛ].

Exercise 1. Slur from [ɩ] to [ɛ].

Exercise 2. Use an interrupted-slur technique to get as many possible subdivisions of the slur in between these two as you can. That is, pronounce [ɩ^, ɩ, ɩ˅, ɛ^, ɛ, ɛ˅].

Exercise 3. Try to get similar results from using a bracketing technique. For example, [ɩ, ɛ, ɛ^].

Exercise 4. In slurring from [ɩ] to [ɛ] did you go through the vocoid quality of [e]? It is possible but not essential to go through [e] in this slur.

Exercise 5. In pronouncing [æ] do you feel any tenseness of the throat? In some dialects of American English [æ] is especially tense.[1]

Notice in Figure 13 that [æ] has a lower tongue position than [e].

There can be a vocoid which is lower than [æ] but still front in the mouth. This may be written with the printed letter [a][2] and is heard, for example, in the pronunciation of Eastern New England half, or in some dialects of southern English at the beginning of the pronunciation of the word eye.

Exercise 1. Pronounce this low front vowel [a]. How does it compare in your speech with the pronunciation of the sound of ma? father? top? past?

We now have the mechanism for classifying the production of many more vocoids. Vocoids can differ in tongue position by being relatively front, relatively back, or relatively central. Likewise the tongue position can be high, or low, or in an intermediate position. For higher and lower varieties within the three divisions high, mid, low, we get close high and open high, close mid and open mid, close low and open low. They can be combined into a chart, as

[1] Foreign speakers who have difficulty with [æ] should try for considerable throat tension, or to mimic the "baa" of a sheep.

[2] Except when it is pertinent to differentiate between [a] and [ɑ], both varieties will for convenience be written elsewhere in this volume as [a].

note Figure 14.

		Front	Central	Back
High	Close	i	ɨ	ɯ̈
	Open	ʟ		ʊ̈
Mid	Close	e	ə	
	Open	ɛ	ʌ	
Low	Close	æ		
	Open	a	ɑ	

Fig. 14.   Tongue Position of Chart
for Certain Unrounded Vocoids

As we have already indicated, tongue
positions are classified for practical
purposes roughly but not accurately in terms
of the highest point of the tongue.[1]   The
grid or chart just illustrated in Figure 14
may be superimposed upon the mouth so that
the relationship between the oral tongue
position and the classification on the chart
can be more clearly seen.   Notice Figure 15
in which the grid is thus superimposed on
the face diagram.

With these variables from high to
low and front to back we can continue to
make many more sounds.   Beginning with [u],
for example, one can retain lip rounding
and lower the tongue gradually to [o] and
[ɔ], and so on.

Exercise la.   Pronounce [u], advance
by interrupted slurs to [ɔ], making as
many intermediate vocoids as you can.

_____

[1]X-ray studies of vowel positions for
English indicate that the rectangle presented
in this volume for the vocoid classification
is not an accurate des-
cription of the place of
the highest portion of the
tongue during the vocoid.
Possibly the rectangle should be modified
somewhat like this.

Notice in this last diagram that
[e] is a bit farther back than [i], and [ʟ]
is likewise farther back than [i].   We will
have occasion to describe the sounds in this
way in the latter part of the volume when
we wish to show that [i] before a back [k]
is likely to be drawn back in tongue position towards [ʟ] or even [e].

There are various other technical
objections to the accuracy of a "Vowel
Triangle" scheme of any kind--but its
practical usefulness seems to be well established.

For a brief discussion of the theoretical problems involved, consult Daniel
Jones, _An Outline of English Phonetics_, 6th
Edition (New York: E. P. Dutton and Co.,
1940), 36-38.

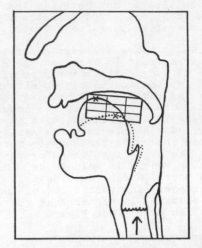

Fig. 15.   Vocoid Grid Super-
imposed on Face Diagram.
Highest Point of Tongue x
Tongue Position for [a]····
Tongue Position for [i]——

Note: For the lower varieties of vocoids,
the lips do not need to be quite so
rounded as for the higher varieties.
lb.   Try, also, to get the intermediate varieties by using the bracketing
technique previously described.

Exercise 2.   Repeat Exercise 1 but
with the lips unrounded, beginning with
[ɨ] and going progressively lower.

Exercise 3.   How much lower can you
go than [ɔ], in producing a low back
rounded vocoid?   Produce the same
vocoid, then unround it.

Exercise 4.   By interrupted slurs or
by bracketing of the vocoids produce as
many low unrounded vocoids as you can
from front to back.   Repeat for rounded
vocoids.

Exercise 5.   Produce as many vocoids
rounded and unrounded as you can, beginning with high close central unrounded
[ɨ] and slurring to low open central unrounded [ɑ].   In this set the central
point between [ɨ] and [ɑ] should be somewhat like one or other of the vowels in
the word _above_.

General flexibility in the producing
of vocoids is highly advantageous, and the
student should have various kinds of drills
to teach him control.   The following exercises
are helpful.

Exercise 1.   Produce as many minute
varieties of [i] as you can--raised,
lowered, backed, fronted, backed and
lowered, and so on.   Repeat for other
vocoid types.

Exercise 2.   Draw a line across the

vocoid chart at any angle. Attempt to pronounce vocoid qualities at each point on the line.

Exercise 3. Dictate a vocoid to one of your colleagues and have him describe the lip formation and tongue position.

Exercise 4. Dictate to a colleague a vocoid glide beginning from one tongue or lip position, or combination, and slurring to a second and third. Have your colleague point out on the vocoid chart the progress of the tongue position during the slur.

Exercise 5. Dictate to a colleague ten vocoids. Have him write them down with appropriate symbols.[1] Repeat, using combinations of two syllables with one vocoid or vocoid glide in each syllable.

Exercise 6a. Try saying all of the English vowels with the teeth together. In terms of the vowel chart, what differences do you hear?
6b. Repeat with the lips spread wide apart.
6c. Repeat with the mouth wide open.
6d. Repeat with the mouth wide open and the lips somewhat rounded.

Speakers of English are likely to utilize vocoid glides[2] from one tongue position to another, or from one lip formation to another, within their words. Thus in the English word boat there is likely to be some lip movement, with more rounding at the end of the syllable nucleus than at its beginning. Speakers of English need to practice assiduously to be able to pronounce nonglided vocoids (that is, "level" and "pure" vocoids) in order that they will not transfer to other languages glides which are undesirable there.

Exercise 1. Pronounce [o] and continue it, timing it for three seconds. During this time watch yourself in a mirror and make certain that no lip movement occurs--especially at the moment that the vocoid ceases, inasmuch as you are most likely to have rounding at that time.

Exercise 2. Practice nonglided [e], beginning with pronunciations of the vocoid for three seconds and then gradually shortening them until they can be pronounced without any tongue or lip movement.

Exercise 3. Dictate to a colleague some nonglided vocoids in contrast to glided vocoids. Have him write them down with appropriate symbols and then attempt to pronounce them as you dictated them.

After exercises of this type the student is ready to practice on actual language material.

Exercise 1. Locate some speaker of a foreign language. Ask him to pronounce words from that language. Mimic his pronunciation.

Exercise 2. Determine the tongue position and lip formation for his vocoids.

Exercise 3. Attempt to record his pronunciation with phonetic symbols. Be especially careful not to give unwarranted glides to the nonglided vocoids which the speaker may pronounce.

Exercise 4. If you have difficulty in pronouncing any of the vocoids, use directed experimental mimicry by starting with the vocoid from your speech which is most like the one he pronounces. Then deliberately make modifications of it by raising, lowering, backing, fronting, rounding, unrounding, gliding, etc., to try to attain a pronunciation which satisfies your ear as being similar--and one which the informant will accept and understand.

Exercise 5. For samples of various sounds indicated here consult the restricted language problems given in Part II, and try to read them.

Vocoid Modification by Retroflexion

When vocoids are produced with the general heights and positions of the tongue as previously described but at the same time with the tip of the tongue curled slightly up (and sometimes back), vocoid types are RETROFLEX: See Fig. 16 for a diagram of retroflex [u].

Exercise 1. Pronounce [e] with a retroflex tongue tip. Pronounce other vocoids similarly.

Exercise 2. To a colleague dictate some retroflexed vocoids in contrast to some nonretroflexed vocoids. Have your colleague attempt to mimic them and record them with appropriate symbols, putting a dot under the vocoid symbol to show its retroflexion.

Exercise 3. Read some paragraph of this textbook, with the tongue tip turned up throughout the entire selection. Note the resultant quality of the vowels and the modifications of the consonants.

---

[1]If you need a symbol not indicated on Chart 1, make one up; or indicate departures from symbols already given you by the modifying symbols [ᐸ], [ᐳ], [^], [ᵛ] or combinations of them.

[2]The term "diphthong" is in general avoided in this book because it causes confusion due to various current usages of the term. See Glossary.

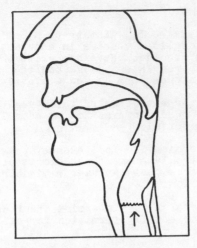

Fig. 16. [u̥]

Exercise 4. Pronounce [ta, na, la]
with the tongue tip retroflexed for the
nonvocoids [t], [n], and [l]. Do the
retroflexed nonvocoids affect the sound
of the contiguous vocoids?

Vocoid Modification by Nasalization

While the tongue and lip positions
are arranged to give any vocoid the passage
through the nose may be open or closed by the
velic. Vocoids which have simultaneous
egressive air through the nose are said to
be NASALIZED, inasmuch as the oral timbre is
modified by nasal resonance. Those vocoids
without this simultaneous nasal egress, but
with air escaping through the mouth only,
are ORAL. See Figure 17. In spite of the
nasalization, the quality still considered
basic to the vocoid is that part of it which
is determined by the mouth and lip positions.
Modifications caused by the mouth are considered secondary. The nasal modification
then is of a lower degree than the oral formation.

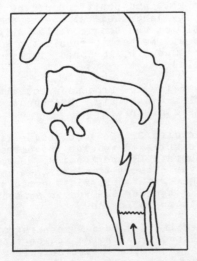

Fig. 17 [e̜]

Exercise 1. Pronounce [a, i, u].
Then lower the velic to leave the nasal
passage open and pronounce [a̜, i̜, u̜].
Repeat for various vocoids.

Exercise 2. Get facility in nasalization by the following exercise which
alternates nasalized and non-nasalized
vocoids. Do not allow a glottal stop or
a pause to come in between the vocoids:
[aa̜aa̜].

Exercise 3a. If you have difficulty
in pronouncing nasalized vowels, get a
colleague to pronounce them for you and
try to learn them by mimicry.
3b. Or say [m], pulling the lips
apart with your fingers and continue trying to say [m]. Once you get a nasalized
vowel in this fashion practice until you
can get the same effect deliberately
without having to use your fingers to
open the lips. Then continue on until
you can pronounce other nasalized vocoids.

Exercise 4. Pronounce the nasalized
vocoid [a̜] and pinch the nostrils closed.
Note that the vocoid continues[1] but that
the quality changes; this vocoid quality
does not occur if the nostrils are closed
during the pronunciation of non-nasalized
[a]. Another test which has been suggested for nasalization is to hold a
mirror in front of the nose during the
pronunciation of the [a̜]. The mirror becomes moistened, indicating that air is
escaping from the nose.

Exercise 5a. Some people have difficulty in pronouncing vocoids which are
not nasalized, since in their ordinary
English speech they tend to "speak
through the nose." For these people exercises are needed to pronounce oral
vocoids rather than nasalized ones. The
following is suggested: Look in a mirror
and yawn. Notice that the soft palate
tends to rise so that the velic closes
the nasal passage. Say [a] with the
velic in this position. Contrast that
with your particular pronunciation of
[a]. Repeat this contrast slowly until
you can get conscious rapid control of
the velic movement for the sequence
[aa̜aa̜a].
5b. If you have difficulty pronouncing non-nasalized [a], practice with
[i]; high vowels are sometimes easier for
the elimination of nasalization. Try
voiced sibilants such as [z] and [ž] before the vowel; these are difficult to
nasalize and may help you to start the
syllable non-nasal. In words or syllables

---

[1]Some people in trying to say [a],
say [an] instead. To correct this, attempt
to say [ŋ] and pinch the nostrils closed.
If the sound is stopped you will know that
the oral passage is closed, since with [a]
both nose and mouth should serve as an escape
for air.

with nasal nonvocoids, however, the difficulty is greatest; practice these syllables slowly; at first you may pause or hesitate between the vocoid and the nonvocoid in order to help prevent nasalization carrying over from the one to the other; then practice for rapid control: [a-n], [an]; [o-n], [on].

5c. Sequences such as [bmbmbm] are said to increase velic control; some transfer might be made to [aạaạ].

Modifications of Vocoids by Changes at the Vocal Cords

The vocoids discussed thus far have all been voiced. Voicing was caused by the "vibration" of the vocal cords during the production of the sound. Vocoids can be produced, however, which have identical lip and tongue positions but during which the vocal cords are far enough apart so that they do not vibrate. If the vowels are pronounced with a light air stream and without strong friction in the throat, one may call them BREATHED. If however, the vocal cords are close enough together so that there is clearly audible friction there, the vocoids are WHISPERED.[2]

A different type of vibration--possibly with shorter total contact time and with smaller movements at the edges of the vocal lips-- is called FALSETTO. Vocoids of various qualities, nasalized or non-nasalized, may be made in falsetto. Most men make falsetto sounds with no difficulty. Fewer women can do so; for some of them falsetto appears as a "squeaky voice" or a "screaming voice."

A further type of vocal cord vibration is TRILLIZATION. It seems to be a glottal trill, and can be produced by most people by trying to sing in a very low voice until their pronunciation degenerates to a "growl" or "rattle."[3] On the other hand, this trillization does not have to be pronounced with low pitch but can be speeded up until the vibration becomes so fast that the separate taps of the trill merge into a continuous hum. This latter is known as the "ventriloqual drone" and may be used for getting the effect of distant voices. For producing it one starts with the slow trillization first referred to and then with extremely tense

muscles of the abdomen and throat, one forces the pitch to ascend.[1] Trillization can be produced in falsetto as well as with regular voice.

LARYNGEALIZATION is a label which may be applied to a type of vocal cord vibration which combines some of the quality of normal voicing with the roughness of trillization.

Exercise 1. Isolate the sounds of hat by first pronouncing the word very slowly. Then pronounce the sounds separately as [h-æ-t]. Now that you have isolated the [h] analyze it phonetically. What is the tongue position for this vocoid? the lip position? Choose ten other English words spelled with [h]; isolate the [h] quality, and analyze the vocoids. Do you observe any relationship between the quality of the vocoid in these instances and the voiced vocoid which they precede?

Exercise 2a. Read some sentence aloud. Then repeat it, utilizing voiceless vocoids instead of voiced ones.
2b. Repeat again with voiceless vocoids with strong friction at the glottis.
2c. Repeat with audible friction but with voiced vocoids.
2d. Repeat with trillization and with laryngealization.

Exercise 3. Pronounce some vocoids; try to analyze their formation. Then whisper them, repeating your analysis. Note that sometimes analysis is easier during the whisper.

Pharyngeal Modifications of Vocoids

In addition to the modifications at the vocal cords, other changes in the throat can affect the vocoids. Regardless of the changes which occur in the throat, the sounds are still vocoids provided that the air stream continues with a nonlateral escape, and provided that there is no friction in the mouth.

All of the vocoids previously described can be modified by amplifying the throat cavity to make them have a different type of resonance--one which sounds "fuller" or "deeper." This amplification may occur (1) by the lowering of the larynx (which can be seen by observing the lowering of the Adam's apple) or (2) by the fronting of the tongue so that the root of the tongue is farther from the wall of the throat and/or (3) by the spreading apart of the faucal pillars at the upper back part of the throat

---

[1]Or open only at the arytenoid cartilages.

[2]Breathed or whispered vocoids are called "voiceless vowels" when they act in phonemic distribution like other vowels or when they constitute nonphonemic varieties of voiced vowels. When, however, the voiceless vocoids are phonemically consonants they are called varying timbers of "h." Those voiced vocoids with audible glottal friction which pattern as consonants are called "voiced h."

[3]Somewhat like a stick drawn along a picket fence.

[1]Data from an unpublished paper presented to the summer meeting of the Linguistic Society of America, August 3, 1946, at Ann Arbor: Kenneth L. Pike, "The Phonetic Basis of Ventriloquism."

behind the mouth.[1]

The lifting of the larynx (observed by noting the Adam's apple rising), the narrowing of the throat (seen by the lifting of some of the muscles above the Adam's apple), and the tightening of the faucal pillars (observable in a mirror by noticing the muscles of the faucal pillars like two curtains being brought close together--see Figure 18), give an opposite effect; these vocoids appear to be "harsh," "thin," and "unpleasing." The tenseness and harshness which comes from the FAUCALIZATION of the vocoids sometimes gives a quality approximating that which comes from nasalization; the various throat changes discussed, however, may be handled independently of the opening or closing of the nasal passage and in each case produce modifications of sound which are distinct from those caused by the lowering of the velic.

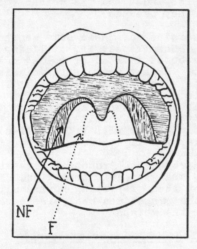

Fig. 18. [a]
Nonfaucalized ——
Faucalized   ....

Exercise 1. Pronounce a long contiguous [a]. Move the back of the tongue further back into the mouth until the vocoid becomes somewhat "choked up" but is still discernably [a]. This type of modification of the sound may be called PHARYNGEALIZATION. (See Figure 19). Pronounce a pharyngealized [o]. Pronounce a pharyngealized [i]; is this more difficult than pronouncing a pharyngealized [o]? If so, how do you account for that fact?

Exercise 2. Look in a mirror, open your mouth wide, pronounce [a] with very tense throat movements--attempting to make the faucal pillars draw together,

and to produce a harsh-sounding vocoid. Try to pronounce the same vocoid quality with voicelessness. Notice that the result is a much higher-pitched whisper than the nonfaucalized voiceless [a].

Exercise 3. Try to pronounce some of the vocoids with the larynx lowered and with the root of the tongue relatively far front in the mouth. How would you characterize the resultant vocoid quality?

Modification of Vocoids by Direction of Air Stream

All the vocoids so far discussed are produced with the air stream proceeding outward from the lungs. In general these same vocoids may be produced by an ingressive air stream drawn into the lungs. The quality of these inverse vocoids is likely to be somewhat different, however, from the egressive ones. Ingressive vocoids seem to appear rarely as regular language sounds.[1]

Vocoid Practice in Sequences

There is considerable difference in the formation or production of some such soun sound by itself in isolation and the same sound in sequences of other sounds. The muscle movements producing it may differ somewhat, and the actual sound itself may be

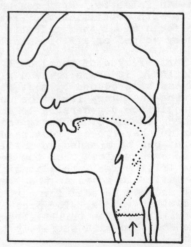

Fig. 19. [a]
Nonpharyngealized——
Pharyngealized   ....

[1]An ingressive lung-air vocoid is commonly used among a number of small tribes, for example the Wazanaki in the Musoma District, Tanganyika Territory, East Africa. It is used in giving assent to a statement or in giving a positive answer to a question. It sounds like a jerky gasp for breath; usually it is voiceless but often it is accompanied by a slight quick raising of the head.

Data from J. Clyde Shenk

---

[1]These observable phenomena affect the tone quality (1) by changing the actual size and shape of the throat and (2) by modifying the tension of certain of the muscles. These latter characteristics will not be discussed here.

modified. Experience shows, however, that
the student who wishes to produce a strange
speech sound can speed up his mastery of
that sound a great deal if he will learn to
produce it in isolation first and then
practice making any modifications necessary
so as to work it into the sequence. One
must not assume that the difference between
sounds pronounced in isolation and sounds
produced as part of a sequence is so great
that there can be no pedagogical connection
in making a transfer from the one to the
other.

For practicing vocoids in successive
syllables utilize the following exercises:

Exercise 1. Select a passage of
English prose. Write it phonetically,
according to your own pronunciation.
Then substitute various types of non-
English vocoids for the ones written,
and read the passage aloud. Repeat with
a different set of substituted vocoids.

Exercise 2. Then write the passage
in reverse, including in it the substituted vocoids. Read the material aloud.

Suprasegmental Modification of Vocoids

Quantitative Modification of Vocoids

Vocoids may be long or short relative
to others in the stream of speech. Whether
or not the length is significant to the
language depends upon nonphonetic factors
such as structure and contrast which will be
discussed later under phonemic procedures.
Meanwhile, however, the student may assume
that [a] represents a rather average-length
vocoid in speech with a vague undefined norm,
but that [a] plus [:] prepesents a vocoid
more than twice as long, whereas [a] with a
raised dot [·] symbolizes a vocoid with
length halfway between them.

Exercise 1. Read aloud the following
material, and in each instance make the
first syllable stressed: ['pa:papa];
syllables for reading aloud. Dictate
some of these sets to a colleague and
have him write them down and mimic them.
Then in turn take dictation from your
colleague.

Exercise 2. Take an English passage
and at various points in it put length
marks following the vocoids. Read the
passage aloud at normal speed but at the
indicated places make the vowels extra
long.

Intensity Modification of Vocoids

Some vocoids may be pronounced with
greater intensity then others. If vocoids
with weak intensity or with average intensity
are written simply as [a] and those with
heavier stress are written as ['a], while
those with extra intensity are symbolized as
["a], the student may obtain initial practice

in pronouncing and recording stress even
though the phonemic interpretation of the
number of significant relative intensities
must await analysis under the phonemic procedures.

Sometimes the vocoid quality tends
to be modified under emphatic stress.
Vocoids under heavy stress are likely to be
longer and clearer and perhaps a bit more
glided (dipthongized) than the same vocoids
without stress. When they become very weak,
vocoids tend to become somewhat obscure in
quality (usually to be interpreted as a shift
of tongue position toward the central mid
classification).

Exercise 1. Practice reading the
following sequences of syllables:
[pa"pa'pa]; ['papa"pa]. Prepare similar
items for reading and dictation to a
colleague.

Exercise 2. Read a passage of
English in your normal voice. How many
degrees of stress do you seem to hear?
Mark them with these symbols. If you
need a fourth symbol, utilize a lowered
stress mark, [ˌa], for an intermediate
degree between [a] and ['a].

Pitch Modification of Vocoids

The frequency of vibration of the
vocal cords during one syllable may be
greater or less than for other syllables in
the same sentence. As with stress and
quantity, the number of significant pitch
levels cannot be determined by instrumental
measurements but must be discovered by means
of phonemic procedures of the types which
will be handled later. Meanwhile, however,
the student should practice pitch control by
setting up a vague norm which he can consider
average height for him, and should then write
syllables which are higher or lower with
symbols ['] and [`] respectively.

Exercise 1a. Read aloud the following items: [pápàpa]; [pápapà]; [pàpapá];
[pápápà]; pàpápà]; [pàpapà]. Make up
other sets for dictation to a colleague
and in turn take dictation from him.

1b. In the following groups, note
the glides: [pápápá]; [pápàpàapá].

1c. In practicing pitch one must be
careful not to confuse it with stress.
In the following exercises notice that
some of the stressed syllables are low-
pitched, and that some of the high syllables are unstressed: ['pàpápá];
[pá'pàpá]; [pápà'pa]; ['pápápá];
[pàpá'pá]; ['pàpàápàá]; [pá'pàápá].

Exercise 2a. Take a passage of
English prose and mark it with tones on
syllables without regard to their stress
or normal pronunciation. Then read the
material aloud. Note: Speakers of English
are used to handling stress in their
speech, and must be careful not to bring
to a tone language their English stress

habits.

2b. Practice reading the material marked for pitch, but without making strong stress differences.

Exercise 3a. Practice hearing pitch by learning to read English marked for intonation;[1] this is the best initial practice for the English speaker.

3b. Practice reading a passage utilizing only one type of intonation contour throughout.

Vocoid Modifications by Placement in the Syllable

Vocoids which are syllabic tend to be relatively more prominent than those which are nonsyllabic. When certain of the vocoids produced by high tongue position--especially [i] and [u]--are nonsyllabic and glide into a following syllabic vocoid, they impress the English hearer as being "y" and "w" respectively. When they are following the syllabic this tendency is less strong. The interpretation of glided or nonglided [i] and [u] as consonantal or vocalic must be determined by the application of the phonemic procedures.

NONVOCOIDS

The previous sections have discussed vocoid sounds, that is, types in which air escapes from the mouth over the center of the tongue without friction in the mouth. Now NONVOCOID sounds will be considered. These include any sound in which the air stream escapes from the nose but not the mouth; sounds in which air escapes from the mouth but over the side of the tongue; sounds in which air escapes from the mouth but with friction localized at some point in the mouth; and sounds during which the air stream has no escape.

Nonvocoid Fricatives with a Pulmonic Air Stream

Nonvocoids with Oral Friction

The first set of nonvocoids to be practiced may well be those in which strong FRICTION is produced at some point in the mouth. Since these sounds are CONTINUANTS (that is, capable of being pronounced so long as one has breath, like the vocoids), they differ from the STOPS in which the air stream is momentarily but completely interrupted.

Of the fricative continuants some are made with FLAT contact so that the air escapes through a narrow slit. Such a flat

narrow opening may be produced by the near contact of the two lips or by the lower lip contacting the upper teeth (in which the air escape may be through the interstices of the teeth, rather than between the lip and lower edges of the teeth), or by the tip, or blade, or middle, or back of the tongue nearly touching some point at the top of the mouth.

Exercise 1a. Place the lips close together but not quite touching; have the corners drawn well back so that the slit between the lips is relatively flat. Blow. Note the fricative sound.

1b. Pronounce this sound before the vowel [a], as in [ɸa]; between vowels as in [aɸa]; following vowels as in [aɸ].

1c. Dictate such items to a colleague and receive dictation in return.[1]

1d. If you have difficulty in making the sound [ɸ], an exaggerated type can be made by thrusting out the lower lip in such a way that upon blowing you can "feel the wind on your nose" or "blow the hair out of your eyes."

Exercise 2a. Pronounce [f] as in English fine.

2b. Make up and practice sets of syllables differentiating [ɸa] and [fa].

2c. If you are not a native speaker of English and have difficulty pronouncing the labio-dental fricative, first place the lower lip deliberately against the upper teeth and then blow. Obtain linguistic control of this pronunciation by combining it with vowels of various types.

Exercise 3a. Place the tip of the tongue between the teeth. Blow. How does this sound compare with the [θ] in your pronunciation of English think? Foreigners who do not have this sound should practice it in different sequences in order to obtain linguistic control of it: [θa], [aθa], [aθ], and so on. See Figure 20.

3b. Keeping the tongue tip flat as it is for [θ], draw it back until it is below the alveolar arch but not quite touching there. Blow. Notice that a duller or lower-pitched variety of the sound is obtained. Make certain that the tongue tip is flat and not grooved, lest a type of [s] will result.

Exercise 4a. Place the middle of the tongue against the top of the mouth as for the [k] in [ka]. Lower the tongue slightly so that there is a small opening between the top of the mouth and the tongue. Then blow sharply. Harsh friction somewhat like a high-pitched whisper should result. See Figure 21.

---

[1]Material for practice may be found in Kenneth L. Pike, The Intonation of American English, University of Michigan Publications in Linguistics, I (Ann Arbor: University of Michigan Press, 1945).

[1]As for the vocoids, so for the nonvocoids, lists of nonsense syllables and language samples for practice may be found in Eunice V. Pike, Dictation Exercises in Phonetics, (Glendale: Summer Institute of Linguistics, 1946).

4b. Continue this friction for at least three seconds to be certain that you have control of it.

4c. Work for linguistic control of this sound by combining it with vowels as follows: [axa], [xa], [ax].

4d. Again pronounce the sound as before, making sure, however, that the tongue is not touching the top of the mouth at the beginning of the sound, in order to be certain that you are not pronouncing [k] plus [x], but merely [x].

Exercise 5a. If you have difficulty pronouncing the sound, start to say [aka] very slowly but as the tongue approaches the top of the mouth for the [k] prevent it from touching so that a small air escape is left.

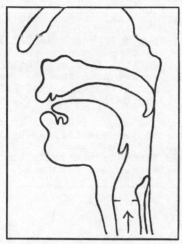

Fig. 20. [θ]

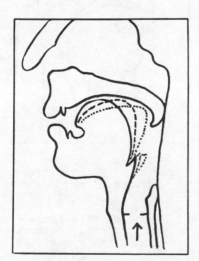

Fig. 21
Tongue Position for [x] ——
Tongue Position for [x̱] - - - -
Tongue Position for [x̣] · · · ·

5b. Or try to say [k] but put on sufficient pressure to "squeeze" the air stream out over the top of the tongue.

5c. Or ask a colleague who can pronounce the sound to do so for you. Then mimic the pitch of the "whisper."

5d. If you have difficulty with [x], say [kakakaka] fast, with increasing speed, until finally the tongue no longer touches the top of the mouth but the air escape continues.

Exercise 6a. Begin with the [x] which you learned in the previous exercise. Make a similar type of sound but with the tongue thrust forward on the hard palate so as to produce a fronted [x̱]. Notice the high pitch of the whisper. Practice for linguistic control of the sound by pronouncing and hearing it with vowels.

6b. Pull the tongue back farther in the mouth (or make near-contact against the velum with a farther back portion of the tongue) for a backed variety of [x], that is [x̣]. Notice the lowered pitch of the fricative whisper. Practice for linguistic control of the sound by pronouncing and hearing it with vowels.

6c. Speakers of English are likely to find it relatively simple to pronounce [x̱] before [i], or [x] before [a], or [x̣] before [u], but find it much more difficult to combine [x̣] with [a] and [x̱] with [i]. Practice pronouncing, hearing and recording drills such as the following: [x̱i, x̣a]; [x̣a, x̱i]; [ix̱, ix̣]; [ax̣ax̱], [ux̣ux̱], etc.

6d. If you still have difficulty in making the sound, pretend that a little piece of paper has stuck to the top of the mouth back on the soft palate. Try to "blow it off" by making friction there between the tongue and the velum.

6e. Or clear the throat as for spitting, with a rising pitch as you progressively scrape with a friction noise. The higher pitch of the scrape is probably some variety of [x].

Exercise 7. Ask a colleague who can pronounce these sounds to give you a far front [x̱] with its high pitch. Then ask him to gradually retract his tongue, a bit at a time, with corresponding lowering of pitch. Mimic the pitch of the "whisper" and by so doing practice minute placement distinctions of the tongue for varieties of [x]. See Figure 21. Continue to lower the pitch of the whisper until the tongue is touching at the back of the soft palate or at the uvula. Caution: Keep the corners of the lips spread apart, since lip rounding will change the pitch of the whisper without giving desired tongue-placement modification.

Instead of having a flat opening, some sounds are produced with a grooved or rounded opening.

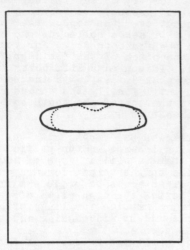

Fig. 22
Cross Section of Shape of
Tongue Tip for [θ] ——
[s] ····

Exercise 1. Round the lips sharply
until there is a small round opening
between them. Blow as you might for putting out a lighted candle. Obtain
linguistic control of the sound by
practicing it with vowels.[1] Thus:·
[Wa, aW, aWa].

Exercise 2a. Move the tip of the
tongue toward the alveolar arch just
below the upper gum. Bring the tip
slowly downward with a small grooved
shape. See Figure 22. Blow, focusing
the air against the back of the teeth.
How does the sound you obtain compare
with your pronunciation of the [s] in
English see? A slight grooving of this
type tends to produce a hissing sound
called a SIBILANT.

_____

[1]The lips should be closed enough
so that there is audible friction at that
point. If there is no friction noticeable
there, but the lip rounding merely contributes to the total shape of the oral
cavity in such a way as to modify the
resonance of the oral chamber, the [W]
would be a voiceless vocoid rather than a
voiceless nonvocoid. Now all of the
voiceless vocoids have a certain amount
of friction, but, (1) this friction is of a
very light type; and (2) it frequently is
not localized at any one point but rather
sounds like the type of friction which one
obtains by blowing through a tube; and (3)
the friction disappears if the sound is
voiced. This type of very light general
friction is here called "frictionless" or
"cavity friction." The term fricative is
used for a stronger friction which can be
localized at some one point such as the
lips or tongue tip.

2b. Contrast this [s] with the
sound produced when the tongue is in the
same position but without the groove.
Can you hear a difference between [s]
and [θ]?

Exercise 3. Maintain the general
tongue formation for [s] but thrust the
tongue farther front into the mouth so
that the tongue tip is against the teeth
or even protruding slightly beyond them.
Blow. Notice that this fronted [s̪] has
a little higher pitch or sharper sound
than the English type of [s]. If
foreigners use this fronted variety instead of our own, we tend to interpret
it as a lisp. Actually, however, this
is quite different from the substituting
of [θ] for [s] which might constitute
lisping in native speakers of English.
Obtain linguistic control of this
fronted [s̪]: [s̪a], [as̪a], [as̪], etc.

Exercise 4. Pronounce [s] while
curling the tongue tip up and back
slightly until a little whistling sound
is superimposed upon the [s] quality.
Obtain linguistic control of this retroflexed [ṣ]: [ṣa], [aṣa], [aṣ], etc.

Exercise 5a. Produce a longer
groove than is used for [s] by lifting
the blade or front part of the tongue
high and front in the mouth but with a
grooved shape. See Figure 23. Blow.

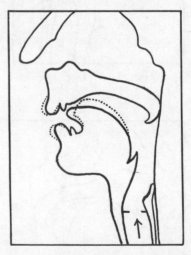

Fig. 23
Tongue and Lip Positions
for [s] ——
[š] ····

5b. How does this sound compare
with the alveopalatal sibilant [š] which
you have in English shame? Note that
the lips tend to be rounded and thrust
forward during the pronunciation of
English [š]. See Figure 23.
5c. Pronounce [š], then push the
tongue farther front so that a higher
pitched variety is heard. Do not let
the tongue have a short enough groove,

however, to change [š] into [s]. Obtain
linguistic control of the sound: [ša],
[aša], [aš].

5d. Curl the tip of the tongue up
and backward during the pronunciation of
[š], until a slight whistling sound is
added to the sibilant. Obtain linguistic
control of the sound: [ša], [aša], [aš].

One other type of voiceless oral
fricative should be mentioned. This is
caused by an escape of air over one or both
sides of the tongue through an orifice which
is small enough to cause friction.

Exercise 1. Put the tongue in position for [l] but do not pronounce it.
Then blow. A voiceless and almost
frictionless [ḷ] should be heard. Now
lift one side of the tongue slowly until
it nearly makes contact with the top of
the mouth. A sharp high-pitched
fricative sound should now be heard.
Obtain linguistic control of it: [ḷa,
aḷa. aḷ].[1]

Exercise 2. Repeat the exercise,
with air escaping over both sides of the
tongue.

Exercise 3. Students are likely to
find difficulty in distinguishing [ḷ],
[š] and [x]. The student therefore
should practice with his colleague to
be sure that he can pronounce, hear, and
transcribe the difference: [ḷa, ša, xa,
xa, ša, ḷa, xa, ḷa], etc.

Oral Fricatives Modified by Voicing

The vocal cords may be made to
vibrate during the pronunciation of all of
these oral fricatives. As a result one may
obtain voiced bilabial flat fricatives,
voiced bilabial rounded fricatives, voiced
alveolar grooved fricatives, voiced velar
flat fricatives, and the like.[2]

Exercise 1. Pronounce [ɸ]. Then
try to pronounce the same sound plus
voicing, that is [β]. See Figure 24.
If you have difficulty, bring the lips
nearly in contact with a flat opening,
and blow. Then "try to say a vowel at
the same time" in order to add voicing.
With the lips in position try to pronounce each of the vowels in turn but

---

[1]Voiceless laterals in actual
language are almost always fricative in type.
Frictionless voiceless laterals are very
rare. For convenience, then, we elsewhere
in the volume leave off the diacritic mark
below the [ḷ] with local friction.

[2]As a test to help the student to
detect voicing, he may place his hands over
his ears, while pronouncing the sounds, and
listen for the "rumbling" noise. Or he may
put his fingers against his larynx and feel
the vibration.

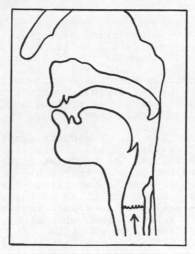

Fig. 24. [β]

utilize considerable breath pressure so
that friction is heard at the lips.
Obtain linguistic control of the sound
[βa], [aβa], [aβ].

Exercise 2. In order to make certain
that the voicing continues, it is helpful
to have a TIME EXERCISE in which one
attempts to maintain the voicing over a
stated period of time. Thus first one
may say [aaaaββββaaaa]. Then the time
may be cut down slightly [aaaβββaaa].
Again the time may be lowered until
finally one may say [aβa] while making
certain that the voicing is maintained.

Exercise 3. It is furthermore helpful to have an exercise with ALTERNATE
VOICING in which the lips are maintained
in one position and the consonants alternate from voicelessness to voicing with
no vowel in between, thus: [ɸβɸβɸβ].

Exercise 4. Place the tongue between
the teeth, blow, and add voicing. Compare the sound with your pronunciation
of the [ð] in English this. Contrast
[θ] and [ð] in thigh and thy. With a
colleague get practice in recording the
difference between the sounds and in
dictating them to one another in nonsense
syllables of various types.

Exercise 5a. In order to pronounce
[g] one may try the following methods:
Pronounce [agagaga] with increasing
rapidity until the air is not completely
interrupted at any point in the sequence.
The sound between the vowels will probably then be [ɣ]. See the tongue position, in Figure 21, which is the same
as for [x].
5b. Pronounce the vowel [a] and
attempt to "squeeze out" the air stream
between the tongue and the top of the
mouth.
5c. Pronounce [x] in accordance
with the methods previously given and
add voicing by "trying to say a vowel"

at the same time.

5d. While trying to say [g], lower the tongue slightly until it is not quite touching the top of the mouth.

Exercise 6. Obtain linguistic control of [g] by dictation to a colleague, and by attempting to pronounce nonsense syllables: [ga], [aga], [ag].

Exercise 7a. Pronounce front and back varieties of [g]. In order to do so, thrust the tongue first farther forward and then farther back[1] in the mouth than for the [g] already obtained.

7b. Mimic the pitch of the sound when a colleague goes progressively from far front to far back with minute articulatory variations of [g].

7c. Practice combinations of the front velar fricative with back vocoids and vice versa: [giga, gigu, gagigu, igagogog], etc.

Exercise 8. For rounded fricative [w̧], say [u], but round the lips further until strong friction is heard between them. Extra breath pressure may have to be added in order for you to hear the friction.

Exercise 9a. The sibilants can likewise be voiced. Say [s], for example, and try to "pronounce" vowels at the same time. If sufficient breath pressure is utilized to guarantee friction at the tip of the tongue, some type of voiced sibilant should be heard. Speakers of English should have little difficulty with [z], which is the voiced equivalent of [s]. They should, however, practice to obtain fronted and retroflexed varieties: [z̧a, az̧a, az̧]; [ẓa, aẓa, aẓ], etc.

9b. Similarly, [š] may be voiced by trying to "pronounce a vowel" at the same time.

9c. Starting with the sound which occurs in the middle of the English word vision, the student should front the tongue and then back and retroflex it in order to obtain the varieties [ž] and [ẓ].[2] He should then practice in order

obtain facility in pronouncing, hearing and recording these sounds: [z̧a, az̧a, az̧]; [ẓa, aẓa, aẓ].

Exercise 10. Practice alternate voicing of fricatives: [szszsz], [xgxgxg].

The voiced lateral continuants can also be heard in fricative varieties.

Exercise 1. Pronounce [l]. Notice that the sides of the tongue are down. Continue to pronounce [l] but gradually lift up the sides of the tongue until they are almost touching the top of the mouth. In this way friction should be heard at the point where the air escapes. Practice this fricative: [ḷa, aḷa, aḷ].

Exercise 2. Practice to distinguish [ģ], [ž], and nonsyllabic [i] (that is [y]): [gi, yi, gi, yi, yi, ži, ži, gi, yi], etc.

Exercise 3. Practice the voiceless fricative lateral after [t]: [tḷ, tḷ].
                                      +   +

Oral Fricatives Modified by Nasalization

The oral fricatives can be modified by nasalization. Such sound types are infrequent in speech.

Exercise. Pronounce [z], then lower the velic so that you nasalize it.

Oral Fricatives Modified by an Additional Nonfricative Articulation

The fricatives can be modified by nonfricative articulation. At the time an [s] or [x] is being pronounced, the lips may be partially rounded so as to modify the timbre of the sound. This is called the LABIALIZATION of that fricative. The lip rounding must not be so severe that local friction is heard at that point, but rather it should merely modify the general timbre of the [s].

If the lip rounding is released at the same time as the alveolar articulation, the labialized [g] will constitute a single segment. If, however, the release of the lips is delayed, then a second segment will result. See Figure 25.

Simultaneous but nonfricative articulation of the mid part of the tongue toward the hard palate gives PALATALIZATION of a fricative. A delayed release of the palatal articulation produces a second segment. If a front variety of [ģ] or [š] is released slowly with a [y] OFF GLIDE, the two-segment sequence [ģʸ] is also sometimes said to be palatalized.

---

[1] A voiced back velar fricative is likely to be interpreted by some students as a variety of "uvular [r]" since this sound is traditionally written [r] in some dialects of certain European languages, or is in nonphonemic fluctuation with a uvular trill, or parallels in one dialect the uvular trill in another.

[2] Speakers of English are likely to think that retroflexed sibilants, especially the voiced ones, sound somewhat like "r". In various languages, as a matter of fact, [r] and certain types of retroflexed sibilants may be substituted the one for the other indiscriminately, or in certain positions in words. In some sections of Latin America, for example, people who have

---

difficulty in pronouncing an alveolar trill may find it quite acceptable to pronounce [ž] for initial "r" but [š] for word-final "r̩."

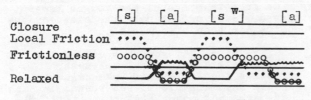

Fig. 25. [s] vs. [sᵂ]

Lip Position: Rounded oooo, Unrounded ⊖⊖⊖⊖
Tongue Tip Position: ••••
Vocal Cords Not Vibrating——,Vibrating ⌇⌇⌇

Less frequent is simultaneous articulation of the back of the tongue toward the velum, producing VELARIZATION.

Exercise 1a. Palatalize [f], [x].
1b. Labialize them.
1c. Practice making a difference between [s̱] as a single segment and [sᵂ] as two segments in sequences such as [s̱a, sᵂa, f̱a, fᵂa] etc.
1d. How does the sequence [sw] in English sweet compare with these sounds? What is the difference between the labiovelar [xᵂ] and the first part of the word wheat?

Exercise 2. Pronounce [s] with the lips spread. Round the lips and pronounce [s] again. What is the difference in the pitch of the sound? Does it appear to be higher or lower?

Exercise 3. Pronounce [z]. Velarize the sound. Can you detect any difference between [z] velarized and nonvelarized?

PHARYNGEALIZATION produces a modification of a fricative by having the root of the tongue make an approach towards the back of the pharyngeal wall but without producing friction there. Frequently pharyngealization is not heard during the actual production of the nonvocoid sound itself, but is most readily heard as a modification of the timbre of vocoids surrounding it.

Exercise 1a. What difference do you hear during the pronunciation of [p] when the tongue is front or back?
1b. Try to pharyngealize [s] and [f]. Pronounce [ѕ] and [f̣] before and after vocoids to see if you hear the pharyngealization more clearly there.

Exercise 2. Dictate a series of nonsense syllables to a colleague and have him dictate to you in return, practicing labialized, palatalized and pharyngealized fricatives with simultaneous and delayed releases.

Nonvocoids with Friction in the Throat

Local friction can be made at various places in the throat.

Exercise 1. Move the tongue backward into mouth until friction is heard at the root of the tongue when air is coming past the pharyngeal wall.

Exercise 2. Whisper down the scale, beginning with a high-pitched [x̱], through [x], and [x̣], and to lower pitches until a pharyngeal fricative [h] is heard; keep the lips spread. Repeat, voiced.

Exercise 3. Tense the vocal cords for friction between them, as for a harsh whisper, for [h̩]. Repeat, with voicing, for [ɦ̩].

Fricatives Modified by an Ingressive Air Stream to the Lungs

The fricatives so far discussed have been produced by air proceeding outward from the lungs. These can be duplicated, however, with air drawn inward to the lungs. The voiceless nonvocoids will not sound very different whether the air stream is ingressive or egressive. The voiced sounds, however, tend to have a somewhat different quality when the air stream is ingressive.

Fricatives Modified by Strength of Articulation

The fricatives may have strong, precise, vigorous articulation; or the movements producing them may be weak. The difference is reflected in louder sounds or sounds with harsher friction. The harsh, loud types with strong articulation are FORTIS; the weak types with softer friction are LENIS.

Exercise 1. Pronounce [p], then [f], [θ], [s], [š], [x], [x̣], first very softly, then with harsh friction.

Exercise 2. While maintaining the vocoids with a constant degree of loudness (so that the relative contrast of loudness between nonvocoid and vocoid may be apparent), practice the fortis [x̱] and the lenis [x̣] so as to obtain linguistic control over the difference: [xaxaxaxa]. Repeat the exercise for other fricatives; repeat again using different vocoids.

Fricatives Modified by Quantity

Just in the same way that the vocoids can be long or short relative to other sounds in a sequence, so the fricatives can likewise have such differences.

Exercise 1a. Practice the following series of sounds. In order to be sure that the items marked with a length sign are actually pronounced long, you may find it advantageous to tap with a pencil. Give one tap for each short element, and two taps for each long element. Once you have made the first initial start with length you should then be able to

control it acoustically, tapping the
time: [s:a'fas:o]; ['x:ixax:u];
[sap̣ip:a'sa].
　　1b. Dictate such elements to a
colleague and take dictation from him.

　　Exercise 2. Practice reading drills
in which length of vocoid and length of
nonvocoid are both present. Pronounce
them, dictate them, and take them from
dictation: ['x:ixa:so]; [xu:'fa:s:i];
[s:os:u'k:i]; ['si:θi:'x:i];
[xo's:o:x:o:].

Fricatives Modified by Pitch

　　Voiceless sounds have their pitch
determined by the size and shape of the
passageways through which the air escapes,
or by the quality of the surfaces of the
passageways, and so on. One cannot hum a
voiceless sound such as a voiceless fricative
without changing the shape of the mouth in
some way.

　　With voiced sounds, however, one can
maintain a single oral formation and get
different pitches just as he can with vocoids.

　　Exercise 1. Pronounce a long [z:].
Hum a tune on the sound.

　　Exercise 2. Pronounce the word
zebra. Can you hear a pitch on the [z]?
How does it compare with the pitch of the
vocoid following it? If you have difficulty in hearing the pitch of the
fricative, pronounce the word very slowly
so that each sound is practically isolated.

Fricatives Modified by Relation to the Syllable

　　When the fricatives occur at the
beginning of a syllable they act as releasing nonvocoids; at the end of a syllable they
act as arresting nonvocoids. The acoustic
characteristic is quite similar in either
case. Fricatives may also serve as syllabics
in such an expression as [pṣt] or in the
isolated pronunciation of a sound such as
[ẓ]. Here, again, the acoustic quality is
quite similar to that which is found when
they are acting as nonsyllabics.

Nonvocoid Sounds with Complete Interruption of a Pulmonic Air Stream

　　The fricatives, since they can be
continued, are relatively easy for the beginner to practice. Turning from these continuant sounds, however, one may now study STOPS,
in which the air stream is completely interrupted.

　　Usually an ORAL stop has the oral
closure released before the nasal closure, so
that air escapes out of the mouth. In
NASALLY-RELEASED stops, however, (e.g. [tn]),
the velic releases rather than the tongue.
In LATERALLY-RELEASED [t], (that is, in [tɬ]),

one side or both sides of the tongue lower
so that air escapes out over the sides of the
tongue rather than over the tip.

　　Exercise. If you have difficulty
making lateral and nasal releases,
practice the following; take pains to
insure that the tip of the tongue in each
case does not move: [tntntn], [tɬtɬtɬ].

Aspirated, Voiceless, and Voiced Stops

　　The first set of distinctions for
the student to practice may well be between
those stops in which there is an ASPIRATION
("puff of breath") following an oral release,
and those in which there is no such aspiration. In the first of these, the aspirated
variety, two segments are present; traditionally, however, they are labelled as single
units, "aspirated stops".

　　Exercise 1a. Say [a], then close the
lips tightly, while interrupting the vibration of the vocal cords. Then open
the lips and allow a long strong puff of
breath to be exhaled. Follow this immediately with [a].
　　1b. Practice this sequence in a time
exercise thus: [a::p::h::a::], tapping
out one beat to each unit of length (each
letter and each colon represent one such
unit). See Figure 26.

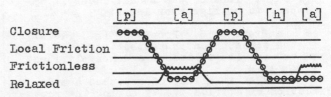

	[p]	[a]	[p]	[h]	[a]
Closure					
Local Friction					
Frictionless					
Relaxed					

Fig. 26. Aspirated and Unaspirated Stops
Lips ⊕⊕⊕⊕
Vocal Cords Not Vibrating——— , Vibrating〰〰〰

　　1c. Reduce the time for each part
of the exercise until one obtains a rapid
but distinct aspiration: [a::p::h::a::],
then [a:p:h:a:] and finally [apha].

　　Exercise 2a. Again practice a time
exercise. In this case, however, eliminate completely the puff of breath:
[a::p::a::], [a:p:a:], [apa]. How does
this compare with the [p] sound which you

---

[1]Except in those instances when
phonemic analysis proves them to be constituted of two phonemes. In these cases,
they are best called consonant clusters.
The phonetic characteristics of [pʰ] may be
identical in either situation but the
phonemic interpretation distinct.·

have in happy? In spy? Most English speakers have difficulty[1] pronouncing voiceless unaspirated stops in stressed syllables. To help eliminate the puff of breath, try the following approaches to them:

2b. Build up heavy pressure from the lungs while the lips are closed for the [p]. In trying to release them very rapidly, try to "begin the [a] in the middle of the [p]" or "before the [p] is finished," taking care not to get a voicing of the stop itself. If the stop is voiced, a rumble will be heard at the opening of the lips; if the stop is voiceless, no sound will be heard.

2c. Draw in the breath: try to hold it lightly until after you begin to pronounce the syllable [pa].

2d. Say the word pepper, noting the unaspirated [p] in the second syllable, and repeating the second syllable several times with increasing loudness: ['pɛprᵽpr]; then space between the first and second syllables: ['pɛ--pᵽ]; finally, say ['pᵽ].

2e. Say [spa], emphasizing the [pa] and weakening the [s]; then "thinking" the [s] and saying the [pa]. The [p] following [s] tends to be unaspirated in many dialects of English. If one can utilize, therefore, some series of sounds such as the following, it frequently proves helpful in trying to pronounce the unaspirated [p]. First pronounce spy at regular speed. Then pronounce it more slowly so that each sound is lengthened: [s:p:a:i:]; elongate the nonvocoid sounds further yet: [s::p::ai]. With the sound thus elongated, one can sometimes maintain the lack of aspiration for the stop and at the same time build up a kind of "feeling" for pronouncing the sound independently. Turn therefore from that exercise to one in which the [s] is followed by a short pause before the pronunciation of the stop and then eliminate the [s] altogether, thus: [s::pa], [s-pa], then [pa].

The student needs to practice a second distinction between types of stops, that is, the difference between voiced and voiceless ones. For speakers of English the pronunciation of fairly long voiced stops proves very difficult even though they may be accustomed to consider English [b] a voiced sound. Some speakers of English actually substitute a lenis voiceless un-aspirated stop for a voiced stop in the pro-nunciation of many of their words.[1] In order to get a fully voiced [b] the follow-ing drills may prove helpful.

Exercise 1a. Try a time exercise: [a::b::a::]. Make certain that the voice "rumbles" throughout the entire long [b:].[2]

1b. Say [b] by itself, with no vocoid before or after it. Keep the lips closed the entire time. Then hum a tune on [b], making certain that one does not make the sound [m] with the velic lowered.

1c. Say [a] loudly, then close your mouth and try to shout [a], while keep-ing the lips completely closed.

1d. Keeping the sound continuous, without stopping the rumble in the throat and without allowing the lips to open, pronounce [bmbmbm]. Do not say merely [ʔmʔmʔm], or the like.

Exercise 2a. Once the aspirated and unaspirated voiceless stops and the unaspirated voiced stops are learned in exercises of this type, they should be practiced assiduously in various types of combinations and contrasts. Hardly any other contrast between sounds is as difficult for English speakers to learn: very few sound types are so widespread in various languages as the unaspirated stops. Read, and take from dictation: ['papʰaba], [ba'papʰa], tʰakʰa'pabal], [pababa'pa].

2b. Practice these same contrasts with the stops [tʰ], [t], [d], [kʰ], [k], [g].

Exercise 3. Except in India, voiced aspirated stops are much less frequent than the voiceless ones. The student begins with the pronunciation of the voiced stop as previously described and follows this pronunciation with a vocoid to which friction is added at the vocal cords as was described earlier for "voiced [ɦ]." Practice this sound sequence with a time exercise: [b::ɦ:a:], [bɦa].

---

[1]Sometimes one hears the statement, "I find aspirated sounds very difficult to pronounce." Frequently, however, this state-ment reflects a misunderstanding of the situation and contributes to the difficulty. In stressed syllables the aspirated sound is likely to be the one which English speakers utilize and therefore is relatively easy for them to pronounce. If English speakers would concentrate on pronouncing the more difficult unaspirated stops, they would usually be better rewarded for their efforts.

---

[1]This is another reason why English speakers are likely to find it difficult to differentiate [pha], [pa], and [ba].

[2]The [b] can be continued for only a limited space of time while the pressure in the mouth builds up. When the pressure gets sufficiently great, the [b] cannot be con-tinued any longer, unless the velic or the oral closures are released. Nevertheless, this time is sufficient to get a clearly audible sound continued long enough to be relatively longer than the average length of sounds in speech.

Fronted and Backed Varieties of Stops

Like the fricatives, the stops may also have various types of modifications. One of the sources of varieties of stops lies in their being fronted or backed in position. [t], for example, may have an interdental closure, or a closure made by the tongue tip against the backs of the teeth, or against the alveolar arch, or turned upward against the hard palate--or with an infinite variety of potential places of contact in between. Acoustically the only voiceless unaspirated stop which is strikingly different from the alveolar type is the retroflexed one. This affects the vocoids before or after it in such a way that they tend to receive a kind of "r" quality since the vocoids partake a bit of the retroflex tongue positions for the stops.

It should be noted in this connection that during the closure itself neither [p], [t], or [k] has any sound, and they are therefore alike acoustically during the closure. They are differentiated by the effect of the APPROACH to their positions or by the RELEASE from their positions--that is by their ON GLIDES or OFF GLIDES. As the tongue approaches the position for retroflexed [t], the vocoid preceding it is affected by that tongue movement so that the ear picks up a difference between [t] and a [ṭ] by these differences in the quality of the approach or release rather than by hearing the differences in the closures as such.

When a so-called dental [t̪] and alveolar [t] are phonemically distinct in languages, dental [t̪] is usually slightly aspirated or affricated, i.e. [t̪ʰ] or [t̪ˢ].

Exercise 1. Practice reading a passage of English prose with the tongue tip curled slightly upward and notice the effect on the quality of the vocoids which precede and follow [ṭ], [ḍ], [n̩], [l̩], [r̩].

Exercise 2. If possible, listen to some person speaking English who is a native speaker of some language in India. Do you detect in his speech any [ṭ]'s of the type you produced in the preceding exercise?

Varieties of [d] may parallel the varieties of [t].

Exercise 1. For [ḍ], [d̪], [ḍ], [dn], and [dl] repeat the exercises which were given above for [t].

Exercise 2. Dictate to a colleague and receive dictation from him exercises designed to differentiate these various sounds. Pattern the drills after the following: [tatatˢat̪ata], [dadadadadada], [tadat̪ˢadaṭada].

The velar stops may be fronted or backed as were the velar fricatives, and the student needs to learn to pronounce various kinds of stops at these points of articulation.

Exercise 1a. Pronounce [x]; back it to [x̱]; blow hard through the aperture above the tongue so that you can clearly feel the back point of articulation. Keeping the tongue at that same back point make it touch the top of the mouth and close off the air so as to produce back [ḵ].

1b. Similarly, front the tongue for fronted [x̟] and then pronounce fronted [k̟].

Exercise 2a. How many varieties of [k] can you make, differentiated only by degrees of forward or back position?

2b. At the same points of articulation, produce the voiced stops [g], [g̟], [g̱], and voiceless aspirated stops [k̟ʰ], [kʰ], [ḵʰ].

Exercise 3. With nonsense syllables practice the rapid pronunciation of these sounds. Dictate them to a colleague and from him receive dictation utilizing simple sound groups like [kʰakaka], [gagaga], [gagaka], [gakʰaga], [kagaga], [kigikigi], [gikigikʰigikʰi].

Exercise 4. For practice in the aspiration and voicing or back stops, utilize the drill types already given you.

Stops Modified by an Additional Nonfricative Articulation

At the time the stop closure is made, an additional modification may be added at the lips (labialization), or at the front of the mouth (palatalization). This articulation may be released either simultaneously with the release of the stop closure or there may be a delayed release. In the one instance a single nonvocoid segment is produced and in the other instance a sequence of one nonvocoid segment and one vocoid segment is heard.

Exercise 1. Say [tʷ] and notice in a mirror the rounding of the lips even before the tongue tip is released. For [pʷ] notice that the lips are pouted, even though they are not open; in this way they parallel lip rounding. In labiovelars the lips are rounded during the velar articulation, as for [kʷ]. The labialized sounds may likewise be comprised of one or two segments, depending upon the timing of the release.

Exercise 2. Compare [py], [ty], [ky]. With all of these note that no sound is heard while the actual closure in the mouth is maintained but that it is the off glide which makes them acoustically distinct from the nonmodified types.

Exercise 3. Prepare nonsense syllables for dictation containing labialized and palatalized stops: e.g. [kᵂa'pᵞokᵞitᵂe].

A simultaneous modification of these stops can likewise be made by a narrowed throat passageway, that is by PHARYNGEALIZATION.

Exercise. Prepare nonsense drills for these sounds.

Stops with Fricative Release

An AFFRICATE[1] is a stop followed immediately by a fricative. If the fricative occurs at the same point of articulation as the closure for the stop, the stop plus its fricative release is called a HOMORGANIC affricate. See Figure 27. If the fricative

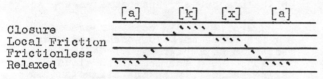

	[a]	[k]	[x]	[a]
Closure				
Local Friction				
Frictionless				
Relaxed				

Fig. 27. A Homorganic Affricate
Tongue Back ````

is at a different point of articulation, the resulting sequence of two segments is called a HETERORGANIC affricate.

Exercise 1. Close the lips, build up pressure behind them, then release the lips very gradually so that one hears [p] and [p̄].

Exercise 2. Repeat this, beginning with [t] at alveolar and alveo-palatal position, but as you release the tongue move it slightly so that you get sequences [ts] and [tš]. Repeat this exercise, releasing to retroflex and fronted varieties of [s] and [š]. Practice differentiating these types.

Exercise 3. Beginning with a closure at one point of articulation have another articulator ready in fricative position so that upon the release of the closure a fricative will be heard at the second point of articulation--as, for example, in [ks], or [px]. How many types of voiceless sequences can you produce?

---

[1]The term is especially useful when the sequence of segments constitutes a single phoneme.

Exercise 4. Repeat exercises one to three with voiced sounds.

Exercise 5. Dictate pertinent nonsense syllables to a colleague and receive dictation for drill in differentiating these affricates.

Exercise 6. Release [t] and [d] laterally, at first making the release voiceless and then making it voiced.

Pharyngeal Stops

Stops may be caused by closing off the air stream in the throat with the root of the tongue.

Exercise 1. Beginning with a high pitched fricative [x] keep the lips spread and gradually move the tongue backwards so that you "whisper down the scale." Do not stop when the tongue touches the uvular position but keep moving backwards down the throat until the friction occurs between the root of the tongue and the back of the pharynx, in order to produce a pharyngeal fricative. Again whisper down the scale in this way, but at each point alternate the whisper with a closure for a variety of [k]. Closure between the root of the tongue and the back of the throat will produce a pharyngeal stop [k̲].

Exercise 2. Repeat for pharyngeal [g̲].

Glottal Stop

The vocal cords can be brought together so as to interrupt the airstream.

Exercise 1. Pronounce Oh! Oh! Do you feel the breath stream choke off between the syllables? Many speakers of English use a glottal stop (that is [ʔ]) in this position. In American English many speakers differentiate "yes" and "no" as ['m̥hm̥] and ['m̓ʔm̓] respectively; other speakers of American English, or the same speakers at different times, make "yes" and "no" as ['ʔə̥hə̥] and ['ʔə̓ʔə̓]. The expression for "yes" tends to be accompanied by rising pitch and the one for "no" by falling pitch.

Exercise 2. Pronounce the glottal stop between the vowels in the following drills, making the glottal stop short and long: [aʔ:a], [oʔ:o], [oʔo], and so on.

Exercise 3. Try to make a contrast between [ʔa] and [a], [ʔo] and [o]. Stressed vowels in English are likely to begin with a glottal stop at the beginning of utterances. If therefore you have difficulty in eliminating this glottal stop before [a], try the following devices. Say [ha] and gradually reduce the length of the [h] until you are "thinking [h]" but saying only [a], or

try to relax and say [a]; or try singing
[a] without an initial glottal stop and
then gradually switch to a speaking
voice.

Exercise 4. Practice this sound
with a colleague extensively. In a
great many languages it is highly important and usually requires much drill
by English speaking students. [ˀa], [a];
[a], [ˀa]; [oˀiˀ], [uˀ], [iˀ], [ˀeˀ],
[ˀeˀeˀ].

Double Stops

For certain sounds, the DOUBLE
stops, there are two closures in the mouth
in addition to the velic closure in the
nasal passageway. One of the oral closures
may be at the lips and another at the velum.
Lung pressure builds up behind the velar
and velic closures. The lips may release
first with or without a little suction in
the mouth, and then the velar closure
releases.

Exercise 1a. Pronounce [a^{k}pa].
Make the closure at the velum come first,
then release the lips and velum simultaneously.
1b. Repeat, releasing the lip
closure first.
1c. Practice the sound in further
sequences such as [^{k}pa], [a^{k}p], [a^{k}pa].

Exercise 2. Practice the sound with
and without a little mouth suction.[1]

Exercise 3. Practice the sound with
different degrees of prominence of the
[k] and [p].
Exercise 4. Repeat exercises 1, 2,
and 3, with voicing during the sound so
as to achieve [a^{g}ba].

Stops Modified by Nasalization

A stop cannot have simultaneous
nasalization or it will cease to be a stop;
that is, if one begins with [b] and drops
the velic so as to open the nasal passage,
the [b] will be changed to [m]. Practice,
however, the sequences of nasal plus stop,
and stop plus nasal.

Exercise. Pronounce [kŋkŋkŋ];
[ŋkŋkŋk].

Stops Modified by Strength of Articulation

Stops may be fortis or lenis.

Exercise 1. Pronounce [apa]. Make
the stop very loud with very tense lip
closure, i.e., [apa]. Repeat the sequence [apa] retaining the vocoid at
the same degree of loudness but making
the stop very weak, i.e., [apa].

---

[1]For a description of mouth suction
see below, Clicks, p. 41.

Exercise 2. Repeat drills for fortis
and lenis stops, voiced and voiceless,
at other points of articulation.[1]

Stops Modified by Length

The stops, like the fricatives and
the vocoids, can be relatively long or short.

Exercise 1. Read aloud the following sequences of stops: ['pap·apa].
Note that the long voiceless stop leaves
"a hole in the air," a hiatus. Notice
also that the first part of the stop
tends to serve as an arresting element
for the preceding syllable, whereas the
second part of the long stop serves as a
releasing element to the following syllable.

Exercise 2. Prepare nonsense
material with different placements of
length; practice reading and dictating
it and taking similar items in dictation:
[b·aba·b·a'bab·a], [pa·pap·a'papa·p·a].

Exercise 3. In some passage of
English prose mark consonant and vowel
length in an arbitrary, miscellaneous
fashion. Read the selection aloud,
taking pains to make the segments long
where they are so marked.

Exercise 4. Practice a length exercise with affricates. In this case,
however, make the stop element long
rather than lengthening both elements:
[ap·sa], [at·sa], and so on.

Stops Modified by Pitch

Voiceless stops during their actual
closures have no pitch at all. Voiced stops,
however, can and do have audible pitch. For
a very brief space of time one can hum a
voiced stop. In language the pitch of voiced
stops is usually not pertinent at the beginning of syllables but sometimes must be
watched carefully in relation to intonation
at the end of syllables, since intonation
contours may be finished on the voiced consonants.

Exercise 1. Pronounce [g]. Make
the voice rise during the pronunciation
of the sound. Be sure that the velic
and the tongue retain their closures.

Exercise 2. Pronounce very slowly
some English words beginning or ending
with voiced stops. Under what circumstances can you detect a change of pitch
during the pronunciation of the stop?

---

[1]A student should be prepared to find
that he will have difficulty differentiating
voiceless unaspirated lenis stops from voiced
lenis stops.

Stops Modified by an Ingressive Airstream to the Lungs

Like the fricatives and the vocoids, stops may be produced with an ingressive airstream to the lungs.

Exercise. With suction from the lungs pronounce [ap⤆a], [at⤆a].

Nonvocoid Frictionless Continuants with Nasal or Lateral Air Escape

Nasals

Nasals are produced by a closure in the mouth but with an opening through the nasal passageway. That part of the oral chamber which is behind the oral closure modified the resonance of the sound. Note Figure 28.

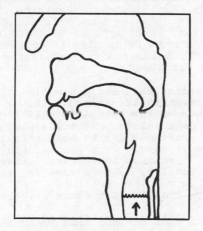

Fig. 28. [m]

Exercise 1. What is the difference between [m] and [n]?

Exercise 2. Arrange the mouth in position for [m], without pronouncing the sound, then blow. By this procedure you should achieve a voiceless [M]. Produce voiceless [N] similarly.[1]

Exercise 3. Practice the difference between voiced nasal, voiceless nasal, voiceless nasal followed by voiced nasal, and voiced nasal followed by voiceless nasal: [ama], [aM], [aMma], [amMa]; [ma], [Ma], [Mma], [mMa]; [m], [M], [Mm], [mM]. Repeat with [n] and [N].

---

[1]Usually the voiceless [M] and [N] are either nonsignificant off glides of voiced [m] and [n] at the end of utterances, or are varieties of [h] nasalized by its contact with a following voiced nasal.

Exercise 4a. Pronounce [k]. Maintain the tongue in the same position but hum through the nose. The result should be [ŋ].
4b. Isolate the final sound of ['hæŋ].
4c. Pronounce the following words backwards: sing (that is, [ŋιs]), rung, tongue.
4d. If you have difficulty pronouncing the [ŋ] at the beginning of words, try the following exercise: Pronounce the word singer slowly, as [sιŋɹ]; then add a brief pause before the last syllable: [sιŋ-ŋɹ], then [sιŋ-ŋɹ-ŋɹ]; and finally [ŋɹ], [ŋa], [ŋe], [ŋi], [ŋo], [ŋu].
4e. Make [ŋ] voiceless, i.e. [N̦].
4f. Pronounce [ŋ] and move the tongue farther back into the mouth so as to make a back velar [ŋ] parallel to the position for [k̦]. Practice this back velar with nonsense syllables.

Exercise 5a. While pronouncing [n], move the front part of the tongue up high until it is touching the palate; then lower the tip of the tongue; the resultant sound should be [ñ]. See Figure 29. Watch in a mirror to be sure that the tip does not remain in contact with the alveolar arch or the hard

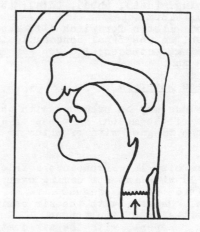

Fig. 29. [ñ]

palate. It will be helpful if you keep the tongue pressed against your lower teeth so that it cannot rise to the top of the mouth. Another way of pronouncing [ñ] is to hold the tongue tip down with the pencil while trying to say [n].
5b. Try to learn to discriminate [n] (with the tongue tip up) from [ny] (with the tongue tip up, and its release followed by [y]), and from [nia] (with syllable division between [i] and [a]), and from [ña] (with the tongue tip down), and from [ñia] (with a syllable division

between [i] and [a]). Practice each of
these sounds or sound sequences between
[a] and [o].

    5c. With the tongue blade touching
on the hard palate or on the alveolar
arch, but with the tongue tip down, blow
so as to produce [Ñ]. Practice drills
to separate [Ña], [Ñĩa], [ñÑa], [Ña],
[Ñya], [Ñia], [Na], [Nŋa].

Nasals Modified in Various Ways

    Nasals, like the stops and fricatives,
can have various types of modification by
the direction of the air stream, by length,
by intensity, and by pitch.

    Exercise 1. Pronounce [m←], [n←],
with an airstream drawn into the lungs.
Give voiced and voiceless types.

    Exercise 2. Practice exercises for
different lengths of nasals, with nonsense syllables: ['n·an·a·na·na],
[n·an·e'neni·na].

    Exercise 3. SYLLABIC NASALS consti-
tute the nuclear part of a syllable.
This nuclear part can be either intense
or weak in its pronunciation. Practice
the following:['n̩.pa] [n̩.'so], [n̩.li'ba].

    Exercise 4a. Pitch contrasts on
nasals are somewhat frequent. Read the
following: [n̄sà], [hbá], [n̄tá; [bõkŋ̀],
[sõtń], [ìɔbm̄].
    4b. Listen for pitch differences in
English, on the final consonants in the
following sentences: Did you say Ann?
I said Ann.

Frictionless Laterals

    Sounds may be produced with the air
coming out of the mouth, over one or both
sides of the tongue, with or without[1]
friction.

    Exercise 1a. Pronounce a friction-
less [l] with the air coming over the
right side of the tongue.
    1b. Repeat, with the air coming over
the left side of the tongue.
    1c. Repeat, with the air coming over
both sides of the tongue.

    Exercise 2. Pronounce a long con-
tinuous [l:]. While doing so, raise the
sides of the tongue so that there is a
much smaller place for the escape of the
air than you normally have for [l] in
led. Make the aperture small enough so
that marked friction is heard during the
pronunciation of this voiced fricative

---

[1] The voiceless frictionless [ɬ]
sounds and the voiceless frictionless nasals
are the only frictionless nonvocoid continuants. The fricative nasals, with audible
friction at the velic, do not seem to be
speech sounds.

nonvocoid [l̩]. Contrast this sound with
[l]. Contrast the voiceless frictionless
and fricative varieties.

    Exercise 3a. Place the tip of the
tongue against the alveolar arch. While
making certain that it is retained there,
try to "pronounce all the vowels" so that
[l]'s result with various vowel timbres:
[l(e)], [l(a)], [l(i)], [l(o)], [l(u)].
Do not pronounce a vowel during this
exercise, and do not drop the tip of the
tongue. The type of [l] with [i] timbre
is called a "clear [l]". The one with
[u] timbre or some other back tongue
position is called a "dark [l]".
    3b. Do you hear a "clear [l]" or a
"dark [l]" in the word leaf? bowl?
bottle? little?

    Exercise 4. Place the tongue tip
against the alveolar arch and make other
vocal adjustments as if to pronounce an
ordinary [l]. Instead of voicing, however, blow. Notice that this sound has
only a very light type of friction of the
cavity as a whole so that it may be
called "frictionless" or containing
"cavity friction".

    Exercise 5a. Place the tip of the
tongue against the lower teeth. Force
the blade of the tongue to make contact
at the hard palate or the alveolar arch.
Try to pronounce [l] in this position.
The result should be a palatal [ʎ].
    5b. Practice the palatal lateral
before vocoids, between vocoids, and
following vocoids.
    5c. Practice the sound voiceless.

Frictionless Laterals Modified in Various Ways

    The laterals can be modified in ways
similar to the nasals.

    Exercise 1. Pronounce [l←] and [ɬ←],
utilizing an ingressive air stream to the
lungs.

    Exercise 2. Practice exercises de-
signed to give control of pronouncing,
hearing, and recording long and short
laterals: [l·a'lal·alala],
['lo·s·o'fol·oso·s·lo].

    Exercise 3. While making the [l]
syllabic, pronounce with different intensity the following: ['l̩ba], [l̩ba].

    Exercise 4. Pronounce the following
items, noting the differences of pitch:
[l̩·sa], [asl̩], ['batl̩], ['fas'l̩].

Nonvocoid Sounds with Flapped or Trilled Articulation

    By a single quick flap of the tongue,
or occasionally by some other part of the
vocal apparatus, a quick flipping noise may
be produced. The alveolar flap should be

made with a single movement in which the tongue tip starts in one direction and touches the alveolar arch in passing, but does not remain there for any appreciable length of time. Instead of being deliberately placed in that position and then deliberately pulled away, the tongue tip flaps rapidly in one direction and merely makes contact in passing.

Exercise 1a. Flap the tongue tip against the alveolar arch. Drop the tongue forward, starting it from a position curled up and back. Let it slap the alveolar arch as it descends downward toward its normal position. See Figure 30.

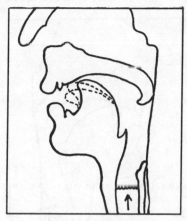

Fig. 30
Successive Points in the
Production of a Forward Moving
Voiced Alveolar Flap

1b. Have the tongue tip make a flap at the same point but in the reverse direction.
1c. Make a flap downward but with an initial starting point further back, and with the contact at the back of the alveolar arch or at the front part of the hard palate.
1d. If you have difficulty making the flap, check to see if you have the sound in the American English pronunciation of the word butter, or bottom, or Betty. Do you make a distinction in your pronunciation of the words matter and madder? If so, how would you describe the difference in terms of flap movement versus nonflap articulation?
1e. If you still have trouble making a flap, the following exercise may be helpful: Pronounce the following sequences, beginning slowly and increasing speed until the central sound of the combination becomes a very rapid flap:[1] ['todo], ['todo], ['todo], ['todo].
1f. An alternate exercise for a similar goal is to start with [tə'da]

and increase it rapidly until you get [tɾa].

Exercise 2. Make a similar flap with the tongue tip, but during the sound do not let the sides of the tongue make contact. Does this flap [l̆] sound to you more like [l] or like [r]?

Exercise 3. Make a labio-alveolar flap[1] by curling the lower lip inward and backward and giving it a single flap outward so that in its outward passage it produces a kind of "pop" as it brushes against the alveolar arch or the teeth.

Exercise 4. Try to produce a ingle flap of the uvula.

For a trill, two or more flaps must follow each other in rapid automatic succession.

Exercise 1a. Let the lips be relaxed and fairly close together. Blow sharply. Can you produce a trill of the lips?
1b. Repeat, with voicing.
1c. With the lips very close together and tense, produce a much higher-pitched rapid trill called "lip voice" such as may be used to initiate sound in playing a cornet.

Exercise 2a. Try to produce a tongue-tip trill in one of the following ways:[2] Let the tongue hang loosely, with the tongue tip a bit closer to the top of the mouth than it would be in a position for [z]. Blow sharply over the tip of the tongue.
2b. Start with a flap produced in one of the ways given in the preceding exercise. Once the flap is being produced easily, the student should attempt to leave the tongue in the general flap position or bring it back rapidly but loosely and relaxed to the same position from which it flapped. If he feels a bit of vibration develop, he should continue to work on the sound until he can get

---

[1] When members of the Mbanza tribe of the northwestern corner of Belgian Congo have followed the custom of removing the four upper teeth they form their regular labio-dental flap against the upper lip instead of against the upper teeth. Data from R. B. Anderson.

[2] Many people find alveolar and uvular trills among the hardest sounds for them to learn. The reason for this is that the sounds must be made automatically; no placing of the tongue can as such make certain the production of the sounds. The student can merely approximate the general tongue position and experiment with mimicry until he feels the first accidental vibrations. Once he does so, he can then by assiduous practice gain control over them.

---

[1] And until it sounds to Spanish speakers like toro.

full control of the trill. Sharp bursts
of breath are more likely to start such
a vibration than a normal breath movement.
    2c. Once the sound has been made for
the first time, the student should continue practicing it in various positions
in relation to vowels and words until he
can control it easily.

    Exercise 3a. For learning the uvular
trill one must adopt similar expedients.
The general tongue position should be
that for [g]. With the tongue relaxed
and in this position sharp bursts of
breath may set the uvula in motion.
    3b. Some people get quicker results
by starting with a kind of gargle--possi-
bly encouraged with a bit of water. If
the gargle starts lower in the throat
than the uvular position, one must
gradually work it up until the vibration
is actually at the point of the uvula.
Practice must be continued until the
uvula can be made to trill without any
water present.

    Exercise 4. A glottal trill--or
trillization--has already been described
in previous paragraphs.[1]

    Exercise 5a. What type of trill is
involved in a snore?
    5b. Most people cannot produce this
trill with the mouth closed. It must
have air coming in from the mouth and
nose simultaneously. A few people can
make this trill with the air coming outward from the lungs.

    Exercise 6a. A few other types of
trilling sounds can be made. With the
larynx lowered, a rather dull-sounding
light trill can be produced which is
probably at the epiglottis.
    6b. With a bit of saliva to finish
the closure, the walls of the pharynx
can be made to trill sounding like a
gargle.
    6c. Using an air stream from the
esophagus, a belch can cause a trill at
the aperture to the esophagus.

    Exercise 7a. Which of the various
trills described can you nasalize?
    7b. Can you produce any of them
with an air stream going into the lungs?
    7c. Practice them long and short,
that is with fewer taps in each trill
or with more. How few of the taps can
you make and still retain an alveolar
trill?
    7d. Pronounce them on different
pitches.
    7e. Can you make the separate taps
on a trill come faster than normal?
slower?

----

[1]See page 20.

Nonvocoid Sounds with a Nonpulmonic Air Stream

    All of the sounds so far discussed
are produced with an air stream leaving the
lungs or--in a few cases--with the air
stream entering the lungs. There are very
important groups of sounds, however, in which
the air stream does not enter now leave the
lungs.

Glottalized and Implosive Sounds[1]

    For one of these groups the air
stream is initiated by the moving of the
larynx up or down like a piston. See
Figures 31 and 32. Once the control of the

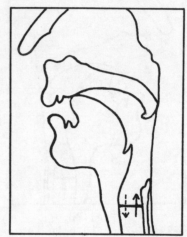

Fig. 31. [t$^{?}$] and [t^{ˤ}]
Movement of the Larynx for
Producing Pharynx Air
(The arrows indicate the direction
of movement of the larynx, and of the
air stream following the release
of the oral closure)
When Egressive ⟶
When Ingressive ⇢

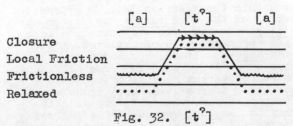

Fig. 32. [t$^{?}$]

Tongue Tip ••••
Vocal Cords Not Vibrating ——, Vibrating ⁓⁓⁓
Rising Larynx Movement ⇉⇉⇉

----

[1]In the classroom there is considerable advantage in starting a course in
phonetics with a lecture on glottalized
sounds, implosives, clicks and nonspeech

larynx is gained so that it can be raised or lowered at will, the various fricatives and stops can be made without much further difficulty.[1] The following type of exercise is highly efficient when accompanied by mimicry of someone pronouncing the sounds. If possible, however, the student should listen to someone who can pronounce these sounds rather than trying to learn them just from a book.[2]

Exercise 1a. First pronounce a long [a::]. Then interrupt the long [a::] with a long glottal stop. Use a timing exercise to be sure that the glottal closure is strongly maintained, thus: [a::ʔ:::a::]. (The purpose of this preliminary exercise is to make certain that the student holds his breath. While he is holding his breath he can be certain that the glottis is closed. If the glottis is closed, he has some possibility of then attaining larynx movement and the production of glottalized or implosive sounds, but if the glottis is open so that air enters or leaves the lungs, the voiceless glottalized and implosive sounds cannot be produced.) During the closure of the glottis, while the breath is being held (and in the middle of the exercise [a:ʔ:a:]) try to pronounce [kʔ]. At first you may find this impossible, since the breath is being held and nowhere can air escape from the lungs to make a [k] audible. If, however, you produce great tension in the throat, and if during the attempt to make the throat tight and smaller you try to squeeze the air out beyond the [k] closure (while still holding his breath), the muscular tension of the throat in general may lift the larynx. This in turn will cause compressed air in the mouth and throat and if the velar closure is at that time released, a [kʔ] is heard. Once you have been successful in pronouncing one

___

sounds. In this way the student gets an over-all picture of the productive mechanisms for vocal sounds, and a broader understanding of the problems involved. For background material of this type, see Kenneth L. Pike, Phonetics, A Critical Analysis of Phonetic Theory and A Technic for the Practical Description of Sounds. University of Midhigan Publications in Language and Literature, XXI Lithoprinted Edition. (Ann Arbor: University of Michigan Press, 1944).

[1]The vocoids, however, demand such a strong air stream that, in general, even though they may be produced in this fashion they remain inaudible except for the percussive transition type which constitute the "pop" upon the release of some pharynx air sounds.

[2]This comment can be applied to all of the sound types listed in the volume, but it is especially true for these, since by speaking English the student has not been trained for voluntary control of the height of the larynx.

glottalized stop, you should attempt to produce a series of these [kʔ] sounds without any vowel between them. You should hear merely the escaping of the compressed air after each velar release. If the sound is being produced correctly --with the glottis closed-- you should be able to start with a full breath and pronounce from 50 to 100 of the [kʔ] sounds without having lost any air at all from your lungs or without having drawn any air into your lungs.

1b. If, however, you have difficulty, you may try to produce first a bilabial glottalized sound, with a lip closure. Then repeat the exercises just given for the [kʔ]. (The [kʔ] is the best glottalized stop to learn first, however, since with it one is not subject to the possibility of substituting an oral click in place of the glottalization.)

1c. If you still have difficulty in getting compressed air to escape, hold your breath, put a bit of paper on your lips and with your tongue between them, try to spit the paper away. (Here, however, you must be certain that you do not blow it off with air from the lungs.)

1d. Once you have achieved mastery over a glottalized stop at any point of articulation, you should then practice to extend control to other points of articulation.

1e. You should then further practice exercises for hearing, recording, and pronouncing these sounds, taking care to distinguish them from regular aspirated or unaspirated stops produced with lung air: [pʔaʹpopʰa], [tʔiʹtʔutʰeto], [kʔikoʹkʔu], [ʹtʃʔutsʔitsʔ].

1f. For an efficient control of the glottalized stops you should further extend this control to the glottalized fricatives [fʔ], [sʔ], [xʔ], and the like.

Exercise 2. Practice also the glottalized affricates [tsʔ], [tʃʔ], [tɬʔ].

Implosive stops are the reverse of the glottalized ones studied in the previous exercises. Voiced implosives constitute a combination (1) of air rarefaction caused by the lowering of the larynx (2) with simultaneous leakage of lung air sufficient to vibrate the vocal cords and ultimately to overcome the partial vacuum in the mouth and throat. The following suggestions may be helpful for producing them:

Exercise 1. Say [a] with ingressive lung air; that is, produce an [a] with suction from the lungs. Then close the lips and continue trying to produce [a] by sucking into the lungs. By so doing you may find that you have induced an implosive [bʕ]. See Figure 33. (In this sound, the lips and velic close the oral and nasal passageways so that no air actually enters the lungs from the outside of the face--but the attempt at ingressive voicing may cause pulmonic

suction which tends to force the larynx
to lower.) Repeat this process but then
open the lips suddenly. Can you feel
or hear air rushing into the mouth? Can
you also feel, just preceding the opening of the lips, the cheeks pulled inward
by the suction? Unless you have unwit-
tingly had pressure from the lungs
forcing the pronunciation of a [g] behind
the velar closure, and unless simultaneously you have at the same time
moved the tongue back[1] so as to form
suction in the mouth, the sound caused
by suction and ingressive voicing may
have been a voiced implosive [bˤ].

Exercise 2. Try to repeat with [dˤ];
with [gˤ].

Exercise 3. Attempt to pronounce a
voiced implosive [bˤ], utilizing the
last two exercises, with voicing added,
as before. Can you see the larynx
lowering the Adam's apple? If you
attempt to continue the sound for a
moment or two, does the suction at the
cheeks change to compression which puffs
them out? (If so, the leakage from the
lungs has overcome the partial vacuum
in the mouth and throat, and filled them
with compressed air. If the lips are
opened at this stage of the sound, the
compressed air will rush from the mouth--
rather than having air rush into the
mouth to fill the partial vacuum which
was existent at the first part of the
sound.)

Exercise 4. Practice nonsense syllables with these sounds: [bˤadˤagˤa].
If you still have difficulty with them,
listen to some child who enjoys attempting to mimic the sound of a frog. Frequently they use voiced implosive sounds
in order to do so, following the stop
with nasalized vocoids.

The voiceless implosive sounds are
quite different from the voiced ones just
described. In them the vocal cords do not
vibrate and there is no leakage of air from

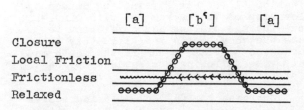

                [a]   [bˤ]   [a]

Fig. 33. [bˤ]

Spread Lips ∘∘∘∘
Vocal Cords Vibrating ∿∿∿
Lowering Larynx Movement with Simultan-
  eous Vocal Cord Vibration ⟨⟨⟨⟨⟨

---

[1]That is, in other words, unless you
have produced a voiced bilabial click.

the lungs. Just as for the voiced type,
however, the larynx must be lowered to cause
the partial vacuum.

Exercise 1. Try to pronounce [pa]
while lowering the larynx. In order to
cause the larynx to lower it may help to
think of sucking air into the lungs--
but do not allow the vocal cords to open;
be certain to hold the breath.

Exercise 2. If you have already
learned to make the glottalized sounds
with the pressure from the larynx, there
is a way for learning the voiceless implosives which is frequently effective:
Produce a [kʔ] so as for force the larynx
to rise; immediately after the tongue
is relaxed, close it again and pronounce
a second [k], trying to suck into the
lungs while keeping the glottis closed,
i.e. while holding the breath. (In this
way the larynx is already lifted for the
[kʔ], and lowers readily to resume its
normal position. Nevertheless while it
is lowering it can create a partial
vacuum in the throat if the tongue has
closed off the oral cavity. This partial
vacuum forms the basis for the implosive
sound which is easily heard at the release of the tongue. If the student can
hear an implosive sound in this way and
can once feel the suction and the strain
on the muscles involved, he may then be
able to pronounce the implosive stop
without first giving the glottalized one.)
In other words train yourself for a ready
control of the raising or lowering of the
larynx by an effort in which it is alter-
nately "push" and "pull": [fʔ], [fˤ];
[fʔ], [fˤ]; [fʔ], [fˤ].

Exercise 3. Can you produce a
[pʔ] and a [ɸˤ] in which the lips do not
open, but for which air is allowed to
escape or enter through the nasal cavity?
These are presumably nonspeech sounds--
velic-released glottalized and implosive
stops.

Exercise 4. Practice drills for
pronouncing, hearing, and recording
glottalized and implosive sounds. [bˤa],
[sʔa], [dˤa], [bˤa], [fʔa], [sʔa], [tʔa],
[kʔa], [sʔa], etc.

Exercise 5. After (or before) having
learned to pronounce implosive stops,
practice making implosive fricatives.

It is quite important for the student
to practice the [kˤ] before practicing [pˤ],
since a glottalized bilabial stop [pʔ] is
acoustically very similar to certain varieties
of bilabial click [pʘ]. If the labial
glottalized stop is uttered by the student
he may not be able to tell whether he has
tongue closure at the velum or not, and hence
may be know whether he is making an implosive
or an ingressive click sound. If, however,
he worked for [kˤ], any suction heard is known
to be implosive, since the mouth formation in
this case does not allow for the formation of

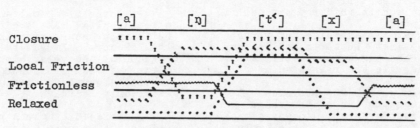

Fig. 34. [aɲt'xa]

Tongue Tip ····
Tongue Back ''''', with Ingressive Movement <·<·<
Velic ,,,,
Vocal Cords Not Vibrating ——— , Vibrating ～～～～

a click.[1]

Clicks

In the formation of clicks the back
of the tongue makes contact with the top of
the mouth. The mouth cavity is then en-
larged by the movement of the tongue backwards or downwards so as to produce a
partial vacuum, or else the tongue is moved
forward and/or upward so as to compress air
in the mouth. If a front oral closure is
maintained during the backward tongue movement, and then the lips are suddenly opened,
air rushes in to fill in the partial vacuum.
While repeating a click it is possible to
have a continuous hum--that is a continuous
[ŋ]. In fact, the [ŋ] may also be produced
by ingressive lung air without preventing
the production of the clicks. The reason
that the hum can be simultaneous with the
click is that the formation of the click has
as its essential characteristic two closures
and movements within the mouth. See Figure
34. The movement behind the mouth for the
nasal sound can therefore be carried on
independently of the clicking sound.

Exercise 1a. Make a closure with
the tip of the tongue against the
alveolar arch. Make a second closure
with the back of the tongue against the
velum. While maintaining this contact,
move the back of the tongue farther
back, and lower the center of the tongue;
then release the tongue tip suddenly.
Do you get, in this way, a sound resembling the noise of commiseration
which is sometimes written in literature
as "tsk-tsk", or "tut-tut?" See Figures
35 and 36.
1b. Repeat the exercise. This time
utilize very tense muscles so as to get

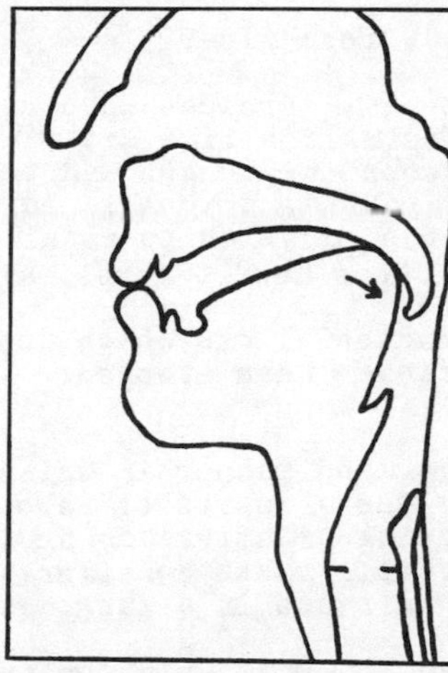

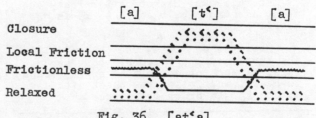

Fig. 35. [p']
The arrow indicates the ingressive
movement of the tongue, and of the
oral air stream following the
labial release.

Closure
Local Friction
Frictionless
Relaxed

Fig. 36. [at'a]
Tongue Tip ····
Tongue Back '''', With Ingressive Move-
ment <·<·<
Vocal Cords Not Vibrating ——— ,
Vibrating ～～～～

_____
[1]Since for the click there must be
both a velar closure and a closure farther
front in the mouth.

an intense sucking movement; then release the front part of the tongue very rapidly. Can you in this way produce a very loud pop?

1c. Repeat the exercise but thrust the tongue against the teeth and release it slowly so the air comes in with a hissing sound; is the result an affricated click?

1d. Again repeat the exercise but this time place the tip of the tongue behind the alveolar arch. Do you get a sound of duller quality or one sharply distinct from the ones you have previously made? If so, you may have produced an alveo-palatal, or cerebral, or retroflexed click.

1e. After again making the oral suction, release the back of the tongue rather than the tongue tip so that the air fills the mouth by way of the throat.

1f. Again repeat the exercise, but this time release one side of the tongue so as to obtain a lateral click, somewhat like the sound used in clucking to a horse.

1g. What is a kiss?

Exercise 2a. Produce an egressive click by closing the lips and making contact between the tongue and the velum following which the tongue is thrust forward in the mouth while retaining its contact. Notice how it forces air out of the mouth.[1]

2b. Produce clicks which are fricative rather than stopped: [fᶜ], etc.

The order and manner in which clicks are affected by the closures or releases of passageways, during or after the production of the click itself, makes considerable difference in their use in a language.

Exercise 1. Form an alveolar click. Release the alveolar closure.

Exercise 2. Repeat, but this time build up pressure from the lungs behind the velic and velar closures before the time for the release so that in the release of the velar closure a [k] is heard.

Exercise 3. Repeat, but release the velar closure slowly so that [x] is heard.

Exercise 4. Delay the pressure from the lungs until the moment that the velar closure opens so that no [k] sound is heard, and follow the click with a strong [h] in order to produce an

aspirated release.

Exercise 5. Simultaneously with the alveolar click make a glottal closure; build up pressure from the lungs behind this closure. Immediately following the release of the velar closure, after the click has been pronounced, release the glottal closure so that a glottal stop is clearly heard.

Exercise 6. Make a hum which begins before the pronunciation of the alveolar click and continues until after the click is made. Then make a different type of nasalization which comes only preceding the click and a third type in which the nasalization stops immediately at the release of the click.

Exercise 7. Simultaneously with one of the various clicks pronounce a [g], so as to produce a "voiced click."

Exercise 8. Practice the following: [atᶜopᶜku], [ipᶜxutᵇ], [omtḷᶜʔu], [ŋtᶜu].

SEQUENCES OF VOCOIDS AND NONVOCOIDS

The difficulties of phonetics are not limited to the pronunciation of isolated sounds but include the pronunciation of sequences of sounds. In some cases individual sounds are pronounced easily but sequences of sound prove difficult. The student needs practice, therefore, in pronouncing, hearing, and recording various kinds of sequences of sounds. Sounds are not produced in static positions of the vocal mechanisms but are the results of a series of fluid muscle movements. Practice with isolated sounds, however, is a very helpful starting point for the practice of sounds of this type in series.

Exercise 1a. Read aloud the data occurring in Restricted Language Problems given later in the book.

1b. Have dictated to you various sequences of sounds.[1]

Exercise 2. Take a passage of English exposition, write it phonetically, then rewrite the data again in reverse order. Read these reverse sequences of English aloud.

Exercise 3a. Take a passage of English exposition; read it aloud while substituting glottalized stops for regular stops.

3b. Repeat, substituting voiceless nasals for voiced nasals.

---

[1] These sounds play little or no part in language systems. It is convenient, therefore, to utilize the term "click" in the remainder of this volume for ingressive clicks.

[1] Sequences for practice both of non-language and language material will be found in Eunice V. Pike, _Dictation Exercises in Phonetics_, (Glendale: Summer Institute of Linguistics, 1946).

3c. Repeat again with various other types of sounds which you have learned, so as to be able to pronounce these sounds in context.

Exercise 4. Practice any tongue twisters which are available to you, such as "She sells sea shells by the seashore." Substitute in them special types of sounds, for example, [s?].

Exercise 5. Take dictation in some foreign language. Try to record it with phonetic symbols, and try to mimic the pronunciation of it.

Chapter 3
SELECTIONS FOR READING

In order that the student might become familiar with phonetic symbols it is helpful for him to read a considerable portion of text. Three types are given here. The first group, Selections 1 through 6, represent English written with symbols designed to represent the sound units of some dialect of that language, rather than phonetic minutiae. The second group, in Selection 7, gives four brief English items arbitrarily modified to give practice in reading length, stress, nasalization, voiceless vowels, and pitch. The third group, constituting Selections 8 and 9, contain foreign language material phonetically written. Before the selections are presented, some discussion is needed about certain of the problems of English transcription and value for the student.

The alphabet used does not indicate all the varieties of pronunciation which one may hear, or which one can train himself to recognize in his own speech. It is planned rather to represent the phonemes (the structural units of sound) of one dialect of American English, or a subtype of that dialect which has been called "General American." There are a great many people in the United States of America, of course, who do not speak in the way indicated in the selections. In fact, the student is almost certain to find a number of differences between this dialect and his own, regardless of the place from which he comes. It is of great value to the student of phonetics and phonemics to study the dialects of people from different sections of his country. By hearing different pronunciations of words with which he is familiar, and by mimicing them, he can learn to pronounce a great many vowel sounds, especially, which would seem very difficult to him were he to meet them in a foreign language, but which as variants of his own speech are not nearly so difficult to imitate.

Some of the main dialects of the United States are those of the Old South, of the New England Seaboard, and of the Midwest, but there are a great many differences which are restricted to smaller sections of the country. These local dialects, as well as the larger regional differences, can all give good experience to the student if he attempts to imitate their sounds. Some of the words which differ from dialect to dialect in English and which may be used as a convenient starting point for mimicry are water, why, huge, pin, pen, can (noun), can (verb), cot, caught, cow, care, book, raw, top, cap, past, farm, marry, merry, Mary, I, wash, city, Betty, Africa, my, more, home, they, bird, poor, morning, mourning, bomb, balm, idea, about. Dialects differ principally according to the geographical location of the speakers, but they also differ according to the occupation of the speakers, their social situation, and so on.

Notice the differences in the following brief samples:

DIALECT SAMPLE A

fə'nɛtɩks 'gæðrz 'rɔ mə'tɩrɩəl. fə'nimɩks 'kʊks ɩt. fə'nɛtɩks prə'vaydz ə 'tɛkˈnik fɔr dɩ'skraybɩŋ 'sawndz ɩn 'tərmz əv 'muvmənts əv ðə 'vokəl æpə-'rætəs, æn fɔr 'raytɩŋ ðɛm ɩn 'tərmz əv ar'tɩkyələtɔri 'fɔrmyuli ('ai 'i, 'lɛtrz əv ðə fə'nɛtɩk 'ælfəbɛt). fə-'nimɩks prə'vaydz 'tɛkˈniks fɔr 'prasɛs-ɩŋ ðə 'rɛf fə'nɛtɩk 'detə, æn træns-'fɔrmɩŋ ɩt ɩntu æn 'ælfəbɛt 'izi fɔr ə 'netɩv tu 'rid. ðə 'pərpəs əv fə-'nimɩks, 'ðɛrfɔr, ɩz tə ri'dus ə 'læng-gwɩʃ tə 'raytɩŋ æn tə pru'zɛnt ðə 'ne-tɩv wɩð ði 'ælfəbɛt əv ðə 'tayp 'izi-ɩst fɔr ɩm tə 'lərn tə 'yuz.

DIALECT SAMPLE B

fʊ'netɩks 'gæðuz rɔ mʊ'tirʊl. fʊ'nimɩks 'kʊks ɩt. 'fnetɩks pru'vaɩdz ʊ 'tɛˈkˈnik fʊ dɩ'skraɩbɩn 'sæʊnz ɳ 'tɩrmz ʊv 'muvmʊnts ʊv ðə vokḷ æpu're-tʊs, æn fʊ 'raɩtɳ dɳ ɳ 'tɩrmz ʊv ɔ'tɩkyulu'tɔrɩ 'fɔmyulaɩ (aɩ i, 'lɛtuz ʊv ðə fʊ'neˀtɩk 'ælfu'beˈt). fʊ'nimɩks pru'vaɩdz ʊ tɛˈkˈnik fɔ 'pro'sɛsɩn ɟ 'rɛf fʊ'netɩk 'deˀtu ɳ 'trænz'fomɩn ɩt ɳtu ɳ 'ælfubeˈt 'izɩ fɔ ʊ 'netɩv tu rid. ɟ 'pɩrpus ʊv fʊ'nimɩks, 'deˀ'fo, ɩz tu rɩ'dʊus ʊ 'læŋgwɩʃ tu 'raɩtɳ æn tu pru'sɛyɩnt ɟ 'netɩv wɩθ ɟ 'æl-fubet ʊv ɟ 'taɩp 'izɩɩs fɔ 'hɩm tʊ 'lɩrn tʊ 'yuz.

Some features of the transcription of the second selection give evidence which suggests that it has not been thoroughly "cooked," or reduced to one symbol for each sound unit. Notice the different transcriptions of the word phonetics. Compare also the transcriptions [ɛ], [ɛˈ], [ɛyˈ], [e], [eˀ], where the first dialect sample had [ɛ]

44

Chart 3. A Tentative Alphabet for English Phonemic Transcription

Key Symbol	Trans-cription	Key Word	Key Symbol	Trans-cription	Key Word
Nonsyllabic Consonants:					
[p]	['pel]	pail	[b]	['æbət]	abbot
[t]	['tek]	take	[d]	['du]	do
[k]	['kærəktɾ]	character	[g]	['gʊd]	good
[č]	['čenǰ]	change	[ǰ]	['ǰorǰ]	George
[f]	['fon]	phone	[v]	['ven]	vain
[θ]	['θɪŋk]	think	[đ]	[đə]	the
[s]	['so]	sew	[z]	[æz]	as
[š]	['šɪp]	ship	[ž]	['vɪžn̩]	vision
[y̱]	['y̱uǰ]	huge	[y]	['yɛs]	yes
[w̱]	['w̱ɛr]	where	[w]	['wɛr]	wear
[h̬]	['h̬u]	who	[m]	['mæn]	man
[l]	['lek]	lake	[n]	['non]	known
[r]	['rat]	rot	[ŋ]	['sɪŋ]	sing
Syllabic Consonants:					
[m̩]	['batm̩] [1]	bottom	[l̩]	['batl̩]	bottle
[n̩]	['bətn̩]	button	[ɾ̩]	['bətɾ̩]	butter
				['bɾ̩d]	bird
Vowels:					
[i]	['fit]	feet	[u]	['but]	boot
[ɪ]	['fɪt]	fit	[ʊ]	['fʊt]	foot
[e]	['met]	mate	[o]	['rot]	rote
[ɛ]	['sɛd]	said	[ɔ]	['kɔt]	caught
[æ]	['kæt]	cat	[a]	['kaləni]	colony
[ə]	['kəp]	cup			
Close-knit Sequences of Vowel Units:					
[aⁱ]	['kaⁱt] [1]	kite	[oⁱ]	['soⁱl]	soil
[aᵘ]	['maᵘs]	mouse			

Suprasegmental Units:

[']	(Innate stress)[2]	["]	(Emphatic stress)
	['tebl̩] table ['haᵘs] house		["tebl̩] table!

[°] (Sentence stress, the beginning of a primary intonation contour)
[°an đə °'tebl̩, nat °'əndɾ ɪt] On the table, not under it.

[|]	(Tentative pause)	[||]	(Final pause)
	[aⁱ °wantəd tu du ɪt |] I wanted to do it,		[aⁱ °wantəd tu du ɪt ||] I wanted to do it.
[‾ ⁻ ₋]	(Four contrastive intonation pitch levels)	[⌐ ⌐]	(Solid line: a single total contour)
	[°'đæt ɪz °'byutɪful ||] That is beautiful.		[aⁱ °'want tu 'go ||] I want to go.

---

[1] Notice that nonsyllabic consonants are unmarked; syllabic ones have a vertical stroke under them. Syllabic vowels are written on the line; nonsyllabic ones are raised above the line. The two systems could be written in analogous ways, but the frequency of syllabic vowels makes the use of a vertical stroke under them impractical.

[2] Weaken all innate stresses considerably or completely unless they are reinforced

or [e]. Probably a further analysis would introduce a more consistent symbolism for these sounds. On the other hand, one or two transcriptions of [e] as [eᵊ] imply a phonetic or sub-unit difference between the unit [e] of Selections A and B. The sound [ɛ] of the first dialect is somewhat glided, ending in a variety of [i] or [ɩ]. The second dialect glides [e], ending it with a sound somewhat like [ə] or [ʊ].

In Samples A and B just given, and in the selections given in Part Two, the reader should not assume that the writing implies that he himself ought to speak in the same way. The selections are illustrating the usage of the symbols and the differences of dialects--not a standard of correctness.

In studying dialects, one observes many differences between them. One may wish to find a basis for determining the "correct" pronunciation. 'It is perhaps as accurate a definition as can be made to say that a pronunciation is correct when it is in actual use by a sufficient number of cultivated speakers.'[1] Pronunciation need not be uniform throughout the country in order to be "correct." Any pronunciation is correct when it is the normal usage of the leaders of that community. In reducing a language to writing, however, the investigator preferably chooses the dialect which has the greatest social, political, or economic prestige and is spoken by the greatest number of people.

As an aid to reading the English selections, a rough KEY to their pronunciation is given in Chart 3. In addition to reading the selections given in Part One, and imitating the dialects of others, the student should attempt to write his own speech with these symbols. He is likely to encounter several difficulties. (1) There may be too few symbols to represent his dialect. For example, some dialects have a difference between the vowels of bomb and balm, and between can (noun) and can (verb). (2) He may find that there are too many symbols and that it would be preferable to eliminate one or more of them. For example, many speakers of English from various parts of the U.S.A. and from Canada do not distinguish between the vowels of cot and caught. (3) Some sound units may be modified by their phonetic environment and these changes sometimes cause difficulty.

For example, it may be difficult to tell whether one is using /o/ or /ɔ/, /i/ or /ɩ/, /e/ or /ɛ/, /u/ or /ʊ/, before /r/. Similarly, there may be a problem in determining whether one uses /s/ or /z/ at the end of such words as adds, or in determining the second element of the vocalic nature of cow, or why, and the like. (4) Another difficulty you may meet is that you do not pronounce some words the same way each time you speak them. In a slow precise style you are likely to use more sounds, or different ones, than in a rapid colloquial style. Compare ['wət are yu 'duɩŋ] with [wət ðə 'duɩn]. (5) In addition, there are certain to be interferences from spelling, so that one may have difficulty in writing words like who, subtle, hiccough, and the like. However, the student should practice transcribing his dialect so as to gain facility in handling technical symbols. If he wishes to write the more intricate phonetic details of his sounds he can utilize the phonetic alphabet provided under Part One.

Even for technicians there remain many severe or unsolved problems of analysis. If one says that phonetic analysis provides the raw material, and phonemics cooks it, then one must add that there are also different cooks. Phonemicists disagree as to the best way of forming a practical or technical alphabet for English.

The differences occur chiefly in symbolizing the vowels and the syllabic consonants. The reason for this disagreement is due to the fact that there are conflicting pressures from the various structural tendencies in English.[1] Bloomfield writes the vocoid glides and certain of the tense vocoid types (including [i], [e], [o], [u], [ai], [au], [oi]) with a vowel letter plus [w] or [j], and the syllabic nonvocoids with a consonant letter plus a syllabic marker.[2] Swadesh writes the syllabic nonvocoids with [ə] plus a consonant letter,[3] and at one time wrote the glides with single symbols, using diacritical marks in order to obtain enough vowel letters. He now uses sequences of vowel symbols.[4] Trager and Bloch use [ə] with syllabic nonvocoids, and [j] and [w] with dipthhongs, but, in addition, use a raised dot (or [h]) to indicate certain long vowels.[5] The system used in this book resembles more that of Kenyon, who writes [i],

ster and Co., 1935).

[1] See Premise Number 4, p. 60-81, 149.

[2] Leonard Bloomfield, Language, (New York: Henry Holt and Co., 1933).

[3] Morris Swadesh, "The Vowels of Chicago English," Language, XI (June, 1935).

[4] Morris Swadesh, "On the Analysis of English Syllabics," Language, XXIII (April-June, 1947), 137-50.

[5] George L. Trager and Bernard Bloch, "The Syllabic Phonemes of English," Language, XVII (July-September, 1941), 223-46.

with sentence stress or emphatic and sentence stresses.

[3] If the contour cannot be completed before the margin is reached, an arrow is added to the intonation line to show that the contour continues below.

[1] John S. Kenyon, "The Guide to Pronunciation," § 5, in Webster's New International Dictionary of the English Language, Second Edition (Springfield: Merriam Webster...

[e], [o], and [u] with single symbols, and
[aı], [au], and [oi] as [aʊ], [au], and
[ɔʊ];[1] in addition, Kenyon includes four
separate symbols for stressed and unstressed
[ə], and for stressed and unstressed [r];
he uses the syllabic consonant signs, and
also [ə] plus a consonant for [l], [m], and
[n] in unstressed syllables.[2] All these
methods of writing English are useful for
the purposes of their authors. For teaching natives to read, there are likely to be
alternative possibilities in the languages
which one investigates. One must be ready
to experiment with different systems in order to determine which is the most satisfactory. One should be prepared, however,
to analyze the technical differences between
them so as to be able to weigh the advantages of each.

SELECTION 1*

ðə °ˈsi ˈsɻpn̩t†

°ˈsi ˈsɻpn̩ts ar °ˈlarj məˈrin
°ˈænəməlz əv ˈmost ənˈyuʒuəl °ˈhæbəts
n̩ əˈpɻn̩ts || ðe ar abˈzɻvd °ˈonli
ɪn °ˈworm °ˈwɛðɻ | °ˈjɛnɻli ɪn °ˈɔ-
gəst ɻ sɛpˈtɛmbɻ | wɛn ðe °ˈsəmtaɪmz
°ˈraɪz tə ðə °ˈsɻfəs | °ˈloŋ əˈnəf tə
gɛt ˈɪntə ðə ˈpepɻz || °ðɛn ðe ri-
°ˈtɻn tə ðɛr °ˈhomz ət ðə °ˈbatəm əv
ði °ˈoʃən | æn °ˈste ðɛr ənˈtɪl ðe
°ˈfil n̩ ðə °ˈmud əˈgɛn || æz °no
°ˈspɛsəmən hæz °ˈɛvɻ bɪn °ˈkæpðɻd |
°ˈsi ˈsɻpn̩ts ʏ °nat bɪn ˈstədid z

---

*Adapted from "The Sea Serpent," by
Will Cuppy, Saturday Evening Post, Vol. 216,
No. 11, (September 11, 1943). Used by per-
mission.

†The student should remember to reduce the intensity of innately stressed syllables unless supported by sentence stress.
He should pause only in the places indicated
by pause markers.

---

[1]The specific analysis given here is
based on the following studies: Kenneth L.
Pike, "On the Phonemic Status of English
Diphthongs," Language, XXIII (April-June,
1947), 151-59; and idem, The Intonation of
American English, University of Michigan
Publications in Linguistics, I (Ann Arbor:
University of Michigan Press, 1945).

[2]John S. Kenyon, American Pronunciation (Ann Arbor: George Wahr, 1935).

°ˈkɛrfli z °ˈmost °ˈəðɻ ˈænəmlz | æn
kəmˈpærɪtəvli °ˈfyu ˈpɻsn̩z ˈno °ˈɛni-
ˈθɪŋ °ˈdɛfɪnɪt əˈbaʊt ðɛm || °ˈðæt ɪz
wɛr °ay ˈkəm ɪn || °ˈsi ˈsɻpn̩ts ar
°ˈbraʊn an °ˈtap | æn °ˈyɛloʊʃ °ˈwaɪt
əndɻˈniθ || ðe hæv °ˈloŋ °ˈslɛndɻ
°ˈnɛks n̩ °ˈtelz | bət ðə °ˈsaɪz n̩
°ˈʃep əv ðə °ˈbadi ɻ prabləmˈætɪkl̩ |
sɪnts °ˈmost əv ɪt ɪz °ˈolwɪz °ˈəndɻ
°ˈwotɻ || °ˈɛstəməts ʏ ðə °ˈtotl̩
°ˈlɛŋθ | °ˈværi frəm °ˈslaɪtli °ˈlɛs
ðṇ °ˈfɪftˈtin °ˈfit tu əˈbaʊt °ˈθri
°ˈmaɪlz n̩ ə °ˈhæf || °ˈaɪwɪtnəs dəs-
°ˈkrɪpʃn̩z əv ðə °ˈsi ˈsɻpn̩t ˈdɪfɻ °so
ˈmɛʃ ðæt °ˈmɛni ˈθɪŋkɻz əv ˈgɪvn̩ əp
ðə °ˈhol °ˈθɪŋ əz °ˈtu °ˈdɪfəkl̩t ||
ðə kənˈflɪktɪŋ əˈkaʊnts | əv ˈkors |
°ˈmɻli °ˈpruv ðæt ðɛr ar °ˈsɛvrəl
°ˈkaɪndz ʏ ˈsi ˈsɻpn̩ts || ðɛr °ˈməst
bi || ðə norˈwiʃn̩ ˈsi ˈsɻpn̩t riˈzɛm-
blz ə °ˈmæs ʏ °ˈflotɪŋ °ˈsiwid || hi
hæz ə °ˈhorslaɪk °ˈhɛd | ə °ˈloŋ
°ˈgrin °ˈmen | °ˈolso riˈzɛmblɪŋ ˈsiwid |
æn °ˈnumɻəs °ˈhəmps ɻ °ˈbɛnðəz əˈloŋ
ɪz ˈbæk ||[1] ðə °ˈwənz wɪd °ˈrɛd °ˈmenz
n̩ °ˈflemɪŋ °ˈaɪz ɻ ə °ˈrɛr °ˈsəbˈspi-
ʃiz || ˈðoz wɪðˈaʊt ˈmenz °me bi
°ˈfimelz || ðə ˈnu °ˈɪŋglənd ˈsi ˈsɻpn̩t
lʊks ɪgˈzækli laɪk n̩ °ˈol °ˈtri
°ˈtrəŋk | °ˈbabɪŋ əˈbaʊt an ðə °ˈwevz|
wɪð ðə °ˈruts ˈstɪkɪŋ əp laɪk °ˈhornz
ɻ °ˈæntlɻz ||[2] ðə mɪsəˈleniəs ˈsi
[1]riˈzɛmblɪŋ °ˈsiwid ||

[2]aɪ kn̩ °ˈjəst °ˈhɪr yu °ˈæskɪŋ |
ðɛn °ˈwaɪ °ˈɪznt ɪt n̩ °ˈold °ˈtrəŋk ||
°ˈhuz °ˈraɪtɪŋ ðɪs ˈartɪkl̩ | °yu ɻ
°ˈaɪ ||

ˈsɹɪpt ɪz ən ɪkˈsɛpʃn̩ tu ˈol
ˈrulz ‖ ðə ˈlak ˈnɛs ˈmanstɹ wəz
əv ˈðɪs ˈtaⁱp ‖[1] ɪn ˈmaⁱ əˈpɪnyən |
ˈsɪ ˈsɹɪpts ɣ sɹˈvaⁱvd frəm ˈpriyɪs-
ˈtorɪk ˈtaⁱmz ‖ wɛn ðə ˈwɹld wz
ˈyəŋ n̩ ˈfulɪʃ ‖ ˈkalɪ ʃ prəˈfɛsɹz
ˈse ət ɪz ɪmˈpasəbl̩ dæt ˈɛni əv ðoz
ˈkriðɹz ʃʊd ˈstɪl ɪgˈzɪst ‖ ðe ˈme
bi məsˈtekn̩ ‖ ay ˈkanstn̩tli ˈmit
ˈpipl̩ | hu ɹ səˈpraⁱzd dæt ˈay stɪl
ɪgˈzɪst ‖ ˈwən ˈθɪŋ əˈbaʊt ˈsi ˈsɹ-
pɹts əˈpɪrz tə bi ˈsɹtn̩ ‖ ˈiðɹ yə
ˈsi ðm̩ ɹ yə ˈdont ‖ ˈmɛni ˈpipl̩
ˈgo ˈθru ðɛr ˈɛnˈtaⁱr ˈlaⁱvz | wɪð-
ˈaʊt ˈsiɪŋ ˈivn̩ ə ˈlɪtl̩ wən ‖ ˈaⁱv
ˈnɛvɹ ˈsin ˈmor ðn̩ ˈtu ɣ ðəm maⁱ-
ˈsɛlf ‖

SELECTION 2
ə ˈsæmpl̩ trænˈskrɪpʃn̩

ˈðɪs ɪz ə ˈtɛntətɪv fəˈnimɪk
trænˈskrɪpʃn̩ əv ˈwən ˈdaⁱəlɛkt əv ə-
ˈmɛrɪkn̩ ˈspiʃ ‖ ɪt ɪz ˈnat ˈrɪtn̩
əˈkordɪŋ tu ˈstændɹd ˈɪŋglɪʃ orˈθa-
grəfi ‖ ˈðɛrfor ɪt wɪl bi ˈslaⁱtli
ˈdɪfəkəlt for ˈyu ˌtu ˈrid ‖ bət
ˈdont ˈwɹri ‖ ɪn ˈtaⁱm ˈyu wɪl
biˈkəm prəˈfɪʃnt ɪn ˈridɪŋ æz wɛl
æz ˈraⁱtɪŋ ˈwɹdz æn ˈfrezəz ɪn fə-
ˈnɛtɪk ˈskrɪpt ‖ ɪf ˈyu wɹ ˈrezd
ɪn ðə ˈsaʊθ | or ɪn ˈnu ˈɪŋglənd |
or ɪn ˈsɹtn̩ ˈəðɹ ˈparts əv ðə ˈyu

---

[1] so wəz ði ˈabjɪkt ˈnotəst bay
ˈfaⁱv ˈnevl̩ ˈofəsɹz | an ə ˈfɪʃɪŋ
ˈtrɪp nɪr ˈhæləfæks ɪn ˈeˈtin ˈθɹ-
ti ˈθri ‖ ˈˌboⁱ | wəz ˈðæt ə ˈpar-
ti ‖

ˈɛs ˈe | ˈyu ˈme ˈfaⁱnd dæt ˈyur
ˈdaⁱəlɛkt ɪz ˈdɪfɹənt frəm ˈðɪs
ˈwən ‖[1] ɪn ə ˈde ɹ ˈtu ˈyu wɪl bi
ˈstədiɪŋ ˈdaⁱəlɛkts əv ˈɪŋglɪʃ ænd
ˈyuzɪŋ yur ˈklæsmɛmbɹz æz ɪnˈform-
ənts ‖ haʊˈɛvɹ | ɪt ɪz ˈnɛsəsɛri
ˈnaʊ for ˈyu tu ˈkansn̩tret an bi-
ˈkəmɪŋ kəmˈplitli fəˈmɪlyɹ wɪð ˈðɪs
ˈmɛθəd əv ˈraⁱtɪŋ | sɪnts ˈyu wɪl
ˈyuz ɪt θruˈaʊt ðə ˈhol ˈkors ˈðɪs
ˈsəmɹ | nat ˈonli ɪn ˈðɪs ˈklæs | bət
ˈolso ɪn ˈol ði ˈəðɹz ‖

ðə ˈsɪmbl̩z wɪč ar ˈyuzd ɪn
ˈðiz ˈfɹst səˈlɛkʃənz | ar ˈfaʊnd ɪn
ðə ˈčart ˈlebl̩d ə ˈtɛntətɪv ˈælfəbɛt
for ˈɪŋglɪʃ fəˈnimɪk trænˈskrɪpʃən ‖
ˈletɹ ɪn ðə ˈkors | ˈyu wɪl bi ˈgɪvn̩
ˈəðɹ ˈridɪŋ səˈlɛkʃn̩z] wɪč wɪl ˈmek
ˈyus əv ˈmor æn ˈdɪfɹənt fəˈnɛtɪk
ˈsɪmbl̩z ‖ ˈðiz ˈsɪmbl̩z wɪl bi ˈfaʊnd
ɪn ðə fəˈnɛtɪk ˈčarts ˈɹlɪɹ ɪn
ˈpart ˈwən əv ˈðɪs ˈbuk ‖

SELECTION 3
ðə ˈfrɛnli ˈwɛst[2]

biˈfor aⁱ ˈlɛft maⁱ ˈhom ɪn
ˈbɔləmor | ə ˈfrɛnd əv ˈmaⁱn ˈsɛd
tu mi | ˈsædlɹ | yu wɛl ˈlaⁱk ðə
ˈpipl̩ ɪn ðə ˈwɛst] ðe ɹ ˈso
ˈfrɛnli ‖ ˈwɛn ðe ˈpæs yu ɔn ðə
ˈstrit | ðe wɪl ˈse ˈhæʊdi | æn
ˈofn̩ ðe wɪl ˈpoz æn ɛnˈgeʃ yu ɪn
kanvɹˈseʃn̩ ‖

aⁱ wəz ˈglæd tu riˈsiv dæt ɪn-

---

[1] Largely that of Donald Stark.

[2] Written for this volume by Wesley
Sadler.

forˈmeš̩ | æn wa¹ ᵒˈrazlən æn ᵒˈkɛzli
æn a¹ wɹ ᵒˈkəmɪn ᵒˈæᵘt ᵒˈhir ɔn ðə
ᵒˈtren | ˈwi ᵒˈpræktɪst ˈseɪŋ ᵒˈhæᵘdi
tu ˈwən əˈnəðɹ || ˈkɛzli ˈhæd ə
ˈlɪt̩l ˈdɪfəkəlti wɪð ðə ˈwɹd | æz ɪt
wəz ᵒˈnu tu hɪm || hæᵘᵒˈɛvɹ | hi kʊd
ᵒˈmænɪǰ ðə ˈprapɹ grɪᵒˈmes æn ᵒˈmošn̩z||

ᵒˈwɛl | ᵒˈwən ˈde ˈæftɹ wi
əˈra¹vd ɪn ᵒˈnormən | ᵒwi ᵒˈθri wɹ
ᵒˈstændɪn an ðə ᵒˈkornɹ | ᵒˈitɪn ᵒˈa¹s
ˈkrim ˈkonz | wɛn ə ᵒˈmæn æn hɪz
ᵒˈwa¹f ᵒˈpozd bɪᵒˈsa¹d əs || ᵒˈhæᵘdi |
hi ˈsɛd || ᵒˈhæᵘdi | hɪz ˈwa¹f ˈɛkod ||
ᵒˈhæᵘdi | ˈrazlən ən a¹ riˈpla¹d ||
ᵒˈkɛzli ˈsɛd ˈsəmθɪn wɪč ᵒˈsæᵘndɪd
ᵒˈla¹k ə ᵒˈkæᵘ ˈpʊlɪŋ hɪz ᵒˈfʊt ˈæᵘt
əv ðə ˈməd | bət wɪč ðə ᵒˈmæn æn
ᵒˈwumən ɪnᵒˈtɹpɹtɪd æz ᵒˈhæᵘdi ||

wi ᵒˈtɔkt ᵒˈkwa¹t ə ᵒˈlɔn
ᵒˈta¹m | ᵒˈfrɛnli ˈla¹k | æn ᵒˈrazlən
æn ᵒa¹ wɹ ᵒˈseɪn tu ɹˈsɛlvz | ᵒˈma¹ |
bət ðə ˈpipl̩ ɪn ðə ˈwɛst ɹ ˈfrɛnli ||
a¹ ᵒˈwɪš ðe wɹ la¹k ᵒˈðɪs ɪn ðə
ᵒˈist || æn wi ˈsma¹ld ᵒˈnoʊnli ˈæt
ˈwən əˈnəðɹ | æn ˈkɛzli ˈgɪɡəld ||
ˈwɛn ðə ᵒˈmæn æn hɪz ᵒˈwa¹f ᵒˈmuvd
ᵒon | wi ᵒˈhɹd hɪm ᵒˈse tu hɹ | a¹
ᵒˈwɪš ðə ᵒˈpipl̩ ᵒˈbæk ᵒˈhom wɹ æz
ᵒˈfrɛnli æz ᵒˈðiz ᵒˈwɛstn̩rz ||

SELECTION 4
ᵒˈbebi ˈtɔk¹

ᵒˈhɛɛlo ˈwɪdl̩ ˈbebi || ᵒˈna¹s
ˈwɪdl̩ ˈbebi || ˈhaᵘ ɪz u ᵒˈfilɪn tu-
ˈde || ˈnaᵘ ɪf u ɪz ᵒˈwiiiil ᵒˈtwa¹-

ət | ᵒˈmami wɪl ᵒˈtɛl u ə ᵒˈnaa¹s
ᵒˈnaa¹s ᵒˈtori || ɪf u ɪz ˈdoɪŋ tu
ᵒˈtwa¹ | ᵒˈmami wɪl hæf tu ᵒˈpæŋk u ||
ᵒˈwɛl | ᵒˈwatsə ᵒˈmætɹ wɪf u || dəz u
ˈwants tu ˈdɛt ᵒˈəp ᵒˈnaᵘ || u ᵒˈdəz ||
ˈtəm ᵒˈan tu ᵒˈmami æn ᵒˈmami wɪl
ᵒˈtɪs u an u ᵒˈwɪdl̩ ᵒˈfesmz-ˈwesmz ||
ᵒˈɔɔɔɔ | u ɪz so ᵒˈtwit || ᵒˈhuz
ˈuzmz-ˈwuzmz ɪz ᵒu || ɪz u ᵒˈmamiz
ˈwɪdl̩ ˈuzmz-ˈwuzmz || ᵒˈššššš ˈbebi |
ˈdəzn̩t u ˈwants tu ˈhir ᵒˈmami ˈtɛl
u ðə ᵒˈnaaa¹s ˈtori || ˈkəᵒˈman naᵘ |
ᵒˈstap u ᵒˈwækət or ᵒˈmami ᵒˈwunt
ᵒˈtɛl u əˈbaᵘt ðə ᵒˈwɪdl̩ ᵒˈgɹl ||
ᵒˈwəns əᵒˈpan ə ᵒˈta¹m ðɛr wəz ə
ᵒˈwɪdl̩ ᵒˈgɹl huz ᵒˈnem wəz ᵒˈwɪdl̩
ᵒˈrɛd ᵒˈra¹dɪn ˈhʊd || ᵒˈwən ˈde hɹ
ᵒˈmami ᵒˈtold hɹ tu ᵒˈdo tu ɹ ᵒˈdræn-
ˈmaz ˈples || æn ˈwɛn ši dat ˈðɛr |
wa¹ ᵒˈləvmz | ˈwat ɪz u ᵒˈtwa¹ɪŋ for ||
ᵒdont ᵒˈtwa¹ kəz ᵒˈmami ᵒˈləvz u so ||
ᵒˈtap u ᵒˈtwa¹ɪŋ ˈnaᵘ ˈpwɛšəs | kəz
ᵒˈhɪmz ɪz ə ᵒˈbɪg ᵒˈmæn ˈnaᵘ | æn
hɪm ᵒˈšudn̩t ᵒˈtwa¹ ᵒˈɛɛɛni ᵒˈmor || ɪz
u ᵒˈtɪl ˈsipi || hɪm ɪz dəst ə
ᵒˈdweeet ᵒˈbɪɪɡ ᵒˈmænz ˈnaᵘ || ᵒˈmm-
hmmm || ˈɛs hɪm ɪz | ænd hɪm ɪz
ᵒˈmamiz ᵒˈpwɛšəs ᵒˈɪti-ᵒˈbɪti ᵒˈbo¹ ||
ᵒˈpwiz ˈtap u ˈtwa¹ɪn ˈbebi || ------
ᵒˈJunyɹ | arn ðu ᵒˈɛvɹ ˈgənə ᵒˈšət
ᵒˈəp ||

SELECTION 5
ᵒˈesaps ᵒˈfiblz (ˈnəmbɹ ᵒˈθri)¹
ᵒˈwe ᵒˈbæk biˈfor ᵒˈkrosɪntən
ᵒˈdɛld ðə ᵒˈwašəwɛr | ə ᵒˈlet ᵒˈbɪg

°ˌgraⁱən wəz ˈdipɪŋ °ˌpisfəli ɪn ɪz
°ˌslɛn | °ˌbimɪŋ ɤ ə °ˌdrif ˈstek |
wɛn hi wɤ °ˌəˈwekɪnd baⁱ ə °ˌmi
°ˌwaᵘs | ˈrənɪŋ °ˌfæk ᶇ °ˌborθ əˈfos
ɪz °ˌkres || °ˌtuzɪŋ ɪz °ˌlɛmpɤ | də
ˈgraⁱən °ˌlæbd də ˈmɪtᶅ ˈlaᵘs baⁱ də
°ˌnef ɤ də °ˌskrɛk | ænd wɤ an də
°ˌkɤʃ ɤ °ˌvɪlɪŋ ɪm || °ˌmur °ˌlɪtᶅ
°ˌpaᵘs || °ˌliz | ˈmɪstɤ ˈplaⁱən | ˈmaⁱd
də ˈkraᵘs | ɪf yə wɪl °ˌonli ˈgɤt mi
°ˌlo | aⁱ °ˌfamɪs °ˌpreθfəli tə ri-
°ˌkaⁱnd yu for yɤ °ˌpenəs || °ˌso | də
°ˌlirs °ˌfaⁱən | hu məst ɤ bɪn ə
°ˌkəb °ˌskoⁱ ˈbaᵘt ɪn ɪz °ˌdəŋgɤ
ˈyez | ˈθot hi wud °ˌdi hɪz °ˌdeli
°ˌgud °ˌdud | æn hi °ˌsɛt də °ˌfraᵘs
°ˌmi || ə °ˌkəpᶅ ɤ °ˌliks ᶜˈwetɤ |
ɛɪs °ˌvɛri °ˌlem °ˌsaⁱən gat °ˌnæŋgᶅd
əp ɪn ə °ˌtɤt | °ˌænd | ɑo hi wɤ
°ˌbɪŋ ɤ də °ˌkists | nat tə bi kᶇ-
ˈfyuzd wɪɤ °ˌkrɔz °ˌbɪŋbɪ | °ˌnoˈwɛn
ˈkem tu ˈæntsɤ ɪz °ˌrɛloɪŋ °ˌborz ||
°ˌbət | ˈčɪr ˈdɪldrən | °ˌpe ɪz də
°ˌhirɔf || ə°ˌlɔŋ ˈkəmz də °ˌmaⁱni
°ˌlɪtᶅ °ˌtaᵘs | ænd | °ˌnoɪŋ də °ˌrops
wɪɤ ɪz °ˌtiθ | hi °ˌfriz də ˈšaⁱən
frəm ɪz °ˌlækᶅz || °ˌtɤn ə°ˌfer ɪz
°ˌbaᵘt °ˌple | ˈmiks də ˈskwaᵘs | æn
wɪɤ °ˌdæt i °ˌhɤnz an ɪz °ˌtil | æn
°ˌhits ɪt fɤ °ˌbom || æn də °ˌstorᶅ
tə ɛɪs ˈmori ɪz | °ˌsəmtaⁱmz ar
ˈbəbᶅz ar °ˌtrɪg | æn °ˌsəmtaⁱmz ar
ˈsməbᶅz ar °ˌtrɔl | bət ɪf wi °ˌtræd
no ˈhəbᶅz | °ˌhaᵘ wud wi °ˌblɛkɪgnaⁱz
ar °ˌrɛsɪnz ||

SELECTION 6

də °ˌskorpiən |¹

°ˌsi də °ˌskorpiən | wɪl də

¶ˌskorpiən °ˌbaⁱt | °ˌno | ɪf yu ar

°ˌkaⁱnd tu də °ˌskorpiən æn °ˌtrit hɪm

laⁱk ə ˈfrɛnd | °ˌhi wɪl nat ˈbaⁱt yu |

hi wɪl °ˌstɪŋ yu || °ˌskorpiənz °ˌstɪŋ

ðɛr ˈpre | kənˈsɪstɪŋ əv °ˌspaⁱdɤz ᶇ

ˈɪnsɛkts | tə °ˌmek ət biⁱ°ˌhev waⁱl

də °ˌit ət || °ˌskorpiənz ᶇ °ˌspaⁱdɤz

ɤ nat °ˌɪnsɛkts | bət əˌ°ˌrækᶇədz | wɪd

°ˌɛt °ˌlegz || °ˌɪnsɛkts hæv °ˌonli

¹Adapted from Will Cuppy, "The Scorpion," Saturday Evening Post, Vol. 216, No. 1, July 3, 1943.

Preceding final pause, symbolized by [||], a phrase ending in pitch [4] tends to fade away a bit, or end with the last vowels extra low and laryngealized; a phrase ending in [°2-4-3 ||] tends to have the final pitch [3] relatively lower than usual. Preceding tentative pause, symbolized by [|], a phrase ending in pitch [4] tends to have the final syllable or syllables held level (or even rising a trifle, but not as high as [3]), without fading lower; similarly, [°2-4-3 |] and [°2-4-2 |] tend to have their final pitches sustained at normal heights.

The student should not assume that this is the only intonation with which the selection could be read; others are equally possible. For selections less difficult to read, see Kenneth L. Pike, The Intonation of American English, University of Michigan Publications in Linguistics, I (Ann Arbor: University of Michigan Press, 1945).

ˈsɪks ˈlɛgz || wunt yu ˈˈtraɪ tə
riˈmɛmbɚ ˈðɪs | ˈskɔrpiənz ˈɔfn̩
ˈstɪŋ ˈpipl̩ an ðə ˈhænz n̩ ˈfit wɛn
əˈnoɪd ɚ dɪsˈtɚbd || ðe ˈɔlso ˈstɪŋ
an ˈɛnɚl ˈprɪnsəplz || ðe ˈkæri
ðɛr ˈtɛlz ˈkɔrld ˈovɚ ðɛr ˈbæks | n̩
ˈɔlwiz ˈstɪŋ ɪn ˈfrʌnt ə ðəm-
ˈsɛlvz || wɛn yur ˈhæŋɪŋ əˈraʊnd ə
ˈskɔrpiən | ˈste ˈnɪr ɪz ˈseɪfɪn
ˈɛnd || yul n̩ ˈdʒoɪ ət ˈmɔr ||² ðə
ˈpoɪzn̩ əv ðə ˈskɔrpiənz ˈstɪŋ ɪz

---

¹ˈwɛl | yu ˈnidn̩t gɛt ˈsɔr
æt mi || ˈˈaɪ hæd ˈnəθɪŋ tə ˈdu wɪð
ɪt ||

²ˈskɔrpiənz kn̩ bi ˈkɛp fr
absɚˈveʃn̩ ɪn ə ˈglæs ˈdʒɑr wɪð ə
ˈlɪd an ət || ˈˈdont fɚˈgɛt ðə
ˈlɪd |

ˈsɛldm̩ ˈfetl̩ tə ˈlardʒɚ ˈmæml̩z | bət
ət ˈhɚts ˈsəmpɪn ˈfirs || ˈwən
ˈkæn | haˈʊɛvɚ | əˈkwaɪr ˈparsl̩
əˈmyunɪti baɪ ˈtekɪn ðə ˈprapɚ
ˈstɛps || ɪf ye ˈlɛt ə ˈskɔrpiən
ˈstɪŋ yu ˈɛvri ˈwənts n̩ ə ˈwaɪl |
ði əˈfɛkts biˈkəm ˈlɛs səˈvir ɪč
ˈtaɪm || ənˈtɪl ˈfaməli | ˈɔl yu
ˈnotɪs ɪz ðə sɛnˈseʃn̩ əv ˈbɪɪŋ
ˈstæbd wɪθ n̩ ˈaɪs ˈpɪk ænd ə
ˈslaɪt ˈdɪzi ˈfilɪŋ fr ˈsɛvrl̩ ˈdez ||
aɪv ˈnat ˈtraɪd ˈðɪs maɪˈsɛlf || ˈwat
wɪð ˈwən ˈθɪŋ n̩ əˈnəðɚ | aɪm
ˈɔlwiz ˈpʊtɪŋ ət ˈɔf ||¹ ðə ˈskɔr-

---

¹ɪf yu ˈθɪŋk yu hæv ˈskɔrpiənz ˈʌndɚ yr ˈbɛdrum ˈflor
ˈdont ˈwʌri || ˈskɔrpiənz ˈlɪv ˈonli
ˈfaɪv ˈyɪrz ||

piən 'lidz ə °'saləteri 'la¹f fɹ ðə

'most 'pɑɹt | æz i hæz ə °'lo ə·'pɪn-

yən ɣ °'ɔl °'ɔðɹ 'skorpiənz || °ðe

°"het ðɛr 'ka¹nd | ɛk'sɛpt ɪn °'me |

°'ɪɹn jə°'la¹ ŋ °'ɔgəst || wɛn ðe 'go

tə ðə °'apɪzɪt ɛk'strim || ɪn °ðiz

°'mənθs ðə °'skorpiən ŋ ðə °'skor-

piənεs 'tek °'lɔŋ °'strolz | °'pɪnsɹ

ɪn °'pɪnsɹ | °'stænd an ðɛr °'hɛdz |

æn °'kæri °an rɪ°'gardləs ||¹ °ðɛn ðə

°'skorpiənεs dɪ°"vɑⁿɹz hɹ 'met | ænd

°ðæts ðə °"læst ðəts 'sin əv °hɪm |

°'simz əz °ðo °ðɪs °'hæbət ɣ hɹz wʊd

'gɛt ə°'raⁿnd ə'mən ðə 'fɛləz | bət

°'ðoz hu 'no °'most ə°'baⁿt ət ɹ ɪn

1°'boθ 'partnɹz ɹ ɛk°'strimli

°'əgli ŋ ri°'pəlsɪv || °'forʧnətli ðe

hæv °'pur °'a¹sa¹t ||

°no kən'dɪʃn tə °'mek ə rɪ°'port ||

°'bebi 'skorpiənz rɪ°'men wɪð ðɛr

°'məðr fɹ ðə °'fɹst °'tu °'wɪks |

'ra¹dɪŋ an hɹ °'bæk | 'frɪskɪŋ °'mɛr-

əli ŋ ðə °'græs | æn 'groɪŋ °'minɹ

°'ɛvri °'mɪnət || a¹ sə°'poz a¹ °"ot

ə bi °'sari fɹ 'skorpiənz | bi'kəz ðe

ɹ so °'ofəl || a¹l °"θɪŋk ət °'ovr ||¹

SELECTION 7

'ɪŋglɪʃ 'madɪfɪkeʃnz for 'præktɪs
'lɛŋkθ:

ðə 'vo·kl 'mɛ·kənɪ·zm ɪz na·t
i·'kwɪpt tə 'gɪv prɪ'sa·¹s rɛpə·'tɪ·-
ʃənz əv 'ɪnɪ· spɛ·'sɪ·fɪk 'saⁿnd or
'saⁿndz wɪ·ð·a·ⁿt vɛr·ɪ·'eʃən || ɪn prə-
'naⁿnsɪŋ 'ɪnɪ· 'wɹd 'twa·¹s ðɛr wɪl
'bi· mɪ·'nut 'dɪ·fɹnsə·z | 'i·vn ɔ·l'ðo

1°'skorpiənz °'nɛvr 'stɪŋ ðm-

'sɛlvz tə °'dəθ | no 'mætɹ °"wat 'ðæt

°'na¹s 'ol 'ʤɛntlmən 'told yu | bət

'go ə'hɛd ŋ bə°"liv ət | ɪf yəd

'ræðr || ðɹz °no °"lo ə'gɛnst ət |

'điz 'dɪfɾnsə·z 'me bi· 'tu 'smɔl
fo·r đi· 'ɪr tʊ· 'hir bət 'nat 'tu·
'smɔ·l tʊ· bi rɪ·'kordə·d ba¹ 'dɛlɪ·-
kə·t 'ɪ·nstrumə·nts ||

'nezłə'zešṇ:

ɪn 'əđɾ 'wɾdz | nọ 'wɾd ɪz 'ɛvɾ
rɪ'pitəd ɛk'sæktlɪ ɪn đə 'sẹm 'we |
nọr wɪd ɛk'sæktlɪ đə 'sẹm 'ta¹p əv
'sɛgmṇts || on đị 'əđɾ hænd | 'wɾdz
'yuẓuəlɪ ạr prọ'na^unst so đət đi 'ɪr
dəz nat 'kæč đə mɪ'nut vɛrɪ'ešṇz
'prɛzṇt ||

'vo¹słɛs 'va^ulz:

ɪt 'səmta¹mz 'hæpṇz ha^uɛvɾ |
đət đə fləkčU'ešṇz ịṇ đə prənənsɪ'Ešṇ
əv wən əv đə 'sa^undz əv ə spɛ'slfɪk
'wɾd aR so 'gret đət đə 'forṇR ịz
'vɛrɪ 'sɛnsɪtɪv tu đɛm || 'đis ịz
ə'spɛšlɪ đə 'kes wɛn đə fləkču'Ešṇ ịz
əz 'grɛt æz Or 'gretɾ đɛn đə 'dɪf-
ɾns bɪ'twIn 'tU əv đə slg'nlfəkṇt
'sɪgnḷlŋ 'yUnɪts ịn đə 'læŋwịǰ əv đə
'fOrṃɾ ||

ton:

ə 'kɔšṇ mэst bị 'gịvṇ đə
'stụdṇt ịn fịld wɾ̄k || ɪt 'səmta¹mz
'hæpṇz đət ạn ịn'vɛstɪgetɾ̄ mэ θịŋk
đət ə wɾd ɪz prọ'na^unst ịn tū 'dịf-
ɾ̞ṇt wêz | 'wɛrэz đə wɾd ɪz 'đkčủlɪ
prọ'na^unst 'yúnə'fŏrmlɪ | bət đị ịn-
'vɛstɪgetɾ̄z pɪ'sɛpšṇ hæz 'vɛ̄rɪd || 'đis
ɪz ə'spɛšlɪ trú wɛn đə sa^und ɪn
'kwɛsčṇ ịz ə'kùstɪklɪ əba^ut 'hæf'wé
bị'twIn tū 'fŏnịmz əv đị ịn'vɛstɪgetɾ̄z
'læŋwịǰ ||

Selection 8
Aztec Text[1]

    'sie tu'nalɪ o'motši   o'yeya
    One   day   it happened there

    'sente 'koyutł 'wa 'sente tła'k^wo-
    was a   coyote and a   possum.

tsi. ini'noŋka tła'k^wotsi la'łɪwɪs
    This   possum   very much

kɪ mahma'tɪya.
knew.

    'sie tu'nalɪ o'yeya 'ikpak
    One   day   he was up in

'sente tsapo'k^wawɪtł kɪk^woh'taya tsa-
a   zapote tree   eating   za-

'potł. 'k^wok 'yaha tłak^wah'taya, a'sɪko
potes. As   he   was eating,   there

    'sente 'koyutł i'tsintła
arrived a   coyote beneath

'k^wawɪtł 'wa o'pie   tłahtła'nek^wɪ.
the tree and he began to sniff.

o'kɪhnek tła'k^wotsi 'wa oahkopa'tła-
He smelled the possum and looked up

tšiš 'ipa tsapo'k^wawɪtł. o'kɪhtak
into the zapote tree. He saw

tła'k^wotsi 'tłakpak 'wa 'koyutł
the possum up there and the coyote

_____

[1]Aztec text, phonetically written.
Data obtained from Richard Pittman, Summer
Institute of Linguistics.

teosᵻh'taya 'wa kᵻl'wᵻya, "'tɬi taš'tᵻka
was hungry   and he said, "What   are you

'taha 'ompau?"
doing there?"

        "'amo 'itɬa. nonᵻtɬahtɬakᵂoh'tᵻka."
        "Nothing.   Here I am eating."

        o'kᵻhto 'koyutɬ. "šᵻmoa'sᵻwᵻ,
        Said   the coyote, "Hurry,

šᵻ'temo. 'naha 'nuᵻhkᵻ nᵻteu'sᵻwᵻ 'wa
come down. I   also   am hungry and

nᵻk'nekᵻ tᵻmᵻts'kᵂɔs. 'ye   nᵻk'pᵻa
I want   to eat you. Already I have

nɔ'wᵻ tu'nalᵻ 'amo nᵻ'tɬakᵂɔ 'wa 'ka
four days   of not eating   and so

'ini 'ɔšɔ la'lᵻwᵻs nᵻteu'sᵻwᵻ."
     now I am very hungry."

        o'nɔwat tɬa'kᵂɔtsi, "'amo 'ᵻhkᵻu
        Replied the possum, "Don't do

šᵻk'tšiwa, 'pᵂes 'amo 'tɬi tᵻmᵻhtši-
that,   because I am not   doing any-

'wᵻlᵻa.   'tɬi i'pampa
thing to you. Why   are you going

tᵻ'nietškᵂɔs?"
to eat me?"

        o'kᵻhto 'koyutɬ,   "tᵻmᵻtsᵻlᵻh-
        Said   the coyote, "I'm telling

'tᵻka la'lᵻwᵻs nᵻteu'sᵻwᵻ. šᵻ'temo
you   I am very hungry.   Come down

i'sᵻhko."
quickly."

        'kᵻhtoa tɬa'kᵂɔtsi, "šᵻ'kᵻhta,
        Said   the possum, "Look,

'amo šᵻnietškᵂɔ. 'naha 'nᵻkɔ nᵻkᵂɔh-
don't eat me.   Here I   am eat-

'tᵻka 'tsapotɬ la'lᵻwᵻs 'wielᵻk 'wa
ing   a very sweet and delicious za-

tsɔ'pielᵻk. 'amo tᵻk'nekᵻ tᵻmᵻts'makas
pote.   Don't you want me to give you

'sente?"
one?"

        "'amo. 'naha nᵻk'nekᵻ tᵻmᵻtskᵂɔs
        "No.   I   want   to eat

'taha."
you."

        'kᵻhtoa tɬa'kᵂɔtsi, "sa si'kiera
        Said   the possum, "But at least

šᵻk'matᵻ 'kienᵻ 'ika 'wielᵻk   'wa
taste   how   delicious it is and

tᵻ'kᵻhtas 'asta tᵻk'nekᵻs ok'sekᵻ."
you'll see that   you'll even want some more.

        yekᵂɔ'kᵻnu 'kᵻhtoa 'koyutɬ,
        Then   said   the coyote,

"'kᵂalᵻ, šᵻhietštɬahka'lᵻlᵻ 'sente."
"All right, throw me   one."

        yekᵂɔ'kᵻnu o'tɬehkok tɬa'kᵂɔtsi
        Then   the possum climbed up

'katš\ 'tłakpak. k\tehte'k\ to 'tłin
higher.   He went and cut a big

'wiey\ 'tsapotł 'wa 'ye oye'k^w\ks\k.
and ripe zapote.

"''ošo, om'paya!"   o'k\hto tła'k^wotsi.
"Now, there it goes!" said the possum.

"š\k\n'tsak^wa mištelo'lohwo 'wa š\kamako-
"Close   your eyes   and open your

'yow\   'ka 'tłakpak. om'paya!"
mouth   upward.   There it goes!"

          yek^wo'k\nu owe'ts\ko 'tsapotł
          Then   the zapote fell

'ihtek i'kamak. 'koyutł   sa'nima
into   his mouth. The coyote quickly

ok\k^wah't\w\ts. ok\'welmat, 'wa o'k\hto
ate it up.   He liked it, and he said,

'koyutł, "me'lowak 'wiel\k.   š\kteh-
          "It sure is delicious. Cut

'tiemo ok'sente 'tłin 'k^wal\ 'wa
down another   as   good   and

š\nietšwoltłahka'l\l\."
throw it to me."

Selection 9
Popoluca Text[1]

'nimpa nak | ni'may't^yaap 'eeši |
says   the toad | the crab is spoken to |

mič ṅaps mi'pak | huut^y mi'ñikpa ||
you are all bone | where are you going ||

'iku'nu'kum 'hiiši meeš ''eeši | 'nimpa|
the crab had an idea | he says |

'ič 'a'nikpa huut^y 'it^y he'm 'piiših
I   I-go   where   those people

'ocho¢wit^y'pa'ap || 'hesam
the-ones-who-walk-by-jumping || then

'nimpa   nak | 'pero he?   huut^y ||
the toad says | but   where (is) that ||

'hesik 'nimpa ''eeši | huu'u't^yit^y he'm
then the crab says | it is where those

'piiših 'wit^yt^yampik 'i'hip || nas
people have big mouths || the toad

''uših 'anhagoy'ñe? nak | ni'may't^yaap
passed by little ahead | the toad is

nak | huut^y mi'nikpa || 'nimpa
spoken to | where are-you-going || says

nak | 'a'nikpa huut^y 'e'¢niimpa ||
the toad | I go   where there is dancing ||

'nimpa | kwi'dao | d^ya 'ii   mik-
he says | be careful | that someone does

'ka'aba || 'hesik 'nimpa nak |
not kill you || then the toad says |

---

[1]Phonemically written. Data from Ben Elson, Summer Institute of Linguistics. The phonemic symbols should be read with the following phonetic notes in mind:
a. Long vowels have a down glide on the second mora.
b. The symbol [t^y] represents a single segment, only, of a palatalized type.
c. Nasals and [y] have a voiceless off glide in utterance-final position.
d. Stops are aspirated in syllable-final position unless they are followed by a sound produced at the same point of articulation; note, for example, [k] in [nak^h] which has no aspiration in /mik.'ka'aba/.

miho'nɨ̈mpa || 'nɨ̈mpa | ʔa'nɨ̈mpa dʸa | hɨ̈ɨ̈ | ʔɨ̈ɣ wɨ̈'ʔaap   ʔanakka'ʔoʔy ||

you-what-say || he says | watch out you | yes | I   I-am-able I can be killing ||

ʔii inik'kaʔaba || 'nɨ̈mpa nak | | hemum ku'yah   heʔ ||

do not kill someone || the toad says | | there it-ends it ||

Part   II

ANALYSIS   AND   DESCRIPTION
OF   PHONEMIC   UNITS

Chapter 4

THE PREMISES OF PRACTICAL PHONEMICS

THE RELATIONSHIP OF PHONETICS
AND PHONEMICS

Phonetics gathers raw material.
Phonemics cooks it. Practical phonetics provides a technique for describing sounds in
terms of movements of the vocal apparatus,
and for writing them in terms of articulatory
formulas, i.e. as letters of a phonetic
alphabet. Practical phonemics provides a
technique for processing the rough phonetic
data in order to discover the pertinent units
of sound and to symbolize them in an alphabet
easy for the native to read.[1] The purpose
of practical phonemics, therefore, is to
reduce a language to writing.

The sounds of a language are automatically and unconsciously organized by the
native into structural units, which we call
PHONEMES. One of these sound units may
have as submembers numerous slightly different varieties which a trained foreigner might
detect but which a native speaker may be unaware of. In fact, if the native is told
that such variation exists in the pronunciation of his sound units he may emphatically
deny it. For a speaker to recognize sub-
varieties of his own sound units, he may need
many hours of training. People are much more
readily made conscious of the distinctive
sound units in their language than they are
of submembers of the units. For this reason
a practical orthography is phonemic. It has
one, and only one, symbol for each sound
unit. These the native soon learns to recognize. He needs no "extra" symbols which
correspond to sub-units in his language.

Once the native learns an orthography
which is closely correlated with his sound
units, there is no "spelling" problem.
Everything is spelled as it is pronounced,
and pronounced as it is spelled. There are
no "silent letters," nor series of words like
cough, hiccough, through, where the same
letters represent different sounds.

Untrained foreigners do not intui-
tively recognize native sound units. On the
contrary they are usually "deaf" to some of
the native sound units and tend to "hear"
only their own, even when the native is

speaking. On the other hand, some sub-units
which the native does not recognize, the
foreigner may notice simply because they
happen to correspond with sound units of his
own. A foreigner for this reason finds it
difficult to reduce a language to writing
in the manner best adapted to rapid learning
by the native. The foreigner is likely to
symbolize some sub-units which should be
left unwritten, but fail to symbolize certain
full units which need symbolization; his
orthography would tend to confuse the native.
Phonemic techniques provide safeguards which
help the foreigner to discover the organization of the native sound units without
undue influence from the units of his own
language. They aid in the prevention of
symbolizing too much or too little detail.
They help prevent the symbolizing of sub-
units, and help insure the symbolizing of
all full units.

In order to arrive at the sound
units pertinent to a language the foreigner
must, therefore, have a methodology which
will allow him to start with his own inadequate reactions but discover significant
sound characteristics which he at first overlooked, or re-classify segments which he at
first handled without reference to their
structural organization in the language.
Such a methodology is valid only if one
assumes that all language structures of the
world are sufficiently uniform to warrant
the application to an unknown language of
those procedures which have given adequate
results in application to known languages.
Phonemic procedures, then, must be founded
upon premises concerning the underlying
universal characteristics of languages of
the world, lest the orthographical conclusions arrived at by the procedures prove
to be both technically and practically inadequate.

The beginning student finds it
difficult to retain in mind at any one time
more than a few premises. For this reason
we have chosen to emphasize four premises
which can be made to serve as central points
of reference for the discussion of almost
all the practical problems of reducing a
language to writing. In this way the student
finds highly numerous details of analysis,
and many lesser premises, integrated into an
easily remembered system.

The premises and procedures leading
to the discovery[1] of the sound units of a

---

[1]In popular usage the term 'practical
phonetics' is often used to include both
practical phonetics and practical phonemics.
For this volume it proves convenient to employ separate labels for these two phases of
linguistic analysis. Similarly, the term
'phonetic alphabet' in popular speech covers
approximately the ground represented here by
'phonetic alphabet' and by 'phonemic alphabet.'

---

[1]It is assumed in this volume that
phonemes exist as structural entities or

language must later be amplified or modified
by social considerations. Local orthographical tradition, governmental rulings,
prevalence of linguistic knowledge, and
available printing facilities must all be
considered before a practical orthography
can be established for any community.

Illustration of the Premises
behind Phonemic Procedures

The procedures of phonemic analysis
as given in this volume are built around
four basic premises and constitute techniques
which can be utilized in the field. The
basic premises contain various implicit or
explicit related assumptions, some of which
will be given near the end of the chapter.

First Premise: Sounds Tend[1] to be Modified by Their Environments

Only a limited number of signals can
be used in any communicating system for
speech since an infinite number would be impossible to remember and too cumbersome to
be of service. Now the sounds which follow
one another in a changing sequence constitute
the signals of speech and these sounds are
produced by movements of the vocal apparatus,
i.e., by movements of the lips, tongue,
throat, lungs, and so on. It is, therefore,
important to understand that these vocal
movements, caused by the various muscles
involved, tend to slur into one another.
Since each variation of movement gives a
variation in sound, the slurring of movements
produces a slurring of sounds. Furthermore,
since a specific sound will have different
slurs of movement depending upon the movement which it precedes or follows, each
sound type resultant from the productive
movements will vary somewhat according to
the sounds which it precedes or follows.

If, for example, the vowel [a] is
followed by a vowel [ə] and then by [æ],
there tends to be in the middle of the series
a rapid movement of the tongue toward the
tongue position which would be given for the
pronunciation of isolated [ə]; but the

relationships; and that our analytical purpose is to find and symbolize them. This
implies that there is only one accurate
phonemic analysis of any one set of data. At
present, however, our phonemic theory is inadequate to lead phonemicists to uniform
conclusions on many problems including many
difficulties in the analysis of English. In
the future, phonemic theory must be amplified
in such a way that workers in the field can
reach agreement in analysis, or the assumption
stated here must be modified so as to allow
alternate analyses of equal validity.

[1]This word could be omitted provided
the student did not conclude that sounds of
one language must always slur into their
environments in the same way or to the same
degree as do the same sounds in similar environments in a different language.

position for isolation may not quite be
reached since the tongue movements partially
anticipate the position for the succeeding
lower and more front sound [æ]. Likewise,
if [a] is followed by [ə] and then by [o],
there is a slurring of the tongue movement
toward the position for [o], without a
clear-cut stationary position for [ə], and
the sound resultant from these movements is
proportionately slurred. The two varieties
of [ə]--say, [ə˅] and [ə˃]--will differ
somewhat depending upon whether they constitute the center of the sequence [aəæ] or
[aəo].

In instances of this type, one must
conclude that the slurred modification is
not a basic part of the structural system of
the communicating signals but is a nonsignificant difference which does not produce a
contrast of distinct signals able to convey
messages. For this reason one would not in
a phonemic alphabet provide special symbols
for the variants of a sound caused by its
slurs to its environment but would provide
only one symbol for all varieties of that
particular unit. From the first premise then
we can deduce the following conclusion:
Sounds tend to slur into one another and the
nonsignificant varieties of a sound so produced must not be symbolized in a practical
alphabet.

This statement must be extended to
include a second kind of environment: sounds
tend to slur into silence. For example,
certain phonemes might occur voiced at the
beginning of sentences or in the middle of
sentences, but become voiceless at the end
of sentences. Preceding or following the
silence or pause at the end or the beginning
of a sentence, a voiced sound may lose its
voiced nature and thus approximate silence
more closely.

Further modifications in sound units
may be caused by a third type of environment:
the borders of various types of larger phonological or grammatical units may also modify
sounds. One might find, for example, that
sound units which are voiced at the beginning
of words become unvoiced at the end of words,
even when these words are in the middle of a
sentence. But nonsignificant modifications
of a sound unit at the borders of those
major phonological or grammatical units which
are symbolized in the orthography (e.g. at
word boundaries symbolized by spaces) should
be treated as slurs into the environment and
should not be given distinct symbols in the
phonemic orthography. Notice, for example,
the following illustrations. In the first of
them, sounds unvoice at the end of sentences
but not at the end of words in the middle of
sentences. In the second, sounds unvoice at
the end of words regardless of their place in
the sentence.

Hypothetical Language A

Phonetic Data:

[gabab mik]	'The pig eats'
[gabab mig vi]	'The pig eats here'
[vug davip]	'The house is burning'
[vug davib mo]	'The house is burning right now'
[vi mo gabab mik]	'At this point right now the pig is eating'

Hypothetical Language B

Phonetic Data:

[gamik zap]	'He cut a tree'
[gamik lof zabs]	'He cut two trees'
[gamigs zabs]	'They cut the trees'

Phonetic writing may for convenience be enclosed in brackets, and phonemic writing in diagonals.[1] The phonetic data for Languages A and B, then, would be rewritten phonemically as follows:

Hypothetical Language A

Data Rewritten Phonemically:

/gabab mig/	'The pig eats'
/gabab mig vi/	'The pig eats here'
/vug davib/	'The house is burning'
/vug davib mo/	'The house is burning right now'
/vi mo gabab mig/	'At this point right now the pig is eating'

Hypothetical Language B

Data Rewritten Phonemically:

/gamig zab/	'He cut a tree'
/gamig lov zabz/	'He cut two trees'
/gamigz zabz/	'They cut the trees'

A fourth type of environment is this: sounds can be affected nonsignificantly by their relation to syllables which are stressed or unstressed, long or short, high or low. Such syllables may cause sounds in or near them to become also stressed, or

long, or high pitched, and so on, or to be modified in other ways. In reverse, sound types may affect the intensity, or duration, or physical frequency of other sounds in the syllables in which they occur. Notice that sounds modified by neighboring sounds or by stress, pitch, or length, tend to become more like their environments, but that sounds modified by a border can not in the same way become "like" a border which is merely a junction of two large phonological or grammatical units and not a phonetic entity[1] in itself.

Second Premise: Sound Systems Have a Tendency toward Phonetic Symmetry

The general phonetic pattern of a language exerts a slight pressure upon the interpretation of sounds, since sound systems have a tendency toward symmetry. If, for example, one finds [p], [t], [b], and [g], and he can prove by unequivocable evidence that [p] is phonemically different from [b] and that [k] is phonemically different from [g], probability is that [t] is phonemically different from [d], even though strong evidence is not found to confirm the fact.

If in a language which he has begun to study the student finds voiceless stops at bilabial, alveolar, and velar points of articulation, and voiced stops at bilabial and velar points of articulation, he should be suspicious of the lack of an alveolar voiced stop, and check his data to see if he has overlooked one, since such gaps of symmetry are less frequent than a full series of stops in the corresponding series. Structural pressures of this type are especially valuable in the early stages of investigation of a language to keep the analyst alert to find sounds which he has not yet heard in that language but which do occur there.

When evidence of symmetry, combined with other evidence, shows that two sounds are in all probability separate phonemes, the two should be written with separate symbols in a practical orthography.

Like the segmental system a tonal or stress system tends to be symmetrical. The comparison of the theoretically possible sequences of postulated tones with the sequences actually encountered is often a helpful clue to the analysis of tone phonemes.

Third Premise: Sounds Tend to Fluctuate

The vocal mechanism is not equipped to give precise unchanging repetitions of any specific sound or sounds. In pronouncing any word twice there will be minute differences

---

[1] A practice which seems to have been initiated in publications of Bernard Bloch and George Trager.

[1] Nor a phoneme as such. This assumption is based on an unpublished paper, Kenneth L. Pike, "Grammatical Prerequisites to Phonemic Analysis." For the practical handling of this problem, see below, Chapter 13.

in the sounds even though these differences
may be too small for the ear to hear;
delicate instruments can, however, record
the fluctuations. Words usually are pronounced so that the ear does not catch the
minute variations present.

It sometimes happens, however, that
the fluctuations in the pronunciation of
one of the sounds of a specific word are so
great that the foreigner notices them. This
is especially the case when the difference
between the fluctuating segments is the same
as the difference between two of the significant signalling units in the language of the
foreigner. If, for example, in Hypothetical
Language C a word [tas] means 'song', but
fluctuates phonetically to [das], a foreigner
from Hypothetical Language D would notice
this fluctuation and be likely to comment
upon it if in Language D there appear words
such as [tof] meaning 'house', and [dof]
meaning 'tree', in which the difference
between the words is only the difference
between the two segments [t] and [d]. The
native of Language C, however, would probably
be completely unaware of the fluctuation
which the foreigner notices, or even deny
that he had such variations if one attempted
to call it to his attention. In instances
like this one the investigator must conclude
that the fluctuation in Language C is not
significant structurally. For this reason
one would not provide separate symbols for
[t] and [d] in Language C but would write
both of the sounds with a single symbol.
This would not be true in Language D where
separate symbols would be necessary because
of the structural contrast between them.
The second premise, then, is the following:
Sounds tend to fluctuate. If this fluctuation
is between noncontrastive segments it is
structurally nonsignificant[1] and should not
be symbolized in a phonemic alphabet.

Fourth Premise: Characteristic Sequences of
Sounds Exert Structural Pressure on the
Phonemic Interpretation of Suspicious Seg-
ments or Suspicious Sequences of Segments.

Each language contains its characteristic types of sequences of sounds. Some
languages have heavy consonant clusters, that
is, sequences of several contiguous consonants. Other languages tend to have no
consonant clusters but rather alternate
consonants and vowels. In some of these
languages the investigator may, at first, be
in doubt whether to write certain segments
(e.g. nonsyllabic [i] and [u]) as consonants
(i.e. "y" and "w") or as vowels. He should
interpret these segments as consonants or as

vowels according to the way in which they
occur in sequences in places parallel to
the occurrence of items which are certainly
consonants, (such as [t] and [s]) or vowels
(such as syllabic [a]). Such a set of conclusions implies several statements which
are assumed to be true: (1) In every
language there are two main groups of sounds
which have sharply different distributions
(seen especially in their different
functions in syllables) and typical articulatory characteristics. (2) Of these two
groups the VOWELS constitute that group
which is most frequently syllabic and is
largely comprised of vocoids.[1] CONSONANTS
comprise the other group, which most frequently (but not exclusively) function as
nonsyllabics and which are largely (but not
exclusively) made up of nonvocoids.

It will not do to define vowel and
consonant exclusively in terms of that
articulatory or acoustic characteristics,
since nonsyllabic [i] may function as a
consonant [y], or in a different language
it may function as an unstressed member of a
sequence of two vowels, and so on. Their
distributional characteristics, especially
in relation to syllables, must be considered.

The definitions of vowel and consonant, then, further necessitate the following assumptions: (1) All languages contain
PHONETIC SYLLABLES which are units of one or
more segments during which there is a single
chest pulse and a single peak of sonority or
prominence. The investigator can begin his
studies of distribution and analysis of
vowels and consonants in terms of the
relationship of various vocoid and nonvocoid
segments to phonetic syllables. Yet even
this will not suffice, since, for example,
by this definition the [s] of string is
syllabic. A further assumption is needed:
(2) All languages contain PHONEMIC SYLLABLES
which are units of one or more segments in
length such that one phonemic syllable
constitutes for that language a unit of
actual or potential stress placement, or tone
placement, or intonation placement, or
rhythmic grouping, or of morpheme[2] structure;
in general (but by no means exclusively),
a phonemic syllable tends to be constituted
of a single phonetic syllable.

When a sound is of a type which
appears suspicious, since it might prove to
be either consonant or vowel, the investigator makes his decision on the basis of its
distribution in phonetic or phonemic syl-

---

[1] In Language D the sounds [t] and
[d] are separate phonemes, as proved the
data just given. If, now, in Language D,
one or two words were found in which [t] and
[d] fluctuated freely, the two sounds would
still have to be written separately because
of the evidence already quoted which proved
them phonemically separate.

[1] Vocoid: a sound during which the
air escapes from the mouth over the center
of the tongue, without friction in the mouth.
See also p. 12.

[2] A MORPHEME is the smallest meaningful unit of linguistic structure, such as
boy and -ish in boyish.

lables, or in morphemes, or its distribution in relation to analogous nonsuspicious items, since characteristic sequence of sounds exert structural pressure on the interpretation of suspicious segments. If the suspicious vocoid [i] parallels in distribution the nonsuspicious nonvocoids [s] and [p], etc., in nonsuspicious sequences, it is to be analyzed as the consonant [y].

For example, in Language C given below, the predominant pattern of the syllable structure is that of one consonant followed by one vowel. The initial [i] of [ia] 'moon' would then have to be interpreted as a consonant, since no nonsuspicious vocoids occur at the beginning of the syllables. The phonemic writing of this word would be /ya/.

Hypothetical Language C

[ma]	'cat'
[bo]	'to run'
[su]	'sky'
[sa]	'leaf'
[ia]	'moon'
[tsa]	'ten'

Structural pressure can be exerted on the interpretation of other types of data. A phonetically long vowel in one language may be interpreted as constituting a single unit. In another language the same phonetic item may be forced apart into two phonemes if the structural pressure of the predominating material forces it in this direction. For example, in Language D, illustrated below, the phonetic form [ska·f] would have to be re-interpreted as /skaaf/ since, apart from these types susceptible to alternate interpretations all of the words of that language contain two vowels.

Hypothetical Language D

[speam]	'dirt'
[plaef]	'limb'
[skoes]	'building'
[ska·f]	'sandal'

A third type of structural pressure may be exerted on groups of contiguous segments. In this case two segments may be forced into one phonemic unit if the nonsuspicious data indicate that a single unit must constitute that part of the structural pattern. Thus, for example, in Language C the phonetic form [tsa] would receive structural pressure which would force the [ts] into a single sound unit which should then be re-symbolized with a ligature or with a new symbol as /t͡sa/ or /ɖa/. There are certain types of sequences which are most

likely to be affected by this kind of pressure. They include, among others, those stops which release to a fricative of a similar point of articulation.

The fourth premise then may be amplified as follows: Characteristic sequences of sounds exert structural pressure in line with the predominant syllable structure, or the word or morpheme structure, which tends to force the interpretation of certain sounds as consonants or vowels, or as phonetically complex phonemic units.

Structural pressure occasionally forces the investigator to interpret a single segment as containing simultaneously a consonant and a vowel; or forces him to consider certain weak vocoids as constituting nonsignificant transition sounds. Structural pressure may affect the phonemic interpretation of single short segments, or sequences of segments, or long segments, or transition segments.

Further Premises:

For the convenience of the students just four major premises have been presented as such. If he understands and remembers these he should not lose his orientation throughout the rest of the book. He should realize, however, that this approach represents an oversimplification of the complexity of phonemic theory. Other premises are utilized in the volume in addition to those four, and will be explained where pertinent to the particular procedures with which they are used. A number of these premises have already been implied or stated as subpremises of the four basic ones.

Some of the more important of these subpremises can be summarized as follows: (1) A phonemic orthography is the easiest one for the native to learn to read and write. (2) Phonemic procedures are based upon universal language characteristics. (3) Phonemes exist. (4) There is only one accurate phonemic analysis for a specific set of data. (5) Borders of major phonological and grammatical units can cause the nonsignificant modifications of sound units. (6) Border types which are utilized for the description of nonphonemic modification of sounds must be symbolized in the orthography. (7) A grammatical or phonological border or juncture is not a phonemic or phonetic entity as such. (8) Stress, pitch, and length can affect or be affected by sound segments. (9) Sounds tend to become more like the environments which modify them. (10) Tonal systems, as well as segment relationships, tend to be somewhat symmetrical. (11) Nonsignificant fluctuation of sound should not be written in a phonemic orthography. (12) Fluctuation can occur between full phonemes. (13) Each language contains characteristic sequences of sounds. (14) Every language has consonants and vowels. (15) Certain kinds of segments may be vowels in one language but consonants in another, and vice versa. (16) The dichotomy between vowel and consonant is not strictly an articulatory one but is in part based on distributional characteristics. (17) Phonetic syllables are determined by physical and/or acoustic criteria. (18) Phonemic syllables are in part determined by distributional criteria, including potential placement of stress, pitch, and length, and in part by the structural shape of morphemes. (19) A long vowel or consonant may in some languages constitute two phonemes. (20) A sequence of two segments may in some languages constitute a single phonetically complex phoneme. (21) Occasionally a single segment may constitute a consonant and a vowel simultaneously. (22) Some segments may be nonsignificant transition sounds.

Closely related to the four basic premises are certain additional ones: (1) Segmental or suprasegmental elements which are predictable are nonphonemic; nonsymbolized elements are PREDICTABLE when the reader can tell where they will occur by following a set of rules which tell him how to modify his pronunciation of symbolized contrastive items. (2) If two segments are submembers of a single phonemes, the NORM of the phoneme is that submember which is least limited in distribution and least modified by its environments. (3) In order to be considered submembers of a single phoneme, two segments must be (a) phonetically similar and (b) mutually exclusive as to the environments in which they occur. (4) Every phonetically distinct segment of a language is a separate phoneme unless it is a part of some more inclusive phonemic unit; each segment is a phoneme unless it is an environmental modification of a phoneme or a nonsignificant fluctuation of a phoneme, or part of a phonetically complex phoneme. (5) When two phonemic conclusions each appear to be justifiable by the other premises, and each seem to account for all the available facts of all types, that conclusion is assumed to be correct (a) which is the least complex, and (b) which gives to suspicious data an analysis parallel with analogous nonsuspicious data, and (c) which appears most plausible in terms of alleged slurs into specific environments, and so on. (6) Once two segments are proved to be phonemically distinct it is assumed that they remain phonemically distinct even if there is fluctuation between them. (7) Two segments are proved phonemically distinct if they consistently constitute the only difference between two words of different meanings; this statement follows from the first major premise, since in such a pair of words the environments for the differing sounds are identical and could not be causing that difference. (8) The native speaker can more easily be taught to recognize and symbolize the difference between two of his phonemes than between two submembers of phonemes. If he has a hard time learning to distinguish between two sounds in his language, they are probably not phonemically distinct. Thus, for English, the native speaker easily learns

to identify the fact that there is a difference between [p] and [b], as in pin and bin, but only with considerable difficulty is he likely to learn to hear a qualitative difference (not a stress difference) between the two vowels of above, or between the heavily aspirated and weakly aspirated (or unaspirated) [p] sounds in paper.

Other premises are less closely related to the basic four. Two of these concern syllables: (1) Where syllable division affects the meaning of an utterance, the syllable border is not symbolized as such, but is indicated by space or hyphen between some grammatical units or larger phonological ones.[1] (2) Syllables may have a complicated structure. The vowel or syllabic usually constitutes a NUCLEUS which serves as a convenient point of reference for describing the consonants clustering around it. The division into consonants and vowels does not represent the entire structural organization of the syllable. COMPLEX NUCLEI are CLOSE-KNIT sequences of two vowels or of a vowel and a consonant, and so on, which in distribution act like a single nuclear phoneme.[2] In English, for example, [aⁱ] appears to be a complex close-knit nuclear sequence of two phonemes which acts in distribution much like /ɔ/; the /a/ is the syllabic, the /ⁱ/ the nonsyllabic.

Three further assumptions can be mentioned about grammatical units: (1) The investigator should assume that a specific morpheme contains the same sequence of phonemes every time and in every environment it appears, until or unless he finds definite evidence, by way of the analytical procedures, which forces him to conclude that there has been a substitution (or loss, or addition) of phonemes. This assumption is helpful, since the morphological data give clues as to the nonsignificant modification of phonemes; it is dangerous, however, since the unwary may be tempted to neglect evidence which should indicate to him that a morpheme has several alternate phonemic forms. (2) Before phonemic analysis can be completed, at least some morphemes must be differentially identified; the investigator needs to know for English, for example, that pin and bin are distinct words so that he could conclude

---

[1]It is not clear whether this is due to convention or to some underlying phonemic principle. Syllable peaks, however, are symbolized by vowel letters for vowels, or by the syllabic indicator (or tone marks) for syllabic consonants.

[2]Premise based on the following material: Kenneth L. Pike, "On the Phonemic Status of English Diphthongs," Language, XXIII (April-June, 1947) 158-59; idem and Eunice V. Pike, "Immediate Constituents of Mazateco Syllables," International Journal of American Linguistics, XIII (April, 1947), 78-91.

that [p] and [b] are distinct phonemes.
(3) In some languages considerable grammatical analysis, based on phonetic data, is prerequisite to phonemic analysis since spaces and hyphens must be written at certain types of grammatical units, and subphonemic modifications may occur at their borders.

One other very important premise[1] has served as a background for the construction of the practice material. Quantitative characteristics, and these only, may serve as suprasegmental phonemes in the structure of morphemes.[2] By a quantitative characteristic is meant some modification of a sound which does not change the basic quality or shape of its sound waves. Thus a sound wave may be repeated over a longer period of time, to give greater LENGTH; or it may be increased in amplitude for greater STRESS; or it may be repeated more times in a given space of time for higher PITCH. By this premise nasalization, labialization, and the like[3] are ruled out as suprasegmental phonemes on a lexical[4] level.

---

[1]Premise based on an unpublished paper: Kenneth L. Pike, "Suprasegmental versus Segmental Phonemes," 1942.

[2]My colleague, Donald S. Stark, when I suggested this premise to him some years ago, added that suprasegmental characteristics cannot modify each other as such but can only modify a qualitative segment.

[3]Glottal stop in some instances might possibly be included as a suprasegmental phoneme quantitatively--as zero, the interruption of quality. This has not been so treated here; rather a close tie between vowels and glottal stop have been handled as close-knit complex nuclear sequences of sounds.

For a differing view of suprasegmental phonemes, see George L. Trager, "Theory of Accentual Systems," Language, Culture, and Personality, Sapir Memorial Volume, Edited by Leslie Spier (Menasha, Wis.: Sapir Memorial Publication Fund, 1941). He states (p. 135) 'It is suggested that any secondary phonetic character--such as glottalization, nasalization, labialization, retroflexion, "throatiness," "weight," etc.--may conceivably function as an exponential in a given language." Also (p. 143), 'Beyond the three main types of prosodemes, it appears that others may exist and function in the same way.'

[4]General modification of total voice quality (general lip rounding, large throat opening, tense vocal cords, etc.) affect utterances as a whole.

Definition of a Phoneme as Based on the Premises

There have been many attempts to define the phoneme. None of them are accepted by all workers in the field. In the phonetic materials of Part One (p. 3) we stated the following:

'It proves difficult or impossible to describe the flavor of a pumpkin pie in such a way that one who has never eaten that kind of a pie may know what it tastes like. One must content oneself with comparing it to other similar flavors, or one must describe it by means of a recipe in which the description is not one of taste as such, but of procedure for combining and cooking them. In practical phonetic work one must follow a similar procedure. Frequently the most adequate available description of a sound, for the purpose of learning to produce it, is a definition which tells a student how to make that sound, rather than telling him what constitutes its acoustic properties.'

Just as for practical phonetics we gave a definition of the sounds in terms of their analysis as produced by various movements of the mouth, nose, and throat, so for practical phonemics we shall use a "recipe" type of definition. Specifically, then, a PHONEME is one of the significant units of sound arrived at for a particular language by the analytical procedures developed from the basic premises previously presented.

Uncertainties in the Application of Phonemic Premises

In phonemic theory today considerable uncertainty remains. In some instances there is doubt as to how the premises should be applied to specific data; in other instances additional premises may be needed; in addition, the validity of all the premises is at times in question. Certain of the difficulties will be mentioned here. The validity of the premises will be discussed in the next section.

In order to be submembers of a single phoneme sounds must be phonetically somewhat similar, or else one could not be considered an environmental modification of the other. Query: Just how similar must the submembers be in order to be similar enough? We do not know. In doubtful cases the investigator must utilize symmetry and structural pressure to help him decide. No pressure seems strong enough, however, to force into a single

---

[1]See, for example, W. F. Twaddell, On Defining the Phoneme, Language Monographs, Vol. 16 (Baltimore: Linguistic Society of America, 1935) where many definitions are discussed.

phoneme English [h], which occurs only at
the beginning of syllables, and English [ŋ],
which occurs only at the end of them.

Symmetrical structure exerts pressure
on the interpretation of sounds. Query:
How strong, or consistent, must the pressure
or symmetry be to force a particular interpretation? Again, we do not know, but must
reach a decision in the light of all other
data available.

Characteristic structural sequences
exert pressure on the phonemic interpretation
of sounds. Query: What should be done when
different types of structural sequences
exert conflicting pressures, or when the
pressures cannot clearly be analyzed as
applied to the suspicious items? We do not
know, and precisely for that reason have
differing interpretations of English vocoid
glides, and the sequence [tš]. We must wait
for further phonemic theory to clarify these
problems. Until such a theory is available,
we must expect to find differing solutions
equally valid within our present premises,
-even though we previously stated that we
assume that, ultimately, only one accurate
analysis can be made of any one set of data.

Although these difficulties are
severe, it is fortunate that one seldom finds
them as strikingly so as in English. The
student can proceed with the assurance that,
once mastered, present phonetic and phonemic
procedures will lead to fairly adequate
solutions of the majority of problems which
he will meet, and that even in the theoretically more doubtful cases a practical working solution can be found. The arrangement
of this book seems to give phonemic theory
a "mechanical" flavor. The uncertainties
mentioned, basic to all phonemic analysis,
emphasize the necessity of careful judgment
and weighing of alternatives.

One other problem may be treated in
this section. We assume that the native
speaker can easily be taught to identify the
difference between two phonemes, no matter
how similar they may be phonetically. Yet
trained English speakers, for example, often
find they have difficulty in deciding whether
they use [o] or [ɔ] before [r] in for, etc.
Query: To which of two phonemes should one
assign a sound which appears phonetically
to be halfway between the two and which is
mutually exclusive in distribution with both
of them? One should first hunt for some
phonetic or symmetrical basis of choice. If
it cannot be found, he should probably
choose to symbolize it with one or the other,
arbitrarily, rather than postulate a third
phoneme and a third symbol for a sound unit
(a) which has highly limited distribution,
(b) which is phonetically similar to and
mutually exclusive with other sounds, and
(c) which is not in contrast with the sounds
to which it is phonetically similar.

The Source and Validity
of the Premises

Phonemicists do not all work with
the same premises. Even the existence of
the phoneme is not granted by some workers.[1]
This conflict of theory forces us to consider
the source and validity of the assumptions
explicit or implicit underlying this volume.

The premises for this volume are
chosen from existing theory, or postulated
for the first time, so as to lead the student
to arrive at an analysis which parallels the
vague or explicit observable reactions of
speakers to their own sounds.

After observing that many English
speakers in phonetic classes have difficulty
in learning to distinguish the vowels of
above, or the [t] sounds of tatter, or the
differences in length of the vowels of bit
and bid, and having observed that the respective pairs of sounds were phonetically
similar and mutually exclusive as to the
environments in which they occur, I, as
others before me, have chosen to set up as
a generalized premise and procedure the
statement that phonetically similar mutually
exclusive sounds are submembers of a single
phoneme.

The fact that English speakers tend
to be unaware of fluctuation in the presence
or absence of an oral release of utterance-
final stop serves as a basis for a generalization about free fluctuation between submembers of phonemes in certain restricted
environments.

The observation that speakers of
English have difficulty in learning to distinguish between the two [p] sounds in paper
leads to the conclusion that in some way the
sounds are "the same" for them. Combined
with this observation are the further ones
that the release, though a vocoid, cannot
carry a stress and so does not function as
a vowel, and the fact that sequences like
[pʰɩn] parallel in morpheme structure words
like [bɩn], whereas [p] without aspiration
does not occur initially preceding vowels in
such words. Following these observations
(a) of speakers' OBSERVABLE REACTIONS to
sounds, and (b) of the STRUCTURAL ARRANGEMENTS
of these sounds, the premises and procedures
here are so designed that in similar situations the student would analyze as a single

---

[1]The existence of a phonemic unit
as an actual structural or configurational
reality which may be discovered by the requisite approach is assumed in the statement
of these procedures. Some investigators,
such as W. F. Twaddell (in a review in International Journal of American Linguistics XII
(April, 1946), 107), seem to deny this possibility. Be that as it may, the practical
goal of an adequate alphabet for vernacular
literatures may be reached by using these
techniques.

phonetically complex phoneme any sequence
which had similar structural relationships.[1]
Evidence for structural unity in conflict
with evidence for phonemic diversity gave
rise to the postulation of close-knit nuclei
of syllables with phonemic diversity but
distributional unity.

Since some of the sound modifications of the type similar to those referred
to above occur at borders of grammatical
units, and since oftentimes no phonetic entity can be detected at the border point
which could as such have been responsible
for the change, it is assumed that borders
can modify sounds. After observing (1) that
speakers of English if given a few general
samples of syllabification and told to syl-
labify other items will pronounce or sylla-
bify skates and lay as one syllable each,
whereas Spanish speakers tend to hear lay,
or cow as two syllables[2] and Chinese speakers tend to hear skates as three,[3] and after
observing (2) that lay in English can carry
only one stress, but [lei] in Spanish occurs
as [léi] (ley) 'law' and [leí] (leí) 'I
read', I have concluded that phonetic syllables and phonemic syllables differ,[4] and
have suggested premises and procedures designed to allow the student by studying only

the structural facts to arrive at a conclusion which will adequately represent potential native reaction also. We conclude:
segments are to phonemes as chest pulses (or
phonetic syllables) are to phonemic syllables.

The support of the premise granting
only stress, pitch, and length as suprase-
mental phonemes is more nebulous. The observable reaction is that linguists in general
seem to consider them "normal," in some way,
as superimposed phonemes, and any other possibility as slightly abnormal or "surprising."
I concur in that reaction, therefore, after
finding the structural unity of the three--
that each of them affects sounds quantitatively but not qualitatively--I have set forth
as a premise the assertion that only the
three should be considered as suprasegmental
phonemes.

Phonemic analysis cannot be made with
phonetic data alone; it must be made with
phonetic data plus a series of phonemic premises and procedures. These procedures, for
practical purposes at least, are best designed to give results, in an unknown language, of a type which would parallel (1) observable native reaction to native sounds,
and (2) structural facts about the phonetic
nature of the sounds and their distributions.
This premise[1] underlies all the other premises given above.

---

[1]For these two types of criteria applied to a much more difficult English problem see Kenneth L. Pike, "On the Phonemic
Status of English Diphthongs," Language,
XXIII (April-June, 1947), 151-9.

[2]Data on Spanish reaction from an
experiment by the author with several gradu-
ate students of the National School of Anthropology, Mexico City, 1944.

[3]Data on Chinese reaction from Y. R.
Chao.

[4]W. F. Twaddell, in his review of
R. H. Stetson's book Bases of Phonology
(Oberlin: Oberlin College, 1945) states
(International Journal of American Linguistics, XII [April, 1946], 107) that 'in the
syllable, then, Stetson finds a fundamental
unit of linguistic analysis. Syllables are
positive; syllables are additive; syllables
are countable; they are marked, in the process of speech events, by a simple physiological correlate, the chest-pulse. It will
be agreed that no such simplicity can be at-
tributed to sounds or phonemes. The number
of phonemes "represented" in a given form or
utterance is not easily determined by observers with a low level of competence.'

If the difficulties of counting phonemes is evidence that phonemes may not be
'positive additive units' then a similar
type of severe difficulty in the counting of
syllables of many languages constitutes evidence that syllables are not positive additive units, either Twaddell and Stetson
oversimplify the situation: observers of
different language backgrounds by no means
"hear" or readily count the same number of

syllables in an utterance, as they would imply. If observers of different language
backgrounds "hear" the identical data differently, the implication must be that syllables
in the linguistic sense are no more immediately apparent, or physical, or countable,
than are phonemes as such. It is interesting to note that Stetson himself (Motor Phonetics, Vol. III of Archives néerlandaises
de phonétique expérimentale, 1928) lists data showing two syllables in a sequence like
[ska] or in [apt] (due, in the first instance,
to the [s] and in the second to the release
of one of the consonants). 'In some cases
[with "stV" etc.] there develops an unvoiced
preceding syllable and a bi-syllabic form
results' p. 121; 'It is to be said, however,
that tracings often betray the fact that
such groups [pf, pn, ps, bd, pt, kt, plus
vowel] often break up into a preliminary silent syllable followed by a voiced syllable;
cf. Fig. 67 p. 124' p. 125 (see also 129,
and Figs. 64-66, 67, 27). He also grants
(p. 58; cf. also p. 14) that syllable division may not always coincide with borders between chest pulses: 'In very rare cases, it
may be that the chest movement is a continuous, slow, "controlled" movement of expiration, and that the syllable is due to the
ballistic stroke of the consonant...it is
possible that "a-la" may be so uttered.
There is no experimental evidence for such a
correlation.'

[1]For articles which utilize observations of this type to support certain items
of phonemic analysis, but without phonemic

The procedures in this book are made for application to linguistic material as spoken by one individual, in a more or less uniform style. It is assumed in this volume (including earlier stated premises) that for practical purposes this analysis will serve for the same person speaking in a somewhat different way, or for other individuals of a somewhat homogeneous community.

Recently, however, Martin Joos, during the Linguistic Institute at the University of Michigan, pointed out on the basis of spectrograph analyses that children may have vowels whose characteristic frequencies do not exactly correspond to the vowel frequencies of older people; an extremely rapid adjustment is made by the hearer soon after an individual of a different age begins to talk to him, so he may interpret properly the vowel pattern.

It appears to me that a similar situation can be encountered within the speech of a single individual: I have heard, for example, sharp changes of vowel quality in a woman using a type of "baby talk" which has a "caressing" quality without mutilating the language structure or suppressing phonemic contrasts. In the instance referred to the vowels seemed to be raised and fronted so that the net result gave a partial paralleling of the smaller vocal cavity of a child. Singers, also, sometimes modify vowel qualities by giving in general a group of fronted, raised varieties of vowels (but with [ʌ] tending toward [a]), while preserving the linguistic contrasts.

For the study of tone we point out (see Chapter 9) that relative pitch is linguistically significant but that absolute pitch is linguistically nonsignificant. A relative high-low contrast may be maintained by a speaker talking either in a high tone of voice, or in a low tone of voice. It is the pitch contrast within the immediate context which is pertinent.

Instead of assuming, then, that pitch contrasts are relative but qualitative ones are absolute, we must set up a premise

axioms or procedures based upon these observations, see Edward Sapir, "La realité psychologique des phonèmes," in Psychologie du Langage, Journal de Psychologie (Normale et pathologique), XXX (1933), 247-65; and Morris Swadesh, "Observations of Pattern Impact on the Phonetics of Bilinguals," Language, Culture, and Personality, 59-65, Sapir Memorial Volume, Edited by Leslie Spier (Menasha, Wis.: Sapir Memorial Publication Fund, 1941).

George L. Trager, of the University of Oklahoma, pointed out to me another kind of observable reaction: The substitution of sound units or sequences in mispronunciations. Thus his daughter once said safe lifers for life savers. William S. Smith suggests to me that some type of observable reaction may be responsible for the widespread postulation of word units in languages.

to explain qualitative differences between speakers of the same dialect, or of one speaker utilizing two different styles of expression: Quality, like pitch, is ultimately relative rather than absolute. Qualitative changes are less troublesome to the analyst than those of pitch, however, since qualitative changes tend to be less severe and the resultant actualizations of phonemes less likely to overlap phonetically. Thus a certain absolute pitch which is phonemically low when a person is talking in a high tone of voice may easily prove to be higher than the absolute pitch of a phonemic high when the same person is speaking in a low tone of voice, whereas the most violent changes of English /z/ due to general style of speech (ignoring the utterance-final modifications of normal speech) would seldom equal phonetically a normal English /s/.

In a tone language the phonemes of tone exist as the structural relationships (see p. 105) of relative pitches in contrast; yet a certain specific absolute pitch level may at one moment belong to one phoneme of tone and at a different moment (when the speaker changes key) to a different pitch phoneme. In this sense, there is so-called "intersection of phonemes." Similarly, segmental phonemes may likewise exist as the structural relationships between relative qualities. One of the most striking of normal shifts of quality of "voiced" sounds is encountered in the change from normal speech aloud to whispered speech. Possibly the total system of quality could so shift that the same number of phonemic contrasts were preserved in the same morphemes, and in similar series of types of qualitative distinctions. For quality (in a way analogous to tone) this allows a single absolute quality to belong in one style of speech to one phoneme but in a different style of speech to a different phoneme. For practical purposes, however, the student should make his phonemic analysis with homogeneous data as regards style. This allows him to avoid the problem of overlapping quality. For pitch he will find special procedures in Chapter 9 to handle unavoidable key changes. If the qualitative changes were harder to identify than in fact they are, then similar procedures would of necessity be used for qualitative analysis also.[1]

---

[1] For further discussion of quality see also fn. 1, p. 124-25.

Chapter 5

PRELIMINARY PROCEDURES

Following the general discussion of the premises in Chapter 4, we now present a methodology for the analysis or discovery of the phonemic units. For each of the procedures there will first be given a set of Directions. After each step in the directions, the Solution will be given to a particular problem presented. Following that there will be given a Discussion of the reasons for this particular procedure and the explanation of the way to apply it.

PRELIMINARY PROCEDURE A:

RECORDING THE DATA

Directions:

Record as best you can with phonetic symbols the language upon which you are working.

Discussion:

When one wishes to analyze the sounds of a language, the first step is to record the phonetic data by means of phonetic formulas which represent the manner by which sounds are produced. The investigator is certain to make numerous errors, however, but if he thinks he hears a certain sound or variety of sound, he writes it. If he thinks he hears a fronted [s], for example, he writes that. Regardless of whether or not he is mistaken, he writes the sounds which he thinks he hears. It is from these data, or these data revised, that he must ultimately deduce the phonemes.

The investigator will also indicate, when he can, the breaks between phonetic syllables. This may be done by some sign such as a dot between them, or preferably he may choose to indicate division between syllables only when it proves impossible to utilize some unwritten convention such as that each nonvocoid syllabifies with the vocoid which follows it unless he indicates otherwise. In addition, he may indicate the syllabics by using vowel letters, or by adding a vertical line under consonant letters, whereas the nonsyllabics may be indicated by using consonant letters or by raising the vowel letters above the line.

The investigator also analyzes the grammatical divisions as fast as he can find them. Some grammatical and lexical observations are necessary before the phonemic analysis can be completed. He signifies the points where utterances begin and end, by marking the pauses or the places where the informant has begun to speak anew. (In the early stages of the investigation these utterances which he records are likely to be very short—perhaps only one or two or three syllables in length.) He attempts to analyze the grammatical structure of the language on the basis of this tentative phonetic data. He hunts for the borders between parts of words, attempts to identify some of the morphemes, and begins to classify the various types of constructions. Phonetic, phonemic, and grammatical analysis should proceed together.

By such a procedure he records utterances in terms of the sounds which he hears. This raises a major question: 'Does the investigator hear the sounds in the same way that the native does, or has he overlooked some distinctions which the native would maintain, or has he used more symbols than necessary because the native does not have the same units of sound which the investigator has symbolized with his phonetic alphabet?' For example, if the investigator hears and writes [tatata], he must ask himself the following questions: 'Do the first two [t] sounds seem alike to the native as they do to me, or did I overlook some slight difference that the native notices?' 'Do the second and third [t] sounds seem different to the native as they appear to be to me, or did I hear a difference that the native ignores because it does not constitute a significant distinction in the structure of his language?' 'If the native ignores any possible difference between the second and third [t] sounds, is there a real phonetic difference there, or did I merely imagine it?' Phonemic theory helps the investigator answer such questions

Preliminary Procedure A is designed for application to data acquired in actual field research. There the data are recorded a bit at a time, some of them accurately and others inaccurately. The investigator in beginning his analysis is certain to have errors in his initial phonetic transcription. He may have failed to hear certain minutiae of sound which are pertinent to that system, or, on the other hand, he may have recorded minor varieties of sound which are nonsignificant to that particular system. If the investigator wishes to reach a practical alphabet with each sound unit represented by one symbol and one symbol only, his analytical procedures must be able to remedy both of these kinds of error.

PRELIMINARY PROCEDURE B:

ASSUMING THE ACCURACY AND COMPLETENESS

OF THE PROBLEMS

Directions:

Assume that, for the problem below, the phonetic data are accurate and complete.

Discussion:

The illustration of the analytical procedures will be given by means of sample problems. Certain of the problems are hypothetical and will be called dialects of KALABA. These hypothetical problems have the advantage of allowing complete control of the data, and the admission of only those data which illustrate the procedures. With this method, the difficulties and the complexity of the procedure may be increased gradually.

Other problems are comprised of data from actual languages. Here, however, there is not space to present all of the information available for any one specific language, and even if space did so permit, the problems would be too complicated for solution by the first procedures given to the student, and they would take too much time for solution. RESTRICTED LANGUAGE problems, then, give actual language material. Such exercises give valuable practice. At the same time they are presented to the student so that he may see that the theoretical procedures are applicable to actual language situations.

For both the Kalaba and Restricted Language problems it is assumed here that the recording linguist has not failed to hear or write any phonetic data pertinent to the analysis required. Such an assumption, of course, would be completely unwarranted for the investigator's field notes since it is very easy to overlook or fail to hear some of the data--in fact, it is precisely to overcome some of these errors that certain of the phonemic techniques are developed. At the moment, however, the requisite procedures can best be mastered by working with controlled data in which such errors are assumed to be absent. Later on, problems will be presented in which a contrary assumption is given.[1] At that time, the student must be prepared to handle possible errors. For the moment, however, the sample dialects are assumed to be accurately presented.

Furthermore, in handling those problems the student is to consider that the data presented constitutes the entire material for the language. Any statements therefore which he can make about the material so presented are pertinent to the entire "language," whether the problems

[1]In Chapter 10.

represent data from the hypothetical Kalaba dialects or from artificially restricted but actual languages.

PRELIMINARY PROCEDURE C:

MAKING A PHONETIC CHART

With the preliminary assumptions now stated, a sample problem may be presented to serve for illustrating the next steps of the technique:

Sample Problem Number 1--

Kalaba Dialect A (a Hypothetical Language)

Phonetic Data:

[mafsa]   'whale'

[tasa]   'walrus'

[mavma]   'house'

[katavsa]   'garden'

Directions for Problem 1:

Make a phonetic chart of all the kinds of segments in the dialect being studied.

Solution to Problem 1:

Phonetic chart of kinds of segments

		t	k
f		s	
v			
m			
			a

Discussion of Problem 1:

One should search his entire data in order to discover all the different kinds of segments which he has recorded for the language being studied. These segments should then be listed in the form of a phonetic chart. In this chart the symbols for the segments are arranged in the general positions in which they occur on the phonetic charts presented in Part One. However, the labels for the columns need not be given, and no more columns should be drawn than are necessary to accommodate the kinds of segments which actually appear in the data. Thus, for example, there is no column given in the solution above for alveo-palatal sounds, nor for voiced stops.

It is important to note that each of these segments listed will ultimately prove to be a separate phoneme unless it is eliminated by one of the later procedures. There will be some resemblance, therefore, between this preliminary listing of segments and the final listing of sound units, the phonemes. The ultimate list of units may have some of these segments eliminated or others (if they have been overlooked so far) added. A preliminary listing of segments serves to foreshadow the phonemic alphabet and to present one part of the data in a way in which it can be most readily studied.

PRELIMINARY PROCEDURE D:

LISTING SUSPICIOUS PAIRS OF SOUNDS

Directions for Problem 1, Continued:

List all pairs of segments which are suspicious because they are phonetically similar and might prove to be submembers of a single phoneme.

Solution to Problem 1, Continued:

Pairs of segments which are suspicious because they are phonetically similar and therefore might prove to be submembers of a single phoneme:

[f] and [v]

Discussion of Problem 1, Continued:

It was noticed in the first premise that sounds tend to slur into their environment, and that therefore some of the sound units have nonsignificant varieties according to the other sounds which they precede or follow, or the places in the words in which they occur, and so on. One of the goals of phonemic analysis must be to eliminate these minor variations of sounds from final practical symbolization. A sound which is modified by its environment is rarely changed drastically--rather it tends to become a little bit more like its environment, so that the original sound type and the modified form of that type are still phonetically similar. To discover whether any such minor variations occur the investigator must study pairs of sounds which are of a type similar to each other phonetically in order to determine whether or not one of them is a variant of the other due to its environment. We ask, then, 'What types of sounds must the investigator study in order to find such variation?' The answer is that he must study carefully any pair of sounds which are phonetically similar to each other. The segments which are most likely to represent submembers of a single phoneme are those which are quite similar phonetically, and when the investigator finds two segments thus similar, he must be suspicious of their phonemic status until he can prove definitely whether or not they are submembers of a single phoneme. He asks himself, 'Are these two similar sounds submembers of a single basic unit of sound or are they actually distinct units in their own right?' If for that particular language he determines that the two phonetically similar sounds are distinct units in the phonemic system, he will keep them distinct in his practical alphabet, but if he concludes that one of them is a minor modification of the other due to its environment he will

indicate both varieties of the one unit with a single symbol in his practical, phonemic alphabet for that language.

Early in his study therefore, it is wise for the investigator to keep before him a list of pairs of sounds phonetically similar, since they are likely to be the chief trouble spots in his analysis. Such sets of words may be called SUSPICIOUS PAIRS. The question now arises, how similar must sounds be for them to be SUSPICIOUSLY similar? Or, phrased in other terms, how similar must two segments be before they can constitute submembers of a single phoneme? Although no known evidence yet exists to indicate exactly the degree of similarity which must be present in submembers of a single sound unit, nevertheless, by experience we can arrive at a fairly useful set of generalizations. These generalizations will be found presented in the form of a chart in which various sounds are given and typical suspicious pairs or suspicious groups of segments are enclosed in circles. (See Chart 4.) For the beginner, this is a fairly adequate indication of the possibilities, but every once in a while the investigator in a strange situation may find the pressures of the phonetic symmetry and/or sequences forcing him to include as submembers of a single phoneme some items not circled here. Thus the beginner may use the chart as a fairly satisfactory guide, but must not consider it as an exceptionless list of all the ultimate possibilities. In fact, in Chapter 10 of this volume some problems will depart from the restrictions of this list precisely to teach the student to be aware of the necessity for alertness in this respect.

If the student studies the chart he will notice that many of the sounds circled differ in one respect only; by type of articulation, for example, but not by point of articulation; or by point of articulation but not by type of articulation, as [m] versus [M], or [n] versus [ṇ]. In addition, some circled items include pairs or groups of sounds which differ not only by adjacent point of articulation, but also by a simultaneous difference in their type of articulation. Compare, for example, [n] and [Ṇ]. A few circles do not reflect parallel articulatory relationships: alveolar and velar stops, for example, are rarely if ever submembers of the same phoneme, so are not encircled, whereas alveolar and velar nasals are submembers of a single phoneme very frequently indeed, and therefore have a circle enclosing these nasals at both points of articulation. In general, also, the larger circles are less significant than the small ones, and indicate a lower degree of suspicion: one large circle is drawn to include [h] with all of the vocoids, since any unvoiced vocoid may prove to be a submember of a general phoneme [h]; yet this circle should not be utilized to make valid the hypothesis that [o] and [i] are to be considered suspicious pairs. A few circles imply the further encircling of analogous

Chart 4. Phonetically Similar Segments[1]

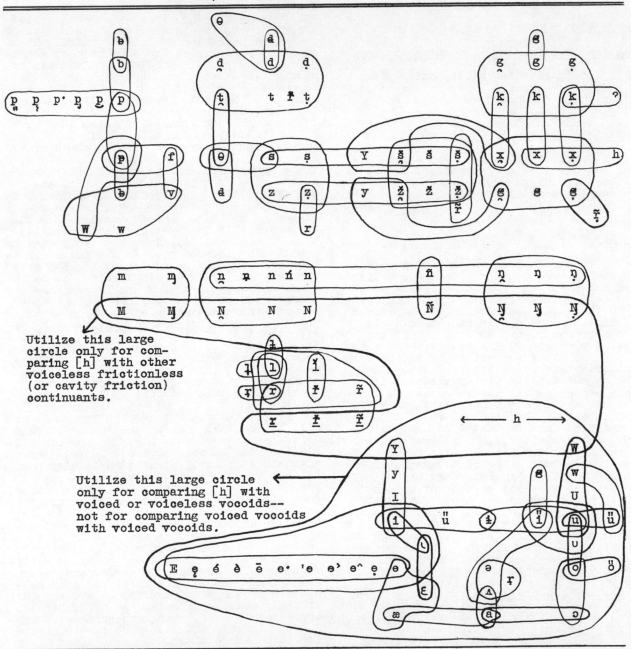

Utilize this large
circle only for com-
paring [h] with other
voiceless frictionless
(or cavity friction)
continuants.

Utilize this large circle
only for comparing [h] with
voiced or voiceless vocoids--
not for comparing voiced vocoids
with voiced vocoids.

[1]Circles enclose selected groups of similar kinds of segments. Other sets
may be determined by analogy with these. Items enclosed by small circles are more
suspicious than those enclosed in larger circles. There is no criterion to tell us
exactly how similar two sounds must be in order for it to be possible for them to be
united into a single phoneme; in general, these suggestions are based on experience.
Sounds made by similar types of production movements at similar points of articulation tend to give similar acoustic effects.

types: the varieties of [p] or [e] could
be duplicated for other sounds.

In many of the problems presented
and in actual language work also, a single
segment will have to be listed several times
since it may be a member of various pairs
of segments. If one had [s], [z], and [š],
for example, there would be the three pairs,
[s] and [z], [s] and [š], and [z] and [š].
The student must not in this procedure ignore the double listing of the sounds in
pairs by substituting a single listing of
the series [s] [š] [z]. Certain errors are
very likely to creep in if he fails he heed
this warning, since in that case the
step-by-step procedure later on is invalid.[1]
It is because of the danger of drawing conclusions contrary to this principle that he
should always treat each suspicious pair of
segments by itself before he attempts to
unite two pairs together or draw conclusions
about the total number of phonemes represented by the various pairs.

PRELIMINARY PROCEDURE E:

LISTING NONSUSPICIOUS SOUNDS

Directions for Problem 1, Continued:

List the segments which do not occur
in suspicious pairs, that is, not listed in
Preliminary Procedure D, and which, therefore, because of dissimilarity of productive
type are probably separate phonemes.

Solution to Problem 1, Continued:

Dissimilar segments not listed in
suspicious pairs and which are presumably
phonemically distinct:

$$[t], [k], [s], [m], [a]$$

---

[1]Let us suppose, for example, that
[s] may be shown to be phonemically separate
from [z], and [z] may be shown to be phonemically separate from [š]. In such a case
one might be tempted to conclude that [s],
[z], and [š] were three separate phonemes.
This conclusion might prove to be inaccurate,
however, since [s] and [š] could still be
submembers of one phoneme. That is to say:

If [s] is phonemically different from [z], and
If [š] is phonemically different from [z],
        this does not prove that
    [s] is phonemically different from [š],
      since [s] and [š] might still be sub-
      members of a single phoneme.

Two segments which are each phonemically
separate from a third segment are NOT necessarily phonemically separate from each other.
Similarly, in the initial stages of analysis
on the field, two segments which are each
phonemically to be united to a third cannot
be united to each other until it is certain
that the phonetic data is accurate. See
p.92.

Discussion of Problem 1, Continued:

Since modifications in sounds caused
by environment affect the sounds only to a
limited extent, it follows that sounds which
are considerably dissimilar in type are not
likely to constitute submembers of a single
phoneme. Sounds thus dissimilar should not
be considered to be members of a single unit
modified according to environment. When the
investigator therefore finds two segments
which are sharply different from each other,
he is justified in assuming tentatively that
they are separate phonemes. If two segments
differ widely in type, there is no necessity
of further proof of the fact that they are
significantly different in the sound system.
Sounds must be similar in order to be submembers of a single phoneme.

As we have already indicated, however, we have no certain proof of just how
similar such segments must be. In border
line cases the investigator may occasionally
be mistaken in his judgment of such dissimilarity. On the field he must be ready to
modify his preliminary conclusions after
other evidence is classified and after the
remaining procedures have been applied to
the data at hand. For the purpose of the
beginning student, however, the hints given
in Chart 4 may be considered adequate, provided he uses it with caution.

In general, then, the criterion of
dissimilarity of sound type produces a rough
classification, with considerable probability
of correctness, which eliminates from early
consideration certain of those sounds which
are probably separate phonemes. In the early
stages of analysis the investigator can in
this way concentrate on the more doubtful
segments.

Problem 2--Kalaba Dialect B

Phonetic Data:

[ʔadzu]	'malaria'	[tezʔo]	'secret'
[pogle]	'world'	[ʔobvu]	'to say'
[akʔat]	'owl'	[kugžeʔ]	'to hire'
[tobže]	'to posess'	[žetuv]	'gourd'
[ʔadzo]	'unlike'	[pazve]	'river'
[ʔobže]	'to insist'	[vazve]	'smell of
[zagza]	'spectacle'		burning hair'
[voʔle]	'to write'	[vapte]	'corral'
[vogle]	'to compete'	[ʔablo]	'family'

Directions:

Follow Preliminary Procedures C, D,
E.

Problem 3--Kalaba Dialect C

Phonetic Data:

['sʌɾʌɾ̌]   'rice'   ['fivɾ̌i]   'next'
['nizdʌs]   'canopy'   ['kivdʌ]   'door'
['sʌvgik]   'seldom'   ['kʌnʌf]   'behind'
['kʌnʌv]   'to rush'   ['digʌs]   'extra'
['kʌznit]   'to breathe' ['sʌtʌɾ̌]   'gnarled'
['ɾ̌igʌs]   'placenta'   ['tigʌs]   'fly'
['fʌɾ̌ni]   'force'   ['ɾ̌ʌfin]   'heel'
['fʌznʌt]   'lightning'   ['tigʌz]   'thumbnail'
['gʌnʌf]   'to blaze'

Directions:

        Follow Preliminary Procedures C, D,
E.

Problem 4--Kalaba Dialect D

Phonetic Data:

[pu.ʔiʔI]   'pineapple' [ka̱.sitI]   'different'
[ke̱.ñikI]   'boat'   [x̱u.ʔakʌ]   'to love'
[ma.xuŋ]   'octopus'   [ʔa.ke̱kE]   'to belong'
[ka.sipI]   'cloth'   [ku.mim]   'brown'
[xi.fupU]   'mango'   [ʔa.siŋ]   'to sing'
[ta.ŋus]   'weeds'   [pu.tix]   'to write'
[nu.ko̱ʔO]   'heel'   [ke̱.ŋaf]   'to drink'
[ki.xaḵʌ]   'to dance'   [ta.ñix]   'juicy'
[xa.ŋaf]   'armpit'   [pu.tis]   'to expect'
[ki.ḵox]   'to exhale'   [ḵo.ñiŋ]   'wine'
[fu.ñikI]   'to see'   [mi.faŋ]   'during'
[sa.kupU]   'leprous'   [ñi.x̱us]   'to scream'

Directions:

        Follow Preliminary Procedures C, D,
E.

Chapter 6

ANALYTICAL PROCEDURE ONE-A:

THE PHONEMIC SEPARATION OF SIMILAR SEGMENTS UPON FINDING THEM

IN CONTRAST IN ANALOGOUS ENVIRONMENTS

Procedures for the analysis of phonemes will be introduced in accordance with the following outline. First there will be procedures which involve the phonemic SEPARATION of segments and therefore their symbolization in the phonemic orthography. Then there will be procedures for the UNITING of the minor varieties of any particular sound unit within a specific language, and the writing of these variants with a single symbol. A third group of procedures involves the INTERPRETATION of certain sounds as vowels or consonants, and certain sequences of sounds as consonant clusters or as phonetically complex but single consonant units, or as vowel clusters or phonetically complex single vowel units, and so on. The first of these procedures will be applied to sound segments such as [p], [o], [s], and [m]. Later the same procedures will be discussed again but amplified by special techniques given for the handling of some of the more difficult problems of linguistic pitch, stress, and length. Chapter 6 illustrates and discusses one procedure for the phonemic separation of segments.

Problem 5--Kalaba Dialect E

Phonetic Data:

[sama]	'man'	[esa]	'leaf'
[ɛḳa]	'stem'	[zama]	'seed'
[tamza]	'pollen'	[tadza]	'branch'
[tatsa]	'flower'	[ksama]	'petal'
[eḳe]	'sap'		

Directions for Problem 5:

Preliminary Procedures:

Make a phonetic chart of the kinds of segments.

List all pairs of segments which are suspicious because they are phonetically similar.

List the segments which are nonsuspicious because they are phonetically dissimilar and do not occur in suspicious pairs.

Separation Procedures: Analytical Procedure I-A (Apply to each suspicious

pair; if several pairs are present, work first with those segments which occur in the environments that are the most similar. Repeat the steps for suspicious differences of pitch, stress, or length):

State the phonetic nature of the difference between the segments of a suspicious pair.

Select samples of the most similar environments in which the segments occur.

State the nature of the differences (1) in the immediate phonetic environments (sound types both preceding and following the segments), and (2) in the larger phonological or grammatical environments (position in syllable, utterance, stress group, word, etc.).

Choose the most plausible[1] hypothesis which you can find as to the way in which certain environments are responsible for the difference between the segments. (Such a hypothesis is most plausible when it can be said of the two sounds that one of the segments occurs only in certain environments, whereas the other segment never occurs in those environments; also, when it can be shown that a sound becomes more like adjacent sounds.)

Refute the hypothesis, if possible, with further contradictory evidence. If the hypothesis chosen has been well refuted, the sounds occur in analogous environments; conclude, therefore, that they are phonemically separate. If no reasonable hypothesis could be made initially, the sounds are likewise in contrast in analogous position.

Concluding Procedures:

If the hypothesis cannot be refuted, and provided it is supported by a careful check of all occurrences of the sounds in every utterance to determine that the one segment occurs only in one set of environments and the other segment

---

[1]Sometimes only an extremely complex or highly improbable hypothesis can be found. In such cases, state that no plausible hypothesis can be found, and pass to the next step of the procedure.

never occurs in those environments, the student should conclude that the segments do not occur in analogous environments. Likewise, if the segments occur only in widely divergent kinds of environments then the student knows that they do not occur in analogous environments. In either case retain the sounds as a residue of suspicious segments to be treated under Analytical Procedure 1-C.

Solution to Problem 5:

Preliminary Procedures:

Phonetic chart:[1]

```
═══════════════════════════
        t            ḳ
        d
        s
        z
  m
              e
              ɛ
            a
───────────────────────────
```

Suspicious pairs:

    [t] and [d]

    [s] and [z]

    [e] and [ɛ]

Nonsuspicious segments:

    [k], [m], [a]

Separating Procedures:

For [s] and [z]:

The phonetic difference between them:

    [s] is voiceless, [z] is
        voiced

The most similar environment in which they occur:

    [sama] 'man

    [zama] 'seed'

The environmental difference:

    Of adjacent segments: none
    Of position in larger phono-
        logical or grammatical
        units: none

---

[1]Notice that the labels to the various parts of the solution are abbreviated once they have been given in an earlier solution. Compare p. 69. The student should, however, be prepared to expand the labels whenever it appears advisable to do so.

Hypothesis as to how environment might be responsible for the change of [s] to [z] or vice versa: none

Phonemic conclusion:

    [s] and [z] are in contrast
        in analogous environments
        and are separate phonemes.

For [e] and [ɛ]:

Phonetic difference:

    [e] is higher than [ɛ], (also
        a bit more tense, and
        front)

Most similar environments:

    [ɛḳa] 'stem

    [eḳe] 'sap'

Environmental difference:

    Of sounds: difference of
        noncontiguous [a] after
        [ɛ] but [e] noncontiguous-
        ly after [e]
    Of general position: none

Hypothesis (weak, but based on this incomplete evidence):

    That [ɛ] occurs only when
        noncontiguous [a] follows
        it, lowering [e] to [ɛ],
        but [e] never appears in
        this position   (implica-
        tion: noncontiguous [a]
        always causes this modifi-
        cation)
    [Note: For an alternative
        hypothesis, based on dif-
        ferent initial evidence,
        see the discussion of this
        problem.]

Evidence refuting hypothesis:

    [esa] 'leaf', in which [e]
        does precede noncontiguous
        [a].

Phonemic conclusion:

    [e] and [ɛ] contrast in
        analogous environments
        and are separate phonemes.

For [t] and [d]:

Phonetic difference:

    [t] voiceless, [d] voiced

Most similar environments:

    [tatsa] 'flower'

    [tadza] 'branch'

Environmental difference:

Of sounds: [t] before
  voiceless segment, [d]
  before voiced segment
Of general position: none

Hypothesis:

That [d] occurs only before
a voiced nonvocoid but
[t] never occurs in that
position (implication:
a voiced nonvocoid always
causes a [t] immediately
preceding it to become
voiced)

Evidence refuting hypothesis:

none (A check of every occurrence of [d] shows that
it occurs only preceding
voiced nonvocoids; this
evidence supports the
hypothesis.)

Phonemic conclusion:

[t] and [d] do not occur in
analogous positions
(and so cannot be in
contrast); they cannot
be proved separate
phonemes.

Concluding Procedures:

Residue of suspicious pairs (to
be treated under Procedure I-C):

[t] and [d]

Discussion of Problem 5:

In the first premise we noticed that
sounds slurred into their environments and
therefore that sounds similar to each other
might actually be submembers of a single
unit of sound, with one (or both) of them
modified slightly and nonsignificantly by
its environment. The investigator may conclude therefore that the two sounds of a
phonetically similar suspicious pair must
be considered as separate sound units if he
can discover data which eliminates the possibility of the environment having caused
the phonetic difference involved in that
pair. The investigator wishes, therefore,
to classify his data in such a way that he
can direct his attention to the environments
of the suspicious pairs of segments. He
wishes to find (providing it exists) such a
pair of sounds, each occurring in environments which are analogous. If he can find
each of them in analogous environments, he
may conclude that the environment is not
causing them to be different, since it would
require different environments to cause different modifications of sound. The discovery of the suspicious pair of segments in
identical environments or in highly similar

environments therefore eliminates the possibility of the environment being responsible
for the modification of one of the segments
in such a way that it becomes the other.
ANALOGOUS ENVIRONMENTS are phonetic and/or
grammatical contexts sufficiently similar
and of such a type that they could not
plausibly be considered as being responsible
for the particular phonetic differences between a specific suspicious pair of segments.
Environments analogous for one suspicious
pair may not be analogous for another pair:
each suspicious pair of segments must be
treated in the light of its own characteristics and its own environments.

It is wise to consider first those
suspicious sounds which occur in the most
similar environments, since sounds in such
environments are more likely to be proved
phonemically separate than are the others.
Once proved separate, they sometimes are
very helpful as points of reference for making hypotheses about remaining suspicious
pairs. In Problem 5, [s] and [z] were for
that reason analyzed before the treatment
of [t] and [d]. It would have been harder
to start with [t] and [d], since in [tadza]
'branch' one might wonder whether it were
preferable to set up the hypothesis that [z]
voiced [t] to [d], or the hypothesis that
[d] voiced [s] to [z]. After [s] and [z]
were proved to be separate phonemes, the
first of these two hypotheses remained the
more probable.

For [s] and [z] the environments
were identical. All identical environments
are analogous, but not all analogous environments are identical.[1]

In analyzing the suspicious pair [e]
and [ɛ], the forms [ɛka] and [eke] were
chosen as the most similar in environment.
A hypothesis might have been made, instead,
around [ɛka] and [esa]; then the investigator would have suggested that it is the
[k] which lowers [e] to [ɛ]. We considered
the first samples to have environments "more
similar," however, and set up the hypothesis
on that pair of words, since the differing
characteristics were farther from the segments in question. The hypothesis that [a]
had modified [e] to [ɛ] was weak in part because it postulated the noncontiguous influence of the [a]. In order for sounds to
affect other sounds most noticeably, they
usually must be directly adjacent to them.
Thus an [m] following an [f] might cause the
[f] to become voiced to [v] by the influence
of its voicing. Less frequently a sound may
intervene between the segments affected and
the segment causing the modification; for
example, a [w] might cause lip rounding of a
[t] in such a sequence as [awst].

---

[1]Special consideration will be given,
in the next chapter, to identical environments, but the student should notice that
they can be analyzed within the broader
framework of the present chapter as well.

The hypothesis was weak for a further reason. One usually expects that any sound modified by other sounds will become more like those sounds of its environment. Thus a front vowel might cause back consonants near it to become somewhat fronted like itself, but could not be expected to cause a consonant to go farther back. Likewise a voiced consonant might force a voiceless consonant next to it to become voiced also, but a voiced consonant could not be expected to cause an adjacent voiced consonant to become voiceless. Silence at the end of an utterance might cause a voiced consonant just before such a pause to become unvoiced but would rarely caused a voiceless consonant to become voiced. In Problem 5, there is no reason why the low vowel [a] should cause vowel [ɛ] to become higher, modifying it to [e]. This type of argument does not apply to sounds modified by border points, since the border points have no consistent phonetic characteristics as such for the modified sounds to reflect. Hypotheses should be checked for apparent REASONABLENESS by such considerations as these just given.

In this respect, the hypothesis that [k] lowered [e] to [ɛ] sounds more reasonable. It implies, however, that [k] lowers every preceding [e] to [ɛ]. This implication will not stand up in the face of the evidence: in [eke] the hypothesis breaks down. One should note, nevertheless, that alternate hypotheses[1] eventually lead the

---

[1]One further possible hypothesis should be mentioned: that [ɛ] occurs only in the sequence [ɛka] and [e] never occurs there; [e] occurs only in the sequences [eke] and [esa], and [ɛ] never occurs there; [e] becomes [ɛ] in the sequence listed. The difficulty with this type of approach is (1) that in actual language situations the statement of conditions might become so extremely complicated that only a list of words could be used to express the details of the hypothesis; no simple statement would suffice; (2) that such a conclusion would not be reasonable in terms of the first premise, that sounds tend to slur into their environments--since no reasonable basis for such a slur could be demonstrated. All items which cannot be found in identical environments are ultimately mutually exclusive, although the conditions of this distribution may be so highly complicated as to leave the sounds, for practical purposes, in contrast in analogous environments. If in some specific instance the student is in doubt as to whether he should consider sounds in contrast even though some statement of mutually exclusive distribution can be made, he must make a practical decision on the basis of (1) the relative complexity of the alternate descriptive statements, (2) completeness of data, (3) analysis of analogous sounds in the same general series, and (4) apparent reasonableness of statement of slurs of the sounds into their environments.

investigator to the same conclusion if he rigorously modifies, accepts, or rejects them in accordance with ALL the facts.

In the analysis of the suspicious pair [t] and [d], a hypothesis was made that [d] occurs only when a following voiced non-vocoid causes [t] to become voiced. When this hypothesis could not be refuted, the student was forced to conclude that the sounds were not in analogous environments, and must remain suspicious until analyzed by other procedures. (By the procedures of Chapter 8 the student would find that the hypothesis would be sustained, and that since the segments [t] and [d] are phonetically similar and mutually exclusive in their environments, they are submembers of a single phoneme.)

The control or selection of data and hypotheses in accordance with Analytical Procedure I-A, Contrast in Analogous Environment, is at times difficult. Several possibilities of error are present which the beginner may overlook. For this reason the next procedure, Procedure I-B (Contrast in Identical Environment), will continue with this same approach but in a restricted usage which is more easily applied and less frequently subject to error. Nevertheless, Procedure I-A (which also includes I-B), is often the only one which will indicate the distinct nature of phonemes in the early stages of one's field analysis, before suspicious segments can be found in contrast in identical environments.

A further sample problem will now be given in order to show how the procedure is applied to stress, pitch, or length.

Problem 6--Kalaba Dialect F

Phonetic Data:

['tomas]   'yellow'
[ta'mof]   'blue'
['tasof]   'black'

Directions:

Same as for Problem 5.

Solution to Problem 6:

Preliminary Procedures:

Phonetic chart:

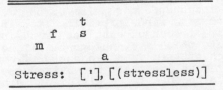

Stress: ['], [(stressless)]

Suspicious pairs:

['] and [(stressless)]

Nonsuspicious segments:

[t], [f], [s], [m], [a]

Separating Procedures:

For ['] and [(stressless)]:

Phonetic difference:

['] represents stress on
    segments
[(stressless)] represents
    stressless segments

Most similar environments:

['tasof] 'black'

[ta'mof] 'blue'

> [Note: Attention and
> discussion here is
> focused on the initial
> syllable.]

Environmental difference:

Of sounds in syllable under
   attention: none
Of sounds in following syllable: [m] follows unstressed syllable, [s]
   follows stressed syllable
Of position: none (both
   initial) etc.

Hypothesis (completely
invalid):

Stress occurs only on a syllable which is followed by
   a voiceless nonvocoid;
   stressless syllables are
   never followed by such a
   sound

Evidence refuting the
hypothesis:

['tomas] 'black'

[ta'mof] 'blue'

Phonemic conclusion:

['] and [(stressless)]
   contrast in analogous environments and are phonemically separate.[1]

In order to solve the problems below, follow the directions given for Problem
5, (p. 72), excepting in those instances
where special abbreviated instructions[2] are
presented.

---

[1] In this volume we call phonemic
stress a phoneme; but do not call the lack
of stress a phoneme.

[2] Note to the teacher: Abbreviated
instructions are given for many of the

For each step make the solution
parallel the style given you in the solution
of the step-by-step procedure.

Problem 7—Kalaba Dialect G

Phonetic Data:

[nisi]	'two'	[saga]	'to mix'
[fabi]	'bath'	[zibi]	'rough'
[niza]	'foreigner'	[vibi]	'nostril'
[taka]	'all'	[daki]	'north'
[sipa]	'chocolate'	[niti]	'gourd'
[kizi]	'dirty'	[zabi]	'palm'
[vapi]	'short'	[kaki]	'thumb'
[faki]	'nine'		

Problem 8—Kalaba Dialect H

Phonetic Data:

[tuŋga]	'stone'	[puŋgi]	'chair'
[mafpi]	'prairie'	[sana]	'turkey'
[siřu]	'mat'	[řamda]	'thunder'
[kanbu]	'fat'	[landu]	'cut'
[tilu]	'heavy'	[faɲa]	'soft'
[kiska]	'jug'	[ŋɑgi]	'melted'
[pusta]	'criminal'	[tadi]	'drum'
[nabu]	'viscous'		

[tuŋga dilu] 'a heavy stone'

[naspi sana ganbu ba] 'the fat
                          turkey was eaten'

Problem 9—Restricted Tabascan Chontal[1] A

Phonetic Data:

[sis]	'cold'	[išim]	'corn'
[šuš]	'bad'	[sum]	'rope'
[šaŋ]	'dried palm'	[šiš]	'corn meal'
[sami]	'earlier today'		

---

problems so that the student may solve more
exercises in the same amount of time which
it would require for him to apply the full
procedure to fewer of them. In general, the
student assimilates the principles of structural pressure and phonetic pattern more
readily by frequent repetition of the application of the procedures on simple exercises
than by occasional labored solution of intricate problems.

[1] Data from Kathryn Keller, of the
Summer Institute of Linguistics.

Problem 10--Kalaba Dialect I

Phonetic Data:

[biǧo]   'ox'
[bιko]   'stream'
[kiki]   'pool'

Problem 11--Kalaba Dialect J

Phonetic Data:

[laga̠]   'cot'
[laxas]   'dog'
[axal]   'mouse'

Problem 12--Kalaba Dialect K

Phonetic Data:

[spafu̠] 'rascal'
[zafu]   'village'
[susa]   'shore'

Problem 13--Kalaba Dialect L

Phonetic Data: (['] represents high tone):

[tóbð]   'all'
[tófó]   'some'
[bófð]   'many'

Directions:

Prove that tone is phonemic.

Problem 14--Kalaba Dialect M

Phonetic Data:

[tomig]	'flea'	[lalaf]	'mosquito'
[ɡitom]	'chicken'	[matum]	'fly'
[lofus]	'bug'	[tomig]	'elephant'
[tukag]	'roach'	[sosus]	'lion'

Directions:

Do the data prove [g] and [ɡ] to be separate phonemes? Answer "yes" or "no".

Problem 15--Restricted Mazateco[1] A

Phonetic Data:[2]

[naǧi]	'cliff'	[naǧa]	'salt'
[sa]	'sour'	[ǧa]	'loose'
[ta]	'hand'	[tǧiǧa̠]	'married'
[tasa]	'cup'	[ǧa]	'lion'

---

[1]Data from Eunice V. Pike, Summer Institute of Linguistics.

[2]Tone is omitted as not pertinent to the problem.

[ti]	'boy'	[ǧo]	'nail'
[natį]	'corn tassel'	[ǧoti]	'paper here'
[tǧiki]	'firewood'	[ǧoto]	'Saturday'
[ki]	'he went'	[ǧolo]	'pitcher'

Directions:

Prove that nasalized vowels and oral vowels are phonemically separate from each other.

Problem 16--Kalaba Dialect N

Phonetic Data:

| [molis] | 'blue' | [tomil] | 'red' |
| [tiliM] | 'green' | [mimoM] | 'purple' |

Directions:

What characteristics of their environments prevent the phonemic separation of [m] and [M]?

Problem 17--Kalaba Dialect O

Phonetic Data:

[tapaŋk] 'tomorrow'
[lomonk] 'yesterday'

Directions:

Prove that [n] and [ŋ] are separate phonemes.

Problem 18--Kalaba Dialect P

Phonetic Data:

[nabuN]	'to wonder'	[ɲabis]	'elbow'
[gizap]	'man'	[mamik]	'to enrage'
[suɲit]	'horse'	[zusap]	'fire'
[gisak]	'anteater'	[ɲugiŊ]	'to walk'
[danaM]	'circular'	[bibap]	'leaf'
[dinaM]	'breath'	[naɲap]	'to seek for'
[busiN]	'to be hurt'	[sudus]	'weeds'
[gazik]	'nose'		

[gizap danam ɲugiŊ] 'the man walks in
                                 circles'
[samak zasuŋ mugat] 'the hornets
                                 swarmed here'

Directions:

Why is it impossible to prove by this data that [p] and [b], [t] and [d], [k] and [g] are phonemically separate? How does the data differ for [m] and [M], [n] and [N], [ŋ] and [Ŋ]?

Are [z] and [s] similar to either?

Problem 19--Kalaba Dialect Q

Phonetic Data:

    [toˑmis] 'oak'
    [fomiˑs] 'elm'
    [ˌfuˑsoˑs] 'maple'

Directions:

Prove that length is phonemic.

Problem 20--Kalaba Dialect R

Phonetic Data:

    ['tapa] 'I am running'
    [ta'pa] 'sour milk'

Directions:

Prove that stress is phonemic.

Problem 21--Kalaba Dialect S

Phonetic Data:

[šųŋǎk] 'heart'   [n̜i̧kis] 'silver'

[ni̧diş] 'anvil'   [mi̧tis] 'ugly'

[pašųn] 'to rotate' [lusam̧] 'to cough'

[ŋ̧alap] 'poultry'   [tatat] 'wheel'

[kašil] 'to ache'   [gašųn] 'house'

[lušam̧] 'picture'   [dalis] 'to scrap'

[ˌsąni̧p] 'afraid'   [šimųl] 'round'

[pali̧n] 'to think'

   [pasųŋ tatat] 'the wheel turns'

   [lušam̧ mi̧tis] 'the picture is ugly'

Directions:

Can you prove that the following suspicious pairs are separate phonemes? (Answer "yes" or "no" for each set.)

    [t] and [d]   [n] and [l]
    [k] and [g]   [d] and [l]
    [n] and [ŋ]   [s] and [š]
    [i] and [i̧]   [a] and [ą]
    [u] and [ų]

Chapter 7

ANALYTICAL PROCEDURE ONE-B:

THE PHONEMIC SEPARATION OF SIMILAR SEGMENTS UPON FINDING THEM

IN CONTRAST IN IDENTICAL ENVIRONMENTS

Problem 22--Kalaba Dialect T

Phonetic Data:

[ténð]   'puddle'   [nùté]   'spider'

[nùté<] 'awkward'   [tènð]   'hiccough'

[tð<té<] 'rough'   [nónó]   'onion'

Directions for Problem 22:

Preliminary Procedures:

Follow instructions as for Problem 5, p. 73.

Separation Procedures: Analytical Procedure I-B: For a suspicious pair of which each segment occurs in identical environments:

List the pair.

State that they occur in identical environments.

Present the evidence.

Conclude and state that they are phonemically distinct.

[Note: This follows Analytical Procedure I-A, with the exception that the student may immediately conclude that suspicious segments found in identical environments are separate phonemes, without attempting to set up a hypothesis about the environments being responsible for the phonetic difference between the sounds. This is, then a special abbreviated form of Procedure I-A, which can be applied to certain types of environments only.]

Analytical Procedure I-A: Apply this procedure to any further suspicious pairs (for directions see p. 73).

Solution to Problem 22:

Preliminary Procedures:

Phonetic chart:

t		
n		
	e< e	o

Pitch: [´] [`]

Suspicious pairs:

[e<] and [e]

[´] and [`]

Nonsuspicious segments:

[t], [n], [o]

Separating Procedures:

For [e<] and [e]:

Environments: identical

Evidence: [nùté<] 'awkward'

[nùté] 'spider'

Phonemic conclusion:

Since the similar segments [e<] and [e] contrast in identical environments, they are separate phonemes.

For [´] and [`]:

Environments: identical

Evidence: [ténð] 'puddle'

[tènð] 'hiccough'

Phonemic conclusion:

[´] and [`] are separate phonemes of tone, since the tones contrast in identical environments.

Discussion of Problem 22:

The problems which are treated in this chapter can be handled adequately by the procedures given in Chapter 6. In fact, certain of the problems treated in the preceding chapter could now be analyzed by this new procedure. In either case the result would be the same, since contrast in identical environment is merely an instance of contrast in a specific kind of analogous environment. For a comparison of similar data treated by the two methods compare the analysis of [e‹] and [e] of Problem 22 with the analysis of [s] and [z] of Problem 5 (p. 74).

The newer procedure is more abbreviated, so is economical to use when it is applicable.

Furthermore, segments should, where possible, be separated by contrast in identical rather than in non-identical but similar environments, since the analysis in identical environments is much less liable to error. If the student uses an inadequate hypothesis to prove sounds separate in non-identical similar environments, he might conclude that the segments were phonemically separate even though the data did not actually warrant that conclusion; if the environmental characteristics which cause the nonphonemic modification of sounds should happen to be complicated, the student might set up a hypothesis which included only part of these conditions--and a wrong conclusion would result.

An incorrect conclusion may result from Procedure I-B, also, if the student's field notes are incorrect. If, for example, a language has a sound [k] which he hears inconsistently, writing it sometimes [k] and sometimes [g], his written data would lead him to postulate two velar phonemes. For this reason the investigator must carefully check with his informant to see that all words which are used for crucial evidence in arriving at phonemic conclusions are properly recorded.

Languages differ as to the segments which they unite into single phonemes. They differ also as to the pertinent distinctions which they make between segments. For this reason, the investigator must find adequate evidence before concluding that any specific set of similar segments are phonemically distinct.

A pair of words in which the first word is the same as the second except for the fact that one segment in the first word is replaced by a different but phonetically similar segment in the second word constitutes proof that the two similar segments are phonemically distinct. This proof goes back to the first premise, since in such a word pair the possibility is eliminated, because of the identical surroundings, that the environment may be responsible for the phonetic difference. In the data above, then, [e‹] is proved to be phonemically different from [e] because the sounds differ in spite of having identical surroundings. Word pairs of this type are said to be MINIMALLY DIFFERENT because no smaller difference in the language can make a difference in the meaning of the words. These

sets of words may be called MINIMAL PAIRS or (MINIMALLY) CONTRASTIVE PAIRS. Three words so differing constitute a MINIMAL TRIPLET. Phonemes of one segment length are the smallest replaceable parts of such pairs of words. For replaceable parts in English notice [s], [p], [n], [h], in seal, peal, kneel, heel, and so on.

For such proof, a single word pair in an actual language situation is not sufficient, since it is very easy for the investigator to be mistaken as to the identity of the remaining sounds in those words. For this reason the investigator should keep a list of a number of minimal pairs proving the phonemic differentiation of each suspicious pair of segments until he is convinced that his data has been correctly recorded. In the sample above, however, one minimal pair is to be considered evidence of phonemic separation, since the data has been kept very limited in order to prevent the problem from becoming unwieldy.

Once minimally different word pairs are discovered in an actual language, they are useful in two other ways: (1) They may serve to convince the investigator that between certain words there is actually a significant phonetic difference which he has previously overlooked. If, for example, the investigator is talking, and suddenly is misunderstood--or if the native seems highly amused at a statement or possibly offended when the statement appears to the investigator to have been completely innocuous--there is a considerable possibility that a word has been utilized of which the investigator is completely unaware because of his inadvertant usage of the wrong phoneme of a similar phonetic type. When misunderstandings arise the investigator should notice carefully the word or words which have caused the trouble. It may be that some one sound was pronounced incorrectly and that that sound caused the word to be different from what he had intended. By such accidents minimally different word pairs are frequently found and by them the investigator may be made conscious of differences between sound units which he has otherwise missed.

(2) The other advantage is that pairs of words of this type may be used by the investigator for practicing purposes, to help him learn to differentiate readily between sounds which to him appear so similar that they cause him difficulty. Once such a difference is found, he can ask to have the words repeated a few times each day until he can hear the difference readily and recognize each of the phonemes in any other words in which they occur. Spanish speakers, for example, have difficulty in hearing the difference between English [i] and [ɩ] since two similar sounds are submembers of the /i/ phoneme in Spanish. For Spanish speakers, therefore, practice with hearing word pairs like beat and bit prove helpful in teaching them the difference between English /i/ and /ɩ/.

In summarizing the values of this procedure, one may state that minimally different word pairs prove to be the beginner's single most important tool for the analysis of phonemic differences, and for giving ear training to foreigners.

Problem 23--Kalaba Dialect U

Phonetic Data:

[tap]	'every'	[tab]	'nerve'
[nat]	'to work'	[gana]	'monkey'
[kana]	'belt'	[tan]	'fruit'
[gan]	'to swim'	[kaka]	'lime'
[sona]	'to sink'	[tazna]	'lemon'
[dan]	'stick'	[dat]	'hard'
[nata]	'purse'	[gaka]	'to sell'
[kos]	'to buy'		

Directions:

For this problem, and for those immediately following, utilize the pertinent Preliminary Procedures, and Procedures I-B and I-A. Utilize I-A only when I-B is not applicable.

Problem 24--Kalaba Dialect V

Phonetic Data:

[šuŋa]	'forest'	[nisu]	'to burn'
[kisu]	'ice'	[sanu]	'corncob'
[tanu]	'to weave'	[kikit]	'his pipe'
[ŋukaš]	'roof'	[ŋisʊ]	'always'
[nʊšit]	'his wife'	[taši]	'to prepare'
[nušit]	'his altar'	[sinʊ]	'hollow'
[suŋa]	'brown'		

Problem 25--Kalaba Dialect W

Phonetic Data:

[biʃɛ]	'earth'	[tebgo]	'paper'
[poti]	'moving'	[aga]	'around'
[kespo]	'tree'	[pisɛ]	'timid'
[bose]	'skin'	[ketpo]	'any'
[dopɛ]	'to hurt'	[tɛbgo]	'squirrel'
[podi]	'parental'	[bosi]	'barren'
[aka]	'to trample'		

Problem 26--Kalaba Dialect X

Phonetic Data (the low dot represents syllable division):

['ma.tɛ]	'cow'	['pa.tɛ]	'lamb'
['mɛ.lšo]	'tree'	['sme.ta]	'here'
['mɛ]	'house'	[pa.'so]	'come'
[ni.'no]	'clear'	[mo.'sti]	'fly'
[ša.'lo]	'red'	['mɛ.nšo]	'open'
[pa.'to]	'climbing'	[mo.'ste]	'inside'
['me]	'fig'	[ni.'ŋo]	'round'
[sa.'lo]	'horse'		

Problem 27--Kalaba Dialect Y

Phonetic Data:

[foxt]	'end'	[vokt]	'pear'
[taθs]	'summer'	[θaθs]	'trough'
[stak]	'man'	[zaz]	'way'
[fokt]	'to wish'	[đoxa]	'four'
[đoga]	'to enter'	[vaz]	'to be'
[θoxa]	'small'	[foxs]	'bread'
[sfaks]	'house'	[kaxk]	'to catch'
[tova]	'checkered'	[kfog]	'hole'

Problem 28--Kalaba Dialect Z

Phonetic Data:

[dřage]	'to bewitch'	[březa]	'father'
[leza]	'tired'	[smode]	'to sit down'
[gedəs]	'hyena'	[beza]	'fire'
[bolo]	'to marry'	[bosel]	'to confer'
[gřamo]	'dented'	[lage]	'soot'
[mezas]	'fetish'	[zem]	'six'
[gedəz]	'bean'	[gřəga]	'to stab'
[lezə]	'drum stick'	[mosel]	'to chant'
[lamo]	'wart'	[bolə]	'scar'

Problem 29--Kalaba Dialect AA

Phonetic Data:

[peze]	'first'	[nẹzep]	'fifth'
[xezeb]	'second'	[pežẹn]	'sixth'
[x̣epe]	'third'	[beze]	'seventh'
[pezẹn]	'fourth'	[benẹ]	'eighth'

Directions:

(1) Give phonetic chart, suspicious pairs, nonsuspicious segments.

(2) List suspicious pairs separated by contrast in identical environment and present the evidence.

(3) List suspicious pairs separated by contrast in analogous environment and explain the evidence.

(4) List residue of suspicious pairs.

Problem 30--Kalaba Dialect AB

Phonetic Data:

[š͜ǐ]	'high'	[pǐ'šu]	'round'
['b͜ǐ͜pu]	'low'	[p͜u'ž͜ǐ]	'big
[žu]	'soft'	[ž͜ǐ]	'small'
[pu'b͜u]	'hard'	[žu'b͜u]	'full'
['b͜upǐ]	'rough'	[š͜ǐ'b͜ǐ]	'empty'

Directions:

(1) Can the following suspicious pairs be proven phonemically separate by the data given? Answer "yes" or "no" for each set: [p] and [b̥], [p] and [p͜], [b] and [b̥], [š] and [ž], [ǐ] and [u].

(2) For those claimed to be separate phonemically, name the procedure or procedures used to prove it.

(3) State the limited kinds of environment in which the voiced stop occurs but in which the voiceless stop does not occur.

Problem 31--Restricted Zinza[1] A

Phonetic Data (high tone [´], low tone unmarked; length [·]):

[kuɽoba] 'to become wet'

[obukó·mbe] 'wedding feast'

[tuke·bwa] 'we forgot'

[obukombe] 'thunderstorm'

[tuké·bwa] 'we were stolen from'

[kuɽóba] 'to fish by line'

Directions:

Prove tone to be phonemic.

Problem 32--Restricted Badaga[2] A

Phonetic Data:

[be·]	'mouth'	[kaṭ·e]	'I learned'
[kaṭ·e]	'ass'	[to·gu]	'wash it!'
[be̥·]	'bangle'	[to̥·go]	'plural of [to̥·]'

Directions:

Prove that [e·] is phonemically distinct from retroflex [e̥·]; [a] from [ḁ], [o·] from [o̥·].

---

[1]Data from Donald H. Ebeling, "Tonal Morphology of Zinza," an unpublished manuscript. Possibly the long vowels should be interpreted phonemically as clusters of identical vowels.

[2]Data adapted from M. B. Emeneau,

Problem 33--Restricted Oaxacan Chontal[1] A

Phonetic Data:

[ku·šax]	'needle'	[tsaʔpa]	'I sifted'
[paŋxa]	'he is able'	[axaʔ]	'water'
[ɛpa]	'sugar cane'	[ṭa·sɛta]	'he is going for a walk'
[saxpa]	'I ate'		
[ṭɛpa]	'he bit'	[paŋxa·]	'slowly'
[kušax]	'bitter'	[tšɛ·pa]	'he went away'
[tsɛ·pa]	'I went away'		
[tɛpa]	'I bit'	[akaʔ]	'bird'
[šaxpaʔ]	'they ate'		

Directions:

Explain the evidence for separating phonemically [s] and [š]; [k] and [x], [t] and [ṭ], [ɛ] and [ɛ·], [u] and [u·], [ʌ] and [a·].

"The Vowels of the Badaga Language," in Language, XV (January-March, 1939), 43-7.

[1]Data from May Morrison, Summer Institute of Linguistics.

Chapter 8

ANALYTICAL PROCEDURE ONE-C:

THE PHONEMIC UNITING OF SIMILAR SEGMENTS UPON FINDING

THEM IN MUTUALLY EXCLUSIVE ENVIRONMENTS

Problem 34--Kalaba Dialect AC

Phonetic Data:

[tofo]	'constella- tion'	[kexɔ]	'snow'
		[xexe]	'fail'
[ose]	'eclipse'	[topo]	'toe'
[pexɔ]	'sun'	[seso]	'estimate'
[efes]	'yesterday'	[fepe]	'sharp'
[tefot] and [tefod]		[xot] and [xod]	
	'I'		'twelve'
[toxos]	'possibly'	[tokox]	'sing'
[foxɔ]	'stump'	[xope]	'bluebird'

[pexɔ ose] 'the sun is eclipsed'

[pexɔ fepe efes] 'the sun was bright
yesterday'

Directions for Problem 34:

Preliminary Procedures: (1) Make a phonetic chart, (2) list suspicious pairs, and (3) list nonsuspicious segments.

Separation Procedures:

For any suspicious pair which can be separated by contrast in identical environment, (1) state the nature of the environment, (2) give the evidence, and (3) draw a phonemic conclusion. (Cf. Procedure I-B.)

For any further suspicious pairs which can be separated by contrast in analogous environments, (1) state the general nature of the environments, (2) give the evidence, and (3) draw a phonemic conclusion. (Cf. Procedure I-A.)

Uniting Procedures: Analytical Procedure I-C: For any further suspicious pairs:

Make a hypothesis as to the mutually exclusive distribution of the segments, stating that one of the sounds occurs only in certain positions, whereas the other sound never occurs in those same positions.

Test the hypothesis by a chart (1) which states the environmental characteristics held responsible for the modifications, and (2) which charts, against all the data available, their

occurrence in the specific restricted set of environments named, and elsewhere.

If the hypothesis is supported by all the evidence, then (1) state that the sounds are submembers of a single phoneme because they are (a) phonetically similar and (b) mutually exclusive in distribution; (2) choose one submember of the phoneme which may best be considered the norm for that phoneme; choose that segment which is (a) least limited in distribution and (b) least affected by its environment. If two or more segments are equally distributed, and so on, choose one of them arbitrarily as a hypothetical norm for a convenient point of reference in making statements about the submembers of that phoneme.

If the hypothesis is not supported by all the evidence, then (1) attempt to modify the hypothesis, by restating the environments in which the least widely distributed submember occurs, so that it can be supported by all the evidence; or (2) reconsider the data under Procedure I-A.

Concluding Procedures:

List any further residue of suspicious segments which must be handled under later procedures.

Make a labeled chart of the phonetic norms of the phonemes. Include any residue of suspicious sounds, but with a question mark beside them.

If the phonetic symbols used to represent the phonemic norms are inconvenient for practical purposes, modify them.

Rewrite the data presented for the dialect, using just one symbol for each phoneme. Enclose phonemic writing in diagonals. Read aloud the material now that it is rewritten; maintain the same pronunciation as indicated in the original phonetic data.

Solution to Problem 34:

Preliminary Procedures:

Phonetic chart:

```
      t      k
      d
  p  f s     x
      e     o
            ɔ
```

Suspicious pairs:

[p̃] and [f]

[k] and [x]

[o] and [ɔ]

[t] and [d]

Nonsuspicious segments:

[ș], [e̦]

Separating Procedures:

For [p̃] and [f]:

Environments: identical

Evidence: [tofo] 'constella-
tion'

[top̃o] 'toe'

Phonemic conclusion:

[p̃] and [f] are separate
phonemes since they con-
trast in identical en-
vironments.

For [k] and [x]:

Environments: analogous

Evidence: [kexɔ] 'snow'

[xexe] 'fail'

[tokox] 'sing'

Phonemic conclusion:

[k] and [x] are phonemically
separate since they con-
trast in analogous en-
vironments.

Uniting Procedures:

For [o] and [ɔ]:

Hypothesis: [ɔ] occurs only
in word-final open syllables following a velar nonvocoid whereas [o]
never occurs in that environment.

Test of hypothesis:

Occurrence of [o] and [ɔ] in Word-Final Open
Syllables after Velar Nonvocoid, and
Elsewhere

Submembers of /o/	In Word-Final Open Syllables after Velar Nonvocoids	Elsewhere
[ɔ].....	̶ ̶ ̶ ̶ (five times)	(never)
[o].....	(never)	̶ ̶ ̶ ̶ ̶ ̶ ̶ ̶ ̶ ̶ ̶ ̶ !! (seventeen times)

Phonemic conclusion:

[o] and [ɔ] are submembers
of a single phoneme,
since they are phoneti-
cally similar and mutual-
ly exclusive in their
distribution.

Phonemic norm: [o]

Concluding Procedures:

Residue of suspicious segments:

[t] and [d] (to be treated
under Procedure III)

Chart of phonetic norms of the
phonemes:

Nonvocoids	Bilabial	Labio-	Alveolar	Velar
Voiceless unaspir-ated stops			t	k
Voiced stops.....			d ʔ	
Voiceless fricatives	p̃	f	s	x

Vocoids		
Mid close............................	e	o
	Front unround	Back rounded

Practical orthography:

Change "p̃" to p; otherwise no
changes:
(dʔ, e, f, k, o, p, s, t, x)

Phonemic rewrite:

/tofo/   'constella-   /kexo/   'snow'
                tion'   /xexe/   'fail'
/ose/   'eclipse'   /topo/   'toe'
/pexo/   'sun'   /seso/   'estimate'
/efes/   'yesterday'   /fepe/   'sharp'
/tefot/? /tefod/?   /xot/? /xod/?
         'I'   'twelve'
/toxos/ 'possibly'   /tokox/ 'sing'
/foxo/   'stump'   /xope/   'bluebird'

 /pexo ose/ 'the sun is eclipsed'

 /pexo fepe efos/ 'the sun was bright
                              yesterday'

Discussion of Problem 34:

In Procedures I-A and I-B the first assumption was applied negatively. By this procedure it could be demonstrated that the difference in certain similar segments could not be caused by slurs into differing surroundings. One concluded that such items were phonemically different.

Procedure I-C is the reverse of I-A. In I-C the distribution of similar segments in relation to their environment is studied. When it can be shown that two similar segments occur in different types of environments, the analyst concludes that the environment has caused the modification of one of the similar sounds to the other, or both of them to their present form from a common or hypothetical norm.

Some sounds are like chameleons, and change a bit so that they take on some of the characteristics of the sounds next to them. Sounds coming together are likely to influence each other. The first may receive some of the characteristics of the second, or the second of the first. For example, English /k/ has a front tongue position before the front vowel /i/ but a back tongue position and rounded lips before the back rounded vowel /u/. One sound unit, therefore—that is, one phoneme—may have several submembers depending upon the sounds which precede or follow it.

In the language of the investigator, two sounds which are phonemically different may in the language of the native be phonemically one. In this case, the investigator is likely to hear in a language differences of sound which to the native himself are nondistinctive. For this reason, the investigator needs a technique which will allow him to determine whether segments which sound similar to him are separate phonemes or submembers of single phonemes in the structure of the language being studied.

Two segments may constitute submembers of a single phoneme only if they are (1) phonetically similar and (2) mutually exclusive. The general procedure attempts to aid the investigator to locate mutually exclusive positions which similar segments occupy, and to conclude from this data that the segments so distributed are members of a single phoneme and should be written with a single symbol. Two sounds are MUTUALLY EXCLUSIVE as to the environments in which they occur when the following can be said about them: 'The first segment of the two occurs only in such and such positions, but the second segment never occurs in these same positions.' If, for example, one finds that in a certain problem [t] occurs only at the beginning of words but [s] never occurs at the beginning of words, the two are mutually exclusive as to the environments in which they occur. That is to say, [t] in such a case could never be found in the same position or type of position phonetically in which [s] is found, since [t], being limited to occurrence at the beginning of words, could not be found at the end of words where [s] may occur; similarly, [s] could not be found at the beginning of words, since it would be limited strictly to occurrence at the end of words in this hypothetical case.

In order to discover whether or not the segments of one of the suspicious pairs are mutually exclusive in the positions which they occupy, it is possible for the student to start drawing up intricate tabulations of the various phonetic environments in which these specific segments are found. In this way he might eventually discover the particular types of environments which were pertinent to the problem at hand, in that they could cause the modification of one segment to the other by its being slurred into such an environment. However, this is a very slow and laborious process, since the possible combinations of environment are many, and the factors which are known to influence sounds comprise a considerable number. Fortunately the student can shorten this process a great deal by careful study of the nature of the particular segments in question.

In order to help locate quickly the environments which limit the occurrence of such segments,[1] the student may ask himself the following questions: If one of the sounds is changed to the other because of its relationship to other sounds in its environment, what kind of environment might have caused such a change?' For example, with a [ķ] versus a [k], if [ķ] were assumed to be the normal phonetic form of the phoneme, but one tentatively advances the hypothesis that the front [ķ] has been backed to [k] by its environment, one might legitimately assume that the probability is that the environment causing such a change must have some phonetic characteristic which partakes of an articulatory position farther back in the mouth than that in which the front [ķ] occurs. On the other hand, if one

---

[1] But not as an essential phonemic criterion or prerequisite.

advances the hypothesis that the [k] with medial point of articulation is the normal phonetic form of a phoneme containing both [k̯] and [k] as submembers, then one might assume that the change from a medial articulatory position to a more front position is most likely to have been caused in an environment which includes sounds which also have a somewhat front articulation. After he has made such an assumption the student may then make a quick perusal of the actual data to see if the sounds in question actually do occur in such postulated environments.

Specifically then, the student should be alert to notice the phonetic differences between the segments of suspicious pairs, and be prepared to find in the environments in which they occur those sounds which might cause them to be modified in one of the following ways:

Fronting or backing

Raising or lowering

Voicing or unvoicing

Complete or partial nasalization

Retroflexion

Stops changed to fricatives, or fricatives to stops

Friction increased, decreased, added, or eliminated

Rounding or unrounding

Palatalization, velarization, pharyngealization, glottal influence (laryngealization) added to sounds

Change of sounds from one syllable to another; the change of the place of syllable division

Changing syllabics to nonsyllabics, or nonsyllabics to syllabics

Lengthening or shortening of sounds

Heightening or lowering the pitch of sounds

Intensification or weakening of the loudness of sounds

Centralization of the quality of voiced central resonant orals

Sometimes, however, it happens that the pertinent environment which modifies the segment in question is not a single sound but a group of sounds which have some phonetic characteristic in common. For example, the student should be prepared to find a nonvocoid fronted when next to a front vocoid, regardless of which particular front vocoid is present, and so on.

One does not find, however, that the sounds in question are necessarily slurred into or modified by certain other sounds regardless of their relationship to them. Sometimes it happens that sounds will be affected by a certain set of other sounds which are followed by this group of sounds, but that the segment is completely unaffected by the same sounds if it is preceded by them. Occasionally one finds a sound affected by a second sound which is not directly next to it, but which has a third sound coming between them. In Problem 34, one should notice that the [o] is lowered when it follows [x] in a word-final open syllable, as in the word for 'stump' [foxɔ], but that the [o] is not lowered when it precedes the same sound instead of following it.

In other words, one must be prepared to advance hypotheses that of two segments of a suspicious pair, one of them has been changed to the other because of a slur into its environment, and that this environment can consist of a sound or group of sounds which might readily cause such a change.

One must also be ready to find modifications of sounds in environments where it is less easy, or impossible, to show a reason for this change in the phonetic characteristic of the pertinent environment. These changes are usually those caused by the position of the segment in some grammatical unit, such as the word.

Once the investigator has set up a hypothesis stating that two segments which are phonetically similar are mutually exclusive in the positions which they occupy he should check this hypothesis very carefully against <u>all</u> of the data (every word and phrase recorded) for that dialect.

If the hypothesis proves to be inaccurate and inapplicable to some of the data, the hypothesis may have to be rejected. First, however, the investigator should attempt to modify the hypothesis slightly so as to make it to apply to the entire problem. Here, for example, in Problem 34, if he should advance a hypothesis that [ɔ] occurs only following the velar nonvocoids, and [o] never occurs in that environment, he would find that that would apply to the word for 'stump' [foxɔ], but that it would not apply to words like [toxos] 'possibly', in which [o] does occur following a velar nonvocoid. Instead of rejecting the hypothesis that the velar nonvocoid is the pertinent item in the environment, however, he should study the data further and note that the hypothesis can be rephrased adequately by stating that the [ɔ] occurs, to be sure, only after velar nonvocoids, but that a further stipulation must be made: [ɔ] occurs only in an open syllable, at the end of a word; the earlier and later elements must be combined into the single hypothesis that [ɔ] occurs only in word-final open syllables following a velar nonvocoid, whereas [o] never occurs in those environments. Now the statement can be applied to all the data without exception, as in [toxos] 'possibly'. When he has tested this statement of the mutual exclusiveness of [o] and [ɔ] and found that it is accurate, he can then conclude that they are submembers of a single phoneme, since (1) they are phonetically similar and (2) they are mutually exclusive in occurrence.

It is instructive to see the appearance of the data on a testing chart for which the hypothesis is pertinent but only partly accurate:

Occurrence of [o] and [ɔ] after Velar Nonvocoids

Submembers of /o/	After Velar Nonvocoids	Elsewhere
[ɔ].....	⊢⊣	(never)
[o].....	' ' ' '	⊢⊣ ⊢⊣ ' ' '

In this chart we see that the occurrence of [ɔ] is limited, but the [o] appears to occur in some of the same positions--i.e. to contrast in analogous environments. Because of the limited distribution of the [ɔ], however, the investigator should recheck the data. If he revises the statement of the distributional limitations of [ɔ], as for the chart given earlier in the solution to the problem, he would then be able to find that the segments are mutually exclusive in their environments.

In describing the varieties of submembers of any specific phoneme it proves convenient to assume that one of the varieties is in some way basic, or the NORM, and that the others are modified from this normal type because of slurs to their respective environments. It is advisable to consider as the norm that segment which has the least limitation in distribution in the language, and appears to be the least affected by surrounding sounds. In Problem 34 it is convenient therefore to consider [o] the norm for the phoneme /o/, since it has a wider distribution than [ɔ]. After calling [o] the norm, it then proves convenient to state that '[o] becomes [ɔ], after velar nonvocoids at the end of words.'

When no good reason can be found which makes the choice of a norm certain, the investigator may arbitrarily choose one segment or another to be called the phonetic norm as convenient point of departure for the description of the phoneme.

Occasionally at this stage in the analysis there are suspicious pairs of segments which are neither proved to be phonemically distinct under Analytical Procedure I-A or I-B, nor phonemically unitary under Analytical Procedure I-C. In such cases their analysis must await the application of further procedures. In Problem 34, the segments [t] and [d] fluctuate freely. Later on the student can analyze them with Procedure III.

One who wishes to learn the number and general phonetic type of phonemes in any language can do so most easily by means of a chart of the phonetic norms of the phonemes, provided that he is acquainted with phonetic symbolization and terminology. It is therefore a great convenience to the reader to have such a chart. Such a chart should be accompanied, in a full description of the language, by a statement of the submembers of phonemes in so far as they have been observed by the investigator. The preparation and presentation of such a statement with other items which enter into it will be discussed under Descriptive Procedures.

A chart of the phonetic norms of phonemes will contain the same sounds as the chart of kinds of segments (which was prepared under one of the Preliminary Procedures), except that some of the segments will have been eliminated, and--if they have been overlooked in transferring the data from the problems, or in hearing data in an actual field situation--others may be added. Label the sections of the chart. Utilize only those columns necessary to contain the data which actually appear in the dialect. If the analysis of certain of the phonemes is still dubious at this point, the student should list them on the chart, with a question mark. For Problem 34, [d̷] is listed in this way.

Once the phonemes are determined, a linguist or educator may wish to use these studies as the basis for the formation of a practical orthography for some specific language area. In this case the symbols chosen need not be the ones used here for technical purposes, but may be modified or have substituted for them any symbols which are easier to print, easier to write, easier to read, or better adapted to the traditional culture of the area. Later in the volume, under Orthographical Procedures, attention will be turned to these practical phases of alphabet formation. Meanwhile, however, the educator studying phonemics needs to keep these goals in mind. In Problem 34 the symbol "ƀ" would probably be changed to "p", for such practical purposes, in many cultural areas. In China or Russia, however, all the symbols might have to be modified.

Following the choice of a practical orthography the data is to be rewritten phonemically using this alphabet. By so doing, the student starts building habits of utilizing a phonemic script which will foreshadow future field activities.

After the material of the problem is rewritten phonemically, the student should practice reading it aloud. There is one strong caution, however: phonemic writing has been modified to eliminate the symbolization of the submembers of the phoneme (other than the norm) but this does not change the pronunciation of the material one iota. The material is still to be read in the identical way as it was from the phonetic transcription given earlier.

The reading of a phonemic script necessitates the foreigner's learning a series of rules instructing him how to pronounce the symbols for that particular language. This may at first seem to him to be somewhat awkward and difficult. With a bit of practice, however, he can learn to do so quite readily. The native, on the other hand, does not meet this particular difficulty since the modification of the sound is automatically conditioned by its environment. Therefore, once he learns the general phonetic value of the phoneme, the conditioned varieties caused by the environment will be pronounced by him automatically whenever the symbol is found in those environments. It is for this reason that a phonemic script is the easiest type for the native to read: he does not have to learn extra symbols which merely indicate modification of his basic units according to their position but can learn instead the minimum of symbols necessary to distinguish all of the basic sound units in his language.[1]

In the solution to Problem 34 the student has seen that the distribution of the segment [ɔ] was in part described in reference to its occurrence at the end of words. Border points of the larger grammatical or phonological units may cause the nonsignificant modification of phonemes. At the boundaries between the grammatical units, large phonological units, or at the beginning or end of utterances (which, of course, begin or end some kind of grammatical unit and phonological unit) such disturbances may occur.

One of the grammatical units most frequently responsible for nonphonemic modification of segments is the word. In the problems at the end of this chapter words are frequently the pertinent unit for the student to watch.

The student may feel that he can recognize a word when he sees or hears one, in his own writing or speech. Yet words are not so readily apparent in many languages. Frequently the investigator may find it difficult to determine the points at which he wishes to separate words. The problem is sufficiently acute that a separate

discussion will be given to it later, in Chapter 13. Meanwhile, for the purposes of solving the problems, the student may assume that words are separated by spaces in the phonetic data. Later on he will learn how to place spaces himself, placing them, usually, but not always, between items which he has heard pronounced by themselves or at the beginning and end of utterances. A WORD, then, is the smallest unit arrived at for some particular language as the most convenient type of grammatical entity to separate by spaces; in general, it constitutes one of those units of a particular language which actually or potentially may be pronounced by itself.

The student should be aware of certain other types of grammatical and phonological units, also. Some of them may be mentioned briefly here.

Immediately following a PAUSE, or preceding one of them, phonemes may have submembers which do not occur elsewhere. An UTTERANCE is a unit of speech which happens to begin and end with a pause. An utterance includes everything that a native says from the time he begins to speak until he reaches a long or short pause. If he says a single word, Tom!, and then pauses, the word Tom! is there a single complete utterance. If he says I want to buy a paper, and then pauses, that also is a single complete utterance. Since special phonetic varieties of the phonemes are likely to occur at pauses, partly because there are likely to be slurs from or to silence, the investigator must give careful attention to these places.

It proves important for the investigator to note the phonetic phenomena at the beginning of an utterance, also, because it is certain to constitute, also, the beginning (1) of a morpheme, (2) of a word, and (3) of a grammatical construction if one is present in that utterance.

The beginning of an utterance is significant to the investigator for another reason; he can be certain that at that point he is also at the beginning (1) of a syllable, (2) of a stress group, if such exist in the language, (3) of a rhythm group, and (4) of an intonation group, if these last two also exist. This is helpful since in the middle of utterances one may find it difficult at times to determine where any of these begin or end. Yet if the phonemes are modified at such points, he needs to know where such modifications occur. Early in the investigation he can be certain of such borders only at the beginning or the end of utterances.

A MORPHEME is the smallest structural unit which is itself meaningful in the language being studied (or in some instances is a meaningless or nearly meaningless[1] unit

---

[1] Many of the earlier problems at the end of this chapter can be solved by the student without reading further in this discussion. For the later problems the student will need the background material to be gained from the remainder of the discussion. For some of the earlier problems, also, the succeeding discussion may serve to prevent errors of procedure.

[1] Some morphemes have grammatical function with but little or no lexical meaning. One of these is constituted of the -er

arrived at by analogy with the meaningful ones). They are the smallest meaningful parts of words, or may constitute complete words by themselves. Thus, the words boy and run are single morphemes. Hyphens separate morphemes in the following words: hunt-ing, run-s, girl-ish-ness. Sometimes morphemes may be fused together so that it is hard to separate them; notice the difficulty of separating do from not in don't-- or did from you in /'dɪʤə/.

Various other grammatical unit types in addition to words and morphemes may sometimes be found. These include words which at certain times are incomplete, and are pronounced with other words. Such items may be called PROCLITICS or ENCLITICS, depending upon whether they are pronounced with the following word or the preceding one. Compare s in s' the truth and m in I'm going. On the other hand, in the house constitutes a unified PHRASE longer than a word but shorter than such an utterance as The book is in the house today.

Whereas GRAMMATICAL units include morphemes, words, clitics, phrases, and utterances, PHONOLOGICAL units include phonemes, syllables, stress groups, rhythm groups, intonation groups, utterances, and so on.

In many instances, especially at the beginning or end of utterances, the borders of phonological and grammatical units coincide. Thus, the beginning of an utterance constitutes, in addition to some of the grammatical units mentioned above, the beginning of certain phonological units as well.

In the initial presentation of the premises in Chapter 4 there was some discussion of the PHONETIC SYLLABLE which phonetically, or physically, is constituted of a chest pulse. Certain sound types--the central resonant orals such as [e] and [o]--are those which more frequently than others constitute the SYLLABIC, or peak of the syllable. Other types--such as [p], [s], and [n], are more likely to be found at the margins of the syllable, as NONSYLLABICS. On the other hand, sound types are not restricted in occurrence exclusively to any one part of the syllable, so that [n], for example, may be found to be syllabic or [i] nonsyllabic. In some languages it proves convenient to define a syllable as a single unit of PROMINENCE, such that each outstanding vocoid forms the center of a new syllable.

For particular languages the student must be prepared to find that the phonetic syllable does not correspond with the most

pertinent structural grouping of segments. Just as segments must be analyzed into the structural phonemes, so phonetic syllables must be analyzed into the structural phonemic syllables. The reason for this difficulty is that the interpretation of syllable units varies from language to language. A speaker of English "hears" fewer syllables in English than a speaker of Spanish is likely to do. Spanish speakers, for example, are likely to think they hear two syllables in the English word cow, since Spanish structural units differ from those of English. One cannot determine in advance exactly what will be the type of unit to which to apply the term phonemic syllable, until he studies the language as a whole, and finds some phonetic unit larger than the phoneme which serves as a unit of stress placement, or of tone placement, or of the timing of vowel length, or of the formation of the morphemes. This discussion of this problem must be delayed until Chapter 11. Meanwhile, the discussion of Procedure I-C continues, utilizing syllable types where these particular difficulties are kept to a minimum. A lowered dot in the phonetic data indicates a division between phonetic syllables. Nonsyllabic sounds at the beginning of syllables tend to differ somewhat from the same sounds at the end of syllables.[1]

Phonetic syllables become modified by a changed speed of utterance. At the moment we lack adequate procedures for analyzing or describing these changes efficiently, and usually give a description of a language spoken at a more or less normal speed, with only occasional but nonsystematic references to changes in slow and fast speech.[2]

Syllables may be united into larger units containing a single heavy stress. Such items may be called STRESS GROUPS. In languages such as English, they tend to constitute simple RHYTHM UNITS[3] and are likely

---

in hammer, river. These can sometimes be ignored in the early analysis, though later they may enter the distributional statement, as in Leonard Bloomfield's "The Stressed Vowels of American English," in Language, XI (June, 1935), 97-116.

[1] R. H. Stetson has concerned himself with changes due to speed. In his researches certain nonsense syllables, such as op, served as the basis of experiment, in which -p passed to the following vowel in rapid syllabification. Yet in such an experiment the syllable op serves as a hypothetical morpheme and as such can be subsumed under the statement below. In his Bases of Phonology Stetson gives (p. 108) formulas for disappearance and reappearance of phonemes, but fails to see that reappearance involves identification in terms of morphemes.

[2] For one of the best, but brief, attempts to show speed changes, see Doris Needham and Marjorie Davis, "Cuicateco Phonology," International Journal of American Linguistics, XII (July, 1946), 142.

[3] For an analysis of the phonemic nature of rhythm units, intonation contours, and pauses in English, see K. L. Pike, Intonation of American English, University of

to be closely related to INTONATION UNITS. Sound units frequently have submembers modified according to the places in which they occur in stress groups or rhythm groups. One variety may be limited to occurrence in the stressed syllable of the group. Another may occur only in syllables preceding the stressed syllable. A third variety may be found only at the boundaries--the beginning or end--of the group, and so on.[1] Sound units tend to have varieties of submembers which are limited to the border spots. For this reason the investigator needs to know where all such borders occur. In the middle of utterances, especially early in this analysis, he may be very dubious as to where phonological or grammatical borders occur. At the beginning of utterances, however, he knows immediately that he is at the beginning of syllable, morpheme, word, and the like. Precisely from this fact streams the great value to the linguist of the study of varieties of sound at the beginning of utterances. For the end of utterances a similar line of reasoning brings similar results.

After he has observed characteristic modifications of sound units at borders initially in utterances, the investigator wishes to know whether or not the same modifications occur at borders of some type within large utterances. This, however, proves much more difficult to do, since borders between rhythm units, intonation units, or stress groups are frequently not readily apparent. Even borders between syllables are often vague.

In actual practice on the field the investigator in early study seldom attempts to symbolize these phonological subdivisions of utterances. Rather (1) he notes (a) the beginning and end of utterances, and (b) the specific grammatical items and borders of items--morphemes, especially--which begin or end at these places; then (2) he watches for these same identical morphemes with their borders--or other grammatical units and their borders--which may recur within larger utterances. He can identify these grammatical units since they have (a) a constant or at least similar sequence of consonants and vowels and (b) constant or at least similar meaning; for example, he can recognize the

---

Michigan Publications in Linguistics, I (Ann Arbor: University of Michigan Press, 1945), especially pages 30-38. Intonation and punctuation are discussed in the present volume, see p. 45, p. 50, p. 105, and Chapter 16.

[1]For a physiological explanation of this phenomenon see R. H. Stetson, Bases of Phonology (Oberlin, Ohio, 1945), and references in his Bibliography. 'The foot includes one or more chest pulses, syllables, grouped by an abdominal-diaphragmatic contraction of expiration. This is the movement which binds the syllables together and gives junctures and the main stress' (p. 57), etc.

morpheme Tom both at the beginning of an utterance like Tom! (as a call to come) and in the middle of the utterance I hear that Tom is here, since in each case it has (a) the sounds [tam] and (b) the meaning of the name of a particular person. Grammatical units can often be more readily identified, even with crude initial phonetic symbolization, than can some of the phonological ones.

Since the larger phonological divisions tend to coincide with grammatical divisions of some types (although syllables, as a smaller type, more frequently cut across such grammatical boundaries), it often proves convenient to describe the environmental modification of sounds as due to their position in the grammatical unit, rather than in a phonological one, when either could be used.

This, at times, also avoids the setting up of duplicate terminology for phonological and grammatical units which are identical. In those instances in which a stress group, for example, is always a word, and a word is always a stress group, it avoids the presentation of two terms for the same unit if one calls it simply a "word." Then one describes modification of sounds at the beginning of that unit as due to changes forced by the environment as a word beginning rather than as due to a special type of phonemic phonological grouping such as "stress group" or "intraspace," or "internal juncture."

Often the use of grammatical terminology is technically helpful even for phonological analysis, since grammatical boundaries frequently serve as the POTENTIAL BORDERS for optional phonological units. In the sentence,

He 'wants to 'go to"morrow,
3-   °2--4||

with heavy stress only on -mor-, only one rhythm unit and one intonational unit are involved. The borders of each word, however, may optionally become the borders of further phonological units. In

'He 'wants to 'go   to'morrow,
°2-3 3-   °2-3-2| 3-°2--4||

there are two rhythm units (because of the extra pause shown by the single vertical bar) and three intonation units (the groups of syllables joined by hyphens). The added rhythm border occurred at the final border of the morpheme go; the added intonation borders occurred at the final borders of the morphemes go and he.

From this data we conclude that the symbolization exclusively of the phonological units, alone, may at times fail to represent the entire phonological structure which includes the potential breaks between smaller units. Since the potential breaks are highly important, and identifiable largely as grammatical borders, the presentation of grammatical environments in a phonological statement is valid and valuable.

Not only do the grammatical boundaries first identified as utterance-initial and utterance-final phenomena prove of value for locating potential phonological borders in the middle of utterances, but they also prove to be convenient points in the environment from which to describe modifications of phonemes by their environments. This proves especially true if and when the subphonemic modifications persist at the grammatical borders even when the larger types of phonological borders are not present.

For purposes of the present volume, then, subphonemic modification will be described in reference to grammatical or phonological environments, or a combination of them.[1]

A further reason for utilizing grammatical data in phonological analysis is seen in abbreviated forms, or in items modified by speed. In fact speech sounds (or even syllables) may be completely lost, or have different sounds substituted for them; in slow speech the original sounds tend to reappear. Now the utterance has to be identified in some way, or else one could not say that the sounds had reappeared--one could merely state that certain sounds occurred, but could not prove that the disappearance and reappearance concerned the same item. This identification must be accomplished by means of grammatical likeness. That is, the same morphemes must be found, and identified (1) by their meaning and (2) by their general phonetic make up. Phonological units as such will not serve for determining the identity of the morphemes and hence the disappearance or reappearance of sounds in them.

Problem 35--Kalaba Dialect AD

Phonetic Data:

[kapi]	'to wear'	[tipi]	'to change'
[piki]	'brain'	[kaza]	'royal palm'
[taku]	'carrot'	[kika]	'to worship'
[kupa]	'southern'	[ziku]	'to blacken'
[pata]	'Polaris'	[taka]	'square'
[kɔta]	'house'	[kata]	'dog'
[tasa]	'hen'	[kaka]	'greasy'
[zuki]	'to deny'	[zapi]	'oak bark'

---

[1]For an excellent description utilizing a different approach--the presentation of phonological terminology only--see William Cornyn, *Outline of Burmese Grammar*, Language Dissertation No. 38, Supplement to *Language* Vol. XX, No. 4, (October-December, 1944).

[kaku] 'to snarl'   [tupu] 'pearl'
[tɔkɔ] 'tree'

Directions for Problem 35:

Present a chart proving that [ḱ], [k], and [ḳ] are mutually exclusive in distribution.

Solution to Problem 35:

Occurrence of [ḱ], [k] and [ḳ] before [i]; before [u], and before [a] or [ɔ]

Submembers of /k/	Before [i]	Before [u]	Before [a] or [ɔ]	Elsewhere
[ḱ]......	'''			
[k]......			ℿℿ ℿℿ	
[ḳ]......		''''		

Discussion of Problem 35:

A set of three phonetically similar segments are mutually exclusive when the following can be said about them: 'The first segment occurs only in such and such positions, but the second and third segments never occur in these positions; the second segment occurs only in a different list of such and such positions, but the first and third segments never occur in this second list of positions; the third segment occurs only in positions not previously listed, whereas the first and second segments never occur in these positions.'

It is only on the basis of such a statement that three items can be considered mutually exclusive. The fact that [ḱ], [k], and [ḳ] are mutually exclusive can be proved as follows: Of the three segments [ḱ], [k], and [ḳ] the front one, [ḱ], occurs only before [i] but the second and third segments never occur in that position; [k] occurs only in a different list of positions, specifically before [a] and [ɔ], whereas [ḱ] and [ḳ] never occur in that position; the third segment, [ḳ], occurs only in positions not previously listed, which in this case happens to be before [u], whereas the first and second segments, [ḱ] and [k], never occur in this third set of positions. Since the segments [ḱ], [k], and [ḳ] are (1) phonetically similar and (2) mutually exclusive in distribution, they are submembers of a single phoneme.

Problem 35 can be used to illustrate a source of error in inadequate charting: It frequently happens that the beginning student in meeting some of the problems will be tempted to chart, without adequate reason for doing so, the various environments in which sounds occur. The charts of a great many environments will yield no data of value for some particular problem. Notice, for example, the following chart of Problem 35:

Suspicious Pairs of Nonsyllabics Which
Follow Vowels

The Submembers of /k/	The Vowels Which are Followed by the Submembers of /k/			
	i	a	ɔ	u
k̯	✓			✓
k	✓	✓	✓	
k	✓	✓	✓	
ḳ	✓	✓		
k̯	✓			✓
ḳ	✓	✓		

From this chart there can no statement of distribution be made which shows mutually exclusive positions for any of the pairs of segments. For example, one cannot say that [k] occurs only after [i] but that [k] never occurs there, since in this chart both [k] and [k] are seen to occur after [i]. There is no evidence from this chart that any one of these pairs of segments are mutually exclusive. The chart as such therefore is of no value for this purpose. On the other hand, this chart does eliminate the possibility of their mutually exclusive occurrence in reference to other sounds. It does not invalidate the chart given earlier in which it was shown that [k] occurs only before [i], but that [k] never occurs before [i]. That statement remains true, with no exceptions, in all the data of the dialect, and it is that statement which proves that [ḳ] and [k] are submembers of a single phoneme. In other words, this chart with [k̯], [k], and [ḳ] following vowels neither supports nor refutes the conclusions based on the data from the previous chart with [k̯], [k], and [ḳ] preceding vowels. In fact, in a complicated problem one might chart his data in various ways in order to check different hypotheses before he discovered the particular situation which will set forth clearly the fact that two items are mutually exclusive in their distribution.

An erroneous conclusion might be drawn from this chart of distributions following vowels: The student might conclude that [k̯], [k], and [ḳ] contrast in analogous environment since these segments may each occur after [i]. The fallacy in this conclusion is that the total environment must be taken into account. It is precisely at this point that the procedure for finding contrast in identical environment is less subject to error than is the procedure for finding contrast in analogous environment. In the latter the student may overlook some important difference in the environment, assuming incorrectly that it is not affecting the sounds which he is seeking to separate phonemically. For these reasons one can save oneself a great deal of work if before one begins to chart data indiscriminately an early guess or hypothesis is

advanced as to the most probable source of conditioning if there is one there. The charts are then used only to support or refute such hypotheses. Indiscriminate charting of the data is likely to produce confusion.

The two difficulties with this particular chart are (1) that the "Elsewhere" column is omitted, so that the sounds might contrast in unlisted environments, unobserved by the student, and (2) that it is designed to test an inadequate hypothesis.

It should also be noticed that the distribution of the phoneme /k/, as a whole, includes the environments in which all of its submembers occur—thus the phoneme /k/ (but not the submember which is phonetically [k]) may occur before all of the vowels /i/, /a/, /ɔ/, and /u/. The full distribution of the phoneme /k/ includes its permitted occurrence before each of these vowels. To discover this full distribution one must add together the distribution of the phonetically defined submember [k], the distribution of the phonetically defined submember [ḳ], and the distribution of the phonetically defined submember [k̯], as in the following chart.

The Distribution of the Phoneme /k/ before
Vowels

The Consonant Phoneme	The Vowels Which Follow the Consonant Phoneme /k/			
	i	a	ɔ	u
/k/	✓	✓	✓	✓

The distribution of any one submember complements the distribution of the others, to make up the total complement of the environments in which the phoneme as a whole may occur. In other words, the submembers are COMPLEMENTARILY DISTRIBUTED. Each submember is in complementary distribution to each other submember in the total distribution of that phoneme in that particular language. Any statement of distribution of the submembers of a phoneme needs to be carefully checked against all available data, lest errors of omission invalidate a hypothesis. In situations which are not too complex the investigator may do this checking mentally. In actual field procedure, however, the data may prove to be sufficiently numerous or complex to prevent doing so. Therefore the student needs to learn to check his distributional hypotheses by listing the data in chart form, where omissions are less likely to pass unnoticed.

The segment [k] is best considered the norm of the phoneme. The [k̯] is limited in occurrence to positions before [i], and [ḳ] is limited to occurrence before [u], whereas [k] occurs before both [a] and [ɔ]. In addition, the [k̯] and [ḳ] are more affected by the surrounding sounds than is [k], since [k̯] is made to partake of the front

nature of the vowel [i] which it precedes,
and [k] is made to partake of the back nature of the vowel [u] which it precedes,
whereas in [k] there is no differentiation
of tongue position indicated for the phoneme
when it precedes [a] and [ɔ]. Furthermore,
it appears to be simpler to state that a
norm mid velar [k] has been fronted to front
velar [ḳ] before front vowels and backed to
back velar [ḳ] before back vowels than it
would be to say that a norm [ḳ] occurs only
before front vowels, is backed somewhat before [a] and [ɔ], and backed still further
before [u]. In addition, the fact that a
certain variety is least limited in distribution also makes the norm likely to be more
frequent in occurrence than the other submembers of the phoneme. In Problem 35 the
[k] occurs more often than the other submembers of the phoneme.

In the discussion of Problem 35 it
has been shown that [ḳ], [k], and [ḳ] are
submembers of a single phoneme. The student
must beware of a false inference from this
data. In algebra, if a = b and b = c then
a = c. The student is likely to assume that
if "x" and "y" are submembers of a phoneme,
and if "y" and "z" are submembers of a
phoneme, then "x" and "z" must be submembers
of that same phoneme. This assumption holds
true for data which are sufficiently detailed and accurate, but proves invalid for
incomplete data, in which the segments supposedly the same in each suspicious pair
are actually different. Thus if one had
overlooked a phonemic-phonetic difference
between [p̣] and [f], and had written both
of them as [p̣], he might conclude that [p],
[p̣], and [v] were submembers of a single
phoneme since [p] and [p̣] were phonetically
similar and mutually exclusive, and [p̣]
(miswritten for [f]) and [v] were similar
and mutually exclusive. Note the hypothetical data [pop] 'deer', [pof] 'tiger', [voṗ]
'lion', [vof] 'jackal'; if 'tiger' and
'jackal' were misheard as [pop] and [voṗ].
The excessive number of false homophones
should give the student a clue as to his
error.

With correct data the student might
from overlapping suspicious pairs gain data
which would lead him to treat as suspicious
and sufficiently similar as to be investigated for possible phonemic unity, two segments not circled on the Chart of Phonetically Similar Segments. If two pairs of
suspicious items are proved phonemically
united, and they contain a common member,
those sounds at first considered nonsuspicious must be considered suspicious, and
the data checked with the informant for
possible error of recording.

The student is much more likely to
fall into error in a slightly different cir-
cumstance. If one segment is proved phonemically separate from a second segment,
and the second from a third, this by no
means constitutes evidence that the first is
phonemically distinct from the third. For
separating three segments phonemically they
must be treated as constituting three distinct suspicious pairs.

Note the following phonetic data:
['famo] 'tree', ['p̃amo] 'house', [lov] 'man',
[loƀ] 'rock'. Of the segments present, [f]
is similar to [v], and also to [p̃], while
[ƀ] is similar to [v], and also to [p̃]. If
one finds in this dialect minimal pairs to
separate [f] from [p̃] and [v] from [ƀ], as.
in the words ['famo] 'tree', ['p̃amo] 'house',
[lov] 'man', and [loƀ] 'rock', the beginning
student is likely to conclude that there
are four phonemes, /f/, /p̃/, /v/, and /ƀ/,
apparently proved by the minimal pairs showing contrast in identical environment since
each of them may be found in these illustrations in one part of a minimal pair. This
conclusion would not be justified, however,
since there is no data which forces the separation of [f] from [v], nor the separation
of [p̃] from [ƀ]. In fact, there is data to
unite [f] to [v] in a single phoneme, and
[p̃] to [ƀ] in a single phoneme, since [f]
and [v] are in mutually exclusive positions,
with [f] occurring at the beginning of words
only, and [v] never occurring at the beginning of words. Likewise [p̃] occurs only at
the beginning of words and [ƀ] never occurs
at the beginning of words. Therefore [f]
and [v] are submembers of one phoneme; [p̃]
and [ƀ] are submembers of a second phoneme.
Although [f] and [p̃] occur in one set of
minimally contrasting pairs and [v] and [ƀ]
occur in another set of minimal pairs, the
relationship between [f] and [v] does not
follow, but must be proved or disproved separately. The suspicious pairs for these data,
then, would have been the following: [p̃]
and [ƀ], [p̃] and [f], [f] and [v], [ƀ] and
[v]. Two of the pairs are to be phonemically
separated, and two phonemically united.

Problem 36--Kalaba Dialect AE

Phonetic Data:

    [sazos] 'roof'

    [zbalo] 'chimney'

    [spalo] 'gable'

Directions:

Prove that [p] and [b] are separate
phonemes.

Solution and Discussion of Problem 36:

(1) [s] and [z] are submembers of a
single phoneme, since they are phonetically
similar and mutually exclusive in distribution; the voiced variety occurs only between
vocoids and preceding voiced stops; the
voiceless variety never occurs in these environments.

(2) Rewritten, with /s/ representing
the submembers [s] and [z], the data now are
/sasos/, /sbalo/? and /spalo/? with only the
[p] and [b] still suspicious.

(3) However, [p] and [b] now occur
in environments with identical phonemes, so
they are phonemically distinct. /sbalo/
'chimney' and /spalo/ 'gable' now are
proved to be written phonemically for the
stops as well as for the fricatives.

Problem 37--Kalaba Dialect AF

Phonetic Data:

['posa] 'buzzard'   [ta·la·pa] 'hen'

[to'pamo·] 'sparrow'   [mo·pa'toma·] 'egg'

[lo·ta'ma·so] 'feather'   ['ma·ma·] 'bread'

   [lo·ta'ma·so 'posa] 'a buzzard's
                              feather'

Directions:

     Are stress and length phonemic?
Rewrite phonemically the last utterance.

Solution to Problem 37:

     No.   /lotamaso posa/ 'a buzzard's
feather'.

Discussion of Problem 37:

     Any item which is completely con-
ditioned or PREDICTABLE is nonphonemic.
Here the student can see that the occurrence
of stress is conditioned by the number of
syllables and by word boundaries: the next
to the last syllable of each of these words
has received a nonphonemic stress. Assuming that any further words in the language
would follow the same pattern, he could predict that the penultimate syllable of such
words would be stressed.

     Length in Problem 37 is also pre-
dictable and nonphonemic: every vowel following a voiced nonvocoid is lengthened,
and long vowels occur nowhere else. A short
vowel and a long vowel of similar quality
are phonetically similar, mutually exclusive
in distribution, and submembers of a single
phoneme.

     In the full procedure it is conven-
ient to describe phonetic characteristics
of stress. If stress is conditioned by the
position of a syllable in the word or utterance, it is convenient in the full procedure
to discuss that fact following the description of the phonemes but before the concluding procedures. Predictable syllable division is nonphonemic and may be discussed at
the same place in the procedure. Nonphonemic stress, length, or pitch which is conditioned by segments may be described at the
time the segments themselves are discussed.

Problem 38--Kalaba Dialect AG

Phonetic Data:

[pó·'moso·] 'cat'   [to'mo·po] 'dog'

['mó·poto] 'cow'   [poto·'mo] 'horse'

[potopo] 'fox'   [tó·po·to·] 'snake'

Directions:

     Are pitch, stress, and length pre-
dictable?

Solution to Problem 38:

     Stress and pitch are predictable.
Length is nonpredictable.

Discussion of Problem 38:

     Stress occurs always and only on syl-
lables beginning with a voiced nonvocoid.
High pitch occurs always and only on syllables containing a long vocoid and occurring
at the beginning of a word. No simple statement of conditions covers the occurrence of
long vowels. They contrast in analogous
positions.

Problem 39--Kalaba Dialect AH

Phonetic Data:

[bap] 'house'   [babop] 'his house'

[bap] 'tree'   [babobis] 'his

[babas] 'my house'   recent house'

Directions:

     Can [b] and [p] be proved to be
separate phonemes? Rewrite the data phonemically.

Solution to Problem 39:

     No.

/bab/ 'house'   /babob/ 'his house'

/bab/ 'tree'   /babobis/ 'his

/babas/ 'my house'   recent house'

Problem 40--Kalaba Dialect AI

Phonetic Data:

[bap] 'house'   [babop] 'his house'

[pap] 'tree'   [babobis] 'his

[babas] 'my house'   recent house'

Directions:

     Can [b] and [p] be proved to be
separate phonemes? Rewrite the date phonemically.

Solution to Problem 40:

     Yes.

/bap/ 'house'   /babop/ 'his house'

/pap/ 'tree'   /babobis/ 'his

/babas/ 'my house   recent house'

Discussion of Problems 39 and 40:

In Problem 39, [b] and [p] were sub-members of a single phoneme since they were phonetically similar and mutually exclusive; [p] occurred only at the end of words and [b] never there; they never were found in contrast in any environment. The norm [b] became unvoiced in word-final position. The words /bab/ 'house' and /bab/ 'tree' are homophonous.

In Problem 40, however, [p] and [b] contrast in identical environment in the words /bap/ 'house' and /pap/ 'tree', and are therefore distinct phonemes, and must be written with separate symbols. Neverthe-less, one sees /b/ of the morpheme /bab-/ 'house' change to /p/ when the morpheme comes at the end of words. In this problem the change from /b/ to /p/ constitutes the substitution of one full phoneme for another under certain stated conditions. It repre-sents a grammatical interchange of phonemes, or CONDITIONED SUBSTITUTION of phonemes, rather than a nonphonemic conditioned occur-rence of the submembers of phonemes.

Specifically, one can say for Prob-lem 39 that [p] occurs only at the end of words and [b] never there. This statement would be untrue for Problem 40, since [p] actually does occur elsewhere than in word-final environments, in the word /pap/ 'tree'. Charts representing the distribu-tion would differ for the two dialects:

Occurrence of [p] and [b] in Word-Final Environment and Elsewhere, in Problem 39

	In Word-Final Environment	Elsewhere
[p]..	...	
[b]..		⊤⊤⊤ ''''

Occurrence of [p] and [b] in Word-Final Environment and Elsewhere, in Problem 40

	In Word-Final Environment	Elsewhere
[p]..	...	'
[b]..		⊤⊤⊤ '''

Notice that on the basis of this last chart the investigator cannot truthful-ly say that [p] occurs only in word-final environment. He can indeed say that [b] occurs only in environments other than word final, but he cannot say that [p] never oc-curs in these same environments, since [p] is once found there. That is to say, [p] and [b] are not mutually exclusive in their environments within Problem 40. It is this difference between the distribution of the segments [p] and [b] in Problems 39 and 40 that makes the phonemic analysis of the problems to be different also.

From this discussion a phonemic prin-ciple may be deduced: When, by contrast in identical environments, two segments are once proved to be phonemically separate, they must each be considered as phonemically distinct wherever they occur, regardless of the mechanical, arbitrary, or grammatical substitutions which they may undergo else-where.

In the following problems, follow the directions given at the beginning of this section on Procedure I-C, except where spe-cial directions are stated. For problems with special directions present in writing only the material requested--although var-ious of the remaining analytical steps may have to be taken in order to reach the proper conclusion:

Problem 41--Kalaba Dialect AJ

Phonetic Data:

[kɪtɪ] 'sand'	[tⁱɪku] 'parrot'
[tata] 'tamarind'	[pɪtɪ] 'waterjar'
[ɛg] 'cross-eyed'	[tɛga] 'macaw'
[ɛka] 'pelican'	[gɪtɪ] 'chili'
[kɪ] 'hair'	[gɛkɪ] 'ankle'
[ɪp] 'mahogany'	[təku] 'chigger'
[pəku] 'yes'	[tatu] 'ten'
[kata] 'palm'	[tɛkɪ] 'straw mat'
[tuku] 'shoulder'	[ɪtɪ] 'fish'
[gɪ] 'shrimp'	[kɛkɪ] 'hand'

Problem 42--Kalaba Dialect AK

Phonetic Data:

['toŋkiš] 'to want to'	['natzon] 'trial'
['kantos] 'beauty'	['sižnak] 'brick'
['zikaŋ] 'oily'	['ʔoŋkiž] 'coral'
['nonsaz] 'cracked'	['natzon] 'tornado'
['sazsoʔ] 'to have'	['toŋkiž] 'to become
['kantoz] 'to wet'	tired'
['sonnat] 'yesterday'	['kiʔnos] 'ropelike'
['ziʔaŋ] 'tidal wave'	['kaŋʔas] 'hopping'

Directions:

Make a chart which shows how [s] is mutually exclusive with [š] and [z] with [ž].

Are [š] and [ž] submembers of the same phoneme? (Answer "yes" or "no".) Pre-sent evidence and name the procedure used to prove it.

Problem 43--Kalaba Dialect AL

Phonetic Data:

| [suŋki] 'treachery' | [giŋgi] 'inside' |

[tuntu]   'meanwhile'   [piman]   'raccoon'
[nusan]   'to remember' [kuminu] 'to leave'
[kiŋgi]   'dry'   [maŋkas] 'stalk'
[duntu]   'to enter-   [nuntu]   'sixteen'
           tain'   [biman]   'to fight'
[puŋgi]   'bride'   [bimkan] 'to sing'
[baŋka]   'charcoal'   [sinbi]   'naked'

Directions:

        Why are [n] and [ŋ] submembers of a
single phoneme? Rewrite the first column of
data phonemically.

        Problem 44--Kalaba Dialect AM

Phonetic Data:

[tindo]   'arm'   [zaska]   'jar'
[saska]   'to weep'   [kotsi]   'four'
[kiksi]   'to smile'   [sakni]   'to wipe'
[nango]   'water'   [totko]   'hound'
[ninda]   'every'   [zosta]   'not yet'
[nossi]   'human'   [singa]   'to want'

Directions:

        Make a labelled chart of the pho-
netic norms of the phonemes.

        Problem 45--Kalaba Dialect AN

Phonetic Data:

[katʋk]   'one'   [takup]   'seven'
[pipat]   'two'   [katuk]   'eight'
[pupat]   'three'   [tʋkat]   'nine'
[pųtut]   'four'   [tipʋk]   'ten'
[kitit]   'five'   [tʋkap]   'fifteen'
[tukak]   'six'   [kukʋk]   'twenty'

Directions:

        Make a phonetic chart of the seg-
ments. List the suspicious pairs of segments. List remaining sounds which are presumably separate phonemes.

        Problem 46--Kalaba Dialect AO

Phonetic Data:

[bimd]   'elbow'   [buggin] 'his ear'
[nigbin] 'his arm'   [dunnų]   'eyes'
[bimmų]   'elbows'   [gid]   'finger'
[dungin] 'his eye'   [mųgnįn] 'his hair'
[mįmd]   'ant-hill'   [nųngin] 'he will eat'
[bugbi]   'ears'   [nųbmų]   'feet'
[dibnųg] 'my head'   [midmįn] 'his nose'
[dibgu]   'hen'

Directions:

        Rewrite the first column phonemi-
cally.

        Problem 47--Kalaba Dialect AP

Phonetic Data:

[nuag]   'paper'   [duan]   'sold'
[pʋus]   'chin'   [taik]   'man'
[suit]   'mountain'   [nuak]   'red'
[baaŋ]   'pear'   [gʋut]   'floor'
[ŋuag]   'yellow'   [tauŋ]   'brush'
[ŋuud]   'wheat'   [bʋus]   'wasp'
[taun]   'mule'   [diid]   'flea'
[nʋup]   'stone'

Directions:

        Make a chart to show the mutually ex-
clusive distribution of [i] and [ʋ]. Make a
statement giving conditions of their mutual
exclusiveness. Rewrite the first three words
phonemically; then read these words aloud.

        Problem 48--Kalaba Dialect AQ

Phonetic Data:

[ifuix]   'thumb'   [asaʋp]   'to work'
[anaʋk]   'to warm up'   [itaʋx]   'melted'
[ipuix]   'to sleep'   [ixiuf]   'truthful'
[usaʋn]   'harness'   [unias]   'to untie'
[ipuik]   'spike'   [utuat]   'charm'
[ukuit]   'to bow down' [apaʋn]   'fifteen'
[asaʋt]   'chile'   [uxuis]   'soot'
[ikiuf]   'right here'

Directions:

        Are [p] and [k] submembers of the
same phoneme? Explain the evidence. Rewrite
the first four words phonemically.

        Problem 49--Kalaba Dialect AR

Phonetic Data:

[mami]   'to weaken'   [sala]   'yard'
[pǘsi]   'lucky'   [suno]   'terrible'
[kino]   'to break'   [tǜmi]   'to grieve'
[nȍki]   'greenish'   [sunu]   'sun'
[soka]   'to believe'   [nǘsi]   'cornfield'
[tȍli]   'grapevine'   [nȍni]   'heart'
[lito]   'board'   [sȍli]   'atoll'
[maso]   'barracuda'   [tȍsi]   'spear'
[timi]   'left-handed'

Directions:

Follow the full procedure on this problem, but note especially that [u] and [ü] are submembers of a single phoneme; be sure to state the conditions.

Problem 50--Kalaba Dialect AS

Phonetic Data:

['miɲi]	'arrow'	[a'boze]	'fearsome'
[di'gonaŋ]	'to work'	[i'nar̃be]	'to judge'
['giñez]	'intestine'	[a'bor̃e]	'for them'
['meñi]	'skirt'	['nizor̃g]	'meteor'
[ge'zano]	'up until'	[zo'r̃ino]	'zebra'
['ɲizor̃g]	'earring'	['giɲez]	'elephant'
[r̃i'gonaŋ]	'crater'	['neñez]	'scorpion'
[i'noɲe]	'to bury'	[o'nidar̃]	'hyena'
[i'ɲone]	'pear'	[e'ñizi]	'his name'
['miñi]	'knotted'		

Directions:

[n] and [ñ] are submembers of the same phoneme. State the conditions.

Problem 51--Kalaba Dialect AT

Phonetic Data:

['tistuɲ]	'slime'	['tiŋkup]	'to weave'
['r̃ugak]	'tearing'	['pubar̃]	'trench'
['ɲinir̃]	'rifle'	['r̃anku]	'parrot'
['ɲir̃ir̃]	'sickly'	['sugi]	'mountain'
['padas]	'to whistle'	['r̃aŋku]	'to dream'
['kanaŋ]	'waterway'	['kur̃am]	'to sing'
['kabir̃]	'sleeping sickness'	['suma]	'pouch'
		['kudam]	'red'
['sisuŋ]	'my head'	['pugar̃]	'outside'
['suba]	'plow'	['r̃istuɲ]	'my house'

Directions:

Rewrite phonemically the first six words. Stress should not be written. Why not?

Problem 52--Kalaba Dialect AU

Phonetic Data:

[tušlu]	'to turn'	[šler̃i]	'to marry'
[kofsor̃]	'emery'	[tušlo]	'to enter'
[r̃ilɲat]	'windstorm'	[flikko]	'white'
[soso]	'never'	[ɲalšo]	'to win'
[nalšo]	'to lift'	[r̃ine]	'charred'
[skaŋ]	'pride'	[par̃o]	'sibling of opposite sex'
[xaso]	'three'		

[sifum]	'spirit'	[xifsor̃]	'hunger'
[r̃ene]	'walnut'	[sipum]	'firstborn'
[r̃ilɲas]	'straw'		

Directions:

Of the following suspicious pairs, which are to be separated into separate phonemes? United into single phonemes? [k] and [x]; [n] and [ŋ]; [s] and [š]; [l] and [r̃]; [i] and [e]; [u] and [o].

Problem 53--Kalaba Dialect AV

Phonetic Data:

[mʌs]	'road'	[ba]	'corner'
[vɛs]	'water'	[mʌz]	'erosion'
[ʌb.sa]	'detour'	[bʌp]	'steep'
[bon] or [boŋ] 'spring'		[nɛv] or [ŋɛv] 'level'	
[be.be]	'mountain'	[sʌz.ma]	'ledge'
[fe.sɛz]	'ditch'	[ɛv]	'near'
[ʌm]	'cliff'	[fɛz]	'curve'
[za.so]	'difficult'	[no] or [ŋo]	'hill'
[sa.zʌp]	'far'	[mɛf]	'here'

Problem 54--Kalaba Dialect AW

Phonetic Data:

[kiv.uk]	'horse'	[tul.if]	'paper'
[zal.ak]	'twined'	[laz.af]	'jokester'
[giv.uk]	'house'	[tit.at]	'three'
[vak.as]	'uncle'	[dal.ak]	'tall'
[dit.at]	'fast'	[guv.ul]	'nine'
[tuz.af]	'to go'	[zid.ik]	'noisy'
[kuv.it]	'pear'	[vig.al]	'to be inside'
[lad.as]	'door'		

[laz.av. guv.ul] 'nine jokesters'

[vak.az. giv.uk. vig.al] 'the uncle is inside the house'

[kiv.uk. giv.uk. tuz.af] 'the horse went home'

Problem 55--Kalaba Dialect AX

Phonetic Data:

[va.lɔ]	'to become'	[la.ðu]	'to become warm'
[la.ɵu]	'to run'		
[ki.ku]	'to climb'	[ti.lɔ]	'to age'
[mu.ʔɔ]	'to hurt'	[ʔa.ði]	'to read'
[ðu.ɵɔ]	'to whisper'	[mu.tɔ]	'to be tired'
[fa.ki]	'to enjoy'	[ka.tu]	'to clap'
[ki.ʔu]	'to pour out'	[fa.lɔ]	'to drink'

[ʔi.ku. mu.ta. ʔam] 'he got tired yesterday'

[lu.θam. ti.lɔ] 'his brother is old'

Problem 56--Kalaba Dialect AY

Phonetic Data:

[ta.θi.-ŋuʔ] 'my arm' [ŋu.xa.-kan] 'his
[ta.θi.-kan] 'his arm'   shirt'
[ʔa.θi.-tot] 'bees' [ti.ŋe.-ʔak] 'her job'
[ka.θi.-tot] 'colors' [ʔi.ŋe.-ʔak] 'her leg'
[nu.xa.-kan] 'his wife'[ta.θe.-ŋuʔ] 'my
[me.θu.-to.-kan] 'his trees'   chair'
[nuk.-ak]   'her dish'[no.xa.-kan] 'he
[ŋo.xo.-to.-ŋuʔ] 'we see'   wants'
[ma.nu]   'house' [ʔat.-ot]   'corn'
[ka.ma.-to.-taŋ] 'your seeds'

   [ŋo.xo.-to.-ʔak. ʔa.θi.-to.-kan] 'they
                             see his face'

   [no.xa.-to.-ŋuʔ. ŋu.xa.-to.-ŋek] 'we
                         want their shirts'

Note: Hyphens in this problem indicate morpheme divisions.

Problem 57--Kalaba Dialect AZ

Phonetic Data:

[nu.kal] 'to see'   [pik.ak] 'corpse'
[piŋ.ak] 'to hit'   [niŋ.up] 'to kiss'
[tuŋ.iŋ] 'worm'   [kal.uŋ] 'star'
[lap.al] 'sweet'   [taŋ.al] 'bull'
[tu.niŋ] 'feather'   [luŋ.ul] 'to revive'
[ku.pap] 'to eat'   [ti.nip] 'box'
[lat.aŋ] 'juicy'   [pu.luk] 'midnight'
[nik.at] 'to cover'

   [tuŋ.in. lat.aŋ] 'a juicy worm'

Problem 58--Kalaba Dialect BA

Phonetic Data:

[bazuf] 'tree'   [mavat] 'stick'
[givas] 'view'   [nimiN] 'rain'
[zavup] 'fox'   [maŋU] 'hut'
[vaniM] 'dirt'   [gizus] 'mat'
[mazuf] 'angry'   [dubA] 'wary'
[zanI] 'easy'   [bugiŊ] 'to look at'
[duzik] 'palate'   [zanI] 'fog'
[duvA] 'cane'   [vunuf] 'waterfall'
[vadiM] 'ball'

   [ŋavus] 'to sell'

   [zani givas nudaM] 'the fog obscured
                             the view'

   [daŋaf duvʌ] 'the chair is made of cane'

   [zavup maŋu bavat nimin gizas] 'the
   fox came into the hut out of the rain'

Directions:

   If you find submembers of a phoneme,
state, in such a way as to show that they
are mutually exclusive, the environments in
which each submember occurs.

   Rewrite phonemically the data of the
last four utterances.

Problem 59--Kalaba Dialect BB

Phonetic Data:

[mu.dɩk] 'rainy'   [da.řaM] 'resin'
[nag.ɩp] 'easy'   [nag.ip] 'rare'
[řu.tiM] 'to hate'   [tu.řaŊ] 'yesterday'
[in.ik] 'house'   [řu.diM] 'to steal'
[nak.ɩp] 'jungle'   [bɩ.mul] 'knife'
[ři.řaɫ] 'elbow'   [kař.ut] 'horn'
[u.biŊ] 'much'   [pɩ.muɫ] 'lily'
[da.nɩk] 'clan'

   [řu.ka.n in.ik] 'they returned home'

   [u.biŋ. dɩ.řu.l an.uŊ] 'many white
                             stones'

   [bɩ.mul. ta.řim. pɩ.kaɫ] 'he lost the
                             knife'

   [tu.řa.n a.maŋ. ři.ɫaM] 'yesterday
                       they shelled peas'

Directions:

   Same as for Problem 58.

Problem 60--Kalaba Dialect BC

Phonetic Data:

[nad̪.ex] 'to be'   [geŋ.em] 'good'
[du.nux] 'man'   [lab̪.aŋ] 'fifteen'
[baŋ.aŋ] 'to run'   [bu.d̪up] 'log'
[me.lab̪] 'circular' [de.d̪un] 'to watch'
[ga.ɡuθ] 'away'   [mu.ɡex] 'ant'
[le.nax] 'to be cold' [ne.naθ] 'tail'
[bed̪.eŋ] 'bottle'   [da.nem] 'black'
[lul.ax] 'green'   [gu.mal] 'quickly'
[ma.b̪uθ] 'streaked' [num.up] 'wing'

   [nad̪.ek. du.nuk. geŋ.em] 'the man is
                               good'

   [baŋ.aŋ. ma.b̪ep. ga.ɡuθ] 'the nephew
                             runs away'

   [le.nak. ma.b̪ut. gu.mal] 'the stove
                         cooled quickly'

   [du.nap. na.luk. lul.ax] 'the grass
                         became green'

Directions:

   Same as for Problem 58.

Problem 61--Kalaba Dialect BD

Phonetic Data:

[zumbᵒus]   'to see'   [pazmuak]   'time'
[tiŋgæip]   'hardly'   [guŋgæin]   'shadow'
[ñinduat]   'oak tree'   [tiŋgᵒus]   'turning'
[diŋgæip]   'knife'   [zazñiat]   'to sweat'
[zamgaam]   'hearth'   [bazmuap]   'to be out'
[kuŋgæin]   'twin'   [guŋgaam]   'night'
[ñimdᵒus]   'acorn'   [dumzuup]   'house'
[punbiis]   'to wait'

Directions:

Note especially the suspicious pairs
[p] and [b], [t] and [d], [n] and [ñ], [n]
and [ŋ], [ñ] and [ŋ], [s] and [z], [æ] and
[a].

For each of those pairs, state whether or not they are separate phonemes or submembers of a single phoneme.

If they are to be separated by contrast in identical environment, present the
evidence.

If they are to be separated by contrast in analogous environment, explain the
evidence.

If they are to be united into single
phonemes because they are mutually exclusive,
state the nature of such environments.

Sounds [a] and [ɔ] are mutually exclusive. Present a chart to prove it; be
sure that the chart is labeled adequately
so the reader can understand it.

Rewrite phonemically the first five
words.

Problem 62--Kalaba Dialect BE

Phonetic Data:

[tipak]   'soap'   [kapit]   'button'
[katιk]   'to dream'   [pupat]   'to receive'
[kitit]   'earthly'   [tukak]   'large'
[kapuk]   'shade'   [pᴜtut]   'cabbage'
[kukup]   'foam'   [tιkᴜk]   'to owe'
[kukιk]   'consistent'   [tikιk]   'beautiful'
[kupuk]   'pointed'   [tikap]   'better'

[tikᴜk putιk] 'he owes money'

[kutιk kupuk] 'a pointed spear'

Problem 63--Kalaba Dialect BF

Phonetic Data:

[sinaki]   'rich'   [tiřaʔ]   'every'
[kiřa]   'slowly'   [kiřa]   'now'

[ka̧ka̧ʌ]   'to make'   [ka̧řiʔ]   'round'
[snataʔ]   'outward'   [řaka̧ʌ]   'to begin'
[sinaki̧]   'woman'   [řiki̧]   'to spin'
[ki̧ta]   'armpit'   [sika]   'short'
[ki̧naki̧]   'to make sad' [saķik]   'to notice'
[tanat]   'before'   [tiřat]   'hound'

[ki̧naki̧ ka̧ sinaki̧] 'he makes the woman
                                        sad'

[řiki̧ ki̧řa] 'to spin slowly'

[tiřaʔ naki̧ ka̧řiʔ] 'every round ob-
                                      ject'

Problem 64--Kalaba Dialect BG

Phonetic Data:

[sra.gat]   'endless'   [sag.ra]   'to taste'
[pa.ban]   'thief'   [pa.bar]   'differ'
[taz.rap]   'storehouse'   [na.bas]   'to know'
[na.dan]   'ease'   [saz.rak]   'hound'
[kab.zrak] 'to argue'   [ta.zas]   'hungry'
[sa.dak]   'eye'   [ka.nan]   'anger'
[tan.zat]   'to flash'   [pa.garṣ]   'right'
[ran.zra]   'ball'

[saz.rak. ta.zas. pa.garṣ. taz.rap.
   kan.da] 'the hungry hound robbed the
                          storehouse at night'

Problem 65--Kalaba Dialect BH

Phonetic Data:

[xi.ṇat]   'to walk'   [ki.ṇat]   'shoe'
[ɲu̧m.ɡa]   'winding'   [ṇaṇ.ɡu]   'to cover'
[sa.xi]   'rapidly'   [ti.ɲi̧f]   'larynx'
[ṇa.tan]   'snake'   [fa̧m.vux]   'to shout'
[fu̧n.zus]   'cousin'   [fu.ṇu̧s]   'to bat'
[ta̧m.ɡi̧n]   'to be drunk' [mi̧.sak]   'owl'
[mu̧ṇ.zis]   'ant-hill'   [faf.ṇan]   'rotten'
[ka.ṇu̧]   'chosen'

[xi.ṇa. ma̧n. za.xi] 'we all walked
                                      rapidly'

[ta̧n.da̧m. ɡu.su. mu̧ṇ.zis] 'the chief
                          destroys the ant-hill'

[ni̧.xan. va.fi] 'red flowers'

Directions:

If you find submembers of a phoneme,
state, in such a way as to show that they
are mutually exclusive, the environments in
which each submember occurs.

Rewrite phonemically the data of the
last three utterances.

Problem 66--Kalaba Dialect BI

Phonetic Data:

[liɓok] 'bowstring'   [nařɑu] ''snake'

[nařgu] 'to sell'   [liriɫ] 'here'

[giɑaN] 'foot'   [daŋgit] 'stone'

[leɓok] 'fast'   [nařgop] 'cactus'

[biɕi] 'to arrive'   [biɕep] 'to turn
                                   around'
[doroɫ] 'pepper'

[nane] 'baby'   [lombiN] 'he did it'

[goɕu] 'wrist'   [benrok] 'to count'

[meɑaM] 'charcoal'   [nana] 'mother'

[birat] 'shoulder'

   [nařgo ɓeɕil ɑaŋgu] 'he likes to sell
                                  eggs'

   [lomiŋ gaŋgal neɓoM] 'a tall black
                                   horse'

   [gedon maril ɓik] 'the child does not
                                  see'

   [naɓob niɕu] 'rainy weather'

   [leɓog liril lomiN] 'horses run fast'

Directions:

If you find submembers of a phoneme, state, in such a way as to show that they are mutually exclusive, the environments in which each submember occurs.

Rewrite phonemically the data of the last five utterances.

Problem 67--Kalaba Dialect BJ

Phonetic Data:

[dasuN̦] 'witch'   [gaŋgU] 'warrior'

[ñižgA] 'to look   [sakI] 'moon'
             for'
                        [tizñiM̦] 'to go out'
[sagI] 'striped'
                        [papiN̦] 'wife'
[pabiN̦] 'cousin'
                        [sinaN̦] 'to feel'
[midup] 'egg-
          shaped'   [mitup] 'dog'

                        [nažgaN̦] 'to howl'
[bañis] 'fast'
                        [kuškis] 'brother'
[muñI] 'own'
                        [kuspis] 'oldest'
[mužgA] 'xiphoid
          process'   [gandU] 'orchard'

                        [tasuM̦] 'cross-aunt'
[siŋkA] 'shield'
                        [saŋkA] 'to pass'

   [naškaŋ kisu pazmI] 'oranges are
                              ripening'

   [nažgan sama tunaM̦] 'the wolf howls
                               loudly'

   [siŋka sagi dusiN̦] 'the shield was
                               striped'

   [papin ñižga kuspiš kuškis] 'the
        oldest brother looks for a wife'

[bañiz bañis tizna gaŋgU] 'the warrior
                            runs very quickly'

[gaŋgu kuspaN̦] 'the warrior is old'

[dasun pusi dasuŋ kažguN̦] 'the witch
                       sees another witch'

Directions:

Same as for Problem 66.

Problem 68--Kalaba Dialect BK

Phonetic Data:

[ker] 'shoe'   [andak] 'my food'

[prot] 'dog'   [aŋker] 'my shoe'

[brot] 'cat'   [aŋger] 'my dress'

[nun] 'man'   [anzin] 'my leg'

[non] 'woman'   [aprot] 'your dog'

[nuŋ] 'child'   [abrot] 'your cat'

[mes] 'ribbon'   [adak] 'your work'

[sak] 'friend'   [adak] 'your food'

[amprot] 'my dog'   [ager] 'your shoe'

[antsak] 'my house'   [ager] 'your dress'

[andzak] 'my hat'   [anzak] 'my friend'

[ambzar] 'my hair'   [antak] 'my work'

[aŋgzaŋ] 'my finger'   [anzin] 'my arm'

[amar] 'my foot'   [anzen] 'my head'

[ames] 'my ribbon'   [iksin] 'her arm'

[iker] 'his shoe'   [iksen] 'his head'

[ikger] 'her dress'   [ikmar] 'her foot'

Directions:

Follow full phonemic analytical procedures, concluding with rewriting the data phonemically.

On the basis of the rewritten data, make a list of the morphemes in the form in which they are unaffected by surrounding sounds or grammar.

What types of substitution of full phonemes do you find, and under what conditions does it occur?

What consonants seen in the basic form of the morphemes are eliminated in some parts of the grammar? Under what conditions does this elimination occur?

Problem 69--Restricted Oaxacan Chontal[1] B

Phonetic Data:[2]

[moyɡiʔ]	'tomorrow'	[paŋɡuy]	'he lives'
[libida]	'his grand-mother'	[fuŋɡuy]	'she grows fat'
[waduy]	'he carries'	[ɛntɛda]	'liver'
[gaʔa]	'that'	[toga]	'thick'
[kanduy]	'he leaves'	[goʔ]	'heron'
[iɲxa]	'wild boar'	[ðiɲ]	'quiet'
[paɡuy]	'she washes'	[faday?]	'they sow'
[apandoʔ]	'lame'	[bamaʔ]	'ten'
[toɡuy]	'I grow'	[nana]	'mother'

Directions:

Under what conditions do voiced fricatives become stops?

State reasons for combining [n] and [ŋ] into one phoneme. Which should be considered the norm? The symbol for the norm? Explain.

Problem 70--Restricted Popoluca[3] A

Phonetic Data:

[pa·ɲʌ]	'put in the ground'	[yo·mo]	'woman'
		[nʌts]	'armadillo'
[noŊ]	'flat'	[tsa·Ň]	'snake'
[hoŊ]	'bird'	[tsa·M]	'very'
[wo·ñi]	'little girl'	[antʌkmʌ]	'my country'
[mok]	'corn'	[ñi·wi]	'chili'
[anʌkpa]	'I go'		

Directions:

Chart the distribution of nasals in the word.

Problem 71--Restricted Aztec[4] A

Phonetic Data:

[ɪłfɪtł]	'feast'	[watsɪnko]	'tomorrow'
[iwa]	'and'	[biebeɪtsi]	'biggish'
[beyak]	'long'	[teusɪbɪ]	'hungry'
[behfeyɪ]	'big'	[tehWɔ]	'we'
[iyołWa]	'yesterday'	[mɪtsʃika]	'he takes you'

---

[1]Data from Viola Waterhouse, Summer Institute of Linguistics.

[2]Stress has been omitted as non-pertinent to the problem.

[3]Data from Ben Elson, Summer Institute of Linguistics.

[4]Data from Richard Pittman, Summer Institute of Linguistics.

Directions:

[f], [b], [W], and [w] are said to be all submembers of a single consonant phoneme. State the conditions under which each occurs. (Proof that [w] is a consonant must await Procedure 3.)

Problem 72--Kalaba Dialect BL

Phonetic Data:

[mimma]	'lobster'	[tfiʔuhp]	'turtle'
[ʔuhki]	'to remain'	[ŋusiNn]	'to spit'
[miMma]	'island'	[řifhaʔ]	'to relate'
[hkafta]	'to snap'	[řifha]	'distance'
[łliřu]	'quietly'	[nusiNn]	'centrally'
[puhsiʔ]	'channel'	[kuhki]	'to present'
[řipha]	'cocoa'	[htunnu]	'sun'
[lliřu]	'to bend'	[Nŋika]	'blood'
[řahři]	'to make'	[htuNnu]	'girlhood'
[lifhaʔ]	'early'	[ŋutiNn]	'toward'
[ŋŋika]	'waterspout'	[tuhki]	'bait'

Directions:

Describe the phonetic varieties of the consonant phoneme /h/, and the environments in which they occur. (Proof that [h] is here a consonant must await Procedure 3.)

Problem 73--Kalaba Dialect BM

Phonetic Data:

[pori]	'bat'	[borta]	'scorpion'
[tsugpa]	'crab'	[rumi]	'mango'
[gřopa]	'tumpline'	[glopa]	'fishnet'
[tumor]	'sad'	[romi]	'eagle'
[tatřa]	'young child'	[lo]	'turtle'
		[apt]	'hen'

Directions:

State the environments in which the phonemic norm [r] is modified to [ř]. (Proof that [r] is a consonant must await Procedure 3.)

Problem 74--Kalaba Dialect BN

Phonetic Data:

[piWsa]	'waterfall'	[waswa]	'papaya'
[soWpo]	'spindle'	[bivzo]	'beard'
[wavzo]	'deaf'	[pavba]	'cookpot'
[bavba]	'cotton'	[wazwo]	'braids of hair'
[bi]	'vine'		
[bivzo]	'thatch'	[zoWpo]	'banana leaf'

Directions:

What are the varieties of the phoneme

/w/, as conditioned (modified) by their environments, and where do they occur? (Proof that [w] is here a consonant must await Procedure 3.) Rewrite the data phonemically.

Problem 75--Kalaba Dialect BO

Phonetic Data:

[ƀaxđu]	'flea'	[ᵽudla]	'house'
[θibla]	'sweat'	[ᵷuᵽza]	'mud'
[đukmu]	'sand'	[đapni]	'thatch'
[zuxi]	'rock'	[xiglu]	'grindstone'
[ƀaga]	'sack'	[naƀi]	'saddle'

Directions:

With what phonetically similar segments is [k] complementarily distributed?

Problem 76--Kalaba Dialect BP

Phonetic Data:

[piḷa]	'well'	[pozḷo]	'lard'
[kalo]	'stick'	[taḷsa]	'money'
[polta]	'chicken'	[losḷo]	'parakeet'
[kiḷsa]	'comb'	[ḷali]	'thumbnail'

Directions:

Are [l] and [ḷ] phonemically distinct?

Problem 77--Kalaba Dialect BQ

Phonetic Data:

[pata]	'foot'	[táʔáʔ]	'this'
[panáʔ]	'river'	[kana]	'which'
[kʔáʔna]	'when'	[nakʔáʔ]	'someone'
[páʔ]	'run'	[napa]	'ear'

Directions:

[a] and [áʔ] are submembers of /a/. Why?

Problem 78--Kalaba Dialect BR

Phonetic Data:

['pi·tiš]	'sorrow'	[si'ta·s]	'cold'
[ka'nu·s]	'table'	[ta'ki·š]	'feather'
[sa'ti·k]	'bear'	['si·siš]	'louse'
[si'si·š]	'himself'	[ki'su·s]	'red'

Directions:

1. Are [s] and [š] separate phonemes? If they are, give proof. If they are submembers of the same phoneme, state the environment in which each may occur.

2. Why is length nonphonemic?

3. Rewrite the first four words phonemically.

Problem 79--Kalaba Dialect BS

Phonetic Data:

['bagʌ]	'man'	[dɩ'zu]	'calf'
['gizʊ]	'banana'	['zugʌ]	'straw'
[zɩ'du]	'leaf'	['badɩ]	'meat'
[bɩ'da]	'horse'	['dizɩ]	'elbow'
[bɩ'bi]	'terrible'	[bʌ'ga]	'to sneeze'

Directions:

1. How many vowel phonemes are there?

2. Explain the conditions under which the variants occur.

Problem 80--Kalaba Dialect BT

Phonetic Data:

['pi·nuf]	'to blow'	[ba'ŋa·]	'to mimic'
[za'na·]	'artful'	[di'ti·ŋ]	'spoon'
['fu·bɪ]	'hot'	['ku·nuf]	'nephew'
['ta·ŋas]	'never'	['vi·ɤʌ]	'to assist'
[bi'su·t]	'tired'	[ga'fu·]	'to wander'
['ka·nup]	'to want'	['ki·dan]	'to cheat'
[na'ni·f]	'to shut'	['fa·bɪ]	'blue'
['ki·vʊ]	'hairy'	['va·bʌ]	'woody'
[sa'na·k]	'to lack'	[ŋa'si·]	'cholera'
[da'ni·]	'to stick'	['za·nʌ]	'hammock'
[ŋa'zi·]	'branch'		

Directions:

What type of nonsegmental phoneme is here?

What is the phonemic interpretation and explanation of [ʌ]?

Problem 81--Kalaba Dialect BU

Phonetic Data:

[nipas]	'to waste'	[kumʌ]	'to recognize'
[stuŋa·]	'nearby'		
[ŋusi·]	'lip'	[spantu]	'rocky'
[ka·ŋi]	'to pray'	[misu·]	'to shine'
[tsu·sʌ]	'to be soft'	[ni·pat]	'tarantula'
[ka·ni]	'knowledge'	[nipat]	'hearty'
[ki·ta·]	'wise'	[pisu·]	'to rain'
[ku·mʌ]	'egg'	[kani]	'spilled'

Directions:

Is length phonemic?

Problem 82--Kalaba Dialect BV

Phonetic Data:

['ru.nunt] 'dog'   ['ka.xump] 'to chant'
['ki.šak] 'red   ['pi.šam] 'driver
          earth'   ant'
['tša.mul] 'plantain'   ['ŋgu.xit] 'wither'
['pu.riŋ] 'a design'   ['ra.mbal] 'malaria'
['mi.θip] 'to think'   ['nda.šiŋ] 'egg'
['tu.ƥik] 'ox team'   ['ta.rutš] 'to enter'
['m̃bu.naŋk] 'to drag'   ['ni.ŋgik] 'daylight'
['ri.ndant] 'cloud'   ['m̃bi.nap] 'to sort'
['ndu.ƥutš] 'shoulder'   ['ku.θul] 'to deny'
['tšu.šamp] 'bitter'   ['ta.ŋgim] 'herd'
['ndi.xant] 'virgin'

Directions:

Is stress phonemic?

Problem 83--Kalaba Dialect BW

Phonetic Data:

[sɩ'fʌt] 'apt'   [ra'mʌŋ] 'to dicker'
['ŋunam] 'small'   ['muša] 'queerly'
['nʌfɩr] 'to apolo-   [ša'šʌ] 'waist'
          gize'   ['ritɩf] 'none'
['minɩt] 'insane'   ['ŋʌfɩr] 'to leak
[su'siš] 'wobbly'   badly'
[tɩ'fʌt] 'heron'   ['ŋʌrʋm] 'wife'
[na'mʌŋ] 'we'   [sʋ'šiš] 'to pay
['funan] 'a black spot'   wages'

Directions:

Is stress phonemic?

Problem 84--Kalaba Dialect BX

Phonetic Data:

[gu'rap] 'wealth'   [ŋi"kib] 'colored'
["pumum] 'to uncover'   ["pumub] 'banana'
[sa'sar] 'treason'   ['risuŋ] 'to dry'
['fudib] 'tail'   [ku'rap] 'to blow'
['fuŋib] 'to go back'   [ba"tup] 'to hoard'
['dasar] 'pus'   [ta'sar] 'horse'
['funib] 'comb'   [da'sar] 'to under-
[ku'raf] 'witch'   stand'
[ba'dup] 'west'   ["pinad] 'four'
[ŋi"kip] 'hardly'

Directions:

How many degrees of phonemic stress
are there?

Chapter 9

ANALYTICAL PROCEDURE ONE

AMPLIFIED FOR SPECIAL APPLICATION TO PROBLEMS OF PITCH

Problem 85--Kalaba Dialect BY

Phonetic Data:

[kòsí˙] 'to try'　　[mótí] 'to sing'

[màlí˙] 'to fail'　　[mò˙tí] 'to read'

[mōtí] 'to throw'

Directions:

Is this a register-tone system or a contour-tone type of language?

Solution to Problem 85:

Problem 85 represents a register-tone language type.

Discussion of Problem 85:

Procedure I-B (Contrast in Identical Environment) is the best one for proving that a language is tonal. When one finds two words which have identical sounds, but in which the pitch differs and the meaning differs also, one assumes that the pitch is significant. This is true, however, only if the investigator has eliminated all other possible conditioning characteristics such as stress, and provided that he has enough such sets of pairs of words to be sure that he has not merely made a mistake in hearing the words or recording them. Nevertheless, Procedure I-B proves inadequate for determining the number and kinds of tonemes which one finds since tonal phonemic differences are contrasts between relative pitches, not between absolute pitches. If the system is complicated, relative contrasts are difficult to analyze by utilizing groups of isolated words only. The only linguistically pertinent pitch phenomena are contrasts between the pitch of one syllable and the pitches of its neighboring syllables. When several level pitches are phonemic, say three or four, it is difficult to determine their number by using minimal word pairs.

There can be considerable variation in the absolute pitch of words minimally different by pitch only. For example, a woman speaking such words would pronounce them in a higher tone of voice than would a man. Yet since the relative pitch contrasts would remain undisturbed, the absolute pitch of a syllable is linguistically nonsignificant. This presents a difficulty which is not encountered to the same extent when one is dealing with segments, since [s] remains phonetically [s] regardless of the person pronouncing it (but see pp. 65-6). It is relative pitch which is pertinent to a tone language.

There are various types of tone languages, and this fact constitutes a further difficulty in attempting to analyze them by minimal pairs. One may find languages with only level tones as basic tone phonemes. Such a language may be said to have a REGISTER system. Another kind of tone language has basic gliding pitches; such phonemes constitute a CONTOUR system. One of the problems of the tone analyst is to determine the basic nature of the system with which he is dealing, and this analysis is complicated by the fact that a register system may have combinations of level tonemes which phonetically become glides. Thus, a mid toneme followed directly in the same syllable by a low toneme might appear as a low falling glide, whereas a contour system may have overlapping phenomena of a register type in that contours may be of different relative levels. These differences of types are not readily analyzed by a study of minimal pairs only.

To complicate the picture still further, one must be aware of the possibility of encountering significant INTONATION CONTOURS which in some cases appear similar to tonal ones. The differences are largely as follows: Significant intonation contours tend to be applied to phrases and to affect the shade of meaning of those phrases, not their basic meanings, whereas tone phonemes tend to be applied to syllables and to affect the lexical or dictionary meaning of the words on which they occur. The analyst must be prepared to find either significant tone or significant intonation, or a combination of the two--or intonation which does not affect meanings at all but which merely represents a type of sentence melody that constitutes a mechanical pitch curve on which all sentences are pronounced.

The tone forms basic to a tone language are usually those which occur on the shortest structural units of that language-- on short vowels, single short syllables, or on short morphemes. On short vowels, in Problem 85, the tones are level. Probably, therefore, a register system is present in such a language.

Problem 86--Kalaba Dialect BZ

Phonetic Data:

[pádà] 'to find'　　[bòpó] 'to lose'

[tótó] 'to regret'

Directions:

Is this a tone language? Rewrite
phonemically the first word.

Solution to Problem 86:

No. /pada/.

Discussion of Problem 86:

Procedure I-C (the Phonemic Uniting
of Similar Segments upon Finding Them in
Mutually Exclusive Environments) is applicable to tone analysis. The investigator must
be prepared to find pitch completely or partially conditioned by its environment. Here,
for example, high pitches occur only following voiceless consonants. When pitch is
conditioned by its environment it is nonphonemic and should not be indicated in a
practical or phonemic orthography. Or, the
pitches might be conditioned by their occurrence in grammatical units such as words or
utterances. Very frequently, for example,
one finds that tonemes tend to be lower at
the end of utterances than at the beginning
of them, or to be raised slightly before a
glottal stop. In all of these details, the
investigator must be prepared to utilize the
steps of Procedure I-C for reaching a proper
analysis. In Problem 86, ['] and [`] are
phonetically similar; ['] occurs only and
always on syllables beginning with a voiceless consonant, whereas [`] never occurs
there; pitch is therefore predictable--it is
noncontrastive and nonphonemic.

Problem 87--Kalaba Dialect CA

Phonetic Data:

[pásá] 'a jar'   [bàsá] 'a hill of
[pásà] 'a spring'   corn'
[bàsà] 'a rock'   [sábà] 'a hen'
[sápá] 'a baby'

Directions:

Is this a tone language?

Why are [p] and [b] submembers of
the same phoneme?

Solution to Problem 87:

Yes. [p] and [b] are phonetically
similar and mutually exclusive in the environments in which they occur--[p] is found
only in syllables with high phonemic pitch,
and [b] is never found there.

Discussion of Problem 87:

Phonemic pitch may cause the modification of certain sounds. A segmental phoneme might have one submember, for example,
in high pitch, but a different submember
with low pitch. After the investigator has
found certain pitches to be phonemically in
contrast with each other, he must be prepared

to find that some of the segmental sounds
are modified by the tonemes.

Problem 88--Kalaba Dialect CB

Phonetic Data:

['pá·dà] 'empty'
[bò'bó·] 'full'
['tá·pà] 'basket'

Directions:

Is this a tone language? Rewrite
the first word phonemically.

Solution to Problem 88:

No. /'pada/.

Discussion of Problem 88:

One may find a phoneme which is neither tone nor stress by itself, but is a
combination of pitch and stress, or pitch,
stress, and length. In such an instance, it
is frequently convenient to call the group
of contrastive characteristics a 'phoneme of
stress with a simultaneous phenomena of
pitch and length.' This kind of suprasegmental phoneme appears in Problem 88.

Problem 89--Kalaba Dialect CC

Phonetic Data:

[nìkátá pópó nì] 'I saw the dog'
[nìkátá tútú nì] 'I saw the house'
[nìkátá sófā nì] 'I saw the man'
[nìkátá pōpō nì] 'I saw the hen'
[nípásā pópó ní] 'I bought the dog'
[nípásā tútú ní] 'I bought the house'
[nìkātā pōpō nì] 'I saw the dog' (spo-
                                  ken quietly)
[nìkātā sōfà nì] 'I saw the man' (spo-
                                  ken quietly)
[nípāsà tūtū ní] 'I bought the house'
                      (spoken quietly)
[nìkātā pōpò nì] 'I saw the hen' (spo-
                                  ken quietly)

Directions:

1. Identify the frames.

2. How many tonemes are there?

3. Rewrite phonemically the first,
fourth, and last utterances.

Solution to Problem 89:

1. Frames: nìkátá...nì
            nípásā...ní

2. Number of tonemes: Two (in any
one frame, at any one time, only two levels

of pitch are found in contrast).

3. Phonemic rewrite:

/nìkátá pópó nì/ 'I saw the dog'

/nìkátá pòpò nì/ 'I saw the hen'

/nìkátá pòpò nì/ 'I saw the hen' (spo-
                   ken quietly, in a
                   low key)

Discussion of Problem 89:

Procedure I-A (Phonemic Separation of Similar Segments by Finding Contrast in Analogous Environment) was not the easiest to apply in the analysis of segments since it was open to considerable possibility of error. Procedure I-B (Contrast in Identical Environment) was much more satisfactory for segmental phonemes because it eliminated a large proportion of such errors. Provided that suitable amplifying techniques are utilized, Procedure I-A is much more effective for finding the number and kind of pitch phonemes, however, than is Procedure I-B. The amplifications of the procedure are designed to give partial control of free variation in the general height of pitch which was referred to in an earlier paragraph in this section, and control of conditioned pitch, and to present the entire gamut of pitch contrasts where they can be seen in a sample set of data rather than in the miscellaneous contrasts of unrelated minimal pairs.

In order to control free variation in the general height of pitch and so to observe pitch contrast in the most advantageous circumstances, as the relative contrast from syllable to syllable (contrasts which constitute the basis of the system) words are studied in context rather than in isolation. The contexts studied are chosen from the data available to the investigator. They are so selected that within a single sentence or single phrase one of the words may be withdrawn and another put in its place. Then, in turn, this word is withdrawn and replaced by a third substitution item, and so on, until all the words are studied which can legitimately be found in that place in the particular sentence chosen. Such a sentence may be called a FRAME. The replaceable words may be called a SUBSTITUTION LIST. The utilizing of frames for pitch analysis is an extremely important tool for the tone analyst.[1]

When the substituted word is placed in the frame its pitch (or pitches) is contrasted by the investigator with the pitches of those syllables of the frame which immediately precede and/or follow it.

[1]This procedure is based on material in Kenneth L. Pike, Tone Languages (Mimeographed edition; Glendale: Summer Institute of Linguistics; 1943, 1945. Printed edition now in process of publication by the University of Michigan Press).

The advantage to this method consists in the fact that by so doing the investigator always has a point of reference to which the items of the substitution list can be compared. If now, the pitch of the entire sentence is raised nonsignificantly, the pitch of the substitution item is raised, but the pitch of the frame is raised along with it so that the pertinent, relative pitch contrasts remain unaffected. By this means then, one is able to control free variation in that he can observe the relative pitch contrasts in terms of the relationship of the substitution item to the pitches of the frame, regardless of the general pitch of the sentence as a whole.

At the same time, the investigator is able to assure himself that the sounds of the neighboring symbols in the sentence are not causing any pitch differences which he may discover in the substitution list in that frame, inasmuch as the sounds remain identical[1] in the frame sentence so that they could not be responsible for any pitch changes of the substitution list.

Likewise the use of frames eliminates the possibility of error introduced by the investigator's overlooking modifications of pitch caused by the position of syllables in larger phonological or grammatical units. The grammatical situation in which the substituted items occur is retained without change, since the frame—the only grammatical environment—tends to remain the same.

In Problem 89 notice the two utterances of the phrase 'I saw the dog'. In the second utterance, spoken quietly, each syllable is lower in pitch than the corresponding syllable of the first utterance. The same is true of the two utterances of 'I saw the man'. Notice especially the relation of the pitch of the substitution items ([popo] 'dog' and [tutu] 'house') to the pitch of the frame: [popo] remains the same height as [kata]. If [kátá] lowers to [kātā], [pópó] lowers with it; if [kátá] lowers to [kàtà], then [tútú] lowers to [tùtù]. Observe (1) that throughout the change of general voice height, the pitch contrasts (in the height of one syllable relative to the height of neighboring syllables) remain unaffected; (2) that within any one of the frames, during any one utterance, no more than two contrasting heights can be found; (3) that two pitch symbols could distinguish all the contrasts of this problem, provided that the change of key in quiet speech is not symbolized.

[1]If in some particular frame the investigator further observes a substitution of the sounds of frame syllables, he should temporarily discard that frame and try different ones until he finds frames with this characteristic. In fact he can only be certain of his results if he uses a goodly number of frames to eliminate the possibility of overlooking some such characteristic which might cause nonphonemic modification of pitch.

Why, then, were the pitches written differently in the various utterances? We assume that the hypothetical analyst of this synthetic problem tended to retain a general impression of a vague "absolute pitch." This auditory impression caused him to write the three levels in this problem, since the pitch was lowered, thus:

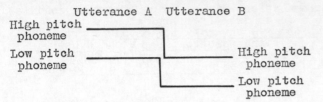

The lowest pitch of the first utterance was approximately the same as the highest pitch of the later utterance.

If the investigator had been able to recognize easily any general change of key, he would have been able to make these analytic compensations easily and automatically. Since, however, the investigator is usually unable to recognize minor changes of this type at the time they occur, (even though gross changes are readily heard) he needs a technique which will allow him to eliminate the effect of unnoticed key changes on his analysis.

It is the use of frames which provides the requisite clue. If the frame changes in pitch, he assumes that the key has changed and he can study the pitch contrasts between the substitution items in the light of that assumption. He may study (1) the number and kind of pitch contrasts between the substitution item and the frame, or (2) the pitch contrasts between the different substitution items themselves.

Thus, for Problem 89, he may observe (1) that certain of the syllables of the various substitution items are on the same level of pitch as the syllables of [kata] in the first frame (e.g. the pitches of the syllables of [pópó] 'dog') and (2) that some syllables of the substitution items are lower in pitch than [kata] (e.g. the pitches of [pōpō] 'hen', but (3) that no syllables are intermediate in pitch, between these two contrasting types, nor relatively lower (in the same frame) than those cited. This proves a maximum and minimum of two phonemic tonemes, since the differences cited contrast in analogous positions and are unconditioned by any other characteristic of the language. The two contrasting pitches of the frame spoken in a high key are thus to be equated with the two contrasting pitches of the same frame spoken in a lower key; the highest pitch of the one key is to be equated with the highest pitch of the same utterance in a lower key, and so on.

Notice, now, the difficulty which would have arisen if the investigator had been recording isolated words, only. The first utterance of 'dog' would have been [pópó], the second utterance of 'dog' would have been [pōpō]; the first utterance of 'hen' would have been [pōpō] (apparently, but--as we have seen--not structurally homophonous at that moment with 'dog'), the second utterance of 'hen' would have been [pòpò]. If he had not detected the basic change of key, his phonemic analysis would then have been erroneous. In an actual language situation this type of difficulty, accentuated by a large number of words and an infinite number of key changes, may become very serious, but the use of frames for analysis aids the investigator in controlling such interference of key changes.

Problem 90--Kalaba Dialect CD

Phonetic Data:

[to]	'horse'	[sof]	'bird'
[bof]	'cow'	[sofas]	'frog'
[oma]	'pig'	[ulo]	'pollywog'
[totaf]	'man'	[pufat]	'flea'
[so]	'cat'	[mo]	'mouse'
[lom]	'hen'		

Directions:

Classify the items into groups which are phonetically similar in syllable structure.

Solution to Problem 90:

CV	CVC	VCV	CVCVC
to	bof	oma	totaf
so	lom	ula	sofas
mo	sof		pufat

Discussion of Problem 90:

Before the investigator has the words of the list pronounced one after another in the frame sentence, he first classifies the words of the list according to their phonetic shape. That is, he puts together into subgroups those words which have similar syllable structure. (He may also make subclassifications of these groups by listing together in one group those words which end with voiceless consonants, and in a different subgroup those words which end in voiced consonants, and so on.) This serves as a control to prevent the investigator from overlooking conditioned variation of pitch by type of syllable, or by some other specific phonetic characteristic of the words in which the pitches occur, and allows for the observing of pitch contrasts in analogous phonetic environments. He must further subclassify the words or morphemes into groups which are grammatically uniform so that a list of substitution items may be permitted in a specific frame.

Once the words are grouped according to their phonetic and grammatical characteristics, and can be placed in a frame, one of these groups and one frame are chosen. The investigator asks the informant to pronounce each of the words of the group within the particular frame. As the investigator hears first one of the words and then another in the uniform context, he asks himself a crucial question: "Are the pitches of these substitution items the same or are they different? If they are the same he puts them together in a list. If they are different, he starts separate lists with them. He then takes another word, hears it pronounced in the frame, and judges whether or not it has the same pitch contour as one of the other two. He lists it with the one it resembles. If it is like neither of the first two, he begins a third list with it.

Once lists are established for all of the words of any one phonetically similar group which is allowed to enter that frame, the investigator then double-checks the words of each list to be sure that the lists are actually uniform within themselves and to be sure that no more lists are present than are needed. The checking of a supposedly uniform list can be done more accurately than the initial classification, since minor differences become much more apparent when the attention can be concentrated on them.

There are two major advantages to be obtained by this approach: First, it eliminates much of the variation which is one of the difficult features of the tonemic analysis, since words by groups are joined together so that they can be studied by groups rather than by highly varying individual occurrences of pitches. Secondly, once such a sublist is established of sounds acting similarly, the investigator can then choose one or two or three words from the sublist to represent the action of the entire list. By this procedure the investigator narrows down the number of words to which he must give his immediate attention. Instead of a very large number, he can concentrate on a relatively small number, since the words chosen from each list as samples may be considered tentatively to represent the action of the entire group. To be sure, there are dangers in this procedure, in that there may be further subgroupings which the investigator is unaware of, and which will prevent a representative word for any one list from showing precisely what will happen to other words of the list. This difficulty is less serious, however, than the problem of the variation of a great many uncorrelated words which this procedure avoids; furthermore, any errors introduced by this procedure can be caught ultimately by checking very carefully in connected text any rules or conclusions postulated about tonemes or tonal action. Once rules are set up for describing tonal action, any exceptions encountered in texts must carefully be studied, to see how the postulated rules should be modified. At the early stages of analysis,

however, the advantages of studying sounds in frames and of listing them according to likenesses and differences are very great indeed.

Problem 91--Kalaba Dialect CE

Phonetic Data:

[pô]	'tree'	[tŭmă]	'bug'
[tôpŏ]	'fly'	[mŭ]	'mosquito'
[tō]	'insect'	[păpū]	'microbe'

Directions:

What type of tone system is present? How many tonemes are present? Rewrite the first three words with a practical orthography.

Solution to Problem 91:

A contour system. Three tonemes. pŏ 'tree', tôpŏ 'fly', tō 'insect'.

Discussion of Problem 91:

After the groups of tonally similar items are prepared, the investigator then studies the representative words from these lists in order to discover the types of pitch contrasts which occur, if any, and the type of system into which these constructive pitches seem to fit. At this stage of the analysis the investigator is utilizing the procedure for discovering contrast in analogous position. The principal difference between his using it at this point and using it on problems earlier is that now, even before he has studied the pitch contrasts in these environments, he has gone to considerable pains to get environments which are quite probably analogous. We may emphasize again that the best procedure for analyzing the number of pitch contrasts in any one language is the procedure for finding contrasts in analogous environments, with the proviso that wherever possible the investigator should control the environments in which he is going to listen to pitch, so that he can more readily discover contrast in analogous environments.

If the language proves tonal the analyst must be ready to determine whether it is of a register type or contour type, or some combinatory type of tone system. In Problem 91, the shortest units of tone placement are the short vowels; glides appear on them; no more than one level tone appears; these facts indicate that Problem 91 constitutes a contour system.

Once the number and kind of tonemes are known they can then be added to the list of phonemes given on the chart of the phonemic norms which has been mentioned in the concluding procedures for Procedure I-C. A practical set of symbols may be chosen to represent the tonemes and the data can be written in a practical orthography.

Problem 92--Kalaba Dialect CF

Phonetic Data:

[mà pótá pū] 'this big tree'
[mà tùtò pú] 'this big house'
[mà pómò pū] 'this big man'
[pótà sòsúfá] 'the tree fell'
[tùtó sósúfá] 'the house fell'
[pómó sōsúfā] 'the man fell'

Directions:

Which syllables would serve as unchanging frame tonemes?

Solution to Problem 92:

[sú] for high; [mà] for low.

Discussion of Problem 92:

One of the difficulties with working with contrast in analogous environments, for tone within frames, is the fact that in many languages the frame tonemes may themselves change and thereby give the investigator a false basis of comparison. In a language which proves to be of a register-tone type, or which the investigator suspects is of this type, the investigator may find it helpful to look for evidence that a certain syllable of the frame has an unchanging toneme. This may be done in the following manner: The investigator experiments with several frames until he finds some one frame syllable which is as high as anything else in the sentence, including the highest tone of the substitution items. If he finds such an item, he knows that it is (a) high in tone, and (b) unchanged within that frame (part [b] is true since if the tone were to change at all, after it began high, it would ultimately go lower than its original high form and in so doing would ultimately be pronounced on a lower pitch than some other items which the investigator would find in the various contexts of that particular language). Once a high toneme is proved unchanging within any particular frame it then serves as an extremely convenient point of reference for studying contrast in analogous position, since the environments of the substitution list can then be equated to or contrasted with it in pitch. The same procedure in reverse may allow the investigator to find a low tone unchanging within a specific frame.

In Problem 92 the frame syllable [sú] is always as high as any other syllables of the frame or any items of the substitution lists within any one utterance. It therefore is phonemically high, and unchanging within that frame. Syllables equal to it in pitch also have phonemically high tonemes.

Problem 93--Kalaba Dialect CG

Phonetic Data:

[tífù mó] 'one house'
[tífù sù] 'one grasshopper'
[tífù mù] 'one lizard'
[tífù pá] 'one worm'
[tífù pó] 'one deer'

Directions:

Why is the syllable [-fù] unsatisfactory as a low-pitched point of reference for analyzing tones?

Solution to Problem 93:

Because it is not always as low as some of the syllables of the substitution list; the investigator could not be sure, therefore, that it was unchanging. According to this data it does at times change to high.

Discussion of Problem 93:

The investigator must discard, as a frame, any syllable which does not meet the stipulations given under Problem 92. [Note: This technique is especially applicable to register-tone systems. For contour systems it is not completely usable, nor as necessary (since substitution of one toneme by another is likely to be more readily apparent because of the change of direction of glides, and so on.)]

Problem 94--Kalaba Dialect CH

Phonetic Data:

[tómò] 'head'
[tómó] 'hand'
[tómómì ʔúmù] 'my head hurts'
[tómómì ʔúmù] 'my hand hurts'
[mómù tómómì] 'he hurt my head'
[mómù tómómì] 'he hurt my hand'

Directions:

Are ['] and [`] separate tonemes?

In what grammatical situations is [`] replaced by [']?

Solution to Problem 94:

Yes.

[`] is replaced by ['] when a word with [`] functions as an object of the verb.

Discussion of Problem 94:

In some tone languages, especially those of North America and of Africa, one of the chief problems is to find the rules

which govern the substitution of one toneme for another in the grammar. Substitution of tonemes may be very complicated in
its patterns of change. The best method for
analyzing tonal substitution is to study
long lists of words which the informant pronounces successively in one frame, then in
a second frame, and so on. In this way he
can watch for tonal substitution in the various types of phonological and grammatical
contexts. The investigator assumes that the
number of actual phonemic tones is already
known, and has been proved by the phonemic
procedures already discussed. The investigator then makes a chart or table showing in
a highly convenient form the changes which
occur in these phonological and grammatical
contexts.[1]

If the informant cannot be taught
to cooperate by giving words in frames, or
if in attempting to do so he gives unnatural
or distorted speech forms (discovered by the
investigator by comparing the utterances
with conversational forms), the investigator
must follow a much more laborious process of
finding contrasts of tone in text material:

Problem 95--Kalaba Dialect CI

Phonetic Data:

[tȍpōmū] 'fire'   [tópōmū] 'water'

[tópómū] 'air'   [tȍpōmȕ] 'sky'

[tópómū] 'earth'   [tȍpōmȕ] 'wind'

Directions:

How many tonemes are there?

Solution to Problem 95:

Two: ['] and [`].

Discussion of Problem 95:

The student might at first assume
that the presence of three pitches in sequence, as in [tópōmū] 'fire', proves the
existence of three tonemes. This is not
the case. Rather ['] and [¯] are phonetically similar, mutually exclusive in the
environments in which they occur (since [¯]
occurs only following a [`] tone, but [']
never occurs there), and are submembers of
a single toneme /'/. In order to avoid error, the student must realize that, in order
to be phonemically distinct, tones must be
in unconditioned contrast in analogous positions in the word (e.g. at the end) and not
merely in sequence. Thus in Problem 95 the
pitch level ['] contrasts with [`] at the
beginning of words; ['], [`], and [¯] each
occur at the end of words, but [¯] occurs
only after [`] whereas ['] occurs only after

---

[1]For a detailed description of these
procedures for the analysis of tonal morphology, and for intricate sample analyses
of tone sandhi, tone fusion, and tone substitution in grammar, see my Tone Languages.

['], so that [¯] and ['] do not contrast at
the ends of words.

Problem 96--Kalaba Dialect CJ

Phonetic Data:

[lomo·so] 'my house over there'

[lopiso] 'my cow over there'

[lopa·so] 'my child over there'

[lobo·so] 'my town over there'

[lomi·so] 'my pencil over there'

Directions:

Is length phonemic?

Solution to Problem 96:

Yes.

Discussion of Problem 96:

Certain of these specialized procedures for tone may be applied with advantage
to the analysis of stress, quantity, and intonation. In each of these, it is also advisable to look for contrasts within sets of
words which are first sorted into uniform
groups according to their phonetic and grammatical structure. In this way, any stress
contrasts which appear are much more likely
to be phonemically in contrast in analogous
environments, rather than being due to some
phonetic or grammatical conditioning characteristic which the investigator otherwise
might ignore. For quantity, likewise, listing by phonetic shape will often prove helpful. For both stress and length, frames can
be of considerable benefit. In English, for
example, the existence of innate stress on
monosyllables is best demonstrated by the
occurrence of these monosyllables in a normal context with normal meaning, such as in
the 'house--a situation which shows that
house is normally (or "innately") stressed,
whereas in and the are normally unstressed.
(Note the parallel of in the 'house to on
the 'table, where lexical stress is maintained in normal pronunciation; note the
further parallels in "in the house and "on
the table wherein the innate stresses of
house and table are reduced partially or
completely.

Problem 97--Kalaba Dialect CK

Phonetic Data:

['nénȁ] 'blossom'   [rȕ'só] 'honey'

['kā?ȕ] 'to try'   ['nēsí] 'to suck'

[tó'só] 'Orion'   ['pī? á] 'to eat'

['sūnȁ] 'woodpecker'   ['nínȁ] 'to succeed'

['pītá] 'braid'   ['?ēsð] 'rotten'

[rȕ'kī] 'to turn'   [rȕ'?ī] 'true'

['ká?ȕ] 'to scare'   ['nētí] 'unkempt'

(Continued on next page)

[tá'ŋō] 'belt'   [nú'rú] 'hairy'

['núrú] 'wily'   [rò'só] 'to stare'

Directions:

Is stress phonemic?

How many phonemic levels of pitch are there? How does stress affect them?

Problem 98--Kalaba Dialect CL

Phonetic Data:

[xéúmà] 'to injure'   [āōráò] 'to charge'

[gáléò] 'infinite'   [θēōθúó] 'to be sad'

[θēōáúò] 'clean'   [mēénì] 'October'

[dúráá] 'road'   [bóábíí] 'to sag'

[nìxúú] 'uvula'   [mūfáè] 'written'

[ēéúmì] 'milk'   [vīrīè] 'to whine'

[fālóò] 'lagoon'   [fēúmá] 'opal'

[gāmáè] 'to repeat'   [nóífēá] 'to insist'

[mēénì] 'ladle'   [θáólēè] 'to live'

[búímú] 'stone'   [gáléò] 'to change'

[gārēò] 'wrong'   [múvāè] 'diamond'

[mūdōò] 'chief'   [θīōθúò] 'to make, do'

[xúérèè] 'fetish'   [dōráá] 'to bark'

[gúáxóÉ] 'to agree'   [líábó] 'open'

[nāgíú] 'hunter'   [vúímá] 'hammock'

Directions:

What type of tone language is this?

How many tonemes are there?

What is the phonemic analysis of long vowels?

Problem 99--Kalaba Dialect CM

Phonetic Data:

["xú·rú] 'dozen'   ["tí·rà] 'to scrape'

['ŋàsí] 'active'   ['mì·mín] 'kapok'

[sí'rà] 'tomorrow'   [rú"nák] 'farther'

['tàsàn] 'to reach'   ["sámà] 'into'

[nà'tú·] 'sickness'   ["kú·rá] 'both'

[fú'rì·] 'salty'   [tà·sàn] 'to recon-
                                    sider'
['sá·nì] 'each'

['xù·nì] 'opal'   ["kú·rà] 'orifice'

[kù"nú·] 'beside'   ['xù·ŋí] 'desirable'

[fú"rà] 'together'   ['ŋàsít] 'horny'

["tàfà] 'to churn'   [fú·'rì] 'hot'

Directions:

How many degrees of phonemic and/or nonphonemic stress are there here? Of tone? Of length?

Problem 100--Kalaba Dialect CN

Phonetic Data:

[xī'né·] 'rainbow'   ['púñà] 'above'

['mérà] 'ostrich'   [kū'pí·] 'to shave'

[xù'pì·] 'to work'   ['xútì] 'glass'

['térē] 'to swirl'   ['mìrā] 'knife'

[lā'kù·] 'unreal'   [lā'nà·] 'egg'

[kī'rí·] 'never'   [nà'kú·] 'to slip'

[mè'xà·] 'to swim'   ['tèsū] 'angry'

['sákē] 'to believe'   [nù'rì·] 'white'

['nímì] 'arm'   ['nùrì] 'native'

['fùrē] 'windy'   ['sérè] 'to arrive'

[pì'fá·] 'hyena'   ['núrí] 'nose'

[tù'pè·] 'to express'   ['nèmì] 'to review'

['lárì] 'to watch'   [xū'fí·] 'sharp'

['nìmì] 'cool'

Directions:

Same as for Problem 99.

Problem 101--Tone Dictation Type A

Typical Phonetic Data:

[sī má tō]   'my red house'

[sī kō tō]   'my red cow'

[sī rò tō]   'my red snake'

[sī lÉ tō]   'my mercurochrome'

[sī psálí tō]   'my red blanket'

[sī pì tō]   'my red hat'

[sī kōmúftīlē]   'my shoe'

Directions for the Teacher:

[Note: This is a sample problem. Others may be prepared by the teacher.]

1. Dictate rapidly the above data-- or preferably substitute data of a similar type with frames--to the students. Other problems can be modelled on the basis of the problems discussed earlier in the chapter.

2. Have them identify the frame.

3. Have them put into groups those words of the substitution list which are alike in phonetic and grammatical form.

4. Working with one of the larger of those groups obtained in (3), have the students subgroup them. Repeat the words as necessary; usually a sample word of a group should be repeated just before a new word is given for classification. Do not allow them to be concerned with an attempt to write the tones, at this stage of analysis, although a rough guess is permissable or helpful; the main purpose is to determine whether two items are the same or different, and to

group them accordingly.

5. Introduce into the dictation some deliberate change of key, and deliberate free modification of the pitch intervals, so that the frame tones must be used for the analysis.

6. If a student cannot at first hear pitch differences, whistle or hum them for him.

7. Have the students check the groups (a) for uniformity in each group, (b) for contrast between them, (c) for the accounting for differences in all tonal minimal pairs.

8. Next have the students determine the number of tonemes (a) by studying the contrasts of the tones of the various groups and/or (b) by studying the contrasts of representative words of the groups in relation to the frame pitches.

9. Have the students determine the type of tone system involved.

10. Let the students choose a practical orthography.

Problem 102--Tone Dictation Type A

Phonetic Data:

[mápì lāsō tî] 'he swims fast'
[mápì lāsō kò] 'he spoke quickly'
[mápì lāsō kàlì] 'he wrote fast'
[mápì lāsō sǎ] 'he runs'
[mápì lāsō ku] 'he ate fast'
[mápì lāsō sǎ] 'he understands readily'
[mápì lāsō tí] 'he works fast'
[mápì lāsō kō] 'he plays fast'
[mápì lāsō kō] 'he punches'

Directions:

As for Problem 101.

Problem 103--Tone Dictation Type A

Phonetic Data:

[nálì ksáp̄šú] 'he saw it yesterday'
[kōp̄ō ksáp̄šú] 'she cooked it yesterday'
[tÉlù ksáp̄šú] 'it was hot yesterday'
[tápí ksáp̄šú] 'yesterday was Tuesday'
[kātǜ ksáp̄šú] 'he came yesterday'
[lÉsì ksáp̄šú] 'he played yesterday'
[másū ksáp̄šú] 'he went home yesterday'

[tÉlù ksáp̄šú] 'he left yesterday'
[lātì ksáp̄šú] 'he finished it yesterday'
[kātù ksáp̄šú] 'he wrote yesterday'
[kásù ksáp̄šú] 'he ran yesterday'
[kātǜ ksáp̄šú] 'he repeated it yesterday'

Directions:

As for Problem 101.

Problem 104--Tone Dictation Type B

Phonetic Data:

A. [ná tànà] 'one tree'
   [ná tílì] 'two trees'
   [ná túná] 'three trees'
   [nà sìtó] 'four trees'
   - - - - - -
B. [tànà fì] 'one over there'
   [tílì fì] 'two over there'
   [túnà fì] 'three over there'
   - - - - - -
C. [tànà sò] 'one man'
   [tílì sò] 'two men'
   [túná sò] 'three men'
   [sìtó sò] 'four men'
   [sànì sò] 'five men'
   [kónì sò] 'six men'
   [lìtò sò] 'seven men'
   [sÉfĊ sò] 'eight men'
   [lÉnò sò] 'nine men'
   [nìlÉ sò] 'ten men'
   [fàtÈ sò] 'eleven men'
   [tÈní sò] 'twelve men'

Directions for the Teacher:

[Note: This is a sample problem. Others may be prepared by the teacher.]

1. Ask the students to find either a high or a low tone which does not change within one context.

2. Dictate the first two or three utterances; have the students locate the frame syllable.

3. Concerning the frame syllable ask the students, "Does anything in this context go higher?" If so, the frame syllable cannot be used as an unchanging high. Ask: "Does anything go lower?" If so, the syllable cannot be used as an unchanging low. If neither possibility is workable, reject the frame, and try another. (Thus, frame A should be rejected; pass to B, and

so on.)

4. When there has been located a syllable unchanging in one frame, then utilize the directions given for Problem 101.

Problem 105--Tone Dictation Type B

Phonetic Data:

A. [káli̱ mōti̱bō] 'men sing'
   [káli̱ nāti̱fḗ] 'men run'
   [káli̱ nɛ́súti̱] 'men jump'
   [káli̱ nɛ́lūfi̱] 'men laugh'

- - - - - - -

B. [sáni̱ mōti̱bò] 'boys sing'
   [sáni̱ kánūfi̱] 'boys try'
   [sáni̱ káli̱ti̱] 'boys walk'
   [sáni̱ tɛ̀lūsà] 'boys work'
   [sáni̱ mìtɛ̀fɛ́] 'boys play'
   [sáni̱ nɛ̀mi̱tú] 'boys cry'
   [sáni̱ làki̱só] 'boys come'
   [sáni̱ làki̱sò] 'boys insist'
   [sáni̱ fɛ́ti̱tū] 'boys talk'
   [sáni̱ fɛ́ti̱tú] 'boys write'
   [sáni̱ láki̱sō] 'boys count'
   [sáni̱ móti̱bō] 'boys swim'
   [sáni̱ nɛ̀mi̱tú] 'boys think'
   [sáni̱ kāli̱ti̱] 'boys act lazy'
   [sáni̱ ŋàsófi̱] 'boys eat'
   [sáni̱ kàli̱ti̱] 'boys sleep'
   [sáni̱ kàli̱tí] or [sáni̱ kàli̱ti̱]
                    'boys help'
   [sáni̱ mɛ̄sōfù] 'boys wiggle'
   [sáni̱ tōni̱lɛ̀] 'boys look'
   [sáni̱ káni̱ti̱] 'boys swing'
   [sáni̱ fóli̱tō] 'boys stumble'
   [sáni̱ mɛ̄sōfù] 'boys hunt'
   [sáni̱ nɛ́māfú] 'boys chew'
   [sáni̱ ŋàti̱ké] 'boys get sick'
   [sáni̱ fɛ̀ti̱tú] 'boys shout'
   [sáni̱ fóli̱tō] 'boys die'
   [sáni̱ mɛ̀sófù] 'boys swallow'

Directions for the Teacher:

As for Problem 104.

Problem 106--Tone Dictation Type C

Phonetic Data:

[spómòfs súpáksf] 'I sing'
[stòmòpf súpáksf] 'you sing'
[štàfápš súpáksf] 'we two sing'

[tsósásf súpáksf] 'we, but not you, sing'
[spómòfs súpáksf] 'we, including you, sing'
[tsósásf súpáksf] 'we, but not you, were singing'
[spómòfs súpáksf] 'I was singing'

Directions for the Teacher:

1. Dictate the data.

2. Have the students determine the number and kind of tonemes.

3. Have the students analyze any types of substitution of one toneme for another.

Problem 107--Restricted Zapoteco of Villa Alta[1] A

Phonetic Tone Data (pitch 1 is high, 4 low):

[de^{4}za^{1}n ya^1] 'a lot of bamboo'
[ḻa^{4}gy̰^{3}ʔ] 'leaf'
[ye^{4}r̰^{w}be^{3}ʔ] 'mist'
[de^{4}za^{1}n ya^2] 'many steambaths'
[go^{4}bi^{4}ẕ] 'noon'
[bo^{2}za^2] 'mulberry'
[ya^{4}g] 'wood'
[za^4 ni^{2}ʔ] 'that bean'
[g^{w}a^{2}ẕy̰^{3}ʔ] 'a fat corncake'
[ẕ̰i^{1}tbo^{2}ʔ] 'his bone'
[ẕe^{2}n] 'big'
[ẕa^2 ni^{2}ʔ] 'that day'
[ba^{4}dy̰^{3}ʔ] 'tumpline'
[ne^{4}ẕa^4] 'today'
[ya^{2}gyi^{2}ʔ] 'firewood'
[de^{4}za^{1}n ya^4] 'a lot of weapons'
[yi^{1}ʔ] 'fire'
[zsa^{4}bo^{2}ʔ] 'his beans'
[ẕna^{3}ʔ] 'mother'
[za^1 ni^{2}ʔ] 'that lard'
[ḻo^{2}ẕy̰^{2}ʔ] 'tongue'
[ẕ̰i^{1}ty̰^{4}b] '(the animal's) bone'
[ẕi^{4}n] 'work'

---

[1]Data from Eunice V. Pike and Otis Leal, Summer Institute of Linguistics.

[z̧i¹so³ʔ]　　　'your water'

[bso¹]　　　'adobe'

Directions:

How many tonemes are there? Explain your conclusion briefly.

Problem 108--Restricted Mandarin[1] A

Phonetic Data (a high line indicates high pitch; a low line, low pitch; a curved line, falling or rising pitch; a long line, extra duration; pitch is given after each syllable):

["tʰa‾ yao‑ nei_ kʰa_ shu⌣]　'"he wants that tree'

[tʰa‾ yao‑ nei‑ kʰa‑ "shu⌍]　'he wants that "tree'

[tʰa‑ "yao⌍ nei kʰa shu]　'he "wants
　‑　　‑　‑ (or ⌍) that tree'

[tʰa‑ yao⌐ nei⌐ ban "shu‾]　'he wants that
　　　　　　　　　　_　　　 "book'

[tʰa‑ "yao⌍ nei ban shu_]　'he "wants
　　　　　　　　　_　　　that book'

[ꞯʰa‑ yao‑ "nei⌐⌍ ban shu]　'he wants
　　　　　　　　　　_　　_　　"that book'

[tʰa‑ yao⌍ nei_ ga_ "ya⌎]　'he wants that
　　　　　　　　　　　　　　"tooth'

[tʰa‑ "yao⌍ nei ga ya⌎]　'he "wants
　　　　　　　　_　_　　that tooth'

[tʰa_ yao⌍ nei_ ga_ "pi⌎]　'he wants. that
　　　　　　　　　　　　　　"brush'

[tʰa_ "yao⌍ nei ga_ pi⌎]　'he "wants
　　　　　　　　_　　　　that brush'

or:

[tʰa_ "yao⌍ nei ga pi]　'he "wants
　　　　　　　‑　‑　‑　that brush'

Directions:

1. What types of situations constitute analogous environments for this problem?

2. What general type or types of nonphonemic modification of tone can you identify?

3. What causes this (these) modification(s)?

4. How many tonemes can you prove to be present?

---

[1]Rough pitch data gathered by the author from the pronunciation of Y. R. Chao. Ignore the segmental writing.

5. Can the tonemes be distinguished in all environments in these data? If so, how? If not, how would you describe the changes?

6. What characteristics of the material might lead you to suspect that the data may be inaccurate in some respects? How would you propose verifying the data?

Problem 109--Kalaba Dialect CO

Phonetic Data:

['ma]	'house'	[ma'sɪ]	'my house'
['nū]	'tree'	[nù'sí]	'my tree'
['tā]	'rock'	[ta'sɪ]	'my rock'
['mɪ]	'basket'	[mɪ'sí]	'my basket'

[mà'nā]	'houses'	[mà'tū]	'little house'
[nù'nā]	'trees'	[nù'tū]	'little tree'
[tà'nā]	'rocks'	[tà'tū]	'little rock'
[mɪ́'nā]	'baskets'	[mɪ́'tū]	'little basket'

[màsi'nā] 'my houses' [mana'tū] 'little houses'

[nùsi'nā] 'my trees' [nuna'tū] 'little trees'

[tàsi'nā] 'my rocks' [tana'tū] 'little rocks'

[mɪ́si'nā] 'my baskets' [mɪna'tū] 'little baskets'

[màsinà'tū] 'my little houses'

[nùsinà'tū] 'my little trees'

[tàsinà'tū] 'my little rocks'

[mɪ́sinà'tū] 'my little baskets'

Directions:

There are two phonemic pitch levels. Explain the nonphonemic variation, and state the conditions under which it occurs.

Problem 110--Kalaba Dialect CP

Phonetic Data:

[pàdá]	'to cry out'	[záká]	'waterfall'
[tàzá]	'mustache'	[tàká]	'moss'
[sàpá]	'smoke'	[vágá]	'sixteen'
[dáfà]	'baby'	[fàvá]	'silly'
[bátà]	'choking'	[zábá]	'to smell'
[sàgá]	'boulder'	[kàfá]	'procession'
[bàdá]	'witch'	[táká]	'one-eyed'

Directions:

Prove that [s] and [z] are submembers of one phoneme.

Chapter 10

ANALYTICAL PROCEDURE TWO:

CLUES FOR ANALYSIS GAINED FROM PHONETIC SYMMETRY

At the beginning of Chapter 4 the student read a brief discussion of four basic premises around which the analytical techniques of this volume were to be built. The first premise stated that sounds tend to be modified by their environments. On this premise were based Procedures I-A to I-C. In Procedure I-A sounds proved to be phonemically distinct when it could be demonstrated that their differences were not simply modifications caused by the environments in which they occurred. Procedure I-B carried this technique further, in certain restricted but simpler situations (with minimally different word-pairs). Procedure I-C was likewise based on the first premise but was the reverse of Procedure I-A; instead of eliminating the possibility of environmental influence, and separating phonemes, it proved the existence of environmental modifications and by so doing united various segments into single phonemes. Chapter 9 introduced techniques for solving, on the basis of the same premise, special difficulties of tonal analysis.

Chapter 10 is based on the second of the four premises emphasized in Chapter 4, that sound systems have a tendency toward phonetic symmetry. The numbers and kinds of phonemes are studied and listed. Then Procedure II-A shows how potential symmetry can be used as a helpful criterion for the analysis of problems which otherwise leave the investigator in doubt. Procedure II-B, however, uses the lack of symmetry as a clue to possible error or incomplete analysis.

ANALYTICAL PROCEDURE II-A:

PHONETIC SYMMETRY AS A SUPPORTING CRITERION FOR SEPARATING OR UNITING PHONEMES

Problem 111--Kalaba Dialect CQ

Phonetic Data:

[tisab] 'work'   [butaŋ] 'to pulsate'

[misab] 'goat'   [tipug] 'to bathe'

[sagak] 'pumpkin'   [fařit] 'epidemic'

[paluf] 'fellow man'   [kusum] 'to groan'

[řaduŋ] 'to falsify'   [řatuŋ] 'to discard'

[nisap] 'heavy'   [lařup] 'gullet'

[binud] 'to kick'   [susak] 'to fade'

[dimis] 'to snore'   [subiŋ] 'shame'

[pinud] 'a dry thing'

Directions:

Prove that [k] and [g] are separate phonemes.

Solution to Problem 111:

One might assume, by contrast in analogous environments, that [k] and [g] are separate phonemes inasmuch as they both occur at the end of words, as in [sagak] 'pumpkin' and [tipug] 'to bathe'. The proof is rather weak, however, since the [k] occurs only after [a] and the [g] only after [u] and because the [g] occurs only once throughout the entire problem.

The proof of the phonemic separation of [k] and [g] is supported by the following fact--namely, that [p] and [b], [t] and [d] are separated phonemically by contrast in identical position. Note the words [pinud] 'a dry thing' and [binud] 'to kick'; and [řaduŋ] 'to falsify' and [řatuŋ] 'to discard', which indicate a pattern of voiceless-voiced contrast in the language which may be assumed to extend to the phonemic separation of [k] and [g].

Discussion of Problem 111:

One makes a phonetic chart of the sounds and looks for nonsymmetrical elements. For Problem 111 the phonetic data would be the following:

Phonetic chart:

p	t	k
b	d	g
m	n	ŋ
	s	
	l	
	ř	
	i	u
	a	

Of these segments, [p] and [b], [t] and [d] are phonemically separate. Since the bilabial and alveolar stops are phonemically separate, it is probable that the velars are, also, on the ground that sound systems have a tendency toward phonetic symmetry.

It should be emphasized, however,

that a language does not have to be symmetrical. Very frequently a sound system is not symmetrical and there are defective series of sounds, or what might be called in this instance "holes in the pattern". In such instances one simply describes the system as it actually is, i.e., as nonsymmetrical. In the data just discussed, for example, the [n] and [ŋ] are not phonemically separate, but are rather submembers of a single phoneme, since the [ŋ] occurs only in word-final position, and the phonetically similar [n] never occurs there. Phonemically, then, there is no existing contrast between alveolar and velar nasals such as occurs for the stops. This particular difference between the nasals and stops is a common one in languages.

Procedure II-A is especially useful to reinforce Procedure I-A (the Phonemic Separation of Similar Segments by Finding Them in Contrast in Analogous Environments). It rarely should be used by itself. The investigator may speed up his work, however, by noting that any proof of phonemic separation of two sounds at one point of articulation gives weight to the phonemic separation of sounds of the same type at other points of articulation.

Problem 112--Kalaba Dialect CR

Phonetic Data:

In this dialect the segments [s], [z], [f], [v], [θ] and [ð] occur. Both [s] and [z] are easily proved to be submembers of a single phoneme; /s/ becomes voiced word medially.

Directions:

What hypothesis should the investigator immediately consider?

Solution to Problem 112:

That there is a phoneme /f/ which becomes [v] word medially; similarly that [ð] and [θ] are submembers of /θ/.

Discussion of Problem 112:

The hypothesis was raised because of the premise concerning the tendency of sound systems to be phonetically symmetrical. In this kind of situation the student should notice that any type of environmental modification which affects one sound of a series is likely to affect other sounds of that series. Since one fricative becomes voiced, in Problem 112, the student should suspect that the other fricatives will do so likewise.

ANALYTICAL PROCEDURE II-B:

LACK OF SYMMETRY AS A CLUE TO POSSIBLE ERROR

Problem 113--Kalaba Dialect CS

Phonetic Data:

[pa] 'roof'	[da] 'basket'
[so] 'waterjar'	[ka] 'skirt'
[ba] 'grinding stone'	[fa] 'ribbon'
[go] 'blouse'	[ko] 'sky'
[ta] 'fire'	[ko] 'tree'

Directions:

What suspicious, nonsymmetrical feature is present in the sound system of this dialect? How should the data be checked with the informant so as to discover a possible error?

Solution to Problem 113:

Labial sounds and alveolar sounds occur for the voiceless stops, the voiced stops and the fricatives. Velar sounds occur only for the voiced and voiceless stops. The lack of a velar fricative constitutes a nonsymmetrical "hole in the pattern."

The investigator should double check on words containing sounds similar to [x] (specifically in this instance the velars [k] and [g]) to find whether by any chance his hearing has been inaccurate and he has written both [k] and [x] with the symbol [k], or both [g] and [x] with the symbol [g]. In this problem, note that 'sky' and 'tree' appear to be homophones, both of them with [k]. Since a source of error is most likely to consist of the fact that the investigator heard [x] as [k], it would be quite possible in an actual language situation of this type that 'sky' and 'tree' were actually not homophonous, but that one of them was actually [xo].

Discussion of Problem 113:

If the investigator fails to hear some particular sound of a series, but does hear the others, the one missed will leave a nonsymmetrical pattern. For this reason any lack of symmetry should be investigated for possible error. "Holes in the pattern" are those nonsymmetrical situations in which one sound is missing to fill in a series.

In general, when an investigator finds a hole in the pattern, he should check his data, listening to words which contain sounds which are similar in point of articulation or in production type in order to make certain that he has not written with a single symbol sounds which actually are phonetically distinct.

If a person wishes to match colors he can do so most readily if he sees samples side by side. In this way slight differences are more likely to be apparent. If he sees one sample today, and then tomorrow he sees a different sample, he can not easily be certain whether they are merely similar or actually identical in shade. So, also, it is with sounds: If words containing similar sounds are pronounced in sequence an investigator has a much better chance of noticing slight differences--or for assuring himself that two sounds are the same.

For this reason the investigator may find it profitable to check groups of words written with the same or similar sounds, even though a hole in the pattern may not be present to make him suspicious of error. Beginning with sounds which occur initially in utterances, he may study all types made at a single point of articulation, for example, bilabials; he has the informant repeat one after another all words beginning with bilabial stops to ascertain if there be more than one type of such stops. For the fricatives, in the same way, he can then check to see how many types are in contrast, and to be certain that the stops contrast with the fricatives, and so on. Then contrasts of sounds differing by point of articulation, such as [n] and [ŋ], may be checked. When all sounds occurring in one environment have been checked for type and for point of articulation, these same sounds (or additional ones, if there be such) may be checked for contrasting pronunciations in other environments to see whether the same number and kinds of contrasts exist in those environments also. These testings are valuable since one can hear with more certainty those contrasts to which one is not accustomed when the utterances containing them are given consecutively by the informant.

Words written as homophones should also be checked to be certain that they are actually pronounced the same. All languages seem to contain homophonous words, but the investigator should be suspicious of them early in his word, since apparent homonyms will result if he has overlooked the phonetic contrast in minimally different words.

It must be emphasized again that systems do not have to be symmetrical, that they merely tend to be symmetrical. Lack of symmetry is an indication that data should be checked against one's hearing, but the data should not be tampered with merely to fill a pattern.

At times a sound may be missing simply because it is rare and the investigator has by chance failed to gather the particular words in which this particular sound occurs. If the data is very limited, therefore, he gathers more words to see if he can encounter the missing sound.

In previous chapters, the phonetic data are assumed to be accurate. Now the student has a procedure for detecting data which appear suspicious in that they may contain an error of transcription.

One of the most interesting nonsymmetrical situations which I have observed occurs in some of the Mayan languages of Mexico. In them a voiced stop [b] is likely to be found, yet in words of native origin no other voiced stops are seen in these languages, even though voiceless stops and affricates do occur at several points of articulation. One might call a situation such as these a "sore thumb" because a single sound seems to fit nowhere.

Problem 114--Kalaba Dialect CT

Phonetic Data:

[bap]   'red'   [nadop] 'to grunt'

[babo]   'to try'   [gagot] 'to sing'

[lap]   'yesterday' [dobik] 'ten'

[dolok] 'two'   [bigod] 'fifty'

Directions:

Are [t] and [d] separate phonemes?

Solution to Problem 114:

The data are not clear. [t] and [d] seem to contrast in analogous environments (cf. [gagot] 'to sing' and [bigod] 'fifty') yet the over-all pattern of symmetry would seem to contradict this hypothesis (since [p] and [b], and [k] and [g], are mutually exclusive submembers of phonemes, with the voiceless submembers occurring word-finally.

Discussion of Problem 114:

A further type of suspicious lack of symmetry is the occurrence of a very few words which prevent the formation of a statement of the mutually exclusive distribution of segments. In such an instance the investigator double checks these words to make certain that no error of hearing is involved. If he finds his hearing has been in error he can then correct his data and arrive at a conclusion about the mutually exclusive nature of the sounds without having these few occurrences invalidate the hypothesis. If, however, his hearing has been accurate, he must either (a) discard his hypothesis and consider the sounds to be separate phonemes, or (b) he must modify his hypothesis in some way so that the statement of mutual exclusiveness will now hold for all of his data without exception.

In Problem 114 it at first appears that one may state that all voiced stops become voiceless in word-final position, so that [b] and [p], [g] and [k], [d] and [t], are submembers of single phonemes. But in the word [bigod] 'fifty' a word-final voiced [d] occurs,--which does not fit such a statement.

Any alternative statement which includes this data is awkward: [d] and [t] would be separate phonemes because of the contrast in analogous word-final positions in the words [gagot] 'to sing' and [bigod] 'fifty', but [b] and [p], [g] and [k], would remain submembers of single phonemes since they are phonetically similar and mutually exclusive in distribution. Because of the second basic premise of Chapter 4 we might expect [p], [t], and [k] to act uniformly. For this reason the statements given in this paragraph appear suspicious since [t] is listed as a separate phoneme but [p] and [k] as submembers of phonemes.

The investigator should conclude, therefore, that the data are suspicious, and check to see whether the word 'fifty' may have been heard incorrectly, and should have been written as [bigot].

Problem 115--Kalaba Dialect CU

Phonetic Data:

[pap]	'wide'	[kap̟]	'deep'
[paθ]	'narrow'	[taθ]	'hungry
[tax]	'shallow'	[kaθ]	'fifty'

Directions:

What pair of segments must be considered suspiciously similar, for this problem, even though they are not specifically circled on the chart of Phonetically Similar Segments (p. 70)?

Solution to Problem 115:

[θ] and [t].

Discussion of Problem 115:

A lack of symmetry may constitute a clue to the investigator that he must consider as suspicious certain pairs of segments which he at first ignored.

As suspicious pairs of segments in Problem 115, the student would at first, according to the chart on p. 70, list [p] and [p̟], [k] and [x]. He would then observe that the stop [p] is mutually exclusive, and in the same phoneme, with its corresponding fricative at the end of words (or syllables, morphemes, and utterances). [k] acts similarly. Since [t] is also a stop, he would then check to see if it becomes fricative under similar circumstances. He would find [t] and [θ] mutually exclusive and assume that they should be treated as suspiciously similar even though not circled on the chart.[1]

---

[1]He should have noted, however, (1) that [t] and [θ] are circled (this might have led him to this hypothesis earlier),

Finally, he would conclude that [t] and [θ] were submembers of a single phoneme, and that these conditioned varieties of the phoneme paralleled the occurrences of the submembers of /p/ and /k/.

Problem 116--Kalaba Dialect CV

Phonetic Data:

[pòfī]	'egg'	[lómā]	'bird'
[tȯsí]	'fox'	[tútū]	'ventrilo-
[lȯlù]	'vibrato'		quism'
[fōpí]	'whistle'	[pópó]	'falsetto'

Directions:

Assuming that there are four tonemes, what type of nonsymmetrical data would you find here, for pitch?

Solution to Problem 116:

Sixteen two-syllable sequences of four tonemes are theoretically possible:

(sequences of tone marks)

Of these, the following occur in Problem 116:

(sequences of tone marks)

This decided lack of the full gamut of symmetrical possibilities should lead the student to look for possible--but not certain--error, since tone languages tend to have symmetrical patterns of permitted tone sequences.

Discussion of Problem 116:

In this problem there appear to have been key changes unrecognized by the one who recorded it, since the data were gathered without frames for testing. Probably no more than two phonemic pitch heights exist in this language. The word [pòfī] 'egg' is perhaps /pòfí/; [lómā] 'bird' might be /lómà/; [tȯsí] 'fox' might be /tósí/; and so on. Only a checking of the data in context could afford an adequate test of such a hypothesis.

Problem 117--Restricted English A

Phonetic Data:

[š] and [ž] occur in English.

Directions:

What data can you show, and what procedures can you utilize, to prove them

---

and (2) that on p. 69 the student was warned that the chart did not represent every possibility which might be encountered.

distinct phonemes in your dialect of English?

Problem 118--Kalaba Dialect CW

Phonetic Data:

[mapʌ]   'radish'

[mapɔ]   'tamarind'

[lomɪsu] 'coconut'

Directions:

What evidence can you find for separating phonemically the segments [ʌ] and [ɪ]?

Problem 119--Kalaba Dialect CX

Phonetic Data:

[damug] 'corn'   [dikab] 'blanket'

[poŋgu] 'kettle'   [bongu] 'camp-fire'

[bukuv] 'tea'   [pokub] 'drum'

[samkuŋ] 'coffee'   [dabob] 'tent'

[pisgo] 'pottery'   [zadgob] 'hunter'

[timug] 'meal'   [tazgo] 'arrow'

Directions:

What lack of symmetry is to be observed in types of stops encountered? What words should be double checked with the informant to see if the sound has been misheard?

Problem 120--Kalaba Dialect CY

Phonetic Data:

[g̊aps] 'every' [magag̊] 'plenty'

[px̩oz] 'some'   [fpav]   'many'

[voxp]   'few'

Directions:.

If [x] and [g] are submembers of a single phoneme, what hypothesis should the investigator consider for [s], [f], [v], and [z]?

Problem 121--Kalaba Dialect CZ

Phonetic Data:

[bɔxá] 'to help'   [zåpá] 'coat'
[tɔzɔ] 'such a'   [kɔbå] 'unhurt'
[påtɔ] 'non-alcoholic' [gàxɔ́] 'seriously'
[zɔká] 'song'   [bɔxɔ́] 'powder'
[gågɔ] 'mackerel'   [g̊åpá] 'to practice'
[g̊ågɔ] 'eat'   [tɔsɔ́] 'to burn'

[dɔká] 'to display'   [tɔsɔ] 'prairie'
[sɔdå] 'to end'   [xádå] 'to cure'

Directions:

How is tone proven to be phonemic by the data as it is represented here?

If two certain syllables have had their pitches recorded incorrectly, the language, however, is not tonal. What are these two syllables? What makes you suspect that they were heard and written incorrectly?

Problem 122--Kalaba Dialect DA

Phonetic Data:

[lařa]   'to play'   [tana] 'lime'

[sipha] 'to point'   [sisa] 'to sleep'

[gati]   'to chew'   [thupi] 'tender'

[khasi] 'follower'   [niřa] 'front

[pukha] 'nightly'   [githu] 'later on'

[lupu]   'shaman'   [tugi] 'stepson'

[nuřu]   'arrowhead' [khusu] 'turtle'

[thaphi] 'blue   [piti] 'a twin'
          squirrel'
[phigu] 'apron'   [gařa] 'embers'

Directions:

What suspicious lack of symmetry do you find? What data should be checked with the informant?

Problem 123--Kalaba Dialect DB

Phonetic Data:

[siŋgu] 'jungle'   [mak·a] 'wagon'

[tupta] 'te be drunk' [sutpu] 'nephew'

[mandza] 'every'   [mandzu]'opening'

[ŋasku] 'tiger'   [tsamka]'beautiful'

[tsup·i] 'liquid'   [kut·u] 'nose'

[samga] 'identical'   [ñispa] 'to select'

[tsinba] 'coconut'   [ŋaŋbi] 'smoke'

[pindi] 'to scream'   [tandzi]'betrothed'

[nasku] 'to attempt'   [kinpu] 'blue'

[sinbu] 'blood'   [katpu] 'skunk'

[ñiŋgu] 'seed corn'

Directions:

There are two errors of phonetic transcription in these data. What do you

think they are? What makes you suspicious
of them? What would be your hypothesis as
to the phonemic transcription of the first
three and last three words, assuming your
guess is correct as to the errors?

Problem 124--Kalaba Dialect DC

Phonetic Data:

[zos] 'fig'   [gam] 'lemon'

[sos] 'orange'   [gax] 'banana'

Directions:

Notice that [z] and [s] are proved
phonemically separate. How?

Notice that [g] and [x] are mutually
exclusive.

Do the data appear to be incomplete?
Why?

Problem 125--Kalaba Dialect DD

Phonetic Data:

[akṣa] 'mine'   [atxa] 'hers'

[atsa] 'his'   [afYa] 'the child's'

[afsa] 'theirs'   [akx̣a] 'the animal's'

[asta] 'ours'   [ax̣ka] 'the girl's'

Directions:

What suspicious pairs would be
noticed early in this problem?

What further pairs would have to be
added? Why?

Problem 126--Restricted Maya A

Data:

Consult the article: Kenneth L.
Pike, "Phonemic Pitch in Maya," International
Journal of American Linguistics, XII (April,
1946), 82-8.

Directions:

In what way does lack of symmetry
affect the analysis of the Maya pitch system?

Chapter 11

ANALYTICAL PROCEDURE THREE:

THE PHONEMIC UNITING OF SIMILAR SEGMENTS UPON FINDING
THEM FREELY FLUCTUATING BUT NEVER IN CONTRAST

Problem 127--Kalaba Dialect DE

Phonetic Data:

  [muŋa] or [muna] 'white'
  [sada] or [sata] 'old'
  [kimu] or [kimʊ] 'wall'
  [laki] or [lagʊ] or [lakʊ] or [lagi]
          'to be ill'
  [zuli] or [zulʊ] or [suli] or [sulʊ]
          'sword'
  [ŋiza] or [niza] 'three'
  [nuga] or [nuka] or [ŋuga] or [ŋuka]
          'rock'
  [tasa] or [taza] 'cup'
  [nisa] or [ŋisa] 'man'
  [kimu muŋa] or [kimu muna] 'white wall'
  [sata nisa] or [sada ŋisa] or
    [sata ŋisa] or [sada nisa] 'the
                      man is old'

Directions:

Preliminary procedures, separation
procedures I-A and I-B, and uniting procedure I-C should be applied mentally according to the steps given in Chapters 6-9. List
any fluctuating pairs which are proved phonemically distinct by the earlier procedures.
List also any suspicious pairs (seen as a
residue from the earlier procedures) whose
segments fluctuate freely in some or all
environments but which never contrast in
any environment. State the environments in
which the fluctuation occurs. Choose a norm
for the phoneme.

Concluding Procedures:

Make a labelled chart of the
phonetic norms of the phonemes.

If the phonetic symbols used to
represent the phonemic norms are inconvenient for practical purposes, modify
them.

Rewrite the data presented for
the dialect, using just one symbol for
each phoneme. Enclose phonemic writing
in diagonals.

Solution to Problem 127:

Fluctuating suspicious pairs proved
phonemically distinct by earlier procedures:

[s] and [z]

Noncontrastive fluctuating suspicious
pairs:

[t] and [d], submembers of a
single phoneme; fluctuating
freely between vowels in the
middle of words (but initially [t], only, occurs); [t]
is best chosen as the norm,
since it is least limited in
distribution.

[k] and [g], submembers of a
single phoneme; fluctuating
freely in environments as for
[t] and [d]; [k] is best
chosen as the norm.

[n] and [ŋ], submembers of a
single phoneme; fluctuating
freely in all environments
in which either segment occurs.
[n] is arbitrarily chosen as
the norm.

[i] and [ʊ], submembers of a
single phoneme; fluctuating
freely at the end of an utterance; [i] is best chosen as
the norm.

[u] and [ʊ], submembers of a
single phoneme; fluctuating
freely at the end of an utterance; [u] is best chosen as
the norm.

Concluding Procedures:

Chart of the phonetic norms of the phonemes:

Nonvocoids	Bilabial	Alveolar	Velar
Voiceless stops......		t	k
Voiced nasals.....	m	n	
Fricatives voiceless..		s	
voiced.....		z	
Voiced lateral....		l	

Vocoids	Front unrounded..	Central unrounded..	Back rounded....
High close..	i		u
Low open....		a	

No modification of symbols needs to be made for convenience in writing them.

Phonemic rewrite of data:

/muna/ 'white'   /niza/ 'three'

/sata/ 'old'   /nuka/ 'rock'

/kimu/ 'wall'   /tasa/ or /taza/ 'cup'

/laki/ 'to be ill'   /nisa/ 'man'

/zuli/ or /suli/ 'sword'

/kimu muna/ 'white wall'

/sata nisa/ 'the man is old'

Discussion of Problem 127:

Notice that two kinds of free variation occur in this problem. The first is free fluctuation between full independent phonemes, that is, between /s/ and /z/. The second is free fluctuation in which the interchange is between submembers of phonemes, as for [t]/[d], [k]/[g], [n]/[ŋ], [i]/[ɪ], and [u]/[ʊ].

One must be careful to delay his conclusion as to whether a particular instance of free fluctuation is between full phonemes or between submembers of phonemes, until one has studied all the data given for the problem. Each instance in which free fluctuation occurs must be checked with the informant, and then the segments so varying must be checked for contrast in identical and analogous environments elsewhere. If the seg-

ments vary freely in certain instances but can be separated phonemically elsewhere by minimal pairs or by contrast in analogous position, the variation is between full phonemes and not between submembers of phonemes. Such segments would have been separated phonemically by Procedures I-A or I-B.

Free variation between full phonemes is shown in [tasa] or [taza] 'cup'. The sounds are proved to be separate phonemes by contrast in identical environments in [nisa] 'man' and [niza] 'three'. This variation is limited to the two words 'cup' just quoted and 'sword', [zulɪ]/[sulɪ], and so on, so that it is found both initially and medially in words, but in other words it does not occur. Note, for example, the words for 'old' and 'man'. There seems to be no structural pattern to define the environments in which this fluctuation occurs.

Under these circumstances the student should retain both pronunciations in his phonemic rewrite. Later, under field procedure, he may decide for practical literature to write one or the other, only, just to be consistent. He should base his choice on general frequency of usage or the extent of the area to which one or the other or both of them is used in neighboring dialects. In scientific writing of text material, however, the student should record a word phonemically as it is pronounced during each specific utterance.

Free fluctuation between submembers of phonemes, however, should not be reflected in the symbolization, since only the norm would be symbolized. Notice also that free variation between submembers is of two general types: Noncontrastive fluctuation of segments occurs in any and every environment in which either submember occurs; or the variation is found only in certain restricted environments. In Problem 127 the unrestricted variety of free fluctuation between submembers of phonemes was seen between the segments [n] and [ŋ] which fluctuated in all environments in which either one or the other occurred. The restricted variety was illustrated by [t] and [d], and by [k] and [g], since [t] and [k] varied freely to their voiced varieties but this variation occurred only between vowels in the middle of words. Similarly, [u] and [i] varied freely to their opener varieties at the end of utterances, but not elsewhere.

A caution must be given the student in field work: it sometimes happens that an investigator may think that a word is pronounced in two different ways whereas the word is actually pronounced uniformly but the investigator's perception has varied. This is especially true when the sound in question is acoustically about half way between two phonemes of the investigator's language. If, for example, an English speaker who is used to unaspirated voiced stops and aspirated voiceless stops hears an unaspirated voiceless stop, he is likely to

124 PHONEMICS

perceive it at one time as a voiced stop and at other times as a voiceless one because it approximates both of his own stop phonemes.

If variation does actually occur in the language, the native speaker is likely to be aware of it if the fluctuation occurs between full phonemes; but if the fluctuation is from one submembers of a phoneme to another submember of that phoneme, the native speaker usually is completely unaware that any such change exists. He may, in fact, vigorously deny it. The investigator can be certain of such variation only by means of trained hearing or by instrumental tests.

The student must be careful to delay his conclusion as to whether the free variation is between full phonemes or submembers of phonemes, on the one hand, or (provided it is between submembers) in limited or unlimited environments, until he has studied all the available data.

Problem 128--Restricted English B

Phonetic Data:

[aⁱ æm] or [aⁱ-m]   'I am'

['ædrɛs] or [æ'drɛs] 'an address'

[ə 'mæn]   'a man'

['mæɾ̌ɽ] and ['mætʰɽ] 'matter'

[barn] or [ban]   'barn'

[fag] or [fɔg]   'fog'

['wʊndo] or ['wʊndə] 'window'

[kat]   'cot'

[kɔt]   'caught'

['pɛnsʊl] or [pɛnsḷ] 'pencil'

['pɽmʊt]   'a permit'

[pɽ'mʊt]   'to permit'

[æn 'æpḷ] or [n̩-'æpḷ] 'an apple'

Discussion of Problem 128:

Notice the free fluctuation between the vowel sounds a] and [ɔ] in 'fog', which are proved to be phonemically separate as shown by the words 'cot' and 'caught'. Note similar proof for phonemic contrast between stress in 'a permit' and 'to permit', but the free fluctuation in stress in 'an address'. Not all speakers of English have these particular fluctuations, but they do occur in at least some dialects.

WEAK forms (or RAPID forms) are alternate pronunciations of a morpheme, especially in fast speech, which omit certain segments customarily heard in slow or in

precise pronunciations of that morpheme; or in which one or more phonemes is replaced by more centrally articulated or obscure phonemes or submembers of phonemes. In Problem 128 notice the central vowel in ['wʊndə], the syllabic consonant in [pɛnsḷ], and the syllabic [n̩] in [n̩-'æpḷ].

Rapid forms frequently involve a change in the syllabification of morphemes. Note [s̩-də-'truθ] 'it is the truth', or ["ɛd-d̩ 'du ɩt] 'Ed would do it', or [ə.'nem] for 'an aim'. Variations due to speed need considerable further study before they can be conveniently treated in terms of a step-by-step procedure such as this. The beginning student will do well, however, for practical orthographical purposes to adopt as a norm that pronunciation of a word which occurs in speech of normal (or slightly slow) speed rather than to consider basic those forms which are extra rapid.

As for ['mæɾ̌ɽ] and ['mætʰɽ] in American English, the type with a quick flap (voiced or voiceless) is more common than the type with aspiration, yet the aspirated type tends to occur in very slow careful speech, as, for example, when one is trying to teach the word to a foreigner.[1] Here the student does well to consider as the normal pronunciation that variety which occurs in normal conversation rather than in the extremely slow style. Here the substitution because of style is from one submember of a phoneme to another submember of that same phoneme.[1]

---

[1] This implies that a certain social importance is attached to items which under the regular procedures of this volume are treated as nonsignificant. At the end of Chapter 4 it was pointed out that quality can be relative, and that sounds can be modified somewhat in different styles of speech used by any one person at different times. Differences of precision in speech, especially when they produce different phonetic effects, should be handled under such an assumption. If one wished to indicate these changes in an orthography it would seem best not to do so by adding new segmental phonemes to the alphabet, but by adding to the phrase concerned a statement somewhat like 'slow and precise', or a symbol defined as meaning that. For such a symbolism see Kenneth L. Pike, The Intonation of American English 101-03, University of Michigan Publications in Linguistics, I (Ann Arbor: University of Michigan Press, 1945).

In the writing of English literature authors frequently indicate qualitative modifications of this type by phrases such as '"...," he shouted', '"...," she moaned', '"...," he muttered hoarsely'. These and related qualitative modifications which affect an entire utterance, or part of an utterance, may be called SUPERIMPOSED CHARACTERISTICS. They are not considered

In ordinary free fluctuation between full phonemes, the substitution of the one phoneme for the other occurs sporadically, and arbitrarily, within a single style of speaking or a uniform speed. Substitution of phonemes which occurs in weak forms or rapid forms reflects a difference in style.

Problem 129--Kalaba Dialect DF

Phonetic Data:

[sainu] or [sæinu]   [zæinu] or [zainu]
  'green'   'sign'

[mauki] 'scroll'   [nuba] 'braid'

[tiuzu] 'hand'   [mupa] 'word'

[sæiki] or [saiki]   [kupu] or [kubu]
  'brown'   'to want'

suprasegmental phonemes, in this volume, since (1) they may affect an utterance qualitatively rather than quantitatively, and (2) they tend to be GRADIENT (i.e., with no clear-cut structural dividing line between one quality and the other) rather than contrastive. The general height of a person's voice, changing from higher to lower, and so on, is a gradient quantitative characteristic but not a qualitative one. In this volume gradient superimposed characteristics, (whether qualitative or quantitative) are not called phonemes, even though they frequently are socially significant.

After I had discussed the problem of ['mæřř] and ['mætⁿř] with Eunice V. Pike, she pointed out to me that the disturbance of the vowel quality of /oᵘ/ in 'common colloquial ['gonə] (gonna), whose vowel is not like that of gunner (ʌ) or bonus (ou)' (quotation from Morris Swadesh, "On the Analysis of English Syllabics," Language, XXIII [April-June, 1947], 142) is presumably to be accounted for in an analogous manner. The pronunciation ['gonə] for 'going to' would appear in my speech only in a style which is to some extent facetious or abnormal.

Special segmental phonemes should not be set up on a par with regular phonemes to account for sporadic instances of this type which are due to lack of uniformity of type of speech. Rather the style should be symbolized. Otherwise the number of alleged contrastive symbols for the care of the unified system would be legion (and so break the provision, asserted for the first basic premise of Chapter 4, that signals must be limited in number) once symbols had been set up for English to place all whispered vowels, whispered "voiced" sounds, sung segments, chanted segments, shouted segments, slow speech segments, fast speech segments, hoarse segments, choked segments, segments uttered with the mouth full, and so forth, on a par with the sound types encountered in a single type of speech.

[nuka] 'pencil'   [diuzu] 'to seem'

[nuga] 'to point'   [suiba] or [suipa]
                        'cow'
[tudu] 'hat'

Directions:

For any free variation between suspicious segments, state whether it is between full phonemes or submembers of phonemes. If free variation occurs between submembers of phonemes, describe the environments in which it is found.

Problem 130--Kalaba Dialect DG

Phonetic Data:

[ta] or [da] 'rope'   [ba] or [pa] 'one'

[gira] or [kira]   [naka] or [naga]
  'stone'   'to wipe'

[ratu] or [radu]   [rupu] or [rubu]
  'wheat'   'all'

Directions:

As for Problem 129.

Problem 131--Kalaba Dialect DH

[nisʌ] or [nisa]   [nasi] or [nasɩ]
  'heavy'   'windy'

[satu] or [satʊ]   [fata] or [fatʌ]
  'strong'   'to earn'

[nufɩ] or [nufi]   [satɩ] or [sati]
  'bright'   'to crush'

[tatɩ] or [tati]   [fitu] or [fitʊ]
  'to beat'   'leaf'

[nisʊ] or [nisu]   [sunu] or [sunʊ]
  'swift'   'forehead'

Directions:

As for Problem 129.
Rewrite the data phonemically.

Problem 132--Kalaba Dialect DI

Phonetic Data:

[kam] or [kʌm]   [siŋa] or [siŋʌ]
  'to ask'   'frosty'

[sikas] or [sikʌs]   [siʔʌs] or [siʔas]
  'roughly'   'soap'

[ŋas] 'to chatter'   [tʌsu] 'arm'

[nupi] 'water'   [ŋʌs] 'to beg'

[sinʌ] or [sina]   [sumam] or [sumʌm]
  'mule'   'house'

[tuʔi] 'dog'   [paʔʌ] 'wasp'

[kʌnu] or [kanu] 'mat'   [mʌʔa] 'cat'

Directions:

      As for Problem 129.   Rewrite the data phonemically.

      Problem 133--Kalaba Dialect DJ

Phonetic Data:

[sel]   'one'   [amil]   'his head'

[nařo] or [nalo]   [řalol] or [řařol]
   'to hate'   'to rob'

[simuk] 'ox'   [mesu]   'to love'

[pakal] 'to buy'   [kapan] 'first day
                                 of month'

[řuso]   'sharp'   [tinis] 'east'

[tesop] 'dog'

   [řama sel pakal] or [řama seř pakal]
                  'one merchant'

   [me luso] or [me řuso] 'dull'

Directions:

         Rewrite the data phonemically.

         Problem 134--Kalaba Dialect DK

Phonetic Data:

[simba] 'letter'   [samdi] 'child'

[numzi] or [numsi]   [panfa] or [panva]
   'middle'   'bear'

[fakpi] 'false'   [kafpu] 'disgusted'

[tiznu] or [tisnu]   [safma] or [savma]
   'new'   'to rescue'

[simgu] 'river'   [sana] 'clean'

[mamu] 'caribou'   [numu] 'calf'

Directions:

         As for Problem 129.

         Problem 135--Kalaba Dialect DL

Phonetic Data:

[lisun] or [lisuŋ]   [luŋgis] or [lungis]
   'to run'   'cat'

[kanzu] 'meat'   [nanduk] 'severe'

[aŋgu] or [angu]   [sapan] or [sapaŋ]
   'dog'   'to sweat'

[nuna]   'dawn'   [pinbal] 'shell'

[kisi]   'horse'   [tulgi] 'oil'

[sildat] 'windy'   [nalza] 'until'

[tatap] 'water'

[lisun angu] or [lisun aŋgu] 'the dog runs'

[sapan gisi] or [sapaŋ gisi] 'the horse
                                  sweats'

Directions:

      As for Problem 129.

      Problem 136--Restricted Mixteco[1] A

Phonetic Data:

[tutu] or [tut·u]   [sutu] or [sut·u]
   'paper'   'priest'

[kata] 'sing!'   [kaka] or [kak·a]
                            'lime'

[kat·a] 'sing!' (If I have to tell you
      again I'll spank you!)

[sana] or [san·a] 'turkey hen'

Directions:

      What hypotheses could you suggest which might ultimately explain the free fluctuation of length here? What type of evidence would be needed to substantiate or to refute these hypotheses?

      Problem 137--Restricted English C

Data:

Ed had "edited it.[2]

Did you eat the crust of the bread?

What is the matter with you?

How is it going to reach them in time?

If you want to, it is O.K.

Directions:

      1. What weak forms do you hear as you read these sentences in your fastest, but normal, speed?

      2. Construct five sentences which contain weak forms in rapid speech.

      3. Read the sentences aloud, five times; utilize a different superimposed quality each time.

---

[1]Data from Donald Stark, Summer Institute of Linguistics. Tone has been omitted as nonpertinent to the problem.

[2]Sentence from Charles Hockett.

Problem 138--Restricted English D

Directions:

1. Name, if possible, three instances in your dialect of free fluctuation between full phonemes.

2. Name and illustrate for your dialect, if possible, three types of free fluctuation between submembers of phonemes.

3. How would you analyze and symbolize the speech of a person

(a) who utilized unaspirated or weakly aspirated stops at the end of phrases in conversation but

(b) who aspirated stops phrase finally in public address?

4. How would you analyze word-final voiced release of voiced sounds of a person who had that particular speech characteristic only in certain types of public address?

5. How would you analyze weak or partial or zero voicing of "voiced" lenis sibilants word finally in normal conversation, but full voicing of the same phonemes when a person was pronouncing the words in isolation for a foreigner to hear a voice contrast between fortis voiceless sibilants and lenis voiced ones (e.g. hiss and his)?

6. What differences can you detect in the sounds of a person smiling, weeping, or talking in his sleep?

Problem 139--Fluctuation Dictation A

Phonetic Data:

['tómð] or ['tōmð] 'desk'

[sð'sðs] or [sð'sðz] 'chair'

[dû'tû] or [tû'tû] 'chalk'

['zðtó] or ['zðdó] or ['zðdō] or ['zðtō] 'pencil'

['sðtð] or ['sðdð] 'pen'

['tðmð] 'eraser'

['tûmð] 'student'

[lð'tû] or [lð'tó] or [lð'tū] or [lð'tō] 'class'

[mðs] or [mðz] 'window'

['nðsó] or ['nðsō] 'floor'

[nð'só] or [nð'sō] 'ceiling'

Directions for the Teacher:

1. Prepare as many problems of this type as can be used in the time available.

2. Include various types of free fluctuation:

(a) between full phonemes,

(b) between submembers of phonemes,

(c) between weak and normal forms,

(d) between various types of superimposed qualities.

3. Dictate them to the students, repeating each word at least three times so as to allow for the fluctuation of segments during the repetitions.

Directions for the Student:

1. Record each utterance of each word as you hear it.

2. Analyze the phonemes.

3. For any free fluctuation recorded

(a) state whether it involves the substitution of one phoneme for the other, or

(b) the replacement of one submember of a phoneme by another submember of that same phoneme.

(c) If it is (b), state the environments in which the fluctuation occurs.

4. Rewrite the data phonemically.

Chapter 12

ANALYTICAL PROCEDURE FOUR:

THE PHONEMIC INTERPRETATION OF SUSPICIOUS SEGMENT TYPES AND SEGMENT
SEQUENCES BY ANALOGY TO NONSUSPICIOUS OR PREDOMINANT
STRUCTURAL TYPES AND SEQUENCES

In order to give the student a technique whereby he can apply the premises of phonemics to actual field data we have in previous chapters presented one or more procedures for the use of each of the first three basic premises discussed at the beginning of Chapter 4. Since sounds tend to slur into their environments, Analytical Procedure I allowed the student to conclude that certain specific segments are or are not nonsignificant slurs into these environments. Since phonetic systems tend to be symmetrical, Analytical Procedure II showed the student how to utilize symmetry or lack of symmetry of sounds in series to find a positive or a negative indication of the accuracy of his analysis. Since sounds tend to fluctuate freely, Analytical Procedure III gave the student a methodology for eliminating nonsignificant free variation from his phonemic orthography.

For the present chapter the fourth basic premise serves as a background, and Analytical Procedures are provided to implement it. Since <u>characteristic sequences of sounds exert structural pressure on the phonemic interpretation of suspicious segments or suspicious sequences of segments</u>, we now set forth the techniques (1) which indicate that certain characteristic types of sequences of sounds are nonsuspicious for some particular type of difficulty and (2) which show how the remaining sequences of segments, the suspicious ones, can be interpreted phonemically by analogy with the nonsuspicious ones.

Analytical Procedures IV-A through IV-C contain the techniques which are the most important for the beginner to master within Analytical Procedure IV. IV-A shows how to determine whether certain doubtful segments are for a particular language consonants or vowels. IV-B shows how to determine whether certain sequences of two segments constitute single phonetically complex phonemes or sequences of phonemes. IV-C shows how to determine whether certain single segments comprise single phonemes or two overlapping simultaneous phonemes. Each of these procedures (IV-A, -B, -C) may be difficult to apply when conflicting pressures arise and clear cut analogies cannot be found.

The remaining techniques given in this chapter treat with special, often restricted situations which usually affect the analysis less seriously, but which sometimes are crucial to the choice of an adequate practical orthography or to the description of the phonemic system. Procedures IV-D and IV-E deal with under-differentiated and over-differentiated phonemic contrasts, respectively. IV-F considers problems arising from bilingualism, and loan words. IV-G and IV-H give hints for handling general quality modifications, and special additions of sounds (as in interjections). IV-I treats a problem of description: the determination of the relation of phonetic syllables to phonemic syllables. Finally, a further problem of structural interpretation, in Procedure IV-J, involves types of sequences which are comprised of separate phonemes, but which act somewhat like single units in distribution.

Analytical Procedures I-A, I-B, and in part II, were separating procedures, designed to show that two segments are separate phonemes. I-C and II were uniting procedures, to join segments into one phoneme. Procedure IV constitutes a series of INTERPRETATION techniques to determine the nature of segments as consonants, vowels, single phonemes or sequences of phonemes, and the like.

ANALYTICAL PROCEDURE IV-A:

INTERPRETING SEGMENTS AS CONSONANTS OR VOWELS

Problem 140--Kalaba Dialect DM

Phonetic Data (the vertical stroke under a symbol indicates that the segment marked is the center of a phonetic syllable; a low dot indicates a division between phonetic syllables):

[pu̯.i̯as]	'dog'	[ii̯.pi̯t]	'daughter'
[ti̯.mu̯f]	'man'	[sa̯.tu̯i]	'girl'
[fa̯.sai̯]	'woman'	[ta̯.fa̯p]	'father'

<u>Directions:</u>

1. What segments of this problem are suspicious because in some languages they may be consonants but in other languages, or even in the same language, they may be vowels?

2. How should these segments be analyzed in the present problem?

3. Rewrite phonemically the third and fourth words.

Solution to Problem 140:

1. Segments suspicious because they might prove to be consonants or vowels: [i] and [ɨ].

2. [ɨ] is a vowel, [i] is a consonant.

3. /fasay/ 'woman', /yipit/ 'daughter'.

Discussion of Problem 140:

Only a few types of segments differ from language to language as to whether they are consonants or vowels. Specifically, the most common ones are the following:

Segment Types which are Suspicious because They Might Prove to be Consonants or Vowels:

High vocoids (e.g. [i], [u], [ʉ])

Retroflexed central vocoid ([r])

Voiceless vocoids of any quality, (e.g. [A], [E], [I], [O], [U], or [h(i)], [h(e)]; or same with local glottal friction --e.g. [ɦ(i)], [ɦ(e)])

Lenis voiced velar fricatives (e.g. [g̬])

The student should notice that the sounds treated as suspicious during this procedure are different from those treated as suspicious during Analytical Procedure I. Segments should be treated as suspicious or nonsuspicious only for the particular procedure under attention, since the list of items which are suspicious vary for the different procedures or subprocedures.

The sound types just listed will function as consonants or vowels according to the place in which they occur in basic phonological and grammatical units of the particular language under consideration, and according to the structural pressure exerted upon them in these positions by structural analogies. Weighing the evidence to determine the structural pressure exerted upon such segments, the investigator needs to study the characteristic types of consonant and vowel sequences in that language, and needs to do so utilizing nonsuspicious data. That is, in determining the structural types of syllables, morphemes, or words, he should utilize only the following nonsuspicious sounds: stops, fricatives, nonsyllabic nasals and laterals, and low or mid vocoids. The stops and fricatives will almost certainly be consonants and the low and mid vocoids will almost certainly be vowels. Nonsyllabic nasals and laterals are also almost certain to function as consonants.

In Problem 140, then, one specific nonsuspicious pattern of a phonetic syllable is CV, as indicated by the nonsuspicious data [fa], [sa], and [ta] (ignoring the syllables [pu], [ti], and [ii] which contain suspicious types of segments). A second nonsuspicious syllable pattern in CVC, as indicated by the nonsuspicious sequence [fap]. Note also that all words in Problem 140 appear to be single morphemes, and that for them the nonsuspicious structure is CVCVC, as in [ta.fap] 'father'. In other words, all of the nonsuspicious data indicate that the final nonsyllabic element of a phonetic syllable is a consonant. Therefore the final elements of [fa.sai] 'woman' and [sa.tui] 'girl' are to be interpreted as consonants, because of the clear structural analogy creating pressure which affects them. Similarly, a nonsyllabic element at the beginning of a syllable is in every nonsuspicious instance a consonant, as in [fa], [sa], and [ta] so that by analogy with them the first element of [ii.pit] should also be interpreted as a consonant. On the other hand, every nonsuspicious vocoid is syllabic, as in [fa], [sa], [ta], and [fap]. These syllabic nonsuspicious vocoids are conveniently called vowels. By analogy, under the pressure of this predominant pattern, the suspicious vocoids which are syllabic should also be considered vowels. Thus in [ti.muf] 'man' the [ɨ] is a vowel. Having reached these conclusions, one can rewrite the words as given above in the solution; 'daughter', for example, becomes /yipit/. Syllable division is noncontrastive and nonphonemic[1] and is therefore omitted from the phonemically rewritten data.

In English, syllable-initial /y/ and /h/ must be analyzed as consonants because of pressures of the types just illustrated.

Occasionally the investigator finds it difficult to decide how to handle certain

[1]Certain investigators (see the discussion of Kickapoo by Charles F. Hockett in "A System of Descriptive Phonology," Language, XVIII [January-March, 1942], 3-21) imply that under circumstances of this kind presyllabic [i] (i.e. [y]) and syllabic [i] are mutually exclusive in terms of the syllable structure, and therefore members of a single phoneme--so they would write the syllable /yi/ as "ii". This conclusion seems to me to be inadvisable on the basis of native reaction to such writing, and therefore is deliberately ruled out, in this volume, by the setting up of Procedure IV-A.

For the detailed handling of an intricate problem in the analysis of [w] and [y], in which various types of evidence are presented, see Kenneth L. Pike and Eunice Pike, "Immediate Constituents of Mazateco Syllables," in International Journal of American Linguistics, XIII (April, 1947), 78-91.

of the nonsyllabic, suspicious vocoids because there are conflicting structural pressures in the language or because the structural pressure is not clear. Such a difficulty occurs in English, with nonsyllabic, postsyllabic [i̯] or [ṷ] in [ai̯], [au̯], [ɔi̯]. It is difficult to determine whether the second element of one of these sequences is a consonant or a vowel. One might affirm that [rai̯] 'rye' is analogous to [rɑt] 'rot', and so the [-i̯] is phonemically /-y/; but one also finds [rai̯t] 'write' in which one sees that the [-i̯] does not actually parallel the [-t], after all, since one does not find *[rɑtt] with [-t-] preceding [-t]—so one may affirm that the [-i̯] is a vowel. Compare also [pænt] 'pant' and [pai̯nt] 'pint'.

Since the data (of which this is merely a sample) indicate that there are conflicting analogies in terms of which the English [-i̯] could be interpreted, it is difficult for investigators of English to reach agreement on this point. (Additional data and conclusions concerning [-i̯] will be given with the discussion of Procedure IV-J.)

Whenever, on the grounds of the phonetic and distributional evidence, the student is unable to decide which of two descriptions is preferable, he should choose the one which allows the simplest description of the grammar. If, for example, in a certain language the word 'tree' is [bi̯], but when followed by the suffix [ɑ] '(plural)', the [-i̯] becomes nonsyllabic, i.e. [bi̯ɑ], the nonsyllabic [i̯] should still be retained as a vowel (and the word written /bia/) unless other evidence forces the student to consider it a consonant. If the [i̯] must be written as a consonant, and the word as /bya/, then in the morphology there must be given a statement describing the conditions in which the phoneme /i/ is replaced by the phoneme /y/.

If the investigator of a language unreduced to writing meets a situation with pressures which are not clear, he will be forced to make an orthographical decision on the basis of the practical situation. Factors to be considered would be prevailing orthographies in the region, the attitude of other investigators, ease of printing, morphological relationships, and the like. We earlier assumed (Chapter 4) that there was only one correct analysis for a given body of data. Where pressures conflict, however, we at present lack adequate theory to bring workers into agreement as to which constitutes the correct analysis. In such instances, however, the acceptance of either of two alternatives is likely to be satisfactory for the preparation of literatures. English [ai̯] can be written adequately as /ay/, or /ai/, or in other ways (cf. IV-J).

Problem 141--Kalaba Dialect DN

Phonetic Data:

[pas̆]	'here'	[tɑm]	'there'
[pʉs̆]	'ten'	[li̯p]	'everywhere'
[s̆as̆]	'under'	[pʉm]	'hunt'
[bi̯s]	'egg'	[sas]	'cyclone'
[mas̆]	'dissolve'		

Directions:

What are the vowel phonemes?

Rewrite phonemically the first two words.

Solution to Problem 141:

/i/, /a/, /u/.

/pis̆/ 'here', /pus̆/ 'ten'.

Discussion of Problem 141:

This problem is similar to the preceding one, with two major differences: (1) nonvocoids here serve as vowels, and (2) certain of the nonvocoids are in complementary distribution with certain of the vocoids. The phonemes /i/ and /u/ are raised until fricativized before /s̆/; thus [s̆] equals [i̯], and [s̆] equals [ʉ]; fronted syllabic [ɑ] and [i̯] are phonetically similar (though not circled on the chart of phonetically similar segments, p. 70), mutually exclusive in distribution, and submembers of a single phoneme, /i/. [ʉ] and [s̆] are similarly submembers of /u/.

Several other conclusions should be drawn from a study of these two problems: (1) The student should notice, for the last two problems, that once segments are analyzed as consonants or vowels, it is convenient, where possible, to represent them by traditional consonant or vowel symbols respectively. Thus consonantal [i̯] was rewritten /y/; vocalic [s̆] was rewritten /i/. (2) Consonantal /w/ and /y/ may be included on a chart of the consonants of the language, and labeled SEMIVOWELS, or NONSYLLABIC VOCOIDS, or CONSONANTAL VOCOIDS, or the like. (3) In some cases it is possible to apply the interpretation Procedure IV-A (to determine whether segments are consonants or vowels) before applying Procedure I-C (to determine whether phonetically similar segments are mutually exclusive and submembers of a single phoneme). Where it is convenient to do so, it may save the student some time if he applies IV-A first.

ANALYTICAL PROCEDURE IV-B:

INTERPRETING SEQUENCES OF SEGMENTS AS SINGLE PHONEMES OR SEQUENCES OF PHONEMES

Problem 142--Kalaba Dialect DO

Phonetic Data:

[pa]	'man'	[tsa]	'cow'
[ta]	'dog'	[ka]	'person'

Directions:

1. Is the suspicious sequence [ts] one phoneme or two? Why?

2. Rewrite phonemically the second column.

Solution to Problem 142:

1. The suspicious sequence [ts] comprises a single phonetically complex phoneme because the nonsuspicious predominant structural pattern consists of a single consonant followed by a single vowel for each syllable. This produces a structural pressure which by analogy forces the [ts] to constitute a single phonemic unit.

2. /ȼa/ 'cow', /ka/ 'person'.

Discussion of Problem 142:

Certain kinds of sequences are likely to be forced by the pressure of the nonsuspicious predominant structural pattern into single phonetically complex phonemes. Sequences of types subject to these pressures should be regarded with suspicion until the nonsuspicious patterns can be ascertained. Such suspicious sequences include the types in the following list. Notice that, in general, the list is constituted of sequences composed (1) of a stop plus some type of off glide or release, or (2) of a vocoid glide (especially a rising or centering one, in which the higher or the central articulatory type is unstressed or without a pitch phoneme), or (3) of pitch glides.

Segment Sequence Types which are Suspicious because They Might Prove to be One or Two Phonemes:

Any stop plus aspiration (i.e. voiceless stop plus voiceless vocoid of varying timbre or voiced stop plus vocoid with local glottal friction): e.g. [ph], [th], [pA], [pE], [bɦ]

or plus voiced rounded or unrounded high vocoid (i.e., followed by labialized or palatalized release): e.g. [kw], [py], [gw]

or plus homorganic fricative: e.g. [pɸ], [kx], [bƀ]; also [ts], [tš], [dž], [pf]; also same plus aspiration: e.g. [tsh]

or plus homorganic nasal: e.g. [pm], [tn]; or [mb], [nd], [nt]

Voiced stop or continuant plus voiced mid central vocoid: e.g. [bə], [mə]

Glottal stop plus voiced stop or nasal or lateral or high voiced vocoid: e.g. [ʔb], [ʔm], [ʔl], [ʔw], [ʔy]

Glottal stop plus voiceless stop: e.g. [ʔt]

Glottal or velar closure as initiator for nonpulmonic sounds, plus release: e.g. [pʔ], [tˤ]

Alveolar stop plus lateral: e.g. [tɬ], [dl], or same plus nonpulmonic initiator: e.g. [tɬʔ]

Velar stop plus labial stop: e.g. [kp], [gb]

Sounds other than stop, plus voiced rounded or unrounded high vocoid: e.g. [xw], [mw], [ny], [ly]

Voiced segments followed or preceded by voiceless segments of the same quality (especially next to silence): e.g. [pb-], [-zs], [ah⁽ᵃ⁾]

Vocoid glides (especially those containing a toneless, unstressed, nonsyllabic end or beginning which is high or mid central in quality; or those whose articulatory position does not glide very far): e.g. [ei], [ou]; [iə], [əee]; [ɨu]

Pitch glides: e.g. [˙]

Pitch plus glottal stop: e.g. [ˊʔ]

Sequences of these types tend to be forced into single phonemes when they occur in kinds of environments which apart from these suspicious types are occupied by single segments only. For example, in Problem 142, apart from the suspicious sequence [ts], syllables consist of a single nonvocoid segment followed by a single vocoid segment. By analogy with them the sequence [ts] of [tsa] is forced into a single phoneme. If now the word [tsa] 'cow' were written phonemically, as /ȼa/, the sequence [ts] would be represented by a single symbol, which in this case is traditionally the letter "c", modified by a diagonal bar. The investigator does not need to be suspicious that every sequence may be a complex phoneme. For his early conclusions he needs to consider closely only the evidence for the types listed here. Later in his study he can compare the other types also to make sure that certain conclusions do not have to be modified by some special distributional character of the segments which he at first overlooked. He may also find it convenient to note certain types of nonsuspicious sequences, which are probably sequences of two phonemes (although a few sequences which are at first

considered nonsuspicious may later have to
be treated as suspicious--cf. p. 119, Chapter 10): fricative plus stop ([sp], [st],
[xb]); vocoid plus stop, fricative, nasal,
or lateral ([ap], [os], [um], [il], [hk],
[wk], [hn]); stop, fricative, nasal, or
lateral plus stressed voiced vocoid ([p'a],
[p'e], [s'a], [n'i], [l'u]); stop plus
sharply heterorganic fricative or nasal
([px], [ks], [kf], [pŋ], [pn])--but tš],
[pf], etc. are suspicious since they are
homorganic or nearly so; nasal plus non-
homorganic stop ([mt]); nasal plus fricative, or vice versa ([mf], [nx], [fm], [xn]);
fricative plus fricative ([sx]); nasal or
fricative plus voiceless vocoid preceding
voiced vocoid ([m̥h(V)], [sh(V)]); long vocoid
glides which in their slurs do not end or
begin at an unstressed or nonsyllabic high
vocoid position or an unstressed or nonsyllabic mid central one, but which cover a
fairly long articulatory range ([ea], [ae],
[eo], [oe]); vocoid glides, with no mid
central end or beginning, which have stress
on the high part ([a'i], ['ia], [a'u]); vocoid glides with no high end or beginning,
but with stress on the mid central part
([a'ə], ['əa]); vocoid glides with a separate phonemic contrastive toneme on the end
and beginning of the glide ([áə̀], [ìə́],
[ōúˋ], [éî]).

Problem 143--Kalaba Dialect DP

Phonetic Data:

[mtos]	'man'	[ftaft]	'uncle'
[smump]	'dog'	[tfoms]	'house'
[tuf]	'child'	[stast]	'father'
[mfofm]	'woman'	[tsats]	'mother'

Directions:

Does the suspicious sequence [ts]
form a single phonetically complex phoneme?
Explain.

Rewrite the last two words phonemically.

Solution to Problem 143:

No, because it is paralleled by
various other analogous nonsuspicious sequences, such as [st], [ft], [tf], [mf].

/stast/ 'father'; /tsats/ 'mother'.

Discussion of Problem 143:

Whenever a suspicious sequence is
paralleled by analogous nonsuspicious sequences, the suspicious phonetic sequence
must be interpreted as a sequence of phonemes and not as a single phonetically complex phoneme. The sequences [sm], [mf],
[st], [tf], and [ft] are nonsuspicious
types, and are therefore presumably sequences
of two phonemes. The presence of these sequences establishes the fact that one of
the predominant patterns in the language is

the sequence of two consonants together,
either preceding or following a syllabic but
in the same syllable with it. Therefore,
this structural pattern exerts pressure upon
the interpretation of [ts] and forces it to
act as a sequence of two phonemes. Phonemically, then, the word 'mother' must be written /tsats/.

A further evidence that in Problem
143 [ts] must be considered a sequence of
phonemes is that in the same language, in
analogous environments (that is, at the beginning of syllables), this sequence is also
found in reverse; note the word [stast]
'father'. If a suspicious sequence is paralleled by a reverse sequence of the same segments in the same relative environments in
the language, the structural pattern is
likely to separate them into sequences of
separate phonemes, since in this case one of
the sequences is usually of a nonsuspicious
type and exerts pressure upon the phonemic
interpretation of the other.

Note further evidence contained in
the sequence [ms] in the word /tfoms/ 'house'.
Whenever the off glide in question occurs
with sounds other than with stops (for example, where [s] follows nasals as well as
[t]), there is less likelihood that such sequences form single phonetically complex
phonemes.

In a complicated problem it is sometimes difficult to observe all the data adequately without actually listing it ahead of
time. It is therefore convenient, in an
actual language situation, to list mechanically all sequences of two or more nonvocoids
and all sequences of two or more vocoids, in
order that the predominant pattern or patterns of nonsuspicious sequences may be
recognized. Sequences of either type may be
called CLUSTERS of nonvocoids or vocoids.
When listing of this type is done, the data
should be subdivided according to the types
of sounds which make up the sequences.
Note, for example, the following listings of
consonants in Problem 143:

Nonvocoid Sequences in Problem 143
(Suspicious Sequences are Preceded by a
Check Mark [✓])

Sequences End	Sequences Begin		
	With Stops	With Nasals	With Fricatives
With Stops.......		✓mp mt	ft st
With Nasals......			fm sm
With Fricatives..	tf ✓ts	mf ms	

Sometimes it is more convenient to classify the sequences according to the last segment in the sequence, and sometimes according to the first one, or to group them in other ways to see further analogies. Notice the same data reclassified so as to make prominent the second segment of the sequences:

```
mp   ft   fm   mf   ms
     st   sm   tf   ts
     mt
```

For the purposes of establishing pertinent structural distributions in order to determine the structural pressure, it is usually more important (and gives more reliable results) to observe the consonant sequences at the beginning or end of utterances than it would be, say, in the middle of utterances, since at the beginning and end of utterances the consonant clusters are likely to be simpler and, therefore, there is less probability of error. In the middle of utterances one tends to get word-final consonants followed by word-initial consonants, or syllable-final and syllable-initial sequences, and so on, which are larger and more complex than the clusters at the beginning or end of utterances where they are not doubled up. Occasionally, however, it is highly valuable for purposes of determining the predominant pattern for a person to study the predominant sequences in the middle of morphemes or between words. The investigator must use his judgment in this regard as problems arise in the particular language. In any case, when sequences are listed they should be identified as to the environments from which they are chosen. For the interpretation of structural pressure, comparison of one sequence with another should be made between sequences which are encountered in similar environments. For Problem 143, notice a re-listing of utterance-initial clusters of nonvocoids (a hyphen following them shows that they are initial):

```
ft-   sm-   mf-   ts-
st-         tf-
mt-
```

The contrast of [st] with [ts], and the parallel of [ts] to [tf] and [ft], remain in this classification and confirm the analysis of [ts] as a sequence of phoneme /t/ plus phoneme /s/.

If a language has sequences of vocoids, they should be listed in ways similar to those illustrated for the nonvocoids. Note the following possibility:

```
ia   ai   oi   ui
io   ao   oa   ua
iu   au   ou   uo
```

In instances where there is no clear cut pattern the investigator may have great difficulty in reaching a satisfactory conclusion. In English, for example, there has been considerable discussion concerning the phonetic cluster [tš]. One investigator may insist that it is a cluster of phonemes, on the ground that it occurs finally in words like catch, analogous to /ts/ as in cats. In this text we have written the phonetic cluster as a single phoneme /č/ for various distributional reasons, among which is the fact that the [ts] cluster has analogous clusters with [ps], [ks], [fs] in tips, backs, cliffs (and similar clusters with /z/ after voiced consonants) but there are no clusters of *[pš], *[kš], *[fš] (nor clusters of *[bž], *[mž], and so on) analogous to the [tš].[1] Supporting this conclusion is the morphological evidence that word-final [ts] tends to be interrupted by a morpheme boundary (i.e. except for loans like ritz) whereas [tš] is not so interrupted.

Several other difficulties in the analysis of English must be handled, if at all, by this procedure. Voiceless [W], for example, varying with the sequence [hw] (with the [w] lenis and rapid) may be considered, as in this volume, (see p. 45), a single phoneme because of the analogy of [b] : [p] = [w] : [W]; or it may be considered a sequence of phonemes because of the conflicting analogy of [k] + [w] = [h] + [w] (as in quail and whale); if [W] is considered a sequence of phonemes it leaves a lack of symmetry in simple phonemes, whereas if it is analyzed as a single phoneme it leaves a hole in the symmetry of consonant clusters.

Problem 144--Kalaba Dialect DQ

Phonetic Data:

[abᵊda] 'man'		[opti] 'cousin'
[omᵊnu] 'father'		[ifto] 'nephew'
[ibᵊgu] 'mother'		[upsu] 'brother'
[isfa] 'girl'		[afso] 'sister'

Directions:

What is the phonemic interpretation of [ə]?

Rewrite the first word phonemically.

---

[1]For a different analysis, see Morris Swadesh, "A Method for Phonetic Accuracy and Speed," in American Anthropologist, XXXIX (October-December, 1937), 731. For an analysis in which [tš] is considered to be constituted of two phonemes on the grounds that 'Medially and finally, the sounds in question behave exactly like such unmistakable clusters as /ts, dz/ and /tr, dr/'; and 'By analyzing these affricates as /tš, dž/ rather than as unit phonemes, we simplify the description of the total structure, which must account for distributions as well as for individual phonemes,' see Bernard Bloch and George L. Trager, Outline of Linguistic Analysis, (Baltimore: Linguistic Society of America, 1942), 49.

Solution to Problem 144:

[ə] constitutes an open transition between voiced consonants. The sequence [bᵊ] is a phonetically complex submember of the phoneme /b/, occurring before other voiced consonants; [mᵊ] is a submember of the phoneme /m/.

/abda/ 'man'.

Discussion of Problem 144:

Again the investigator seeks for the nonsuspicious predominant structural pattern of the language. In this instance, however, he is looking for numbers of syllables in morphemes or in minimal utterances or the like. Here, for example, apart from the morphemes with the segment [ə], which is suspicious because it occurs between voiced consonants and might prove to be merely a sound of open transition, the predominant pattern is VCCV. Here, also, each morpheme has only two syllables. No morpheme has three syllables with the exception of those morphemes containing [ə]--and provided that it is interpreted as a separate syllable. Since, however, the handling of [ə] as a syllabic pertinent to the structure of the language would give morphemes of a size not analogous to the predominant dissyllabic pattern of the language, the investigator concludes that [ə] is merely a type of phenomenon which links together two syllables when the one syllable ends and the other begins with a voiced consonant, but which is not present when the consonants are voiceless. A fact substantiating this conclusion is the absence of any other vowel type occurring between consonants. There is no contrast, for example, between a theoretically possible *[aboda], *[abida], and *[abəda]. In the absence of such contrast, the [ə] has no signalling value and therefore is nonphonemic. Sounds which must be handled in this general way include the following:

Voiced vocoids of a rather neutral or central quality, such as [ə].

Voiceless vocoids such as the aspiration of an aspirated stop.

Problem 145--Kalaba Dialect DR

Phonetic Data:

[pha]   'beaver'   [sapa]   'tree'

[phapa] 'radish'   [phasa] 'to swim'

Directions:

What are the submembers of the phoneme /p/, and what are their distributions?

Solution to Problem 145:

The phoneme /p/ has an aspirated submember initially in words but an

Discussion:

A phoneme may have submembers some of which are phonetically simple and others which are phonetically complex. In the present instance, for example, the /p/ becomes phonetically complex at the beginning of words and simple in the middle of them. The reasons for uniting into a single phoneme the phonetically simple unit [p] and the phonetically complex item [ph] is that they are mutually exclusive, and phonetically similar (inasmuch as the [h] following [p] merely constitutes a different type of release of the stop). The aspirated release and the unaspirated release occur in different environments.

In English the problem is made more complex by the fact that [h] occurs as a separate phoneme in words like /hæt/ 'hat', but that the /h/ is phonetically similar to the aspiration following the [p] in /pæt/ [pʰæth] 'pat'. Nevertheless the nonphonemic aspiration [ʰ] and the phonemic /h/ must not be equated, since the /p/ does not occur at the beginning of heavily stressed syllables unaccompanied by [ʰ]. The stressed /p/ at the beginning of syllables occurs only in the phonetic sequence [pʰ]. This essential association tends to force the two into a single phoneme. In addition, the pressure of the nonsuspicious sequences in the language is to permit the occurrence of a single consonant preceding single vowels in monosyllables such as /sæt/, /bæt/, /mæt/, /ræt/, etc. Yet if [pʰ] is considered to constitute a sequence of two phonemes, then /p/, /t/, and /k/ do not so occur by themselves at the beginning of such monosyllables. Furthermore, there is no parallel for consonant clusters which include [h] when these clusters constitute the first part of a syllable,[1] so that a cluster initially with */ph/ would not fit any nonsuspicious pattern whatsoever; this is additional evidence that in English [pʰ] is a single phoneme. At the end of utterances there is free variation between [pʰ] and [p] as in [pʰapʰ] or [pʰap] 'pop'. Elsewhere, [pʰ] and [p] tend to be in complementary distribution with each other (one of them occurring only in certain types of environments and the other never occurring there); for example, the [pʰ] before syllabics is largely limited to the beginning of stressed syllables, an environment in which the unaspirated [p] is not found. Thus by a combination of

---

[1]In ['lup.hol] 'loophole', note that a syllable division occurs between the [p] and the [h], and a morpheme division occurs at the same point. These two border phenomena prevent this item from being parallel to the [pʰ] in [pʰai] 'pie'. The [h] of loophole is to be identified with the [h] of /hæt/ 'hat' as a phoneme distinct from the [pʰ] = /p/ but following it after the border phenomena referred to.

Procedures III, I-C, and IV-B, the sounds [pʰ] and [p] are analyzed as submembers of a single phoneme /p/.

Problem 146--Kalaba Dialect DS

Phonetic Data:

    [vat.sa] 'horse'

Discussion of Problem 146:

    Single phonemes tend to occur in single syllables and not to be divided between two syllables. In the data for Problem 146, one would suspect that [ts] constituted a sequence of two phonemes, inasmuch as the syllable division occurs in the midst of the cluster of segments. Whenever this principle comes in conflict with the principle of structural pressure, however, structural pressure should be considered the more potent of the two.

Problem 147--Kalaba Dialect DT

Phonetic Data:

[pwa]	'horse'	[two]	'cow'
[tyo]	'dog'	[pya]	'sheep'

Directions:

    Are [py], [ty], [pw], and [tw] single phonemes or sequences of two phonemes?

Solution to Problem 147:

    [py], [ty], [pw], and [tw] are sequences of two phonemes.

Discussion of Problem 147:

    If only two types of sequences of consonants occur at the beginning of utterances, and one of these consists of labialized stops and the other of palatalized stops in each of which the off glide to [w] and [y] is quite clearly delayed until after the release of the stop itself, it seems best to consider that the contrasting pattern causes a separation of these items into sequences of two separate phonemes. Nevertheless, with only two series of sounds, especially when they are confined to items like stops, the structural pressures are not strong enough to make such a conclusion absolutely certain, and one must watch carefully for other types of data to swing one's judgment one way or the other. Specifically, one can watch for evidence of syllabicity, as to whether the [y] and [w] are prominent in their off glide, and so on.

    In addition, the problem is raised as to whether or not the [y] and [w] should be handled as consonants or whether they should be handled as nonsyllabic vowels and be written /pua/, /pia/, and so on. Here again the evidence given in Problem 147 is not detailed enough to make any certain decision. The investigator must look for other clues for reaching an adequate decision. If, for example, there is a morpheme division between the second and third segments of [pya], and the first two segments elsewhere constitute a distinct morpheme /pi/, the investigator is likely to conclude that there is considerable pressure for analyzing the second segment of these groups as vocalic rather than consonantal, and write the word /pia/.

    We have now seen three types of situations in which two or more segments may be united into a single phoneme:

    (1) If interchanging, phonetically similar segments fluctuate freely, and never occur in contrast, they are united by Procedure III.

    (2) If noncontiguous segments are phonetically similar and mutually exclusive in the environments in which they occur, they are united by Procedure I-C.

    (3) If contiguous suspicious segments (especially if the second is the release of the first) are unique in distribution, and are not paralleled in the language by analogous nonsuspicious sequences, they may be united by Procedure IV-B.

    When sequences of segments constitute single phonemes, a technical phonemic orthography symbolizes them with single symbols. Symbols are considered to be single, for this purpose, (1) if a single or unit letter is utilized (either as a special symbol, as "¢" or "c" for [ts], "z" for [dz], "č" for [tš], "ǰ" for [dž], "λ" for [tɬ]; or by deleting one of the two parts of the phonetic symbolization of the sequence, when this does not leave ambiguity in the particular language, as "p" for [pʰ]--in a language in which [p] does not contrast with [pʰ]--"p" for [py], "z" for [zs], "b" for [bᵊ], "e" for [ei]); or (2) if one of the letters (usually the second, except for combinations with initial nasal) is raised above the line, as "pʰ" for [ph], "kʷ" for [kw], "pʸ" for [py], "tˢ" for [ts], "tⁿ" for [tn], "ʔⁿ" for [ʔn], "kᵖ" for [kp], "eⁱ" for [ei]); or (3) if a ligature joins the two phonetic symbols, as "tš" for [ts].

Problem 148--Kalaba Dialect DU

Phonetic Data:

[po]	'yesterday'	[si]	'frog'
[mo]	'spittle'	[ndza]	'foam'
[ni]	'handkerchief'		

Directions:

    How should [ndz] be interpreted?

    Rewrite the word 'foam' phonemically with technical symbols.

Solution to Problem 148:

As a single phonetically complex phoneme.

/ⁿza/ 'foam'.

Discussion of Problem 148:

Just as a two segment sequence may be forced into a single phonemic unit by its distribution analogous to that of phonetically simple single phonemes, so occasionally a three segment sequence may constitute a single phoneme. In this problem the sequence [ndz] parallels in distribution the simple consonants /p/, /s/, /m/, and /n/, and is therefore a single phoneme.

By experience we set up a brief list of sequences of three segments which should be suspicious, since they might constitute single phonemes. This would include the following types of sequences:

Three-Segment Sequence Types which are Suspicious because They Might Prove to be a Single Phoneme:

Nasal plus homorganic alveolar affricate: e.g. [nts], [ntš], [ndz], [ndž]

Homorganic alveolar affricate plus aspiration: e.g. [tsh], [tšh]

Homorganic alveolar affricate with velar or glottal release (and nonpulmonic mechanism): e.g. [tsʔ], [tsˤ], [ts<], [tš?], [tɬʔ], [tɬʔ]

Problem 149--Kalaba Dialect DV

Phonetic Data:

[ʦsha]	'when'	[nta]	'whether'
[hto]	'where'	[tna]	'whence'
[to]	'why'	[tsna]	'wherefore'
[tho]	'who'	[ha]	'whenever'
[tsa]	'which'		

Directions:

Why must [ts] be analyzed as /ɸ/?

Rewrite the first column phonemically.

Solution to Problem 149:

[ts] must be analyzed as a single phoneme because it is analogous to single phonemes in distribution.

/ɸha/ 'when', /hto/ 'where', /to/ 'why', /tho/ 'who', /ɸa/ 'which'.

Discussion of Problem 149:

There is a pitfall in this problem, for the unwary beginner. The [ts] of [tsa] 'which' may at first seem to be analogous to the [th] of [tho] 'who', and so constitute a sequence of two phonemes. Further examination of the data, however, would show him that in [tsha] 'when' the [ts] occurs before another consonant--a position which with respect to nonsuspicious data is filled only by nonsuspicious unit phonemes and not by sequences of nonsuspicious segments. Thus the [ts] of [tsha] must form its analogies with the [t] of [tho], and the [ts] of [tsa] is analogous with the single [t] of [to]. The full distributional symmetry of a system must be considered before structural pressures and analogies can safely be postulated.

Problem 150--Kalaba Dialect DW

Phonetic Data:

[xudapA]	'to squeeze'	[kudikI]	'state'
[nisikI]	'rock'	[nafatA]	'hard'
[tamakA]	'brother'	[xamupU]	'fifty'
[nafutU]	'tower'	[maxas]	'brown'
[tigitI]	'soft'	[famukU]	'pigeon'
[subipI]	'sturdy'	[kinuf]	'ham'
[masix]	'feather'		

Directions:

1. What would seem to be the phonemic analysis of [A], according to Procedure I-C?

2. What would seem to be the phonemic analysis of the same segment according to Procedure IV-B?

3. How would you resolve the difficulty?

Solution to Problem 150:

1. [A] is phonetically similar to [a], and mutually exclusive with it (since [A] occurs only word finally, whereas [a] never occurs there), so by Procedure I-C the segments would seem to be submembers of a single phoneme.

2. The sequences [pA], [kA], and [tA] are suspicious. The nonsuspicious structure of words and morphemes in this language is CVCVC. If the suspicious sequences are phonemically sequences of consonant plus vowel, it would break this nonsuspicious pattern (a) by adding a third syllable to morphemes, and (b) by adding word final vowels to the language. So, by analogy with /mapas/, the utterance [xudapA] should be interpreted as /xudap/, in which [A] is analyzed as a nonsignificant release of the [p].

3. It should be noticed that the result of (2) can be achieved, also, by Procedure I-C, beginning with the stops: the phoneme /p/ has a voiceless unaspirated submember initially in words, a voiced unaspirated submember word medially, and a voiceless

aspirated submember word finally--with the [A], [I], etc., constituting the aspiration. It should further be noticed that the analysis of [A] as /a/, according to (1), gives a peculiar distributional result: word final /a/ would be found only after stops, and only after a stop which was preceded by /a/. Similar statements must be made for the other vowels. Neither of these two restrictions seems natural to languages as we have observed them (i.e., it does not "make sense"). The analysis of [A] as /a/ should, therefore, be discarded in favor of the analysis of [A] (and other voiceless vocoids) as aspiration-- a solution which our experience tells us is satisfactory.

Discussion of Problem 150:

The particular problem has been solved here. In a manner similar to that for earlier procedures (see footnote on p. 76) the student must be prepared to choose between alternate solutions on the basis of (1) the relative complexity of the alternative descriptive statements, (2) completeness of data, (3) analysis of analogous sounds in the same general series, and (4) apparent reasonableness of the statements in the light of all the distributional facts.

The question arises, however, as to which procedure should be applied first. Notice that Procedure I-C must now have a restriction added if it is to be applied before IV-B: Two sounds are submembers of a single phoneme provided (1) that the submembers are phonetically similar, (2) that the submembers are mutually exclusive in the environments which they occupy, and (3) that the total distribution of the submembers united into a single phoneme does not give a heavily nonsymmetrical result out of balance with the pressures of nonsuspicious sequences in the language.

From this we gather that I-C can be applied tentatively before IV-B, if the student is careful to check for symmetry of the system as a whole before making his tentative conclusions final. In some instances, perhaps in all,[1] it would save some time if Procedures II-A, II-B and IV-B were applied before Procedure I-C.

---

[1]This possibility has only recently been called to my attention by our teaching staff. We have not yet had time to test the approach adequately in the classroom, and locate the theoretical restrictions which presumably will be found to modify its use. In general, students find Procedure IV more difficult to apply than they do earlier procedures. This seems to make it convenient to delay Procedure IV until late in the course, if possible.

Problem 151--Kalaba Dialect DX

Phonetic Data:

[tsab.zes]	'hot'	[dzef.sap]	'artery'
[po.iadz]	'arm'	[gak.dzon]	'jumpy'
[bo.tsef]	'to be'	[sob.dzeg]	'son'
[fats.tšoi]	'ink'	[dou.iei]	'baby'
[tsas.gat]	'red'	[beg.vou]	'wolf'
[kag.zedž]	'wet'	[tei.notš]	'chair'
[tšo.iets]	'man'	[tou.nedz̧]	'thirsty'
[ua.tsab]	'good'	[džob.von]	'sold'
[nai.zes]	'uneven'	[džok.sau]	'trail'

Directions:

1. What words in this language contain only nonsuspicious sequences?

2. How should [ts] be interpreted phonemically?

Solution to Problem 151:

1. None.

2. [ts] = /¢/.

Discussion of Problem 151:

When it is inconvenient or impossible to utilize entire words for setting up the patterns of nonsuspicious sequences, it frequently is helpful and valid to study nonsuspicious sequences of a more limited type. In Problem 151 there is no word which is composed exclusively of sequences simultaneously nonsuspicious for Procedures IV-A and IV-B. That makes it difficult to analyze [ts]. At the ends of words, however, there are nonsuspicious sequences of vowel plus consonant: /-es/, /-ef/, /-at/, /-ap/, /-on/, /-eg/, etc. Without exception these establish a word final nonsuspicious predominant pattern of /-VC/. By analogy with this pattern, word final [-Vts] must be interpreted as /-V¢/. Word initially a similar procedure gives similar results. Word medially similar results are obtained, provided one charts his distribution in terms of syllable borders there. By analogy with the same nonsuspicious patterns, [i] and [u] must be analyzed as /y/ and /w/.

Problem 152--Kalaba Dialect DY

Phonetic Data:

[póʔ]	'blue'	[tù]	'sky'
[sǒ]	'red'	[pǒ]	'sunset'
[pò]	'cloud'	[súʔ]	'atmosphere'

Directions:

Rewrite the first two words phonemically.

Solution to Problem 152:

/pó/ 'blue', /tù/ 'sky'.

Discussion of Problem 152:

Rising, falling, and falling-rising tones are found in contrast. Glottal stop appears only on syllables with rising tone; it does not occur initially in syllables, nor freely at the end of them, but only when rising pitch is present. Rising tone never appears without glottal stop. No final consonants appear (other than the [ʔ], with the limited distribution just mentioned). It seems convenient, therefore, to consider the rising pitch plus glottal stop to be united into a complex of phonetic characteristics which constitute a single suprasegmental phoneme, symbolized by /'/.[1] In studying tones or sequences of tones the student must watch for structural symmetry (cf. Procedure II, Chapter 10) and structural analogies (cf. also Chapter 9) for clues toward their interpretation.

ANALYTICAL PROCEDURE IV-C:

INTERPRETING SINGLE SEGMENTS AS SEQUENCES OF PHONEMES OR SINGLE PHONEMES

Problem 153--Kalaba Dialect DZ

Phonetic Data:

[toef] 'man'	[moas] 'uncle'
[pá·s] 'boy'	[su·f] 'aunt'
[saot] 'girl'	[fiot] 'niece'
[feom] 'woman'	[fo·p] 'nephew'
[pi·t] 'cousin'	[tuim] 'father'

Directions:

Does [a·] constitute one or two phonemes? Explain.

Rewrite the first two words phonemically.

---

[1]It would not be satisfactory to consider the [ʔ] a phoneme with the rising pitch conditioned by the glottal stop, since pitch must be analyzed as independently phonemic, on the evidence of contrasts like [pó] 'sunset' and [pò] 'cloud'. Once pitch is thus proved phonemic, the treatment of ['] as a phoneme of tone introduces no new type of phonemic entity, whereas [ʔ] postulated as a phoneme would introduce postsyllabic consonants.

Solution to Problem 153:

[a·] constitutes a sequence of two short vowel phonemes, since phonetically long vowels are structurally parallel to sequences of two diverse vowels, as in the words [moas] 'uncle', [toef] 'man', and so on.

/toef/ 'man', /paas/ 'boy'.

Discussion of Problem 153:

In Analytical Procedure IV-B we studied sequences of two (or three) segments which might prove to be single phonemes. In IV-C we consider single segments which may prove to be sequences of two phonemes.

When a long vowel is phonemically in contrast to a short vowel and is structurally analogous to clusters of diverse vowels, the long vowel must be considered as a sequence of two short identical vowel phonemes.[1] The investigator wishes, therefore, to establish the nonsuspicious pattern or patterns of vowel sequences in the language. We have already indicated, on p. 133, how these can be lined up. In Problem 153 relatively nonsuspicious sequences of vowels such as [oe] and [oa] contain two vowels. With the establishment of this pattern, therefore, the long vowels may be interpreted as being composed of sequences of short identical vowels by analogy with them.

Problem 154--Kalaba Dialect EA

Phonetic Data:

[mot] 'monkey'	[la·m] 'to sing'
[mo·t] 'parrot'	[mo·l] 'to eat'
[laf] 'to talk'	[mam] 'coconut'

Directions:

Rewrite the first two words phonemically.

Solution to Problem 154:

/mot/ 'monkey', /mo·t/ (or /mott/) 'parrot'.

Discussion of Problem 154:

If long vowels are phonemically in contrast with short vowels but fill the same structural position as is filled by single short vowels, the investigator may conclude that the long vowels represent single long vowel phonemes. (In such an instance, one would not expect to find vowel sequences of the type which appear in the problem just

---

[1]For my first interest in this principle I am indebted to Morris Swadesh, "The Phonemic Interpretation of Long Consonants," Language, XIII (January-March, 1937), 1-10.

preceding this one.) Thus the [o·] in [mo·t] is analogous to the [o] of [mot], with which it is phonemically in contrast.

For a technical orthography, phonemic long vowels of this type may be symbolized with a raised dot or with a macron (but nonphonemic length should not be symbolized).

Long consonants are analyzed in a manner similar to the analysis of long vowels. When long consonants are phonemically in contrast to short consonants and are structurally analogous to clusters of diverse consonants, the long consonants constitute sequences of identical short consonants. It would appear that long consonants are usually sequences of short phonemes, and only rarely single long phonemes.

In English one finds long consonants in such utterances as [əbɪg·us] 'a big goose' or [kʰæt·ʰeⁱl] 'cat-tail'. Several types of evidence force these into sequences of phonemes: (1) There are analogous diverse clusters, as in [əbɪgboi] 'a big boy' and [tʰɪptʰap] 'tiptop', etc. This is the principal evidence; the remaining data support the same conclusion. (2) The long consonants have syllables dividing somewhere in their midst (i.e., [ə.bɪg.·us], [kʰæt..ʰeⁱl]. (3) By the techniques of Chapter 13, spaces would separate the two halves of the long consonants, since word divisions come in the middle of them ([bɪg ·us], [kʰæt ·ʰeⁱl]). The phrases should be rewritten phonemically thus: /ə 'bɪg 'gus/, /kæt tel/. When a word or morpheme border interrupts a long consonant, that long consonant is usually composed of two short phonemes in sequence.

Problem 155--Kalaba Dialect EB

Phonetic Data:

[táf] 'money'   [tá˙f] 'thatch'

[tàf] 'whisker'   [tà˙f] 'donkey'

Directions:

Rewrite the last two words phonemically.

Solution to Problem 155:

/táàf/ and /tàáf/.

Discussion of Problem 155:

Occasionally a further type of evidence may cause long vowels to be phonemically interpreted as constituting a sequence of identical short vowels. In a tone language some type of unit must carry the tone. Frequently such a unit will be a short vowel. If every short vowel has one toneme and one toneme only, but every long vowel has two tonemes, the investigator should conclude that the long vowels are sequences of two identical vowel phonemes rather than constituting single long phonemes with a complex

tone.

Similarly, contrasting stress on each of the long vowels (i.e., ['a·] and [a·'·]) tends to show that they are a sequence of phonemes (i.e., /'aa/ and /a'a/).

Problem 156--Kalaba Dialect EC

Phonetic Data:

[nas] 'man'   [sos] 'mother'

[pǫ] 'father'   [sap] 'girl'

[nap] 'woman'   [pạ] 'boy'

Directions:

Present the data and conclusions pertinent to the analysis of the nasalized vowels.

Rewrite the last two words phonemically.

Solution to Problem 156:

Segments which are suspicious because they might prove to be composed simultaneously of a consonant and a vowel:

[ạ] and [ǫ].

The nasal vowels [a] and [o] are to be interpreted as sequences of a vowel plus the consonant [n] since the nonsuspicious and predominant pattern of the language indicates a morpheme and syllable structure of CVC, as in the nonsuspicious sequences [sap], [sos]. Each syllable and morpheme ends with a consonant except for the suspicious sequences previously indicated.

Phonemic rewrite of data:

/sap/ 'girl', /pan/ 'boy'.

Discussion of Problem 156:

Sounds may be interpreted as containing both a vowel and consonant if the structural pressure from nonsuspicious data warrants that conclusion. In the light of this possibility, the following segment types may be so interpreted:

Segment Types which are Suspicious because they Might Prove to Contain Both a Vowel and a Consonant:

Nasalized vowels

Retroflexed vowels

Laryngealized vowels

Syllabic nasals

Syllabic laterals

Syllabic [ɹ̩]

In a problem of this type the student should notice (1) a lack of symmetry, in that the consonant /n/ is missing from word-final position, where it would be expected to occur in analogy to other word-final consonants, and (2) a lack of symmetry in that nasalized vowels and oral vowels do not contrast preceding consonants. This dual lack of symmetry should make him suspicious of the nasalized vowels (or retroflexed, or laryngealized ones). If nasalized vowels are analyzed as phonemic oral vowels plus the phoneme /n/, both nonsymmetrical characteristics of the language would disappear, since /n/ would then occur word finally, and no phonemic nasalized vowels would exist.

In English one occasionally hears a pronunciation of a word in which [n] disappears but leaves the preceding vowel nasalized. Situations of this type would have to be analyzed in some such way as indicated above--or with [-an] and [-ã] in free or stylistically conditioned variation.

In American Indian languages there is frequently variation of some type in the sequence of vowel plus glottal stop; /Vʔ/ may vary from [Vʔ] to [V̰ʔ] or to [V̰]. Similarly, /VʔV/ tends to vary from [VʔV] to [V̰ʔV] or to [V̰·].

Problem 157--Kalaba Dialect ED

Phonetic Data:

[ļmǫs] 'philosopher'   [ǝslǫs] 'absolute'

[ļlsļs] 'reality'   [ǫssǝl] 'abstract'

[ļsǫm] 'implied'   [ǫllļl] 'unknown'

[ļsmǝs] 'postulated'

Directions:

Write the last two words of the first column phonemically.

Solution to Problem 157:

/ǝlsom/ 'implied', /ismǝs/ 'postulated'.

Discussion of Problem 157:

In the two previous problems we have a vowel phoneme which could simultaneously contain a consonant phoneme. In this new problem the reverse is true: we find a consonant phoneme which can simultaneously contain a vowel phoneme.

Notice the lack of symmetry in Problem 157. /i/ and /o/ both occur initially in words, before /l/; /ǝ/ does not so occur. Nonsyllabic /l/ occurs following initial /o/ and /i/; syllabic [ļ-] never follows these vowels. If [ļ-] is analyzed as containing the phoneme sequence */ǝl-/, the nonsymmetrical characteristics of this problem disappear.

[ļ-] is to be analyzed as /ǝl-/ on the analogy with /il-/ and /ol-/. Syllabic consonants may be analyzed as containing a consonant and vowel simultaneously, if there are analogies giving structural pressure in that direction, and if the nonsymmetrical characteristics of the resultant phonemic system are decreased by that analysis. The vowel concerned tends to be of a somewhat obscure or mid central type.

Such an analysis is strengthened if there is free variation between the types [Ç] and [VC].

In English there are conflicting pressures which affect the analysis of the syllabic consonants. Some writers analyze English syllabic consonants as containing the vowel /ǝ/,[1] and write them as [ļ] = /ǝl/, and so on--partly because of structural symmetry, partly because of free or nearly free fluctuation of [ǝl] and [ļ], and partly for economy of symbols. In this volume I have chosen to write English [ļ] as /ļ/, although the other analysis has much to commend it and may prove to be preferable. Tentative reasons for the analysis here include (1) the fact that some words seem to use [ǝ] plus /l/, /n/, or /m/ preferably or consistently, and others tend to use the syllabic consonants preferably,[2] provided that the style and quality of speech is kept uniform[3] (contrast /'ʤɛntļmǝn/ 'gentleman' and /'ebļ/ 'able'); (2) the symmetry or lack of symmetry, which would have to be responsible for forcing [ļ] to /ǝl/, is not clear enough; (3) the resolution of [ļ] to /ǝl/ does not give a system of parallels which is readily applied to other syllabic consonants which may develop in phrase abbreviations of normal speech (cf. /'brɛd ŋ 'bǝtɾ/ 'bread and butter', /'ş ǝ̀ə 'truθ/ 'it's the truth', /ǝ̀ə ki d̩ du/ 'the key would do', /'taim ɣ 'de/ 'time of day'); (4) it seems to me to work a bit more satisfactorily in our classes in practical phonetics and practical phonemics, although either of the analyses is adequate for that purpose. Instead of analyzing English [ļ] as /ǝl/, therefore, I have chosen

---

[1] Cf. Morris Swadesh, "The Vowels of Chicago English," Language, XI (June, 1935), 150. He does so "even in those cases where syllabic r, n, m, l, are nominally pronounced, because the vowel discussed above (that is [ǝ]) has a range of values that shades off to mere syllabicity in some instances."

[2] See suggested list in Y. R. Chao, "The Non-uniqueness of Phonemic Solutions of Phonetic Systems," in Academia Sinica, Bulletin of the Institute of History and Philology, IV (1933), 375-5.

[3] It is still possible, however, that style may be responsible for the difference or the variation between the two types, under Procedure IV-G.

to symbolize the peak of syllabicity[1] of forms: (1) by a syllable marker, [,]; (2) by regular vowel letters on the line [a], [o] (but with nonsyllabic vowels written above the line,--cf. /aⁱ/ as a sequence of /a/+/i/).

ANALYTICAL PROCEDURE IV-D:

INTERPRETING SEGMENTS AS UNDER-DIFFERENTIATED PHONEMES

Problem 158--Kalaba Dialect EE

Phonetic Data:

[pito] 'fetish'   [pɛto] 'ghost'

[potʊ] 'demon'   [tɛpʊ] 'taboo'

[topo] 'worship'   [titʊ] 'idol'

Directions:

Rewrite phonemically the first two words.

Solution to Problem 158:

/pito/ 'fetish', /póti/ (or, provided it is written thus consistently, /potɛ́/) 'demon'.

Discussion of Problem 158:

Notice (1) that /i/ and /ɛ/ are proved to be phonemically separate by contrast in identical environments ([pito] 'fetish', [pɛto] 'ghost'); (2) that [i] and [ɛ] are both phonetically similar to [ʊ]; (3) that [i] and [ʊ] are both mutually exclusive with [ʊ]; (4) that according to Procedure I-C [i] and [ʊ] would be submembers of a single phoneme, as would [ɛ] and [ʊ]; (5) that this leads to a contradiction, since [i] and [ɛ] are separate phonemes, and could not each have [ʊ] as a submember in the same environment. In this environment, in this language, /i/ and /ɛ/ are under-differentiated. An UNDER-DIFFERENTIATED phonemic contrast is constituted of the occurrence, in some environment, of a segment which is phonetically similar to but mutually exclusive with each of two phonemically contrasting segments.

To solve this difficulty we can either (1) state that [ʊ] is a third, separate phoneme, or (2) assign [ʊ] to /i/ or /ɛ/, according to which it resembles the more closely in its phonetic characteristics, or (3) assign it to one of them arbitrarily. Solution according to suggestion (1) is impractical for literatures, and is not followed here, since (a) it sets up extra phonemes for highly limited environments, and incidentally necessitates extra symbols, and since (b) the consistent symbolization of the suspicious segment, by either of the symbols

for the phonemes phonetically similar to it provides an unambiguous, practical orthography. Solution (2) should be adopted where possible (e.g. in this problem [ʊ] should be written /i/ if the investigator thinks that he can demonstrate that [ʊ] is more like [i] than it is like [ɛ]). If solution (2) cannot be applied, then solution (3) must be utilized, making an arbitrary decision for one symbol or the other, until phonemic theory gives us a more refined method of analysis.

These decisions for [ʊ] can be expressed in a generalization: When a segment is phonetically similar to but mutually exclusive with two other segments which contrast phonemically with each other, the first segment should be assigned as a submember to that phoneme to which it is phonetically most similar (provided that the one segment is not in contrast, in any other environments, with this or any other submember of the phoneme to which it is assigned), or, if that be impossible, it should be assigned to one or the other of them arbitrarily.

This type of problem occurs in English. The segment [t] occurs after [s], and is phonetically similar to and mutually exclusive with both aspirated [tʰ] and voiced [d]. Because the [t] seems more closely related to [tʰ] than to [d],[1] and because it proves convenient to continue the traditional spelling of "t" after "s", we assume that 'stay', for example, is phonemically /ste/.

A situation in English which gives much more trouble to the average student of phonetics and phonemics is the occurrence of vowels before postsyllabic /-r/ in dialects in which /-r/ is clearly heard as a retroflex vocoid. The difficulty consists in the obscuring of the contrast between close and open vowel types in that environment. Specifically, it is hard to determine, for many English dialects, whether /i/ or /ʊ/ is pronounced in bier and/or near; whether /e/ or /ɛ/ is pronounced in their and/or pair; /o/ or /ɔ/ in four and/or for; /u/ or /ʊ/ in boor and/or poor. For some speakers the decisions may be quite simple--/i/, for example, is pronounced clearly in near. Other speakers seem to find it impossible to decide the question for their own dialects; the vowel sound, say, of four, is acoustically about half way between the sounds of /o/ and /ɔ/. For these speakers last mentioned, /o/ and /ɔ/ are under-differentiated before /-r/. For them an arbitrary choice may have to be made as to writing one or the other sound.

---

[1]This implies the presence of a PHONEME OF SYLLABICITY. The implication for phonemic theory is not clear.

[1]As pointed out by Bernard Bloch and George L. Trager, in their Outline of Linguistic Analysis (Baltimore: Linguistic Society of America, 1942), 43-44, [tʰ] and [t] are both fortis; [d] is lenis.

ANALYTICAL PROCEDURE IV-E:

INTERPRETING SEGMENTS AS OVER-DIFFERENTIATED
PHONEMES

Problem 159--Kalaba Dialect EF

Phonetic Data:

[bo] 'to run' (normal speech of adults)

[bo] 'to sing' (normal speech of adults)

[bo] 'to run' (precise speech of school
          teacher at the time she is
          teaching spelling)

[po] 'to sing' (precise speech of school
          teacher at the time she is
          teaching spelling--but other-
          wise she pronounces the word
          as [bo])

Directions:

        Rewrite the words phonemically, for
purposes of normal literature.

Solution to Problem 159:

        /bo/ 'to run', /bo/ 'to sing'.

Discussion of Problem 159:

        In some types of speaking, espec-
ially in precise or schoolroom speech, phonemic contrasts are present which do not
exist in normal speech. This constitutes a
type of over-differentiation of phonemes,
since OVER-DIFFERENTIATION of phonemes is
constituted of a phonemic contrast (or of a
phoneme) which appears only in speech (or in
single morphemes) representing abnormal or
special style. If similar situations are
found in a language as yet unreduced to writing, the extra contrasts should probably not
be symbolized in the writing of ordinary
literature. I do not know, however, of any
such instance.[1]

        In Mexican Spanish there is a phoneme
/b/ which varies from [b] to [ƀ] in normal
speech; it tends to be actualized as [b] in
initial stressed syllables, or after nasals
or laterals, but as [ƀ] in unstressed inter-
vocalic position, and so on. In extra precise speech, however, as when a school
teacher is demonstrating the difference

_____

[1]The closest kind of parallel I have
found is perhaps a situation in which a phonemic contrast (1) is in use by many speakers
but (2) in many words either phoneme can be
used, and (3) speakers disagree as to which
phoneme they use in a particular list of
words. Compare your pronunciation with mine
in the following list: /fag/ or /fɔg/ 'fog',
/lɔg/ 'log', /bag/ 'bog', /hag/ 'hog', /frag/
'frog', /tagz/ 'togs', /rat/ 'rot', /dɔg/
'dog'.

between the sounds of the letter "b" and the
letter "v"--both of which occur in the spell-
ing--an artificial phonemic contrast may be
introduced between bilabial stop [b] and
sharply labio-dental [v], with minimal pairs
such as botar 'to fling' and votar 'to vote'.
On the other hand the teacher may use an expression such as [be de buro i be de baka]
'"b" de "burro" y "v" de "vaca"' ([b] of
burro 'donkey' and [b] of vaca 'cow') to tell
the children which letter should be used in
a particular instance. The phonemic contrast
between /b/ and /v/ is an artificial one, in
such instances, but actually present. The
knowledge as to which words may be pronounced
with the one sound or the other must be gained
from the traditional orthography. For a
suggestion for a different approach to this
same problem, see p. 143, Procedure IV-H.[1]

ANALYTICAL PROCEDURE IV-F:

INTERPRETING THE SEGMENTS OF LOAN WORDS
OR OF NATIVE WORDS UNDER PRESSURE FROM
A TRADE LANGUAGE

        Problems with regard to the spelling
of loan words will be treated in Chapter 16,
but a few general rules may be mentioned here:

        (1) When sounds present in the trade
language but not in words of native origin
are introduced to the native language through
loan words, symbols for these sounds should
be added to the native language, and the additional phonemes treated as more or less parallel to the native ones, if the loans appear
to be thoroughly assimilated. In doubtful
instances we have at present no way of proving that words are or are not thoroughly
assimilated. As a general rule-of-thumb we
may assume, however, that words have been
assimilated if they are used naturally by
monolinguals (or, where there are few monolinguals, by women when they are speaking the
native language in the home).[2]

        (2) Loan words should be respelled as
pronounced by speakers of the vernacular, and
not as pronounced by speakers of the trade
language, unless strong social or governmental
pressure prevents one from doing so.

_____

[1]I.e., Interpreting Sporadic Special
Segments. William Wonderly, of the Summer
Institute of Linguistics, suggests that over-
differentiated phonemes may be said to occur
in a special style--say that of precision--
and so can be handled as extra-systematic
(under our assumption that analysis of the
phonemes must be made in a uniform style inasmuch as quality is relative).

[2]Viola Waterhouse, of the Summer
Institute of Linguistics, suggests that extra
sounds introduced only through names borrowed
from foreign languages could technically be
treated as parallel to the sporadic special
segments of Procedure IV-H, for which see p.
143; this would show them to be extrasystematic, with a special style or special social
situation.

(3) When assimilated loan words bring in sounds which contrast with each other but which parallel mutually exclusive submembers of a native phoneme, the newly developed phonemic contrast must be interpreted as separating the segments previously constituting submembers of a phoneme into distinct phonemes.

ANALYTICAL PROCEDURE IV-G:

INTERPRETING SEGMENTAL CHANGES DUE TO A SHIFT OF GENERAL QUALITY

Problems with regard to the phonemic interpretation of a general shift of quality do not usually disturb the analyst seriously. The following brief general statements may be made concerning it and related problems. (Compare Chapter 11, pp. 124-5 [especially the footnote], and Chapter 4, p. 66).

(1) A shift of the general quality of the voice may modify each segment in any given phrase, yet if the same relative contrasts of segments in sequence are preserved, the practical orthography does not need to be affected by such changes. That is to say, quality is relative, and a shift of the system of contrasts, as a whole, leaves the systematic relationships undisturbed.

If qualitative changes need to be indicated for special purposes, this may be accomplished by the use of special symbols or statements covering the change of an entire sentence or conversational interchange.

(2) Similarly, if a general change of pitch occurs, so that a sentence as a whole is raised or lowered in pitch, the intonation phonemes or tone phonemes retain their contrasts undisturbed, and the practical alphabet need not be modified. So, also, a general change in intensity does not affect a practical alphabet for a literature.

Special techniques for the locating of regular phonemic contrasts of lexical pitch, in the presence of unrecognized changes of the general height of the voice, have already been outlined in Chapter 9, and need not be repeated here.

(3) A general change of quality (or specific qualitative changes in a few segments) from speaker to speaker, or from dialect to closely related dialect does not need symbolization in a practical orthography.

ANALYTICAL PROCEDURE IV-H:

INTERPRETING SPORADIC SPECIAL SEGMENTS

Problem 160--Kalaba Dialect EG

Phonetic Data:

[topa] 'baseball'   [toto] 'first base'

[patop] 'home run'   [abˤ] 'ouch!!'

Directions:

Should [bˤ] be considered part of the normal phonemes of this language? If it is in some other sense significant, place it between dotted diagonals.

Solution to Problem 160:

No. ⫶bˤ⫶

Discussion of Problem 160:

The initial analysis of the phonemes of a language must be performed (1) with data from a single speaker, and (2) with data of a uniform style. If additional styles entail further sounds outside the systematic relationships they should be analyzed as EXTRA-SYSTEMATIC phonemes, or given some other label which seems appropriate.

In Problem 160 the exclamation of 'ouch!!' constitutes a different style of speech from the normal utterances of 'baseball', and the like. The word [abˤ] 'ouch!!' carries with it, furthermore, a segment not found in normal speech,--and this segment utilizes an air mechanism which does not produce any of the normal sounds of this language. [bˤ] must be considered socially significant, for this language, but on a different basis from the significance of, say, the regular /t/. The ⫶bˤ⫶ constitutes an extra-systematic phoneme.

Expanding this principle further, we find that special extrasystematic phonemes may be restricted (1) to specific styles of speech, or (2) to specific types of social situations, or (3) to specific morphemes which in turn are restricted in usage. In English, for example, /tˢtˢtˢ/ may be used for commiseration, or for reproof; /tˢ/ for urging a horse to go; the morpheme /m̃ʔm̃/ for negation; ʃˈüˈu· (whistled with these general tongue and lip positions) for surprise, etc.; /ˈgʲoʲnə/ (with short nondiphthongized [o]) 'going to' for facetious style (cf. p. 125); /m̃·ˈetə mʊnʊt/ 'wait a minute', with the /w/ pharyngealized and lengthened for lugubrious style; /Wʌˀt f/OR/ 'what for', whispered; ⫶kᵉⁱmf ifrf⫶ 'come here', with deliberate harshness from faucalization symbolized by superscript [f].

Possibly the over-differentiated phonemes treated under Procedure IV-E[1] could be handled as extrasystematic phonemes, also, since they both represent special social situations. If so, the added phoneme (the one differing from the phonetic norm of the phoneme spoken in normal style) would be enclosed in dotted diagonals. The over-differentiated ones differ from those of IV-H, however, in that they apply to word lists determined by traditional writing rather than being in special morphemes, or applied equally to all morphemes.

---

[1]Also special segments in foreign names; cf. footnote 2, p. 142.

ANALYTICAL PROCEDURE IV-I:

INTERPRETING PHONETIC SYLLABLES IN RELATION TO PHONEMIC SYLLABLES

In Chapter 4 (p. 65) we stated that phonetic syllables were sometimes not equivalent to phonemic syllables, since speakers of two different languages might, because of their disparate linguistic backgrounds, hear a different number of syllables in a specific utterance. We will now study various methods of identifying the pertinent structural units which it may be convenient to call phonemic syllables in particular languages.

Problem 161--Kalaba Dialect EH[1]

Phonetic Data (lowered dot indicates syllable division as it might seem to English ears):

[p'ai.]   'today' [pa.'i] 'tomorrow'

[pai.p'i.a] 'yester- [pia.pi.'a] 'sometimes'
             day'

[p'ai.pia] 'always'

Directions:

What is the basic structural unit which serves best as a point of reference for describing the distribution of phonemes in this language?

Solution to Problem 161:

A unit of potential stress placement--here equivalent to a single vowel with or without a preceding consonant.

Discussion of Problem 161:

The contrast of permitted stress in [a'i] versus ['ai] forces ['ai] to be analyzed as comprising two syllables. The reverse clusters [i'a] and ['ia] substantiate this conclusion. Therefore, it is convenient to emphasize the structural balance or parallel between ['ai] and [a.'i], in spite of the apparent difference in syllabification. (Speakers of English tend to hear this data with ['ai] constituting one syllable but [a.'i] two.)

Once he has reached this conclusion, the investigator may choose for his starting point in description one of three units which are equivalent to each other in this dialect: (1) a unit of potential stress placement, (2) a minimum unit of timing (i.e., a MORA, usually comprising a short vowel or half a long vowel), or (3) a minimum unit of vowel quality. If he so desires, he can then state

that he will call each vowel the nucleus of a phonemic syllable--in contrast to the phonetic syllables which he first recorded--and describe consonants in relation to them. Thus /p'ai/ 'today', and /pa'i/ 'tomorrow' each contain two phonemic syllables; the first syllable of each set begins with a (nonsyllabic, presyllabic) consonant; the first word is stressed on the first (phonemic) syllable, and the second word is stressed on the second (phonemic) syllable.

Problem 162--Kalaba Dialect EI[1]

Phonetic Data (1 indicates high tone spread over all vowels immediately preceding it; 2 indicates low tone similarly):

[pia^2.pi^1]   'gentleman'

[paoi^1.poa^1] 'woman'

[pa^2.pi$^{1-2}$] 'child'

[pi^2.pai^2]   'snob'

[pa$^{1-2}$.pia^2] 'man'

[pia^2.pi^2]   'baby'

Directions:

What is the basic structural unit which serves best as a point of reference for describing the distribution of phonemes in this language?

Solution to Problem 162:

The phonetic syllable, which is here equivalent to a phonemic syllable.

Discussion of Problem 162:

Permitted tone placement does not correspond to units of vowel length since one tone can be spread over one, two, or three vowels; nor does a single vowel correspond to either tone or phonetic-syllable length, since a single short vowel may have one or two tones, and from one to three rapid short vowels may constitute a single phonetic syllable (two or three vowels in sequence are pronounced with approximately the same timing as a single short vowel). Every phonetic syllable must have at least one tone occurring upon its nucleus.

Every phonetic syllable begins with a consonant and ends with a short vocalic nucleus comprised of from one to three vowels and containing from one to two superimposed

---

[1]For illustration of a language of this type, and its description, see John B. McIntosh, "Huichol Phonemes," _International Journal of American Linguistics_, XI (January, 1945), 32-5.

[1]For a language of this type--with, however, some initial nasals which constitute nonphonemic but phonetic syllables--see Kenneth L. Pike and Eunice V. Pike, "Immediate Constituents of Mazateco Syllables," in _International Journal of American Linguistics_, XIII (April, 1947), 78-91.

tones. The phonetic syllable proves the most convenient unit to serve as a point of reference for describing the distribution of phonemes in the language.

Problem 163--Kalaba Dialect EJ[1]

Phonetic Data: (['] indicates high tone; [ˇ] indicates low tone):

[tó.tò] 'tomato'   [tó.à] 'corn'

[tô·]   'potato'   [tā.ō] 'wheat'

[tō.tō] 'squash'   [tō·] 'bean'

Directions:

What is the basic structural unit which serves best as a point of reference for describing the distribution of phonemes in this language?

Solution to Problem 163:

A unit of tone placement, here equivalent to a single vowel mora, or a short vowel.

Discussion of Problem 163:

Speakers of English tend to hear [tōtō] 'squash' as two syllables, but [tō·]--with a long level nonrearticulated vowel as one. The diverse clusters [ao] and [oa] force [o·] to be interpreted phonemically as [oo]. The high-low tone pattern on [tó.tò] parallels that of [tô·], so that it likewise must be analyzed as containing a high and a low toneme.

The balance or parallel between [tó.tò], [tó.à], and [tō·] is structurally more important to this language than the difference of syllabication which may be heard by ears of speakers whose native language is English. The investigator does well, therefore, to describe distribution of consonants in relation to one of the following units which are equivalents in this dialect: (1) a unit of tone placement, or (2) a single minimum unit of vowel length, a mora. If he so chooses, he can then define a phonemic syllable for this language so that it will constitute a mora; in that case, the phonemic syllable and the phonetic syllable will not completely coincide.

A general principle may be observed in the discussion of the last two problems: The phonemic structure of a language can usually be described most readily if the investigator takes as his starting point the unit of permitted tone placement or permitted stress placement. The task is easiest when these units coincide with the nuclei of phonetic syllables; if the nuclei of phonetic syllables do not coincide with such units of tone or stress placement it is frequently helpful to postulate for descriptive purposes phonemic syllables which are structural units, related to phonetic syllables, but whose nuclei do so coincide.

Problem 164--Kalaba Dialect EK[1]

Phonetic Data (Numbers indicate contour tones):

[pa·²] 'sea'   [kaⁱl¹] 'sky'

[kⁱa²] 'land'   [poᵒ²] 'air'

[kⁱa¹] 'breeze'   [pʰat²] 'tornado'

Directions:

What is the basic structural unit which best serves as a point of reference for describing the distribution of phonemes in the language?

Solution to Problem 164:

The morpheme, here equivalent to the phonemic syllable and to a single unit of tone placement.

Discussion of Problem 164:

A unit of vowel length is not a convenient starting point for describing the distribution of phonemes in this language, since there is not a one-to-one correlation between them and either tone or syllables.

The status of the phonetic syllable here is not clearly indicated in the transcription; [kaⁱl¹] might represent one chest pulse or two. For this reason the phonetic syllable is inadequate for a descriptive reference point.

The unit of tone placement (a vowel, or vowels, plus adjacent presyllabic or postsyllabic consonants) is seen to occur in a one-to-one correlation with morphemes. Either the unit of tone placement, or the morpheme unit, then, might conveniently serve for a descriptive starting point. If, now, the phonemic syllable for the language is defined as constituting one group of sounds which serves as a single unit of tone placement--e.g., [kaⁱl¹] whether it is one or two phonetic syllables--then the phonemic syllable, also, can be conveniently utilized in descriptive statements.

---

[1]For a detailed description of a tone system of this type, see the discussion of Mixteco, in Kenneth L. Pike, Tone Languages, (Mimeographed edition; Glendale: Summer Institute of Linguistics 1943, 1945).

[1]In G. Edward Roffe, "The Phonemic Structure of Lao," one may see a language situation similar to that presented here. Journal of the American Oriental Society, LXVI (October-December, 1946).

In the present problem, then, the unit of tone placement coincides with a grammatical unit, the morpheme. In this case, the distributional description may be made in terms of the grammatical unit since in this way a single label--morpheme-- serves in both phonological and grammatical description, so that (1) needless duplication of terminology is avoided (the "phonemic syllable" does not then have to be postulated) and (2) some of the more important interrelationships between phonology and grammar may be immediately perceived by the reader. Since the ultimate goal of description should include a complete statement of the language as a whole, the foreshadowing of the grammar in the phonology is advantageous.[1]

With these things in mind, the student should first analyze the relationships of occurrence between phonemes of tone, stress, length, vowel quality, and the relationship between these and phonetic syllables, and morphemes, utterances, words, and/or other grammatical units. Second, he should determine the most suitable starting point for his description. Third, he should label the units in useful ways--for example, the phonemic syllable. Fourth, he should describe the distribution of the individual phonemes in relation to the larger units he has postulated (see Chapter 14). Fifth, he should choose a practical orthography for the system.

Problem 165--Kalaba Dialect EL

Phonetic Data:

[ŋdoto] 'house'   [psota] 'to run'

[psata] 'moon'   [dniti] 'knife'

[spoto] 'door'   [snito] 'river'

Directions:

Should the syllabic [ŋ] be treated as a full syllable within the structure of this language?

Solution to Problem 165:

Syllabic [ŋ] should not be treated as a separate syllable in this language, because the morpheme structure permits only two syllables each and this doubtful type does not act according to that pattern.

---

[1]This conclusion appears highly unacceptable to some contemporary phonemic investigators who attempt to keep phonemic and grammatical terminology rigorously separate. Note, for example, Charles F. Hockett, "A System of Descriptive Phonology," Language, XVIII (January, 1942), 38-41. To me it seems that the advantages which they claim to gain are not sufficient to warrant the loss of clarity in description of the total language. See below, Chapter 13, for grammatical prerequisites to phonemic analysis.

Discussion of Problem 165:

In some of the problems discussed under Procedure IV-B (pp. 131-8) there were some extra syllables phonetically, which were due to transition sounds. In Problem 165, extra syllables phonetically are again under observation, but this time are due to the fact that in certain sequences, continuants are more syllabic than stops. In [ŋdoto], therefore, the [ŋ] comes closer to being a syllabic peak than does the [d]. For this reason there is inevitably at least a weak phonetic syllable in [n], since the [d] separates it from the vowel [a]. Nevertheless, if one studies the nonsuspicious data, each morpheme in this language contains two and only two syllables. Therefore, the pressure exerted by this predominant pattern is for the light phonetic syllabicity of the [ŋ] to be considered nonpertinent, or else the pattern would be broken and a three-syllable morpheme result. In tone languages a doubtful point of this type may be frequently resolved in terms of permitted tonemes or tone placement. If, for example, [ŋdoto] has tonemes on each of the vowels and these tonemes may contrast with words which are identical except for the tonemes, but no such tonal contrasts occur on the nasals (e.g., if one does not find [ŋ́doto̅] in minimal contrast with [ŋ̀doto̅]), then one must conclude that the nasal, even though phonetically syllabic, is not structurally parallel to the vowels which do have contrastive pitch. In such a tone language it is convenient to state that every phonemic syllable must have one contrastive tone.

Three further illustrations will be given briefly:

In English, a phonemic syllable seems to be related to a unit of permitted stress placement. The /s/ of /ste/ 'stay' may be a phonetic syllable (see p. 65, footnote 4) but not a phonemic one.

In Sierra Popoluca, for example, the [n] following a vowel but with intervening glottal stop sounds to English ears quite syllabic, yet the structure of the language forces it to be considered as a normal nonsyllabic consonant.[1]

The most striking difference between phonetic and phonemic syllables which has come to my attention is contained in the Mixteco word [ŋdạ̄·] 'is going to go up'. The word constitutes two phonetic syllables, that is, two chest pulses. The first of these is the nasal [ŋ]; the second is [dạ̄·], with a long level vowel on a mid tone. The syllabic nasal cannot be considered a phonemic syllable, however, (1) since the [ŋ] carries no

---

[1]For a discussion of phonemic syllables in that language, see Ben Elson, "Sierra Popoluca Syllable Structure," International Journal of American Linguistics, XIII (January, 1947), 13-17.

contrastive pitch even though the language is tonal, and (2) since the [ŋ] must be analyzed as part of a complex phoneme /nd/ (since no analogous consonant clusters occur morpheme initial, and so on).

On the other hand, every morpheme in isolation which contains no suspicious elements has two phonetic syllables and two vowels, each with a tone, as in the word /tōtō/ 'rock'. Long vowels always have two units of tone and never occur as the first syllable of such a two-syllable unit. For these reasons, and others,[1] a long vowel must be considered structurally parallel to two short vowels and to two phonetic syllables. The [-ā·] is phonemically /-āā/, and each of the identical vowels constitutes the nucleus of a permitted unit of tone placement. If, now, a unit of tone placement in Mixteco is called a phonemic syllable, then /ⁿdāā/ contains two phonemic syllables, /ⁿdā-/ plus /-ā/. The word /ⁿdāā/ contains two phonetic syllables, [ŋ-] plus [-dā·], and two phonemic ones, /ⁿdā-/ plus /-ā/, with the borders between the syllable types not coinciding.

In general, the types of sequences which tend to constitute phonetic syllables but which in a particular language may or may not constitute phonemic syllables are usually those in which a continuant is separated from surrounding vowels by stops and/or word borders.

Finally, the student should observe that Procedure IV-I is designed more for preparing descriptions of the structure of material than it is for the finding of the phonemes themselves. The next procedure is somewhat similar to this one, but may be more important for solving some of the difficulties in locating the phonemes.

ANALYTICAL PROCEDURE IV-J:

INTERPRETING SEQUENCES AS CLOSE-KNIT
SYLLABLE NUCLEI

Problem 166--Kalaba Dialect EM

Phonetic Data:

[pos]	'tea'	[puʔs]	'sip'
[poʔs]	'leaf'	[moʔp]	'relax'
[sum]	'painting'	[pom]	'society'
[ʔom]	'scroll'	[som]	'sociable'

Directions:

How is the postvocalic [ʔ] related

in distribution to the vowel preceding it?

Solution to Problem 166:

Vowel plus /ʔ/ constitutes a close-knit nuclear sequence of two phonemes which acts as a unit in distribution.

Discussion of Problem 166:

Notice that [ʔ] in this problem is a consonant phoneme, appearing initially in words, as do other consonants. Notice further that every word begins with a consonant and ends with a consonant; in between these two consonants there may appear (1) a vowel, or (2) a vowel plus glottal stop. The glottal stop differs distributionally from all other consonants since no other consonant occurs in these environments.

Four interpretations of this data should be considered.

(1) That /ʔ/ is like any other consonant phoneme. We have already eliminated this possibility by showing that /ʔ/ differs from other consonant phonemes in distribution.

(2) That any vowel plus a following [ʔ] coalesce into a single phonetically complex phoneme (according to Procedure IV-B). This solution seems legitimate, though in such an analysis the sequence [ʔVʔ] must presumably also be considered a single phoneme. Yet the analysis of initial [ʔ-] remains awkward. This solution has the advantage of emphasizing the structural distributional unity of [Vʔ]; but the disadvantage of postulating additional phonemes (/oʔ/, /uʔ/) paralleling each vowel quality. More important, the solution does not set a precedent for an analysis which is the most helpful in certain other difficult problems (e.g., for English diphthongs, to be discussed presently).

(3) That [ʔ] constitutes a suprasegmental phoneme. This would have the advantage of accounting for all the data (provided word-initial glottal stop were analyzed as a nonsignificant method of beginning a vowel, which is awkward in the face of clear CVC pattern), and of adding only one symbol superimposed on the pertinent vowels, e.g., /ŏ/, /ŭ/. As disadvantages we note the fact that [ʔ] as a suprasegmental phoneme does not readily fit the premise that suprasegmental phonemes are all quantitative (although it could be argued that [ʔ] is quantitatively zero); word-initial glottal stop remains awkward to describe (but could be discounted, as for [2]); such a questionable analysis is unnecessary, since [ʔ] can be described merely as a regular consonant with special distribution; but, most important, this analysis (like [2]) fails to set a precedent which is as useful elsewhere as is (4).

(4) That the vowel and glottal stop in the sequence /Vʔ/ are each separate, legitimate phonemes, but that they are joined together in a special type of close-knit

---

[1]Based on rules for the substitution of tonemes in the grammar and in tonal sandhi, and so forth. For more detailed evidence, see Kenneth L. Pike, Tone Languages (Mimeographed edition; Glendale: Summer Institute of Linguistics, 1943, 1945).

sequence which as a unit acts in further distribution like a single vowel. This has the advantages (a) of accounting for all phonetic and distributional data; (b) of allowing the [ʔ-] to be analyzed as a regular initial consonant; (c) of allowing a simple symbolization of the data; (d) of postulating no new or strange phonemes; (e) of leaving premises concerning suprasegmental phonemes undisturbed; (f) of providing for simple statements concerning morpheme structure (morphemes = CNC, in which N = nucleus, composed of V or Vʔ); (g) of leading to a premise which proves helpful in other instances where analysis is difficult.

The NUCLEUS of a syllable is the prominent part of a syllable, or the part which (1) is the domain of phonemic pitch or stress, or (2) is the inner structural part of the syllable distinct in distributional characteristics from the MARGINAL elements, the consonants, which precede and/or follow it.

A syllable may have a CLOSE-KNIT nucleus composed of two vocoids, or of a vocoid plus a nonvocoid, which acts in distribution (in the syllable) like a single simple nuclear phoneme. In the problem just discussed, /Vʔ/ constitutes a close-knit nucleus.

For the purposes of a practical orthography it would be unnecessary to symbolize the nuclear tie between /V/ and /ʔ/ in this particular problem. For technical purposes the unity could be shown by one of several devices--e.g., by a ligature (/V͡ʔ/), the raising of the second element (/Vʔ/), or by some bracketing device (/poʔs/), provided these symbols are so designed that the reader does not confuse them with similar symbolization of phonetically complex but unitary phonemes.

In Totonaco[1] the glottal stop should be in a close nuclear tie with the vowel which it precedes, for the following reasons: (1) The glottal stop occurs much more frequently than any other consonant--in fact, following the vowels of about 40 percent of the syllables. (2) If considered a part of regular consonant clusters, the number of clusters would be doubled. (3) The distribution of most of the voiceless stops, nasals, and semivowels would then appear highly strange, since they occur finally in words

singly, only, or following /ʔ/--that is to say, following syllable nuclei of any type, whether simple ones or the close-knit sequences with /Vʔ/. (4) Loans from Spanish are often adopted with /Vʔ/ substituted for the Spanish vowel. This is most easily explained as a nuclear modification (paralleling the lengthening of some vowels in loans--which is also nuclear); other types of additions to loans are rare. (5) In various places in the grammar, the appearance of certain alternate forms of morphemes is determined by the ending of the word preceding them. If the first word terminates in a vowel, one form is used for the second word. If the first ends in a consonant, a different form of the second word is found. The sequence /Vʔ/ (or /V·ʔ/) acts like /V/ (or /V·/) in such cases rather than like /VC/. Note, for example, that /-niʔ/ loses its nucleus when it comes directly after syllable nuclei of types /V/ and /Vʔ/, but not after a regular consonant: /ška/ + /niʔ/ > /škan/ 'it hit you'; likewise /či·ʔ/ + /niʔ/ > /či·ʔn/ 'he tied it'; but contrast /nik/ + /niʔ/ > /nikniʔ/ 'he hit you'.[1] All of these facts taken together show that the [ʔ] is more closely united to the vowel which it follows than it is to the consonant which it precedes. Distribution of other consonants is best handled in terms of margins clustered about nuclei of types /V/ and /Vʔ/.

In some languages it proves convenient to make a description in terms of close-knit syllable nuclei, even though the glottal stop is not part of those nuclei. It is evident, then, that the postulation of close-knit nuclei can be utilized for the two types of languages (those with glottal stop intimately linked to the vowel, and those with other consonants or vowels intimately linked to the main vowel), whereas the postulation of glottal stop as a prosodic phoneme would be useful in only one of these instances. It is partly for this reason, then, that we have chosen to make descriptions in terms of close-knit nuclei.

In Mazateco, for example, close-knit nuclei include one, two, or three vowels, with one, two, or three tonemes; two tonemes may be found on one vowel, or on two; one toneme may be distributed over one vowel, or two, or three, and so on. For this language the premise about close-knit nuclei is helpful for descriptive purposes--whereas a theory of glottal stop as a suprasegmental phoneme would not be applicable.

In Mazateco, suborganization and special distributional characteristics can be detected not only in close-knit nuclei, but also within the syllable margins. The data,[2] however, need not be given here.

---

[1]See Herman P. Aschmann, "Totonaco Phonemes," in International Journal of American Linguistics, XII (January, 1946), 34-43 (especially 41-42). I am using Aschmann's data, which I have checked with his informant. He, however, interprets [Vʔ] as a single laryngealized vowel phoneme; whereas I interpret the [Vʔ] as a vowel phoneme followed by a glottal stop phoneme in a close nuclear tie with it--mentioned but not discussed in his argument.

[1]Aschmann gives other evidences (p. 42) which I shall not summarize.

[2]For the details, see Kenneth L. Pike and Eunice V. Pike, "Immediate Constituents

In English the sequence [aɪ] (or [ɑi]) in buy seems to be a sequence of two phonemes because of the contrasts with [aʊ] of bough and [ɑ] of pa. Yet the sequence [aɪ] seems to have a unity in distribution somewhat parallel to [ɛ], as in [bɛt] bet and [baɪt] bite, but lacks the parallel of [baɪ] buy to *[bɛ], which does not occur. The English sequence [aɪ], then, contains unity in diversity,[1] in some respects it acts as two units, and in other respects as one. It functions as two units because it is a sequence of two phonemes; it functions, in part, as a single unit in distribution because it constitutes a close-knit nucleus.

The close-knit nucleus may carry only one stress--which further emphasizes its unity; this stress falls most strongly on the first element of the sequence (as ['ɑi]).

The symbolization of the English close-knit sequence can be given in several ways. Note the following one: /'baɪt/ bite. In this volume, however, it has been indicated by raising the second element above the line, as /'baᶦt/ (see p. 45).

Before giving exercises in the form of problems for the student to solve, we return again to the difficulty which he must face in interpreting data if each of two solutions for a particular problem seems to be legitimate.

In general, when two alternate analyses of data are possible, the best analysis is the most CONVENIENT one. Convenience may be caused by technical or practical considerations. It may consist of neatness of analytical statement, or the practical results, such as the provision of a practical alphabet for natives to use. Thus, the SIMPLEST analysis may be considered to be the best one. Judgment here may be based upon simplicity of descriptive statement, or simplicity of symbolization, or simplicity of some other type. However, there must be two cautions applied: (1) No analysis may be considered correct if it gains simplicity by repressing data, or by failing to explain or classify some of the data. (2) Simplicity is not to be interpreted as a mere matter of fewer symbols. Simplicity of description applies rather to the simplest but most adequate statement of the structure of the language as it functions--not a system of symbols as such.

---

of Mazateco Syllables," _International Journal of American Linguistics_, XIII, (April, 1947), 78-91.

[1]This seems to be one of the sources of differences in the analysis of English vowels. For the one utilized here, see Kenneth L. Pike, "On the Phonemic Status of English Diphthongs," _Language_, XXIII (April-June, 1947), 151-59.

Problem 167--Kalaba Dialect EN

Phonetic Data:

[naʔas] 'turkey'	[mʌpits] 'tiger'
[tsukam] 'basket'	[kaʔup] 'calf'
[zitaŋ] 'to whinny'	[tutsak] 'eyelash'
[ŋaʔas] 'to cough'	[kaʔʌs] 'to throw'
[ʔazis] 'cockroach'	[zʌpit] or [zʌpid] 'roof'
[paʔut] or [paʔud] 'buzzard'	

Directions:

What is the analysis of [ts]? Of [d]?

Problem 168--Kalaba Dialect EO

Phonetic Data:

[motek] 'grass'	[kapax] 'angry'
[taias] 'idol'	[pasek] 'cheese'
[xonap] 'whip'	[kanam] 'other'
[waxau] 'to sneeze'	[nayau] 'to lend'
[patet] 'to want'	[koiou] 'to show'
[sekai] 'hard'	[saman] 'from'
[yeman] 'rain'	[xewoi] 'manly'
[yoiai] 'to sift'	

Directions:

Is the final phoneme in the word 'to sneeze' a consonant or a vowel? Explain.

Problem 169--Kalaba Dialect EP

Phonetic Data:

[toza·k] 'boat'	[kaneoz] 'child'
[lesaep] 'chance'	[zusoun] 'whoever'
[kinis] 'to die'	[sune·l] 'neck'
[tosa·k] 'rid'	[nozo·k] 'boiling'
[papeat] 'meat'	[kakuas] 'he is'
[natup] 'pencil'	[lali·n] 'dew'
[penu·s] 'world'	[sapiak] 'green'
[ziliat] 'water'	

Directions:

Is the long vowel [a·] a single phoneme or a sequence of two vowel phonemes? Explain.

Problem 170--Kalaba Dialect EQ

Phonetic Data:

[kusu]	'then'	[tšuki]	'cheek'
[faŋi]	'cloud'	[tšatsi]	'uvula'
[fani]	'that one'	[ŋata]	'cross'
[tsupa]	'seed'	[sana]	'female'
[ŋatša]	'woman'	[kunu]	'trouble'
[tusu]	'squash'	[tsatšu]	'earring'
[tsitsi]	'mouth'	[nisa]	'beef'
[kafi]	'under'	[putsi]	'shoe'
[nutsi]	'hairy'	[tisa]	'short'

Directions:

What is the predominant type of sequence which allows one to interpret phonemically [ts] as /ø/?

Problem 171--Kalaba Dialect ER

Phonetic Data:

[sakhif]	'aunt'	[piwau]	'floor'
[tunui]	'wolf'	[nathin]	'heat'
[fapas]	'vein'	[khanus]	'chief'
[thuwaph]	'ink'	[phakhath]	'cousin'
[kanak]	'moon'	[wanai]	'flaming'
[thunuu]	'thin'	[faphis]	'thirsty'
[khuyau]	'vertically'	[sisaf]	'belief'
[fuphuth]	'paint'	[nikukh]	'spark'
[phisau]	'black'	[pakhii]	'boulder'

Directions:

Are aspirated stops single phonemes or clusters of two phonemes? What evidence gives you your conclusion? Rewrite phonemically the word for 'boulder'.

Problem 172--Kalaba Dialect ES

Phonetic Data:

[tsaŋi]	'to hit'	[fafi]	'to turn'
[peŋo]	'to see'	[spoia]	'to unroll'
[tšufa]	'to heat'	[nuŋe]	'to reap'
[kiŋo]	'to believe'	[kseue]	'to skin'
[tasa]	'to ask'	[šuša]	'to keep'
[nute]	'to wish'	[pseko]	'to save'

[špafi]	'to doubt'	[stifa]	'to fight'
[suša]	'to halve'	[tsoŋe]	'to be quiet'
[šiŋa]	'to stare'	[stifa]	'to be well'
[wusa]	'to change'	[tšofa]	'to untie'
[kšopo]	'to walk'	[yašu]	'to yellow'
[pšake]	'to get dark'	[skaŋa]	'to sneeze'

Directions:

Is [ts] one phoneme or two? What evidences can you adduce for your conclusion?

Problem 173--Kalaba Dialect ET

Phonetic Data:

[ketkebəd]	'table'	[soggeit]	'to turn'
[tasoiz]	'to enter'	[dasagz]	'thunder'
[yunodz]	'heart'	[yonzist]	'hard'
[nodəbeit]	'knife'	[pakseup]	'to sit'
[wabəgind]	'every'	[kitnauz]	'to eat
[paktiud]	'beside'	[tosoib]	'to try'
[kebbait]	'paper'	[daktogəd]	'lightning'
[yigəbask]	'liver'	[nidəgain]	'chance'
[gebbaut]	'to leave'	[bugədekp]	'hurricane'
[weddoiz]	'tent'	[baktaŋg]	'to see'

Directions:

Write the first and second words phonemically. Explain any changes made.

Problem 174--Kalaba Dialect EU

Phonetic Data:

[tak·uur]	'rainy'	[nuuptip]	'skirt'
[riftą]	'sticky'	[siksap]	'to paint'
[saapniif]	'to taste'	[niiŋgus]	'to enjoy'
[nuptąą]	'daughter'	[sapnų]	'fork'
[puus·ik]	'forward'	[tirfaap]	'parallel'
[runbųų]	'almost'	[kaanzį]	'to will'
[kaan·at]	'well'	[piinduk]	'opened'
[raf·ų]	'healthy'	[siiksuur]	'strange'
[far·at]	'feather'	[nastįį]	'to cause'
[kunvaak]	'punishment'	[put·į]	'boiling'
[nuptą]	'loud'		

Directions:

Same as for Problem 173.

Problem 175--Kalaba Dialect EV

Phonetic Data:

[koo.fei] 'snake'   [to.seek] 'to laugh'

[se.naal] 'boulder'   [wa.waau] 'cat'

[na.rok] 'shoe'   [ke.rai] 'to walk'

[yo.taau] 'thin'   [pa.yeu] 'ring'

[paa.yeel] 'round'   [roo.faai] 'second'

[ree.wau] 'water'   [fa.sek] 'to cook'

[noo.pef] 'to get'   [nee.soi] 'to seem'

[ra.roou] 'male'   [te.tep] 'loose'

[fu.wuuu] 'bird'

Directions:

Write phonemically the word for 'bird'. Explain at least three problems involved.

Problem 176--Kalaba Dialect EW

Phonetic Data:

[tšą̄nǫu] 'beard'   [stšǫskǫu] 'to squabble'

[stęrą] 'wooden'   [skęrʌ] 'to be frightened'

[stšʌnęi] 'bridge'   [nr̨ęi] 'hip'

[tęręi] 'patella'   [tšrʌstšą̄] 'to gyp'

[sʌdžǫu] 'to fish'   [nǫgą] 'wheel-barrow'

[stǫrą] 'storm'   [kąksą] 'wildcat'

[sʌtą] 'hidden'   [skęnęi] 'picturesque'

[tšʌdʌ] 'first'   [kątšą] 'to seize'

[stąstǫu] 'marketplace' [tšątšǫ skr̨ęi] 'long beard'

Directions:

Write phonemically the words for 'to fish' and 'hip'. Explain.

Problem 177--Kalaba Dialect EX

Phonetic Data:

[masąŋk] 'to capsize'   [napas] 'to stay'

[pindamp] 'pants'   [tumbam] 'drum'

[katšup] 'tomato'   [ŋgasin] 'root'

[ndiŋgas] 'to curse'   [patšup] 'to mend'

[mbaputš] 'hound'   [nindžak] 'to ride'

[tšakik] 'big toe'   [ndžupit] 'to spit'

[nanan] 'to deny'   [ndžisup] 'food'

[mbapint] 'to drink'   [sutaŋk] 'container'

[sakantš] 'to punch'   [tšimatš] 'expensive'

[ndapuntš pasik] 'to climb a mountain'

[pindant panaŋk] 'to sell oranges'

Directions:

Write phonemically the utterances 'to ride', 'to climb a mountain' and 'to sell oranges'. Explain any deviations from phonetic writing.

Problem 178--Kalaba Dialect EY

Phonetic Data:

[kolo] 'poultry'   [lawi] 'churned'

[pali] 'tree'   [yoʔya] 'tent'

[naŋo] 'country'   [pini] 'pig'

[ʔwana] 'wavy'   [ʔyoma] 'mountain'

[saʔa] 'to make'   [ʔomi] 'to sleep'

[laʔwi] 'mask'   [ʔwoʔya] 'cabbage'

[wuki] 'turning'   [saka] 'to fall'

[niʔwa] 'bed'   [tawo] 'elbow'

[niʔyo] 'to love'   [ʔawa] 'water'

Directions:

Write phonemically the word for 'tent' and 'to make'. Explain.

Problem 179--Kalaba Dialect EZ

Phonetic Data:

[phuga] 'flea'   [khadzi] 'witch'

[tsali] 'doll'   [hpusu] 'to send'

[kasi] 'almost'   [tshabi] 'difficult'

[tumu] 'load'   [htina] 'aged'

[pina] 'apple'   [lasu] 'male'

[thadu] 'to soak'   [kaga] 'liver'

[thadza] 'ink'   [hkuma] 'arm'

[kini] 'to see'   [taga] 'day'

[suba] 'to enter' [tshuna] 'always'

Directions:

Write phonemically the words for 'witch' and 'difficult'. Explain.

Problem 180--Kalaba Dialect FA

Phonetic Data:

[maA] 'lamb'   [dabp] 'girl'

[bagk] 'man'   [gadt] 'fly'

[mazs] 'horse'   [mal] 'gnat'

[rar] 'dragon'   [zamM] 'river'

[baA] 'to sneeze'   [bar] 'soap'

Directions:

What are the submembers of the phoname /d/? Rewrite the first three words phonemically.

Problem 181--Kalaba Dialect FB

Phonetic Data:

[ipˀˀakwa] 'sea'   [akˀˀuˀu] 'toward'

[apaˀu]   'dove'   [akitša] 'speckled'

[ukwani]   'eyelid'   [aˀnasu] 'nervous'

[iˀiša]   'to cheat'   [astšuka] 'skirt'

[iˀiša]   'knuckle'   [akwitša] 'to be
                                     crazy'

[atakwi]   'space'   [ifˀˀusa] 'to sing'

[aˀšuku]   'clove'   [ufušu]   'to stab'

[atšˀˀafa] 'oyster'   [akwˀˀuki]'servant'

[usaˀi]   'toenail'   [aˀmafi] 'fifteen'

[atšuki]   'egg-   [uˀtimi] 'to sweep'
           shaped'

[utˀima]   'flat'   [amatši] 'to be hot'

[išˀˀumu] 'termite'   [iˀkwuša] 'lumpy'

[isˀˀufi] 'to scream'   [iˀtšatši]'shadow'

[inata]   'thumb'   [uspufu] 'to handle'

[aˀkaˀa]   'flame'   [aftšikwi]'garbage'

[iˀsami]   'to hunt'   [uskwanu] 'mud'

[afpana]   'fisherman'   [uˀfukwi] 'ball'

[uˀpama]   'torch'   [astatši] 'marshy'

Directions:

Write phonemically the words for

'sea', 'shadow', 'termite'. Explain

Problem 182--Restricted Shipibo[1] A

Phonetic Data:[2]

[mwɨru] 'castor oil'   [paka] 'fish'

[vwɨru] 'eye'   [kapwɨ] 'alligator'

[pwɨru] 'name'   [yamwɨ] 'night'

[makɨ] 'piranha'   [yuvwɨ] 'wizard'

[vakɨ] 'child'   [muru] 'bead'

[vuna] 'ant'   [ruvu] 'monkeys'

[yapa] 'wood'   [tapu] 'shelf'

[vwɨkɨ] 'he brought'   [numa] 'dove'

Directions:

Write phonemically the word for 'wizard'. Explain.

Problem 183--Kalaba Dialect FC

Phonetic Data:

['Wawa] 'one'   ['bɨWu] 'seven'

['bɨwu] 'two'   ['řapɨ] 'eight'

['Wupɨ] 'three'   ['pɨwa] 'nine'

['wuWu] 'four'   ['wařɨ] 'ten'

['pɨbɨ] 'five'   ['pɨWu] 'fifteen'

['wuwa] 'six'   ['wařu] 'twenty'

Directions:

Explain the reasons for the following phonemic writing: /Wawa/ 'one', /wɨwu/ 'two', /WuWɨ/ 'three'.

Problem 184--Kalaba Dialect FD

Phonetic Data:

[mǫivf] 'white'   [kǫnN] 'paper'

[zǫt]   'loud'   [vǫik] 'soap'

[pętš] 'to under-   [tęmM] 'son-in-law'
        stand'

[tšęzs] 'to reward'   [mįt]   'to see'

[kąup] 'to drink'   [nąup] 'chile'

[mǫmM] 'to weigh'   [zętš] 'vertically'

---

[1]Data from James Lauriault, South America Indian Mission.

[2]Tone is omitted as not pertinent to the problem.

[mẹp]   'moon'   [tšǫizs] 'black'

[nẹzs]   'mountain' [pạt]   'papaya'

[vạivf]   'brush'   [tǫk]   'wild'

[mụp]   'to know'   [zạik]   'to squeeze'

[tšẹnN]   'chin'   [nạzs]   'floor'

Directions:

Write phonemically with technical symbols the words 'white' and 'chin'. Explain.

Problem 185--Restricted Oaxacan Chontal[1] C

Phonetic Data:

[faḍui]   'he sows'   [maiyui] 'he is going away'

[šoxta]   'I'm tired'   [moipa]   'late'

[šoxtoʔ]   'are you tired?'   [fiškui] 'he squeezes it'

[fonsal]   'fly'   [tišmu]   'shrimp'

[paʔta]   'he will come'   [kandui] 'he leaves it'

[xoipa]   'nowʔ'   [maxpa]   'it cooked'

[malpaʔ]   'they went away'   [laxaʔ]   'the water'

Directions:

Write phonemically the word 'he is going away'. Explain.

Problem 186--Restricted Bolivian Quechua[2] A

Phonetic Data:

[ḳolḳai]   'silver'   [kʔasa]   'a hole'

[wisa]   'stomach'   [kʔaitu] 'string'

[kantšis] 'seven'   [ḳasi]   'in vain'

[thuta]   'old rag'   [lixřas] 'wings'

[řumi]   'stove'   [pansa]   'stomach'

[wařmi]   'woman'   [halʸpʔa] 'land'

Directions:

Write phonemically the words for 'seven', 'old rag', 'string', 'land'. Explain.

[1] Data from May Morrison, Summer Institute of Linguistics.

[2] Data from author's field notes, 1943.

Problem 187--Restricted Huichol[1] A

Phonetic Data:[2]

[karu]   'banana'   [takita]   'in our house

[kyɛta]   'foot'   [nɛkyɛmaɣi] 'my father'

[kiriwa]   'basket'   [ʔikḭ]   'this'

[kḭmḭ]   'come on'   [kakai]   'huaraches'

[ʔileu]   'corn'   [ʔaki]   'your house'

[kyɛpɛtitɛwa] 'what is your name?'

Directions:

Is the sequence [ky] one phoneme or two? Why?

Problem 188--Restricted Aymara[3] A

Phonetic Data:

[pata]   'a high plain' [lakʔo] 'warm'

[xaksu]   'to vomit'   [phutša] 'daughter'

[laka]   'mouth'   [tʔantʔa] 'bread'

[lʸulʸu]   'green, unripe'   [tšoxlʸo] 'dried corn on the cob'

[phutšʔu] 'a well'   [kʔulkʔu] 'narrow'

[kʔaxa]   'whooping cough'   [tšixma] 'the head of'

Directions:

Write phonemically the words 'dried corn on the cob', 'a well'.

Problem 189--Restricted Oaxacan Chontal[4] D

Phonetic Data:

[a.sans]   'person'   [iš.ʔaiʔ] 'edge'

[fʔans]   'palpitate' [i.maŋkʔ] 'you (pl.)'

[nu.šans] 'twenty'   [xoŋkʔ]   'light weight'

[i.yaŋkʔ] 'we'   [lo.ʔaiʔ] 'your teeth'

[1] Data from John McIntosh, Summer Institute of Linguistics.

[2] Stress is omitted as not pertinent to the problem.

[3] Data from author's field notes, 1943.

[4] Data from May Morrison, Summer Institute of Linguistics.

[xai⌐]   'friend'   [a.xiŋkⁿ] 'hiccough'

[pamfⁿ]   'short'

Directions:

  Write phonemically the words 'pal-pitate', 'hiccough'.

   Problem 190--Restricted Aztec[1] B

Phonetic Data:

[ko.yutł]   'coyote'   [tłíł.tɩk] 'black'

[i.tu.nał] 'his   [tłɔ.katł] 'man'
     shadow'

[ku.lutł] 'scorpion'   [tłi.ka]   'why'

[tłak.pak] 'up'   [sa.katł] 'grass'

 [we.lɩ.tɩ.lɩs.tłɩ] 'freedom'

 [ye.ka.tsoł.tłɩ]   'nose'

 [no.ne.ne.pɩł]   'my tongue'

 [pɩł.tsin.tłɩ]   'baby'

 [la.le.bɩsˌ]   'very'

 [po.po.sok.tłɩ]   'lung'

 [ɩł.fɩtł]   'feast'

 [nah.koł.wa]   'my shoulders'

Directions:

  Write phonemically the words for 'black', 'coyote'.

  Problem 191--Restricted Oaxacan Chontal[2] E

Phonetic Data:

[panta] 'bag'   [ai̯wala]   'horse'

[šai̯mu] 'spearmint'   [miyu̯iyaⁿ] 'I say'

[um·a]   'firefly'   [šimpa]   'he saw'

[sañyuⁿ] 'people'   [san·a]   'imitation
            star'

[awa·ta] 'girl'   [aspala]   'alligator'

[pɛnla] 'nine'   [iŋkoⁿ]   'who knows'

[ⁿɾiya] 'there is'   [ⁿɛ·x]   'wood'

[ku·šax] 'needle'   [paŋxa·]   'slowly'

[mo̯igi]   'tomorrow' [iŋkoxmaⁿ] 'yet

[po·sopa] 'he bathed'[kušax]   'bitter'

[pagimbamaⁿ]   [awixi·]   'sleepy'
    'marigold'

[ma̯iyu̯i] 'he goes'   [on·ɛ]   'meal'

[kuš]   'curly'   [fuŋgu̯i]   'he gets fat'

[iŋxa]   'wild boar'[pi·xpa]   'he mashed
              it'

Directions:

  Rewrite phonemically words 'firefly', 'marigold', 'horse', 'wood', 'who knows', 'slowly'. Explain briefly the problems encountered.

  Problem 192--Restricted Lenzburg German[1] A

Phonetic Data:

[ḻi·m]   'glue'   [ʌḻi·də] 'to suffer'

[ḻaxə]   'to laugh'   [ḻawp]   'foliage'

[ⁿi·ḻ]   'rush,   [ḻa·p]   'rennet'
    hurry'

[ḻiəxt] 'light'   [ⁿa·lə] 'awl'

[baḻt]   'soon'   [tsi·ḻə]'to take aim'

[ⁿa·ḻpə]'alps'   [saḻbi] 'salve'

[hæiḻə] 'to heal'

Directions:

  Is vowel length phonemic? Give evidence to support your conclusion.

  Rewrite phonemically the words for 'to suffer', 'foliage', 'to take aim'.

  State the conditions under which [l] and [ḻ] occur. Choose a symbol for use in a practical orthography.

  Problem 193--Restricted Tabascan Chontal[2] B

Phonetic Data:

[taneth] 'hello'   [teřom] 'sterile'

[semeth] 'griddle'   [telom] 'maiden'

[benoŋ] 'give me'   [nath] 'far'

[aŋkře] 'run'   [pam]   'head'

[taŋ]   'lime'   [pataŋ] 'work'

---

  [1]Data from Richard Pittman, Summer Institute of Linguistics.

  [2]Data from Viola Waterhouse and May Morrison, Summer Institute of Linguistics.

  [1]High German, dialect of Lenzburg, Switzerland. Data from Dr. Fritz Frauchiger.

  [2]Data from Kathryn Keller, Summer Institute of Linguistics.

[paph] 'father'   [beth] 'debt'

[kokh] 'my foot'   [bakh] 'bone'

[řahleve] 'noise of spanking'

Directions:

    Rewrite phonemically the words for 'hello' and 'work'.

Problem 194--Restricted Chol[1] A

Phonetic Data:

[tyhan]	'lime'	[mis]	'cat'
[bɛkˀ]	'spill'	[tyˀan]	'word'
[khukhu]	'go'	[huˀbɛn]	'get down'
[phɛkˀ]	'short'	[haph]	'drink'
[huhpˀɛn]	'fat'	[biˀbiˀ]	'dirty'
[pˀɛhtyh]	'pot'	[phusikˀal]	'heart'
[bih]	'road'	[bakh]	'bone'

Directions:

    What lack of symmetry is seen on a phonetic chart of the stops?[2]

    Rewrite phonemically the words for 'lime', 'short', 'pot', 'drink'.

Problem 195--Kalaba Dialect FC

Phonetic Data:

[mǫf]	'fireplace'	[sǫm]	'chimney'
[Aą̈p]	'lamp'	[pą̈ü]	'candle'
[lǫO]	'log'	[üą̈A]	'coals'
[Oǫs]	'ashes'		

Directions:

    Write phonemically the words for 'candle' and 'log'. Explain.

Problem 196--Kalaba Dialect FD

Phonetic Data:

[kxo]	'bridge'	[so]	'water'
[pAa]	'river'	[ma]	'bubble'
[kxa]	'creek'	[la]	'stone'
[pOo]	'rapids'		

---

[1] Data from Evelyn Aulie, Summer Institute of Linguistics.

[2] The data represent the field situation. This lack of symmetry is actually present in words of native origin.

Directions:

    Rewrite phonemically the words for 'bridge' and 'river'. Explain.

Problem 197--Kalaba Dialect FE

Phonetic Data:

[bˤokp]	'brush'	[tiəꬶ]	'forest'
[mõˀ]	'pigmy'	[sam]	'elephant'
[ꞣpat]	'lion'	[tiꞣ]	'water hole'
[ꞣos]	'roars'	[kobˤ]	'screech'
[pãˀ]	'gulp'	[ˀit]	'arrow'
[ˀop]	'death'		

Directions:

    Rewrite the data phonemically.

Problem 198--Kalaba Dialect FF

Phonetic Data:

[sol]	'fan'	[bą]	'fire'
[rob]	'hot'	[tg̑s]	'sparks'
[lot]	'burn'	[sal]	'scorch'
[sg̑b]	'sizzle'		

Directions:

    Rewrite the data phonemically. Explain.

Problem 199--Kalaba Dialect FG

Phonetic Data:

[pot]	'tree'	[top]	'sing'
[kot]	'man'	[tot]	'leaf'
[kap]	'to run'	[xxxpˤ]	'putrid'

Directions:

    Describe the system of sounds in this language.

Problem 200--Kalaba Dialect FH

Phonetic Data:

[tòmò]	'near'	[tómò]	'home'
[ńká]	'far'	[ǹká]	'sent'

Directions:

    What would be the unit which would serve as a basis for defining phonemic syllables in this language?

Problem 201--Sapir's Language[1] A

Phonetic Data:

['pakuy]   'horse'   ['kayæ]   'cylindrical'

['pa·kuy]   'tent'   ['xayæ·]   'to call'

[pʰa·ke]   'hoe'   [ʔaŋ'ko]   'water'

[yæzi'fo]   'he turns'   ['mu·xitʰ] 'cousin'

[yæ'sifo]   'white'   [ʔu'hat]   'meat'

['yæsifo]   'chief'   ['laʔi·n]   'woman'

['kʰawɔ]   'he runs'   ['tupe]   'chicken'

['kawɔ·]   'sleeping'   ['kawɔ·]   'leg'

   ['laʔi·ŋ 'kawɔ·] 'the woman is sleeping'

   ['θubi 'wɔza 'mo·] 'once upon a time'

   ['paguy 'kʰawɔ] 'the horse runs'

   ['paguy 'kawe] 'the warriors were asleep'

   ['utʰaw 'kawe·] 'the men are sleeping'

   [ʔu'had a'ʔaye·] 'they wanted the meat'

   [ʔu'had a'ʔaye·] 'they wanted the beans'

   ['wɔgi 'æfu·lo] 'the charred tree stump'

   ['tubi 'kawɔ·] 'the chicken is asleep'

   ['yæsivu 'kʰawɔ] 'the chief runs'

   ['yæsibu 'kʰawɔ] 'the elk runs'

   ['ma·ɨi 'lusi·ʔ] 'I killed the bear'

   ['ma·θi ælu'xo] 'the large bear'

Directions:

      Rewrite the data phonemically.

      Problem 202--Sapir's Language[1] B

Phonetic Data:

['hoo.sekh] 'she is   ['nææ.om] 'smoke'
              tired'

['hɔɔ.sex] 'bear'   ['ŋææ.om] 'working'

['nɔɔ.zex] 'onion'   [ʤw.'ath] 'horse'

[bo.'gif] 'to   ['ʔeg.nɔkh]'bloody'
            answer'

──────────────────
   [1]Linguistic forms constructed for this volume by Donald Stark, of the Summer Institute of Linguistics, from data suggested in Edward Sapir, "Sound Patterns of Speech," Language, I (June, 1925), 37-51.

[po.'gin]   'dish'   ['voo.eθ]   'man'

['gaa.yph] 'round'   [ʔum.'bif] 'four'

['gaa.na]   'tarantula' ['ʔeŋ.go]   'fire'

['ʔal.ba]   'white'   [hil.'duu] 'cloudy'

[ʔal.'baa] 'knife'   ['taa.ha]   'square'

['ʔæl.bas] 'radish'   ['daa.os]   'water'

['duu.e]   'two'   ['kaa.ŋoph] 'acrid'

['ʔel.bas] 'three'   ['haa]   'you'

['ʔiŋ.gɔ]   'even though'[po.'gin]   'I wash'

   [mæk.'soth. 'al.ba] 'white stones'

   [ˌzɔl.gi. um.'bif] 'four houses'

   ['daa.oz. ɔ.'keθ] 'she carries water'

   ['hɔɔ.zeg. 'duu.e] 'two onions'

   ['voo.eʤ. 'ŋææ.om] 'the man is working'

   [ʤw.'ath. um.'biv. am] 'his four horses'

   [po.'gil. 'gaa.yph] 'round dish'

Directions:

      Rewrite the data phonemically.

      Problem 203--Phonemic Quiz Type[1] A

Phonetic Data:

['kí.mʉ̀g] 'cute'   ['sɔ̄.rɛ̂b] 'junebug'

[šɔ̄.'láž] 'shoestring' [Mmã.'kʉ̀d] 'hypo-
                                     crisy'

['rɛ́.pðg] 'sack'   ['plɛ̂.kóu] 'guess'

[Mã.'kʉ̀n] 'irrelevant' ['rū.θɔ̄r]   'to ex-
                                     pect'

['swɔ̄.kʉ̀b] 'skeleton' ['θɛ́.sðd]   'to drip'

['lí.nʉ̄m] 'upstart'   [Nnɛ̄.'séb] 'gossip'

['šɛ́l.rǐg] 'putrid'   ['θɛ́.sɔ́l]   'relief'

[šɔ̄.'ráz] 'colossal'   ['lí.nʉ́m]   'finished'

Directions:[1]

      Write yes or no before each statement from 1-8. Fill in blank in 9.

   ____ 1. Tone is phonemic.

   ____ 2. There are three phonemic tone levels.

──────────────────
   [1]Note to the teacher: This type of problem was developed by Evelyn G. Pike for quick quizzes in the classroom; they prove very useful.

_____ 3. Contrast in identical environment proves [e] and [ɛ] to be separate phonemes.

_____ 4. [ɔ] and [o] are separate phonemes because [ɔ] occurs in initial syllables of the word and [o] in final syllables of the word.

_____ 5. [p] and [b] are mutually exclusive.

_____ 6. [k] and [g] are submembers of the same phoneme.

_____ 7. Stress is phonemic.

_____ 8. The sound [u] is phonemically in some positions a consonant and in others a vowel.

9. Because of pressure of phonetic symmetry, one assumes that "ɵ" might represent a sound which was recorded incorrectly. This sound was probably [ ].

Problem 204--Phonemic Quiz Type[1] B

Phonetic Data:

['pota·m]	'tree'	['ki·za·u]	'straw hat'
['kitso·ž̌]	'mountain'	['ia·mᵊna̧]	'long'
['b̧itša̧]	'canoe'	['da·uǯi·ģ]	'wash'
['na·dzoķ]	'kill'	['b̧i·gᵊdas]	'eat'
['wa·bᵊdi̧]	'scorpion'	['žistaš]	'snake'
['bota·z]	'saddle'	['ko·ģᵊbiķ]	'obey'
['lapb̧i̧] or ['rapb̧i̧]	'donkey'	['la·uši·ģ] or ['ra·uši·ģ]	'funny'
['wa·bti̧]	'this'	['zikpas]	'rotten'
['bitša̧]	'muddy'	['woķtas]	'beer'
['wo·nᵊmi·l] or ['wo·nᵊmi·r]	'alligator'		
['gi·lo̧] or ['gi·ro̧]	'rope'		

Directions:

A. Is the free variation between [r] and [l] variation between full phonemes or between submembers of the same phoneme?

_____

B. Using the phonetic symbol of the phonemic norm, how would you write the following?

[a̧] _____   [ķ] _____

[ts] _____   [b̧] _____

C. Are the following suspicious pairs of segments separate phonemes?

[t] and [d] _____

[š] and [ž̌] _____

[s] and [š] _____

D. Is length phonemic? _____

E. Rewrite phonemically:

_____ 'scorpion'

_____ 'long'

_____ 'wash'

Problem 205--Phonemic Quiz Type C

Phonetic Data:

['ta.bukʰ]	'to run'	['na.lm̩]	'barn'
['su.tsʌd]	'boy'	['ku.ŋid]	'weeds'
['sʌ.pupʰ]	'dog'	['pa.kn̩]	'to ride'
['ŋa.mn̩]	'hat'	['kʌ.dab]	'grass'
['bi.lig]	'cow'	['na.lʌs]	'car'
['lu.mats]	'horse'	['bi.dam]	'earth'
['di.bal̩]	'to throw'	['da.bukʰ]	'to eat'
['li.ŋʌl̩]	'rock'	['ka.niŋ]	'nice'
['ka.tn̩]	'spider'	['sʌ.bul̩]	'rabbit'
['tsu.sʌtʰ] or ['tsu.šʌtʰ]	'house'	['mi.šan] or ['mi.san]	'cat'
['di.bal 'su.tsʌd 'li.ŋul̩]	'the boy throws a rock'		
['da̧.bukʰ 'bi.lig 'kʌ.dab]	'the cow eats grass'		

Directions:

Present a phonemic statement[1] that includes the following:

I. Description of the phonemes
   A. List of phonemes
   B. List of their submembers
   C. Phonetic description of their submembers
   D. Occurrence of all submembers if there are more than one
   E. At least one example for each submember

---

[1]By Evelyn G. Pike. Time--fifteen minutes.

[1]The student will find this kind of statement easier after studying Chapter 14.

II. Distribution of the phonemes

    A. General (the consonant-vowel pattern of the major phonetic or grammatical units of the language, word markers, etc.)

    B. Specific (the specific sounds that can occur in the consonant and vowel positions in the units described in A.)

Problem 206--Phonemic Quiz Type[1] D

Phonetic Data:

[fatšA]	'I run'	['evatš]	'run!'
[mękA]	'I think'	['ęmęk]	'think!'
[pesA]	'I sweep'	['ebes]	'sweep!'
[sexA]	'I speak'	['ezex]	'speak!'
[kaṇA]	'I sit'	['egaṇ]	'sit!'
[fakA]	'I eat'	['evak]	'eat!'
[sopA]	'I fall'	['ezop]	'fall!'
[topsA]	'I climb'	['edop]	'climb!'
[rakfA]	'I worship'	['elak]	'worship!'
[xamA]	'I bathe'	['egam]	'bathe!'
[tšęṇA]	'I drink'	['edžęṇ]	'drink!'
[kęṇA]	'I stab'	['egęṇ]	'stab!'
[taskA]	'I read'	['edas]	'read!'
[toṇA]	'I die'	['edoṇ]	'die!'
[ṇelA]	'I hide'	['ęṇel]	'hide!'
[kopkA]	'I sing'	['egop]	'sing!'
[roṇsA]	'I sleep'	['eloṇ]	'sleep!'
[tasɫA]	'I wash'	['edas]	'wash!'
[natsA]	'I walk'	['ęnat]	'walk!'
[noksA]	'I work'	['ęnok]	'work!'
['komvatš]	'racetrack'	['kommęk]	'brain'
['komzex]	'word'	['kombes]	'broom'
['kombaṇ]	'chair'	['komvak]	'food'
['komzop]	'trap'	['kombop]	'ascent'
['komlak]	'idol'	['komgam]	'bath'
['komdžęṇ]	'drink'	['kombęṇ]	'knife'
['kombas]	'book'	['komboṇ]	'poison'

['kommęl]	'town'	['kombop]	'song'
['komloṇ]	'bed'	['kombas]	'soap'
['kommat]	'path'	['kommok]	'job'

Directions:

    Given the preceding data by your informant:

    1. List the stems.

    2. Identify the affixial morphemes and give them appropriate names.

    3. Describe the phonological processes.

---

[1] By Donald Stark, Summer Institute of Linguistics. Time--fifteen minutes.

Chapter 13

ANALYTICAL PROCEDURES FURTHER AMPLIFIED FOR APPLICATION

TO SPECIAL PROBLEMS OF BORDER PHENOMENA

Problem 207--Kalaba Dialect FI

Phonetic Data:

[topik] 'the big horse'

[top] 'horse'

[iktop] 'the horse is big'

[ik] 'big'

Directions:

At what point would you write spaces in the data above?

Solution to Problem 207:

Spaces should be written in the first and third utterances between the items [top] and [ik].

Discussion of Problem 207:

To arrive at this conclusion one first identifies some or all of the morphemes involved, by assuming that a morpheme maintains a somewhat constant phonetic form, and somewhat constant meaning.[1] In Problem 207 the morphemes are as follows: [top] 'horse', and [ik] 'big'.

Next, note that each of these morphemes may occur also by itself. It is frequently convenient to write spaces between items which themselves may be found elsewhere as constituting complete utterances. Furthermore, notice that within utterances an item which occurs before a space is of the same type which occurs at the end of an utterance. In reverse, notice that an item which follows a space within utterances is of the same type as those which may begin an utterance.

---

[1] Both form and meaning may vary considerably, however. Note the substitution of /v/ for /f/ in /laif/ 'life', and /laiv-/ 'lives'; and the meanings of 'table' in 'an office table' and 'table land'. At present, we have no criterion to tell us just how similar in form and how similar in meaning items must be before we can be certain that they represent utterances of the same morpheme; occasionally one may be quite perplexed as to whether two items represent one or two morphemes. It is seldom, though, that this difficulty affects a practical conclusion as to spacing.

A supporting criterion[1] of a related type, but not a conclusive one, is that any morpheme or close-knit sequence of morphemes which can occur at the beginning, end and middle of utterances should be preceded and followed by a space.[2] In this problem notice that [ik] occurs at the end of an utterance in /top ik/ 'the big horse', but at the beginning of the utterance in /ik top/ 'the horse is big'. The statements for [top] are similar. These data support the conclusion that spaces should be written after and before /top/ and /ik/.

Problem 208--Kalaba Dialect FJ

Phonetic Data:

[op] 'horse'   [basop] 'the big horse'

[bas] 'big'   [opzuMbas] 'the horse
                    is big'

[zuM] 'is'

[ma] 'his'   [opmazuMbas] 'his horse
                    is big'

Directions:

1. Rewrite phonetically the last three utterances, adding spaces in the appropriate places.

2. Rewrite the same data phonemically.

Solution to Problem 208:

1. The utterances rewritten phonetically, but with spaces:

[bas op] 'the big horse'

[op zuM bas] 'the horse is big'

[op ma suM bas] 'his horse is big'

2. The data rewritten phonemically:

---

[1] This criterion came to my attention through Archibald A. Hill, of the University of Virginia, at the 1947 summer meeting of the Linguistic Society of America, Ann Arbor, Mich. Professor Hill was using the criterion, however, to establish boundaries of "phrase words" rather than items customarily called words.

[2] Unless, as a result, further bound morphemes are left between spaces. This exception will be taken care of later in this chapter, p. 162.

/baz ob/ 'the big horse'

/ob zum baz/ 'the horse is big'

/ob ma zum baz/ 'his horse is big'

Discussion of Problem 208:

Notice that this problem in many respects is the same as the preceding one, and that the criterion of occurrence in isolation applies here.

A further criterion, however, may be observed: that preceding the space in this rewritten material, the same types of modification of phonemes occur as are found also at the end of utterances: voiced nonvocoids become voiceless.

Two observations can be made concerning these data:

1. That if no spaces were given, then the segments [z] and [s] could not be considered submembers of phoneme /z/, because they might contrast in analogous environments, namely, in the middle of utterances. If, however, spaces are introduced, then one may make a statement of the mutually exclusive distribution of these submembers as follows: Segment [s] occurs only preceding space or at the end of an utterance; segment [z] never occurs in these environments; inasmuch as segments [z] and [s] are phonetically similar and mutually exclusive, they are submembers of a single phoneme. That is to say, the investigator advances the hypothesis that at certain points in the language a border occurs which is pertinent to the phonemic system of the language. He then may test this hypothesis by attempting to analyze his phonemes by utilizing these borders as points of reference from which the distribution of certain of the submembers may be described. Such a procedure would show [b] and [p], [m] and [M], to be submembers of their respective phonemes. If he finds that the introduction of the symbolization of such a border makes a simpler phonemic statement, he concludes that this border represents an actual functioning phonological border in the language. He should notice, however, that a hypothesis of this type is not spun out of thin air but parallels phonological or grammatical data.

2. Space was utilized as a point of departure for describing the varieties of submembers of the phonemes /z/, /b/, and /m/. With the data rewritten phonemically, based upon such an analysis, a further investigator may read this data, pronouncing it as it was originally given, provided that he has available a description of the phonemes which can serve as a set of rules telling him how to modify the phonemic norms preceding spaces. If such a set of rules were not given him, or if the spaces were omitted after the analysis had been made, he would be helpless and could not read the data as it is pronounced

by the native. It is clear, therefore, that such a postulation of a significant border and a phonemic analysis of submembers of phonemes based upon this postulation becomes legitimate only when the border thus postulated is actually represented by some symbol such as, in this case, a space. No type of border should be referred to as conditioning the occurrence of specific submembers of phonemes unless it is represented in the phonemic rewrite by some symbol.

These actions are based upon the further assumption that native speakers react to languages in some such way[1] as reflected by this symbolization, namely, that they respond to the writing of their language as

---

[1] As we pointed out at the end of Chapter 4, our establishment of phonemic principles and procedures must ultimately rest upon our observations of native reactions to the phonetic data. This statement must not be construed to mean that the untrained native can discourse learnedly and accurately about border phenomena, but rather that his unconscious physical, linguistic or social reactions to the structural unity of his phonemic system may be analyzed by the observer. Phonemic procedure must be based upon (1) phonetic data, and (2) upon the investigator's observation of native reaction to the facts of a wide variety of languages. A procedure which ignored either of these facets of reality would be just an arbitrary type of "algebra" which does not analyze the facts of the language as a structural system functioning as a medium of communication.

It is further interesting to note that even in arithmetic and algebra (which to laymen often appear to have rules set up and established by pure reason without reference to desired ends as such) that many of the most basic postulates and equations are arrived at by intuition, or stated so as to get a specific desired result which seems to "make sense" or to parallel daily experience. So the procedures given in this chapter are deliberately designed for finding word units useful for purposes of introducing a literature to languages hitherto unwritten. For intuition in mathematical discoveries and procedures see Richard Courant, and Herbert Robbins, What is Mathematics An Elementary Approach to Ideas and Methods (London, New York, Toronto: Oxford University Press, 1941). Thus they state (concerning a formula for arithmetical progression, p. 15) 'It should be remarked that although the principle of mathematical induction suffices to prove the formula (5) once this formula has been written down, the proof gives no indication of how this formula was arrived at in the first place.' And 'The question of the origin of the hypothesis (5) belongs to a domain in which no very general rules can be given; experience, analogy, and constructive intuition play their part here.' When dealing with parallel lines, and an "ideal"

if the units between spaces and the like are structurally functioning entities within the stream of speech. They tend to ignore or find it very hard to become aware of modifications of phonemes at the borders of such units. The units between the spaces are grammatical entities of some kind, and may usually best be called WORDS.

Places at which grammatical units come together are GRAMMATICAL BORDER POINTS or JUNCTURES. Places at which words come together constitute one of the most important types of grammatical border points. If special phonetic modifications occur at these points, or if they must be used as a point of reference for describing or defining submembers of phonemes, the border point may be called a PHONOLOGICAL BORDER POINT or juncture, or a "phonemic"[1] one.

point which is common to all lines parallel to any given line, the statements are so set up that 'every pair of lines in the plane will now intersect in a single point' (p. 182); but parallel lines thus intersect in only one direction by virtue of the fact that only one such ideal point is set up for each line. The explanation of this limitation follows: 'The reason for adding only one, as we have done, is that we wish to preserve the law that through any two points one and only one line may be drawn.' (p. 182). As a further instance of rules set up with desired goals in mind, note that numbers can be multiplied by zero, but not divided by zero 'For if division by 0 were permitted, we could deduce from the true equation 0·1 = 0·2 the absurd consequence 1 = 2 (p. 56). Finally, the authors state: 'True, the element of constructive invention, of directing and motivating intuition, is apt to elude a simple philosophical formulation; but it remains the core of any mathematical achievement, even in the most abstract fields' (p. xvii).

[1]In this volume the phonologically pertinent junctures are handled as combined grammatical-phonological border points, rather than as strictly or exclusively phonological ones, for various reasons which I have presented in an unpublished article entitled "Grammatical Prerequisites to Phonemic Analysis." Some of these reasons can be summarized as follows:

(1) Field procedure in the practice of those linguists whom I have observed at work, makes use of grammatical facts for the recognition of such junctures--and this volume is designed to reflect field procedure so that the student may himself learn the best methods of working.

(2) The student should learn to study all the facts of a language, and their interrelationships. Since the grammar and phonology of a language affect each other (especially in border modifications, in length of intonation units, in rhythm char-

Problem 209--Kalaba Dialect FK

Phonetic data:

[nibap] 'horse'   [zabas] 'man'

[bazis] 'town'   [zinin] 'to run'

[bibip] 'to sing'

[nibapbazis] 'the horse is in town'

[nazapzabasbazis] 'the man travels to town'

_____

acteristics, and the like) he must not ignore grammar while attempting to analyze the phonemes lest he arrive at incorrect conclusions.

(3) In order to establish phonemic contrasts between phonetic elements of only two morphemes, he must be certain of the identity (or, as a minimum, of the differential identity) of each morpheme; he must be able to recognize through similarities of phonetic form and of semantic character the repetition of a morpheme or its substitution by another morpheme. This prerequisite differential identification of morphemes is essentially a grammatical (or at least a semantic) process, not a phonetic one as such.

(4) The student must be trained to hear sounds in environments which he knows are somewhat analogous. This often can most easily be done at the beginning of utterances where he knows that any initial sound is simultaneously beginning an utterance, a morpheme, a word, a sentence, an intonation group, a rhythm group, a stress group, a syllable, and so on. The grammatical certainties in such environment are important, as are the phonological ones.

(5) Repeated occurrences of some certain juncture type in a specified language are not necessarily all characterized by the identical phonetic phenomena, or by related ones. They may lack (a) the requisite phonetic similarity, and (b) the requisite mutually exclusive distribution, which are essential for postulating the phonemically unitary nature of two phonetically diverse items. This prevents a "juncture" from being analyzed a phoneme as such.

(6) Many of the word junctures important to phonemic analysis are identifiable phonetically only a part of the time, and not during every repetition of the same sequence of words. The potential for a normal pause, or the potential for the end of an intonation contour, or the potential for a rhythm break, may be important to establishing grammatical border points or phonological ones (and the writing, say, of spaces from which point submembers of phonemes can be described) even though the potential is not actualized at every utterance of that sequence of words.

[nibapzabasbazis] 'the man and the horse
                  are in town'

Directions:

Rewrite the data phonemically.

Solution to Problem 209:

/nibab/ 'horse'   /zabaz/ 'man'

/baziz/ 'town'   /zinin/ 'to run'

/bibib/ 'to sing'

/nibab baziz/ 'the horse is in town'

/nazab zabaz baziz/ 'the man travels to
                     town'

/nibab zabaz baziz/ 'the man and the horse
                     are in town'

Discussion of Problem 209:

Note that stops and fricatives are
found voiceless at the end of isolated words
and at the end of longer utterances; those
words which occur in isolation retain the
voiceless final nonvocoid when the words
occur in phrases.

There is one voiceless nonvocoid,
however, which is found in the middle of an
utterance even though the morpheme [nazap]
'travel' in which it is seen does not occur
in isolation.

If, on the basis of the larger part
of the evidence, (or nonsuspicious evidence),
we set up the hypothesis for Problem 209
that [b] and [p] are both submembers of the
phoneme /b/, since the two segments are
phonetically similar and mutually exclusive
in their distribution, (with [b] replaced by
[p] at the end of words), there remains a
residue of data which does not fit the hypothesis. Since [nazap-] has not been proved
a separate word by occurrence in isolated
position, the [p] would not have been accounted for. If, however, one assumes the
previous hypothesis to be correct, then the
occurrence of the voiceless [p] could serve
as a criterion for the occurrence of a word
border at the end of [nazap-]. Then one
would conclude that [nazap] is a separate
word, to be written /nazab/ and to be followed by a space, even though it is not found
in isolation. This conclusion should be
checked further against the grammatical characteristics of that item to be certain that
the newly postulated word is grammatically
analogous to other units assumed to be words
in that language. Here the verbs /zinin/
'to run' and /bibib/ 'to sing' are grammatically analogous to /nazab/ 'to travel'. If
most of the phonetic data of a certain type
can be described (a) in terms of the predominant pattern of words which can be identified in isolation, and (b) in reference to
spaces between these items in context, then

similar phonetic data can be used as a criterion for determining word boundaries and
for the writing of spaces in doubtful instances, provided that the additional words
so postulated are grammatically analogous
to words found in isolation. In the writing
of spaces, as in the interpreting of sequences, one first finds the predominant
nonsuspicious pattern and then utilizes it
as a criterion for interpreting the items
whose analysis is more difficult.

Problem 210--Kalaba Dialect FL

Phonetic Data:

[barI]   'house'   [barikO] 'his house'

[parI]   'cat'   [korO]   'dog'

[barimI] 'my house' [ripA]   'mouse'

[korokO] 'his dog'   [parikO] 'his cat'

[rabI]   'I see'   [rabA]   'you see'

[rabO]   'he sees'

  [rabIbarI] 'I see the house'

  [rabObarikO] 'he sees his house'

  [barikOpanO] 'he goes to his house'

Directions:

Rewrite the last three items phonemically.

Solution to Problem 210:

/rabi bari/   'I see the house'

/rabo bariko/ 'he sees his house'

/bariko pano/ 'he goes to his house'

Discussion of Problem 210:

Notice that the item /bari/ occurs
by itself as 'house'. Therefore, one might
at first expect that spaces would be legitimately placed before and after it each
time the morpheme occurs. In this problem
such a conclusion would be erroneous, however, since the morpheme [kO], which at times
is directly after it, never occurs by itself.
In placing spaces one must never have as the
sole item between spaces any morpheme (or
series of morphemes) of a general grammatical
type which never occurs by itself as constituting a complete utterance. In this language, morphemes grammatically somewhat parallel to /-ko/ are /-mi/ 'my', /-i/ 'I',
/-a/'you', and /-o/ 'he'. None of these
occur in isolation. Thus /-ko/ 'his' must
not be preceded by a space, since it (a)
neither occurs in isolation, nor (b) is
paralleled by isolated morphemes grammatically similar to it. Items like /-ko/ which
never occur in isolation are called BOUND
FORMS in contradistinction to FREE FORMS

which may occur by themselves.

Substantiating evidence for this decision is found in the distribution of the phonetic modification of the vowel phonemes in the grammar: One may state that all vowels unvoice at the end of words provided that he grants that the pronominal morphemes are suffixes rather than separate words. This would explain why the /i/ of the morpheme /bari/ unvoices in isolation, as in [barI], but not when it constitutes part of a longer word, as in [barikO] 'his house'.

Problem 211--Kalaba Dialect FM

Phonetic Data:

['babab] 'a fish'   ['masas] 'yonder'

['mosos] 'line'   ['sobam] 'catch!'

   ['sobam'babab] 'catch the fish!'

   ['masas'bomam'babab] 'see the fish
                        yonder!'

Directions:

Rewrite the last utterance phonemically.

Solution to Problem 211:

   /masas bomam babab/ 'see the fish yonder!'

Discussion of Problem 211:

In this problem each utterance begins with a stressed syllable. Every word which occurs in isolation is stressed initially and retains its initial stress when it occurs in the middle of an utterance. Because of this predominant pattern one tentatively assumes that stress is for this language a mechanical, noncontrastive characteristic of the beginnings of words. Before accepting this conclusion as accurate, however, the student should note that there is a residue of morphemes undescribed: the morpheme ['bomam] 'see!' does not occur here in isolation; it is, nevertheless, grammatically analogous to ['sobam] 'catch!' which is found isolated as well as included in phrases. Therefore (1) by analogy of the grammatical type and (2) by the fact that it follows the word-stress rule postulated earlier, the student may legitimately conclude that ['bomam] is a separate word. In special instances, nonphonemic stress may be utilized as a criterion for word borders if it gives a conclusion consistent with all the grammatical and phonological data. Provided that spaces are now placed between words, the occurrence of stress is PREDICTABLE and may be omitted from the phonemic orthography.

Substantiating the conclusion reached for /bomam/ is the evidence of the occurrence of characteristic STRUCTURAL SEQUENCES OF SOUNDS. Notice (1) that all the utterances end with a consonant and (2)

that when a morpheme which occurs at the end of an utterance is found in the middle of an utterance the consonant is retained. Since every morpheme also begins with a consonant the result is that two consonants occur together whenever two morphemes are juxtaposed in an utterance. In the last long utterance, however, one finds the consonant cluster [-mb-] but without having seen the morpheme [-bomam-] in isolation. On the ground that the predominant pattern of the language entails a word border in the middle of any cluster of consonants, one assumes also that space should occur between the consonants [-mb-] and that /bomam/ is a separate word even though it is not found in isolation. Any type of sequence of sounds which in the predominant nonsuspicious pattern is restricted in occurrence to a place at the juncture of two words, may be used as a criterion for word division in doubtful instances.

Problem 212--Kalaba Dialect FN

Phonetic Data:

   ['tato'lala'lo'tomo'mara] 'I saw Tom and
                            Mary'

   ['tato'lala'lo|'tomo'mara] [repeated]
        'I saw Tom and Mary'

   ['lo]   'I'   ['mara]   'Mary'

   ['tomo]   'and'   ['lala]   'saw'

Directions:

Rewrite the first utterance phonemically.

Solution to Problem 212:

   /tato lala lo tomo mara/ 'I saw Tom and
                            Mary'

Discussion of Problem 212:

Notice that in the second utterance, which was a repetition of the first, a vertical bar was given as part of the phonetic data. This symbol was used to represent a pause. Spaces should be written in normal utterances at points where pauses occur, since pauses in natural speech tend to occur only between large grammatical and phonological divisions which are highly pertinent to the language.

There were alternate pronunciations of the first sentence--one with pause and one without pause. In either case one should normally write a space at points where pauses may optionally be given, that is, at POTENTIAL PAUSE POINTS, since with few exceptions a place where pause may optionally occur is a division, between important grammatical and phonological parts of the utterance, which is best symbolized for practical orthographical purposes by a space. (Certain hesitation forms do not follow this rule. A speaker might say in English, for example, 're..re.. re..rehabilitation', with pauses between the 're..'s', yet this type of utterance is not considered a normal linguistic form. Apart from such situations, however, pauses or optional pause points are very pertinent criteria for the placing of spaces.)

In addition, such places need to be symbolized if nonphonemic modifications of phonemes, (such as prepausal lengthening of vowels) need to be described with pause as the environmental characteristic causing the modification. Pauses which affect the phonetic actualization of the neighboring phonemes should be symbolized in some further way--say by a comma or period. If pauses are of two significantly different types, different symbols should be used to represent them. If, for example, one pause indicates a tentative implication by the speaker and is recognizable (a) by its shortness or (b) by its effect on preceding sounds, whereas a second type implies an attitude of finality in the speaker and is recognizable (a) by its extra length or (b) by a different set of nonphonemic modifications of preceding sounds, the tentative pause could be written with a comma and the final one with a period.[1] The sequence of sounds between any two consecutive pauses constitutes a RHYTHM GROUP.

In the problem just given, notice that the criteria of occurrence in isolation and of nonphonemic stress placement support the decision for the placing of a space after the word /lo/ 'I'.

In a language where intonation contours are important or well marked, the investigator may frequently use them as helpful or supporting criteria for the placing of spaces. Intonation contours tend to begin and end (but do not always do so) at the borders of important grammatical units or of actual or potential phonological ones. Therefore if one finds the end or the beginning of an intonation contour, it gives evidence pointing toward the presence of a border which should be symbolized by space. This evidence is not to be considered conclusive, however, since in special situations this criterion may be overruled; except in hesitation forms a space should not be written before bound forms, nor within the middle of a morpheme. Thus in the word vaccination
                                    2--3 2-4
there are optionally two intonational contours, but a space should not be written there since -ation is a bound form.

---

[1]Tentative and final pauses are phonemic in English (see Kenneth L. Pike, The Intonation of American English, University of Michigan Publications in Linguistics I, [Ann Arbor: University of Michigan Press, 1945], 30-40). Traditional English orthography, however, tends to follow grammatical criteria rather than phonemic ones.

Frequently the borders of intonation groups are parallel to the borders between rhythm groups; intonation units often begin and end with pause. Many times, however, languages contain sequences of several intonation contours in series, between which no pause occurs, as for example in the following English sentence pronounced fairly rapidly:

I'd like to do it tomorrow.
3- 2-   -4--3 3 2--4

Usually spaces should be written between the intonation contours of such a series, also. Exceptions are of the same type as indicated at the end of the preceding paragraph.

At intonation borders there may be a change of speed. A sharp increase of speed is likewise usually indicative of the need for a space at the point where the increase begins.

Problem 213--Kalaba Dialect FO

Phonetic Data:

[mob]	'man'	[mim]	'fast'
[ma]	'tiger'	[ki]	'to see'
[po]	'hair'	[nob]	'to fall'
[bo]	'nose'	[libpa]	'to run'
[labmo]	'tooth'	[mapmi]	'eye'

[bimopma] 'the man sees the tiger'

[noppo] 'the hair falls'

[piplabmomim] 'the tooth aches strongly'

Directions:

Rewrite the last three utterances phonemically.

Solution to Problem 213:

/bi mop ma/ 'the man sees the tiger'

/nop po/ 'the hair falls'

/pip labmo mim/ 'the tooth aches strongly'

Discussion of Problem 213:

/p/ and /b/ are separate phonemes, as proved by contrast in identical environments in the words [po] 'hair' and [bo] 'nose'. It is evident, then, that when the segment [b] is replaced by the segment [p], it does so as a part of a phonological process: /p/ and /b/ remain separate phonemes, but one replaces the other in certain instances. Notice that /b/ is not always replaced by /p/; in the center of [libpa] 'to run' and of [labmo] 'tooth' the /b/ remains. The substitution of /p/ for /b/ is found only at those places which one might assume are ends of words on the basis of isolated utterances. Sometimes the systematic substitution of one set of phonemes for another set of phonemes is limited to certain places in nonsuspicious words, and gives clues for word division in doubtful instances.

Problem 214--Kalaba Dialect FP

Phonetic Data:

['pok] 'book'   ['lof] 'big'

['pokna] 'my book'   ['mo] 'over there'

[pok'mona] 'my book   [pok'sa] 'it is a
        over there'   book'

[pok'lof'mona] 'my   ['sim] 'blue'
  big book over there'

['sana] 'it is mine' [pok'lof] 'a big book'

  ['pok'sa'lof] 'the book is blue'

  ['pok'lof'sim'mona] 'my big, blue
            book over there'

Directions:

        Rewrite the last utterance phonemically, placing spaces between the words, and hyphens before semi-free morphemes.

Solution to Problem 214:

   /pok lof sim mo-na/ 'my big blue book
                       over there'

Discussion of Problem 214:

        With the exception of the morpheme /-na/ all morphemes in this language occur in isolation and are stressed. They may be separated by spaces, therefore, and presumably constitute separate words.

        The morpheme /-na/ never occurs in isolation; that fact, plus its lack of stress and its pronominal meaning, make it appear like a suffix. One should notice, however, that it does not always occur close to the main noun stem which it modifies: other morphemes come between the modified noun and the pronominal element; the intervening morphemes /lof/ 'big', /mo/ 'over there', and /sim/ 'blue', are themselves free forms and separate words. /-na/ clings to the last word in any particular sequence of which it is an integral part. If one considered /-na/ to be a suffix, it would force items like ['pok'lof'sim'mona] to be analyzed as single words. This conclusion appears unconvincing because of the free forms contained in the utterance, and because the /-na/ appears to be grammatically more closely related to /pok/ which is far removed from it, than to /mo/ beside which it is found. In such situations one may best conclude that the language contains a layer of morphemes, called CLITICS, inter-

mediate between words and affixes, when these morphemes are grammatically loosely bound, but phonologically tightly bound to a free word to which they are adjacent. Thus /-na/ 'I' is grammatically loosely bound to /mo/ 'over there' but is phonologically tightly bound to it since, in lacking a stress of its own, /-na/ must be pronounced with /mo/. A clitic is a SEMI-FREE word.

Problem 215--Kalaba Dialect FQ

Phonetic Data:

 ['toma] 'I'   ['sulo] 'you'

 ['tapa] 'loudly'   ['polu] 'today'

 ['saso] 'house'   ['putu] 'road'

 ['moma] 'sky'   ['mulu] 'he is singing'

 ['toma'lamo] 'it is I' or ['lamo'toma]

 [tom'mulu] 'I am singing' or ['mulutom]

 ['sulo'saso] 'it is your house'

 [sul'polu'tapa'putu'moma'mulu] 'you are
                singing loudly upwards today'

Directions:

        Rewrite the last two utterances phonemically.

Solution to Problem 215:

 /sulo saso/ 'it is your house'

 /sul-polu tapa putu moma mulu/ 'you are
                singing loudly upwards today'

Discussion of Problem 215:

        All isolated morphemes in this langauge contain two syllables with a stress on the first syllable. These constitute free morphemes, or words. Each of the morphemes is found in isolation. Two of the morphemes, however, have abbreviated forms (a) which never occur in isolation, (b) which have no stress, and (c) which are monosyllabic.

        At first these forms /tom-/ and /sul-/ would appear to be verbal prefixes, and one might expect to join them, without spaces, to the words which they precede. Yet this would be unsatisfactory for several reasons:

        (1) Free morphemes such as 'today', 'loudly', 'road', and 'sky' may come between the alleged prefix and the verb which it modifies.

        (2) The alleged verbal prefixes may be phonologically dependent upon words like 'today' rather than upon the verbs upon which they are grammatically dependent.

        (3) One of them, /tom-/, may either

precede or follow its verb just as the independent possessive pronoun /toma/ 'I' may
precede or follow its verb. This would turn
the "prefix" into a "suffix" with the same
meaning and use.

(4) /tom-/ is closely related to the
free form /toma/.

(5) If /tom-/ were written as a prefix, without stress, and if stresses were
omitted from the free forms, then one could
not predict the syllable on which the stress
would fall in an unfamiliar sequence CVCVCV,
since the first or the last syllable might
be an unstressed prefix (or prefix turned
suffix).

If, however, a hyphen were written
following a procliticized /tom-/ or preceding
it when encliticized, then the ambiguity of
(5) would be avoided, and the stress would
be predictable even though it were not written. This solution is probably simpler than
it would be (1) to join /tom-/ and /sul-/,
without spaces or hyphens, to the words preceding or following them, and (2) to write
stresses everywhere they occur.

Whenever semi-free items are phonologically dependent, but contain some characteristics of free words, the student must
consider the possibility of hyphenating them
in a phonemic or a practical orthography. In
any event, the pronunciation of a sentence
must be predictable from its orthography.

In many languages there are more
than two degrees of forms which must be
joined or separated in some way for technical
accuracy--even though in traditional writing
one seldom sees more than space, lack of
space (and an occasional hyphen for compounding, for which see the next problem). The
investigator should consider each case on
its own merits, and weigh it in the light of
the criteria:

(1) of freedom of occurrence, or
lack of such freedom

(2) of phonetic relationship to
specific free forms

(3) of presence or absence of structural and prosodic characteristics of free
forms

(4) of grammatical close or loose
connection with adjacent morphemes to which
it is phonologically united

(5) of freedom of position of occurrence

(6) of freedom with which other morphemes may come between it and the morphemes
it modifies most directly

(7) of the effect of the analysis
upon the rules for the writing of stress in
the language

(8) of the resultant size of word
units.

Sometimes the use of hyphens next to clitics
in a practical orthography will be advantageous.

Problem 216--Kalaba Dialect FR

Phonetic Data:

[po'los]   'blue'   ['mosal]   'big'

['sapol]   'yellow'   ['sotop]   'green'

[so'map]   'bird'   [tiso'map] 'birds'

  [so'map'mosal] 'a big bird'

  [so'map'sapol] 'a yellow bird'

  [so'mappo'los'sotop] 'a bird which is
        blue and green'

  [tipo'losomap'mosal] 'big bluebirds'

  [tiso'mappo'los'sapol] 'big birds
        which are yellow'

Directions:

Rewrite the last three items phonemically.

Solution to Problem 216:

  /so'map po'los 'sotop/ 'a bird which is
        blue and green'

  /tipo'losomap 'mosal/ 'big bluebirds'

  /tiso'map po'los 'sapol/ 'big birds
        which are yellow'

Discussion of Problem 216:

In this language, stress patterns
are in contrast in analogous phonetic environments, and hence stress is phonemic. The
morpheme /ti-/ has no stress; it lacks the
two syllables which a free form in this language must have; it never occurs in isolation; it does not parallel grammatically any
free morphemes, but as a pluralizer of nouns
appears to be an inflectional element. /ti-/
is best considered a prefix.

The free morpheme /po'los/ 'blue' is
a separate word, as is the morpheme /so'map/
'bird'. Yet /tipo'losomap/ must be considered a single compound word (even though two
of the morphemes contained in it are elsewhere free) for various reasons: (1) Only
one stress occurs in the combination; since
/-somap/ here has no stress, it does not in
this combination act like a free morpheme,
each of which contains a stress. (2) The
/-s/ of /po'los/ and the /s-/ of /so'map/
have coalesced to a single /-s-/; this re-
duction of an /-ss-/ cluster does not occur
between distinctly separate words, as may be
seen in the phrase /so'map po'los 'sotop/

'a bird which is blue and green'. (3) The order of the morphemes is different from that of free morphemes; in an ordinary sentence, the noun precedes its adjectival modifier, but here the modifier precedes the noun. (4) The plural prefix is attached to the total combination, which begins with the adjectival morpheme. These evidences show /po'losomap/ to be a compound. Two free forms may combine into a single free form which then acts more or less like a single free morpheme. The criteria used may be summarized as follows:

(1) Special arrangements of stress patterns.

(2) Special phonological changes.

(3) Special orders in which the morphemes occur.

(4) Morphological inflection of the total combination.

There are further, negative, criteria, which can sometimes be utilized, with an informant, as supporting evidence:[1]

(5) The indivisibility of words by inflectional elements normally permissible for related sequences of free words: greenhouse but not *greener-house; thoroughbred but not *thoroughly-bred.

(6) The omission of certain words normally expected in a related sequence of free words: cutthroat but not cut the throat.

(7) The impossibility of using some compounds in syntactic positions where the principal member of the compound could itself occur: castaway serves as a subject, not as a predicate.

(8) The impossibility of modifying

some element in the compound by words which could be used to modify that morpheme in a normal phrase: a big greenhouse but not a very greenhouse.

(9) The lack of occurrence elsewhere of one of the morphemes: a berry, and a cranberry, but not a *cran.

Occasionally a phrase of several words may be united by an affix;[1] note, for example, the King of England's (daughter). In such instances it appears wise not to join the parts of the phrase without space, as /ðə 'kɪŋ əv 'ɪŋləndz 'dɔtɹ/, but either to leave spaces or else to separate the units by hyphens, as /ðə 'kɪŋ əv 'ɪŋləndz 'dɔtɹ/ or /ðə-'kɪŋ-əv-'ɪŋləndz 'dɔtɹ/. In neither case should the affix be separated by a space.

Many of the problems involving the joining of two or more free forms can be very difficult to solve in a practical way. Orthographical decisions regarding any one language must be carefully considered in the light of all available phonological and grammatical data for that language, and decisions reached for that one language alone.

Problem 217—Kalaba Dialect FS

Phonetic Data:

['bŏmŏ]	'a song'	[mŏ'bŏˇ]	'to hide'
['bŏmó]	'a girl'	['bóbó]	'a chair'
[bŏ'mŏ]	'to sing'	[bó'bóˇ]	'to sit'
[tó'tóˇ]	'to fret'	['mótŏ]	'a storm'
[bŏ'mŏˇ]	'to be singing'	[bó'tŏˇ]	'to be running'

Directions:

1. Is stress phonemic?

2. Is tone phonemic?

3. Are the pitch glides phonemic?

4. Rewrite phonemically the last two utterances.

Solution to Problem 217:

1. Yes.

2. Yes.

3. Yes.

4. /'mótŏ/ 'a storm', /bó'tŏˇ/ 'to be running.'

---

[1]The illustrations for these negative types are taken from Eugene A. Nida, Morphology, the Descriptive Analysis of Words, University of Michigan Publications in Linguistics, II (Ann Arbor: University of Michigan Press, 1946), 152-6. For further discussion and details, see Leonard Bloomfield, Language (New York: Henry Holt and Company, 1933), 227-37.

Negative criteria of any kind, however, must be used with caution, since some omissions may be determined by semantic limitations without structural implications. Furthermore, a native speaker may consent to utter some word combinations, at the request of the investigator, which he would never utilize in normal conversation. For this latter reason it is best to draw negative conclusions on the basis of amassed natural speech. Here, again, is a difficulty since some permissible but rare forms may happen not to have been collected.

---

[1]For various levels on which forms may thus be bound, see Robert A. Hall Jr., "A Note on Bound Forms," The Journal of English and Germanic Philology, XLV (October, 1946), 450.

Discussion of Problem 217:

Stress is proved phonemic by contrast in identical environments: [ˈbòmó] 'a song' versus [bòˈmó] 'to sing'. Tone is similarly proved phonemic: [ˈbòmó] 'a song' versus [ˈbòmó] 'a girl'. Glides are phonemic, since they contrast in analogous environments: [tóˈtó`] 'to fret' versus [bóˈtó`] 'to be running' versus [bòˈmó`] 'to be singing'.

In a problem of this type students are likely to suggest that stress should be considered nonphonemic since all nouns are stressed on the first syllable but verbs are never stressed there.

In reply to such a suggestion it should first be admitted that an unambiguous, though undesirable, orthography can sometimes be made by symbolizing specific subtypes of words. Here, for example, the stress of all words would be unambiguously known if a check mark [√] preceded each noun, but no such mark occurred on verbs, thus: /√bòmó/ 'a song', /bòmó/ 'to sing', /bòmó´/ 'to be singing', /√mótó/ 'a storm', /bótó´/ 'to be running', and so forth. By this device the reader would know that each word marked with [√] was a noun, and a rule for reading the sign would be to stress the first syllable of each noun. All other words in this particular language are verbs and should be stressed on the last syllable which begins with a consonant.

When, for this volume, we state that such an orthography is undesirable, we imply (1) that it is possible for an unambiguous orthography to be nonphonemic, and (2) that major or minor form classes (verb, noun, adjective, etc.) as such, should not be symbolized.[1]

In summary of the procedures for symbolizing borders of grammatical units.

---

[1]There must be further assumptions behind the conclusion that one should not symbolize a noun-verb dichotomy as such. Just what these assumptions consist of is not yet clear, however. The problem is still somewhat academic, rather than practical, since no case has come to my attention in which the data would warrant such a symbolism; there occasionally are tendencies to a differentiation of noun and verb (as when in English stress is frequently found at the beginning of a noun but at the end of a verb--compare 'permit, per'mit), but in the instances known to me there are always exceptions which rule out a mark for, say, 'verb' instead of stress (thus, for English, Ju'ly is stressed finally, and 'indicate is stressed initially). Perhaps it is this lack of specific known examples which leads us to rule out the possibility for unknown ones. For symbolization of grammatical borders, however, see Chapter 16.

note the following general rules:[1]

(1) Phonemes must be defined, in so far as varieties conditioned by grammatical position are concerned, only in terms of those grammatical borders which are symbolized in some way--such as by space, or by hyphen.

(2) Symbols for grammatical borders should be utilized only for those types of border points by which the analyst wishes to define subphonemic variation, or for highly important nonphonetic potentials such as ability to occur in isolation or next to pause.

(3) Once a certain kind of border point is symbolized at one place in the language, the investigator must write that same symbol at every occurrence of the same kind of border, even though no phonetic modification is there observed.

(4) The investigator should avoid utilizing small or (even large) specific grammatical categories for these purposes. Although one may conceive, for example, of a situation in which the symbolization of every noun in a way different from every verb would reduce the number of phonemes postulated, this type of transcription should be avoided.

(5) When the analyst (a) has accounted for all his phonetic data by symbols for the phonemes themselves, or by symbols for those grammatical border points which are responsible for the modification of the phonemes and so produce subphonemic phonetic phenomena, and (b) has symbolized all highly important and widespread potentials such as possibility of occurrence in isolation, he needs no further analysis of the grammar for purposes of phonemic analysis.

Problem 218 --Kalaba Dialect FT

Phonetic Data:

[veʔena] 'my house'   [sinisuka] 'big tree'

[veʔei] 'his house'   [veʔesukani] 'your
                             big house'

[sakanaveʔei] 'I go   [tanisini] 'the tree
   to his house'   fell'

[sakaiveʔei] 'he   [veʔesukanasaʔa] 'this
   goes home'   big house of mine'

Directions:

List the morphemes and their meanings.

---

[1]Abstracted from an unpublished paper, Kenneth L. Pike, "Grammatical Prerequisites to Phonemic Analysis."

Problem 219--Kalaba Dialect FU

Phonetic Data:

[sašnatu] 'Do it tomorrow!'   [kimunkui] 'She was there'

[kutaškua] 'I am here'   [saškutamku] 'He will be here tomorrow'

[kutanšak] 'She will live here'   [makmnatui] 'She did it yesterday'

[makkutaškui] 'I was here yesterday'   [kimuššaka] 'I live there'

[kutamuši] 'Bring it here'   [saškimušnatu] 'I will do it there tomorrow'

Directions:

List the morphemes and their meanings.

Problem 220--Kalaba Dialect FV

Phonetic Data:

[davagusan] 'my house is red'   [gugus] 'it's a house'

[gusandava] 'my red house'   [gusdava] 'the red house'

[vakzat] 'the tree is tall'   [zatvakufgusandavaat] 'the tall tree is near my big red house'

[guzat] 'it's a tree'

[gusat] 'the big house'

Directions:

Copy the phonetic data; draw a vertical line between each morpheme.

Problem 221--Kalaba Dialect FW

Phonetic Data:

[kupaŋatapatʌ] 'my sister went'   [kunapatapu] 'my brother will go'

[napatapʌ] 'his brother went'   [tatiŋatapitʌ] 'her mother is going'

[kinʌatapuku] 'I will go tomorrow'   [kinʌtiŋataputʌ] 'tomorrow his mother will go'

Directions:

1. Rewrite the first and last utterances phonemically; add spaces where necessary.

2. Draw a vertical line between each morpheme.

3. What is the meaning of [tʌ]?

Problem 222--Kalaba Dialect FX

Phonetic Data:

[soki]   'vine'   [pu]   'long'

[sokipu] 'long vine'   [pusoki] 'the vine is long'

Directions:

Rewrite the data, putting spaces between words.

Problem 223--Kalaba Dialect FY

Phonetic Data:

[sak] 'this one'   [ma] 'man'

[sap] 'that one'   [masak] 'this man'

[masap] 'that man'   [nat] 'tall'

[manatsap] 'that tall man'   [manatsak] 'this tall man'

Directions:

Rewrite the data, putting spaces between words.

Problem 224--Kalaba Dialect FZ

Phonetic Data:

[mana] 'horse'   [nana] 'cat'

[maŋa] 'dog'   [ŋana] 'good'

[na]   'my'   [manana] 'my horse'

[maŋana] 'my dog'   [nanana] 'my cat'

[manaŋana] 'good horse'   [maŋaŋana] 'good dog'

[nanaŋana] 'good cat'   [maŋaŋanana] 'my good dog'

[nanaŋanana] 'my good cat'

Directions:

Rewrite the data, putting spaces between words.

Problem 225--Kalaba Dialect GA

Phonetic Data:

[axut] 'fire'   [dagu] 'shirt'

[iš]   'hot'   [axutiš] 'the hot fire'

[dagudak] 'the white shirt'   [isaxut] 'the fire is hot'

[dakdagu] 'the shirt is white'

Directions:

Rewrite the data phonemically.

Problem 226--Kalaba Dialect GB

Phonetic Data:

[gunita] 'he sees'   [naŋ] 'house'

[naŋdiduk] 'the   [gunit] 'to see'
    big house'

[diduk] 'big'   [naŋak] 'that house'

[naŋa] 'his house'   [gunitunaŋdiduka] 'you
                            see his big house'

[ak] 'that one'

[u] 'you'   [a] 'he'

Directions:

Rewrite the data phonemically.

Problem 227--Kalaba Dialect GC

Phonetic Data:

[tučiN] 'water'   [imap] 'he goes'

[čitiø] 'he bought' [nuø] 'away'

[upuM] 'five'   [nuøimap] 'he goes
                                    away'
[saMpačiøimap] 'he   [nuøisuNut] 'he lives
    goes to the plaza'   over there'

[upuManuNčitiøimat] 'he bought five
    bananas yesterday'

Directions:

1. Rewrite the last four utterances
phonemically.

2. How do you know that [saM] is a
word?

3. Can you identify its meaning with
certainty from this data?

Problem 228--Kalaba Dialect GD

Phonetic Data:

[táŋgín] 'to work'   [sún]   'man'
[kūnbŭ] 'storm'   [tā̃ŋgín] 'to see'
[nȧp]   'water'   [nap]   'food'
[pándȧs] 'bear'
[súntā̃ŋgínpándȧs] 'the man will see the bear'
[nȧpsā̃ŋȧp] 'he will drink water'
[kūnbŭtánkūnbú] 'the storm destroyed many
                                    things'
[nánkúŋgȧnáp] 'she prepared meals'
[tùsándánkūnȧstȧ] 'why did he leave the
                                    house?'
[kŭku] 'nut'

Directions:

Rewrite the last six utterances
phonemically.

Problem 229--Kalaba Dialect GE

Phonetic Data:

[tukʊ] 'meat'   [tugʊ]   'roof'
[sidɩ] 'charcoal'   [sudigɩ] 'my arm'
[dukʊsufɩkusugɩ] 'I ran one kilometer'
[nifunʊkitɩdinu] 'they used to live here'
[sɩsitɩtukunigʊ] 'where is the hamburger?'

Directions:

Rewrite the last three utterances
phonemically.

Problem 230--Kalaba Dialect GF

Phonetic Data:

[mok]   'tree'   [zon]   'house'

[džom] 'to see'   [natš] 'woman'

[nadžił] 'your wife'   [logot] 'his tree'

[zonas] 'my house'   [anatš] 'women'

[zonaza] 'our house'

[nadžotdžomił] 'you see his wife'

[zonilnanoda] 'they build your house'

Directions:

Rewrite the last two utterances
phonemically.

Problem 231--Kalaba Dialect GG

['paka] 'marrow'   ['sap] 'healthy'

['kanaf] 'hurt'   ['satpa] 'he chose'

['talnafa] 'idiot'

['tansa'kanal'fasan] 'the horse ran fast'

['laka'fatapna'pafa] 'why did you go?'

['naklaka'fap'tanasa] 'when did the man
                                    leave?'

Directions:

Rewrite the last three utterances
phonemically.

Problem 232--Kalaba Dialect GH

Phonetic Data:

['stanih] 'man'   ['yunuh] 'tree'

['kayuʔ] 'road'   ['nisaʔ] 'to command'

['sustih] 'axe'

['saya?'stanih] 'I see the man'

['yunuh'nasah'sustih] 'he cut down the tree with his axe'

['kuyuta?'kayu?] 'we all are walking along the road'

['nisastanih'puyih] 'the chief is here'

Directions:

Rewrite the last four utterances phonemically. What types of criteria did you use for determining word boundaries?

Problem 233--Kalaba Dialect GI

Phonetic Data:

[kat] 'moon'   [tsuŋ] 'fast'

[tis] 'chance'   [suts] 'shirt'

[nits] 'to hunt'   [pak] 'wing'

[sutšip] 'your shirt'   [sutsaŋ] 'weary'

[tsundaksuts] 'the shirt was torn to shreds'

[nitšiskunbaŋ] 'he hunts every day'

[tsungutstšinuts] 'I ran fast yesterday'

[paptukkuŋ] 'I was sick'

[nitsakatpap] 'it is hunting season'

[tšinzutšip] 'you ate fish'

Directions:

Rewrite the last six utterances phonemically.

Problem 234--Kalaba Dialect GJ

Phonetic Data:

[zabonamagu‿?aza] 'he went home today'

[zabonamagu] 'he went home'

[mabonamagu] 'you went home' (do you really mean it?)

[zabonadozamu‿valu] 'he went, but he will return'

Directions:

Rewrite the first three utterances phonemically.

Problem 235--Kalaba Dialect GK

Phonetic Data:

[ka'nu] 'animal'   [niš'pa] 'yellow'

[šaš'ki] 'flower'   [xa'ka] 'black'

[xakaka'nu] 'black panther'

[xakanišpaka'nu] 'tiger'

[šaš'kiniš'pa] 'buttercup'

Directions:

Rewrite the last three utterances phonemically.

Problem 236--Kalaba Dialect GL

Phonetic Data:

[mazaɓ] 'bird'   [ðakin] 'house'

[bafu] 'white'   [mazabafu] 'swan'

[nasu] 'postage stamp'   [ðakinasu] 'post-office'

[mazabbafu] 'the white bird'   [ðakinax] 'palace'

[nᴜx] 'king'   [ðakinnax] 'the king's house'

Directions:

Rewrite the last column phonemically.

Problem 237--Kalaba Dialect GM

Phonetic Data (vertical bar indicates pause):

[kᴜn] 'man'   [tisuk] 'water'

[sula] 'he comes'   [lan] 'road'

[?akaŋ] 'birds'

[kunsula|tus?akaŋ] 'the man comes to see the birds'

[sapsula|maktisuk] 'the woman comes to get water'

[?akaŋsanus|lantisuk] 'the birds fly toward the water'

Directions:

Rewrite the last three utterances phonemically.

Problem 238--Restricted Mixteco[1] B

Phonetic Data:

['ñā̧?ā̧] 'woman'   ['ká?nū] 'big'

['sáná] 'turkey'   ['šā̧ā̧] 'very'

---

[1]Data from Donald Stark, Summer Institute of Linguistics. For discussion of

['níí] 'you'   ['kūtū] 'nose'

['kēē] 'to go away'   ['kɨ̄tɨ̄] 'animal'

['kɨ̄tɨ̄'káʔnuš̥ą̄ą̄nɨ́] 'your very big animal'

['sánánɨ́] 'your turkey'

['sánáñā̠] 'her turkey'

['kūnɨ̄nɨ́'kūtū'kánɨ̄nǎ] 'you will see my long
nose'

['sānā̠'sánánɨ́] 'your turkey will get lost'

['kɨ̄tɨ̄'káʔnūnɨ́] 'your big animal'

Directions:

Rewrite the last six utterances putting spaces or hyphens where appropriate.
The data as presented are phonemically written except for word division.

Problem 239--Restricted Zoque[1] A

[heksu] 'he hurried'   [pʌngʌsi] 'on the man'

[hekspa] 'he hurries'   [ʔunekʌsi] 'on the
child'

[hekskeʔtpa] 'he
also hurries'   [kungeʔtpa] 'he
also falls'

[ʔunetaʔm] 'children'   [kukyʌsi] 'on a tree'

[kunu] 'he fell'   [pʌndaʔm] 'men'

[kunba] 'he falls'   [kuy] 'tree'

[teʔpʌnkunu] 'the
man fell'   [teʔkuykunu] 'the
tree fell'

[pʌn] 'man'   [hʌyu] 'he cried'

[teʔunekunu] 'the
child fell'   [maŋbakyunu] 'he is
going to fall'

[minba] 'he is coming'   [maŋba] 'he is going'

[hʌpya] 'he cries'   [hʌkyeʔtpa] 'she
cries too'

[ɸʌʔpya] 'it stays'   [ɸʌʔyu] 'it stayed'

Directions:

What criteria can be used in this
problem to determine word boundaries? Rewrite phonemically, placing spaces at appro-

---

priate places.

Problem 240--Restricted Cuzco Quechua[1] A

Phonetic Data:

['kaɖi] 'salt'   ['laka̠] 'a (certain)
white worm'

['čaki] 'foot'   ['lak̠ʔa] 'thief'

['čaka] 'bridge'   [mi'xuni][2] 'I eat'

['wikʔar] 'belt'   ['mikhuy] 'come!'

['lak̠ha] 'shadow'   [mixu'šani] 'I am
eating'

[mixuči'šani] 'I am giving (to someone)
to eat'

Directions:

What phonetic characteristic of
these words might help to find word boundaries in connected Quechua speech?

Problem 241--Restricted Mazateco[3] B

Phonetic Data:

['ska·¹]   'foolish'
[si¹'ska·¹]   'he plays'
[ma³ska¹'ya·³]   'it is a mistake'
[ma³ska¹'ya·³li²] 'you make a mistake'
[ma³ska¹'ya·³na³] 'I make a mistake'
[si¹'ska·¹ni¹]   'he plays indeed'
['se·⁴⁻³]   'he sings'
[ti¹'se·⁴⁻³]   'he is singing'
[b̥ʔe¹'se·⁴⁻³]   'he whistles'
[ti¹si¹'se·⁴⁻³]   'he is teaching singing'
[si¹'se·⁴⁻³li²]   'he teaches singing to
you'
[b̥ʔe¹'se·⁴⁻³ni¹] 'he whistles indeed'
[ti¹si¹'se·⁴⁻³na³] 'he is teaching singing
to me'
['se·³]   'thick'
['ska·⁴]   'he will fall'
['na·⁴li⁴]   'your mother'
['se·¹]   'he will sing'

---

[1]Data from author's rough field
notes, 1943. Exclamatory utterances tend to
form a different pattern, not indicated here,
with utterance-final stress.

[2]The velar fricative in this verb
varies freely to a corresponding velar stop--
which is a distinct phoneme; other informants in pronouncing this word use only the
stop.

[3]Data from Eunice V. Pike, Summer
Institute of Linguistics.

---

the problem, see Kenneth L. Pike, "Analysis
of a Mixteco Text," _International Journal of
American Linguistics_, X (October, 1944),
128-32.

[1]Data from William Wonderly, Summer
Institute of Linguistics. Recent loan words
from Spanish now force a reinterpretation of
Zoque phonemic structure. The conclusion to
be gathered from this data is valid only for
the Zoque pre-loan situation.

['ka·$^{4-3}$na^3]	'I am able'
['ye·^{4}]	'snake'
[ƀa^3'ne·^{1}]	'he washes'
[ki^3'sʔe·$^{4-3}$]	'he obtained'
[ƀa^{3}ne·^{1}ni^1]	'he washes indeed'

Directions:

Where are hyphens needed and why? What are the alternatives to the utilization of hyphens; and how would these alternatives affect the phonemic analysis of stress?

Problem 242--Restricted Mazateco[1] C

Phonetic Data:[2]

['ye·^{4}]	'snake'
[ye^{4}na^4'ṣi̥·^{4}]	'rattlesnake'
[na^4'ṣi̥·^{4}]	'seeds'
[ti^1'ti·^{2}]	'it is burning'
[na^3'nda·$^{1-3}$]	'water'
[nda^1'ti·$^{2-3}$]	'kerosene'
['khoa·^{4}]	'abstract thing'
[khoa^{4}tṣi^4'ne·^{4}]	'wisdom'
['ya·$^{1-3}$]	'wood'
[tṣi^{4}ne^4'ya·$^{1-3}$]	'carpenter'
[tṣi^{4}ne^{4}na^{4}Nni·$^{1-3}$]	'orchestra leader'
[na^4'Nni·$^{1-3}$]	'stringed instrument'
[lao^{4}tṣi^3'ko̥·$^{3-4}$]	'grave stone'
[na^{4}tṣi^3'ko̥·$^{3-4}$]	'godmother'
[ni^{4}ndo^{3}tṣi^3'ko̥·$^{3-4}$]	'smallpox'
[la^{4}hao·^{4}]	'stone'
[htsi^1'lao·^{4}]	'hailstone'
[hko^4]	'his head'
[tshe^2]	'clean'
[na^4'ṣi̥·^{4}'Mma·$^{2-3}$ṣi^3-'ʔndo·$^{3-4}$]	'the black rotten seed'

[1]Data from Eunice V. Pike, Summer Institute of Linguistics.

[2]When two or more syllables are stressed in a single phrase, all but the last have their length and intensity considerably decreased; this modification is not symbolized in the present data. Hyphens indicate proclitics; sufficient evidence is not presented for their inductive analysis here.

[na^{4}tṣi^3'ko̥·^{3}'ʔndi·$^{1-3}$]	'little godmother'
[na^{4}tṣi^3'ko̥·^{3}'ʔndi·$^{1-3}$ṣi^3-htṣi^1'nga·$^{3-4}$]	'the little old godmother'
[htsi^1'lao·^{4}'he$^{3-4}$ṣi^3-'ʔndži·^{4}]	'the big wet hailstone'
['ye·^{4}ʔndi·^{1}ṣi^3-'to̥a·^{2}]	'the little poisonous snake'
[ye^{4}na^4'ṣi̥·^{4}ʔndi·$^{1-3}$]	'the little rattlesnake'
[tṣi^{4}ne^4'ya·^{1}nda·$^{4-3}$]	'the good carpenter'
['yao$^{3-4}$]	'meat'
[yao^3'ʔndi$^{1-3}$]	'tenderloin'
[yao^3'ʔndi^1'ʔndi$^{1-3}$]	'the little tenderloin'

Directions:

List the compounds. Explain the criteria utilized for determining word boundaries in this set of data.

Problem 243--Restricted Mazateco[1] D

Phonetic Data:

[ƀa^3'koi·$^{2-3}$]	'you show'
[ƀa^{3}ko^2'yai·^{3}]	'you teach'
[ƀa^{3}ko^2'ya·nai$^{1-3}$]	'you teach me'
[ƀa^{3}ko^{2}ya^3'nga·^{1}nai$^{1-3}$]	'you teach me again'
[tṣo^{1}tʔai·$^{4-3}$]	'you try!'
[tṣo^{1}tʔa$^{4-3}$'yai·^{3}]	'you study!'
[tṣo^{1}tʔa$^{4-3}$ya^3'so̥i̥·$^{2-3}$]	'you review!'
[ha^4'tʔa·$^{4-3}$]	'against (it)'
[ha^4'ya·^{3}]	'inside (it)'
[ha^4'so̥·^{2}]	'on top (of it)'
[tṣo^{1}tʔa$^{4-3}$ya^3'so̥·^{2}lai^4]	'you review it!'
[tṣo^{1}tʔa$^{4-3}$ya^{3}so̥^{2}'nga·^{1}lai^4]	'you review it again'
[tṣo^1'tʔai·$^{4-3}$'Nngoi·^{3}]	'you try one!'
[tṣo^1'tʔai·$^{4-3}$tṣa^1'hƀa·^{3}]	'you try John!'
[tṣa^1'hƀa·^{3}]	'John'

Directions:

Rewrite the data phonemically; supplement the data with that from the two previous problems. List the compounds. What types of criteria determine word boundaries?

[1]Data from Eunice V. Pike, Summer Institute of Linguistics.

Chapter 14

TYPES   OF   DESCRIPTIVE   STATEMENTS

Once the investigator has made an analysis of the phonemes of a language, he should make a written statement describing them and the types of phonological and grammatical sequences in which they occur so that his information will be available to other persons. If the language has previously not been reduced to writing it may well be that other individuals wish to learn to speak the language or to prepare written materials for it. If so, it is a great convenience to them to have an analysis of the phonemes. With a phonemic statement adequately prepared in advance, a person can come into a study of a strange language and learn it more rapidly. This is especially true if a grammatical statement and a dictionary accompany the phonemic statement.

Students of linguistics in general also need to have precise, accurate, and detailed descriptions of the sound systems of all languages. They wish to make general studies of the types of structural relationships which are found around the world, in the hope of discovering various language characteristics of a universal nature which will increase their understanding of basic language types. For this purpose they need statements about the large number of languages of which there are as yet no technical materials available.

The audience for which one is writing will determine to considerable extent the form in which the descriptive statement will appear. In writing for people who are technicians, for example, much of the technical nomenclature does not need to be defined. On the other hand a description prepared for a lay audience must have no undefined linguistic terms at all. This difference may affect appreciably the succinctness with which the data can be presented and the total size of the resultant manuscript. Also, it will modify the form in which the data will be given and, to some extent, the data which will be included.

For the investigator himself it is important that he prepare a written statement of the phonemic data. This helps (1) to clarify his ideas, (2) to check the completeness of his materials, (3) to assemble evidences which help him reach phonemic conclusions, and (4) to provide a technically accurate foundation which may serve as the basis for practical orthographic decisions.

DESCRIPTIVE STATEMENT TYPE A:

A BRIEF TECHNICAL STATEMENT

The simplest and shortest technical statement of the phonemes of the language is likely to be found as a footnote to an article on grammar, or as a very brief paragraph within some morphological statement of a language. In this type of presentation the audience is assumed to be a technical one familiar with phonemic and phonetic terminology and needing only a brief statement of the data in order to understand it.

The purpose of such a note is (1) to explain the phonetic implication of the symbols, especially any unusual symbols, so the reader can pronounce the forms listed, and (2) to give a short introduction to the system of sounds so the reader can understand substitution of phonemes in the grammar in terms of the symmetry of the phonemic system as a whole.

In a note of this type the sounds may be listed in groups (1) according to their general phonetic type and (2) according to the groups which function uniformly or in similar ways in distribution in phonemic and grammatical units of the language. A brief descriptive word or two states the type of segments represented by these groups, with additional comments for prominent varieties which are modified according to environments. Note, for example, the following statement of the sounds of Mixteco:

'The phonemic symbols are used in general as in traditional phonetic alphabets: voiceless unaspirated stops: [p, t, č, k, k^w, ʔ]; prenasalized voiced stops: [^{m}b, ^{n}d, ^{n}ǰ, ^{n}g] (these tend to unvoice the occlusion in morpheme-medial position); voiced nasals: [m, n, ñ] (postsyllabic nasal is actualized as phonetic nasalization of the preceding syllabic, or in morpheme structure CVV, CVʔV, CVhV, of the two preceding syllabics--it occurs only morpheme final, and is the only consonant so to occur); voiced fricatives: [b, d, ž] ([b] varies freely from a stop, especially initially in morphemes, to a flat fricative in the same position, and to a [w], especially morpheme medially; [ž] varies freely from a sibilant to [y]); voiceless fricatives: [s, š, ṧ, h] ([š] is rare with this informant, whereas the retroflex phoneme [š] is more frequent; some informants from the same village use only one phoneme which phonetically is usually of the nonretroflex variety; [h] varies from little to considerable friction on the velum); lateral: [l] (slightly fricative after [i]); the trill: [r] (fricative trill in all positions except enclitic initial, where it becomes a single flap); the vowels: [i, e, a, o, u, ə] (fairly close varieties of the first five, with [ə] somewhat back, high, unrounded, or centering); Spanish loans bring in some other sounds and problems. There are three level tonemes; of these, high is written ['], low [`], and mid is given no symbol here.'[1]

DESCRIPTIVE STATEMENT TYPE B:

A BRIEF NONTECHNICAL STATEMENT

With a less technical audience in mind a brief statement of the data may ignore all sounds which are symbolized by letters familiar to a lay audience, and may ignore all conditioned varieties of these sounds, but mention only those symbols with which the lay readers might not be familiar. For unfamiliar sounds, a brief description can be given by comparing them to the sounds of some language familiar to those lay readers who are most likely to be reading the article. On the other hand, a brief phonetic--but nontechnical--description can be made of the sounds. For this type of description of the same material as given above for Mixteco, notice the following:

'The symbol [č] is be read approximately like ch in English change; [ž] as z in azure; [nÿ] as nj in can joke; [š] as sh in ship, with a slight added whistle; [ʔ] as the catch in the throat in the middle of Oh Oh!; [ə] as the vowel of book, but with the lips spread apart; [n], after a vowel, as the nasalization of that vowel.'[2]

DESCRIPTIVE STATEMENT TYPE C:

A KEY TO PRONUNCIATION

In various types of practical literature (in a small dictionary, for example), there may be needed a brief key to pronunciation for laymen who will be using the volume. In such a note one is likely to list first those sounds and symbols which are familiar to at least some of the people--presumably bilinguals--whom the writer expects will utilize the volume. These sounds need not

be given much or any comment (except, perhaps, to say that they are like the sounds of the trade language of the area). Then sounds which differ from those of the trade language are given with samples from the vernacular being described; further illustrations may be given in terms of other languages which are also presumably known to the readers--possibly, for example, Spanish, or French, or German, or Russian, in areas where those languages are well known. (Instead of this definition in terms of samples of well-known languages there may be a very brief, but nontechnical, articulatory description such as the following: 'The symbol [x] represents a fricative sound made by air passing through the narrow space between the palate and the back of the tongue which is raised toward it...').

A very brief statement of this latter type and representing Mixteco, which was previously described for Statement Types A and B, is the following: '[ʌ] is the sound which occurs in [kʌtʌ] 'animal'; [x] is the sound which occurs in [xini], 'head'; ['] is a high tone as in [kuchí] 'pig'; [¯] is a low tone as in [tutū] 'paper'.'[1] This is even more abbreviated than an ordinary key to pronunciation. The readers in this case are the speakers of the language being described; some of them are bilinguals and once these people can identify the words of the vernacular by means of the translation into Spanish (the trade language), the pronunciation of the letters would be immediately known to them.

DESCRIPTIVE STATEMENT TYPE D:

A MONOGRAPH ON PHONEMICS

In addition to the routine phonemic statements and to the highlighted articles (for which see most of the remainder of this chapter), longer technical studies may be made. A long published study may be called a MONOGRAPH. A research monograph attempts to give in detailed analysis some phase of some problem or situation in the phonemics field. Its preparation is quite similar to that of a highlighted article; it represents a special treatise[2] on a particular subject, but is likely to be longer and more detailed.

---

[1]Kenneth L. Pike, "Analysis of a Mixteco Text," International Journal of American Linguistics, X (October, 1944), 115.

[2]Kenneth L. Pike, "Tone Puns in Mixteco," International Journal of American Linguistics, XI (July, 1945), 129.

[1]From cuendú ñanga, Mixteco, San Miguel el Grande, Oaxaca, México, 1946. The data here is translated from the Spanish. Some of the symbols are modified to meet the practical situation.

[2]For sample monographs in the field of phonemics, see Kenneth L. Pike, The Intonation of American English, University of Michigan Publications in Linguistics, I (Ann Arbor: University of Michigan Press, 1945); and Harry Hoijer, Navaho Phonology, University of New Mexico Publications in Anthropology, I (Albuquerque: The University of New Mexico Press, 1945).

DESCRIPTIVE STATEMENT TYPE E:

A TEXTBOOK ON THE PHONETICS OF
SOME LANGUAGE.

A textbook is not limited to a single
topic but covers a wide range of data and is
likely to include a large proportion of material which is the result of the research
of other investigators. In some instances a
phonetic textbook dealing with a single language is prepared for beginners in the field.
In this kind of presentation each technical
term has to be defined and a general background in phonetics and phonemics must be
given to prepare students for understanding
the statements which must be made about the
specific language to be described. For this
reason the descriptive statement of the phonetics and phonemics of one particular language actually tends to turn into a textbook
for phonetics in general, or for some portion
of the field. Two books which represent this
approach and are widely known are the discussion of English phonetics by Jones[1] and
Kenyon,[2] presenting British and American
speech respectively.

DESCRIPTIVE STATEMENT TYPE F:

A HIGHLIGHTED TECHNICAL DESCRIPTION

A HIGHLIGHTED phonemic paper is one
which attempts to present the data so that
some one phase of the phonemic system is
brought forcibly to the reader's attention.
It marshalls all available facts about the
system in such a way as to make one interesting characteristic prominent. The title, the
progression of the outline, and the choice of
material are all designed to make clear the
nature of a new or interesting contribution
to the science of linguistics.

In general, a highlighted paper
should have all the data included in it so
arranged as to contribute to the one point at
hand, but should exclude data which are not
pertinent to that analysis.[3] In this way the
reader finds immediately the most important
parts of the paper without having to work
through a great mass of detail which affects
neither the particular theory nor the general
methodology of the science.

---

[1]Daniel Jones, An Outline of English
Phonetics, Sixth Edition (New York: E. P.
Dutton and Company, 1940).

[2]John Samuel Kenyon, American Pronunciation, A Textbook of Phonetics for Students of English, Sixth Edition (Ann Arbor:
George Wahr, 1935).

[3]The student must not interpret this
to mean that he may with impunity omit certain data which disprove or cast doubt on his
argument. All pertinent data must be recorded, whether they help to support or to
refute the author's conclusions.

A ROUTINE phonemic description (for
which see the next section of this chapter),
on the other hand, is designed to present all
the available phonemic data regarding a language in a clear concise manner, without
calling special attention to any one part of
the data. However, the audience which reads
this type of paper is somewhat limited inasmuch as there is nothing to indicate to the
casual reader that there is anything of particular interest to him in the discussion.
It appeals rather to the person who is interested in languages in general, and therefore
is interested all languages; or it appeals
to the individual who is going to make a further study of that language for technical or
practical purposes. Sometimes the identical
data or parts of those identical data can be
lined up in a different way, so as to be
given a wider appeal.

Wherever possible, a routine paper
should be reworked into a highlighted one
which is designed to present to the reader
some particular part of the information which
may interest him. The writer should highlight material if he knows it will be of interest on the ground that (1) nothing of that
type has ever been described previously, or
that (2) some problem is solved by using a
new approach or new theory. In this case,
readers who wish to be familiar with all
types of language phenomena find the paper
one which is essential for them to read since
it presents information--not of new detail,
but of actual new type--which is not available elsewhere. In other words, it contributes to linguistic theory, as well as to
linguistic knowledge.

It is difficult for a beginner to
write a paper of this type inasmuch as he
may not be aware of the type of articles
which are at present existent in the literature. The advanced student should, however,
be acquainted with all of the pertinent literature in the field, and especially with
those articles which deal with technical approaches and types of interpretation of data.
If he is not certain of the existence or non-
existence of material on the point of issue,
he should search in all available publications which might possibly contain it. Thereafter he is in a position to note what kinds
of items represent (1) data new to the field,
(2) new approaches to linguistic data, or
(3) new linguistic theory. An article which
presents new approaches to data or new types
of interpretation of data is of interest to
many more workers than an article which presents new data only. Nevertheless, before
preparing such a paper, even the advanced
student would usually do well to line up the
complete distributional and descriptive material in a routine way in order to be certain that he is not overlooking facts pertinent to his analysis or to that particular
part of the data which he wishes to present.

The TITLE of a highlighted paper should
reflect its contents so that anyone observing
the title in a bibliographical list will be

likely to find in the title itself the evidence that the paper is of interest to him. If a paper is highlighted, but the title fails to show this fact, even potential readers who search bibliographies of the field may fail to realize that the paper would be of interest to them. The title to a highlighted article should be kept as short as possible, consistent with these aims. A title which is too long cannot readily be printed or used as a running head. As a general rule, a title should not be over thirty-five letters in length. The shorter the title, the better, provided that it indicates the nature of the highlight.

Similarly, a brief table of contents or a brief introductory paragraph should give in very concise form the nature of the highlight in more detail than can be done in the title alone. In this way the reader can go directly to the parts of the article in which he is interested, or he may be convinced that the article as a whole will interest him and read it rather than just glance at it and lay it to one side.

As a usual thing, every article—whether it is of a highlighted type or of a routine type giving data only—should include supplementary material which indicates the source of the information, the time during which it was gathered, informants used, the linguistic family to which the language belongs, and any other data of the linguistic material which the reader needs for his orientation. However, if this information is placed at the beginning of the text, it tends to defeat the purpose of the highlighted approach, since the reader's first attention must then be given to background statements which, as such, have no direct bearing upon the linguistic principles being presented. For this reason the beginner should place all such nonlinguistic information in a footnote or in some inconspicuous place where it will not interfere with the smooth reading of the highlighted material.

In general, one may state that if the student is acquainted with the literature in the field, and then meets a problem in a particular language which he has seen duplicated in the literature, but which is difficult to handle, then if he can solve the problem and describe the results and method of solution, a highlighted article will result. The first person to solve a particular type of problem is a pioneer in that section of the field, since he blazes a trail for others to follow, using the same approach or the same type of solution in the face of similar difficulties. A paper of this type is always a welcome addition to the field.

As a sample article which is well highlighted note the one on Zoque in Chapter 15.[1] This paper is of particular interest

in that it gives discussion of the practical handling of loan words both for linguistic statements and for the preparation of practical orthographies.

DESCRIPTIVE STATEMENT TYPE G:

A DETAILED ROUTINE TECHNICAL STATEMENT

In order to get the phonemic data stated in its simplest, most concise form, the investigator should early aim to make a routine description of the sounds of the language. The audience may be assumed to consist of persons acquainted with phonetics and linguistics in general, so that the technical terminology does not need detailed explanation. The paper may be concerned exclusively with a presentation of the facts about the language without taking time to lay a background for the readers to understand the terms in which it is presented.

Such a ROUTINE statement should include two basic parts: the first of these is a description of the phonetic nature of the phonemes and the second is a description of the environments, sequences, syllable patterns, phonological patterns, and grammatical patterns in which the phonemes occur.

The first of these sections describes the phonetic nature of the norms of each phoneme and the phonetic nature of other submembers of the phonemes. In addition it gives a statement of the particular places in the phonological or grammatical units which may be occupied by the various submembers of these phonemes. For each phoneme, then, there is presented (a) a description of the way in which its submembers are physiologically produced, and (b) the mutually exclusive environments in which they occur.

This descriptive material should be illustrated with words from the language being described. Such illustrations allow the reader to visualize the linguistic pattern much more readily, and to absorb the data faster than he could do with no illustrations. With the illustrations he is able to practice the pronunciation of the phonemes including the various varieties of their submembers and so to fix them in mind. Without such illustrations the statements tend to become a very uninteresting series of facts which are hard to remember. By having practiced on the illustrations, the reader not only understands the material more easily but at the same time is better prepared to read accurately, with the pertinent phonetic modifications, a text written phonemically. When the submembers of phonemes form an intricate pattern so that they are hard to visualize then it is convenient to write each

---

[1] For an article highlighting a small part of the total phonemic data of a language,

but supported by a brief routine description, see Nadine D. Weathers, "Tsotsil Phonemes with Special Reference to Allophones of B," International Journal of American Linguistics, XIII (April, 1947), 108-11.

illustration twice--once in brackets, phonetically, and then immediately following that a repetition of the data written phonemically and enclosed in diagonals. If the material is to be written once only, it should be written phonemically. For a sample of this type of statement which shows complicated submembers written phonetically and phonemically, with technical symbols, notice the following paragraph:[1]

'When the short vowels are contiguous to /y/, they are drawn toward a palatal position. /tiyay/ [ti^yə^yY] he gets it; /ɬkuyuy/ [ɬku^‹yu^‹yY] he burns it; /tancayan/ [tʌnd^{z}ə^yə^n] eight animals.'

Statements concerning the phonetic formation of the phonemes should be arranged neatly and concisely so that the reader may follow them easily. This can be done in one of two ways: in paragraph style, or with lists.

For the paragraph type notice the following excerpt from a description of Huichol.[2]

'There is a series of voiceless unaspirated stops at bilabial, dental, velar, labialized velar and glottal points of articulation, with affricates at alveolar and alveopalatal points of articulation. These are [p, t, k, k^W, ʔ, c, č] as seen in /pizʌ'zʌi/ 'chick', /tai/ 'fire', /ne'ki/ 'my house', /'ʔik^Wai/ 'food', /nemu'ʔu/ 'my head', /'ʔeci pukuri'ʔʌa/ 'it smells bad', and /'ʔeči pu'tewi/ 'he is short'. The velar stop [k] is palatalized when occurring before the mid front vowel [e] as seen in /neke'maci/ [nek^Ye'maci] 'my father' and /neke'ta/ [nek^Ye'ta] 'my foot'. Wnen the alveolar affricate [c] occurs in clusters it is varied to the alveolar grooved fricative [s] as in /nemacta'zeiya/ [nemasta'zeiya] 'I will see you'.'

The beginner will find it easier to utilize a more schematic arrangement of the data concerning the phonetic formation of phonemes. This presentation is constituted of a number of lists: (1) the phonemes, (2) the prominent submembers of the phonemes, (3) brief physiological characterizations of the formation of these submembers, (4) statements of the distribution of these submembers,[3] If there are two or more listed, and (5) illustrations of these data (with phonetic writing paralleling the phonemic writing if the two differ considerably). It is often helpful to use minimally different word pairs as illustrations for phonetically similar phonemes to show their phonemic separation. Phonemes of stress, tone, or length; pertinent border types or modifications; and any further interesting phonetic data which is nonphonemic and which has not been mentioned in the lists, may be listed following the segmental phonemes or handled in a separate section. For illustrations of this arrangement see Problem 245 at the end of this section,[1] p. 186.

Turning now to the second part of the phonemic description, we find that it is constituted of a statement of the distribution of the phonemes in phonological and grammatical units. There are several reasons why a statement of distribution is needed:

(1) It gives a picture of the phonemic structure of the language since phonemic structure largely consists of the permitted sequences of sounds in syllables, the number of syllables within words, types of syllables within words or morphemes, and various other limitations of groups of characteristic sequences. Ultimately, the description of a language has as its goal the presentation of STRUCTURE, not a mere listing of unassociated uncorrelated facts. Therefore, it is desirable to have a statement of these sequences since they constitute a significant part of the phonemic structural pattern.

(2) If some other investigator wishes to check the conclusions of a writer as to the phonemic interpretation of his phonetic data, he must have available a statement of the distribution of submembers of phonemes. Conclusions regarding the mutually exclusive nature of submembers of phonemes are dependent upon observations regarding their occurrences (see Procedure I-C). Likewise, interpretation of certain doubtful sequences (under Procedure IV-B) is dependent upon the analysis of structural pressures from nonsuspicious sequences. If a second investigator wishes to check the conclusions of the first investigator he must, therefore, have available the data concerning distribution which were originally the evidence upon which the first investigator based the conclusions presented in his article. For these reasons technical readers who wish to read the paper critically or who wish to be assured of the accuracy of the phonemic conclusions must have before them statements of distribution of the phonemes and their submembers.

---

[1]Quoted from Herman P. Aschmann, "Totonaco Phonemes," International Journal of American Linguistics, XII (January, 1946), 35.

[2]Quoted from John B. McIntosh, "Huichol Phonemes," International Journal of American Linguistics, XI (January, 1945), 31.

[3]Notice that the distributional statement about submembers is based upon data as it occurs before it is rewritten phonemically.

[1]Or see material on Hungarian Phonemes, by Robert A. Hall, quoted in Chapter 15. The first part of the solution to Problem 245 is modeled after this description by Hall.

(3) Certain of the distributional characteristics of sounds are almost as important for the teaching of pronunciation of a language as are the actual phonetic characteristics of the sounds themselves. If a speaker of Language A has a certain phoneme in his own language, this is no guarantee that he will be able to pronounce the identical sound with ease in Language B if the sound occurs in different types of sequences or in different places in the phonological and grammatical units of that second language. For example, English speakers have no difficulty pronouncing their phoneme /ŋ/ at the end of words nor the phoneme /h/ at the beginning of words, as in 'hang', but English speakers frequently find it very difficult indeed to pronounce in a second language the same sounds when they occur in different orders as, for example, *[ŋæh], which is merely 'hang' in reverse. The reason for this is that /h/ in English occurs only at the beginning of syllables and /ŋ/ occurs only at the end of syllables; this limitation of distribution affects the ease with which English speakers may pronounce these same sounds in sequences unfamiliar to them. Similarly, Spanish speakers have a phoneme /m/, a phoneme /p/, a phoneme /s/, a phoneme /t/, and two kinds of /r/ phoneme, yet they meet extraordinary difficulty in trying to pronounce a sequence of consonants together, such as /mpststr/. Now English speakers also would have difficulty in pronouncing this sequence at the beginning of a word such as */mpststro/, but have no difficulty in pronouncing it when it is divided between two words such as in the phrase 'glimpsed streams'. That consonant cluster which would cause difficulty for English speakers at the beginning of utterances but which causes them only minor difficulty in the middle of an utterance causes Spanish speakers a great deal of difficulty at any place whatsoever, since they are unaccustomed to such long sequences. In other words, the person who wishes to learn a language practically as well as one who wishes to check its analysis needs to have available a statement of the types of sequences which may be encountered in that language.

(4) The grammarian who wishes to utilize a phonemic statement as a basis for his grammatical analysis needs to have available a statement of the structural sequences in the language. This is true for various reasons:

The structure of his grammatical units such as morphemes and words are directly affected or limited by characteristic permitted sequences of sounds. In order to describe his grammatical units, he must have a knowledge of the sequences permitted. If this has been partly prepared for him by the phonemicist, it saves him time. Furthermore, the grammarian may find considerable difficulty in determining the places at which boundaries occur, say, between words. Certain of the criteria which he may wish to use are precisely the phonological ones which are used by the phonemicist to set up phonemes. For example, certain types of sounds may be found to occur only in certain grammatical environments in a certain language. The phonemicist may have interpreted these grammatical environments to be the ends of words and therefore have concluded that these special characteristic sounds are submembers of phonemes which are modified by this word-boundary environment; for example /z/ might become unvoiced at the end of words. The fact that [s] occurs only at certain types of grammatical junctures or boundaries may then be the clue which gives to the phonemicist the basis for uniting [s] and [z] into a single phoneme, and to the grammarian the clue for deciding that a word boundary occurs at such points. If, therefore, the phonemicist presents the data which he has utilized for reaching such conclusions, the grammarian is then able to check all the data and use them for grammatical purposes.

Stress placement in terms of units of words and the like is one of the criteria which are used most frequently by grammarians and phonemicists alike in determining word boundaries, submembers of phonemes, and so on.

Many morphemes are likely to have certain phonemes eliminated and others added or substituted within the course of their usage in a particular language. Often these changes in the phonemic content of morphemes— the contraction, loss of consonants, and the like—can most easily be explained in terms of permitted occurrences of phonemes and permitted occurrences of characteristic sequences of phonemes at certain types of phonological and grammatical borders in the language. If, for example, all utterances end with vowels but certain morphemes basically end with consonants, then these morphemes must inevitably lose their final consonant at the end of utterances. This disappearance of the consonant may be more readily explained as a mechanical loss due to nonpermitted occurrence of utterance-final vowel-consonant sequences than as some type of grammatical process significant to the meaning of the language. If the phonemicist has already lined up permitted occurrences and sequences of phonemes, these frequently can be used by the grammarian for his statement of the morphological structure and morphological action of his units.

After the phonemes have been found and their phonetic characteristics described and their distribution charted in detail, it often is helpful to give some kind of chart or simple series of statements which summarize the distribution data and, if possible, correlate it with groups of phonetically similar sounds. Usually, therefore, some relationship exists between the kinds of sounds which are found and the places in which these groups of sounds may occur in the characteristic sequences of the language. Note, for example, that in the following problem the vowels form a uniform group; they are syllabic and they alone may occur at the ends of words. The stops form a uniform distribution group since they alone may be the second consonant of a consonant cluster. The fricatives all occur word initially but the velar fricatives form a distributional subgroup since they are the only fricatives occurring singly in word-medial position. When the listing shows differences in permitted occurrence of sound types, it constitutes a DIFFERENTIAL DISTRIBUTION chart.

Problem 244--Kalaba Dialect GN

Phonetic Data:

[so.xi]   'fish'   [spo.xpi] 'window'

[ti.pa]   'mouse'   [xta.go] 'dirt'

[sto.gpo] 'to jump'   [pxa.ti] 'sky'

[gti.go] 'grace'   [to.xto] 'cloud'

Directions:

Present a chart combining phonetic characteristics and differential distributional characteristics of the phonemes of this language.

Solution to Problem 244:

Distributional Chart for Kalaba Dialect GN

Syllabics: The Vowels:

/i/, /a/, /o/

Nonsyllabics: The Consonants:

Consonants which may occur as the second element of clusters:

The stops: /p/, /t/

Consonants which may occur between vowels in word-medial position:

The fricative velars: /x/, /g/

Consonants which may occur word initially:

The consonants previously listed, plus the sibilant /s/

Syllable patterns (C = any consonant: V = any vowel):

CV, CCV

Morpheme or Word Patterns:

CVCV, CCVCCV, CVCCV, CCVCV

Notice that the list of syllable patterns gives only the salient characteristics. It does not mention the specific consonant clusters nor the specific single consonants that precede each vowel nor any noncontiguous relationships in distribution.

It does not pretend to present all the detailed data but gives a convenient schematic statement of the patterns.

In a general statement for technical purposes, there are several degrees of detail which one may give, depending upon the purposes of the author or the audience which he has to reach. He chooses to give just enough detail to suit his particular purposes. A large grammar, for example, can include more phonemic detail than a short one and still preserve an effective proportion between the phonological statement and the grammatical statement. A complete statement of the distribution of the phonemes of a language would indicate every place or environment that every phoneme might occur for that entire language and reduce the description of these occurrences to generalizations which are easily understood and remembered. This aim of completeness would ultimately demand an entire lexicon and the form would be too bulky for easy study. For this reason, various types of abbreviated statements have to be considered.

The minimum statement, if any distribution data is to be given at all, should include a presentation of those single consonant phonemes which may occur at the end of syllables, at the beginning of syllables, at the end, beginning and middle of utterances (or words, etc.); similar statements should be made for consonant clusters and for single vowels and clusters of vowels; the clusters should be further analyzed so as to show what kinds of sounds serve as the first, second and third members of the clusters, and so on.

An expanded description would include the distribution of sounds within syllables. It might delineate phonemic occurrences in utterances, morphemes, sentences, affixes, proclitic words, compounds versus noncompounds, stressed and unstressed syllables, syllables of various contrastive relative pitches, distribution of nonsyllabics in relation to syllabics, or the reverse; distribution of noncontiguous vowels or consonants: distribution of clusters in relation to syllable boundaries, morpheme boundaries, word boundaries, utterance boundaries.

The student may wish to have a check list to give him suggestions as to what environments to study for distribution. If so, he may consult the Working Outline for Determining Distribution of Phonemes in Phonological and Grammatical Units (p. 182). Although the Outline is suggestive, it is neither complete nor essentially in the order which must be followed in the analysis or description. Specifically, for example, the student should notice that in the Outline the larger phonological and grammatical units are listed first, and the smaller ones, such as the syllable, are listed last within any one section. This order is usually best reversed in description. The reason for this difference is that analysis in terms of utterances can be made before one knows syllable boundaries and the like within utterances, whereas at the beginning and end of utterances the investigator knows that syllable boundaries, word boundaries, and morpheme boundaries and so on, must be coincidental with the utterance boundaries (cf. pp. 89, 161).

Although the preceding paragraphs imply that distribution is to be described in reference to syllables, it frequently happens that the investigator will have considerable difficulty in doing so. Sometimes the syllable divisions are not readily apparent; the investigator may be in doubt, for example, as to whether a sequence of vowels such as [ai] constitutes one syllable or two; or he may locate easily the syllabic but be in doubt as to whether the syllable break occurs before, after, or within the consonant in such a sequence as VCV. When difficulties of this type are encountered, and the phonetic data do not become sufficiently clear after some time to allow a distributional description in terms of phonetic syllables, or if description in terms of phonetic syllables seems not to be pertinent to or in close correlation with the structure of the phoneme sequences, the analyst should then adopt one of two expedients for description: (1) he should analyze the language in terms of phonemic syllables according to the methods of Analytical Procedure IV-1 (pp. 144-7); or (2) he should choose as the basic unit of reference for his description some other entity, such as the word (as is done, in part, in Problem 245, p. 186).

For a language type in which certain features of distribution are best described in terms of morphemes of a different type, note Mixteco. In Mixteco[1] there is an intricate series of limitations which controls which types of identical or diverse vowels may appear first or second in morphemes of type CVCV. If, for example, /e/ appears in the second syllable, the first vowel will always be either /e/ or /o/ but never /i/ or /a/ or /u/ or /ə/; /i/, /a/, and /u/ may occur in any order together in the pattern, but the noncontiguous sequences with two vowels of the set /e/, /o/, and /ə/ are limited to CeCe, CoCe, CəCə, and CoCo--i.e., the noncontiguous sequences of identical vowels and the very rare pattern CoCe. A different and more highly restricted set of limitations appears with the pattern CVV or CVʔV; one finds only the contiguous or noncontiguous geminates or sequences /ia/, /ua/, /ai/, /io/, and /au/, as for example, /žaú/ 'century plant', but not *Ceu except in loan names (e.g., /teú/ 'Matthew').

These distributional facts are highly pertinent to the phonological structure of Mixteco, but can only be best described as

limitations imposed by the structure of the morpheme.[1] In situations of this kind, the phonemic statement should utilize grammatical terminology such as 'morpheme', 'word'.

In some languages the Procedures of Chapter 13 fail to give an easily definable unit which can be called a word. Mixteco is of this type, and that is in part the reason why distribution there may better be described in terms of the morpheme rather than of the word.[2]

In order for the investigator to present a statement of the distribution of the phonemes, he needs to have the material gathered together in some pertinent way. The most satisfactory is to list tentative material in the form of CHARTS. Certain of those already illustrated for other purposes may be used here also. Note, for example, the charts on page 132-3. In them the sequences of consonants are listed and divided according to the types of consonants entering the sequence, and subdivided according to their points of articulation. The vowels are similarly illustrated. Notice that they can be classified according to the first or second element of the sequence.

The data for the charts may be subdivided in many ways. Hints for these can be obtained from the Working Outline for Determining Distribution (p. 182). Note the following sample, which is one of the most important:

Environment of Consonants in Relation to Position in Utterances

Consonants	Final[3]	Initial	Medial
Single p...... m...... s...... r......			
Clusters sp..... st..... sk.....			

[1] The only alternative is to attempt to set up some type of two-mora phonological unit and give it some such label as a 'mora couplet,' defined phonologically as a two-mora sequence in which the first--but not the second--mora may receive an optional nonphonemic stress. A very awkward description results if one attempts to handle the material from this starting point, since it does not allow for the reappearance, under some conditions, of vowels and tone which may be suppressed under other conditions.

[2] See Kenneth L. Pike, "Analysis of a Mixteco Text," International Journal of American Linguistics, X (October, 1944), 113-38.

[3] Final consonants are listed first,

---

[1] Data by the author from an unpublished paper presented to the summer meeting of the Linguistic Society of America, in 1939.

It proves difficult or impossible to tell a person in advance exactly what material he can profitably chart. Certain general rules apply, however: (1) Determine the best starting point for the description (i.e., the phonemic syllable, or word, or utterance). (2) Determine the general pattern of syllables, or words, or morphemes (i.e., note sequence types such as CVC, CV, and so on). (3) Make charts which will indicate clearly the specific distribution of vowels and consonants, or clusters of vowels and consonants, in these positions. (4) Then make further charts to find the details of distribution in large units such as the word, or stress groups, and the like.

To help the student to be aware of positions or environments which he wishes to check for distribution, a Working Outline for Determining Distribution will be given presently. This is intended to be suggestive, and not to be slavishly followed.

If the investigator has prepared a FILE of morphemes or of words, some of the data for charting may be abstracted directly from it. Specifically, initial consonants and vowels and their clusters will already be arranged alphabetically. They need only to be rearranged to show groupings according to phonetic and distributional interrelationships. Some people prefer to work with files rather than with charts. They can do so for phonemic distribution (1) provided that the compartments of the file are divided and labelled so as to have separate sections for the types of distribution being studied, and (2) provided that the sections are subdivided according to phonetic type rather than alphabetically.

There remains one very severe disadvantage to the utilization of files rather than charts for the studying of distributions: The student needs to see all at one time, in a glance, a set of distributional relations. This cannot be done conveniently while slips are in a file--and spreading them out on a desk is awkward, though by no means impossible. A gap in distribution--e.g., /sp/, /st/, but not /sk/--can be seen more readily in charted form than when each item is on a separate slip.[1] On the other hand, in a filing arrangement more illustrations may be immediately available; but in initial charts an adequate number of illustrations--say two for each item--can be included so as to off-

set this disadvantage of isolated lists of sounds.

If a student works with filed material, he should be prepared to break the file, and reshuffle the slips in some form pertinent for charting. This data should then be copied on a chart. Next, the slips should be shuffled into another outline and the data charted again. Successive reworking of the order of the slips may help provide the data for the charting.

Once the data is gathered in charts, lists, files, or in some other way, the student must then be prepared to condense his material so that all important limitations or permitted permutations of consonants in sequence, or vowels likewise, may be clearly and succinctly presented.

In order for the reader to visualize readily the structural types of sequences which have been presented in this distribution study, it is sometimes advisable to supplement a description with a short text. The value of this in a distributional statement is that it then allows the reader to see at a glance the general way in which these structures occur within the language without his having to remember each item mentioned in the detailed description. In a sense, such a text serves the way a photograph does for a book. It cannot serve as a substitute for the book since the descriptive material must be presented, but it makes the statements more interesting. So also a short text sometimes makes it easier for the reader to absorb the statements given in the description and to practice applying the rules for points of submembers of phonemes. However, a long text is expensive to publish and as such likely to be uninteresting to the reader. Therefore, if a text is to be presented at all, it should (1) be short and (2) be annotated in such a way that other values are present besides those of mere illustration; that is, the text should be footnoted to show how the principles in the text are proved valid by it, or grammatical notes should be given so that the text at the same time constitutes a brief grammatical paper.

The remainder of this chapter will consist (1) of the Working Outline for Determining Distribution, (2) Problem 245, giving a sample of detailed routine description of the phonetic nature of phonemes and their distribution, and (3) a few exercise problems.

A WORKING OUTLINE FOR DETERMINING DISTRIBUTION OF PHONEMES IN PHONOLOGICAL AND GRAMMATICAL UNITS

I. General Distribution (to establish the size or appearance of units in general and to determine general types of sequences, which are to be expressed by using C for any consonant, V for any vowel, and so on):

---

and initial second, so that one may the more easily see whether or not medial clusters (-CC-, etc.) equal -C + C-.

[1]In addition, rules for tonal interchange in the grammar are likewise best reduced to tables or charts. For samples and discussion of them, see Kenneth L. Pike, Tone Languages, Mimeographed edition (Glendale: Summer Institute of Linguistics, 1943, 1945).

A. Structural types of phonemic syllables (whether or not equated to moras)

B. Structural types of morphemes (or of various kinds of morphemes)

C. Structural types of words (or of various kinds of words)

D. Structural characteristics of utterances

II. <u>Specific Distribution</u> (to establish the occurrence of specific sounds within the specific units in the general types of permitted structural sequences given under I):

A. Single vowels (in relation to basic phonological and grammatical units)

   1. In relation to utterances

      a. final
      b. initial
      c. medial, within utterances
      d. medial, between utterances

   2. In relation to words[1]

      a. final
      b. initial
      c. medial, within words
      d. medial, between words

   3. In relation to morphemes (or in relation to special types of morphemes--e.g., proclitics or enclitics)

      a. final
      b. initial
      c. medial, within morphemes
      d. medial, between morphemes

   4. In relation to syllable structure

      a. final
      b. initial
      c. medial

   5. In relation to specific consonants

      a. following consonants
      b. between consonants
      c. preceding consonants

   6. In relation to nonsegmental characteristics

      a. stress
      b. length
      c. tone
      d. intonation

---

[1]Note: One may be unable to handle description in terms of words until after considerable study to determine what items should be considered words. See Chapter 13.

B. Clusters of vowels

   1. In relation to utterances

      a. final
      b. initial
      c. medial, within utterances
      d. medial, between utterances

   2. In relation to words

      a. final
      b. initial
      c. medial, within words
      d. medial, between words

   3. In relation to morphemes

      a. final
      b. initial
      c. medial, within morphemes
      d. medial, between morphemes

   4. In relation to syllable structure

      a. as nonsyllabic
      b. first vowel syllabic
      c. second vowel syllabic

   5. In relation to specific consonants

      a. following consonants
      b. between consonants
      c. preceding consonants

   6. In relation to nonsegmental phonemes

      a. stress

         (1) each vowel stressed
         (2) first vowel stressed
         (3) second vowel stressed

      b. length

         (1) each vowel long
         (2) first vowel long
         (3) second vowel long

      c. tone (subdivide according to permitted tone patterns: for example, high high, high mid, high low; mid high, mid mid, mid low; low high, etc.)

      d. intonation

C. Single vowels or clusters of vowels in relation to close-knit nuclei (vowels followed by phonemes such as y, w, r, l, h, ?, having special distributions and forming with them nuclear sequences)

D. Single consonants

   1. In relation to utterances

      a. final
      b. initial

       c. medial, within utterances
       d. medial, between utterances

   2. In relation to words

       a. final
       b. initial
       c. medial, within words
       d. medial, between words

   3. In relation to morphemes

       a. final
       b. initial
       c. medial, within morphemes
       d. medial, between morphemes

   4. In relation to syllable structure

       a. final
       b. initial
       c. medial, between syllables

   5. In relation to specific vowels

       a. following vowels
       b. between vowels
       c. preceding vowels

   6. In relation to nonsegmental pho-
      nemes

       a. in stressed syllables versus
          unstressed syllables.
       b. in syllables with various
          vowel lengths; (or constitut-
          ing various consonant lengths)
       c. in syllables of various
          pitches (as carriers or non-
          carriers of contrastive tone
          or intonation)

E. Consonant clusters

   1. In relation to utterances

       a. final

       b. initial
       c. medial, within utterances
       d. medial, between utterances

   2. In relation to words

       a. final
       b. initial
       c. medial, within words
       d. medial, between words

   3. In relation to morphemes

       a. final
       b. initial
       c. medial within morphemes
       d. medial, between morphemes

   4. In relation to syllable structure

       a. final, initial, medial
       b. ambisyllabic

          (1) between words
          (2) between morphemes
          (3) within words

   5. In relation to specific vowels

       a. following vowels
       b. between vowels
       c. preceding vowels

   6. In relation to nonsegmental pho-
      nemes

       a. in stressed syllables versus
          unstressed syllables
       b. in syllables with various
          vowel lengths; (or constitut-
          ing various consonant lengths)
       c. in syllables of various
          pitches (as carriers or non-
          carriers of contrastive tone
          or intonation)

Problem 245--Kalaba Dialect GO

Phonetic Data:

[ótswàtsókO]	'she runs'	[wúwàtsókO]	'he runs'	[wàtsóktṧì]	'we run'	[ànwàtsókO]	'you run'
[ótsráni̇]	'she stabs'	[wílání̇]	'he stabs'	[ráni̇tṧì]	'we stab'	[ànráni̇]	'you stab'
[ótṧíwóʔ]	'she yells'	[wúwóʔ]	'he yells'	[íwótṧì]	'we yell'	[àníwóʔ]	'you yell'
[ótskóyi̇tṧ]	'she returns'	[wíkóyi̇tṧ]	'he returns'	[kóyi̇štṧì]	'we return'	[àngóyi̇tṧ]	'you return'
[ótspóyi̇ts]	'she possesses'	[wípóyi̇ts]	'he possesses'	[póyi̇stṧì]	'we possess'	[ànbóyi̇ts]	'you possess'
[ótssóyą̇]	'she sings'	[wítsóyą̇]	'he sings'	[tsóyàndž̇ì]	'we sing'	[àndzóyą̇]	'you sing'
[ótswòndáʔ]	'she dances'	[wúwòndáʔ]	'he dances'	[wòndátṧì]	'we dance'	[ànwòndáʔ]	'you dance'
[ótsnàpA]	'her house'	[wísnàpA]	'his house'	[snàptṧì]	'houses'	[ànznàpA]	'your house'

[ótšíwð]	'her cow'	[wúwð]	'his cow'	[íwðtšî]	'cattle'	[ǎníwð]	'your cow'
[ótšínzóí]	'she eats'	[wínzóí]	'he eats'	[ínzóítšî]	'we eat'	[ǎnínzóí]	'you eat'
[ótsópìs]	'she carries'	[wísópìs]	'he carries'	[sópìstšî]	'we carry'	[ǎnzópìs]	'you carry'
[ótsyą́]	'her fire'	[wíyą́]	'his fire'	[yándžî]	'fires'	[ǎnyą́]	'your fire'
[ótšìpá?]	'she sleeps'	[wípá?]	'he sleeps'	[ípátšî]	'we sleep'	[ǎnìpá?]	'you sleep'
[óstšìù]	'her nose'	[wítšìù]	'his nose'	[tšìùtšî]	'noses'	[ǎndžìù]	'your nose'
[ótsyápó̧]	'her uncle'	[wíyápó̧]	'his uncle'	[yápóndžî]	'uncles'	[ǎnyápó̧]	'your uncle'
[óstšítI]	'she cooks'	[wítšítI]	'he cooks'	[tšítšî]	'we cook'	[ǎndžítI]	'you cook'
[óstsátš]	'her spear'	[wítsátš]	'his spear'	[tsáštšî]	'spears'	[ǎndzátš]	'your spear'
[ótsró?]	'she burns'	[wíló?]	'he burns'	[rótšî]	'we burn'	[ǎnró?]	'you burn'
[ótsnàpâî]	'her paper'	[wínàpâî]	'his paper'	[nàpâîtšî]	'papers'	[ǎn·àpâî]	'your paper'
[ótsàlí?]	'her ball'	[wísàlí?]	'his ball'	[sàlítšî]	'balls'	[ǎnzàlí?]	'your ball'

Directions:

Write a technical description of the phonetic nature and the distribution of the phonemes of this language.

Solution to Problem 245:

I. Formational Statement of the Phonemes:

A. Consonants: All nonvocoids; all vocoids preceding a more syllabic vocoid; the second vocoid of a vocoid cluster in which each seems to be equally syllabic.

Phoneme:	Allophones:	Description: Occurrence: Example:
/p/	[p]	Voiceless bilabial unaspirated stop. Occurs except word final or after /n/. /wípóyi¢/ [wípóyìts] 'he possesses'.
	[pʰ]	Voiceless bilabial aspirated stop, with aspiration actualized with the voiceless quality of the preceding voiced vowel. Occurs word final. /ansnap/ [ǎnznàpA] 'your house'.
	[b]	Voiced bilabial stop. Occurs after /n/. /anpóyi¢/ [ǎnbóyìts] 'you possess'.
/t/	[tʰ]	Voiceless alveolar aspirated stop, with aspiration actualized with the voiceless quality of the preceding voiced vowel. Occurs word final. /óschít/ [óstšítI] 'she cooks'.
	[d]	Voiced alveolar stop. Occurs after /n/. /wontáči/

[wðndátšî] 'we dance'.

/¢/	[ts]	Voiceless alveolar unaspirated grooved affricate. Occurs except after /n/. /ó¢yán/ [ótsyą́] 'her fire'.
	[dz]	Voiced alveolar grooved affricate. Occurs after /n/. /an¢óyan/ [ǎndzóyą̀] 'you sing'.
/č/	[tš]	Voiceless alveopalatal unaspirated grooved affricate. Occurs except after /n/. /snapči/ [snàptšî] 'houses'.
	[dž]	Voiced alveopalatal grooved affricate. Occurs after /n/. /yápónči/ [yápóndžî] 'uncles'.
	[š]	Voiceless alveopalatal grooved fricative. Occurs before /č/. /¢áčči/ [tsáštšî] 'spears'. (Note: [š] could be considered a separate phoneme. Such an interpretation would be based on the extreme limitations of clusters in the language and on the analogous pattern of /s/.)
/k/	[k]	Voiceless velar unaspirated stop. Occurs except word final and after /n/. /wa¢ókči/ [wàtsóktšî] 'we run'.
	[kʰ]	Voiceless velar aspirated stop, with aspiration actualized with the voiceless quality of the preceding voiced vowel. Occurs word final. /anwa¢ók/ [ǎnwàtsókO] 'you run'.
	[g]	Voiced velar stop. Occurs after /n/. /ankóyič/ [ǎngóyìtš] 'you return.'

/s/ [s] Voiceless alveolar grooved fricative. Occurs except after /n/. /póyisči/ [póyìstšì] 'we possess'.

[z] Voiced alveolar grooved fricative. Occurs after /n/. /ansópis/ [ànzópìs] 'you carry'.

/n/ [n] Voiced alveolar nasal. Occurs except before velar stop. /wínsóy/ [wínzóí] 'he eats'.

[ŋ] Voiced velar nasal. Occurs before velar stop. /ankóyič/ [àŋóyìtš] 'you return'.

[(ṽ)] Actualized as a nasalized vowel. Occurs only word final. /oṣ¢óyan/ [óstsòyą] 'she sings'.

/r/ [r] Voiced mid close central unrounded retroflexed vocoid. Occurs except contiguous to /i/. /ránıči/ [ránìtšì] 'we stab'.

[l] Voiced alveolar lateral. Occurs contiguous to /i/. /ó¢arí/ [ótsàlí?] 'her ball'.

/y/ [y] Voiced high close front unrounded nonsyllabic vocoid. Occurs preceding a syllabic. /yánči/ [yándžì] 'fires'.

[(V)i] Voiced high close front unrounded syllabic vocoid. Occurs as second member of a vocoid cluster in which both are phonetically equally syllabic. /óčinsóy/ [ótšìnzóí] 'she eats'.

/w/ [w] Voiced high close back rounded nonsyllabic vocoid. Occurs preceding a syllabic. /wíwondá/ [wùwòndá?] 'he dances'.

[(V)u] Voiced high close back rounded syllabic vocoid. Occurs as second member of a vocoid cluster in which both are phonetically equally syllabic. /ósčiw/ [óstšìù] 'her nose'.

B. Vowels: All single vocoids; the most syllabic vocoid of a vocoid cluster; the first vocoid of a vocoid cluster in which each seems to be equally syllabic.

Phoneme:	Allophones:	Description: Occurrence: Examples:

/i/ [i] Voiced high close front unrounded vocoid. Occurs except between two /w/s. /wísópis/ [wísópìs] 'he

carries'.

[ü] Voiced high close rounded vocoid. Occurs between two /w/s. /wíwa¢ók/ [wùwàtsókO] 'he runs'.

/o/ [o] Voiced mid close back rounded vocoid. Occurs except before /n/ in word-final position or before /y/. /wíwo/ [wùwò] 'his cow'.

[ɔ] Voiced low close back rounded vocoid. Occurs before /y/ /wí¢óyan/ [wítsòyą] 'he sings'.

[(ǫ)] Voiced mid close back rounded nasalized vocoid. Occurs before /n/ word final. /wíyapón/ [wíyápǫ] 'his uncle'.

/a/ [a] Voiced low open central unrounded vocoid. Occurs except before word-final /n/. /ó¢wontá/ [ótswòndá?] 'she dances'.

[(ą)] Voiced low open central unrounded vocoid. Occurs before /n/ word final. /wíyan/ [wíyą] 'his fire'.

C. Suprasegmental Phonemes:

/'/ ['] High tone. Occurs on all vowels except in word-final position. /wí¢áč/ [wítsátš] 'his spear'.

['?] High tone followed by unaspirated glottal stop. Occurs word final. /wíró/ [wíló?] 'he burns'.

/(zero)/ [ˋ] Low tone. Occurs on all vowels. /ansnap/ [ànznàpA] 'your house'.

D. Additional Nonphonemic Phonetic Phenomena:

Pitch on syllabic consonantal vocoids is the same as the tone of the preceding vowel. /wíčiw/ [wítšìù] 'his nose'.

(Possible alternate treatment of [?].) Glottal stop occurs word final following a vowel on high tone. /anipá/ [ànìpá?] 'you sleep'.

II. Distributional Statement of the Phonemes.

A. General distribution in relation to the word.

1. There are no vowel clusters. /róči/ 'we burn'.

2. Each word has two or three vowels. /an¢óyan/ 'you sing'.

3. These two or three vowels are combined with from two to four consonants in the following patterns:

a. C may or may not occur before or after any vowel. /číči/ 'we cook', /íwóči/ 'we yell', /wíčiw/ 'his nose' /wísarí/ 'his ball'.

b. CC may or may not occur before or after any vowel, except in word-final position. /snapči/ 'houses', /yápónči/ 'uncles'.

c. CCC occurs only following a word-initial vowel /ansnap/ 'your house'.

4. Each word is composed of two morphemes only, a stem and an affix. Affix patterns are:

-CV /-či/ 'first person plural actor-plural of objects'

CV- /wí-/ 'third person singular masculine'

VC- /óȼ-/ 'third person singular feminine'

5. When two vowels come together at morpheme boundaries, the vowel of the stem is lost. /wípá/ [wí + ipá?] 'he sleeps'.

B. Specific distribution in relation to the word.

1. Vowels: There is no limitation within the general patterns of A.

2. Consonants:

a. Single consonants may occur as follows:

Word final: all consonants except /r/. /ansópis/ 'you carry'.

Word initial: all consonants except /t/. /napayči/ 'papers'.

Word final: all consonants.

b. Clusters of two:

Stop plus stop:
pč /snapči/ 'houses'
ȼp /óȼpóyiȼ/ 'she possesses'
ȼk /óȼkóyič/ 'she returns'
kč /waȼókči/ 'we run'
čč /kóyičči/ 'we return'

Stop plus continuant:
ȼn /óȼnap/ 'her house'
ȼr /óȼró/ 'she burns'

ȼy /óȼyápón/ 'her uncle'

Continuant plus stop:
sȼ /ósȼóyan/ 'she sings'
sč /ósčít/ 'she cooks'
np /anpóyiȼ/ 'you possess'
nt /anwontá/ 'you dance'
nȼ /anȼáč/ 'your spear'
nč /ančít/ 'you cook'
nk /ankóyič/ 'you return'
yč /ínsóyči/ 'we eat'
wč /čiwči/ 'noses'

Continuant plus continuant:
sn /wísnap/ 'his house'
ns /ansarí/ 'your ball'
nr /anró/ 'you burn'
nw /anwontá/ 'you dance'
ny /anyán/ 'your fire'

c. Clusters of three:

nsn /ansnap/ 'your house'

Problem 246--Kalaba Dialect GO continued

Directions:

1. Make a phonetic chart of the phonemic norms of Problem 245.

2. Present the evidence and discuss the conflicting pressures for the analysis of [š] as /s/ or /č/.

3. Present the evidence and discuss the conflicting pressures for the analysis of [ʔ] as /ʔ/ or part of /'/.

4. Prove that [-Vi] = /Vy/.

5. Prove that [dž] = /č/.

6. Prove that [tI] = /t/.

7. Prove that [k^h] = /k/.

8. Prove that [g] = /k/.

9. Prove that [z] = /s/.

10. Prove that [ŋ] = /n/

11. Prove that [ɣ] = /Vn/.

12. Prove that [l] = /r/.

13. Show from the evidence in the description that [ü] is a submember of /i/. Prove that it is not a submember of /u/.

14. Why is it strange that /o/ > [ɔ] here?

15. Why are tone symbols omitted from /ansnap/ 'your house'?

16. Why is tone omitted from the phonemic rewriting of [-ù] of [wítšiù] 'his nose'?

17. Rewrite all the data phonemically. Then practice until you can read it aloud, rapidly and correctly from the rewritten material.

18. Make a Key to Pronunciation for this language, assuming that it is spoken where English is the trade language.

19. What phonetic/phonemic problems would a native of Kalaba Dialect GO meet in trying to learn English?

20. What types of facts would appear in a differential distribution chart for this language?

Problem 247--Kalaba Dialect GP

Phonetic Data:

[sugap]	'hammer'	[kagas]	'coffee'
[kasan]	'pumpkin'	[suguk]	'horse'
[pabus]	'ear'	[nasup]	'bread'
[pudan]	'mother'	[nuban]	'valley'
[tusut]	'few'	[sadat]	'cousin'
[kubup]	'basket'	[tasut]	'coat'
[naban]	'smoke'	[padas]	'thunder'
[tugak]	'wet'		

[padaŋ kusan] 'tall tree'

Directions:

Rewrite the first column phonemically.

Describe the phonemes as for a brief footnote in a technical article.

Problem 248--Kalaba Dialect GQ

Phonetic Data:

[kan.ba]	'dog'	[nas.ka]	'stupid'
[pa.sa]	'squash'	[ka.ka]	'cat'
[tas.sa]	'to bleed'	[sa.ta]	'to forget'
[saŋ.ga]	'to dance'	[tan.za]	'to sit'
[na.pa]	'dark'	[pa.ta]	'slow'
[pas.ta]	'happy'	[nas.pa]	'cheat'
[san.da]	'eel'	[kas.pa]	'to bury'
[taŋ.ga]	'buzzard'		

[san.ba ta.ta] 'his father is here'

Directions:

Rewrite the first column phonemically.

Describe the phonemes briefly in a note to laymen.

Problem 249--Kalaba Dialect GR

Phonetic Data:

[to.dox]	'onion'	[not.sok]	'tame'
[kos.kop]	'box'	[kos.toN]	'good'
[not.sot]	'moss'	[tok.sop]	'backbone'
[to.sox]	'pear'	[no.got]	'sober'
[sos.tok]	'scar'	[to.dok]	'flat'
[sos.koN]	'muskrat'	[tok.sos]	'bone'

[no.don so.dox] 'he eats apples'

Directions:

Rewrite the second column phonemically.

Prepare a brief Key to Pronunciation for a lay dictionary.

Problem 250--Kalaba Dialect GS

Phonetic Data:

[nabikh]	'horse'	[tagiph]	'udder'
[kubaM]	'liver'	[kibith]	'grape'
[magus]	'flower'	[ŋabis]	'pin'
[padax]	'blood'	[pubuɬ]	'cabbage'
[lugaN]	'magic'	[niduN̦]	'son'
[ligif]	'enough'	[nudakh]	'doctor'
[tudaN̦]	'cookpot'	[kaguɬ]	'axe'
[piduth]	'wood'		

[laban pigikh madaN̦] 'a woman cut herself'

[mugux nudiŋ pagaɬ] 'the man uses a fire'

Directions:

Prepare, in list format, a routine description of the phonetic formation of the phonemes.

Problem 251--Kalaba Dialect GT

Phonetic Data:

[nupas]	'smoke'	[gubif]	'wild'
[gafaM]	'to twist'	[bavap]	'to watch'
[nagup]	'dry'	[bifut]	'tree'
[bitif]	'to warp'	[dudus]	'green'
[makik]	'to believe'	[mutuk]	'unkempt'
[dadik]	'underneath'	[mivas]	'to be there'
[gusuN]	'water'	[nasuM]	'hollow'
[gikap]	'yesterday'	[daḵuf]	'yellow'
[bašit]	'to paste'	[gukuN]	'outside'
[buzuN]	'hardened'	[gižiM]	'to give'
[gapat]	'tame'	[nipap]	'to resound'

[magit] 'polite'   [gagak] 'to spin'

[dipuN] 'to stink'   [babap] 'nothing'

Directions:

Same as for Problem 250.

Problem 252--Kalaba Dialect GU

Phonetic Data:

[pe.džomM] 'table'   [ku.žiŋN]   'leg'

[da.setš]   'section'   [dži.mas]   'summer'

[to.məp]   'drum'   [be.džomM] 'hat'

[tši.mas]   'to be blue'   [na.zok]   'to hinder'

[gi.džat]   'hair'   [tšu.duzs] 'to learn'

[no.suzs]   'toenail'   [ga.buk]   'steep'

[džu.ñis]   'to suffer'   [mi.minN]   'to comb'

[me.notš]   'to swallow'   [bo.džes]   'square'

[nu.gat]   'firefly'   [pa.zetš]   'chin'

[di.daŋN]   'husband'   [ka.buk]   'rice'

[bo.šip]   'to meet'

[mi.miŋ gi.džat po.džomM] 'the woman
                           combs her hair'

[džu.ñiz be.džom nu.žik] 'the uncle buys
                           hats'

[gɐ.mus džĭ.mazs pɐ.zeŋN] 'the dog runs
                           away'

[tša.man to.miŋ ku.šitš] 'the bees
                           swarmed here'

Directions:

Make a descriptive statement of the general and specific distribution of the phonemes.

Problem 253--Restricted Gulf Aztec[1] A

Phonetic Data:

['te·]   'what'   ['ša·]   'go'

['tɛ·t]   'stone'   [no·.tɛŋ]   'my mouth'

['tsi·.ka]   'ant'   [no·.pi]   'my aunt'

[no.'ku·]   'uncle!'   ['ko·.mit]   'clay pot'

['mo·.tan]   'your   ['ta·.yol]   'grain of
             tooth'   corn'

['na·.kat]   'meat'   ['ta·.gat]   'man'

['ʔi·.ga]   'for, by   ['ʔa·.kon]   'water
             means of'   pot'

['ʔi·s.tak] 'white'   ['ke·.taš]   'leather'

['nɛ·š.ti]   'ashes'   [no·.ma·]   'my hand'

['ʔu·m.pa]   'there'   ['ʔa·.ʔ.kon] 'who?'

[no.'tso·.tsol] 'my clothes'

[no.'sa·.ya] 'my skirt'

[i.'yʊ·k.ni] 'his brother'

['tso·h.mit] 'blanket'

['ni·.wi] or ['ni·.gwi] 'I come'

['si·.gwat] or ['si·.wat] 'woman'

[te.tʊk.'tsi·.wa·] 'what are you doing?'

[wɛl.'ki·.saʔ] 'he was able to leave'

[ki.'te·.ki] 'he cuts it'

[ki.'nɛ·.ki] 'he wants it'

[nʊk.'pa·.ka] 'I am washing it'

[no.'ta·ŋ.kwa] 'my knee'

[to.'ta·.tsin] 'our dear father'

[tša.'po·.lin] 'grasshopper'

[ʔa.wa.'ši·.kal] 'acorn'

[ʔe.'hɛ·.kat] 'wind'

[no.'ma·h.pil] 'my finger'

[ʔa.'ĺi·m.pa] 'little'

[pi.yam.'pa·.ĺe] (a greeting)

[ti.ko.tšis.'nɛ·.ki] 'are you sleepy?'

[no.'ko·.ko] 'my throat'

[no.'ko·.ku] 'my uncle'

[wɛl.'ki·.ʂa] 'he is able to leave'

['ki·.taʔ] 'he saw it'

['ʔi·.kwa] 'until'

[ʔi.'no·n] 'that'

[ki.'tši·.wa·] 'he is doing it'

['ki·.ta] 'he sees it'

['ko·.tši] 'he sleeps'

['tši·.tšik] 'bitter'

[te.tʊk.'tši·.wa. ne.mi. nʊk.'pa·.kaʔ]
    'What are you doing? I am washing it.'

[ʔi.'no·n. 'ta·.gat. 'ki·.taʔ] 'the man
                               sees it'

[ši.ne.'ma·.ka. 'ʔi·s.taʔ] 'give me the
                           salt'

['ʔi·s.taʔ. 'ʔi·s.tak] 'the salt is
                       white'

Directions:

Write a technical phonemic statement about this language.

Problem 254

Directions:

Select five problems given under Analytical Procedures, and give for each a technical description of the phonemes and their distributions.

---

[1]Aztec of Veracruz. Information obtained from Howard Law, Summer Institute of Linguistics. Phonemic conclusions implied by this data may be altered in a few minor points when further data from the language are obtained.

Problem 255--Kalaba Dialect GV

Phonetic Data:

['má·.pá] 'cold'   [má.'på•] 'hot'

[må.'pá•] 'hungry'   ['mó⁝] 'thirsty'

['pǻ] 'rested'   [pð'⁝] 'rested'

Directions:

What is the basic structural unit
(or units) which serves best as a point of
reference for describing the distribution of
phonemes in this language?

Problem 256--Restricted English E

Directions:

1. Prepare a formational statement
of the phonemes of your dialect of English.

2. Discuss any differences between
the list given by you, and the list on Chart
3, p. 45.

Chapter 15

SAMPLE DESCRIPTIVE STATEMENTS

In Chapter 14 mention was made of several kinds of descriptions of the sounds of a language, differing according to the purpose of the author, the kind of material presented, and the audience for which he was writing. This chapter consists of three such technical descriptions. All of them are written for an audience somewhat acquainted with linguistic principles, and give a concise but quite full treatment of the sounds of the language described. The first two present the sound systems of Hungarian and Portuguese, respectively. The third discusses a special problem in the analysis of Zoque.

The paper on Hungarian illustrates a neat but effective way of presenting a list of phonemes, submembers of phonemes, the distribution of those submembers, and illustrations. This general format is probably the easiest for the beginner to follow, and was used as a model for part of the preceding chapter.

The paper on Portuguese shows a different method of presenting similar data, and is especially useful to the beginner for demonstrating the use of minimally different words in supporting a phonemic analysis, and the initial assembling of consonant clusters (whereas the cluster presentation for Hungarian is much more condensed).

The Zoque material is given here to afford the student a more thorough discussion than could be given in the text of the problems raised by loan words. The student should also note carefully how it is successfully highlighted: one general type of problem (that of the loans) is presented; the outline is all designed with that one problem in view; all data chosen are included or excluded according to whether or not they contribute to that end; it tends to get reader interest because it deals with an unsolved difficulty which confronts many workers.

SAMPLE DESCRIPTIVE STATEMENT A:

HUNGARIAN PHONEMES,*
by
Robert A. Hall, Jr.

1.1. THE PHONEMES are: /i, e, a, o, u, ø, y; p, t, k, b, d, g, m, n, ɲ, f, v, s, z, c, ź, ť, ɟ, š, ž, č, ǧ, r, l, h, j, w/. All

---

*Extracted from his Hungarian Grammar, Language Monograph No. 21, (Baltimore: Linguistic Society of America, 1944), 13-17; used by permission.

phonemes may occur single or in geminate clusters (phonetically long).

The individual phonemes are here listed together with their chief allophones and examples of their occurrence. The examples are given in phonemic transcription, followed by English glosses and phonetic transcription.[1]

1.2. VOWELS show, in some cases, contrasts in quality correlated with contrasts in quantity. For this reason, single vowels and geminate clusters will be listed separately.

Stressed vowels, single and geminate, may occur with an additional element of length, which is not of phonemic significance (as it does not affect the meaning) but indicates extra emphasis, emotional connotation, etc. (called by some an 'Emphatikum'[2]); symbol /ˑ/. Vowels occurring with this added element of length have the same quality as for the normal vowel, and extra length.

Phoneme	Allophones	Examples
/i/	[i]	/hit/ 'belief' ['hit]; /aɲagi/ 'material (adj.)' ['o|ɲɔ|gi].
/ii/[3]	[i:]	/hiid/ 'bridge' ['hi:d]; /iirta/ 'he wrote it' ['i:r|tɔ].
/e/	[ɛ][4]	/lehet/ 'it is possible' ['lɛ|hɛt]; /eɲhe/ 'mild, gentle' ['ɛɲ|hɛ].

---

[1] The phonemic transcription is enclosed in solidi, the phonetic transcription in square brackets; the symbol | indicates syllable division. Stress is indicated by '.

[2] Cf. Gy. Laciczius, 'Probleme der Phonologie', Ungarische Jahrbücher 15.495-510 (1936); T. Sebeok, 'Notes on Hungarian Vowel Phonemes', Lang. 19.164 (1943).

[3] In the speech of the younger generation, the geminate vowel clusters /ii, uu, yy/ have dropped out of use, and have been replaced by the corresponding single vowels. Cf. Sebeok, Lang. 19.162-4 (1943), and references there given.

[4] There was also formerly a short close /e/ phoneme, as in /ember/ 'man' ['ɛm\|ber]; /nekem/ 'to me' ['nɛ\|kem], etc., which is often mentioned in Hungarian grammars (e.g. Simonyi 194; Várady 3). In the standard language, however, the short close [e] sound has been replaced by [ɛ]. In the Danube-Tisza dialect, this phoneme is represented

191

/ee/   [e:]   /teel/ 'winter' ['te:l];
/dičeerni/ 'to praise'
['di|t^{s}e:r|ni].

/a/   [ɔ]   /hat/ 'six' ['hɔt];
/tapas/ 'adhesive tape'
['tɔ|pɔs]; /pillantani/
'to glance' ['pil|lɔn|
tɔ|ni].

/aa/   [a:]   /aaltal/ 'by means of'
['a:l|tɔl]; /baar/
'although' ['ba:r];
/pohaar/ 'glass, gob-
let' ['po|ha:r].

/o/   [o]   /bokor/ 'bush' ['bo|kor];
/bolond/ 'crazy' ['bo|
lond].

/oo/   [o:]   /hoo/ 'snow, month'
['ho:]; /soolni/ 'to
speak' ['so:l|ni].

/u/   [u]   /ruha/ 'clothes' ['ru|
hɔ]; /tanulni/ 'to
study, learn' ['tɔ|
nul|ni].

/uu/[3]   [u:]   /tuul/ 'beyond' ['tu:l];
/ǯuuč/ 'summit'
[t^{s}u:t^s]; /ifjuu/
'young man' ['if|ju:].

/ø/   [ø]   /øt/ 'five' ['øt]; /øl-
teni/ 'to put on
(clothes)' ['øl|te|ni].

/øø/   [ø:]   /øøs/ 'autumn' ['ø:s];
/føøzøø/ 'boiling'
['fø:|zø:].

/y/   [y]   /ytni/ 'to strike, hit'
['yt|ni]; /neemetyl/
'in German' ['ne:|mɛ|
tyl]; /ezyšt/ 'silver'
['ɛ|zyšt].

/yy/[3]   [y:]   /tyy/ 'needle' ['ty:];
/hyyš/ 'cool, fresh'
['hy:š].

1.3. CONSONANTS include the following:[5]

/p/   [p]   /part/ 'shore, beach'
['pɔrt]; /apa/ 'father'
['ɔ|pɔ]; /pap/ 'priest'
['pɔp].

/b/   [b]   /bor/ 'wine' ['bor];
/saboo/ 'tailor' ['sɔ|
bo:]; /hab/ 'foam'
['hɔb].

/t/   [t]   /taaj/ 'region' ['ta:j];
/baator/ 'bold, daring'
['ba:|tor]; /hit/ 'be-
lief' ['hit].

/d/   [d]   /deel/ 'south' ['de:l];
/ladik/ 'rowboat'
['lɔ|dik]; /luud/
'goose' ['lu:d].

/k/   [k]   /kar/ 'arm' ['kɔr];
/tykør/ 'mirror' ['ty|
kør]; /seek/ 'chair'
['se:k].

/g/   [g]   /gazdag/ 'rich' ['gɔz|
dɔg]; /egeer/ 'mouse'
['ɛ|ge:r].

/m/   [m]   except before consonants
of the labio-dental
series: /meerni/ 'to
measure' [me:r|ni];
/emleek/ 'memory'
['ɛm|le:k]; /šem/
'neither, nor' ['šɛm].

    [M]   (labio-dental voiced
nasal continuant) be-
fore labio-dental con-
sonants: /hamvaš/
'full of ashes' ['hɔM|
voš].

/n/   [n]   before vowel or dental
consonants, or in word-
final position: /naɟ/
'large' ['nɔɟ]; /beena/
'crippled, lame' ['be:|
nɔ]; /byyn/ 'sin,
crime' ['by:n].

    [ŋ]   before velar consonant:
/zengeni/ 'to ring'
['zɛŋ|gɛ|ni]; /hang/
'sound' ['hoŋg].

/ɲ/   [ɲ]   /ɲak/ 'neck' ['ɲɔk];
/čuɲa/ 'homely, ugly'
['t^{s}u|ɲɔ]; /guuɲ/
'irony, sarcasm'
['gu:ɲ].

/f/   [f]   /feel/ 'half' ['fe:l];
/žufolni/ 'to crowd'
['žu|fol|ni]; /čuuf/
'ugly, nasty' ['t^{s}u:f].

/v/   [v]   /van/ '(there) is' ['vɔn];
/leveš/ 'gravy, soup'
['lɛ|vɛš]; /eev/ 'year'
['e:v].

/s/   [s]   /saam/ 'number' ['sa:m];
/isap/ 'mud, mire'
['i|sɔp]; /ees/ 'in-
tellect' ['e:s].

/z/   [z]   /zaarni/ 'to close'
['za:r|ni]; /ezer/
'thousand'.

/c/   [t^s]   /cim/ 'title, address'
['t^{s}im]; /kaceer/
'flirt, coquette' ['kɔ|
t^{s}e:r]; /šarc/ 'con-
tribution' ['šɔrt^s].

/ʒ/   [d^z]   /eʒeni/ 'to sharpen'
['ɛ|d^{z}ɛ|ni]; /boʒa/
'elder tree' ['bo|d^{z}ɔ].

/č/   [t̬]   (unvoiced alveolar-
palatal affricate):

_____

by /ø/, appearing in alternate forms of certain words in the standard language, e.g.
/fønn/ = /fenn/ 'above'.

[5]For the phonemic interpretation of long
consonants, cf. M. Swadesh, Lang. 13.1-10
(1937).

/tuuk/ 'hen' ['tu:k];
/faatol/ 'veil' ['fa:-
tol]; /fit/ 'half a
pint' ['fit].

/ɹ/	[ɹ]	(voiced alveolar-palatal affricate): /ɹakran/ 'often' ['ɹok|ron]; /raɹogni/ 'to beam' ['ro|ɹog|ni]; /heɹ/ 'mountain' ['hɛɹ].
/š/	[ʒ]	/šaar/ 'mud' ['ša:r]; /eššik/ 'it rains' ['ɛš|šik]; /vaš/ 'iron' ['voš].
/ž/	[ž]	/žeb/ 'pocket' ['žɛb]; /rooža/ 'rose' ['ro:|žɔ]; /varaaž/ 'magic' ['vɔ|ra:ž].
/č/	[č]	/čuuč/ 'summit' ['tšu:tš]; /koči/ 'carriage' ['ko|tši]; /kovaač/ 'smith' ['ko|va:tš].
/ǧ/	[dž]	/ǧida/ 'lance' ['dži|dɔ]; /laanǧa/ 'lance' ['la:n|džɔ].
/r/	[r]	(dental flap or trill): /riini/ 'to weep' ['ri:|ni]; /haarom/ 'three' ['ha:|rom]; /koor/ 'malady' ['ko:r].
/l/	[l]	(dental voiced lateral): /lap/ 'page' ['lɔp]; /falu/ 'village' ['fɔ|lu]; /feel/ 'half' ['fe:l].
/h/	[h]	(simple aspiration) in syllable-initial position: /haaz/ 'house' ['ha:z]; /teher/ 'burden' ['tɛ|hɛr]; /koɲha/ 'kitchen' ['koɲ|hɔ].
	[χˀ]	(unvoiced velar fricative), in syllable-final position after back vowels, only in certain proper names: /'dohnaaɲi/ 'Dohnányi' ['doχˀ|na:|ɲi].
	[χˁ]	(unvoiced palatal fricative), in syllable-final position after front vowels, only in the word /ihlet/ 'inspiration' ['iχˁ|lɛt] and cognates.

The syllable-final vari-
ants of /h/ formerly
occurred, and are
still written, in
word-final position:
/če/ 'Czechish' ['čɛ]
cseh.

| /j/[6] | [j] | in syllable-initial |

position, and after
voiced consonants:
/juhaas/ 'shepherd'
['ju\|ha:s]; /juk/
'hole' ['juk]; /hajoo/
'ship' ['ho\|jo:]; /ho-
maajoš/ 'obscure'
['ho\|ma:\|još]; /dobj/
'throw!' ['dobj].

	[i̯]	after vowels: /taaj/ 'region' ['ta:i̯]; /ho-maaj/ 'darkness' ['ho|ma:i̯].
	[q]	(unvoiced alveolar-palatal fricative), after unvoiced consonants: /leepj/ 'step!' ['le:pq].
/w/	[u̯]	only after vowels in certain loan-words: /awtoo/ 'auto' ['ou̯|to:].

1.4. OCCURRENCE OF PHONEMES is according to the following pattern:

1.41. THE SYLLABLE is the minimum unit of word-structure. Every word consists of one or more syllables. Every syllable contains one highest point of sonority, which is (except in certain short conjunctions and interjections) a vowel (phonetically short or long, phonemically single or geminate). The vowel may be preceded in the same syllable by one, two, or three consonants; but clusters of two or three consonants preceding the vowel occur only in word-initial position. The vowel may also be followed in the same syllable by one or two consonants. The following types of syllable-structure, therefore, occur in normal words (V = vowel, short or long; C = consonant):

V	/a/	'the'
CV	/ha/	'of'
CCV	/plee|baa|noš/	'parson, priest'
CCCV	/štraa|ža/	'guard'
VC	/az/	'that'
CVC	/baab/	'doll'
CCVC	/flot|ta/	'fleet'
CCCVC	(apparently no examples)	
VCC	/elv/	'principle'
CVCC	/fent/	'above'
CCVCC	/frišš/	'fresh'
CCCVCC	/štrucc/	'ostrich'

In the conjunction /š/ 'and', and in certain interjections (e.g. /šš/ 'sh!'; /pst/ 'pst!'), a consonant may be the highest point of sonority in the syllable.

1.42. VOWELS occur only as the highest point of sonority in a syllable; two adjacent vowel sounds always form separate syllables: /kee\|pe\|im/ 'my pictures' ['ke:\|pɛ\|im].

<hr>

[6]The sound [ʎ] formerly existed as a sepa-rate phoneme, but in standard Hungarian speech it has disappeared and become en-tirely fused with /j/; it is, however, still kept distinct in conventional orthography (cf. §1.71).

In final position, the vowels /o/ and /ø/ occur only geminate.

1.43. CONSONANTS occur as follows:

1. One consonant:

a. In syllable-initial position: all consonants except /w/.

b. In word-final position: all consonants except /h/ (cf. §1.3).

Before the initial consonant of a following syllable in the same word, all consonants may occur except as stated in the rules for sandhi (§1.62).

An intervocalic single consonant belongs to the syllable of the following vowel: /e|ɹe|dyl/ 'singly, alone' ['ɛ|ɹɛ|dyl]; /kee|pe|i|met/ 'my pictures (acc.)' ['ke:|pɛ|i|mɛt].

2. Two consonants:

a. In syllable-initial position (only word-initial):

i. Stop, /f/ or /š/ + /r/: /draaga/ 'dear, expensive'; /šroof/ 'screw'.

ii. Labial or guttural stop, /f/ or /š/ + /l/: /flotta/ 'fleet'.

iii. /š/ + unvoiced stop or /m/: /špaarga/ 'asparagus'.

b. In syllable-final position:

i. The following combinations:

/m/ + homorganic plosive or /v, j/: /hamv/ 'ashes'.

/n/ + /t, d, k, g, c, č, ǧ/: /ujonc/ 'recruit'.

/ɲ/ + /v, t́, ɹ/: /koɲv/ 'book'; /roɲɹ/ 'rag'.

/d́/ + /v/: /kedv/ 'mood'.

/s, š/ + /t/: /kost/ 'board (food)'; /fyšt/ 'smoke'.

/z, ž/ + /d/: /kyzd/ 'he struggles'.

/r/ + /t, d, k, v, ɹ, c, č, ǧ, š, j/: /harc/ 'battle'; /kard/ 'sword'; /terv/ 'plan'; /taarɹ/ 'object'.

/l/ + /p, t, d, k, v, ɹ, č/: /talp/ 'sole'; /vølɹ/ 'valley'; /bølč/ 'wise'.

/j/ + any consonant that may occur in syllable-final position: /majd/ 'soon'; /šajt/ 'cheese'; /rajz/ 'drawing'; etc.

These combinations may occur in word-final position or before another syllable in the same word beginning with a consonant; when they occur intervocalically, the first consonant of these combinations belongs to the syllable of the preceding vowel, the second to that of the following vowel.

ii. In word-final position only, the following combinations:

/p, b, d, k, g, f, v/ + /j/: /bukj/ 'fall!'; /døfj/ 'stab!'; etc.

Any double consonant except /hh/, /ww/: /ešett/ 'fell'; /fenn/ 'above, up'; /ujj/ 'finger'.

3. Three consonants, in syllable-initial position only: /štr/: /štraaža/ 'guard'.

SAMPLE DESCRIPTIVE STATEMENT B:

THE SEGMENTAL PHONEMES OF BRAZILIAN PORTUGUESE: STANDARD PAULISTA DIALECT*
by
David W. Reed and Yolanda Leite

1 Introduction

1.1 Background of the study

During the academic year of 1942-43 we studied some of the general problems involved in teaching English to Latin Americans, particularly Brazilians, in connection with the program of the English Language Institute at the University of Michigan. It became increasingly apparent to us that a thorough linguistic analysis of Brazilian Portuguese was necessary as a foundation upon which to build sound teaching procedures. Accordingly, we have attempted an analysis of the segmental phonemes of that language, which we are setting forth here in the hopes that it will prove helpful not only to teachers of English to Brazilians, but also to teachers of Brazilian Portuguese to Americans.

1.2 The dialect studied

We have studied the dialect of one

*[This paper is included in the present volume in order that the student might see a full phonemic statement in a style somewhat different from that given for Hungarian. The manuscript was finished in the spring of 1943. About that time Hall published a paper on Portuguese phonemics which utilizes the same format as that quoted above for his Hungarian Grammar. Students interested in comparing the two styles should consult Robert A. Hall, "The Unit Phonemes of Brazilian Portuguese," in Studies in Linguistics I, No. 15 (April, 1943). I requested Hall to comment on the Reed-Leite analysis. In reply he discussed his objection to the interpretation of nasalized sounds as consisting of vowel phoneme plus nasal consonant phoneme, with Reed's reply to it. His comment is given on p. 197. Reed still feels that his own interpretation is slightly preferable; his reasons are given at the same place. This provides the student with a very instructive illustration of the problems of conflicting patterns in the interpretation of sequences (cf. p. 130). K.L.P.]

of the authors, Miss Yolanda Leite, who is a native of the city of Sao Paulo. Her speech does not differ appreciably from that of most other cultivated speakers in the populous sections of central and southern Brazil, with the exception of those living in the immediate vicinity of Rio de Janeiro. The principal difference between the Standard Paulista dialect we have studied and the Carioca dialect, of Rio de Janeiro, is that the /s/ phoneme of Paulista is replaced by the /š/ phoneme in Carioca when final in a syllable before a voiceless consonant, and that the /z/ phoneme of Paulista is replaced by the /ž/ phoneme when final in a syllable before a voiced consonant in the Carioca dialect. There is also some regional variation in the distribution of the variants of the /ř/ phoneme, but all such differences are noted at the proper points in the following description.

2 The phonemic norms

2.1 Chart of phonemic norms:

Phoneme	Key Word	Transcription	Translation
/p/	pala	/'pala/	'poncho'
/t/	tão	/tauñ/	'so' or 'as'
/k/	cume	/'kumi/	'summit'
/b/	bala	/'bala/	'bullet'
/d/	dão	/dauñ/	'they give'
/g/	gume	/'gumi/	'edge' (knife)
/m/	mato	/'matu/	'woods'
/n/	nato	/'natu/	'born'
/ñ/	unha	/'uña/	'fingernail'
/l/	halo	/'alu/	'halo'
/ľ/	alho	/'aľu/	'garlic'

			Labial		Alveolar	Alveo-palatal	Velar		
			Bilabial	Labio-dental					
Non-Syllabic	Stop	Voiceless	p		t		k		
		Voiced	b		d		g		
	Nasal		m		n	ñ			
	Lateral				l	ľ			
	Flap				r				
	Trill				ř				
	Fricative	Voiceless		f	s	š			
		Voiced		v	z	ž			

		Front	Central	Back
Syllabic	High	i		u
	Mid	e		o
	Low	ɛ	a	ɔ

2.2 List of phonemes[1] with illustrative key words

/r/	caro	/'karu/	'dear'
/ř/	carro	/'kařu/	'cart'
/f/	faca	/'faka/	'knife'

---

[1] Notice that Brazilian Portuguese does not have the fricatives /θ/, which occurs in Castilian Spanish, and /tš/ and /x/, which occur in all dialects of Spanish. (In Brazilian Portuguese, [tš] is an allophone of /t/, 3.1 (1), and [x] is an allophone of /ř/, 3.1 (5).) Brazilian Portuguese, however, has the voiceless fricative /š/ and the series of voiced fricatives, /v/, /z/, and /ž/, which are not phonemic in Spanish. Likewise, two of the Brazilian Portuguese vowel phonemes, /ɛ/ and /ɔ/, are not phonemic in Spanish. Brazilian Portuguese /ľ/ is phonemic in Castilian, but not in Spanish American.

/s/	sêlo	/'selu/	'stamp'
/š/	chá	/ša/	'tea'
/v/	vaca	/'vaka/	'cow'
/z/	zêlo	/'zelu/	'zeal'
/ž/	já	/ža/	'already'
/i/	sino	/'sinu/	'bell'
/e/	sêca	/'seka/	'dryness'
/ɛ/	seca	/'sɛka/	'dries' (vb.)
/a/	sala	/'sala/	'room'
/u/	escuro	/i'skuru/	'dark'
/o/	escôva	/i'skova/	'brush' (n.)
/ɔ/	escova	/i'skɔva/	'brushes' (vb.)

3 Production of the phonemes

3.1 The non-syllabics

There is a series of unaspirated stops at bilabial, alveolar, and velar points of articulation. Three of them are voiceless, /p/, /t/, /k/, and three of them are voiced, /b/, /d/, /g/.

There is a series of voiced nasals at bilabial, alveolar, and alveo-palatal points of articulation, /m/, /n/, and /ñ/.

There are two voiced laterals at alveolar and alveo-palatal points of articulation, /l/ and /ľ/.

There is a voiced alveolar flap, /r/.

There is a voiceless alveolar trill, /ř/.

There is a series of fricatives at labio-dental, alveolar, and alveo-palatal points of articulation. Three of them are voiceless, /f/, /s/, /š/, and three of them are voiced, /v/, /z/, /ž/.

(1) Of the stops, /p/ and /b/ do not have any marked variants in different situations of distribution. Examples are pé, /pɛ/, [pɛ], 'foot'; bola, /'bola/, ['bɔlə], 'ball'. The /t/ and the /d/ phonemes are normally the pre-alveolar stops described, but when they occur before /i/ in the same syllable, they undergo affrication which approaches [tš] and [dž], respectively. Some speakers of Standard Paulista retain the stop even in this position, however. Examples of the normal stops are tenho, /'teñu/, ['teñuˇ], 'I have', and lado, /'ladu/, ['laduˇ], 'side'. Examples of the affricated variants are tive, /'tivi/, ['tšiviˇ], 'I had', and verdade, /ver'dadi/, [ver'dadži], 'truth'. The /k/ and the /g/ phonemes are normally the velar stops described, but when they occur before a front

vowel in the same syllable they become the pre-velar stops [kˤ] and [gˤ]. Examples of the normal velar stops are culpe, /'kulpi/, ['kul'piˇ], 'blame'; and guarda, /'guarda/, ['gwardə], 'guard'. Examples of the pre-velar variants are que, /ki/, [kˤiˇ], 'which'; and guia, /'gia/, ['gˤiə], 'guide'.

(2) Of the nasals, /m/ is the voiced bilabial nasal described when initial in syllables. When final in syllables, it is an extremely brief closure before one of the homorganic stops /p/ or /b/ in the following syllable of the same word. An example of the normal nasal is mão, /mauñ/, [mõũn], 'hand'; while an example of the brief post-vocalic closure is lembrar, /lem'brař/, [lẽm'brař], 'remember'. The /n/ phoneme is the voiced alveolar nasal described, when initial in syllables. When final in syllables, it is an extremely brief closure before one of the homorganic stops /t/ or /d/ in the following syllable of the same word. An example of the normal nasal is nada, /'nada/, ['nadə], 'nothing'; while an example of the brief post-vocalic closure is entre, /'entri/, ['entri], 'between'. The /ñ/ phoneme is the voiced alveo-palatal nasal described, when initial in syllables. When final in the syllable medial in the word after a front vowel and not followed immediately by /k/ or /g/, it is an extremely brief closure at alveo-palatal position. When final in a syllable medial in the word before one of the homorganic stops /k/ or /g/ or when final in the syllable following a central or back vowel there is a nasal closure at velar position. When final in the word, it is nasalization without closure. An example of the normal nasal is unha, /'uña/, ['uñə], 'fingernail'; an example of the brief alveo-palatal closure is tem, /teñ/, [teĩñ], 'has'; an example of the brief velar closure is um, /uñ/, [uŋ], 'one'.

(3) Of the laterals, /l/ is the voiced alveolar lateral described, when initial or medial in syllables, or when final in syllables preceding immediately a vowel in the same word. When final in a syllable and followed immediately by a consonant in the same word, or when final in the word, the phoneme is retracted slightly to [lˠ] and the contact of the tongue with the roof of the mouth becomes optional. An example of the normal alveolar lateral is lado, /'ladu/, ['laduˇ], 'side'; an example of the retracted variant is Brasil, /bra'zil/, [bra'zilˠ], "Brazil". The /ľ/ phoneme is the voiced alveo-palatal lateral described, in all positions. It has no marked variants. An example of the occurrence of this phoneme is milho, /'miľu/, ['miľuˇ], 'corn'.

(4) The voiced alveolar flap, /r/, does not have any marked variants. An example of its occurrence is quatro, /'kuatru/, ['kwatruˇ], 'four'.

(5) The voiceless alveolar trill, /ř/, has a variant [Я], a voiceless, slightly retroflexed, alveo-palatal fricative

which is interchangeable in all positions and dialects in Brazilian Portuguese. Other allophones, [x] a voiceless velar fricative and [R] a voiceless uvular trill, are interchangeable with the norm in all positions in the Carioca and Northern dialects, but do not occur finally in a syllable directly preceding a consonant in the same word in Paulista. Still other allophones, [řˇ], a voiced alveolar trill, and [Яˇ], a voiced, slightly retroflexed, alveo-palatal fricative, are interchangeable in all dialects when not final in words. Examples of the occurrence of this phoneme and its interchangeable variants are carro, /'kařu/, ['kařuˇ], ['kaЯuˇ], ['kaxuˇ], ['kaRuˇ], ['kařˇu], or ['kaЯˇu], 'cart'; carta, /'kařta/, ['kařtə], ['kaЯtə], ['kaxtə] (Carioca and Northern), ['kaRtə] (Carioca and Northern), ['kařˇtə], or ['kaЯˇtə], 'letter'; dar /dař/, [dař], [daЯ], [dax], or [daR], 'give'.

(6) Of the fricatives, /f/ and /v/ do not have any marked variants. Examples are faca, /'faka/, ['fakə], 'knife'; vaca /'vaka/, ['vakə], 'cow'. The /s/ and the /z/ phonemes likewise do not have any marked variants in different situations of distribution. Examples are saga, /'saga/, ['sagə], 'legend'; zêlo, /'zelu/, ['zeluˇ], 'zeal'. The /š/ and the /ž/ phonemes do not have any marked variants. Examples are chaga, /'šaga/, ['šagə], 'ulcer'; gêlo, /želu/, ['želuˇ], 'ice'.

3.2 The syllabics

There is a series of unrounded front vowels at high, mid, and low tongue positions, /i/, /e/, and /ɛ/, respectively.

There is an unrounded central vowel made at the low tongue position, /a/.

There is a series of rounded back vowels at high, mid, and low tongue positions, /u/, /o/, and /ɔ/, respectively.

(1) The /i/ phoneme is normally [i]. This phonemic norm is replaced by a slightly lower variant, [iˇ], when unstressed in a final syllable of a word and not followed in the same syllable by one of the nasal phonemes. This same variant also occurs interchangeably with the phonemic norm in all other unstressed positions, when not followed in the same syllable by one of the nasal phonemes. When the /i/ phoneme is followed in the same syllable by one of the nasal phonemes, it is nasalized to [ĩ].[1] When /i/ is unstressed immediately preceding

[1] Hall disagrees with this analysis and comments as follows:

> Brown University
> Providence 12, R. I.
> September 21, 1945.

"If one considers simply complementary distribution within individual words, nasalization is indeed in c.d., not only

or following another vowel in the word, it is non-syllabic [j]. Examples of the norm and its two variants are rí, /ři/, [ˌři], 'I laughed'; irmão, /iř'mauñ/, [iř'mẽũn] or [iˇř'mẽũn], 'brother'; parte /'pařti/, ['pařtši], 'part'; fim, /fiñ/, [fĩñ], 'end'.

(2) The /e/ phoneme includes the phonemic norm [e] and a number of interchangeable variants ranging from [Iˇ] to [eˇ],

---

with ɲ, but with n and m as well. But in the phrase, ɲ is not in c.d. either as a free or a conditioned variant of nasalization (or the other way around). As I mentioned when we were talking about it this summer, in some dialects of Braz. Port., sióɲ may alternate with siɲóɲ; but siótru 'without another' is always that, and never *siɲótru. To analyze sĩ 'without' as *siɲ one would have to set up a hypothetical special type of juncture between it and any following word which began with a vowel, to justify considering nasalization as representing ɲ in syllable-final position, and one would write siɲ-ótru. But such a procedure would be quite artificial, as it would involve setting up a special kind of juncture with no phonological justification, and would be a circular proceeding, introducing the deus ex machinâ of a special juncture to justify the analysis that one wanted to make. If you wanted to follow Prague school procedure, I suppose you could set up an archiphoneme N representing ~, m, n, and ɲ in syllable-final position, since there is 'neutralization' in that position; but my own feeling is that wherever you get an 'archiphoneme' it's an indication there's something wrong with the analysis."

[Note: For a complete presentation of Hall's analysis, see "The Unit Phonemes of Brazilian Portuguese," in Studies in Linguistics I, No. 15 (April, 1943). Particularly pertinent to the present point are the notes by George L. Trager, at the end of this article and appended to Hall's "Occurrence and Orthographic Representation of Phonemes in Brazilian Portuguese" in SIL II, No. 1 (May 15, 1943), in which an analysis similar to the present one is suggested.

I agree with Trager's criticism that the treatment of nasalization as a suprasegmental phoneme (frequently followed by a nasal consonant on-glide to a stop) is artificial. In addition I should like to point out that it is not necessary to set up a "hypothetical special type of juncture" to describe occurrences like /siɲ 'outru/. Word boundaries can obviously be set up on a basis of potential occurrence in isolation, and once this has been done, such boundaries can legitimately serve as a juncture. Such juncture is, of course, present before all words, not merely before words beginning with a vowel. Indeed, recognition of this juncture provides the only adequate means of analyzing such a phrase as /duñ 'pulu/, where my phonetic data indicates no [m] consonantal nasal on-glide. D. W. R., August 6, 1947.]

which occur in all positions except when followed in the same syllable by a nasal phoneme. When followed in the same syllable by a nasal phoneme, this sound is nasalized to [ẽ] in the initial and medial syllables of words, but is nasalized and diphthongized to [ẽɪ̃] in the final syllables of words. Examples of the norm and its variants are voce, /vo'se/, [vo'se], [vo'sɪ̌ˇ], [vo'se^], or [vo'se˅], 'you'; lembrar, /lem'braɾ/, [lẽm'braɾ̃], 'remember'; bem, /beñ/, [bẽĩñ] 'well'.

(3) The /ɛ/ phoneme is normally [ɛ], but has the variants [ɛ^] and [ɛ˅], which are interchangeable with the norm in all situations of distribution. An example of the norm and its variants is ela, /'ɛla/, ['ɛlə], ['ɛ^lə], or ['ɛ˅lə], 'she'.

(4) The /a/ phoneme is normally [aˤ]. When followed immediately within the word by a back vowel, or when followed in the same syllable by /l/ or by /w/, and not followed in the same syllable by a nasal phoneme, the sound is retracted to [ɑˤ]. When unstressed in the final syllable of a word and not followed within the word by a nasal phoneme, the sound is raised to [ə]. When followed in the same syllable by one of the nasal phonemes, or when stressed and followed immediately within the word by one of the nasal phonemes, the sound is raised and nasalized to [ɐ̃]. When unstressed and followed immediately within the word by one of the nasal phonemes, this nasalized variant is interchangeable with the norm. Examples of the norm and the variants of this phoneme are lá, /la/, [laˤ], 'there'; alto, /'altu/, ['ɑˤlˤtuˇ], 'high'; ela, /'ɛla/, ['ɛlə], 'she'; lã, /lañ/, [lɐ̃ñ], 'wool'; ano, /'anu/, ['ɐ̃nu], 'year'; banana, /ba'nana/, [baˤ'nɐ̃nə] or [bə'nɐ̃nə], 'banana'.

(5) The /u/ phoneme is normally [u]. When unstressed in the final syllable of a word and not followed in the same syllable by a nasal phoneme, the sound is lower and less round, [uˇ]. This variant is also interchangeable with the norm in all other unstressed positions where it is not followed in the same syllable by a nasal phoneme. When followed in the same syllable by a nasal phoneme, the sound is nasalized to [ũ]. When /u/ is unstressed immediately preceding or following another vowel in the word it is non-syllabic [w]. Examples of the norm and its variants are nú, /nu/, [nu], 'naked'; unido, /u'nidu/, [u'niduˇ], or [uˇ'niduˇ], 'united'; untar, /un'taɾ/, [ũn'taɾ̃], 'anoint'.

(6) The /o/ is normally [o]. When followed in the same syllable by one of the nasal phonemes the sound is nasalized to [õ]. Examples of the norm and the variant are avô, /a'vo/, [a'vo], 'grandfather'; tom, /toñ/, [tõñ], 'tone'.

(7) The /ɔ/ is phonetically [ɔ] in all situations of distribution; it has no marked variants. An example of this phoneme is hora, /'ɔra/, ['ɔrə], 'hour'.

3.3 Stress

Although stress is non-segmental, it is clearly phonemic in Brazilian Portuguese, and will be briefly considered here for the purpose of completeness. The stress may fall on the ultimate syllable, the penultimate syllable, or the antepenultimate syllable. Examples are macã, /ma'sañ/, 'apple'; menino /mi'ninu/, 'boy'; árvore, /'aɾvori/, 'tree' respectively. If a plurisyllabic suffix is added to a full word, the stress of the derived form falls on the suffix, but a secondary stress may be retained on the syllable which is normally stressed in the full word. An example is macãzinha, /ma,sañ'ziña/, 'little apple'. This is one of the few types of secondary stress that occurs in Brazilian Portuguese.

4 Construction of syllables

Syllables in Portuguese may consist of a single syllabic, such as the word é, /ɛ/, 'it is', or the first syllable of the word aberto, /a'beɾtu/, 'open'. A more frequent type of syllable is composed of any single syllabic preceded by any single non-syllabic, such as both syllables of the word nato, /'natu/, 'born'. Syllables may also consist of any single syllabic followed by /m/, /n/, /ñ/, /l/, /ɾ̃/, /s/, or /z/. An example of this type is the first syllable in estes, /'estis/, 'these'. A more complex type of syllable is composed of any single syllabic preceded by any single non-syllabic and followed by any single non-syllabic from the above list. An example of this type of syllable is the word mar, /maɾ̃/, 'sea'. A limited number of clusters of non-syllabics may serve the same functions in syllable construction that are served by single non-syllabics. These clusters are described under Clusters of Non-syllabics in the following section.

5 Distribution of phonemes

5.1 Single non-syllabics

(1) Initial: All single non-syllabics can be initial in syllables. All except /r/ can be initial in words, morphemes, and phrases.

/p/	pé	/pɛ/	'foot'
/t/	ter	/teɾ̃/	'have'
/k/	casa	/'kaza/	'house'
/b/	bala	/'bala/	'bullet'
/d/	dedo	/'dedu/	'finger'
/g/	gato	/'gatu/	'cat'
/m/	mar	/maɾ̃/	'sea'
/n/	nó	/nɔ/	'knot'

/ñ/	Nhonhô	/ño'ño/	(proper name)
/l/	lei	/lei/	'law'
/ĺ/	lhe	/ĺi/	'him' (dative case)
/r/	caro	/'karu/	'dear'
/ř/	rosa	/'řoza/	'rose'
/f/	faca	/'faka/	'knife'
/s/	sopa	/'sopa/	'soup'
/š/	cha	/ša/	'tea'
/v/	vaca	/'vaka/	'cow'
/z/	zero	/'zɛřu/	'zero'
/ž/	gêlo	/'želu/	'ice'

(2) **Medial**: No single non-syllabic can occur medially in syllables, but all of the single non-syllabics occur medially in morphemes, words, and phrases.

/p/	opor	/o'poř/	'oppose'
/t/	ótica	/'otika/	'optics'
/k/	oco	/'oku/	'hollow'
/b/	obeso	/o'bezu/	'fat'
/d/	ódio	/'odiu/	'hatred'
/g/	agora	/a'gora/	'now'
/m/	amigo	/a'migu/	'friend'
/n/	ano	/'anu/	'year'
/ñ/	unha	/'uña/	'fingernail'
/l/	alem	/a'leñ/	'beyond'
/ĺ/	olho	/'oĺu/	'eye'
/r/	area	/'aria/	'area'
/ř/	carro	/'kařu/	'cart'
/f/	afim	/a'fiñ/	'related'
/s/	asseio	/a'seiu/	'cleanliness'
/š/	achar	/a'šař/	'find'
/v/	ave	/'avi/	'bird'
/z/	asa	/'aza/	'wing'
/ž/	ajuda	/a'žuda/	'help'

(3) **Final**: The number of single non-syllabics that may occur in final position in syllables, morphemes, words, and phrases is limited to the nasals, the trill, and /l/, /s/, and /z/. The /z/ phoneme never occurs in phrase-final position because its postvocalic occurrence is always conditioned by a following voiced sound within the phrase, and the /m/ and /n/ phonemes never occur in word- or phrase-final positions because their postvocalic occurrence is always conditioned by a following homorganic stop within the word.

/m/	lembrar	/lem'brař/	'remember'
/n/	entre	/'entri/	'between'
/ñ/	tem	/teñ/	'has'
/l/	mil	/mil/	'thousand'
/ř/	mar	/mař/	'sea'
/s/	salas	/'salas/	'rooms'
/z/	salas há	/'salaz a/	'there are rooms'

5.2 **Clusters of non-syllabics**

(1) **Initial**: A fairly large number of clusters of non-syllabics occur initially in syllables, morphemes, words, and phrases. These usually consist of one of the stops or /f/ followed by /l/ or /r/. Alveolar stop plus /l/ does not occur.

Voiceless stop + /l/ or /r/

/pl/	plano	/'planu/	'plane'
/pr/	prato	/'pratu/	'plate'
/tr/	tratar	/tra'tař/	'treat'
/kl/	claro	/'klaru/	'clear'
/kr/	cravo	/'kravu/	'carnation'

Voiced stop + /l/ or /r/

/bl/	blusa	/'bluza/	'blouse'
/br/	branco	/'branku/	'white'
/dr/	drama	/'drama/	'drama'
/gl/	gloria	/'gloria/	'glory'
/gr/	grosso	/'grosu/	'thick'

/f/ + /l/ or /r/

/fl/	flor	/floř/	'flower'
/fr/	fraco	/'fraku/	'weak'

(2) **Medial**: Clusters of non-syllabics do not occur medially in syllables. The clusters of non-syllabics that occur medially in morphemes and words are identical with those that occur initially in syllables. Any single non-syllabic or cluster of non-syllabics that occurs finally in words may directly precede any single non-syllabic or cluster of non-syllabics that occurs initially in words, thus forming new clusters of as many as four non-syllabics medially in phrases. Because of the large

number of clusters occurring in this position, examples have been omitted, but many of the phrases given in other connections contain examples of this type of cluster.

(3) Final: Clusters of non-syllabics occur finally in syllables only when also final in words. /ñz/ occurs only medially in phrases. Both of the clusters in the following list cross morpheme boundaries.

| /ñs/ | irmãs | /if'mañs/ | 'sisters' |
| /ñz/ | irmãs há | /iř'mañz a/ | 'there are sisters' |

5.3 Single syllabics

(1) Initial: All of the single syllabic phonemes occur initially in syllables, morphemes, words, and phrases.

/i/	ilha	/'iĺa/	'island'
/e/	êle	/'eli/	'he'
/ɛ/	ela	/'ɛla/	'she'
/a/	asa	/'aza/	'wing'
/u/	uva	/'uva/	'grape'
/o/	ôvo	/'ovu/	'egg'
/ɔ/	hora	/'ɔra/	'hour'

(2) Medial: All of the single syllabic phonemes occur medially in syllables, morphemes, words, and phrases.

/i/	mil	/mil/	'thousand'
/e/	verde	/'veřdi/	'green'
/ɛ/	mel	/mɛl/	'honey'
/a/	tal	/tal/	'such'
/u/	azul	/a'zul/	'blue'
/o/	cor	/koř/	'color'
/ɔ/	costa	/'kɔsta/	'coast'

(3) Final: All of the single syllabic phonemes occur finally in syllables, morphemes, words, and phrases.

/i/	aquí	/a'ki/	'here'
/e/	você	/vo'se/	'you'
/ɛ/	café	/ka'fɛ/	'coffee'
/a/	lá	/la/	'there'
/u/	tatú	/ta'tu/	'armadillo'
/o/	avô	/a'vo/	'grandfather'
/ɔ/	avó	/a'vɔ/	'grandmother'

5.4 Clusters of syllabics

(1) Initial: A number of clusters of syllabics occur initially in morphemes, words, and phrases. Some others that cross word boundaries occur initially in the phrase only. The following list is partial.

/ia/	ia	/'ia/	'went'
/io/	Ione	/i'oni/	(proper name)
/iɔ/	Iola	/i'ɔla/	(proper name)
/ai/	Aida	/a'ida/	(proper name)
/aɛ/	aedo	/a'ɛdu/	'aedes'
/ao/	aonde	/a'ondi/	'where'
/aɔ/	aorta	/a'ɔřta/	'aorta'
/oa/	oasis	/o'azis/	'oasis'
/i e/	e êle	/i 'eli/	'and he'
/i ɛ/	e ela	/i 'ɛla/	'and she'
/i u/	e uma	/i 'uma/	'and one'
/ɛ i/	é isso	/ɛ 'isu/	'that's it'
/ɛ e/	é êle	/ɛ 'eli/	'it is he'
/ɛ a/	é alto	/ɛ 'altu/	'it is high'
/ɛ o/	é hoje	/ɛ 'oži/	'it is today'
/ɛ ɔ/	é hora	/ɛ 'ɔra/	'it is time'
/ɛ u/	é uma	/ɛ 'uma/	'it is one'
/a e/	há este	/a 'esti/	'there is this one'
/a u/	há uma	/a 'uma/	'there is one'
/u i/	o hino	/u 'inu/	'the anthem'[1]
/u a/	o avô	/u a'vo/	'the grandfather'
/u o/	o ôvo	/u 'ovu/	'the egg'
/u ɔ/	o ódio	/u 'ɔdiu/	'the hate'

(2) Medial: A number of clusters of syllabics occur medially in morphemes, words, and phrases. /aɛ/ occurs medially in the phrase only. The list is again partial.

---

[1] Notice that no phoneme */w/ is set up, although there is a minimal pair in school pronunciation, not attested in normal speech:

| */iw/ | riu | */řiw/ | 'laugh' (third, singular, preterite) |
| /iu/ | rio | /'řiu/ | 'river' or 'laugh' (first, singular, present) |

/ie/	Viena	/vi'ena/	'Vienna'
/iɛ/	viela	/vi'ɛla/	'small street'
/ia/	diario	/di'ariu/	'daily'
/iu/	viuva	/vi'uva/	'widow'
/io/	miôlo	/mi'olu/	'brain'
/iɔ/	viola	/vi'ɔla/	'guitar'
/ea/	meandro	/me'andru/	'meander'
/eo/	Leoncio	/le'onsiu/	(proper name)
/eɔ/	beocio	/be'ɔsiu/	'stupid'
/ai/	tainha	/ta'iña/	(a type of fish)
/ae/	baeta	/ba'eta/	'baize' (a type of cloth)
/au/	balaustre	/bala'ustri/	'post in a balustrade'
/ao/	caolho	/ka'oḽu/	'half-blind'
/aɔ/	caotico	/ka'ɔtiku/	'chaotic'
/ui/	ruido	/řu'idu/	'noise'
/ue/	poeira	/pu'eira/	'dust'
/uɛ/	poeta	/pu'ɛta/	'poet'
/ua/	boato	/bu'atu/	'rumor'
/a ɛ/	ja é	/ža ɛ/	'it is already'

(3) **Final**: A limited number of clusters of syllabics occur finally in morphemes, words, and phrases. /iɛ/ and /aɛ/ occur finally in phrases only.

/ia/	dia	/'dia/	'day'
/ai/	daí	/da'i/	'from there'
/au/	baú	/ba'u/	'trunk'
/oa/	atoa	/a'toa/	'insignificant'
/ua/	lua	/'lua/	'moon'
/i ɛ/	e é	/i ɛ/	'and it is'
/a ɛ/	lá é	/la ɛ/	'it is there'

6 Transcribed text

In order to demonstrate our phonemic writing of Brazilian Portuguese we have chosen the following text from Lobata, Monteiro, _Historias de Tia Nastacia_, "O Macaco e O Coelho," 1941, pp. 121-2. The first line is written in Portuguese orthography, the second line in phonemic transcription, and the third line in literal English translation. The punctuation of the Portuguese orthography

has been preserved in the phonemic transcription to serve as a limited intonation guide. A more literary English translation follows the body of the text.

Um macaco e um coelho fizeram
/uñ ma'kaku i uñ ku'eḽu fi'zɛrauñ
A monkey and a rabbit made

a combinação de um matar as borboletas
a combina'sauñ di uñ ma'tař az bořbo'letaz
the combination of one to kill the butterflies

e outro matar as cobras. Logo depois
i 'outru ma'tař as 'kɔbras. logu di'poiz
and the other to kill the snakes. Soon after

o coolho dormiu. O macaco veio e
u ku'eḽu doř'miu. u ma'kaku 'veiu i
the rabbit slept. The monkey came and

puxou-lhe as orelhas.
pu'šou ḽi az o'reḽas.
pulled to him the ears.

--Que é isso? gritou o coelho,
--ki ɛ 'isu? gritou u ku'eḽu,
"What is that?" cried the rabbit,

acordando dum pulo.
akoř'dandu duñ 'pulu.
awakening with a jump.

O macaco deu uma risada.
u ma'kaku deu 'uma ři'zada.
The monkey gave a laugh.

--Ah, ah! Pensei que fossem
--a, a! pen'sei ki foseñ
"Ha, ha! I thought that they were

duas borboletas . . .
'duaz bořbo'letaz . . .
two butterflies."

O coelho danou com a brincadeira
u ku'eḽu da'nou koñ a brinka'deira
The rabbit was mad at the joke

e disse lá consigo: "Espere que te curo."
i 'disi la kon'sigu: "is'peri ki ti 'kuru."
and said to himself: "Wait until I cure you."

    Logo depois o macaco se sentou
    'logu di'poiz u ma'kaku si sen'tou
    Soon after the monkey sat down

numa pedra, para comer uma banana.
'numa 'pɛdra, 'para ko'meř 'uma ba'nana.
on a stone, to eat a banana.

O coelho veio por trás, com um pau
u ku'eǐu 'veiu poř tras koñ uñ pau
The rabbit came from behind, with a club

e lepte! pregou-lhe uma grande paulada
i 'lɛpti! pre'gou ǐi 'uma 'grandi pau'lada
and whack! he gave him a big club-stroke

no rabo.
nu 'řabu.
on the tail.

    O macaco deu um berro, pulando
    u ma'kaku deu uñ 'beřu, pu'landu
    The monkey gave a yell, jumping

para cima duma árvore a gemer.
'para 'sima 'duma 'ařvori a ži'meř.
toward the top of a tree, whining.

    --Desculpe, amigo, disse lá de
    --dis'kulpi, a'migu, 'disi la di
    "Excuse me, friend," said from

baixo o coelho. Vi aquele rabo torcidinho
'baišu u ku'eǐu. vi a'keli 'řabu tořsi'diñu
below the rabbit. "I saw that twisted tail

em cima da pedra e pensei que
eñ'sima da 'pɛdra i peñ'sei ki
on top of the stone and I thought that

fosse cobra.
'fosi 'kɔbra.
it was a snake.

Foi desde aí que o coelho,
foi 'dezdi a'i ki u ku'eǐu
It was from then on that the rabbit,

de medo do macaco vingar-se,
di 'medu du ma'kaku viñ'gař si,
for fear of the monkey to revenge himself,

passou a morar em buracos.
pa'sou a mo'rař eñ bu'rakus.
started to live in holes.

    Following is the more idiomatic
English translation:

    A monkey and a rabbit made an agreement for one to kill butterflies and the other snakes. Soon after that the rabbit fell asleep. The monkey came and pulled his ears.

    "What is that?" cried the rabbit, awakening with a start.

    The monkey laughed heartily.

    "Ha, ha! I thought that they were two butterflies."

    The rabbit was mad at the joke and said to himself: "I'll fix you."

    Soon after that the monkey sat down on a stone to eat a banana. The rabbit crept behind him with a club, and whack! he gave him a heavy blow on the tail.

    The monkey yelled and jumped into a tree, whining.

    "Excuse me, friend," said the rabbit from below. "I saw that twisted tail on top of the stone and thought that it was a snake."

    It was from then on that the rabbit, in fear of the monkey's vengeance, began living in holes.

SAMPLE DESCRIPTIVE STATEMENT C:

PHONEMIC ACCULTURATION IN ZOQUE*
        William L. Wonderly
        Indiana University

1. The problem
2. Analysis A
3. Analysis B
4. Text with analysis A transcription
5. Text with analysis B transcription
6. Conclusions

*Quoted in full from International Journal of American Linguistics, XII (April, 1946), 92-95; used by permission.

1. This paper presents two alternate phonemic analyses of the Zoque language as spoken in Copainalá, Chiapas, Mexico.[1] In analysis A the language is regarded as a 'mixed' or heterogeneous language, consisting of a Zoque part and a Spanish part. In analysis B, it is stated as a single or homogeneous language.

Copainalá Zoque as actually spoken includes an indefinite number of Spanish loans. Many of these retain their Spanish phonemes unchanged phonetically. Some of these loans are, however, subject to modification when occurring in sequences with Zoque morphemes.

2. Analysis A. In this analysis, Zoque as it is actually spoken is transcribed with two sets of symbols: lower case letters corresponding to the phonemes of a Zoque formulation (= Zoque exclusive of Spanish loans) and small capitals to those of a Zoqueized Spanish (= Spanish loans in Zoque).

2.1. The following are the phonemes of the Zoque formulation:[2]

Stops: p, t, t^y, k, c, č. (The affricates c and č are counted as stops).

The stops are voiced after nasals within a word: mpama [mbama] my clothing, minpa [minba] he comes, mintamu [mindamu] you (pl.) came, ʔəntʸoʔyu [ʔəndʸoʔyu] he got sleepy, minkeʔtu [mingeʔtu] he also came, ncin [ndzin] my pine, ňcehcu [ňdžehtsu] you cut brush.

In other positions the stops are voiceless: pet centipede, petpa he sweeps, tatah father tʸetʸəy little, kəʔ hand, təpkeʔtu he jumped, tək house, cehcu he cut brush, nəc armadillo, čehčahu they cut it, ʔanemuč toasted tortilla.

Spirants: s, š, h. These are voiceless in all their positions; the h is assimilated to the tongue position of a contiguous high vowel: saʔsa beautiful, winsaʔu he came to life, nas earth, šohšahu they cooked it, hahku he crossed over, sah wing, tuh [tux] rain, wihtu [wiχtu] he walked.

Nasals: m, n, ñ, ŋ. Examples: men pain, maŋu he went, kom post, nəmu he said, ñihpu he planted it, keñahu they looked, can snake, kaŋ jaguar.

Lateral: l. Examples: liŋpa [liŋba] to slash, wilo mico de noche.

Glottal stop: ʔ. Examples: təʔŋkuy [təʔŋguy] bell, ʔaci older brother, ʔyaci his older brother (contrast yaci wicked), poʔk knot (contrast pok water-gourd), kuʔtpa he eats, nəʔ [nəʔ·] water, poʔkis [poʔºkis] of the knot, huʔki [xuʔᵘki] vulture.

Semivowels: w, y. Examples: win face, powa burn it!, wyin [bʸin] his face, yoyah pig, ʔuy don't!

Vowels: a, e, i, o, u, ə. The vowel ə is an unround back vowel varying from mid to high position; the other vowels are similar to the corresponding Spanish vowels: haya husband, həyə flower, peka old, piŋu he picked it up, pyoŋu he burned it, pyuŋu he scattered it, pyəŋu he broke it.

2.2. The following are the phonemes of the Zoqueized Spanish:

Voiceless stops: P,* T, T^Y, K, Č. (The affricate Č is counted as a stop). Examples: PALOMA bird, KOMPAGRE compadre, TIA aunt, TYENDA store, KWANTO how much, T^YIA his aunt T^YENDA his store, KAMPO airport, SINKO five cents, ČAKETA jacket, R·ANCO ranch.

Voiced stops: B, D, D^Y, G, J. (The affricate J is counted as a stop). Note that in addition to the occurrence of B, D, G, as in Spanish, the voiced stops occur in clusters where a voiceless stop of Zoqueized Spanish is preceded by a Zoque morpheme ending in a nasal consonant. Examples after Zoque prefix n-~ m-~ñ-~ŋ-: mBALOMA my bird, nDIA my aunt, ñD^YANTEAcəkpa you measure, ŋGOMPAGRE my compadre, ñJAKETA my jacket. Examples occurring as in Spanish: BUR·U burro, SABADO Saturday, DYOS God, KWANDO when, DURAcəhku it lasted, nə D^YURAcehku it is lasting, GAYU rooster, MANGO mango.

Spirants: F, S, Š, H. These are voiceless; H is assimilated to a contiguous vowel as is the h of the Zoque formulation above. (This therefore equates the Spanish j with Zoque h). Examples: FALTA it lacks, FINKA plantation, SEGIcəkpa you follow, GISPIN Crispín, TINAHA water-jar, R·ELOH clock.

Nasals: M, N, Ñ. These are voiced; N is velar [ŋ] before velar consonants and word-finally; otherwise it is alveolar [n]: MULA mule, LAMPARA lamp, NASIMYENTO Nativity, KINKE [kiŋke] kerosene flare, PAN [paŋ] bread, ÑABAHA his razor, MAÑOSO tricky.

Liquids: L, R, R·. (R· is the trilled rr of Spanish). Examples: LOKO angry,[3] KOLA

---

[1]The data on the Zoque language were collected in several field trips from 1940-45 which the writer made under the auspices of the Summer Institute of Linguistics, Glendale California. The paper itself was written at Indiana University while the writer was in residence as an All-University Fellow.

[2]This part of analysis A is essentially in agreement with the analysis given in my Notes on Zoque Grammar (mimeographed for the Summer Institute of Linguistics, 1943).

*[These are printed with small capitals. K.L.P.]

[3]This word retains its Spanish meaning crazy when used in Spanish context by the

glue, MIL thousand, PERO but, LIBRU book,
R·EY king, SYER·A saw, SENOR· sir.

Glottal stop: ʔ. Examples: ʔULI rubber,
ʔYULI his rubber.

Semivowels: W, Y. Examples: WAHE spring,
HWAN John, LEY law, ČYAPAS Chiapas.

Vowels: A, E, I, O, U. Examples: ʔANIMA
soul, SEGIcǝhku he followed, POGRE poor, MULA
mule.

2.3. In the above Zoqueized Spanish system
there are five new or pseudo-Spanish phonemes:
TY, DY, Š, J, ʔ. The first four of these
appear in Spanish morphemes when influenced
by a Zoque morpheme in the same sequence.

TY, DY, Š result from sequence of Spanish
T, D, S, and Zoque y. Compare TIA aunt with
TYIA his aunt; DURAcǝkpa it lasts with nǝ
DYURAcǝhku it is lasting; SEGIcǝkpa he follows with nǝ ŠEGIcǝhku he is following. Š
also appears in certain modified Spanish
morphemes (GIŠPIN Crispín).

J appears in clusters where č is preceded
by a Zoque morpheme ending in a nasal consonant (ñJAKETA my jacket).

ʔ appears initially in loans whose Spanish
form begins with a vowel (ʔANIMA soul, ʔULI
rubber); its phonemic presence is attested
when Zoque y is inserted (ʔYULI his rubber).

2.4. On the basis of analysis A, many Spanish loans, including some which are modified
to fit the Zoque pattern, may be phonemically
accommodated by either the Zoque formulation
or the Zoqueized Spanish. Examples show both
methods of transcription for a few such forms:

As Zoque:	As Zoqueized Spanish:	
mula	MULA	mule
mesa	MESA	table
maŋko [maŋgo]	MANGO	mango
waŋku [waŋgu]	WANGU	bench
kayu	KAYU	horse
lawus	LAWUS	nail
wakas	WAKAS	cow
sanawenes	SANAWENES	pants (Sp. zaragüelles)
ʔakuša	ʔAKUŠA	needle
lahpa	LAHPA	Raphael

same speakers. Two of my informants, remi-
niscing of their boyhood, remembered as a
huge joke that one of them had once used the
Zoque meaning in Spanish context and said,
"Ahí viene un toro loco!" there comes a crazy
bull when he meant to say, "Ahí viene un toro
bravo!" there comes an angry bull.

Certain modified Spanish loans (as well as
the unmodified ones) may be phonemically accommodated only by the Zoqueized Spanish
transcription. Examples are: GISPIN Crispín,
ÑEMPE- ∼ YEMPE- -ever (prob. < Sp. siempre),
LOKTOR· doctor, GINIA banana (Sp. guinéo).

A few other modified Spanish loans may be
phonemically accommodated only by the Zoque
formulation. Example: šapun soap (in the
Spanish transcription final -N = [-ŋ]).

One rarely used word remains which is not
phonemically accommodated by either system.
This is written phonetically [ʔǝŋkǝ] emphatic particle. It has Zoque vowels ǝ (not in
Spanish) and a cluster [ŋk] (not in the Zoque
formulation). If this were written according to analysis A, we should have *ʔǝNKǝ;
this would be misleading, however, because
it would suggest a sequence of three morphemes: Zoque *ʔǝ-, Spanish *-NK-, Zoque
*-ǝ.

3. Analysis B. In this analysis, Zoque
(including all Spanish loans) is transcribed
with a single set of symbols.

The following are the phonemes of Zoque
under analysis B:

Voiceless Stops: p, t, tY, k, č.· Examples: pama clothing, kape cane, cap sky,
kompagre compadre, tatah father, pet centipede, kwanto how much, tYǝtYǝy little, nǝ
tYuhu he is shooting, tǝk house, heke then,
siŋko five cents, čǝhku he did it, čaketa
jacket, r·ančo ranch.

Voiced stops: b, d, dY, g, J.[4] Examples:
bur·u burro, mbama my clothing, sabado
Saturday, dañi Daniel, ndatah my father,
kwando when, nǝ dYuracǝhku it is lasting,
ʔǝndYoʔpya he is sleepy, gišpiŋ Crispín,
maŋgo mango, ñJehcu you cut brush, ñJaketa
my jacket, kaʔnJi turkey.

The phoneme c (affricate [ts]∼[dz]) is
listed separately because it remains a single
non-contrastive phoneme with voiced allophone
after nasals. It does not occur voiceless
in Spanish after nasals (as does č) so as to
provide a contrast. Examples: cin pine,
ncin [ndzin] my pine, puci trash, nǝc armadillo.

Voiceless spirants: f, s, š, h. Examples:
fwera outside, fiŋka plantation, saʔsa beautiful, kǝsmǝ above, nas earth, šohšahu they
cooked it, šegicǝkpa he follows it, hehu he
rested, kahwe coffee, hača axe, tinaha
water-jar.

[4]While the contrast of b, d, dY, g
and the corresponding voiceless stops is
freely made in Spanish loans, that of č and
J is restricted to sequences in which the
latter follows a Zoque nasal morpheme.

Nasals: m, n, ñ, ŋ. Examples: miʔšu cat, kom post, mbama my clothing, nanah mother, cin pine, mingeʔtu he also came, ñanah his mother, suñi pretty, maŋu he went, ŋgəʔ my hand, kaŋ jaguar, paŋ bread, maŋgo mango.

Liquids: l, r, r·. (The r· is the trilled rr of Spanish.) Examples: lahpa Raphael, wilo mico de noche, mil thousand, pero but, pogre poor, r·ey king, señor· sir, bur·u burro.

Glottal stop: ʔ. Examples: ʔaci brother, ʔyaci his brother, ʔuli rubber, ʔyuli his rubber, nəʔ water, poʔk knot, poʔkis of the knot.

Vowels: a, e, i, o, u, ə. Examples: čahku he left it, cəhku he did it, čehcu he cut it, čihku he husked it, cohcu it began, cuʔ night.

4. The following sample text illustrates a transcription using analysis A:

KWENTO DE HWAN SOLDADO[5]

1. ʔihtu tumə pən HWAN SOLDADO. 2. təhkəyu DE SOLDADO makmaktaskuʔ ʔamewə, 3. ʔI DESPWES yohsu BATAYOʔNohmo ʔips ko mak ʔame.

4. ʔI DYAY ʔABUR·Icəhku R·EPUBLIKA, KE teʔšeʔŋa waʔy yohsu ʔEN EL BATAYON. 5. mawə HWANSITO, ñəhayu. 6. teʔšeʔŋa SERBIcəkə.

7. ʔENTONSES nəmu HWAN, KE ciʔəʔəh SIKYERAS DOSYENTOS PESOS. 8. PWES ENTONSES KONTESTAcəhku R·EPUBLIKAʔS, maŋpaʔsmih nciʔu mohsis PESU. 9. ʔI nəmaŋpəʔə mis mBARKE nhučeʔŋ nəʔihtu. 10. ʔI mawə, ʔuʔyaʔsmih ŋkenu, 11. PORKE HUSILAcəkpaʔsmih. 12. yəy ʔihtu mis mohsiʔs PESU. 13. pəkə mis mBARKE ʔI mis ʔARMAS. 14. ʔI ʔuʔyaʔsmih ŋkenu.

Story of John the Soldier

1. There was a man, John the Soldier. 2. He entered as soldier at fourteen years, 3. and afterward worked in the batallion thirty years.

4. And then the commanding officer became bored that he worked so long in the batallion 5. "Go, Johnny," he told him. 6. "Only this long serve."

7. Then said John that, "Give me at least 200 pesos." 8. Then answered the commanding officer, "I am going to give you 200 pesos." 9. And take all your equipment, as much as you have. 10. And go, that I may never see you; 11. because I will shoot you. 12. Here is your 200 pesos. 13. Take your equipment and your gun. 14. And may I never more see you."

5. The following is a continuation of the same text, transcribed according to analysis B:

15. ʔentonses maŋu hwaŋ, maŋu montañaʔohmo 16. hyuyu kyanah waʔy kyuʔtu. 17. ʔi total. 18. pihčeʔka dilatacəhku mohsaʔ poyah.

19. ʔi ʔentonses minu pyaʔtu ʔel dyablo. 20. ʔi tiya meʔcpamis, ñəhayu teʔ dyabloʔs. 21. pikčeʔka ʔaŋcoŋu hwaŋ, nəʔs meʔcu dyablo, nəmu hwaŋ.

22. ʔentonses nəmu dyablo, huka mbyəndeʔ, cəhkisə. 23. ʔentonses preparacəhku ʔəʔwəʔs ʔyarmas. 24. ʔi huntamente čiʔu mohsaʔ tiro. 25. ʔentonses nəmu dyablo, ŋgonosecəhkuʔsmih, ke mbyənmih. 26. pwes yətih sunbaha waʔyʔsmih masaʔnuneʔahu, nəmu dyablo. 27. ʔentonses ʔyaŋcoŋu hwaŋ, bweno, nəmu. 28. huka ciʔpamisɔh miyones de plata. 29. pwes mbagrinoʔahpaʔsmih.

Translation continued

15. Then went John; he went into the forest. 16. He bought his salt to eat. 17. Well. 18. Then he stayed five months.

19. And then he came to find the devil. 20. "And what seek you?" said to him the devil. 21. Then answered John, "I am seeking the devil," said John.

22. Then said the devil, "If you are a man, prove it." 23. Then prepared he his gun. 24. And immediately he gave five shots.

25. Then said the devil, "I know you, that you are a man." 26. Now then, do you wish that I make you godchild?" said the devil. 27. Then answered John, "Good," he said. 28. "If you give me millions in silver, 29. then I shall make you godfather."

6. Conclusions. Of the two alternate analyses, analysis B is preferable for the language as a whole from a descriptive standpoint, and is the one which I propose to use in future publications.

However, analysis A has been worked out experimentally because it permits a simpler distributional statement within the purely Zoque part of the language; a statement which preserves more of what is apparently the basic phonemic structure of Zoque as an Indian language. Certain of the correlations thus preserved may be of significance also for the historical and comparative study of Zoque.

On the side of Zoqueized Spanish, analysis

---

[5]This text is the first part of a story dictated by Miguel López of near Copainalá. The percentage of Spanish words in López's Zoque is considerably higher than that of the average bilingual speaker of the language.

A demonstrates the changes in the phonemic
structure of Spanish when used in Zoque context, and the extent of assimilation to the
Zoque pattern.

Analysis A leaves a practical difficulty
of deciding how to transcribe certain of the
partially assimilated Spanish forms (see 2.4
above).

From a theoretical as well as a practical
standpoint, analysis A is virtually a re-
ductio ad absurdum, inasmuch as the very
extent of assimilation of Spanish loans to
Zoque which it reveals demonstrates that the
Spanish loans are, in effect, Zoque words
and must accordingly be treated as such.

ORTHOGRAPHICAL PROCEDURES

Chapter 16

THE FORMATION OF PRACTICAL ALPHABETS

Directions:

Be prepared to make a practical alphabet of any of the problems already given. This practical alphabet should be chosen in such a way as to obtain an acceptable balance between phonemic principles and general sociological situations.

Discussion:

In forming a practical orthography the investigator is constantly disturbed by a dilemma or series of dilemmas. He wishes to make his orthography scientifically adequate in order to get the best and fastest results in the teaching of reading; he wishes his alphabet to reflect the actual linguistic structure of the vernacular spoken by the people. But he wishes also to have an orthography which will not be offensive to the people in the region in which it is spoken or to the national government of the area. He wishes it to be adapted to traditional alphabets of the region and at the same time to be easy to write and print. These two general types of principles, the phonemic and social ones, do not coincide. The investigator is therefore likely to find himself engaged in debate with people who wish to emphasize the one or the other without due regard for a fine balance between them. Frequently also he will be considerably perplexed himself as to the wisest adjustments to make.

No specific set of rules can be given which will cover the multitude of different situations to be found in the field. The investigator will be better equipped to meet the problems, and to reach a solution which may prove adequate, if he will consider carefully the following principles for the formation of practical orthographies.

GENERAL PHONEMIC GOALS

A practical orthography should be phonemic. There should be a one-to-one correspondence between each phoneme and the symbolization of that phoneme.[1]

---

[1]Some orthographies are based upon the syllable and have a one-to-one correspondence between each syllable and the symbol representing it. Syllabaries have proved to be effective, and in areas where syllabaries are traditionally acceptable a syllabary may still prove to be the most adequate solution. If, however, the investigator has the choice, he should probably set up a phonemic script with one symbol to each phoneme.

(1) A phonemic alphabet has a separate symbol for each unit proved to be phonemically distinct by the Analytical Procedures. Specifically, every sound unit which may replace other sound units and thereby cause a change of meaning should be represented in the orthography.

If a person has too few symbols, some sound units will represent two distinct sounds. Words which are actually different in phonemic form and meaning may then turn out to be written identically. In such cases the native finds it impossible to know what words are being represented except as he may be able to guess them from the context. It would be unfortunate, for example, if English /p/ and /b/ were both written simply as "p" on the grounds that the investigator did not like the looks of the letter "b". Native speakers of English would then find considerable confusion between words like 'pile' and 'bile'.

Occasionally one hears a person say: 'The natives do not need the extra symbols since they can guess what the words mean without them; the context makes it clear.' To be sure, the native may be able to guess what a word means from the context, provided he can read the context and does read it first. This, however, encourages bad reading habits by forcing the beginner to read ahead for contextual clues and then turn back to guess the meaning of earlier words. Furthermore, if too many spellings are obscure he may be unable to read the context itself. For bilingual speakers who have learned to read a trade language it is quite true that at the first stage of transfer to the vernacular the extra symbols of the vernacular do not contribute to ease of reading. It would be erroneous to conclude that the special symbols for extra phonemes would never be of value. At first the reader might guess as well--or better--without as with them. As soon as he learns through association with some words containing them what the phonetic value of the symbols is, however, he can then replace guessing with reading. This then lends itself to easier, faster, and more accurate absorption of the material. Some people contend that English can be read even though it is not written with phonemic consistency. This is true--though the English students pay a heavy cultural price for the inconsistency. Children seem to require two or three times as long to learn to read English as comparable children do to learn to read Spanish, which is written unambiguously.

There should be no more symbols than there are phonemes. It is very confusing to natives when a single phoneme is arbitrarily written with two or more letters without any way of knowing which words are to be written with the one symbol or the other. In the Spanish of Latin America, for example, many students have great difficulty in remembering whether to write words with "b" or "v" since in the dialects of many of them the two units are no longer phonemically distinct. (This ambiguity applies to the writing of Latin-American Spanish, but not to the reading of it, since both symbols can be read alike without causing difficulty.) They have no choice, therefore, but to try to remember which symbol is to be written in any specific word. In the same way these speakers in many areas of Latin America have difficulty in remembering whether to write "y" or "ll" since in certain of the dialects the two symbols represent a single phoneme. In addition, for most of these speakers the letter "h" at the beginning of words represents no sound at all, and school children find it very hard to remember which words are written with "h" and which words are written without. A practical orthography should have one symbol only for each phoneme lest the student learning to read have difficulty in remembering which one to use when they do not reflect any distinction of sound which he can hear.

In a phonemic orthography, spelling does not have to be "remembered" as an arbitrary set of rules. A sound is heard, and the symbols for that sound written. Spelling is then merely the symbolizing of the sounds. Once the memory correlation has been made for the symbol, no further memory burden is entailed.

(2) Submembers of phonemes should rarely receive distinct symbolization since the native tends to be unaware of these differences. Mutually exclusive varieties of a phoneme should not have separate symbols to represent them. The representation of submembers of phonemes by different symbols, when these submembers occur in distinct environments, however, is not as serious an error as the representation of sounds which are not so limited by environments. The native, even though he may not hear the difference, can nevertheless build up a mechanical rule which tells him when to use the one symbol or the other; it does not demand the memorization of an arbitrary list of words. The only case, nevertheless, in which a conditioned variety of a sound should receive a separate symbol is one in which certain variants of a vernacular phoneme constitute separate phonemes in the trade language. In such a case, the pressures from the social situation may be very strong, and may at times force the investigator to depart from phonemic practices in order to get popular support for his orthography, or may modify his phonemic analysis in such a way through the inclusion of loan words in the vernacular.

(3) Freely fluctuating varieties of a phoneme should not receive separate symbolization but should be written with a single symbol as indicated in Chapter 2. The reasons for this are the same as those which have just been given for not writing conditioned varieties of sound.

(4) When the investigator finds free variation between two full phonemes, however, the recommendation is different; in scientific publications of texts, a word should be written the way it is pronounced at each utterance so that readers may see for themselves the proportionate occurrence of the one phoneme or the other. When, however, a practical orthography is being proposed, it is preferable for the investigator to represent one of the phonemes or the other in each particular word and to write that one consistently regardless of which of the two phonemes the speaker may use at any particular moment.

The basis for decision as to which phoneme to represent in these latter instances may be either frequency or dialectal distribution. If one of the phonemes is used more often than the other, he should presumably use the more frequent one. If over a wide area, including a number of minor dialects, one of the phonemes is used in certain regions where the other is not found, the investigator will do well to choose for consistent writing the one which has the widest dialectal distribution; in this way, his published material will be acceptable in more dialects, since it represents a form current over a wider area.

(5) As for abbreviated forms, the words should in general be written as they are pronounced, and not according to the constituent parts of words which the investigator may recognize by morphological analysis.

One should write, for example, 'I'm going' rather than 'I am going.' The fact that one knows that 'I'm' is an abbreviation of 'I am' is not sufficient evidence to force the writing of the longer form. Similarly one should write 'wives' with "v" and not with "f"; the fact that 'wives' is derived from 'wife' is not sufficient evidence to force one to write "f" in both the singular and the plural. The reason for these decisions is that the goal of learning to read rapidly and easily is achieved by making a conscious or unconscious association between sound and symbol. Therefore, the symbols given should represent the sounds as pronounced. The presentation of forms "filled out" on the basis of other information, such as morphology, usually appears to hinder rather than to help this establishment of sound-symbol association.

(6) When, however, forms differ according to whether they are pronounced fast or slow, the choice may be a bit different. Pronunciations which are given only in extremely rapid speech are best avoided in

symbolization because people do not tend to read with that same rapidity--at least not in the early stages of learning. The slow reading of an extremely rapid form is certain to produce an unnatural result which may be misunderstood by the native learning to read. On the other hand, pronunciations which are used for extremely slow speech should also be avoided. Many of these are likely to include extra sounds, or pauses, or extra stresses, or extra lengths of vowels, which are totally unnatural to the speaker in any normal linguistic context; here again intelligibility will be affected and the result will be much less desirable to the native than would a different style. In general then, the choice should be for the consistent writing of pronunciations which are neither extremely fast nor extremely slow. The most satisfactory choice seems to be a somewhat slow but normal style. First reading efforts are likely to be slow and this allows written pronunciation and spoken style to be parallel.

(7) When the analysis shows that sounds must be interpreted as consonants or vowels, or as long or short vowels, or as phonetically-complex phonemes, it is preferable for them to be written so as to reflect this analysis. The complex ones should in general be written with single symbols rather than with combinations of symbols. Prevailing orthographies and available type may, however, force one to use combinations of symbols.

(8) Symbols for tone and stress should reflect an adequate analysis of the language. Where tone and stress are phonemic, and affect the meanings of words, they should be symbolized at each occurrence of the units. One should not content oneself with writing tone merely on those words which may be misunderstood if the tone is given inaccurately. Tone should be written on each of the words of the tone language, wherever the tones occur. In this way the native learns the meaning of the tone symbols, and how to read them, within the words where the consonants and the vowels and the context make these particular words unambiguous. Once he has learned the meaning of the tone symbols in unambiguous contexts of this type he should then be able to utilize these symbols to distinguish words where the tone is the only distinctive characteristic.

In English, for example, we have the phonemes /p/ and /b/, and /s/ and /z/. At times the meaning of words is dependent upon the occurrence of these phonemes; at other times one is able to guess the meaning of words regardless of which phoneme is symbolized. In 'peel' and 'beal', 'pile' and 'bile', 'pay' and 'bay', 'cap' and 'cab', 'seal' and 'zeal', 'hiss' and 'his', the difference is dependent upon the choice of one or the other of these sounds. In some words, however, no such contrast can be

found. Note, for example, the words 'bite' (with no '*pite'), 'bishop' (with no '*pishop'), 'boyish' (with no '*poyish'), 'pineapple' (with no '*bineapple'), 'pilot' (with no '*bilot'), 'zebra' (with no '*sebra' or '*sepra', or '*zepra'), 'zone' (with no '*sone'), 'zig-zag' (with no '*sig-sag'), 'zero' (with no '*sero'), 'save' (with no '*zave'), 'sacred' (with no '*zacred'). In these last instances it would not do for the investigator to say to himself, 'There is no contrast here between /p/ and /b/, nor between /s/ and /z/; we will, therefore, decide to write all of these words with "s" and "p" so as to save writing "b" and "z" so many times.' The result would be that the words 'bite', 'bishop', 'boyish', 'pineapple', 'pilot', 'zebra', 'zone', 'zig-zag', 'zero', 'save', 'sacred', would be written 'pite', 'pishop', 'poyish', 'pineapple', 'pilot', 'sepra', 'sone', 'sig-sag', 'sero', 'save', 'sacred'. Yet this would be unfortunate since then the native would find an inconsistent representation of these sounds; at times, both /p/ and /b/ would be written "p", and at times /b/ would be symbolized with "b".

This type of inconsistency is difficult for the native to write since he must memorize an arbitrary list of words which contain the one or the other symbol; he is likely to make many mistakes in doing so. It is much more economical of time and effort to write more symbols, if necessary, in order to keep a consistent and distinctive representation of the sound phonemes. This applies to tone as well as to segmental sounds. It has been illustrated here with segmental sounds to give the English reader a better opportunity to see how such inconsistency would affect his own language which does not have tonemes. Tones affect the native speaker of a tone language, however, much as do his consonants and vowels.

(9) Borders between certain types of units may need symbolization. It is customary to write spaces between words. This breaks up the line into smaller units which are more readily grasped than is possible if spaces are not used at all. It seems easier for the native to read short units than long ones provided that these short units constitute actual isolatable types. It will not be helpful, but, on the contrary, a hindrance to break up the lines into more or smaller units, however, than represent the actual language structure. An arbitrary writing of spaces just "to make words shorter" slows up reading and the understanding of the material since it is likely to leave many items between spaces which the native never pronounces in isolation in normal speech. In this case he may try to pronounce, and actually succeed in pronouncing by themselves, those items separated by spaces, but if they are not words, but only parts of words, bound morphemes, and the like, they carry too little meaning to him as total units to be intelligible. It is preferable to use units

which are large enough to carry significance to the native.

The method for determining the advisable length of units has already been given in Chapter 13 Occasionally more than one type of break must be recognized. These may be symbolized by hyphens or by some other device. The technical discussion of these possibilities will be found in the same place as the handling of spaces.

(10) One of the severe problems in the preparation of a practical orthography consists in the adequate representation of words borrowed from other languages. Such loan words are most likely to represent the trade language, or national language of that area. Various kinds of words are likely to be brought over into the language-- words for objects of trade (such as 'chocolate', 'tobacco', 'oranges', and so on) which were not originally in the area, as well as governmental terms, legal terms, and many others.

If these loan words have been completely assimilated to the native language, then they will not contain sounds which the native language lacks, nor will they contain familiar sounds in unfamiliar sequences. In these instances assimilated loans should be spelled as they are pronounced by the native, and spelled with the symbols utilized for the native language and not with the traditional spelling of the second language. If the spelling of the trade language were utilized rather than the spelling and pronunciation of the assimilated form, there would be further interference in the attempt to set up an adequate correspondence between sound and symbol within materials placed in the native hands. If the pronunciation of the loan words is highly inconsistent, however, then one may at times best utilize that form which is identical with or closely approximates the source from which it was borrowed.

When loans are not completely assimilated, and contain sounds which words of native origin do not contain, then the problem is more severe and frequently the investigator must add to his alphabet symbols to represent these extra sounds. See Chapter 12 Preferably these symbols should be the ones used to spell the sounds of the trade language.

At other times an investigator may himself wish to prepare literature in the vernacular and in these instances he may desire to bring in from the trade language certain words which have never been in current use in the vernacular. Such items may include names of individuals or cultural objects and the like. In this situation, the investigator should deliberately modify the spelling to make it conform to the way in which the loans which are actually in the native language have been modified in pronunciation by the natives. He should

not hesitate to eliminate sounds from the loans which he is introducing if those sounds are not found in the native language. In addition, he should modify large consonant clusters or sound sequences which are difficult for the native to pronounce, and if at all possible should leave these words fitting into the types of sequences of sounds which actually occur in words of native origin. This type of deliberate adaptation makes the words easier for the native to learn to read and yet does not change the meaning or usage of the words as such. One caution, however, is in order. In bringing in new words, or in modifying them to fit the native pattern, one must be careful to check to see that he has not created a word which actually is identical with a native word which has some objectionable meaning.

GENERAL SOCIAL GOALS

(1) A practical orthography should be acceptable to the people of the region where it is to be introduced. It should receive popular support and approval. In order to learn to read people must first desire to learn to read if they are to do so with relative ease. The most important single attribute of materials for beginners is that they create in the learner the strong urge to master them. Within any large area, there are almost certain to be one or a number of people who have already learned to read some alphabet. If there is no alphabet in the vernacular, they will have learned to read the alphabet of the trade language or of a national language of some type. These people are likely to be bilingual, speaking the language which they can read as well as having their own language. Furthermore, they are usually the leaders of their communities since their education gives them opportunities for representing their neighbors in official ways. If, therefore, these bilinguals object to the vernacular alphabet they can persuade illiterates that it is not worth the effort to try to learn to read it. In the face of such discouragement many beginners will not even try to learn, and if they do not try they are unlikely to succeed. It is important, therefore, that an alphabet receive popular support, and specifically some support from bilinguals.

Administrators who do not speak the language but who have control of the territory in which the vernacular is being spoken are likely to be very insistent that the alphabet be the same as that of the national culture. They usually desire that any minorities be rapidly absorbed into the linguistic stream of the larger community so as to make administrative problems less severe and to give unity to the nation, and they are likely to conclude that a unified alphabet is a prerequisite to such cultural and administrative unity. Nationally appointed administrators of small areas, therefore, are likely to give more approval to an alphabet which reflects the national one that to an alphabet which is divergent from it. Any divergence from the national symbols must, therefore, be explained carefully to local or central administrators, since approval or lack of approval by them may affect the practical goals concerned. This does not eliminate the utilization of essential symbols which do not occur in the national language, provided that the authorities can be made to see the value of them.

(2) For these reasons, the investigator will find it preferable, if possible, to introduce no strange letters; that is, he will avoid symbols which are not found in the trade language or the national language of the area. Unfortunately this principle (and some others) comes into conflict with the phonemic goals which we have mentioned earlier. This creates various dilemmas which will be discussed after the general social goals are outlined.

(3) Similarly, diacritic marks are to be avoided where possible inasmuch as they are likely to constitute strange additions to the national symbols. Diacritics which are already in use in the area are likely to be less offensive. English speakers, for example, are likely to be unaware of the fact that the dot over "i" is a diacritic addition to a basic mark; they take for granted that it is a part of the letter itself. Likewise in Latin America a tilde over "n" in the letter "ñ" passes without comment. The diacritics which are likely to cause more difficulty are those which are unfamiliar to the administrators and bilingual speakers of an area.

A profusion of diacritics is undesirable for a further reason: they are likely to be left off by natives in writing. One or two diacritic marks are not likely to cause much trouble--compare English "i" and Spanish "ñ"; if a number of them occur in any one language, however, the speed of writing is slowed up, and some of them at least are likely to be omitted in writing; readers may then have some difficulty in re-reading the material which has been so written.

(4) Symbols should be chosen which are easy to print. If one is in a country whose printing establishments do not have the symbols chosen for the orthography, then books cannot be printed there with that alphabet, or else special types must be secured from abroad or made to order. It is improbable that all of the print shops of an area will introduce new type unless there is a wide demand for it, so that new letters or strange letters in an alphabet are likely to limit the number of presses which will print the material. Such a limitation is undesirable since it is likely to restrict the ease with which the orthography will spread and the speed with which the vernacular will become a medium of written communication.

(5) In order to avoid strange

symbols, and in order that the material might be readily printed, the investigator will want to utilize to the best advantage all of the letters which are actually within the Roman alphabet, and therefore available to most presses. This is the principle of FLEXIBILITY of usage of letters. If he finds that he has one letter left over which he has not used, he may consider utilizing this letter for some sound other than the one which it would normally represent in traditional alphabets. This type of modification has been used to good advantage, for example, in Africa where certain types of letters, such as "c", "q", and "x" have been used for clicks. Nevertheless if the difference is too striking--especially if these same letters are used for other sounds in neighboring dialects--it may not be practicable. For the clicks, for example, new letters are now being introduced for certain of the African languages.

There is likely to be difficulty if letters are utilized with one phonetic quality in the vernacular but a strikingly different one in the trade language or national language. Minor differences may be ignored, but one should hesitate to use "m", say, for [š]. In general, one should be ready to use the letter "t" for any variety of [t], [tʰ], and so on.

(6) The investigator will want to form an alphabet which is adequate for teaching illiterates to read. He will be especially sympathetic toward the problems of the monolinguals who do not have access to the literature of a trade language. He will want his alphabet to be adapted to their needs so that they can learn to read in the shortest possible space of time.

(7) The investigator will also be very desirous that the alphabet be adapted to the needs of bilinguals in the same area so that a native who with great effort has learned to read the trade language, but perhaps does not understand it well, may be able to utilize the same alphabet in reading his own language which he can understand once he hears it. For this purpose, then, the alphabet should conform as closely as is practicable to the trade language. When sounds are the same in the native language and in the trade language he will want the symbols to be the same for each language so that those who have learned to read the one set of symbols will not then find themselves forced to learn a second set of symbols for the same or similar sounds. Individuals who have learned to read the one may be discouraged from trying to read the other if the two are not parallel.

Likewise, the investigator will want to have an easy transfer from the vernacular alphabet to the alphabet of the trade language so that once a monolingual speaker of the vernacular has learned to read his language he can utilize that knowledge in the easiest way for obtaining a knowledge of the trade language. Unfortunately, both of these principles come into conflict with other desiderata, and a practical compromise between them must be obtained.

(8) The alphabet chosen should represent insofar as possible a wide area. When dialects differ it may be impossible to have a single alphabet represent the phonemes of more than a small geographical section of the country. But if possible the symbols decided upon should serve more than one dialect. When the two dialects differ so much that it proves impossible to have a single alphabet represent them, then the best solution is to have a basic alphabet in which the majority of the letters can be used in all dialects and from this basic set of symbols to depart where necessary for specific areas by eliminating certain of the letters or by adding further ones. If then literature is prepared in the various dialects, natives may learn to read in their own particular speech. Once they have learned to read, however, dialect differences are less of a barrier and they may then be able to cross over such boundaries and read the literature of surrounding related tribes. If in one of these dialects a lay writer begins to create a literature which proves so interesting to the speakers of the other dialects that they all demand it, then a standard dialect may develop by that dialect achieving prominence and becoming the accepted medium for literary production throughout the entire area. It seems preferable to let a standard literary dialect develop in this way, wherever possible, rather than trying to force the growth of one artificially before there are readers who are interested in crossing such dialect barriers.

If lay authorship is developing in the vernacular, that increases the desirability of an alphabet which is easily printed in available presses, since the size of the reading public is apt to be larger if some of their own writers publish material which appeals to them strongly. This might increase the demand for literature and for literature which could be produced locally without dependence upon foreign presses.

(9) One needs to observe the strength of a tendency to incorporate loan words from the trade language. Some languages resist the acceptance of loan words. Other languages readily absorb a great number of them. If many loans are assimilated by the language they may carry with them some of the sounds of the trade language, or some special distribution of those sounds, and in this way modify the phonemic system of the vernacular.

In such a situation the decision for symbols may well be toward the direction of the trade language. If many words are being introduced from the trade language this fact gives intensity to the desire to make the

vernacular alphabet coincide with that of the trade language. Similarly, if bilingualism is increasing rapidly, the pressure would be toward utilizing the symbols used in the trade language.

(10) Increasing government sponsorship of reading campaigns in the vernacular for the monolinguals may affect the alphabet. The officials might decide, on the one hand, to utilize alphabets which are best for the monolinguals, or they might decide to utilize alphabets which are as close as possible to that of the national language.

Their decision may in part be modified by a further tendency: a trend toward accepting linguistic principles. In Africa, for example, there seems to be growing movement toward the adoption of the symbols proposed by the International Institute of African Languages and Cultures. Such tendencies make it easier to introduce a phonemic script which is best suited to the first reading efforts of the monolinguals.

(11) The more primers being introduced in vernaculars, the greater is the pressure towards using adequate phonemic alphabets, especially if there is a concerted attempt to carry on literacy campaigns for adult monolinguals, for whom primers need to be readily teachable with alphabets which are easily absorbed.

With people learning to read, however, one must remember that motivation is highly important. People can be taught to read any alphabet (1) provided ample time is given and (2) provided they desire to read strongly enough. For English the spellings are not easy to remember, since there are a tremendous number of exceptions to phonemic writing. For this reason it takes a considerable period of time for the average child or adult to learn to read it. Nevertheless, a large proportion of speakers of English learn to read because they desire to, or because social and official pressure is placed upon them to force them to do so. Likewise in the vernacular people will learn to read if social or official pressures supply a strong enough incentive.

CONFLICTS BETWEEN PHONEMIC AND SOCIAL GOALS

The goals outlined in the preceding sections of this chapter frequently come into conflict with each other. In many cases it proves impossible to reach all of the goals at the same time. Some of these conflicts must be noted here. The desire to write phonemically may conflict with the desire to indicate all the sounds. For example, two sounds may be submembers of a single phoneme in the vernacular, but separate phonemes in the trade language. In such an instance there is bound to be considerable pressure to write these submembers of the vernacular with separate symbols paralleling those of the trade language. For example, in Aztec of

Morelos,[1] [v] and [w] are submembers of a single phoneme, with [v] occurring before front vowels and [w] occurring before central and back vowels. Yet in Spanish /w/ and /v/ are separate phonemes. Similarly in Cakchiquel[2] of Guatemala, [v] and [f] are submembers of a single phoneme, with [v] occurring initially in words and [f] finally in words--but in the trade language of the area, Spanish, the two are separate phonemes. It is sometimes necessary to write submembers of phonemes with distinct symbols under this type of cultural pressure.

The desire to use no new letters comes into conflict with the desire to write all sound units with distinct symbols. If, however, there are more sounds than there are available letters, one must adopt some expedient to represent them.

The desire to use single unit symbols, only, conflicts with the desire to avoid diacritics. Yet if not enough letters are available the only way to obtain new symbols is to create new ones or to modify traditional ones with diacritics. Likewise, one wishes to avoid new letters, yet to do so demands the use of diacritics or digraphs, both of which it is advisable to avoid.

One wishes to obtain popular approval for one's alphabet in order that it might be accepted, and this may involve restricting oneself to letters of the trade alphabet. Yet one wishes to provide for all sounds with unit symbols, but to do so may offend people who maintain traditional attitudes.

Similarly one wishes to use the letters of the trade alphabet to the most possible advantage by using them where necessary with flexible values, or with values different from those seen in the trade language. Yet one wishes to avoid conflicting values for the letters in the two languages.

One wishes to provide the alphabet which will be easiest for the teaching of monolingual illiterates. Yet at the same time one wishes to provide an alphabet which will most easily serve as a bridge for the transfer from the vernacular to the trade language, or which will be most easily handled by people who have already learned to read the trade language without being able to understand it adequately.

Finally, one wishes to be able to make an alphabet from the point of view of the psychology of the native, that is, reflecting his phonemic system. Yet one also

wishes to have his alphabet acceptable to the psychology of the people who speak the trade language.

The balancing of these conflicting goals and principles is a highly difficult undertaking, especially since people are likely to become emotionally attached to the particular alphabet which they have previously been using, and to be unshakeably convinced that no other orthography is satisfactory. In many instances no really satisfactory solution can be reached--and the best which can be done is to adopt the least objectionable of several awkward possibilities.

The analyst must consider carefully the nature of the public to be reached with the alphabet.

If it is (1) people who have never learned to read anything at all, the problem has several phases: need of (a) an alphabet suitable for primers and the teaching of reading, (b) an alphabet suitable for literature, (c) an alphabet suitable for vernacular writing, unless all writing is to be done in the trade language, (d) an alphabet suitable for transfer to the national culture. If it is (2) people who do not understand the national language, but have been taught to read it by the tremendous efforts of the local teachers in the Federal system, then these people have been provided (a) with an alphabet for primer usage, but (b) with no literature, since that available in the national language is unintelligible to them.

Now since this second group has all the culture needs of Group 1 for literature, and the group is very large (in some tribes far larger, and growingly so, than any group which nontechnitions will teach to read as adults in the non-trade language group) it is exceedingly important to meet their needs, even if it be slightly at the cost of some details which are easier for Group 1.

This duplicate set of goals demands an alphabet which does not go to extremes in any direction. If the goal were to provide for primers only, any symbols could be used which were clear (say, Chinese signs, or Egyptian ones) but the necessity of national unity and cultural absorption prevents such a course. Likewise, Group 2 is accustomed to a trade-language alphabet, and any sharp departure from it slows up their use of the literature, especially by lowering their morale; such morale cannot be legislated but must be wooed.

On the other hand, a severe attempt to adapt to exclusive trade-language signs puts too great a burden on Group 1 by making the task too intricate and nonsystematic in relation to their own internal sound relationships.

The orthographical innovations which

---

[1] Data from Richard Pittman, Summer Institute of Linguistics.

[2] Data from W. Cameron Townsend, Summer Institute of Linguistics.

can be introduced to an area are to a considerable extent proportionate to the prestige of the persons sponsoring them. Private individuals cannot complete with the prestige of local chieftains and their opinions, even when the opinions are but prejudices. Central government sponsorship can go much further, since it cannot so readily be accused of following antinational measures.

Ultimately the problem cannot be solved through the formation of an alphabet by fiat, but by a literature being read. A good alphabet with no motivation will not be read; a poor one with good motivation will allow the absorption of much learning even by people who find reading difficult.

SPECIFIC SYMBOLS

The specific letters which the investigator will choose may vary according to the area in which he is working. In territory where Chinese is the official language, symbols might be quite different, for example, from those chosen for usage in Russian-speaking territory or in Latin America, or in Africa. Any suggestions given here, therefore, must be subject to modification according to the cultural environment. Nevertheless it may be convenient to present certain possibilities for general consideration.

(1) Voiceless Stops

For unaspirated /p/,[1] /t/, and /k/ there is usually little difficulty in deciding what letters to use--that is, "p", "t", and "k". Even in Latin America the symbol "k" is probably preferable in spite of the fact that for Spanish the traditional symbol is "c" before /a/, /o/, and /u/, but "qu" before /i/ and /e/. The fact that in Spanish one does find a small number of words such as kilo and kilometro spelled with "k" would seem, however, to constitute sufficient precedent to warrant the utilization of that letter in order that the phoneme can be represented consistently.

If there are two "k" phonemes, one front and the other back, possibly the use of "k" for the front one and "q" for the back one is usually the best solution.

If the government of a country in Latin America insists on a very close adherence to Spanish usage, the best compromise which one can make is to use "c" and "qu" for /k/, but "k" for /k̲/. This is not completely satisfactory, since the use of "c" and "qu" for submembers of the one phoneme would not meet completely the principle of having a one-to-one correspondence between symbol and

---

[1]Brackets enclose phonetic symbols, diagonals indicate phonemic ones, quotes represent practical orthographical suggestions.

phoneme. However, inasmuch as the two submembers are conditioned by occurrence before vowels, it is not completely arbitrary. Further difficulties are involved, however, inasmuch as "c" in Spanish orthography is also used in certain words for /s/.

The glottal stop can be written either with a large symbol such as [ʔ] (a question mark without the lower dot), or it may be written with an apostrophe. If the glottal stop is strictly parallel to a full consonant and acts in distribution like them, the larger sign may be preferable. If, however, the glottal stop acts differently and seems to be more closely related to a close-knit nucleus, then the apostrophe is probably better, since it would interrupt the words less and indicate closer unity with the vowel.

If aspirated stops are unit phonemes, and no other stops occur in the language, they may be written as "p", "t", and "k". If, however, aspirated stops are single-unit phonemes which contrast with unaspirated voiceless stops, then the aspirated ones may well be written (in an area where English is the trade language) as "p", "t". and "k", and the unaspirated ones with "b", "d", and "g". In English-speaking countries this solution is acceptable and has given good results, since English "p" tends to represent an aspirated sound [pʰ] while unaspirated [p] in stressed syllables sounds to English ears somewhat like "b". In Latin America, however, this solution would be completely unacceptable inasmuch as the normal phonetic interpretation of "p" would be an unaspirated voiceless variety. Thus if it were written "b" it would cause misunderstanding for those bilinguals who read Spanish.

If the contrast, on the other hand, is between a series of voiceless unaspirated stops and voiced unaspirated stops, then the voiceless ones would be written "p", "t", and "k", and the voiced ones "b", "d", and "g". If three series are phonemically present, then the voiced ones could be written "b", "d", and "g", the voiceless unaspirated ones "p", "t", and "k", and the voiceless aspirated series in some other way.

When the voiceless aspirated stops must be distinguished from the others--so that the symbols "p", "t", and "k" are not adequate--several possibilities must be considered. As for diacritics, a reversed apostrophe may be used, such as "p‘". This has the advantage of appearing like a unit symbol, but has the disadvantage of containing a diacritic. A second possibility is to use italics. This has the strong advantage of being a unit symbol which is similar to the non-italicized form. It has the disadvantage that in manuscript italics are represented by underlining "p", "t", and "k" rather than by different-shaped letters. In some foreign print shops, italic letters are difficult to obtain in the proper type fonts. In general, however, italics must be considered a legitimate type of orthographical device when no other satisfactory solution can be found, provided there is little probability of much literature being prepared in manuscript form by native writers.

Underlining on the printed page may be a further possibility, but proves suficiently awkward to print to make its usage inadvisable. Small capital letters would be technically excellent, but again the printing difficulty prohibits their usage.

In the face of these difficulties the only alternative sometimes is to use a digraph composed of the stop symbol plus "h"--that is, "ph", "th", "kh".[1]

Digraphs can be utilized advantageously only when there exists in the language no actual clusters comprised of a sequence of two unit phonemes whose symbols are also used to represent the phonetically-complex phoneme. The symbols "ph" can be used for a unit phoneme /ph/ provided that there is no sequence of phoneme /p/ plus phoneme /h/ which is phonemically distinct from /ph/ as a single phoneme but which would be written identically with it.

(2) Voiced Stops

Voiced unaspirated stop phonemes are usually best written with "b", "d", and "g" respectively.

A back-velar variety of [g] may cause difficulty if it must be distinguished from ordinary [g]. Here one might consider the advantages of "g" italicized, or some type of diacritic mark.

Voiced aspirated stops could probably be written with symbols "b", "d", and "g" in italicized form, or by a digraph entailing "h" following the stop symbol.

Phonemes which are phonetically comprised of nasal plus stop, such as [ⁿd], are usually written on the line as "nd", and so on. Sequences with [ᵐb] and [ᵑg] may be handled similarly. This solution is not unsatisfactory unless it conflicts with actual sequences of phonemes in the language. Alternate suggestions are simply to use "b", "d", and "g" for phonemic /ᵐb/, /ⁿd/, and /ᵑg/, provided that the symbols "b", "d", and "g" are not used for anything else in the language, and provided that bilinguals do not object to the unit symbol on the grounds that in the trade language such a phonetic element would be phonemically written with two letters.

(3) Double Stops

Certain double stops are conveniently written as "kp", "gb", and so on, when there is is no contrast with actual clusters of /k/ + /p/ and /g/ + /b/ (or /p/ + /k/, and /b/ + /g/) in the language.

(4) Glottalized Stops

Glottalized stops seldom if ever occur by themselves but usually are in contrast with other voiceless stops. If they constitute unit phonemes--that is, phonetically-complex single phonemes--in contrast to unaspirated /p/, /t/, and /k/, the glottalized ones are probably best written with an apostrophe mark as a diacritic. The next best solution, and in some instances possibly still preferable if one does not contemplate the preparation of manuscripts or local printing by the natives, is to use "p", "t", and "k" in italic form. If aspirated, unaspirated and glottalized stops must all be contrasted, it would appear inadvisable to use regular apostrophe for glottalized types and reversed apostrophe for the aspirated ones, since the two symbols are so similar that they would tend to cause confusion. In such a case, one would probably utilize "ph" or "p" italicized for the aspirated sound and "p'" for the glottalized one.

(5) Implosive Stops

On the North American continent implosive stops are very rare. In Guatemala certain voiceless ones occur: /pˤ/ and /kˤ/ are in the same series with the glottalized sounds /t'/ and /k'/. Since together they constitute one series, they have been written alike--all of them italicized, or all of them followed by an apostrophe. Voiced implosive stops seem to be quite common in the southern part of Africa. There they may be written in various ways: either with an apostrophe preceding them, "'b", or with special forms of letters, namely "ɓ", "ɗ". The latter are recommended by the International Institute of African Languages and Cultures.[1] Retroflex [ṭ] and [ḍ] are also found in Africa, and by the same Institute are being written with vertical strokes which extend below the line and curve toward the right: "ṭ", "ḍ". If these particular letters could not be used, one would have to consider italics or some type of digraph.

(6) Click Stops

Click stops have been written in various ways. [tˢ<] has sometimes been written as "/", or "c", or "ʇ"; [t<] has

---

[1]Notice that this solution would be awkward in Latin America if one were to use it combined with "c" and "qu" for /k/, inasmuch as "ch" for /kh/ would then become ambiguous with that "ch" which equals /č/.

---

[1]The student of African languages should have some of their publications for reference, for example, their Practical Orthography of African Languages. Memorandum I, Revised Edition. (London: International Institute of African Languages and Cultures, 1930).

been written as "ǂ", or "q", or "ʗ". A
lateral click has been written as "//", or
"x", or "ʖ". Retroflex click has been
written "/" and possibly other ways.

(7) Flat Fricatives

As for the fricatives, the labio-
dental voiceless one is conveniently written
"f". Bilabial [ɸ] could likewise be written
"f" unless there were a contrast between
them, in which case one might want a new
letter. The solution adopted by the International Institute of African Languages and
Cultures is to use an "f" with a vertical
stroke extended below the line for the
bilabial variety: "ƒ".

For voiceless interdental fricative
[θ] one may consider the following alternatives: The Greek letter "θ", or italic
"t", or "z" in Latin America reflecting
Castillian pronunciation,[1] or "th". The
digraph "th" should be considered only if
it does not conflict with an actual sequence
of "t" plus "h", and provided that "th"
has not been used for anything else in the
language such as an aspirated stop.

A velar-fricative phoneme /x/ is
best represented in Latin America by "j".
Elsewhere, "x" would appear to be preferable.
"h" might sometimes be acceptable provided
that it is not phonemically distinct from
/x/ in the particular language being studied.

The voiced counterparts of these
fricatives cause problems which are quite
different from those arising with voiceless
fricatives. The symbol "v" is conveniently
used for a labiodental fricative, or for a
bilabial fricative if there is no phonemic
contrast between /v/ and /β/. Where these
last two must be differentiated, the bilabial
one may have to be given a special type of
symbol, either a new shape of "v", or
italics or some other modification.

The interdental voiced fricative is
conveniently written with "d" in Latin
America provided that it is not in contrast
with a voiced alveolar stop. Where /d/ and
/ð/ are phonemically separate the fricative
would need a modified symbol such as "d"
italicized, or Greek "δ", or it might be
represented by some digraph such as "dh".
The voiced velar fricative /g/ can be
represented by "g" provided that the symbol
does not have to be used for a voiced stop
in the same language. Otherwise the
fricative may be represented by Greek "γ"
or possibly by some such digraph as "gh"
provided in turn that it does not conflict
in that language with an actual sequence

of phonemes /g/ plus /h/.

Occasionally one finds glottalized
fricatives as unit phonemes. The writing of
these may parallel the writing of /t'/ as
"t'"; that is, glottalized /f'/ may be
written "f'", and so on.

(8) Grooved Fricatives: Sibilants

The sibilants cause various problems.
Voiceless [s] can be written simply as "s".
Dental [s̪], alveolar [s], or retroflexed
[ʂ] can be written simply as "s" unless
there is a phonemic contrast between any two
of them. In that case they may be distinguished in some way, such as by italics,
or the second one may be written "z" if that
letter does not need to be used for a voiced
sibilant. A phoneme /š/ may be written with
elongated "ʃ", or as "š", or--where neither
of these is acceptable--with the digraph
"sh", if no actual sequence of /s/ plus /h/
exists in the language. In many parts of
Latin America the most convenient way of
writing this phoneme, however, and one which
has considerable precedent in the actual
materials published, is the use of "x".
This has the advantage of being a unit
symbol easily printed and with some support
for it from traditional usage. If in addition to /s/ and /š/ a third voiceless
phoneme /ʂ/ is found, the three might be
written respectively as "s", "š", and "ʃ";
or "s", "š", and "x"; or "s", "sh", and "x".

A voiced alveolar sibilant may be
represented with the letter "z". An
alveopalatal one may be represented with the
letter "ʒ" or "ž" or with the digraph "zh".
In parts of Latin America the most convenient
way of writing /ž/ is to use the letter "y"
(since pronunciation of Spanish "y" and "ll"
in some areas are both represented by this
sound [ž]) provided that [y] and [ž] are not
in phonemic contrast in the language.

Retroflexed [ẓ] and [ʐ] may be represented simply by "z" and by the symbols
previously given for [ž], provided that they
are not in contrast with those sounds respectively. If, however, they must be
distinguished, various expedients may have to
be used for a complicated system: [ẓ] might
be italicized, or written with a digraph
"zr", or handled in some other way; [ʐ] in
Latin America is frequently written most
conveniently with "r", provided that "r" is
not used for some other phoneme.

(9) Affricates

The affricates [tˢ] and [tˢ] are
best written with simple symbols if the
cultural pattern of the area makes it
feasible. In such a case one or the other
may be written with the letter "c" (or "ȼ",
for Latin America, to save conflict between
"c" as /k/ and "c" as /tˢ/), and [tˢ] may be
written "č". Frequently, however, this is
unacceptable for nonlinguistic reasons. In
such an instance one may employ a PHONETIC

---

[1]Or even "d" for Latin America (reflecting the final unvoicing of "d" in
verdad)--if "d" has not been used for other
sounds, and provided that its usage does not
conflict with usage of "d" elsewhere or cause
confusion with bilinguals who read Spanish.

DIGRAPH in which the two phonetic elements making up the phoneme are each symbolized. Thus [t^s] would be written "ts" and [tš] (that is, /č/) would be written as "tš" or "t/"--or if "x" is being used for [š], then "tx". In Latin America "ch" must usually be used rather than "č" or "tš" since "ch" is established in the culture for /č/.

Aspirated varieties of these affricates should be written in ways paralleling those aspirated stops previously described.[1] Glottalized affricates should be similarly parallel, thus: "ch'". Labialized and palatalized affricates[2] may have parallel handling to the labialization and palatalization of the regular stops.[3]

The voiced affricates [d^z] and [d^ž] present similar problems to the voiceless ones. A digraph may be employed for the [d^z] unless some single symbol such as "z" can be utilized. The alveopalatal affricate is easily written "j" in English-speaking areas. In Latin America this is inadmissible since it conflicts with the use of Spanish "j" to represent /x/. In Latin America, therefore, the affricate must be written with a digraph such as "dy".[4]

The affricates with a nasal item in the same phoneme are probably best written with an "n", thus: "ndz", and so one, even though these trigraphs are highly undesirable.

Laterally-released affricates may usually be written "tl" and "dl". For unit symbols, however, one may consider "ƛ" or "λ".

(10) Nasals

The nasals /m/ and /n/ can be written by the traditional symbols. A palatal [ñ] may be written either as "ñ" or "n".

In some areas the investigator must be careful to write differently three types of sequences which are actually distinct phonemically in the pronunciation of the natives. These are /ña/, /nya/, and /nia/. The first of these begins with a palatal /ñ/, which is phonemically distinct from alveolar /n/, and which has little or no audible off glide; during its production the blade--but not the tip--of the tongue touches the alveolar arch, and in its release a weak y-like off glide may sometimes be heard. The second, that is /nya/, begins with the tip of the tongue touching the alveolar arch and has an appreciable /y/ off glide. The third, /nia/, begins with alveolar /n/, then passes to a pronunciation of /i/ which is longer than that of the /y/ of /nya/ and is possibly slightly syllabic. When the three types are phonemically distinct they should be kept distinct in the orthography. It is in African languages, especially, that one must be alert to notice this series of contrasts.

Retroflex [ɳ] might be symbolized by a new letter, or diacritic, or digraph. The International Institute of African Languages and Cultures suggests "ɳ".

A velar phoneme /ŋ/--but not an [ŋ] which is a submember of the phoneme /n/--may be written with the unit symbol "ŋ", or occasionally it may be more convenient to utilize the digraph "ng". As with other digraphs, it shares the disadvantages of lengthening words and increasing the difficulty of learning to read by preventing a direct one-to-one correspondence of single sound unit with single unit symbol. If /ŋ/ and back-velar [ɴ] are in phonemic contrast in the language some other expedient would be necessary to distinguish them.

Voiceless nasal phonemes are extremely rare. When [Nn] represents a phonemic sequence /hn/, the sequence should be written "hn"--or in Latin America "jn", paralleling the spelling of "j" for /x/. When, however, [N] represents a single phoneme /N/, a similar digraph, or italics, might be the best solution, writing [N] as "hn" or "n". When it is a phoneme separate from "h" or "n", a unit symbol would have to be employed if it conflicted with the phoneme sequence /hn/. Italics would then be a preferable solution.

When /m/ or /n/ are preceded or followed by a quick glottal closure and the resultant combination constitutes one phoneme, two solutions may be adopted: (1) An apostrophe may precede the consonant symbol so as to parallel the phonetic structure of the phoneme, or (2) the apostrophe may follow the consonant symbol, if the investigator feels that these so-called "glottalized" continuants are in a series which parallels the glottalized stops. This is, one could write such an /ʔm/ phoneme

---

[1]This makes unwieldy trigraphs, such as "tsh" and "chh", provided that one chooses to write /č/ as "ch" and provided that aspiration is written with "h" etc. This is very unfortunate. Trigraphs are even more objectionable than digraphs since they depart farther from the principle of having a one-to-one correspondence between phonemic unit and orthographic unit. Frequently however, due to the cultural pressures involved, one is helpless to adopt a solution which is technically preferable.

[2]Affricates other than the alveolar and alveopalatal ones are less likely to cause trouble. Probably digraphs would have to be used to represent them in most instances where they do occur as phonetically-complex single phonemes or as sequences of phonemes.

[3]See below, paragraph (14).

[4]Or with some unit symbol, such as "ǰ".

as "'m" or "m'". Italicis might also be
considered provided italicis had not already
been chosen in the language to represent
other kinds of phenomena.

(11) Laterals

"l" can represent a voiced alveolar
lateral phoneme in the language. If in
addition one finds a voiceless /ł/ phonemically distinct from voiced /l/, one may
consider writing a digraph "hl" or "lh"--
provided again that such a digraph does not
conflict with an actual sequence of phonemes
/h/ plus /l/--or one may utilize a new
letter such as "ł", or italicis, or some
other expedient. Where fricative /ł/ is a
phoneme to be distinguished from regular
voiced /l/, a similar type of solution
could be reached. A palatal /lʸ/ in phonemic contrast with an alveolar /l/ might have
to be written either with a strange symbol
such as "ʎ", or with a digraph such as "ly"--
provided it did not contrast with a true
sequence of /l/ plus /y/--or for Latin America the palatal /lʸ/ might best be written
"ll" if no long /l·/ or sequence of /ll/
occurred.

(12) Flaps and Trills

The voiced alveolar retroflex flap
can usually best be written as "r". A
voiced trill at the same position may be
written with "r" provided it is not in contrast with any other sound which should be
written with that symbol. If both the
alveolar flap and trill are phonemic in the
language, the flap may be written "r" and
the trill either with a digraph "rr"--espec-
ially for Latin America--or with some diacritic, such as "r̃". A uvular trill may
likewise be written "r" if it is not in contrast in that particular language with either
of the ones mentioned. Otherwise, a further
digraph or diacritic must be utilized.

The letter "r" is sometimes used for
the voiced back velar or uvular fricative
[g̃]. There is no objection to this provided
that the sound is strictly parallel to other
types of /r/ or /l/. If, however, the sound
is in a series [f, s, x, x̣, v, z, g̃, g̣],
then probably the "r" symbol would be less
convenient than some letter or modified
letter paralleling the [x] and [g̃].

A flap [l] can cause considerable
difficulty since acoustically it is somewhat
like [l], [r], and [d]. It makes little
difference whether the sound be written "l",
"r", or "d", provided that it is kept distinct from these others if they are also
phonemes, and provided that it does not conflict seriously with prevailing orthographies
in the region.

A heavily retroflexed or alveopalatal
flap occasionally has to be distinguished
from a mildly retroflexed or alveolar one;
possible symbols include: a new letter, e.g.
"ɽ" (elongated r), italic "_r_".

(13) Nonsyllabic Vocoids

When the vocoids [i] and [u] are
functioning as consonants, especially if
they are nonsyllabic, they are usually best
written "y" and "w" respectively. Where
social pressure does not prevent its usage,
"w" is preferable to "hu-" in Latin America
inasmuch as it constitutes a single symbol
and is receiving growing usage for foreign
names or expressions, whereas the writing
"hu-" is not phonemically consistent and
cannot be used at the end of words. In many
areas the symbol "j" is preferred to "y" for
nonsyllabic high close front unrounded
vocoid glide; this would not do for Latin
America, however, because of the conflict
with "j" for /x/.

The phonemes /ʔy/ and /ʔw/ may be
written in ways already described for the
sequences with /m/ and /n/; as "'y" and "'w",
or as "y'" or "w'", or by some other device.

When voiceless vocoids are functioning together as a single nonsyllabic phoneme
/h/, the preferable writing for English-
speaking regions would be "h". For areas
where Spanish is the trade language the symbol "j" is usually preferable. Wherever in
Latin America [h] and [x] are phonemically
in contrast, however, the first may best be
written "h" and the second "j".

(14) Labialized, Palatalized, and Pharyngealized Consonants

The labiovelar [xʷ] may be written
"xw", or, where "j" is used for /x/, as "jw";
labiovelar /g̃ʷ/ may receive similar consideration. Labiovelar /kʷ/ and /g̃ʷ/ are usually
best written as "kw" and "gw". Occasionally,
however, it is possible and advisable to
write "kua" and "gua" for /kʷa/ and /g̃ʷa/
without causing ambiguity with /ku/ and /gu/.
But nonphonemic writing of this type should
be avoided. In some instances, also, it may
be possible to write /kʷ/ as simply "q".
This would be much simpler. It would utilize
a single symbol for the phoneme, and would be
preferable in areas where it would not cause
confusion for any other reason.

Palatalized consonants such as [tʸ]
which are sequences of two phonemes, that is
/ty/, should have the "y" written on the line,
as "ty". When, however, the [tʸ] constitutes
a single phoneme, the solution is more difficult. One would prefer to write either "tʸ"
or utilize some special modified "t" symbol
so as to have a single letter. Frequently,
however, this is impossible, and one must
write the single phoneme as "ty"; this solution should not be adopted if /tʸ/ and /ty/
are in phonemic contrast.

Pharyngealized consonants which are
phonemically distinct from nonpharyngealized
consonants would need either a special symbol such as "θʷ", or some other diacritic
mark, or some type of digraph.

(15) Consonants Modified by Length, Pitch, and Intensity

The consonants which are long may be phonemically distinct from those which are short. If a long consonant is phonemically to be interpreted as a sequence of two identical consonants in a particular language, then it should be written with a repeated symbol: for example, a [t·] which is phonemically /tt/ should be written "tt". In rare cases a phonetically-long consonant may be a single phonemic unit; here the preferable solution might be to write "t·". In those instances in which the phonetically-long consonant is a conditioned or free variant of the short one, the lengthening would not of course have to be indicated in the phonemic orthography.

A few of the consonants may be modified by phonemic pitch and thus made syllabic If contrast of pitches is found on consonants the tones should be written in some way, e.g. thus: "ḿ" and "m̀". The pitch of nasals should not be written, even in a tone language, unless the pitch is unconditioned. The investigator should be wary of writing tone on consonants unless he can find actual pairs differing only by the pitch of the consonants.

Consonants differing by intensity (that is fortis versus lenis phonemes), need distinct symbolization to represent the phonemic contrasts. In some situations it proves convenient to represent the fortis consonants with those symbols previously discussed for voiceless consonants ("p", "s", etc.), but to write the lenis sounds with symbols suggested for the voiced consonants ("b", "z", etc.), since lenis consonants seem to have some tendency toward voicing and may even have free variation between lenis voiceless and lenis voiced submembers of the lenis phonemes.

(16) A System of Five or More Vowels

In a language with the five vowel phonemes /a/, /e/, /i/, /o/, and /u/, there is usually little difficulty in writing them as "a", "e", "i", "o", and "u". In a language with a sixth vowel which is somewhat high, back and unrounded, the vowel may be written as "ə", or "ʌ", or "ɨ"; the "ʌ" is advantageous in this respect in that it is less easily confused with "e" and "o" in printing than is "ə", and lacks the disadvantages which "ɨ" has because it contains a diacritic mark. If the sixth vowel is a low back rounded variety, then "ɔ" may be utilized. If the sixth vowel should be a very low front unrounded vowel, either "ɛ" or "æ" might prove best. With seven or eight vowels, one may be able to use "a", "e", "i", "o", "u" supplemented by "ʌ", "ɔ", "ɛ", or "æ" where necessary.

For a high front rounded vowel, it may be preferable to utilize "ü"--or it may be written with "y", if the downgliding high close front vocoid has been written with "j" in accordance with the alphabet of the International Phonetic Association rather than with the "y" which has been used in this volume.

For a mid front rounded vowel one may use "ø", and for a lower variety an "œ" digraph--or one may consider other digraphs or diacritic marks such as "ö".

(17) A System of Four Vowels

A language with four vowel phonemes, say /i/, /e/, /a/, /u/, needs only one of the letters "u" or "o". The letter may be chosen which represents a phonetic sound closer to the native variety. In an area where the trade language has five vowels, it may be awkward to decide whether to use "o" or "u" for the vernacular since in that case there is likely to be nonphonemic free variation in the vernacular between [o] and [u], or the sound may be acoustically half way between them. In such circumstances bilinguals are likely to insist--inconsistently, however--that sometimes the letter "u" should be used and sometimes "o" should be written, so that it may be difficult to implant a consistent policy.

(18) A System of Three Vowels

In a three-vowel system these problems are accentuated, since in such a structure there are likely to be found the three phonemes which can be symbolized as "i", "a", and "u" but with considerable difficulty caused by great variation phonetically within each of these phonemes. Thus /i/ might be found as [i^], [i], [iˇ], [ɪ], [e^], [e], [eˇ], and so on; whereas /a/ might be found as [a], [ɑ], [aˁ], [æ], [aˀ]; and /u/ as [u^], [u], [uˇ], [ʊ], [o^], [o], [oˇ], and [ɔ], and the like.

This tends to cause confusion, and one may be tempted to write the language with more than the three vowel letters, so as to record the different phonetic varieties of the phonemes. If, however, one succumbs to this desire, he is likely even so to find inconsistencies in his spellings of identical words, or he is likely to find himself in strong argument with the native bilinguals as to which vowel is present. If on the other hand he writes only three vowel letters, bilinguals who have learned to distinguish five or more phonemes on the basis of a trade language are likely to be disturbed by the consistent phonemic writing since sometimes a phoneme will sound to them like one of the phonemes of the trade language and at another time a free variant of that same vernacular phoneme will sound to him like a different phoneme of the trade language. There is no easy or complete solution to this problem, yet in such a situation one should try to write phonemically, using just the three vowels rather than subjecting oneself to the inconsistencies of an attempted recording with five.

The problem is considerably heightened when certain of the submembers of the three phonemes are in some environments free varieties but in other environments conditioned varieties of the phonemes. This is especially likely to be the case when back-velar phonemes occur in the language. In such a system the phonemes /i/ and /u/ are likely to have only their lower varieties occurring directly before or after the back-velar sounds. In this case speakers of a trade language with five vowels or the investigator himself may "hear" the vowels [e] and [o] consistently next to the velar sounds and desire to write them that way, even though they are submembers of the phonemes /i/ and /u/. If the bilingual pressure is sufficiently strong and if loan words are coming into the language rapidly and threatening to modify the phonemic system by causing the phonemic separation of [i] and [e], [u] and [o], one may find it desirable to write the conditioned variant of /i/ as "e" next to the back-velar sounds. This policy has been adopted for some of the Quechua dialects of Peru.

This will not solve all of the investigator's difficulties, however, since he will then have to determine at exactly what distance from the back-velar sounds he will write "e" and "o"-- since these sounds may affect vowel phonemes at some distance from them--but also he will be troubled since the free variation mentioned a bit earlier for a three-vowel system in a language without such back-velars may very well persist in environments where these back-velars do not happen to occur. In these latter environments there will again be argument as to which of the symbols should be written--or there may be other sounds than the back-velars which also give a partial conditioning of /i/ toward [e] or /u/ toward [o]. If the investigator finds it essential to write the conditioned variants [e] and [o] at all, he should try to make some rule, even though it be partially arbitrary, as to when these should be written; for example, he should limit himself to writing them when they occur next to the back-velars but should elsewhere write consistently "i", "u", regardless of which variety of the phoneme happens to occur at the moment.

(19) Nasalized Vowels

Nasalized vowels which are phonemically distinct from non-nasalized vowels may be written in one of three ways: They may have a tilde over them, thus: "ã" and "õ"; or may have a reversed hook under them, thus: "a" and "ǫ". The first type seems to be more in use in Africa and the second style has received more usage in American Indian languages. An easier type to print where these two symbols cannot be obtained, is the use of an "n" raised above the line: "aⁿ", "oⁿ". (This type of symbol is being used advantageously in Mazateco of Mexico.) In rare cases--in certain languages which have every syllable beginning with a consonant and no syllables ending with consonants--

the "n" for nasalization can most conveniently be written on the line as "an", "on". (This is being used successfully in Mixteco of Mexico.) Usually, however, this type of writing would cause much ambiguity and would be highly disadvantageous, since /ąo/ and /ano/ would then both be written "ano".

(20) Retroflexed Vowels

For retroflexed vowel phonemes one might consider the use of a dot under the letters, or italics, or some other device.

(21) Voiceless Vowels

Voiceless vowels are rarely phonemic. If one finds them one might consider writing them with diacritic symbols or with some other marker.

(22) Laryngealized Vowels

Laryngealized ("glottalized") vowels are usually to be interpreted as sequences of vowel plus glottal stop; or of vowel, glottal stop, vowel; or of glottal stop, vowel; that is, phonetic [å] is usually to be interpreted as /aʔ/ or /aʔa/, or /ʔa/. If laryngealized vowels as such should prove to be phonemically distinct from /VʔV/, one might still choose to write them in one of these ways as a digraph, rather than attempt to utilize a new symbol.

(23) Long Vowels

Long vowels, when they are phonemically composed of sequences of identical vowels, should be written with double vowel letters: thus [a·] would be phonemically /aa/ and orthographically "aa". In those instances where the long vowels must be considered as single phonemes one may still write them with double vowel letters, as digraphs, unless it causes difficulty in interpreting syllable division, or tone, or produces vowel clusters which are extra long and hard to read. In these instances one may write long vowels either with a raised dot following them, as "a·", or with a macron, "ā".

(24) Stressed Vowels

If stress is phonemic, so that stressed and unstressed vowels must be distinguished in orthography, there are at least two acceptable ways of doing so: An acute accent may be placed over the stressed vowel, as "á"; or a vertical stroke above the line may be placed immediately preceding the stressed vowel or the stressed syllable, thus: "'pa" or "p'a",(though confusion would be caused by this system if a type-written apostrophe is used for glottalization of consonants). Sometimes one or more additional degress of stress are phonemic and need symbolization. A second degree of stress can be indicated conveniently by a grave accent mark over the vowel, "à", or by a vertical stroke on the line, thus: "ˌpa" or "pˌa". The use of acute and grave accent

marks would be unacceptable in a language
where pitch also was to be written by those
same symbols.

(25) Tone

In a tone language of a register type,
two levels of pitch are most easily distinguished by acute mark versus zero mark on the
vowel: "á" versus "a". Note that in a register tone language one of the tones need
not be indicated. If one of the tones occurs
much more frequently than the other, it saves
marking só many vowels if the tone is marked
over the least frequent type. In a three-
register system a second mark is needed. A
macron is probably the most convenient symbol for this purpose: "á", "ā", and "a".
Again, the tone mark should be omitted from
the most frequent tone if that proves convenient; the macron should then be used for
mid or low tone, depending upon the particular language. In a four-register system a
grave accent mark could be utilized for the
extra symbol which is needed.

The reason that the macron rather
than the grave mark was suggested for the
second symbol in a three-tone system is that
acute and grave marks appear quite similar
to native speakers.learning to read and it
appears difficult for them to remember which
is the high one. The macron is sufficiently
different from the acute mark to make it
more easily distinguished.

A vertical bar over the vowel can
also be used, but the type in general seems
more difficult to secure and the type faces
containing a vertical mark are likely to be
made less strongly than those with a macron.

In a contour system one can utilize
the same marks: for example, acute for high
rising, grave for low falling, macron for
high level, and so forth. They may be
placed over the vowel, or if one chooses,
at the beginning of the syllable and in different places in relation to the syllable;
for this latter type, note the following:
high rising, "´a"; low rising, "ˏa"; high
level, "ˉa"; low level, "ˍa". Further types
of symbolization are also possible--for example, a numbering of the tones or the placing of a degree sign or some other symbol
at different points in relation to the
letter.

(26) Intonation and Rhythm

Many languages have some intonational or rhythmic characteristic which
helps indicate the end of a full sentence.
This can be symbolized with a period. If
there is a further intonation or pause indicator consisting of a pitch pattern or a
rhythm grouping this can be symbolized with
a comma. One may also find intonational
units which indicate the presence of questions of one or more types; these should be
symbolized with the question mark or, if
two types of intonation are involved, with
inverted question mark for the second type.

Further intonational types might be indicated with semicolon, colon, or other markers.
It should be emphasized, however, that in a
language where no significant intonational
units, that is where no intonation phonemes
(or morphemes) differentiate questions from
statements, one should not slavishly follow
the punctuation of material being translated
from a trade language.[1] Nor should one limit
oneself to placing the intonation signs at
the end of the sentence merely because he is
accustomed to seeing them there. In a language where intonation is as complicated as
that of English the practicality of writing
in general literature all of the distinguishing characteristics of the intonation has not
yet been proved. It would be a very valuable
and interesting experiment if someone should
try to indicate such intonational characteristics for a language hitherto unreduced to
writing, and report on native response to
learning the symbols.

(27) Capital Letters

If the cultural pressure does not
force their usage, capital letters can be
omitted. This saves duplication in two sizes
of any extra phonetic characters in the orthography chosen, and in this way eliminates
some inconvenience and expense. The use of
capital letters has certain advantages, however, in that they keep the printed page of
a local vernacular more like the traditional
format of many national languages. In addition, they serve to identify foreign names,
and the like, introduced by the educator, so
that the beginner can learn to identify one
of these items by its orthographical form.
This helps prevent his being confused by
loan words which have no ordinary lexical
meaning.

(28) Border Points (Junctures)

Spaces should be written between
words. The borders between words may be
determined according to the procedures given
in Chapter 13. Short words may be easier to
read than long ones, but a single long
grammatically unified word should not be
broken by a space merely to have shorter
orthographical words, lest the difficulty
introduced artificially by the two somewhat
meaningless resultant "half words" more than
overbalance the advantages gained from
shortness.

The investigator must be prepared to
utilize hyphens next to clitics. This may
prove much more advantageous than separating
them by spaces or joining them without space
or hyphen to the items upon which they are
phonologically dependent. See Chapter 13
for their analysis.

---

[1]For this suggestion I am indebted
to Eugene A. Nida, Bible Translating, An
Analysis of Principles and Procedures, with
Special Reference to Aboriginal Languages
(New York: American Bible Society, 1947),
127-29.

LANGUAGES AS UNITS

After reading the bewildering variety of alternatives presented in the preceding pages, one may well ask why it should not be possible to propose a single alphabet which would be used under any circumstances for all languages and save the type of discussion presented here. There are several reasons why such a uniform alphabet is highly impractical and, at the present stage of knowledge, impossible.

(a) In various parts of the world there exist different cultural traditions for the use of certain orthographies. Regardless of the scientific value of such alphabets it is impossible to get everyone to agree to abandon his own system for a universal one.

(b) It is highly desirable to have a relatively small number of letters which can be used to the best advantage so that these letters can be readily obtained by printing plants around the world. This implies that the use of the letters must be flexible, since otherwise there would have to be thousands upon thousands of signs to indicate the minute shades of sound which actually exist. Once the principle of FLEXIBILITY[1] has been granted as valid for this reason, however, one is confronted with the problem of utilizing this flexibility to the best advantage. If in an area where English is the trade language a certain vernacular has two phonemes distinct, namely [t'] and [t], and another language has [t] and [d], it is convenient to use only the letters "t" and "d" in each instance. If, however, a third language has the distinct phonemes [t'], [t], and [d], then a third sign is necessary. If one had previously decided to utilize these symbols for particular sounds he would not be able to use the letters conveniently and flexibly for the first two systems. If he had set up three symbols which were to be universally applied to all languages because of the distinctions of the third type, then he would be likely to introduce diacritics into the first two systems where they are not needed at all.

(c) In other words, each language as a whole must be considered in relation to the cultural traditions surrounding it and the trade language of the area. An adequate alphabet can only be prepared in the light of the facts about its internal system of sounds and its external relationships to the community. It is for these reasons that no one set of rigid rules will give a single uniform practical solution for all languages.

For any particular language it is not sufficient to discuss the individual sounds. Each language must be considered as while, in order that that orthography can be chosen which allows for the most efficient flexible use of available letters but at the same time symbolizes all phonemic contrasts. At the same time the symbolization must be adapted to the cultural needs of the area, varying according to the trade language used and other characteristics of the culture which have previously been discussed.

Problem 257--Restricted Bolivian Quechua[1] B

Directions:

Following this paragraph there will appear a list of Spanish phonemes heard in certain varieties of Latin American Spanish, with a brief mention of some of the more important submembers of these phonemes; for Bolivian Quechua[1] a similar list is given. Explain the reasons for the orthography suggested for the Quechua.

Mexican Spanish[2]

Phonemes	Selected Prominent Submembers	Orthography in Use
/p/	[p]	"p"
/t/	[t]	"t"
/č/	[č]	"ch"
/k/	[k] (before front vowels)	"qu-" (before /e/ or /i/)
	[k] (before central or back vowels)	"c" (before /a/, /o/ or /u/)
		"k" (in a few loan

---

[1] For technical publications the principle of flexibility can frequently be carried even farther to good advantage. Small caps, for example, can be utilized for a variety of sounds so as to avoid the necessity of having special sound types made. Those persons who wish to publish for technical journals in linguistics should, before sending in articles to the editors, consult the data about available types for these journals. Note, for example, Special Types in Ten and Eight Point Sizes Available for Scientific and Other Journals, edition for the Linguistic Society of America (Baltimore: Waverly Press, Inc., 1941).

[1] Data from author's notes, taken on a field trip for the American Bible Society (November-January, 1943-4), and incorporated in the mimeographed report by the Society, "Linguistic Problems Connected with the Translation of the Scriptures into the Languages and Dialects of Ecuador, Peru and Bolivia" (New York: September, 1944).

[2] For a more detailed treatment of Spanish sounds, see Navarro Tomás, Manual de Pronunciación Española, Fourth Edition, (Madrid: Publicaciones de la Revista de Filología Española, 1918).

Phonemes	Selected Prominent Submembers	Orthography in Use
		words such as 'kilo')
/b/	[b], [ꞵ] (freely variant; or stopped utterance-initially or after nasals and laterals; in "careful" or "school" pronunciation, [b] and [v] are sometimes phonemically distinct)	"b" and "v" (inconsistently within present pronunciation)
/d/	[d], [đ] (as for /b/; but [đ] word finally) [θ] (freely variant from [đ] word finally)	"d"
/g/	[g], [ǥ] (as for /b/)	"g" (before /a/, /o/, or /u/) "gu-" (before /e/ or /i/)
/f/	[ꝑ]	"f"
/s/	[s]	"s" and "z" "c" (before /e/ or /i/) "x" (rarely)
/x/	[x]	"j" "g" (before /e/ or /i/) "x" (rarely)
/m/	[m]	"m"
/n/	[n] (or sometimes [-ŋ] word finally)	"n"
/ñ/	[ñ]	"ñ"
/l/	[l]	"l"
/ḷ/	[ḷ] (or in some dialects this phoneme disappears; it is then replaced with /y/)	"ll"
/r/	[-ř-]	"-r-"
/ř/	[ř] (or freely variant to [ž̌]	"r-" and "-r" but "-rr-"

Phonemes	Selected Prominent Submembers	Orthography in Use
	or variant to [ř̃] or [š̌] in word-final position)	
/w/	[w]	"hu-" (possibly "(C)u" and "(V)u" et al.)
/y/	[y] (or in some dialects [ž̌])	"y" (and possibly "(C)i"
/a/	[a] (This and the other vowels tend to have centralized un-stressed varieties, and others.)	"a"
/e/	[e]	"e"
/i/	[i]	"i"
/o/	[o]	"o"
/u/	[u]	"u"
/'/	[(stress)]	"´" (Applied by morphological, orthographical conventions on the last syllable of CVCV but not on CVCV nor on CVCV + C as a separate morpheme; applied to CVCVC but not to CVCVC; applied to CVCVCV, etc.)
/#/	[(space)]	(between words with some clitic problems; occasionally a nonphonemic "silent h" is written following space before a vowel)

Bolivian Quechua

Phonemes	Selected Prominent Submembers	Suggested Orthography
/p/	[p]	"p"
/t/	[t]	"t"
/č/	[č]	"ch"

Phonemes	Selected Prominent Submembers	Suggested Orthography
/k/	[k]	"k"
/ḳ/	[ḳ]	"q"
/pʰ/	[pʰ]	"ph"
/tʰ/	[tʰ]	"th"
/čʰ/	[čʰ]	"chh"
/kʰ/	[kʰ]	"kh"
/ḳʰ/	[ḳʰ]	"qh"
/pˀ/	[pˀ]	"p'"
/tˀ/	[tˀ]	"t'"
/čˀ/	[čˀ]	"ch'"
/kˀ/	[kˀ]	"k'"
/ḳˀ/	[ḳˀ]	"q'"
/m/	[m]	"m"
/n/	[n]	"n"
/ñ/	[nʸ]	"ñ"
/s/	[σ]	"s"
/š/	[š]	"sh"
/x/	[x̣-], [-x-], [-x̣]	"j"
/l/	[l]	"l"
/ḷ/	[ḷ]	"ll"
/ř/	[ř]	"r"
/w/	[w]	"w"
/y/	[y]	"y"
/i/	[i] (varying freely to [e] and intermediate varieties; limited to [e] next to back velars)	"i" (except that "e" should be used next to back velars)
/u/	[u] (varying freely to [o] and intermediate varieties; limited to [o] next to back velars)	"u" (except that "o" should be used next to back velars)
/a/	[a]	"a"
/ˈ/	[(stress)] (in most cases falls on penult; sporadic instances elsewhere)	"ˊ" (to be written only on stressed syllables other than the penult)

Phonemes	Selected Prominent Submembers	Suggested Orthography
/#/	[(space)] (Words tend to be quite long, determined by criteria of isolatability, grammatical unity, and stress occurrence.)	(space to separate words)

Additional Spanish Phonemes in Loans to Quechua

Phonemes		Suggested Orthography
/b/		"b"
/d/		"d"
/f/		"f"
/g/		"g"
/ř̃/		"rr"

Problem 258--Kalaba Dialect GW

Phonemic Data (This dialect of Kalaba is spoken in an area where Spanish is the trade language. A chart of the phonetic norms of the phonemes is given below.):

$$p^ʿ \quad\quad t^ʿ \quad\quad č^ʿ \quad\quad\quad k^ʿ$$
$$f \quad\quad σ \quad\quad š \quad\quad\quad x$$
$$l$$
$$ř$$
$$\quad\quad\quad\quad i \quad\quad\quad\quad u$$
$$a$$
$$\quad\quad\quad ɨ̧ \quad\quad u̧$$
$$a̧$$

/pʿsixa/ 'flower'   /fčʿu̧ši̧/ 'green'

/čʿxačʿi/ 'red'   /řakʿfu̧/ 'llama'

/lustʿu/ 'potato'

<u>Directions:</u>

Rewrite the five words with the alphabet which you would suggest for use in practical literature for the native speakers of the language.

Problem 259--Kalaba Dialect GX

Phonemic Data (This dialect of Kalaba is spoken in an area where Spanish is the trade language. A chart of the phonetic norms of the phonemes is given below.):

$$p^ʿ \quad\quad t^ʿ \quad\quad k^ʿ$$
$$p \quad\quad t \quad\quad k$$
$$ᵽ \quad θ \quad s \quad\quad\quad\quad\quad ˀ$$
$$m \quad\quad n \quad ñ \quad ŋ \quad\quad\quad h$$
$$\quad\quad\quad i \quad\quad\quad\quad u$$
$$\quad\quad e \quad ʌ \quad o$$
$$a$$

/pʌt'oh/   'donkey'   /ɓsit'kʌŋ/ 'spider'
/k'eɸiθ/   'cactus'   /ʔmʌsθaɓ'/ 'fish'
/tʌpθut'/   'coyote'   /θañan/   'possum'
/sk'iɳeʔ/   'buzzard'   /hoʔuñ/   'tick'

Directions:

Rewrite the eight words with the practical alphabet which you would suggest for use.

Problem 260--Kalaba Dialect GY

Phonemic Data (This dialect of Kalaba is spoken in an area where English is the trade language. A chart of the phonetic norms of the phonemes is given below.):

<pre>
pʰ   tʰ   ȼʰ   č̌ʰ   kʰ
     d   z̦   ǰ   g
ɓ   s   š̌   h
     l
     ɬ

               i   ɨ
             e   o
                  a
</pre>

/pʰʸɨshač̌/   'why'   /ȼʰč̌ʰedsez̦/ 'when'
/š̌pʰiɓoš̌/   'does'   /tʰsasȼʰil/   'whose'
/š̌hɨǰlad/   'format'   /č̌ʰšiɓǰiɾ/   'radio'
/htʰoš̌č̌ʰikʰ/   'atom'   /sč̌ʰegeǰ/   'spell'
/shosɨh/   'velar'   /diz̦loȼ/   'snore'

Directions:

Rewrite the ten words with the practical alphabet which you suggest. State the reasons for your choice.

Problem 261--Kalaba Dialect GZ

Phonemic Data (This dialect of Kalaba is spoken in an area where English is the trade language. A chart of the phonetic norms of the phonemes is given below.):

<pre>
p   t   k   ʔ
pʔ   tʔ   kʔ
ɓ   d̶
          ɬ
          l
          ɬ̵
          ř
               i   u
             e   o
                  a
</pre>

stress: /'/

/'pealiř/   'one'   /dlo'pʔukʔ/   'six'
/kʔig'potʔ/   'two'   /'geʔařɓiʔ/   'seven'
/di'aɾoʔul/   'three'   /ɗtʔaʔʔi/   'eight'
/'tʔkaɾoɗ/   'four'   /dko'ɬoɓaʔu/ 'nine'

/ɬoʔabkʔie/ 'five'   /řiɸʔal'teř/ 'ten'

Directions:

Rewrite the ten words with the practical alphabet which you suggest.

Problem 262--Kalaba Dialect HA

Phonemic Data (This dialect of Kalaba is spoken in an area where English is the trade language. A chart of the phonetic norms of the phonemes is given below.):

<pre>
pʰ   tʰ   kʰ   ʔ
      tʔ   kʔ
b   d   g
ɓ   ɗ
m   n
mʔ   nʔ
      s   x

                 i   u
Tone: high ´ e   o
       mid ̄   a
       low ˎ
</pre>

/pʰtʔiná/   'mine'   /dūpʰɓòʔ/   'his'
/ɓẽmʔõ/   'yours'   /kʰlʔðɗ/   'hers'
/góʔukʔ/   'ours'   /màsxūtʰ/   'theirs'
/nʔidˆsū/   'someone's' /tʔ̀ðxíʔ/   'any'
/xtʰ꞊akʰ̄áb/   'anyone's' /sòbãm/   'some'

Directions:

Rewrite the ten words with the practical alphabet which you suggest.

Problem 263--Kalaba Dialect HB

Phonemic Data (This dialect of Kalaba is spoken in an area where Spanish is the trade language. A chart of the phonetic norms of the phonemes is given below.):

<pre>
pʰ   tʰ   kʰ
b   d   g
ɓ   s
m   n

               i   u
                  a
</pre>

/pʰsag/   'tomorrow'   /nudikʰ/   'today'
/sido/   'not'   /gdikʰan/ 'so'
/sani/   'where'   /ɓimis/   'yester-
/nitʰiɸʰ/ 'sometime'   day'

Directions:

Rewrite the words with the practical alphabet which you suggest. The phoneme /s/ becomes [š̌]; and the phoneme /n/ becomes [ñ], when contiguous to /i/; state the reason for your choice of symbols for these phonemes.

APPENDIX

The problems of learning a language differ according to whether a person has material ready for absorbing or whether he must first analyze the material which he wishes to absorb. The analysis, in turn, will vary according to whether or not he has bilingual informants or monolingual informants. We will consider these various possibilities very briefly.

The most important single rule for absorbing language material already analyzed is that a person should utilize every bit of information which he knows. In the first days when he learns how to say "good morning" or its equivalent, he should determine that thereafter he will say "good morning" only in the vernacular and not in his own language which he may try to teach to the native, nor in the trade language or national language of the region if it differs from the vernacular. It is extremely important for a person to utilize from the very beginning the data which he has once attempted to learn, since by so doing he gradually increases the amount of material known and over which he has mechanical control, and this soon grows to sizable proportions until he can speak the language readily. Where a trade language is in partial usage in the vicinity, a person may be tempted to utilize only that means of communication, looking for interpreters on those occasions when he must deal with people who speak nothing but the vernacular. In this way a trade language can become a crutch to keep him from learning the vernacular. Such a problem does not arise in the community where only one language is spoken. In a partially bilingual community, however, the first principle is that the learner should utilize the words of the vernacular as far as he possibly can.

The next principle is that his attitudes will determine to a considerable extent the way in which he ultimately will learn the language. If he is self-conscious, hesitant to look queer to himself or if he readily tires of utilizing strange linguistic forms, he may never attain a fluent control of the vernacular. The student should train himself to the point that he does not care whether he looks queer, provided he is learning. He should not be afraid of making errors, even vulgar errors, but should rather try by every possible means to push forward his actual daily use of the language. In conversation with the natives he should be courageous to try the language material, rather than hesitate lest people think him queer. If all day long he speaks a language other than his mother tongue he may find it rather tiring, but he should not allow this to deter him from utilizing it. Morning, noon, and night he should insist upon speaking the vernacular and not his own language or a trade language.

In memorizing data the student should not attempt to absorb items in complete isolation but should rather attempt to memorize words or the like within the framework of actual sentences. SUBSTITUTION FRAMES prove exceedingly valuable for this purpose. Such a frame consists of a sentence or a phrase, one word of which may be deleted and another word substituted for it. The items which constitute the replaceable list will tend to be of a single grammatical type--for example, all nouns, or all verbs, or all pronouns, and so forth. Note the following:

'The boys are hungry.'
'The dogs are hungry.'
'The men are hungry.'
'The cats are hungry.'

Here the place for replaceable parts demands a noun plural represented in this instance by 'boys', 'dogs', 'men', and 'cats'. The same sentence could be used for a different kind of frame. Note the following:

'The boys are hungry.'
'The boys are going to be hungry.'
'The boys will be hungry.'
'The boys have been hungry.'

In this instance the drill is on various parts of the verb. By similar types of frames all kinds of words can receive drill.

The value of this type of drill is that the items substituted are learned within normal contexts. They become mechanically used within actual sentence types and are more readily called to mind in the middle of a sentence than are items which are drilled without reference to any context. Furthermore, the speed is more likely to be given at a normal pace. The student should plan to keep his speed at approximately five syllables a second. By these procedures the student obtains fluency and facility with grammatical items in context, rather than having a miscellaneous knowledge which is not welded into a constructive system.[1]

---

[1]For a detailed outline of this approach see Thomas F. Cummings, How to Learn a Language, (New York: privately published, Press of Frank H. Evory and Company, Albany, New York, 1916); or Ida C. Ward, Practical Suggestions for Learning an African Language in the Field, International Institute of African Languages and Cultures, Memorandum XIV (London: Oxford University Press, 1937)

A somewhat different type of frame is also valuable and may be called a TWO-PART SENTENCE FRAME.[1] For these drills a set of five sentences more or less is chosen in which the first half of each sentence can go with the second half of each of the other sentences, and vice versa. In this way advantages are gained similar to those for frames with simple replaceable items, but with the further advantage that longer elements are practiced. Note the following sample:

'The boy wants to buy a car.'
'The man wishes to sell his auto-
    mobile.'
'The young teacher is going to visit
    the university.'
'The man in the blue suit has decided
    to go swimming.'
'The beautiful girl thinks it will
    be wise to join the Red Cross.'

Notice that the first part of each of these sentences can be used with the second half of the others.

'The boy wants to buy a car.'
'The boy wishes to sell his auto-
    mobile.'
'The boy has decided to go swimming.'
'The boy thinks it will be wise to
    join the Red Cross.'

The second half of each sentence can be used with the first half of each of the others.

'The boy wants to buy a car.'
'The man wants to buy a car.'
'The young teacher wants to buy a
    car.'
'The man in the blue suit wants to
    buy a car.'
'The beautiful girl wants to buy a
    car.'

Sentences of this type can be so arranged that they afford practice in the entire grammatical structure of the language and for any particular type of words or semantic area which the student wishes. If the frame sentences are wisely chosen the student can soon pass to conversational exercises upon the frame material, and in a relatively short time can discuss quite a number of topics.

---

[1] This type of frame was called to my attention by Professor Joseph Yamagiwa, University of Michigan.

For a third but related type of frame--a grammatical one for exercises in sentence construction and absorption of grammatical material--see Charles C: Fries, and Staff, An Intensive Course in English for Latin-American Students, Vols. I-VI (Ann Arbor: English Language Institute, University of Michigan, 1943).

Following such types of drill the student may memorize a story or a legend told in colloquial speech. Having memorized this legend and having had frames built upon its vocabulary and sentence structure he can then retell the story from various points of view--that is, telling it in the first person as if he himself had seen the events, or in the third person as if someone else had seen the events, and the like. This gives drill in various types of verb forms, and the like, which vary with the person of the subject.

Early in his study the student should memorize well several sample conversations which represent daily situations. If these conversations are well chosen, they will give him a number of advantages: (1) They allow him to make immediate contacts with the people around him. (2) It encourages the natives to talk to him so that he will actually hear much of the language. (3) The memorized greeting formulas get him started in the first part of any conversation so that the native reaction is likely to be friendly, cooperative and helpful; a sizable percentage of our actual conversation concerns itself with routine formulation of greetings, discussion of the weather, of crops, of one's family, and the like, and if these typical situations are thoroughly mastered in their details, the student has become adept in a portion of the language which is by no means negligible.

A person who wishes to learn a language must have much contact with the people who speak that language. There is no substitute for this part of the language-learning process. The student who by nature is socially inclined has better possibilities for easy learning of the language than has anyone who is naturally phlegmatic, retiring, and shy. Specifically, for example, a student who makes good grades by studying books but is nonsocial has less chance of learning a language well than does a person with somewhat lower grades out who is highly sociable and likes to talk. The student of language should not underestimate the value of meeting people frequently and chatting with them. Since ultimately he studies a language in order to meet people and talk with them, he should begin early by deliberately cultivating their friendship.

The student should realize that in every type of situation he should mimic as well as he can the gestures, speech, tone of voice, and manner of native speakers of the language. In his own culture the student is likely to find it impolite to mimic the tone of voice and manner of his colleagues and therefore he trains himself not to do so. When he is in a foreign language environment, however, the situation is strikingly different. In this new situation he looks queer if he fails to mimic; the better he can mimic, the more normal he appears. He may offend as a foreigner if he fails to act and talk like those to whom he is speaking, but he will please them if he does as they do. The

closer he can come to their actions, the
happier they are as they see him being assimilated to their language and culture.
The student should not be afraid to mimic
but rather should do so to the best of his
ability.

The person learning a foreign language and entering a foreign culture is desirous of learning to analyze the psychology
of the people with whom he is working. He
wishes to know "how they think," and to be
able to appreciate these thought processes.
He wants to be able to understand them, their
reactions, their feelings and thoughts, and
emotions. To a very great extent the
thoughts and cultural reactions of a people
reflect their language structure. If one
knows the language thoroughly, he does know
much about how people think. If he knows
the language well he does know in many ways
how people are going to react. If he knows
the language well he knows the psychology
of the people.

The thoughts of any people are molded
and restricted by the patterns of a limited
series of sounds, a limited series of arbitrary morphemes, a limited number of rigid
syntactic constructions. People cannot
break away from these patterns and are even
unaware of the fact that they are limited by
them. If one speaks the language well, then
one knows the way people think because he
himself thinks in the language; he himself
uses the same thought processes; he himself
voluntarily limits himself to their phonemes,
morphemes, and sentence types.

Furthermore, all languages include
words which are meaningful only in terms of
the cultural background of the community.
For example, a foreigner coming to English
may hear a statement like this: "He has
cried, 'Wolf, wolf!' once too often." To
him, the expression may be meaningless. To
us, as speakers of English the expression
"Wolf, wolf!" means not only, 'C. lupus, C.
lupus,' but also something like this: 'A
person must not raise false alarms lest at
some time his genuine alarm be disregarded.'
This latter meaning is derived from a story
which is well known to most of the speakers
of the language. A speaker of Quechua who
had learned some English but had not read the
story would not understand our "thought processes" or the potent warning conveyed to
someone else when we say, "Better not cry
'Wolf, wolf!'" On the other hand, if he
understands these terms, he will have heard
the story and will react to the warning conveyed by the words. In order to understand
people's reactions we must understand their
statements. In order to understand their
statements we must understand their culture.
In order to understand their culture we must
know the stories and legends, which contribute to that culture. The student of language must know not only the words but the
cultural background and the traditions which
help to give them meaning. He cannot understand the language without knowing the cul-

ture of its speakers. If he understands the
customs and traditions of the people, he will
automatically have gone a long way toward
understanding their psychology and their
thought processes.

Each of these various points which
have been mentioned for the absorbing of linguistic material are applicable to a student
who is studying a language through the traditional textbooks available for the better-
known languages. He can make up his own exercises and studies to supplement the material which he gets from such texts. They do
not, however, supplant textbooks: the grammar must be studied in order to determine
what are good frame sentences for the learning of the language structure; the dictionary
must be consulted to determine what words or
morphemes are best used for replaceable parts
in such situations; and an analysis of the
sounds has presumably preceded the choice of
the practical orthography which he will be
using.

When grammars, dictionaries, alphabets
and the like are available to the student, he
can focus his attention on the actual absorbing of the available material in ways which
we have just discussed. When, however, these
linguistic aids are lacking, the student must
first analyze the language for himself. The
procedures for arriving at a suitable orthography are presented in this volume. Those
which should be utilized for analyzing the
grammar of the language are presented elsewhere.[1]

In analyzing a language, two basic
situations may confront the student--either
he will have available a bilingual informant
who can speak the vernacular and some other
language known to the investigator, or else
no such helper will be available.

In the first case the investigator
can in the trade language ask for linguistic
forms and receive the rough translation
equivalents in the vernacular. This has certain advantages. The initial analysis of the
grammar can be done very rapidly by means of
the translated forms, and the investigator
may arrive at a fairly adequate knowledge of
the meanings of the words except in the more
difficult spots, and can even get helpful
clues as to the meaning of some of the more
obscure morphemes.

Although the bilingual approach is
the easiest for the student, it has two disadvantages: (1) He may find himself tempted
to continue using the trade language long

---

[1]By Eugene A. Nida, Morphology: The
Descriptive Analysis of Words, University of
Michigan Publications in Linguistics, II
(Ann Arbor: University of Michigan Press,
1946). The method of presentation is similar
to the one given here for phonemics. Theory
is paralleled by practical exercises with
hypothetical languages.

after he could have made a transfer to the
vernacular. If one of his goals is to speak
the language concerned, the use of the trade
language may then serve as a pitfall to prevent him from reaching his goal. The anti-
dote to this, however, is to work earnestly
to utilize immediately with the natives all
of the material insofar as he has gathered
it and understands it. In some respects
this first difficulty is a psychological one
rather than a technical one. (2) A second
difficulty is linguistic. Ultimately the
most difficult problems of a language cannot
be solved by any translation procedure. The
analysis of intricate form classes, the analysis of orders of morphemes and delicate semantic problems must all be handled by a comparison of one item of the vernacular with
other items of the vernacular. The difficult
problems must be analyzed by a comparison of
the internal structure of the material, not
by trying to hire someone to translate words.
We are well acquainted with this fact, if we
but stop to realize it, when we notice that
as speakers of English we go to an English
dictionary to find out about the most minute
shades of differences of meaning in English.
In order to find meanings, we speakers of
English do not consult, let us say, an Eng-
lish-Spanish dictionary--rather we go to the
large historical dictionaries in the language.[1] Essentially, the most difficult
problems of the language cannot be treated
merely by a translation of forms, even though
translations may give hints as to meanings.

An alternate method of approach is
to study a language without an interpreter
at all. In some parts of the world this is
the only technique possible, since in out-of-
the-way places there exist tribes in which
there are no speakers of European languages
or other languages likely to be known to the
investigator. Under these circumstances the
student is forced to utilize a technique
which begins with the language material itself and analyze it in terms of linguistic
forms heard in various social and physical
contexts. For example, he may begin by
pointing at various objects and presumably
saying the name in English--until the natives
understand that he is interested in the names
of things, whereupon they may proceed to give
him names of a great many objects. Or he may
get his first start by hearing a parent speak
sharply to a child when the child is being
chided in some way. Or he may say, "Hello,"

in English and by friendly gestures receive
a friendly reply which he assumes is a greeting. Following up the achieving of the names
of things he may continue by getting the
linguistic labels for the sizes for these
things, taking, for example, small rocks and
big rocks, or small leaves and big leaves,
and contrasting them. Similarly he can proceed to get the names of actions by jumping,
walking, singing, and the like--provided that
the native has by now seen that he wishes to
communicate and is trying to help him learn
the language. Labels for ownership such as
'mine', or 'yours', may then frequently be
achieved without great difficulty by gesture
or by pointing to objects which are in the
possession of one individual but not in the
possession of others. Much error will, of
course, creep into the first rough guesses as
to these meanings, yet the situation is by no
means as difficult as it appears.

The advantages of this monolingual
technique are: (1) That it allows the work
to be done when it could not be done in any
other way, and (2) that it avoids some of
the temptation for a person to learn only a
trade language without learning the vernacular. The disadvantages are as follows: (1)
It gets under way much more slowly for grammatical analysis. (2) The investigator usually cannot direct his research so readily
to any one part of the language, but must
follow up lines of information wherever it
appears possible at that time, and must be
content to delay until some later date the
investigation of any point upon which he cannot get information at the moment. (3) The
investigator may find it awkward to arrange
his living conditions until he has some
language to utilize.

Whatever method is employed, the student should be very careful to handle his
informant wisely lest he obtain inaccurate
information or treat his informant in such a
way that the helper will not care to work
with him any longer. This, of course, implies patience and courtesy on the part of
the investigator--but also care that he
neither tires the informant by requiring endless repetition nor encourages the informant
(especially if he is using the bilingual
approach) to philosophize about his grammar
in such a way that it wastes one's time.[1]

---

[1]E.g., The New Dictionary on Histori
cal Principles, edited by Sir James A. H.
Murray, Henry Bradley, W. A. Craigie and C.
T. Onions, Vols. I-X (Milford: Clarendon
Press, and others) 1889-1915. This is the
most important English dictionary with which
the student should be acquainted for technical purposes. Note that the definitions are
arrived at by comparing the usage of the
words in various contexts of the language
itself and not by etymologies or translation
or any other device.

[1]For discussion of these problems
see Leonard Bloomfield, Outline Guide for the
Practical Study of Foreign Languages (Balti-
more: Special Publications of the Linguistic
Society of America, 1942); Eugene A. Nida,
Morphology: The Descriptive Analysis of
Words, University of Michigan Publications
in Linguistics, II (Ann Arbor: University
of Michigan Press, 1946), 162-163; Jules
Henry, "A Method for Learning to Talk Primi-
tive Languages," American Anthropologist,
XLII (October-December, 1940), 635-41; Carl
F. Voegelin, "Anthropological Limits of Lan-
guage," in the Proceedings of the Indiana
Academy of Science, XLVI (1937), 57-64.

THE INTERNATIONAL PHONETIC ALPHABET.
(Revised to 1945.)

		Bi-labial	Labio-dental	Dental and Alveolar	Retroflex	Palato-alveolar	Alceolo-palatal	Palatal	Velar	Uvular	Pharyngal	Glottal
CONSONANTS	Plosive	p b		t d	ʈ ɖ			c ɟ	k g	q ɢ		ʔ
	Nasal	m	ɱ	n	ɳ			ɲ	ŋ	N		
	Lateral Fricative			ɬ ɮ								
	Lateral Non-fricative			l	ɭ			ʎ				
	Rolled			r						ʀ		
	Flapped			ɾ	ɽ					ʀ		
	Fricative	ɸ β	f v	θ ð s z ɹ	ʂ ʐ	ʃ ʒ	ɕ ʑ	ç j	x ɣ	χ ʁ	ħ ʕ	h ɦ
	Frictionless Continuants and Semi-vowels	w ɥ	ʋ	ɹ				j (ɥ)	(w)	ʁ		

		Bi-labial		Front	Central	Back	
VOWELS	Close	(y ʉ u)		i y	ɨ u	ɯ u	
	Half-close	(ø o)		e ø		ɤ o	
					ə		
	Half-open	(œ ɔ)		ɛ œ	ɜ	ʌ ɔ	
				æ	ɐ		
	Open	(ɒ)		a	ɑ ɒ		

(Secondary articulations are shown by symbols in brackets.)

OTHER SOUNDS.—Palatalized consonants : ƫ, ᵭ, etc.   Velarized or pharyngalized consonants : ɫ, đ, ẕ, etc.   Ejective consonants (plosives with simultaneous glottal stop) : p', t', etc.   Implosive voiced consonants : ɓ, ɗ, etc.   ɼ fricative trill.   σ, ҫ (labialized θ, ð, or s, z).   ʆ, ʓ (labialized ʃ, ʒ).   ʗ, ʇ, ʖ (clicks, Zulu c, q, x).   ɹ (a sound between r and l).   ʍ (voiceless w).   ɩ, ɣ, ɷ (lowered varieties of i, y, u).   з (a variety of ə).   ɵ (a vowel between ø and o).

Affricates are normally represented by groups of two consonants (ts, tʃ, dʒ, etc.), but, when necessary, ligatures are used (ʦ, ʧ, ʤ, etc.), or the marks ͡ or ͜ (t͡s or t͜s, etc.).   ͡ also denote synchronic articulation (m͡ŋ = simultaneous m and ŋ).   c, ɟ may occasionally be used in place of tʃ, dʒ.   Aspirated plosives : ph, th, etc.

LENGTH, STRESS, PITCH.— : (full length).   · (half length).   ' (stress, placed at beginning of the stressed syllable).   ˌ (secondary stress).   ˉ (high level pitch) ;   ˍ (low level) ;   ′ (high rising) ;   ˌ (low rising) ;   ˋ (high falling) ;   ˏ (low falling) ;   ^ (rise-fall) ;   ˇ (fall-rise).

MODIFIERS.— ~ nasality.   ̥ breath (l̥ = breathed l).   ̬ voice (ş = z).   ʻ slight aspiration following p, t, etc.   ̣ specially close vowel (ẹ = a very close e).   ̦ specially open vowel (e̦ = a rather open e).   ̫ labialization (n̫ = labialized n).   ̪ dental articulation (t̪ = dental t).   ʻ palatalization (ż = ʑ).   ̝ tongue slightly raised.   ̞ tongue slightly lowered.   ̹ lips more rounded.   ̜ lips more spread. Central vowels ï (= ɨ), ü (= ʉ), ë (= ə̈), ö (= ɵ), ɛ̈, ö̈.   ̩ (e.g. n̩) syllabic consonant.   ̯ consonantal vowel.   ʃˢ variety of ʃ resembling s, etc.

By courtesy of the International Phonetic Association.

Note: The statements and definitions in this glossary are provisional ones and not completely adequate. The meaning of the term can be satisfactorily determined only from its usage, and the student can find this usage only in terms of the actual working procedures of which they are a part. The student must not consider, therefore, that he understands terms well merely by memorizing a glossary, nor must he be too highly disturbed if these definitions do not cover all the usage found in the book. The glossary is merely given for the convenience of the student as a rapid mnemonic device and for convenience in reference.

Items preceded by an asterisk are used infrequently or not at all in this volume, but are given for the convenience of students who may find them in other writings.

The letter "a" or "b" after a number refers to the first or second column, respectively; "n" refers to a footnote.

Abbreviated forms, in orthography, 208b

ACCENT: (1) Stress; or (2) a foreign pronunciation which gives a general strange impression to the native (see also Pitch Accent), 12

AFFIX: A morpheme which is phonologically and grammatically dependent upon some other adjacent morpheme; affixes do not occur in isolation; usually the meaning of affixes is not highly concrete, but rather modifies the basic meaning of the morpheme or sequence of morphemes upon which it is dependent, 162b-63a

AFFRICATE: A two-segment sequence which consists of a stop followed by a fricative, 33a

aspirated, 136a

heterorganic, 33a

homorganic, 33a

lateral, 131b

orthography for, 216b-17a

as a single phoneme, 131a

Air stream, direction of, 3b

*ALLOPHONE: A submember of a phoneme; a nonsignificant variety of a phoneme, or a conditioned variant of a phoneme, 185a

ALPHABET: A system of symbols to represent the separate sounds of a language (see also Syllabary, Orthography, Symbol, Phonetic Alphabet)

for English phonemic transcription, 45; differences in symbolization, 46b: Bloch, 46b; Bloomfield, 46b; Kenyon, 46b-47a; Swadesh, 46b; Trager, 46b

phonemic, goals in, 208a-23b

Alternate descriptive statements, 76an, 130a (see also Conflicting Evidence), 137a

Alternate hypotheses, 76

Alternate voicing exercise, 27b

ALVEOLAR ARCH: The teethridge; on diagram, 4b

*ALVEOLO-PALATAL: See Alveopalatal

ALVEOPALATAL: With point of articulation near the teethridge and front part of hard palate, 7

American English, phonemic alphabet for, 45

Analogy

in interpretation of phonemes, 128a-49a

in interpretation of sequences, 132

ANALOGOUS ENVIRONMENT: See Contrast in Analogous Environment, 73a-77a

including identical environments, 75b

sample problem for, 85

*APICO-: Made with the tip of the tongue as articulator

APPROACH: The articulatory movements preceding the formation of some sound; or the movements closing a passageway, 32a

*ARCHIPHONEME: A special type of phoneme of limited distribution, postulated to account for under-differentiation of phonemes, which see (see also Neutralization), 197bn

Articles (see also Highlighted Article), interesting types, 176b

ARTICULATOR: A movable part of the vocal organs which impedes or directs the air stream, 3b-4a

definition of, 4a

movement of, symbolized in sequence diagrams, 10

Aschmann 148an, 178an

ASPIRATED: With (voiceless, or occasionally voiced) aspiration as the second segment of a two-segment sequence, 7

ASPIRATION: A puff of breath; a voiceless (or, rarely, voiced) vocoid following a sound

*ASSIBILANT: A sequence comprised of a stop followed by a sibilant

ASSIMILATED LOAN: A loan word which has become adapted to the sound system of the language (see also Loan)

Aulie, 155an

Aymara, 153b

Aztec, 53b-55a, 102a, 154a, 189an, 213b

Charts
> data for, 182
>
> distributional, 85b, 181b
>
> value of, 181b-82

Chest pulse, 91an

Chol, 155a

*CITATION: The representation of a word of some language in its traditional orthography

CLEAR L: An [l] with [i] timbre, i.e., with relatively high front tongue position

CLICK: A sound produced by ingressive mouth air (see also Ingressive), formation of, 41a

CLITIC: A word which is phonologically dependent upon some other word; (1) a bound form of an independent word, or (2) a morpheme unrelated to an independent word, but sufficiently independent in grammatical structure from those words to which it is phonologically dependent that it cannot be conveniently analyzed as an affix; a semifree word; nature of and criteria for, 165-66

CLOSE-KNIT NUCLEUS: A sequence of two vocoids, or of one vocoid plus a nonvocoid, which acts in distribution in the syllable like a single simple nuclear phoneme, 62b, 65a, 147a-49a

> with glottal stop, 147b-48
>
> of vowel units in American English, 45

CLOSE VOCOID: A variety of vocoid which has the articulator, whether tongue or lips, more nearly in a state of closure than do open varieties, 5a

CLOSED SYLLABLE: One ending in a consonant

CLUSTER: A sequence of two or more sounds; especially applied to vowel clusters, consonant clusters, vocoid clusters, or nonvocoid clusters, 132b

> of consonants in Brazilian Portuguese, 199b
>
> in distribution, 183b-84

CLUSTER OF IDENTICAL VOWELS: Two vowels in sequence, with the first the same as the second, 138b

COLLOQUIAL: Informal usage or familiar conversational style

COMPLEMENTARY DISTRIBUTION: Submembers of a phoneme which are mutually exclusive in their distribution so that the total of the distributions of each submember make up the total distribution of the phoneme as a whole, 93b

Completeness of data, 76an, 76b, 137a; in checking distribution, 87b

COMPLEX PHONEME: A phoneme comprised of two (or sometimes three) segments in sequence

> analysis of, 131ab

in orthography, 210a

COMPOUND: A grammatically close-knit unit of two free forms functioning like a single free form; criteria for, 167ab

CONDITIONED SUBSTITUTION OF PHONEMES: The replacement of one phoneme by another because of its grammatical or phonological environment (see also Conditioned Variation), 96

CONDITIONED VARIATION: In phonemics: the nonphonemic modification of a phoneme by its environment; in morphology: the mechanical substitution of one phoneme for another in certain types of environment (see also Conditioned Substitution of Phonemes), 86a, 96

CONDITIONED VARIETY: A submember of a phoneme which occurs in limited environments and is modified from the norm by that environment

Conflicting criteria, 62a

Conflicting evidence (see also Alternate Descriptions), 76an, 130a, 137a; in orthography, 130a

Conflicting pressures, 65a; in English, 46b

CONSONANT: A member of one of the two main distributionally determined groups of sounds (consonants versus vowels) found in every language; for a particular language the consonants comprise that one of the two groups whose members most frequently function as nonsyllabics, and which is largely, but not exclusively, made up of nonvocoids

> clusters, in Brazilian Portuguese, 199b; in Hungarian, 194
>
> distribution of, 182b-84
>
> long, phonemic analysis of, 139a
>
> nature of, 60b
>
> in relation to vowels, 128-30
>
> with simultaneous vowel, 139b

*CONSONANTAL VOWEL: The less prominent part of a diphthong, 130b

CONTEXT: Phonetic: sounds surrounding another; or its position in a larger phonological or grammatical unit; grammatical: position of an item in a construction

CONTIGUOUS SOUNDS: Sounds adjacent to each other

CONTINUANT: A sound during which there is no stoppage of the air stream, 24a

*CONTOID: See Nonvocoid

CONTOUR TONE SYSTEM: A system in which some of the basic tone units are gliding tones which cannot be analyzed into phonemically smaller units, 105b

CONTRAST: A consistent, persistent difference between two sounds in analogous environments

CONTRAST IN ANALOGOUS ENVIRONMENT: A persistent difference between two sounds in environments which are sufficiently similar and of such a nature that the phonetic environment could not plausibly be considered as being responsible for the differences between the sounds, 73a-77b

CONTRAST IN IDENTICAL ENVIRONMENT: A difference in sounds which persists in environments which are the same both as to neighboring sounds and as to positions in phonological and grammatical units, 80a-82a

Contrastive pairs, 81b

*CONTRASTIVE STRESS: Sentence stress utilized in a contrastive context (by some writers: a phoneme of contrastive stress)

CONVENIENT STATEMENT: That description of the data which accounts adequately, but most simply, for all the facts, 149a

Cornyn, 92an

CORRECT PRONUNCIATION: Any pronunciation which is the normal usage of a relatively large number of leaders of a relatively large dialect; of American English, 46a

Courant, 160bn

CREST: The peak of movement of a moving articulator

Cuicateco, 90bn

Cummings, 228bn

Cuppy, 47an, 50bn

CVC: Formula implying a sequence of consonant, vowel, consonant; or nonvocoid, vocoid, nonvocoid

DARK L: An [l] with a high back tongue position

Davis, 90bn

DEGREES OF CLOSURE: The relative openness of a passageway: (1) closure; (2) partial closure, producing strong audible friction at some localized point; (3) partial closure, or wide openness, with no audible friction (other than light cavity friction in voiceless sounds), 10a; illustrated, 10

DENTAL: With point of articulation at the back of the upper teeth, 4a

DESCRIPTION: See Highlighted Description, and Convenient Statement
    convenience in, 148a
    of distributions, 177b-80a
    minimum unit for, 145
    of the phonetic nature of phonemes, 177b
    sample statements for, 191-206
    simplicity in, 149a

DESCRIPTIVE PROCEDURE: Principles for the presentation of data, 174-84

Descriptive statements, 174-87

detailed routine type, 177b-80a

highlighted, 176-77b

including all data, 176an

monograph, 175b

nontechnical, 175b

routine, 176b

sample of, 185-87, 191-206

starting point in, 146a

structure in, 178b

technical, 174b; brief, 174b-75a

textbook, 176a

title of, 176b-77a

value of, 174a, 178b-79a

*DEVOCALIZED: See Unvoiced

DIACRITIC MARK: Some mark added to a letter in order to indicate the modification of a sound type, 212a

DIAGONALS: Used to enclose phonemic notation, 59a

Diagrams
    sequence, 9a-11b
    static, 8

Dialect, in orthography, 213a

*DIAPHONE: A phoneme of one dialect corresponding to, but phonetically slightly different from, the corresponding phoneme of another dialect, 14a, 44

Dictation, exercises for, 14n

DIFFERENTIAL DISTRIBUTION: Characteristics of permitted occurrence which make one set of phonemes differ from another set, 180a

DIFFERENTIAL DISTRIBUTION CHART: A listing of phoneme groups according to their differences of permitted occurrences, 180a

DIFFERENTIAL DRILL: An exercise designed to help the student learn to distinguish difficult sounds, 14an

DIGRAPH: A sequence of two symbols representing a single phoneme (see also Phonetic Digraph), 217a

*DIPHTHONG: A sequence of two vocoids; usually restricted to such a sequence when it serves as a single phoneme and when one element is more prominent than the other; rising diphthongs have the second element prominent; falling diphthongs have the first element prominent, 19an

*DIPHTHONGIZED: Given a vocoid glide

DISSYLLABLE: A word of two syllables only

DISTINCTIVE: Contrastive

DISTRIBUTION: Permitted occurrence of segments or phonemes (see also General Distribution, Specific Distribution, Differential Distribution, Complementary

sound by the partial contraction of the faucal pillars, 22a

File, use of, 182a

FINAL ENVIRONMENT: Position at the end of some specified phonological or grammatical unit such as an utterance, a word, or a syllable

FINAL PAUSE: A pause, in English, usually long, but sometimes short, preceded by pitches which tend to drop off slightly lower than they would preceding a tentative pause; the meaning that this English pause type conveys is one of a finished utterance or a finished implication, 45

FLAP: A sound produced by a single, rapid, unidirectional articulatory movement in which an articulator taps some part of the vocal apparatus as it passes by; orthography for, 219a

FLAT ARTICULATOR: One which is relatively ungrooved from side to side;

Flat fricative, 24a

FLEXIBILITY: In orthography, the principle of utilizing a letter even though the vernacular sound is not quite like that represented by that letter symbol as a traditional phonetic formula, 18b, 212b, 223

FLEXIBILITY OF MIMICRY: The ability of the student to modify his pronunciation readily by experimental mimicry (which see); value of, 13b

FLUCTUATING SUSPICIOUS PAIRS: See Suspicious Sounds

FLUCTUATION: See Free Fluctuation; dictation types, 127ab

FORMATIONAL STATEMENT: A description of the phonetic nature and distribution of the submembers of the phonemes of a language, 177b-78b

FORTIS: A nonvocoid sound made loud or precise by the tenseness of the articulators, 34a; phonetic symbol for, 6a

FRAME: An utterance, one part of which can repeatedly have substituted for it each of a list of items such that the various members of that substitution list can be contrasted with the frame and with each other as they enter the frame (see also Two-part Sentence Frame), 107-11

changing tones of, 110a

for tone substitution, 111a

unchanging, 110a

use of, 107b

Frauchiger, 154bn

FREE FLUCTUATION: The occurrence of one segment in one utterance of a word but a different segment upon some repetitions of that word; if these segments do not contrast elsewhere in the language, the freely variant sounds are submembers of the same phoneme; if the freely variant sounds contrast elsewhere in the language, the variation is between full phonemes (see Free Variation), 59b-60a, 122-25a

between full phonemes, 123a

noncontrastive, 60a, 123b

in practical orthography, 209

in restricted environments, 123b

between submembers of phonemes, 123a

FREE FORM: A linguistic entity which in a particular language is sometimes pronounced by itself, 162b-63a; free morpheme, 165b

FREE VARIATION: See Free Fluctuation

FRICATIVE: A sound during which friction can be heard and identified at some point of articulation (where the term *frictional is used, fricative may be restricted to sounds with friction in the mouth)

changed to stops by environment, 87a

flat, 24a, orthography for, 217a

with ingressive air stream, 29b

lateral, 27a

modified by pitch, 30a; by quantity, 29b; by syllable position, 30a; by strength of articulation, 29b

oral, modified by further articulation, 28b; modified by nasalization, 28a; modified by voicing, 27a

phonetic symbol for, 6a

Friction (see also Cavity Friction, Local Friction)

audible, 26an

modified by environment, 87a

types of, 4b

*FRICTIONAL: A sound during which friction can be heard and identified at some point of articulation (see Fricative)

FRICTIONLESS: Pertaining to a sound during which no friction can be heard; or, for voiceless sounds, one in which the friction is very light and cannot be recognized readily at any one point (the latter is cavity friction, which see), 4b

Fries, 229an

Front vocoid, 16a

FRONTING: The forward movement of the tongue during the production of some sound, or the resultant modification of the sound itself

by environment, 87a

phonetic symbols for, 6a

General American, 44

GENERAL DISTRIBUTION: The study of typical types of sequences which can be expressed in general formulas, such as CVC (see also Distribution), 182a–83b

Gerstung, 8bn

GLIDE: (1) A tongue or lip movement which results in a vocoid of changing quality, a vocoid glide; or (2) a change of frequency so that one hears rising or falling pitch, a pitch glide; *(3) nonsyllabic vocoids, such as [w], [y], [r]; vowel, in American English, 46a

GLIDING TONE SYSTEM: A tone language with basic gliding tones; a contour tone language, 105b

GLOTTAL: Involving articulation at the glottis

GLOTTAL STOP: The complete interruption of the pulmonic air stream by closure of the vocal cords

exercises for, 33b

in close-knit nucleus, 147b

orthography for, 215b

as part of a pitch phoneme, 138an

as phonetic laryngealization, 140a

in phonetically complex phonemes, 131b

as suprasegmental phoneme, 63an, 147b–48a

in Totonaco, 148

GLOTTAL TRILL: See Trillization

*GLOTTALIC CLICK: See Implosive

GLOTTALIZED SOUND: Sounds produced by egressive pharynx air; that is, sounds produced by pressure from the rising larynx (but see Laryngealized Vowel)

affricates, 136a

stops, 38b

GLOTTALIZED VOWEL: See Laryngealized Vowel

GLOTTIS: The opening between the vocal cords

Gradient characteristics, 125an

Grammar

analysis concomitant with phonemics, 161

borders in, symbolized, 168b

in relation to phonemic syllable, 146a; to phonology, 146a

GRAMMATICAL BORDER POINT or JUNCTURE: See Border Point, 161a

Grammatical categories, symbolization of, 168b

Grammatical criteria, in English orthography, 164an

Grammatical divisions, 91b; in early analysis, 67a

GRAMMATICAL ENVIRONMENT: The position at which sounds occur in relation to units of grammatical structure, 87b

GRAMMATICAL UNIT: A linguistic structural entity such as morpheme, word, clitic,

phrase, utterance, 90a; in descriptive statement, 146a

GRAMMATICALLY DEPENDENT: (1) Items which do not occur by themselves; (2) items modifying other items

GROOVED ARTICULATOR: One in which the sides of the tongue are higher than the center of the tongue (in labial articulation, rounding), 26a

*GUTTERAL: See Velar

HALF-LONG: Sounds which are shorter than the longest sounds in some language, but longer than the shortest ones

Hall, 167bn, 178bn, 191a, 194b, 197an, 197bn

Height, of pitch, modified by environment, 87a

Henry, 231bn

HESITATION FORM: A sentence or word interrupted before the speaker completes it in a normal way

HETERORGANIC AFFRICATE: A two-segment sequence during which the first segment is a stop which has a point of articulation and articulator distinct from that of the fricative to which it releases, 33a

*HIATUS: A brief cessation of a sequence, or weak spot in it, less than normal pause during an utterance

HIGH VOCOID: One in which the tongue is relatively near to the top of the mouth, 17a

HIGHLIGHTED DESCRIPTION: The presentation of data in such a way that some one phase of it most likely to be interesting to the reader is brought immediately to his attention; the organization of data around some specific characteristic of those data, 176a–77a

Hill, 159bn

Hockett, 126bn, 129bn, 146an

Hoijer, 175bn

Hole in distribution, seen in charts, 182a

HOLE IN THE PATTERN: A nonsymmetrical feature of an observed system, 117b

HOMORGANIC AFFRICATE: A two-segment sequence comprised of a stop and a following fricative which has the same articulator and point of articulation, 33a

Huichol, 144an, 153b, 178a

Hungarian, 178bn, 191–94

HYPOTHESIS AS TO THE CONDITIONING OF PHONETIC DIFFERENCES: A useful initial guess as to the manner in which the environment might have affected sounds

modified or rejected, 87b

origin of, 160bn

HYPOTHETICAL LANGUAGE: An artificial problem of linguistic analysis constructed to simulate a language situation and to be analyzed as an entire language unit, 68a

*LINGUO-: Made with the tongue

Lip rounding

  degrees of, 15

  exercises for, 15

*LIQUID: Voiced continuant nonfricative nonvocoid sounds such as [n], [r], and [l]

LOAN: A word taken from one language and utilized by a second (see also Assimilated Loan)

  assimilated, 143a

  interpretation of, 142b-43a

  in practical orthography, 213a

  in Zoque, 199a, 203-06

LOCAL FRICTION: Friction noise which is readily identified as being produced at some point in the vocal apparatus, 4b, 26an

LONG: See Length

LOOSE POSITION: A morpheme adjacent to other morphemes, but grammatically not closely dependent upon them, 165b

LOW VOCOID: A central resonant oral produced by a tongue position which leaves the vocal cavity relatively wide open

LOWERING: (1) The dropping of the position of the tongue during the production of some sound, or its effect upon the sound so modified; (2) a decrease in pitch

  by environment, 87a

  phonetic symbol for, 6a

LUNG AIR: Rarefaction or compression of an air stream initiated by the lungs

Mandarin, 115a

Margin, of syllable, 148a

Mathematics, 160bn

Maya, 121a

Mazateco, 129bn, 144bn, 172b, 173ab; nucleus of syllable, 148b

McIntosh, 144an, 153bn, 178an

Meaning (see also Minimal Pair), of intonation, 105b

*MEDIAE: Lenis voiceless sounds, especially lenis voiceless unaspirated stops

MEDIAL ENVIRONMENT: A position in the middle of a word, phrase, morpheme, syllable, or utterance, etc.

MID VOCOID: A central resonant oral produced with a tongue position which is relatively halfway between the most open and the most close varieties of vocoids

MINIMAL PAIR: A set of two words differing the least amount possible phonetically and yet contrasting in meaning; i.e., by the substitution, addition, or subtraction of one segment, 81ab; three items so differing: minimal triplets, 81b

  for practice, 81b

  usefulness of, 81b

MINIMAL TRIPLET: See Minimal Pair, 81b

MINIMALLY CONTRASTIVE PAIR: Two words which differ only by the substitution of one sound segment by another sound segment, or by the addition or subtraction of one sound segment (see also Minimal Pair)

MINIMALLY DIFFERENT WORDS: See Minimal Pair

Mixteco, 126b, 171b, 174b, 181bn, 221b

  distributional limitations in morphemes of, 181a

  sounds of, 174b-75

  syllabic consonants in, 146b-47a

  syllables in, 146b-47a

Modification

  segmental, 14b

  suprasegmental, 14b

MONOLINGUAL: A person speaking only one language; orthography for, 212b

MONOLINGUAL APPROACH: Learning a language without an interpreter, 231b

MONOSYLLABLE: A word of one syllable only

MORA: A unit of timing, usually equivalent to a short vowel or half a long vowel, 145a; in relation to phonemic syllable, 144a

MORPHEME: (1) The smallest meaningful unit of linguistic structure; (2) a unit arrived at by analogy with minimal meaningful units, or by separating various meaningful morphemes and leaving a small residue which can then best be handled as analogous morphemes, 60bn

  characteristic of, 89b

  as a descriptive unit, 145b

  differentially identified, 62b

  identified by meaning and form, 92a

  identification of in phonemics, 161b

  persistent sounds in, 62b

  in relation to space, 159b

  sounds restricted to special types, 143b

*MORPHOLOGICAL PROCESS: Some type of grammatical modification of a stem form: reduplication, affixation, prosodic modification, compounding, suppletion, etc.

*MORPHOPHONEMICS: The study of the replacements, losses, and additions of phonemes in the morphology of a language (see Phonomechanics, and Tonomechanics)

*MORPHOTONEMICS: Meaningless substitution of one tone phoneme for another (see Morphophonemics)

Morrison, 83b, 153an, 153bn, 154an

MOUTH AIR: An ingressive or egressive air stream initiated by the lowering and

backing or by the fronting and raising
of the tongue

*MUTE: See Voiceless

MUTUALLY EXCLUSIVE ENVIRONMENTS: Positions
differing in such a way that the first
of two sounds occurs only in one of the
positions and the second sound occurs
only in the second position or set of
positions in phonological and/or grammatical units; two sounds so distributed
that the first of them occurs only in
such and such positions but the second
never occurs in those same positions
(see also Complementary Distribution),
62a, 84-104

as essential for phonemic relationships,
86

in relation to space, 159a

sample problem for, 85

Names

foreign, 142bn

technical order of, 8

NASAL: A sound during which air escapes out
the nose but not the mouth, 35a-36a

in Brazilian Portuguese, 197bn

modified, 36a

orthography for, 218a-19a

in phoneme with affricates, 136a

voiceless, 35an

NASAL CAVITY: The nasal passageway, including velic closure

*NASAL PLOSION: The nasal release of a stop

NASALIZATION: The modification of some
sound by nasal resonance due to a relaxed velic and open nasal passageway,
20a

appearance of by faucalization, 22a

combined with stop phonemes, 131b

by environment, 87a

modifying stops, 34a

in phonemic analysis, 139b

phonetic symbols for, 6a

practice text marked for, 53a

in relation to suprasegmental phonemes,
63a

of vocoids, 20a

of vowels, in orthography, 221a

NASALIZED CLICK: A sound made with ingressive mouth air, accompanied by a simultaneous nasal produced by egressive
lung air with velar closure but with
velic opening; differences in timing of
the various releases give different
varieties of nasalized clicks, 42b

*NASALIZED STOP: The sequence of a nasal
followed by a stop, or the reverse,
serving as a single phoneme

NASALLY RELEASED STOP: A two-segment sequence in which a stop is followed by a
release of air at the velic

Native reaction

as source of premises, 64b

in relation to spaces, 160b

Navaho, 175bn

Needham, 90bn

*NEUTRAL VOWEL: A mid central vocoid

NEUTRALIZATION OF OPPOSITIONS: The occurrence in some environment of a segment
phonetically similar to and mutually exclusive with two other contrasting segments (see also Under-Differentiation of
Phonemes, and Archiphoneme), 141-42

Nida, 222bn, 230bn, 231bn

Noël-Armfield, 14bn

NONCONTRASTIVE VARIETY: Any submember of a
phoneme other than the norm; the submembers of a phoneme do not contrast one
with another, but any submember of one
phoneme contrasts with any submember of
any other phoneme

NONFLUCTUATING SUSPICIOUS PAIR: Two similar
segments which have no perceptible variation in repeated pronunciations of the
same words or phrases

NONSENSE SYLLABLE: A syllable which is produced without relationship to the actual
words of any language

NONSIGNIFICANT VARIETY: Submember of a phoneme; noncontrastive (see also Slur),
58ab

*NONSPEECH SOUND: Any sound of a type which
has not been reported to occur in speech;
speech sounds of normal individuals are
limited to those produced by lung air
(possibly egressive lung air only), by
egressive and ingressive pharynx air,
and by ingressive mouth air

NONSUSPICIOUS PAIR OF SOUNDS: Two segments
which are not likely to constitute submembers of a single phoneme in any language

NONSUSPICIOUS SEQUENCE: A sequence of
sounds concerning which the investigator
need not be in doubt as to their analysis; applicable only to a specific sequence with one specific characteristic
under attention (a sequence or pattern
may be suspicious for one purpose and
nonsuspicious for another), 128-49a; as
separate phonemes, 71a

NONSYLLABIC SEGMENT: A segment which is not
the prominent part of a phonetic syllable (which see; or which is not the nucleus of a phonemic syllable (which see),
90a

consonants, in American English, 45

vowels, in American English, 45n

NONSYLLABIC VOCOID: A central resonant oral
which is not the prominent part of a

types in any language (see also Stress-Timed and Syllable-Timed Rhythm); in orthography, 222

RHYTHM GROUP: An entity comprised of that part of speech which occurs between any two consecutive pauses, 90b-91, 164a

RISING: (1) Of frequency which is increasing, giving a rise in pitch; or (2) of tongue position during the production of a vocoid

Robbins, 160bn

Roffe, 145bn

ROOT OF TONGUE: That part of the tongue which faces the back wall of the throat; on diagram, 4b

ROUNDED VOCOID: A central resonant oral during which the opening between the lips is rounded; or a vocoid during which the lips are relatively parallel, but touching for a considerable portion at each side of the lips so that a small hole is left

ROUNDING: The modification of a sound by the rounding of the lips (see Labialization)

indicated in sequence diagrams, 10

modified by environment, 87a

phonetic symbol for, 6a

SANDHI: The mechanical substitution, addition, or dropping of one or more phonemes in a morpheme, caused when two words come together in phrases (internal sandhi: phonological process within words; external sandhi: phonological process between words); tone in, 146an

SECONDARY ARTICULATOR: Any articulator in the nasal cavity; the velic, 9b

*SECONDARY PHONEME: Significant units of stress or pitch which occur only with combinations of morphemes

SECONDARY STRESS: A phonemic or nonphonemic stress which is louder than unstressed syllables and either less loud than primary stressed syllables or with a stress which is less permanent on the word than that of primary stress

SEGMENT: A single sound caused by the movement of a single articulator or the synchronous movement of several articulators; a sound (or lack of sound) having indefinite borders but with a center that is produced by a crest or trough of stricture during the even motion or pressure of an initiator

explained and illustrated, 11a

kind of, 11a

listed as phonemes, 68b

over-differentiated, 142

separated phonemically, 73-77a, 80-82a

special sporadic types of, 143a

as submembers of phonemes, 69a

united phonemically, 84-96

SEGMENT DIAGRAM: See Sequence Diagram

SEGMENTAL PHONEME: A significant unit of qualitative sound; to be contrasted with suprasegmental phoneme

Selections for reading, 44-56

SEMANTICS: The study of meanings

*SEMI-CONSONANT: A vocoid patterning as a consonant

Semi-free morpheme, 166a

Semi-free word (see also Clitic), 165b

*SEMI-VOWEL: A vocoid patterning as a consonant; place on chart, 5b

Separation of segments, 73a

in analogous environments, 73a-77b

in identical environments 80-82a

SEPARATION PROCEDURE: An analytical technique used to prove that two phonetically similar sounds are phonemically distinct

SEQUENCE DIAGRAM: A schematic representation of sounds and sequences symbolized by the relative openness and closure of a passageway by the articulators (contrast Static Diagram), 9-10

reason for, 9a

illustrated, 9b

Sequence types, suspicious as one or two phonemes, 131-38a

Sequences of sounds

as a criterion for spaces, 163b

in descriptive statement, 177b

interpretation of, 131a-38a

as one phoneme, 61

subword, 137b

Shenk, 22bn

Shipibo, 152b

Short form, in orthography, 209b

Short vowel, in relation to long vowel, 138b

SIBILANT: A fricative sound of a hissing type formed by a grooved tongue position, 26a; orthography for, 217b

Signals of speech, defined, 58a

Silence, slurs into, 58b

Similarity, as essential in phonemic relationships, 71b

Simonyi, 191bn

SKILL DRILL: An exercise designed to help the student hear and produce sounds in difficult sequences, 14a

Slow form, in orthography, 124b, 209b-10a

SLUR: (1) The gradual change of one position of an articulator to another position of that articulator, or the blending of the movements of two articulators; (2) a pitch glide; of sounds into their

especially when they serve as a single phoneme

TROUGH: The point at which a moving articulator reaches its most open position; of movement, 9b

Tsotsil, 177bn

Twaddell, 63bn, 64bn, 65an, 65bn

TWO-PART SENTENCE FRAME: A series of sentences, each of which can have its first part utilized preceding the second part of the others for drill purposes, 229a

TYPE OF ARTICULATION: The general method by which a stricture is made by some vocal organ of speech

*UNACCENTED: Unstressed

UNCHANGING TONEME: A toneme which is not replaced by another toneme in any grammatical sequence, 110a

UNDER-DIFFERENTIATION OF PHONEMES: The occurrence, in some environment, of a segment phonetically similar to but mutually exclusive with each of two phonemically contrasting segments (see Archiphoneme, and Neutralization of Oppositions), 141

UNILATERAL: With air escaping over one side of the tongue or organ of speech

UNIT OF TONE PLACEMENT: The smallest type of segment or segment sequence in the language which can carry a single tone, usually a short vowel (see also Mora), 105a, 145b

UNITING PROCEDURE: A technique used to prove that two similar sounds are submembers of a single phoneme because they are freely fluctuant and noncontrastive, or because they are mutually exclusive in distribution, 73a

interchanging types, 123a-25a, 135b

noncontiguous types, 84a-96a, 135b

UNROUNDED VOCOIDS: Central resonant orals during which the lips are spread apart and are open for approximately their entire length

UNVOICED: A voiceless sound; or a sound unit which is voiced at one point in the language but voiceless elsewhere

Unvoicing

at borders of phonological or grammatical units, 58b

by environment, 87a

UTTERANCE: A grammatically unified linguistic statement preceded and followed by pause (this definition is not completely satisfactory since it is not certain what should be the relationship of an utterance to conversational interchange, or to a full spoken paragraph, or to unitary sentences interrupted by pause)

significance of in phonemic analysis, 89b

study of phonetics in, 89a

usefulness of in phonemic analysis, 91a

UTTERANCE-FINAL POSITION: A sound occurring at the end of an utterance

UVULA: The fleshy lobe hanging from the back part of the soft palate; on static diagram, 4b

UVULAR: With articulation at the uvula

"Uvular [r]," 28an

Várady, 191bn

VARIATION: See Free Fluctuation and Conditioned Variation

VELAR: With articulation at the soft palate

*VELARIC CLICK: See Click

VELARIZATION: The modification of some sound by a tongue position which approximates that of the vocoid [u]

modified by environment, 87a

phonetic symbol for, 6a

VELIC: The nasal side of the soft palate, 22a

on static diagram, 4b

indicated in sequence diagrams, 10

VELUM: The soft palate; on static diagram, 4b

VENTRILOQUIAL DRONE: High-pitched trillization (which see), 21a

VENTRILOQUISM: See Trillization

*VIBRANT: Flapped or trilled

VIBRATING: The rapid automatic opening and closing of the vocal cords in such a way that the separate closures cannot be heard, and so that voice is produced

VOCAL CORDS: The folds of membrane which project into the larynx and which by vibrating cause voice

as initiator, 3b

modifying vocoids, 21a

in sequence diagrams, 10

on static diagram, 4b

VOCOID: A sound during which the air escapes from the mouth over the center of the tongue without friction in the mouth, i.e., a central resonant oral (friction elsewhere than in the mouth does not prevent a sound from being a vocoid; syllabic function or phonemic interpretation of a segment does not affect its interpretation as a vocoid or nonvocoid), 5a, 13bn-14an

chart of symbols, 5

chart of tongue position, 18

diagram, 18an

exercises in pronunciation of, 14

front, 16a

glide of, 19a, 131b

high, 17a

ingressive, 22bn

modification of, by lips, 14b-15; by air stream direction, 22b; by intensity, 23a; by nasalization, 20a; by pharyngealization, 21b; by quantity, 23a; by retroflexion, 19a; by stress, 23b; by syllable placement, 24a; at vocal cords, 21a

nonsyllabic, orthography for, 219b

open, 17a

percussive transition of, 39an

practice in sequences, 22b

in sequence, 42b

tongue modification, exercises for, 15b-19

value of term, 13bn-14an

Voegelin, 231bn

VOICE: The sound produced by the vibration of the vocal cords (see Voicing); harsh, 22a

VOICED CLICK: A sound with ingressive mouth air plus simultaneous egressive lung air with velic and velar closures; differences in the timing of the various releases give different varieties of voiced clicks

Voiced h, 21an

VOICELESS: Without vibration of the vocal cords; symbols for, 6a

Voicing

description of, 4b

by environment, 87a

special (phonetic) symbol for, 6b

test for, 27an

VOWEL: 'In the characteristic segment sequences of all languages there are two main groups of sounds, which have sharply different distributions and a tendency to different functions in phonetic syllables; a sound of that group which is largely comprised of vocoids and is most frequently syllabic is a vowel, 13bn-14an

in American English, 45; nonsyllabic, 45n; glided, 46a

clusters of, in Portuguese, 200

differences by age, 66a

distribution of, 182b-84

general qualitative differences, 66a

length, minimum unit of, 144a

long, phonemically analyzed, 138b

nature of, 60b

orthography for, 220b-21

quality, special types of, 125an

in relation to consonant, 128-30; to vocoid, 14an

with simultaneous consonant, 61b, 139b

voiceless, 21an; in orthography, 221b; text marked for practice, 53a

VOWEL TRIANGLE: An arrangement of vocoid symbols in a triangular pattern with both front and back high varieties, but with only central low ones, 18an

Ward, 228bn

Waterhouse, 102an, 142bn, 154an

Wazanaki, 22bn

WEAK FORM: An alternate pronunciation of a morpheme, especially in fast speech, which omits certain segments customarily heard in slow or in precise pronunciations of that morpheme, or has some of the phonemic norms replaced by less precise or more centrally articulated submembers of the phoneme, 124

Weathers, 177bn

WHISPER: Voiceless vocoids with friction at the glottis; or voiceless speech in which such vocoids serve as the syllabics, 21a

Wonderly, 142bn, 172an, 202

WORD: The smallest unit arrived at for some particular language as the most convenient type of grammatical entity to separate by spaces; in general, one of those units of a particular language which actually or potentially may be pronounced by itself (see also Clitic), 159-68b

characteristics of, 89b

in description, 181a

difficulty in finding, 181b

in orthography, 222b

WORD-FINAL POSITION: Occurring at the end of words

Yamagiwa, 229an

Zapoteco, of Villa Alta, 114b

Zinza, 83an

Zoque, 172a